This major contribution to Ottoman
paperback in two volumes: the orig
(1994) has been widely acclaimed as a
of the most enduring and influential e₁
authors provide a richly detailed accoun.. .. ... social and economic
history of the Ottoman region, from the origins of the Empire
around 1300 to the eve of its destruction during World War I. The
breadth of range and the fullness of coverage make these two volumes
essential for an understanding of contemporary developments in
both the Middle East and the post-Soviet Balkan world.

The text of volume one is by Halil İnalcık, covering the period
1300–1600. The second volume, written by Suraiya Faroqhi, Bruce
McGowan, Donald Quataert and Şevket Pamuk, continues the story
to 1914. Each volume examines developments in population, trade,
transport, manufacturing, land tenure, and the economy, and extensive apparatus and bibliographic information is provided for students
and others wishing to pursue the subject in more detail. Both volumes will be fundamental to any future discussion of any aspect of
Ottoman history.

AN ECONOMIC AND SOCIAL HISTORY
OF THE OTTOMAN EMPIRE
Volume 2: 1600–1914

AN

ECONOMIC AND SOCIAL HISTORY

OF THE

OTTOMAN EMPIRE

EDITED BY
HALİL İNALCIK

WITH
DONALD QUATAERT

Volume 2: 1600–1914

Suraiya Faroqhi
Munich University
Bruce McGowan
United States Foreign Service
Donald Quataert
Binghamton University
and Şevket Pamuk
Boğaziçi University

CAMBRIDGE
UNIVERSITY PRESS

PUBLISHED BY THE PRESS SYNDICATE OF THE UNIVERSITY OF CAMBRIDGE
The Pitt Building, Trumpington Street, Cambridge, United Kingdom

CAMBRIDGE UNIVERSITY PRESS
The Edinburgh Building, Cambridge CB2 2RU, UK
40 West 20th Street, New York, NY 10011–4211, USA
477 Williamstown Road, Port Melbourne, VIC 3207, Australia
Ruiz de Alarcón 13, 28014 Madrid, Spain
Dock House, The Waterfront, Cape Town 8001, South Africa

http://www.cambridge.org

First published 1994
First paperback edition (see below) 1997
Reprinted in paperback 1999, 2000, 2004

Printed in the United Kingdom at the University Press, Cambridge

A catalogue record for this book is available from the British Library

A catalogue record for this book is available from the Library of Congress

A note on the paperback edition

An Economic and Social History of the Ottoman Empire was first published in hardback
as a single volume. For its paperback appearance the work has been divided into two,
the original Part 1 (by Halil İnalcık) constituting the first paperback volume, and Parts
2 to 4 (by Suraiya Faroqhi, Bruce McGowan, Donald Quataert) and the original
Appendix, now Part 5 (by Şevket Pamuk) constituting the second paperback volume.
Although the arabic pagination remains continuous between the two volumes, for the
convenience of readers common material (like the glossary and chronology) are printed
in both volumes, and each has its own index.

Volume 1: 1300–1600
HALİL İNALCIK
ISBN 0 521 57456 0 paperback

Volume 2: 1600–1914
SURAIYA FAROQHI, BRUCE McGOWAN, DONALD QUATAERT, and
ŞEVKET PAMUK
ISBN 0 521 57455 2 paperback

Single-volume hardback edition
(1300–1914) still available
ISBN 0 521 34315 1 paperback

CONTENTS

PART II CRISIS AND CHANGE, 1590–1699   411

Suraiya Faroqhi, Institut für Geschichte und Kultur des Nahen Orients, Munich University

PART III THE AGE OF THE *AYANS*,
1699–1812

Bruce McGowan, U.S. Consulate, St. Petersburg

PART IV THE AGE OF REFORMS,
1812–1914

Donald Quataert, Binghamton University, State University of New York

PART V MONEY IN THE OTTOMAN
EMPIRE, 1326–1914

Şevket Pamuk, Bosphorus University

ॐ

MAPS

FIGURES

゜

TABLES

GENEALOGY OF THE OTTOMAN DYNASTY

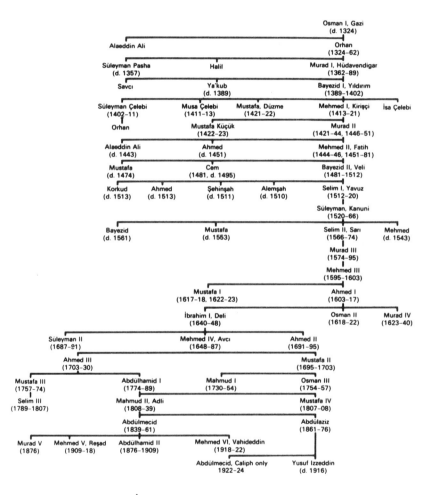

Reproduced from H. İnalcık (1973). *The Ottoman Empire: the classical age, 1300–1600*, London.

·ۈ·

CHRONOLOGY OF OTTOMAN
HISTORY, 1260–1923

1261–1300	foundation of the *gazi* principalities of Menteşe, Aydın, Saruhan, Karesi and Osmanlı (Ottoman) in western Anatolia
c. 1290–1324	**Osman I**
1324–62	**Orhan**
1326	Ottoman conquest of Bursa
1331	Ottoman conquest of Nicaea (İznik)
1335	fall of the Mongol Empire in Iran
1354	Ottoman occupation of Ankara and Gallipoli
1361	Ottoman conquest of Adrianople
1362–89	**Murad I**
1363–65	Ottoman expansion in southern Bulgaria and Thrace
1371–73	Ottoman victory at Chermanon; Byzantium, the Balkan rulers recognize Ottoman suzerainty
1385	Ottoman conquest of Sofia
1389	Ottoman victory at Kossovo-Polje over the coalition of the Balkan states
1389–1402	**Bayezid I, Yıldırım**
1396	battle of Nicopolis
1402	battle of Ankara, collapse of Bayezid I's empire
1403–13	civil war among Bayezid's sons for sultanate
1413–21	**Mehmed I**
1421–44, 1446–51	**Murad II**

1423–30	Ottoman–Venetian war for Salonica
1425	Ottoman annexation of İzmir and the reconquest of western Anatolia
1439	Ottoman annexation of Serbia
1443	John Hunyadi invades the Balkans
1444	revival of Serbian Despotate, battle of Varna
1444–46, 1451–81	**Mehmed II, Fatih**
1448	second battle of Kossovo-Polje
1453	conquest of Constantinople; fall of Pera
1459	conquest of Serbia and the Morea
1461	conquest of the empire of Trabzon
1463–79	war with Venice
1468	conquest of Karaman
1473	battle of Başkent
1475	conquest of the Genoese colonies in the Crimea
1481–1512	**Bayezid II**
1485–91	war with the Mamluks of Egypt
1499–1503	war with Venice; conquest of Lepanto, Coron, and Modon
1512–20	**Selim I**
1514	Selim defeats Shah İsmail at Çaldıran
1516	conquest of Diyarbekir; annexation of eastern Anatolia; defeat of the Mamluks at Marj Dabık
1517	battle of Ridaniyya, conquest of Egypt; submission of the sharif of Mecca
1520–66	**Süleyman I, Kanuni**
1521	conquest of Belgrade
1522	conquest of Rhodes
1526	battle of Mohács; Hungary becomes a vassal
1529	siege of Vienna
1534	conquest of Tabriz and Baghdad
1537–40	war with Venice

1538	siege of Diu in India
1541	annexation of Hungary
1553–55	war with Iran
1565	siege of Malta
1566–74	**Selim II**
1569	French capitulations; first Ottoman expedition against Russia; siege of Astrakhan
1570	Uluç Ali captures Tunis; expedition to Cyprus; fall of Nicosia
1571	battle of Lepanto
1573	peace with Venice and the emperor
1574–95	**Murad III**
1578–90	war with Iran, annexation of Azerbaijan
1580	English capitulations
1589	Janissary revolt in İstanbul
1591–92	further Janissary uprisings
1593–1606	war with the Habsburgs
1595–1603	**Mehmed III**
1596	Celali rebellions in Anatolia
1603–39	Iranian Wars
1603–17	**Ahmed I**
1606	peace of Zsitva-Török with the Habsburgs
1609	suppression of the Celalis in Anatolia
1612	extension of capitulations to the Dutch
1613–35	rebellion of Ma'noğlu Fahreddin
1618	peace with Iran, Ottoman withdrawal from Azerbaijan
1618–22	**Osman II**
1621	invasion of Poland
1622	assassination of Osman II
1617–18, 1622–23	**Mustafa I**
1623–40	**Murad IV**
1624–28	rebellion in Asia Minor; anarchy in İstanbul

1684	Holy League against the Ottomans between the emperor, Polish king and Venice
1686	fall of Buda, Russia joins the coalition; Venetians in the Morea
1687	second battle of Mohács; army's rebellion; deposition of Mehmed IV
1687–91	**Süleyman II**
1688	fall of Belgrade
1689	Austrians at Kossovo; Russians attack the Crimea
1689–91	Köprülü Fazıl Mustafa's grand vizierate; tax reforms
1690	recovery of Belgrade from Austrians
1691–95	**Ahmed II**
1691	battle of Slankamen; death of Fazıl Mustafa
1695–1703	**Mustafa II**
1695	fall of Azov
1696	Ottoman counter-attack in Hungary
1697	Ottoman defeat at Zenta
1698–1702	Köprülü Hüseyin's grand vizierate
1699	treaty of Karlowitz
1700	peace with Russia
1703	army's rebellion; deposition of Mustafa II
1703–30	**Ahmed III**
1709	Charles XII, king of Sweden, takes refuge in Ottoman territory
1711	battle of Pruth, Ottoman victory over Peter I of Russia, insurrection at Cairo, realignment of Mamluks; Shihabi supremacy over Mount Lebanon
1713	peace treaty with Russia: Azov recovered, Charles XII returns to Sweden; introduction of Phanariote rule in principalities
1714–18	war with Venice, recovery of the Morea
1716	war with Austria
1717	fall of Belgrade
1718–30	Damad İbrahim Pasha's grand vizierate

1718	peace treaty of Passarowitz with Austria and Venice: Morea recovered, large parts of Serbia and Wallachia ceded to Austria
1723–27	war with Iran, Ottoman occupation of Azerbaijan and Hamadan
1730	Patrona Halil rebellion; deposition of Ahmed III; end of Tulip period
1730–36	Iran's counter-attack; loss of Azerbaijan and western Iran
1730–54	**Mahmud I**
1736–39	war with Russia and Austria
1739	peace treaty with Austria and Russia; recovery of Belgrade
1740	extension of French capitulations; Ottoman–Swedish alliance against Russia
1743–46	war with Iran under Nadir Shah
1754–57	**Osman III**
1757–74	**Mustafa III**
1768–74	war with the Russian Empire
1770	Russian fleet in the Aegean; Ottoman defeat on the Danube
1771	Russian invasion of the Crimea
1773	Ali Bey's rebellion in Egypt
1774–89	**Abdülhamid I**
1774	treaty of Küçük Kaynarca, independence of the Crimea and northern coasts of the Black Sea from the Ottoman Empire
1783	Russian annexation of the Crimean khanate
1787	war with Russia
1788	Sweden declares war against the Russian Empire
1789–1807	**Selim III**
1792	treaty of Jassy
1798	Napoleon invades Egypt
1804	Serbs revolt

1805–48	Mehmed Ali as ruler of Egypt
1807	Selim's reform program crushed by revolt
1807–08	**Mustafa IV**
1808–39	**Mahmud II**
1808	Document of Alliance
1811	Mehmed Ali massacres Mamluk remnant in Egypt
1812	treaty of Bucharest
1826	destruction of the Janissaries
1832	battle of Konya
1833	treaty of Hünkiar-İskelesi with Russia
1838	Anglo-Turkish Convention
1839	battle of Nezib
1839–61	**Abdülmecid I**
1839	Tanzimat begins with Imperial Rescript of Gülhane
1853–56	Crimean War
1856	Imperial Rescript
1856	treaty of Paris
1861–76	**Abdülaziz**
1875	*de facto* Ottoman bankruptcy
1876	first Ottoman Constitution
1876–1909	**Abdülhamid II**
1878	treaty of Berlin
1881	formation of Public Debt Administration
1885	occupation by Bulgaria of eastern Rumelia
1896–97	insurrection in Crete; war with Greece
1908	Young Turk Revolution and the restoration of the Constitution of 1876
1909–18	**Mehmed V**
1911	war with Italy
1912	Balkan War
1914	World War I begins
1918–22	**Mehmed VI**
1920	establishment of French mandate over Syria and Lebanon and British mandates over Iraq and Palestine
1923	proclamation of the Republic of Turkey

◌̇

PREFACE

HALİL İNALCIK AND DONALD QUATAERT

These volumes are intended for students and, more generally, the informed reader. They are also addressed to the specialist who should find much new material of interest. The authors are specialists in their fields and of the respective time periods on which they have written. The work was first planned by Halil İnalcık, who then invited the best-known scholars to participate, including Mehmet Genç and Halil Sahillioğlu. Generally, the authors of each chronological section survey political events before proceeding to the study of economy and society.

Some subjects of inquiry were not included either because research materials were lacking or because of space considerations. In the latter case, the authors make references to existing literature to guide readers. Thus, to keep volume 1 within manageable limits, Halil İnalcık left the history of urban life and industry before 1600 for another occasion and provided readers with sufficient bibliography on the subject.

This project was begun in 1985 and, inevitably, there were delays in its completion. Some sections were finished in late 1989 while others were prepared in Spring 1992. In some cases, new publications have appeared and are not discussed. For personal reasons, Mehmet Genç and Halil Sahillioğlu found it impossible to continue. And so, Bruce McGowan assumed sole responsibility for the eighteenth-century section and we invited Şevket Pamuk to write the monetary history. We are very grateful to Professors Genç and Sahillioğlu for allowing us to use their unpublished materials.

We have sought to respect the longevity and complexity of Ottoman history in our spellings of personal and place names and technical terms. Thus, we have used the spellings most appropriate to each particular time period and area. Otherwise, we have sought to use modern Turkish spelling whenever possible. We use the English terms for Arabic, Turkish and Persian words that have come into English. In the text, we have sought to minimize the number of technical terms, but have had to use some to maintain accuracy. Hence, for example, *timar* is preferred to fief.

Halil İnalcık thanks his colleagues for agreeing to participate in this project. He is especially grateful to Donald Quataert for all his labours in helping to bring the project to fruition. In addition, he thanks C. Max Kortepeter for his generosity in taking considerable time to make stylistic suggestions.

Suraiya Faroqhi thanks Rifaʿat Abou-El-Haj, İdris Bostan, Linda Darling, Neşe Erim, Cornell Fleischer, Daniel Goffman, Ronald Jennings, Gülru Necipoğlu, Cemal Kafadar, Heath Lowry and Leslie Peirce. She wishes to thank Halil İnalcık and Donald Quataert for commenting on the manuscript as well as Engin Akarlı, Halil Berktay, and Nükhet Sirman Eralp. And finally, for their help with historiographical issues, she thanks Rifaʿat Abou-El-Haj, Chris Bayly, Huri İslamoğlu-İnan, Ariel Salzmann, Sanjay Subrahmanyam and İsenbike Togan.

Bruce McGowan wishes to thank, above all, Professor Mehmet Genç of Marmara University, who generously shared his expert advice on several historical concepts employed in Part III. The writer is well aware that the fit between this section and others is far from perfect. His own conception from the start was to provide a brief and interesting review of the literature which would be useful for students. The writer is, above all, grateful to have had access to the Regenstein Library of the University of Chicago, the collections of the Oriental Studies Department of the University of Vienna, and the American Research Institute in Turkey.

Donald Quataert thanks Cem Behar, Alan Duben and Judith Tucker for providing manuscript versions of their research findings. He is especially grateful to Tom Dublin for his careful reading of an early draft. Thanks also to the Ottoman reading group of the Fernand Braudel Center and Faruk Tabak at Binghamton University as well as Rifaʿat Abou-El-Haj for invaluable comments on various portions of the manuscript. Binghamton University has been very generous in providing the staff support, without which this volume could not have been completed. Marion Tillis has been the very model of efficiency in typing substantial versions of each of the four major contributions. Faruk Tabak has been invaluable for his editing and proofreading assistance.

Şevket Pamuk acknowledges the indispensable work of Halil Sahilli-oğlu over the last three decades as well as the extensive discussions in the summer of 1990. He also thanks Cüneyt Ölçer, Mehmet Genç, Zafer

Toprak, Yavuz Cezar, İsa Akbaş, Mehmet Arat, Linda Darling, Reşat Kasaba, Faruk Tabak, Oktar Türel and Halil İnalcık.

Halil İnalcık provided the chronology up to c. 1700 while Bruce McGowan and Donald Quataert respectively prepared most of the entries for the eighteenth and nineteenth centuries. Halil İnalcık prepared the genealogical table, and the glossary.

̇ↄ

ABBREVIATIONS

AA	Auswärtiges Amt
A&P	Parliamentary Papers, Accounts and Papers, GB
AAH	*Acta Historica Academiae Scientiarum Hungaricae* (Budapest)
AAS	*Asian and African Studies* (Jerusalem)
AE	Archives du Ministère des affaires étrangères, Quai d'Orsay, Paris, Fr.
AHR	*American Historical Review*
AIESEE	*Association Internationale d'Études du Sud-Est Européen,* Bulletin
Annales, ESC	*Annales: Economies, Sociétés, Civilisations*
AOr	*Acta Orientalia* (Budapest)
AO	*Archivum Ottomanicum* (The Hague)
AS	Annual Series, GB
ASI	*Archivio Storico Italiano*
Aus	Austria
B	*Belleten* (Ankara)
BAN	Bılgarska Akademia na Naukite, *Istoria na Bılgaria*
BBA	Başbakanlık Arşivi, now Osmanlı Arşivi, İstanbul, Turkey
BCF	*Bulletin consulaire français. Recueil des rapports commerciaux adressés au Ministère des affaires étrangères par les agents diplomatiques et consulaires de France à l'étranger*
BEO	Bab-ı Ali Evrak Odası, BBA
Bel	Belediye, BBA
BF	*Byzantinische Forschungen*
Bl	*Belgeler* (Ankara)

BN	Bibliothèque Nationale, Paris
BN, MS	Bibliothèque National, Paris, MS fonds turc
BSOAS	*Bulletin of the School of Oriental and African Studies*
BS	*Byzantinoslavica*
BSt	*Balkan Studies* (Thessaloniki)
BTTD	*Belgelerle Türk Tarihi Dergisi* (İstanbul)
BuHI	*Berichte über Handel und Industrie*. Deutsches Reich (Germany)
CC	Correspondance commerciale, Fr
CED	*Coğrafya Enstitüsü Dergisi* (İstanbul)
Cev	Cevdet Tasnifi, BBA
CIEPO	*Comité International d'Études Pré-Ottomanes et Ottomanes* (İstanbul)
CMRS	*Cahiers du Monde russe et soviétique* (Paris)
CSP	*Calendar of State papers and manuscripts relating to English affairs existing in the archives and collections of Venice and in other libraries of northern Italy: Venice*, 38 vols., London 1864–1947.
Dah	Dahiliye, BBA
DII	*Documenta Islamica Inedita* (Berlin)
DO	*Dumbarton Oaks* (Washington, D.C.)
EB	*Études Balkaniques* (Sofia)
EI²	*Encyclopaedia of Islam*, 2nd edition
EcHR	*The Economic History Review*
EHR	*English Historical Review*
EUQ	*East European Quarterly*
FO	Foreign Office, GB
Fr	France
GB	Great Britain
GDAD	*Güney Doğu Araştırmaları Dergisi* (İstanbul)
Ger	Germany
HEMM	*Histoire économique du monde méditerranéen, 1450–1650, Mélanges en l'honneur de Fernand Braudel*, I–II, Toulouse 1973
HH	Hatt-ı Hümayun, BBA
HHSt A	Haus-Hof und Staatsarchiv, Vienna, Politiches Archiv (PA), Austria
HUS	*Harvard Ukrainian Studies* (Cambridge, Mass.)
İ	İradeler, BBA
IA	*İslâm Ansiklopedisi* (İstanbul)

IFM	*İstanbul Üniversitesi İktisat Fakültesi Mecmuası*
IHR	*The International History Review* (Canada)
IJMES	*International Journal of Middle East Studies*
IJTS	*International Journal of Turkish Studies* (Madison)
ISN	*Istorija Srpskoga Naroda* (Belgrade, 1986)
JAH	*Journal of Asian History*
JAS	*Journal of the Royal Asiatic Society*
JAOS	*Journal of the American Oriental Society*
JEEH	*The Journal of European Economic History*
JEH	*The Journal of Economic History*
JESHO	*Journal of the Economic and Social History of the Orient*
JMH	*Journal of Modern History*
JOS	*Journal of Ottoman Studies (Osmanlı Araştırmaları)* (İstanbul)
JRAS	*Journal of the Royal Asiatic Society*
JSAH	*Journal of South Asian History*
JTS	*Journal of Turkish Studies*
Kepeci	Kamil Kepeci Tasnifi, BBA
k und k	*Berichte der k. u. k. Österr.-ung. Konsularämter über das Jahr . . .*, Austria
Mal	Maliye, BBA
MD	Maliyyeden Müdevver, BBA
MES	*Middle Eastern Studies*
MHR	*Mediterranean Historical Review* (London)
MM	Meclis-i Mahsus, BBA
MOG	*Mitteilungen zur osmanischen Geschichte* (Vienna)
MOI	*Mediterraneo e Oceano Indiano, 1970*: Atti del VI colloquio Internl. di storia marittima, 1962, Florence
MTM	*Milli Tetebbu'lar Mecmuası* (İstanbul)
MV	Meclis-i Valâ, BBA
PP	*Past and Present* (Oxford)
R	*Review: A Journal of the Fernand Braudel Center* (Binghamton)
RC	*Rocznik Orientalistyczny* (Warsaw)
RCC	Rapports commerciaux des agents diplomatiques et consulaires de France
RCL	*La Revue commerciale du Levant, bulletin mensuel de la chambre de commerce française de Constantinople, 1896–1912*

RESEE	*Revue des Études du Sud-est Européennes* (Bucharest, 1924–42)
RH	*Revue Historique*
RHES	*Revue d'Histoire Économique et Social*
RIR	*Revista Istorica Romana*
RMMM	*Revue du Monde Musulman et de la Méditerranée* (Paris)
ROMM	*Revue de l'Occident Musulmane et de la Méditerranée* (Aix-en-Provence)
RRJTS	"Raiyyet Rüsumu, Essays presented to Halil İnalcık," *Journal of Turkish Studies*, X-XI, 1986
SB	*Studia Balkanica* (Sofia)
ŞD	Şura-yı Devlet, BBA
SF	*Südost-Forschungen*
SI	*Studia Islamica* (Paris)
SR	*Slavonic Review*
TA	*Türkologischer Anzeiger, Turkology Annual* (Vienna)
TAD	*Tarih Araştırmaları Dergisi* (Ankara)
TD	*Tarih Dergisi* (İstanbul)
TED	*Tarih Enstitüsü Dergisi* (İstanbul)
THİM	*Türk Hukuk ve İktisat Tarihi Mecmuası* (İstanbul)
TİTA	*Türkiye Iktisat Tarihi Üzerine Araştırmalar, ODTÜ Gelişme Dergisi* (Ankara, Middle East Technical University)
TOEM	*Tarih-i Osmani Encümeni Mecmuası*
TM	*Türkiyat Mecmuası* (İstanbul)
TSAB	*Turkish Studies Association Bulletin*
TTD	Tapu Tahrir Defterleri, BBA
TV	*Tarih Vesikaları* (İstanbul)
Ü	*Ülkü* (Ankara)
UPA	University Publications of America
USCR	Consular Reports of the United States
VD	*Vakıflar Dergisi* (Ankara)
VS	Vilayet Salnameleri
VSWG	*Vierteljahrsschrift für Sozial- und Wirtschaftsgeschichte*
WI	*Die Welt des Islams*
WZKM	*Wiener Zeitschrift für der Kunde des Morgenlandes* (Vienna)
ZDMG	*Zeitschrift für der Deutschen Morgenländischen Gesellschaft*
ZstA	Zentrales Staatsarchiv, Potsdam, Auswärtiges Amt, Ger., former Democratic Republic

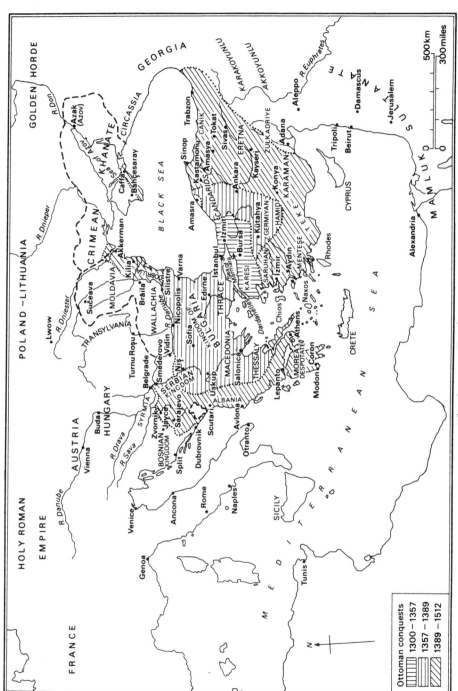

Map labels:

HOLY ROMAN
EMPIRE

FRANCE

GOLDEN HORDE

POLAND–LITHUANIA

R.Don

R.Dnieper

R.Dniester

GEORGIA

CIRCASSIA

Azak (Azov)

Sea of Azov

CRIMEAN KHANATE

Caffa
Bahçesaray

BLACK SEA

Amasra
Sinop
Trabzon

KARAKOYUNLU

AKKOYUNLU

R.Euphrates

Aleppo

Damascus
Jerusalem

MAMLUK SULTANATE

Tripoli
Beirut

CYPRUS

Alexandria

Rhodes

TEKE
KARAMAN
Konya
HAMID
GERMIYAN
Kütahya
Ankara
Kayseri
Sivas
Tokat
Amasya
Kastamonu
CANIK
CANDARLDS
ERETNA
ZULKADRIYE
Adana

Izmit
Bursa
SARUHAN
KARESI
AYDIN
Izmir
MENTEŞE

Istanbul
Gallipoli
Dardanelles
Manisa
Chios
Naxos

THRACE
Edirne
Varna
Nicopolis
Silistre
DOBRUJA

BULGARIA
KINGDOM
Sofia
Vidin
Niš

Kilia
Akkerman
Braila
WALLACHIA
R.Danube
MOLDAVIA
Sučeava
TRANSYLVANIA
Turnu Roşu
Lwow

MACEDONIA
Üsküp
Salonica
THESSALY
Athens
Coron
Modon
MOREA DESPOTATE
Lepanto

SERBIAN KINGDOM
Smederevo
Belgrade
SYRMIA
R.Sava
R.Drava
Zvornik
Jajce
Sarajevo
BOSNIAN KINGDOM
Split
Dubrovnik
Scutari
ALBANIA
Avlona
Otranto

Buda
HUNGARY
Vienna
AUSTRIA
R.Danube

Venice
Ancona
Rome
Naples
Genoa

SICILY

Tunis

MEDITERRANEAN SEA

CRETE

AEGEAN SEA

1 The Ottoman Empire, 1300–1512

N

Ottoman conquests
1300–1357
1357–1389
1389–1512

500km
300miles

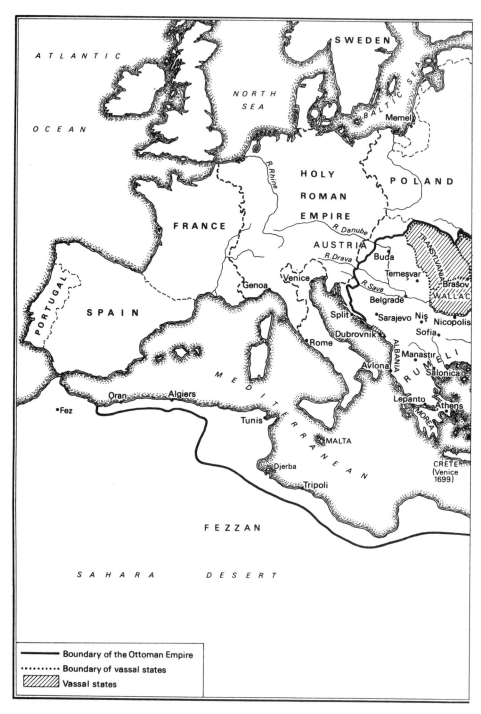

2 The Ottoman Empire, c. 1550

Kazan

Moscow

R U S S I A

N O G A Y S

Aral Sea

R. Dnieper

C O S S A C K S

R. Don

R. Volga

Astrakhan

MOLDAVIA

CRIMEAN KHANATE

Azak (Azov)

Sea of Azov

KABRDA

C A S P I A N   S E A

HIA

Akkerman

Kilia

Caffa

CIRCASSIA

DAGHESTAN

SHIRVAN

Suhum

GEORGIA

BLACK SEA

Sinop

Trabzon

Erivan

AZERBAIJAN

GILAN

Edirne

Istanbul

Erzurum

L.Van

Tabriz

L.Tabriz

Bursa

Ankara

Sivas

R U M

Foçalar

Kütahya

Kayseri

Diyarbekir

Mosul

Hamadan

Izmir

Ayasoluk

Konya

A N A T O L I A

R. Tigris

I R A N

Antalya

Aleppo

I R A Q

R. Euphrates

Baghdad

Candia

RHODES

CYPRUS (Venice 1570)

Tripoli

Beirut

Damascus

SYRIA

Basra

PERSIAN GULF

Bandar-Abbas

Hormuz

AL–HASA

Bahrain

Katif

S E A

Alexandria

Jerusalem

Cairo

Suez

E G Y P T

A R A B I A

O M A N

Kusayr

R E D   S E A

R. Nile

SHARIFATE OF MECCA

Medina

Jidda

Mecca

Suakin

INDIAN OCEAN

0   500   1000 km
0   500 miles

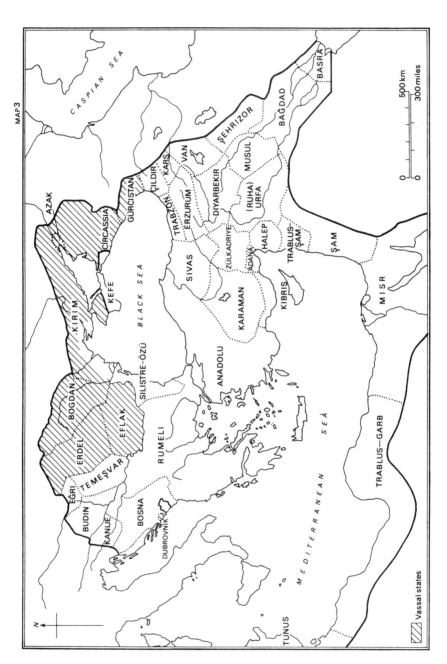

MAP 3

3 Ottoman provinces and vassal states, 1609

CASPIAN SEA

AZAK

CIRCASSIA

GÜRCISTAN

KIRIM

KEFE

ÇILDIR

KARS

VAN

ŞEHRIZOR

BAĞDAD

BASRA

ERZURUM

TRABZON

DIYARBEKIR

MUSUL

(RUHA) URFA

SILISTRE–ÖZÜ

BLACK SEA

SIVAS

ZÜLKADRIYE

ADANA

HALEP

TRABLUS–ŞAM

ŞAM

BOGDAN

ERDEL

EFLAK

KARAMAN

KIBRIS

TEMEŞVAR

ANADOLU

EĞRI

BUDIN

KANIJE

RUMELI

BOSNA

DUBROVNIK

MISR

MEDITERRANEAN SEA

TRABLUS–GARB

TUNUS

N

500 km

300 miles

Vassal states

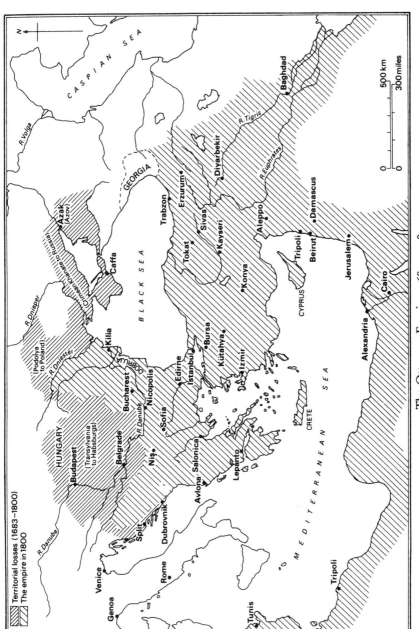

CASPIAN SEA

R.Volga

R.Dnieper

R.Dniester

(Podolya
to Poland)

Kilia

Crimea (Khanate to Russia)

Azak
(Azov)

GEORGIA

Caffa

BLACK SEA

Trabzon

Erzurum

R.Tigris

Baghdad

Diyarbekir

R.Euphrates

Sivas

Tokat

Kayseri

Aleppo

Damascus

Konya

Tripoli

Beirut

Jerusalem

Cairo

CYPRUS

Alexandria

HUNGARY

Budapest

Transylvania
(to Habsburgs)

Belgrade

Niş

Sofia

Nicopolis

Bucharest

R.Danube

R.Danube

DOBRUJA

Edirne

Istanbul

Bursa

Kütahya

İzmir

Avlona

Salonica

Lepanto

Dubrovnik

Split

Venice

Rome

Genoa

CRETE

MEDITERRANEAN SEA

Tunis

Tripoli

500 km

300 miles

N

4 The Ottoman Empire, 1683–c. 1800

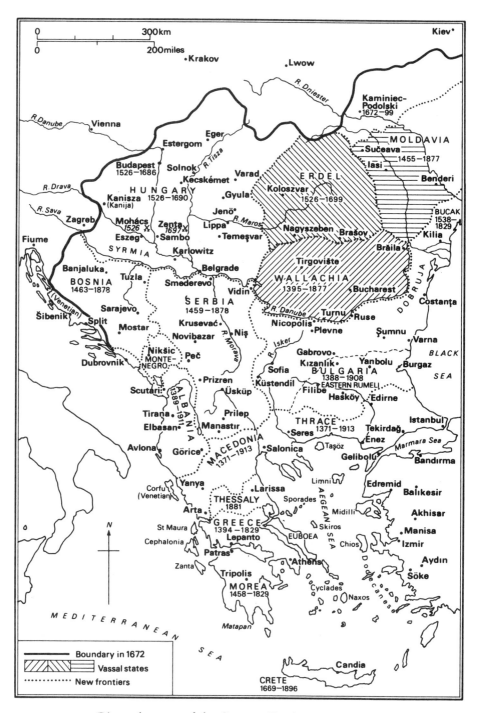

5 Dismemberment of the Ottoman Empire, 1672–1913

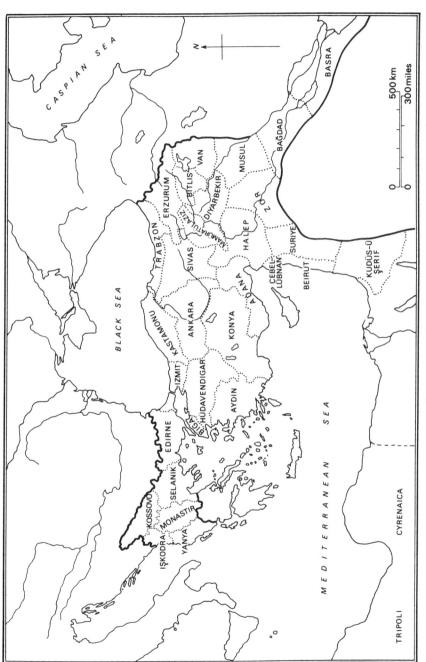

6 Ottoman provinces, c. 1900

ۿ

GENERAL INTRODUCTION

HALİL İNALCIK AND DONALD QUATAERT

These volumes summarize the field of Ottoman social and economic history and, at the same time, offer new findings and perspectives. They build on a half-century tradition of scholarship and present an area of study still in its infancy. Simultaneously, the various authors offer their own research, pushing beyond synthesis into new inquiries and analyses.

In organizing the six centuries of Ottoman history, the classical period 1300–1600 is taken as a well-defined, distinct period with an autocratic centralist government and a command economy, while in the following "decline" period, underpinnings of this traditional polity entered a process of transformation. The seventeenth century became in fact a period of transition, witnessing thorough-going changes. The Köprülüs' attempt to restore the traditional autocratic centralist system totally failed during the disastrous war period from 1683 to 1699. The eighteenth century saw a radically changed Ottoman Empire with the rise of local powers under provincial notables and "dynasties," decentralized, so to speak. The central government followed "liberal" policies not only in the administration of the empire but also in landholding and economy in general. Also, there occurred a radical change in the attitude of the Ottomans toward Europe and its civilization. The Ottomans, for the first time, now admitted the Europeans' superiority and began to imitate and borrow western ways. This led to increasing Ottoman dependence on Western powers for survival. The nineteenth century witnessed gaining momentum in Ottoman dependence on the West, both politically and economically, and in radical westernization reforms.

In our volumes, these four periods – 1300 to 1600 and the seventeenth, eighteenth and nineteenth centuries respectively – have each been prepared by one specialist independently; but the unity of approach is

xxxvii

secured by a common plan presenting the period in its political, economic and social aspects.

The individual chapters are substantially expanded with tables providing detailed statistical data. A genealogical table, general chronology, a list of weights and measures (in volume I), and a glossary (in transcription) are also included. Bibliographies at the end of each author's section are designed to provide the basic literature on the period discussed. In the books, the authors hope the reader will be able to follow the metamorphosis of an empire as a whole, as viewed in its basic aspects.

Hopefully, our volumes will be invaluable for a time and, by the force of its own syntheses and new research, be superseded in the not too distant future. Their publication makes clear the accomplishments and shortcomings of a maturing field that is exploring the social and economic structures of an empire whose legacy has been overlooked for much of the twentieth century. This neglect has been part of a more general attitude that has ignored the Ottoman influence on the present, however powerful it may have been. The decades-long neglect seems doubly odd since the work of some eminent earlier historians, such as William Langer's *The diplomacy of imperialism* (1935) placed the İstanbul-based empire at the very center of European history (in this case political). Recently, the Ottoman past has begun to receive the attention merited by its actual historical role. Take, for example, the commercial success of the flawed *Peace to end all peace* (1989) by David Fromkin, that examines the Middle East regions of the empire during the World War I period. The accelerating interest in the Ottoman experience should be reinforced considerably by the events of the early 1990s, including those in southeastern Europe and the emergence of Turkey as an international power astride Europe, the Middle East and Central Asia. Empires do fall but the residues of their influence linger on.

Until World War II, studies of Ottoman history dealt almost exclusively with military and political events. This focus generally derived from the emphasis then prevailing in European historiography. More particularly, the Ottomans represented for Europeans primarily a military intrusion, requiring latter-day crusades that haunted the Western memory. After c. 1945, interest shifted to the economic and social aspects of the Ottoman historical experience, in part because of better access to the Ottoman archives. The new focus also derived from the growing emphasis on social and economic history in the West. That is, as before, trends in Ottoman historiography followed those set in other areas of historical research.

Fernand Braudel's *La Méditerranée et le monde méditerranéen à l'époque de Philippe II* (1949) can be taken as a watershed, presenting the Ottoman Empire as an integral part of the Mediterranean world, not only in the struggle for hegemony but also in economic relations. In earlier works, notably in Wilhelm Heyd's classic, *Histoire du commerce du Levant* (1936), the Ottomans' role in Mediterranean trade is viewed solely from its European (in this case, Italian) partner's vantage point; thus, developments affecting their position in the Levant are judged negatively without taking into account positive effects that might have accrued to people in the region itself. Little note was given to the fact that the Ottomans did not aim to destroy the Italian trade in the Levant, but rather sought to control and profit from it, which meant eliminating the Latin domination and exploitation that had been established during the period of Byzantine decline. That is, among its other contributions, this work attempts to present events from the Ottoman perspective. It offers the Ottomans as agents capable of independent and internally consistent actions and not, as had been the case for too long, as passive spectators of a European drama.

Also, it can be said, without exaggeration, that the Ottoman superpower in the East substantially contributed to the shaping of modern Europe. For example, when a decisive struggle developed against Venice and its powerful Habsburg allies who then dominated Europe, the Ottomans did not hesitate to extend the same capitulatory commercial privileges to France, England and the Dutch that it earlier had bestowed on the Venetian Republic. This Ottoman re-orientation proved to be a decisive turning point for the initial mercantilist–capitalist expansion of these rising Western nation-states. (It also, obviously, was important for the Ottoman economy.) From then on, every European country aspiring to mercantilist expansion, as a prerequisite for its economic development, sought these economic privileges from the sultan. The West depended, at least at the beginning, on supplies from or through the Ottoman Empire for its newly rising silk and cotton industries. The first successful chartered companies in the West were the Levant companies.

The Ottoman Empire's economic significance in world trade, so far understated by historians, is dramatized in this study. The various authors, on the one hand, trace trade patterns long forgotten by historians in the West. For example, while the horizontal trade route in the Mediterranean through the Middle East to Venice or Genoa was considered the main trade link with Arabia and India, a vertical south–north international trade route through Damascus – Bursa – Akkerman – Lwow had

also developed through Ottoman territories, beginning c.1400. The so-
called oriental goods, including spices, silks and cotton goods, reached
Poland, the Baltic countries and Muscovy through this route. Further to
the east, Hungary and Slovakia through the Danubian ports and Brašov
in Transylvania were another market for the south–north trade. At times,
Hungary received more spices through this route than through Venice.
On these points, Ottoman customs registers were found to have fully
supported the findings of Polish, Hungarian and Romanian historians.

The authors, on the other hand, track the shifting importance of the
trade in its global context. In the sixteenth century, the Ottoman Empire
played a determining role in world trade. The empire's far-flung adventures – on the Volga river, in the Mediterranean, in Azerbaijan and the
Caspian Sea, in Yemen, Aden and Diu, in Sumatra and Mombasa – all had
economic implications. Ottoman military actions were closely connected
with economic – fiscal issues, such as the control of the Tabriz – Bursa
silk route, the Akkerman – Lwow route, the Black Sea sources of food
and construction materials for İstanbul, and Yemen and Aden for the
Indian trade. The battle of Lepanto (1571), and the advent of the English
and Dutch in the Mediterranean (1580–90), marked the beginning of the
empire's reduction to a regional state. At the same time, the rise of the
Atlantic economy, with America's huge supplies of cheap silver, cotton
and sugar, and above all Europe's aggressive mercantilism, caused the
collapse of the Ottoman monetary system, triggering dramatic changes
in the seventeenth century. Subsequently, the relative importance of
Ottoman foreign trade to the global economy declined although, after c.
1750, its volume actually rose, especially during the period 1750–1850.
International trade rose to greater heights than ever before in Ottoman
history. Thus, by 1914, the Ottoman and Western economies were intertwined to an unprecedented degree. But, in terms of economic significance, the Ottomans had slipped from first to second-rate status.

Our examination of foreign trade justifiably stresses the dynamic Ottoman role in the world economy. At the same time, the various authors
spend considerable time examining the importance of trade within the
Ottoman frontiers, an activity that too often has been overlooked in
favor of the foreign trade. To a degree not sufficiently highlighted in the
previous literature, this intra-Ottoman trade played a vital role in the
economic life of the empire, even during its final years. Overall, tracing
the history of these domestic trade patterns over time, an emphasis that
derives from our concern to present the story from the Ottoman vantage

point, makes apparent their centuries-long continuity. And, as a corollary, we more clearly can see the disruptive impact of the territorial losses of later Ottoman times that diverted, truncated or altogether destroyed well-established domestic trading networks.

Similarly, the authors have placed considerable emphasis on the study of landholding patterns and forms of agricultural exploitation. As a result, a comprehensive picture of the crucial agrarian sector over the entire Ottoman period begins to emerge. We explain and trace the impressive continuity in small landholding patterns while also illustrating how and when large estates did emerge. Generally, we found that over time and space, large estates tended to appear in areas being brought under cultivation rather than on already settled lands. This trend was especially marked in the nineteenth century, when the state settled refugees and reluctant tribes on once nearly vacant lands. In the focus on agriculture, we contribute to a debate that has engaged historians and historical sociologists for the past several decades. The debate centered on the issue of the Ottoman social formation and the utility of the paradigms of Marx and Weber. Some of the research in our volumes suggests limits to the usefulness of these models: the Ottoman village generally was not a self-sufficient social entity independent from the city. A money economy was quite developed in the Ottoman world from an early date, and then expanded considerably in the nineteenth century. Further, smallholdings – not large estates – generated most of the marketed surplus throughout the Ottoman era. Thanks to the meticulously detailed tax and population surveys of the bureaucracy, we now see an Ottoman social formation based on the *çift-hane* in rural areas, a social system that is fully described for the first time by İnalcık in volume I. Indeed, this is the "peasant family labor farm" discussed by A. V. Chayanov as an independent mode of production.

Our treatment of manufacturing activities during the period c. 1600–1914 (we ignore the earlier period for reasons stated in the preface), extends and sometimes breaks with existing accounts in several important respects. First, the contributions by the various authors collectively offer a comprehensive account that points to remarkable continuities in the loci of manufacturing. In many cases, industrial centers flourishing c. 1600 were still active in 1914. Second, in common with the commercial and agricultural sectors, Ottoman manufacturing is seen to have possessed its own internal dynamics, creatively adapting to shifts in domestic and international conditions. Thus, sometimes new production centers but more often new production methods and/or new products appeared to retain markets or capture new opportunities. And, as in the case of trade and agriculture, the declining political fortunes of the state and the concomitant territorial losses are seen to have played a vital role in the story of Ottoman manufacturing.

In these volumes, much attention is placed on the relations of the empire with the West which intensified after the sixteenth century. The Ottoman state was the first Asian empire to experience the impact of the phenomenal rise and expansion of Europe in the economic and military fields. While the mercantilist West was keenly interested in the preservation and exploitation of this market so vital for its economy, the Habsburg and Russian empires, taking advantage of new advanced war technology, started an aggressive policy for the conquest and dismemberment of the Ottoman Empire. Thus, already in the first decades of the eighteenth century, the so-called Eastern Question appeared in European politics, putting on the agenda the issue of the very existence of the empire. In the new period, European hegemony changed the Ottoman Empire's position from dominance to mounting dependency. In an attempt to find a way out of the crisis, the Ottomans sought to alter first their military, and then their administrative organizations. So, there appeared for the Ottomans what we may call the Western Question, in the sense of a traditional Muslim society trying to determine to what extent it should follow European ways.

These military and administrative changes accompanied and accelerated increasing imports from the West, not only in weaponry but also in the artifacts of everyday life. In the eighteenth century, the substantial reduction in transport and manufacturing costs in Europe led to an unprecedented trade expansion with the Ottoman territories. During the nineteenth century, additional innovations in transportation technologies further changed the face of the land and densities of populations.

A most interesting development in the post-classical period was Ottoman "liberalism" in culture and economic issues. Capitulatory privileges were extended to all European nations. As the authors show, a liberal policy was also manifest in land possession rights, in *vakfs* and tax-farming; these entailed administrative decentralization and brought about the rise of the provincial notables and loss of the central bureaucracy's control in the provinces. In the final Ottoman century, liberalism resumed with the 1826 destruction of the Janissary protectors of guild privilege and the 1838 Anglo-Turkish Convention. Government efforts to direct the economy, after nearly wrecking it in the late eighteenth century, steadily diminished thereafter. In the nineteenth century, however, the state still attempted to intervene and protect. Administrative centralization, marked by a vast expansion in the numbers and responsibilities of bureaucrats, accompanied military changes that resulted in a state apparatus vastly larger and more powerful than that of the previous era. Wars and territorial losses, however, continued to shatter trade networks and forge new ones, profoundly affecting agricultural as well as manufacturing activities in their wake.

In brief, we have attempted to present an interpretation of the Ottoman social and economic reality in its global context from, whenever possible, new perspectives, based on original archival materials and the most recent studies derived from these same sources.

Part II

⁛

CRISIS AND CHANGE, 1590–1699

SURAIYA FAROQHI,
INSTITUT FÜR GESCHICHTE
UND KULTUR DES NAHEN ORIENTS,
MUNICH UNIVERSITY

15

·ᴄ·

THE PRINCIPAL POLITICAL EVENTS

The financial crisis of the 1580s and 1590s, with which we begin our
account of the seventeenth century as experienced by the Ottoman world,
is commonly regarded as ushering in a period of political decline, demographic crisis and economic difficulties. A distinguished Ottoman writer
of the time, Mustafa Ali of Gelibolu, wrote about the later sixteenth
century in terms of a declining efficiency of the Ottoman ruling class,
and down to the very recent past Ali's verdict has not been challenged.[1]
Other authors, when dealing with the seventeenth century in the chronological sense of the term, have dwelt upon the disadvantages of rule by
inexperienced sultans and palace ladies, even though it is generally admitted that, from 1654 onward, the grand viziers of the Köprülü family
brought about a measure of recovery. However, the gains in political
stability made during the Köprülü period did not survive the long and
exhausting Ottoman–Habsburg War of 1683–99, which is generally
regarded as the beginning of a definitive political decline.

Recent research has, however, modified this picture in certain important respects. Where "Ottoman observers of Ottoman decline" are concerned, we know today that the theme of decline was popular among
certain writers of even the late fifteenth or early sixteenth century, a
period which twentieth-century historians generally view as a time of
expansion and florescence. We are also less inclined to regard the reign
of Süleyman the Magnificent (1520–66) as a standard by which all later
history must be measured, and the system of tax grants (*timar*, *zeamet*),
the holders of which performed military or administrative services to the
Ottoman central government, as the optimum solution of all problems
affecting the empire. Feminist research has also questioned previous blan-
ket denunciations of the "Sultanate of Women."[2] As a result the seventeenth century is now regarded as a time in which significant changes

413

a time of
CHANGE, not decline!
414   *II Crisis and change, 1590–1699*

took place, changes that permitted the Ottoman polity to survive in an increasingly hostile political environment. We are at present concerned not so much with the fact that the Ottoman Empire ultimately lost its cohesion and disappeared from the political arena, as with the mechanisms which allowed Ottoman state and society to survive the first major crisis by over three hundred years. In this context, political changes which occurred during the seventeenth century played a crucial role.

COURT FACTIONS AND MILITARY REBELLIONS

Our period begins with a major military rebellion, the causes of which were economic and financial, and which Ottoman historians of the period described as the "Beylerbeyi Incident" (1589). Janissaries in İstanbul revolted when their pay was handed over in the form of much debased coin (see Ch. 16). As the officials responsible, the governor (*beylerbeyi*) of Rumelia and the chief treasurer were singled out by the rebels, and the reigning Sultan Murad III acquiesced in their execution. Thus court factions built contacts with the soldiery, either with the Janissaries or else with their rivals, the mounted soldiers attached to the central government (*sipahi*). These revolts and alliances were to repeat themselves throughout the seventeenth century. Thus when Murad IV (1623–40) was very young and the government still to a certain extent in the hands of his mother Kösem Sultan, the Grand Vizier Hüsrev Pasha attempted to regain the city of Baghdad, which Shah Abbas had conquered only a few years earlier. The grand vizier's campaign was unsuccessful; when he sent his sovereign a rhymed letter asking for reinforcements, the young sultan showed his literary skill in using the same rhyme and meter in his reply. But the contents of this poetic rescript were scarcely veiled threats, and when Hüsrev Pasha returned from the frontier, the sultan deposed him. This caused an uprising of Anatolian provincial soldiers, who finally left the places where they were stationed and marched into the capital, where they demanded the heads of seventeen people who were known to be close to the young ruler. Murad IV was forced to hand his new grand vizier, Hafız Pasha, over to the rebels, and change a number of high-level officials. But the sultan assumed that the former grand vizier had fomented the rebellion of the provincial soldiers, and got his revenge by having him strangled in Tokat (1632).

Alliances of factions within the Ottoman ruling establishment with soldiers stationed in the capital also occurred during the months of crisis which preceded the dethronement of İbrahim I (1640–48). In this case, the increasing mental deterioration of the sultan had permitted various officials enjoying the ruler's good graces to secure considerable material advantages. Finally, the commanders of the military corps felt that they had reason to fear for their own safety, and with ulema support started a rebellion. The latter began with the murder of the current grand vizier and ended with the dethronement of the sultan himself, who was killed a few days later. The rebels appointed their own candidate to the position of grand vizier. But even after the sultan's young son had been brought to the throne as Mehmed IV (1648–87), alliances of soldiers and palace factions were able to bring about sweeping changes in personnel. Thus, rebellious *sipahi*s in 1651 allied themselves with the Black Eunuchs of the Harem, arranged for the murder of the Valide Kösem Mahpeyker, who had herself relied upon Janissary support, and many Janissaries perished with her.[3] But after Mehmed Köprülü had established himself as grand vizier, he in turn used Janissary and ulema support to eliminate what he regarded as the beginnings of a *sipahi* conspiracy (1657).[4]

Particularly in those rebellions in which Ottoman rulers were deposed and/or killed, Janissaries regularly played a crucial role. An early and dramatic example was the deposition and murder of Sultan Osman II in 1622, brought about by a Janissary rebellion. The grand vizier who obtained office as a result of this rebellion was so deeply involved in palace intrigues that he even threatened the life of the young prince who in 1623, gained the throne as Murad IV. However, when after a long minority Murad IV established control over the Ottoman state apparatus in 1632, he broke the coalition of Janissaries, cavalrymen of the Porte and courtiers which for a while had threatened the sultan's political control. At a later stage, the deposition of Mehmed IV in 1687 was preceded by rebellions of front-line troops whose pay was in arrears. But the revolt only gained political momentum when the rebels allied themselves with various representatives of the Köprülü family, whom Mehmed IV apparently was trying to oust from power in order to take the reins of government into his own hands. In the same way, Sultan Mustafa II was removed from the throne in 1703 by a military rebellion of the Janissaries and armorers (*cebeci*), with allies among ulema and military-administrative officials.[5]

STUDENT REVOLTS, C. 1570–90

In the Anatolian provinces rather a different type of rebellion can be observed, whose political consequences remained more limited due to the remoteness of the rebels from all centers of power. In the second half of the sixteenth century, there had been a considerable increase in the number of students enrolled in theological schools (*medrese*), with a view toward entering a scribal, judicial or teaching career. However, opportunities were never great enough to accommodate all candidates. Moreover, inflation reduced the income of many theological schools and made material conditions extremely difficult for the poorer students. Many were driven to augment their meager resources; while poor students were permitted to beg for alms (*cerre*), collective begging from wealthy provincials easily turned into brigandage. Provincial governors mobilized troops of irregular soldiers to disperse the students, a policy resulting in great loss of life.[6]

At the same time the authorities in İstanbul alternated between wholehearted support for a policy of repression and halfhearted attempts at accommodation. Certain students in İstanbul were appointed "representatives" and were expected to maintain a liaison between their constituency and government authorities. Particularly in 1579 an attempt was made to coopt a certain section of the rebels. On the other hand, the rank and file were offered only amnesty, provided they settled down to a peasant existence. This offer was in no way inviting, and as a result, there were several resurgences of student rebellion, especially between 1579 and 1583. However, in the long run, the central government apparently eliminated the movement by sheer exhaustion of the insurgents, and the closing down of many provincial *medrese*s probably made it more difficult for low-income students to even aspire to an ulema career.[7]

CELALİ CAMPAIGNS AND THE CANBULAD REBELLION, 1590–1610

Much more serious, from a military point of view, were the uprisings of provincial administrators and the irregular soldiers, armed with musketry, which the former were expected to recruit (see Ch. 16). In the closing years of the sixteenth century, certain leaders of mercenary troops were able to traverse all of Anatolia, set siege to major fortified towns, and even take some of the most important ones, such as Bursa and Urfa. Thus Kara Yazıcı (the Black Scribe), who had started his career as a household officer in a pasha's service, began his rebellion in 1599, gaining a major victory over the government forces that had been sent against him. After taking over the fortress of Urfa in southeastern Anatolia, he obtained legitimation by appointments to various official positions. But at the same time his enemies among Anatolian provincial administrators forced him first to abandon Urfa for central Anatolia and later flee to the hills near Samsun, where he died after a short time.[8]

Kara Yazıcı's rebellion demonstrates the divisions within the central government with respect to policy *vis-à-vis* the major Celali chiefs; for without the support of İstanbul, Kara Yazıcı could not possibly have held out as long as he did. However, from the viewpoint of certain viziers, it seemed practical to pacify individual Celali chiefs in order to deal with them piecemeal. At the same time, important Celalis such as Kara Yazıcı, whose main pretext for rebellion was the need to feed their mercenaries, easily could be integrated into the system, for, when they were given public office, the need of rebellion disappeared. In the long run, the policy of pacification was successful with respect to the more prominent rebels. However, given the basic demands and needs of the mercenaries, which constituted the driving force in these rebellions, the defeat of a particular leader did not preclude future risings.

Among the other Anatolian military rebellions of the period, that of Kalenderoğlu was one of the more dangerous from the administration's point of view. Kalenderoğlu did not operate alone, but had gained an ally outside of Anatolia, namely Canbuladoğlu Ali Pasha, a provincial governor turned rebel. Ali Pasha had made preparations for the establishment of a separate state in northern Syria with the help of the duke of Tuscany, to whom he promised significant commercial privileges in return for support. A fully-fledged campaign, led by the Grand Vizier Kuyucu Murad Pasha, finally suppressed this rebellion in 1607.[9]

THE REBELLION OF MA'NOĞLU FAHREDDİN, 1613–35

The pattern of Canbuladoğlu Ali Pasha's Syrian uprising was replicated, a number of years later, in the rebellions of his one-time ally, the Druze leader Fahreddin Ma'n. After having obtained control over the two port towns of Beirut and Sayda (Sidon), the latter put considerable pressure on the Ottoman governors of Damascus and Trablusşam (Tripolis in Syria). In order to maintain his semi-independent power against Ottoman political and military action, Fahreddin established good relations not only with the duke of Tuscany, but also with the Pope and the Spanish viceroy of Naples.[10] In 1613 Fahreddin visited Italy in person to inaugurate an offensive alliance against the Ottomans, which did not, however, materialize. The Druze leader returned to Lebanon in 1618; further disputes with Ottoman governors, in which he was abandoned by his Florentine allies, eventually led to his capture and execution in 1635.[11] The defeat of the Ma'n family spelled the end of "indirect rule" through local families in Ottoman Syria, and ushered in a period of intensified central control (see also Ch. 18).

THE AGE OF REBELLIOUS GOVERNORS

Later rebellions of provincial governors include those led by Abaza Mehmed Pasha, a life-long enemy of the Janissaries. When deposed from his governorship of Erzurum in 1623, he mounted a campaign to avenge the murder of Sultan Osman II which had occurred the previous year. In terms of the power politics of the day, Abaza Mehmed Pasha was fighting Janissary dominance over İstanbul and the Ottoman central administration, which was well-nigh absolute between 1622 and 1656. Tensions between the capital and the provinces during this period were therefore often acted out as conflicts between the İstanbul Janissaries and their opponents in the provinces. It is probable that Abaza's rebellion should be seen in this context. Mehmed Pasha's campaign traversed all of Anatolia; he succeeded in taking Bursa but failed to enter the capital.[12] Retreating once again into central Anatolia, he lost a battle against the grand vizier near Kayseri, but was pardoned and reappointed governor of Erzurum. However, his continuing hostility to the Janissaries led to a further rebellion in 1627, which was defeated by Hüsrev Pasha on his way to the Iranian frontier.[13] After a second pardon, Abaza Mehmed Pasha was transferred to various Rumelian posts, where he continued his struggle against the Janissaries until his execution by Murad IV in 1634.

Another rebellious governor of the time was Abaza Hasan Pasha. His power base was located among the Turkomans of Anatolia, whose governor (*voyvoda*) he became several times at different stages of his career. Moreover, Abaza Hasan Pasha had tied his fortunes to those of İpşir Mustafa Pasha, also of Abaza background, who in 1654 was appointed to the grand vizierate, because it was hoped that this would prevent him from causing further trouble in the provinces.[14] After the execution of his patron within a year of his appointment (1655), Abaza Hasan Pasha continued his struggle in the provinces, which now was directed principally against Grand Vizier Mehmed Köprülü. Hasan Pasha finally was killed, shortly after having gained a major victory against government forces in 1658.[15] His defeat ushered in a period of comparative calm, which lasted until the upheavals of the 1683–99 war. In the rebellions of this governor, involvement with Abaza patronage networks and ties to Anatolian nomads overlaid the normal pressures originating with his mercenaries.

Rivalries between the Janissaries and other members of the recognized military corps on the one hand, and mercenaries of peasant background (*sekban*) on the other, reached a culmination point during the rebellions associated with the name of Yeğen Osman Ağa.[16] When the Janissaries who had been defeated on the Rumelian front marched upon İstanbul in 1687, demanding the deposition of Sultan Mehmed IV, the latter tried to neutralize his opponents by appointing Yeğen Osman Ağa, a self-made commander of *sekban*, to hold them in check. This proved beyond Yeğen Osman's powers, and Mehmed IV was deposed. However, Mehmed IV's successor, Süleyman II (1687–91), continued the same policy, appointing Yeğen Osman Pasha governor-general of Rumelia and commander of the crucially important anti-Habsburg front. Yeğen Osman Pasha then made a determined bid for the grand vizierate. The incumbent grand vizier countered this move by having all *sekban* corps outlawed, and those soldiers unwilling to disperse were threatened with execution. In Anatolia local militias already had begun a battle of their own against the mercenaries, and civil war ensued. By a sudden change in their political fortunes, the *sekban* regained the upper hand in Anatolia, thus allowing Yeğen Osman Pasha to prepare for another march on İstanbul. This was followed by a further *volte-face* of the Ottoman central administration; Yeğen Osman Pasha was captured and killed. However, this did not mean the end of the *sekban* rebellions, which in 1698 even led to a short-lived agreement by which the sultan extended guarantees to the *sekban* in exchange for future good behavior. The agreement speedily was broken; and rebellions of musketeer mercenaries continued, under a variety of names, throughout the eighteenth century.

POLITICAL CRISIS IN İSTANBUL AND THE KÖPRÜLÜ RESTORATION, 1654–91

Apart from the internal tensions described above, the Venetian menace to the Dardanelles during the early stages of the Cretan war led Valide Turhan to arrange, in 1654, the appointment of Köprülü Mehmed Pasha as grand vizier. The latter had built a long but not particularly outstanding career for himself as an administrator, but nevertheless possessed a reputation for extraordinary energy. As a precondition for his appointment he demanded that both the valide and the sultan himself grant him extraordinary powers: all measures advocated by him were to be accepted by the sultan, the suggestions of lower-level officials, even other viziers, to be automatically rejected if they conflicted with his own. Moreover, the new grand vizier was to be given a free hand where appointments were concerned, and was to a certain extent protected in his tenure of office by the stipulation that the sultan was not to listen to his grand vizier's enemies. Köprülü Mehmed Pasha then defeated the Venetian navy blockading the Dardanelles, reestablished the central government's control over Anatolia, and, with a great deal of bloodshed, broke all opposition to his policies on the part of the Porte cavalry.

After the grand vizier had died in 1661, his son Fazıl Ahmed assumed the office and held it until his own death in 1676. The latter was able to continue the sequence of military successes by which the Köprülü period is known. Thus the conquest of Podolia, by which the Ottoman Empire reached its greatest territorial extension, was achieved under this grand vizier (1672–76), who completed the conquest of Crete by the taking of Candia (1669). The power of the Köprülü as a major political household continued after Fazıl Ahmed Pasha's death in 1676, with the appointment of his younger brother Fazıl Mustafa Pasha as grand vizier in 1689; Fazıl Mustafa Pasha held this office until his death in the battle of Slankamen in 1691. Moreover, in the intervening years the most influential grand vizier had been Kara Mustafa Pasha, raised in the Köprülü household and married to a daughter of Köprülü Mehmed Pasha. After Fazıl Mustafa Pasha's death, a Köprülü grand vizier once again was appointed, namely Amcazade Hüseyin Pasha, who held the office between 1698 and 1702 and thus presided over the negotiations of Karlowitz, even though he did not himself participate in them. It also appears that some of the surviving Köprülüs were active in the rebellion which led to the deposition of Mustafa II in 1703, and in the eighteenth century, certain members of this family continued to be appointed to high office.[17]

IRANIAN WARS, 1603–39

On the Iranian frontier, a long war had ended in 1590, leaving Azerbaijan in Ottoman hands. However, in the closing years of the sixteenth century, Shah Abbas had consolidated his power recruiting an army of *gulam*, modeled upon the Ottoman *kul* or "servitors" of the sultan to supplement and ultimately supplant the tribal levies of the Kızılbaş.[18]

With this force he captured Tabriz in 1603, taking advantage of the fact that the Celali rebellions greatly limited Ottoman capacity for retaliation.[19] After the Iranian conquest of Erivan (Revan) a few months later, Cigalazade Sinan Pasha was appointed commander of the Ottoman armies, but lost the battle of Van and later that of Lake Urmiye (Nov. 1605), which permitted Shah Abbas to reconquer Ganja and Shirvan.[20] Thereby the shah of Iran had reestablished control over the area which had been lost to the Ottoman Empire between 1555 and 1590. Moreover, Shah Abbas was able to increase his military strength by granting hospitality to an army of about 15,000 Celalis, among others the famous Kalenderoğlu, who had fled from the Grand Vizier Kuyucu Murad Pasha. However, these troops, who caused considerable problems to the Iranian authorities due to their lack of discipline, for the most part returned to Anatolia after an amnesty had been proclaimed by Nasuh Pasha in 1610. In 1612, hostilities officially were terminated, and Shah Abbas was able to retain his recent conquests, which were guaranteed to him against payment of a yearly tribute of 200 loads of silk. This peace was renewed in 1618, after a campaign commanded by the Ottoman vizier Halil Pasha had resulted in a major defeat for the latter's army.[21]

Peace only lasted for five years. In 1623 the *subaşı* of Baghdad, Bekir Pasha, after a revolt, placed himself under the protection of Shah Abbas, but after a short while returned to his Ottoman allegiance. Shah Abbas used this opportunity to besiege Baghdad, which he took in 1624; a large part of the Sunni population was murdered and the sanctuaries of Abu Hanifa and Abdulkadir Gilani, which were particularly venerable to Ottoman Sunnis, suffered wholesale plundering.[22]

Shah Abbas' forces conquered Mosul a few weeks later, and thus the Ottoman presence in Iraq was limited to a small garrison in Basra. However, an epidemic and a revolt of some Arab tribes soon led to a reversal of military fortunes and Mosul again passed into Ottoman hands. But an Ottoman siege of Baghdad in 1626 ended in complete failure.[23] The rebellion of Abaza Pasha in Erzurum, moreover, furnished an opportunity for bringing Iranian influence to bear on Ottoman internal affairs; Abaza Pasha had at one time proclaimed his allegiance to the shah, and an armed contingent was sent out from Iran to support him.[24]

After Sultan Murad IV had reached majority, the recovery of Baghdad was pursued with renewed urgency. A second Ottoman siege in 1630 produced no results, and Shah Abbas' successor Shah Safi even conquered the fortress of Hille. Once he had established political control in his capital, Murad IV therefore took the field in person against the Iranians;

the campaign of 1635 resulted in the conquest of Erivan, which was, however, retaken by an Iranian force in the following year. A second campaign, undertaken in 1638, led the Ottoman forces to Baghdad, which surrendered just before the final assault. Restoration of the mausolea of İmam Azam and Abdülkadir Gilani marked the Ottoman takeover. A peace concluded in Kasr-ı Şirin in 1639 determined the Ottoman–Iranian borders, and the demarcation agreed upon at this time was in later centuries frequently used as a basis for peace negotiations.[25]

THE "LONG WAR" AND THE PEACE OF ZSITVA-TÖROK, 1593–1606

Older accounts of the Celali rebellions have often linked the beginning of these uprisings to the major Ottoman victory in the "Long War" between Habsburgs and Ottomans (1593–1606): those soldiers who had fled from the battlefield of Mezsokerestes in 1596 were deprived of their livings, and supposedly initiated the Anatolian rebellions. But it now is generally recognized that the Celali uprisings were well under way before the fugitives from the Hungarian war returned to Anatolia. Rather the war in Hungary, if anything, provided an at least temporary solution for political problems in Anatolia; thus one of the major rebels in 1603 was appointed governor-general of Bosnia and set out for the Rumelian front, thus making further repressive measures unnecessary.[26]

Apart from the battle of Mezsokerestes, the "Long War" consisted of a series of sieges. Thus the Ottomans conquered Raab in 1594, but the Habsburg armies retook the place in 1598. Szekesfehervar was lost to the Habsburgs in 1601 and reconquered the following year.[27] International conflict was complicated by civil war when Hungarian nobles, led by the prince of Transylvania, Stephen Bocskai, rose in rebellion against Habsburg rule over those Hungarian counties which remained in Christian hands after the conquests of Kanuni Süleyman. Bocskai refused to call himself king of Hungary in the Central European context; however he accepted this title from Sultan Ahmed I in 1605 and was crowned by the Grand Vizier Lala Mehmed Pasha.[28] Bocskai made his peace with the Habsburg emperor shortly before his death the following year; but the event proved the fragility of Habsburg rule in the Hungarian borderlands.

The peace of Zsitva-Török, concluded in 1606 and extended a number of times between 1615 and 1663, has given rise to varying interpretations among diplomatic historians.[29] Thus it has been debated whether this agreement did in fact embody recognition of the Habsburg ruler as the diplomatic equal of the Ottoman sultan. Divergent interpretations are encouraged by differences between the Hungarian and Ottoman Turkish texts of the agreement, which involved, among other things, the question of tribute: the Habsburg side offered 200,000 florins as a once-and-for-all payment, while the Ottoman text foresaw that tribute was merely to be interrupted, and resumed after three years. However in seventeenth-century practice, tribute payments were allowed to lapse in favor of more or less equal exchanges of gifts between the two rulers. More important than the details of the agreement was apparently the fact that a cessation of hostilities served the interests of both parties. The Habsburgs in the following years faced serious domestic opposition, while from the Ottoman viewpoint, conflicts with Poland and Iran, in addition to internal rebellion, made a cessation of hostilities on the Hungarian front appear desirable. As a result, the peace of Zsitva-Török stabilized conditions on the Habsburg–Ottoman frontier for half a century.

THE CRETAN CRISIS, 1654–69

Compared to the level of activity of the Ottoman navy in the sixteenth century, the number of naval campaigns declined during the post-1590 period. The conquest of Crete constituted the one major naval action of the seventeenth century. The largest Mediterranean island yet remaining in Venetian hands, Crete was inhabited by an Orthodox peasantry under the control of a "Latin" aristocracy who professed Roman Catholicism. The duality of religion increased the distance between rulers and ruled on the island. From the Ottoman point of view, Crete in Venetian hands threatened communications with Egypt, particularly since the corsairs of the Order of Malta in certain instances received support from the Venetian authorities on the island. Moreover, the difficulties experienced by Venice after the drastic downturn of her trade in the early seventeenth century must also have been known in İstanbul. However, political tensions within the Ottoman government during the reign of the young Mehmed IV hampered the conduct of the war; at the same time the Venetian navy was still well led and reasonably efficient. Thus, while the greater part of the island was conquered in 1645–46, the siege of the fortress of Candia itself continued until 1669. Since both sides were forced to supply and replenish the forces which they entertained on the island, the war also turned into a trial of strength between the two navies. In 1656 a major battle was fought within sight of Çanakkale, in which the Ottoman fleet was decimated and the islands of Limni and Bozcaada (Tenedos) were briefly occupied by the Venetians. The breaking of the Venetian blockade of the Dardanelles was Köprülü Mehmed Pasha's first achievement as grand vizier. Venice was able to sustain the expenditure of war due to subsidies from the Popes and intermittent aid from the corsair state of Malta. Unofficial help moreover was sent by the French king Louis XIV; an illegitimate descendant of Henry IV of France for a while commanded the French contingent, shortly before the conquest of Candia was completed by Grand Vizier Köprülüzade Ahmed Pasha.[30]

THE HABSBURGS, TRANSYLVANIA AND HUNGARIAN POLITICS BEFORE 1683

During the "Long War" of 1593–1606, a role of some importance had been played by the rulers of Transylvania, one of the buffer states between the Ottoman and Habsburg empires, which had remained an Ottoman tributary state ever since the campaigns of Mehmed the Conqueror and Kanuni Süleyman. However Transylvania, with its population of Hungarian nobles, German mining towns and a depressed Rumanian Orthodox peasantry, also maintained ties to Habsburg-held Hungary, and during the Long War sided with the Habsburgs. In the early stages of the Thirty Years' War (1618–48), the Transylvanian ruler Bethlen Gabor, himself a Protestant, emerged as a contender for major political power.[31] Bethlen Gabor could count upon a sizable number of sympathizers among the Protestant nobility of Hungary, discontented by the succession of Ferdinand II to the imperial dignity, as the latter was known for his intense and militant support for the Catholic religion.

Bethlen Gabor persuaded Sultan Osman II to accept a protectorate over the Hungarians still under Habsburg rule (1620). The sultan was to side with the rebellious Hungarian estates and support them by the dispatch of troops, which were to attack not only the emperor's lands, but Poland as well.[32] In exchange the border fortresses of Vác (Waitzen) were to be surrendered to the Ottomans. Moreover, due to Bethlen Gabor's efforts, the Ottoman Empire became the one and only ally of great-power status which the rebellious Bohemian estates could muster after they had shaken off Habsburg rule and elected Frederick V as a Protestant king. Frederick offered an Ottoman ambassador dispatched to Prague both faithful allegiance and yearly tribute payments, and these offers were confirmed by a full-scale embassy to İstanbul (Nov. 1620).[33] However, Ottoman commitments to a war in Poland, in addition to concerns about the Iranian frontier, militated against rapid aid to the Bohemian rebels. By November 1620, the battle of the White Mountain, which resulted in the annihilation of Frederick V's and the Bohemian estates' army, had rendered pointless any plans for Ottoman military intervention.

Thus, throughout the beginning years of the seventeenth century, the Ottoman Empire was deeply involved in the politics of the Christian states of Central Europe. This involvement lapsed between 1620 and 1660, only to be resumed when the restoration of Ottoman power under the Köprülüs once again made an expansive policy seem feasible. In Transylvania, Prince George Rakoczi attempted to engage in European power politics on a fairly grand scale: he participated in the Northern War, maintained close links to Mazarin's France, and in 1657 invaded Poland. This invasion did not possess the authorization of Rakoczi's Ottoman suzerain. When the prince returned from Poland without having achieved any conquests, he found himself confronted with a punitive expedition on the part of the Crimean Tatars, who carried out the sultan's commands and at the same time made use of a welcome opportunity to gain booty in Hungary. Rakoczi's military adventures were no more agreeable to the Habsburg ruler than they were to the Ottomans, for they raised the specter of an Ottoman–Habsburg war, for which the emperor and his ministers were in no way prepared. The Transylvanian prince was ultimately forced to abdicate, but it was too late to stave off an Ottoman campaign, which resulted in the annexation of a number of fortress towns (1658). The situation in Transylvania remained explosive; after a further Ottoman campaign in 1660, a fifth Ottoman governorship (*vilayet*) was instituted on Hungarian territory, which confirmed Habsburg suspicions: not only would a Transylvania fully integrated into the Ottoman Empire increase the probability of noble rebellions in Habsburg Hungary, it was also assumed that this was only the prelude to an Ottoman conquest of whatever Hungarian territory the Habsburgs still controlled.[34]

A full-scale Ottoman campaign against the Habsburg domains was undertaken in 1663. The emperor had hastily assembled allies from among the German princes. Limited support also came from France, juridically disguised as a contingent from the "Rhine Federation," an organization formed by the French king and certain princes on the western borders of the Reich. A battle ensued near the monastery of St. Gotthard on the Raab, in the area where the passage from Ottoman into Austrian territories was easiest. The Ottoman army's attempt to cross the river miscarried and the resulting losses induced the grand vizier to conclude a twenty-year peace in 1664, which did in fact last until the Vienna campaign of 1683.[35]

Where Hungarian affairs in the narrower sense of the word were concerned (Transylvania's nobility and peasantry contained a strong Hungarian component, but the country was not considered part of Hungary proper), Ottoman intervention was invited by certain nobles of Habsburg-held Hungary. The latter, for the most part Protestant, were concerned about the Habsburg emperor's abolition of the privileges which their estate had possessed since the Middle Ages. In 1667–68, these "Malcontents," as they are called, asked the Ottoman grand vizier, Köprülüzade Ahmed Pasha, for aid in a projected rebellion, which the grand vizier refused due to his involvement with the conquest of Candia. The Hungarian conflict was exacerbated by the fact that the Habsburg emperor, Leopold I, in line with the traditions of his dynasty, attempted to enforce the Counter Reformation in the Hungarian territories under his control. By abolishing the right of his Protestant subjects to maintain schools and preachers, the emperor and his bishops aimed at eliminating Protestantism as a religion from the eastern Habsburgs' domains. Thus the religious question gave the rebellions of certain Hungarian magnates a popular backing. Particularly the Protestant nobleman E. Tokoly engaged in guerrilla resistance. However in 1681, already under the impact of an impending Ottoman–Habsburg war, Leopold I was persuaded to make substantial concessions both in constitutional and in religious matters. This left Tokoly isolated in Hungary, whereupon he gave his full backing to an Ottoman invasion of Habsburg-held territory, while also receiving French aid due to the diversion that he caused on the Habsburgs' eastern frontiers. Only after the collapse of the Vienna campaign in 1683 did Tokoly lose his value as an ally and instrument of Ottoman politics.[36]

POLAND, THE UKRAINE AND MUSCOVY, 1600–81

While the Habsburgs always remained the principal opponents of the Ottomans in Europe, the expansion of Poland into the Ukraine, and the conflict between Cossacks recognizing Polish suzerainty and their Tatar opponents, provided opportunities for Ottoman intervention in Eastern Europe. The Cossacks were frontiersmen, at times serving the Russian or Polish-Lithuanian rulers, and at other times living the lives of free-booters in the open steppe. During the early stages of Cossack history, Tatar princes seeking political asylum in Muscovy after internecine quarrels within the ruling families of the various khanates often turned into Cossack leaders. By the sixteenth century, Cossacks were usually Ukrainians and Russians; the upper stratum frequently consisted of impoverished noblemen. The rank and file were of peasant background, and enserfed Russian or Polish peasants often sought a better life in escaping to the Cossacks.[37] For summer campaigns, troops of well-armed and mounted men left for the border areas. They elected their chiefs (*hetman*); while on campaign, supplies and arms were shared whenever necessary. From the nobles' point of view, the Cossacks remained a constant challenge to generalized peasant serfdom and thus were a force to be contained as much as possible, even though they remained indispensable for frontier warfare.

On the other hand, the campaigns of the Cossacks, who attacked the southern coasts of the Black Sea and even villages in the immediate vicinity of İstanbul in small and fast ships, tended to embroil the Polish kings with the Ottoman Empire. In 1621 such a conflict resulted in major warfare: Sultan Osman II appeared before Hotin, one of the principal towns of Podolia, at that time a Polish possession. He was unable to take the town; yet the peace treaty stipulated that the depredations of Cossacks against Ottoman territory were to cease. This agreement did not end Cossack marauding. Apart from further attacks on the Bosphorus area in 1624 and 1626, the Ottoman navy in 1634 was forced to fight a major battle with a Cossack flotilla near Varna.[38]

Other long-term tensions between the Cossacks and the Polish king and nobility were of a religious nature. In Poland, during the first half of the seventeenth century, the ruler and magnates, similar to the Habsburg rulers, attempted to establish Roman Catholicism as the dominant religious faith; in the Ukrainian territories the peasantry was generally Orthodox. An enforced "union" between the two churches in 1596, which served as a pretext for bringing newly established Orthodox schools and printing presses under Catholic control, led to considerable friction and in the long run constituted one of the reasons for a major Cossack uprising in 1648. The leader of the Cossack rebellion, the *hetman* Chmelnickij, at first attempted an alliance with the Tatars and the Ottoman sultan. But in 1653 he accepted the overlordship of Muscovy, so that, in a battle fought in 1655, a Polish–Tatar and Russo-Cossack alliance confronted one another.[39] In the long run, this constellation permitted the Czars to obtain control of the Ukraine, oust the Crimean Tatars, eliminate the Ottoman Empire as the Tatars' suzerain, and eradicate the Polish–Lithuanian presence in the area.

But in the short run the armistice of Andrussowo, which ended the Russo-Polish War in 1667, established a division of the Ukraine into a western (Polish) and an eastern (Russian) area. In the following year, the *hetman* of the "Polish" Cossacks, Doroshenko, opted for Ottoman protection. A war ensued between the Ottoman Empire and Poland, in which Grand Vizier Köprülüzade Ahmed Pasha led an army into Podolia and conquered the key fortress of Kaminiecz-Podolski. An armistice concluded in 1672 foresaw the establishment of an Ottoman province in Podolia, a continued Ottoman protectorate over the Cossacks of the western Ukraine, Polish tribute payments and removal of most of the Polish population from Ottoman-held territories.

However, the newly elected Polish king Jan Sobieski refused to accept these conditions and the war continued, until large parts of the Ukraine were turned into a virtual desert. A peace treaty, concluded in 1676, returned a minor part of Podolia to the Polish king and eliminated the tribute.[40] War between Russia and the Ottoman Empire for control of the eastern Ukraine continued until 1681; in this case the desertification of the area under dispute was recognized by the terms of the treaty itself. A no-man's-land was to separate Russian and Crimean territories, and neither side was permitted to either settle or fortify it.[41]

THE OTTOMAN-HABSBURG WAR, 1683–99

The peace of Zuravno between Poland and the Ottoman Empire had been concluded at least partly through the mediation of French diplomats. It was the aim of French diplomacy during these years, in which the regime of Louis XIV arrived at a stage of maturity, to free the Ottoman Empire from entanglements with European states other than the Austrian Habsburgs. Ottoman–Habsburg conflict was beneficial to the interest of Louis XIV by diverting Habsburg attention from the frontier zone between France and the German territories, where Louis had embarked on a policy of piecemeal annexations. Sobieski had been elected king of Poland as head of the French faction within the Polish nobility, and thus represented an anti-Habsburg policy. But in a *coup d'état*, Sobieski in 1678 eliminated some of the more prominent members of the French faction from political life, discontinued support for Tokoly's Protestant rebels in Hungary, and in the hope of changing the terms of the peace of Zuravno, effected a rapprochement with the Habsburg side. Papal diplomacy had played a considerable role in encouraging this reorientation, for the Pope attempted to achieve an alliance of Christian states against the Ottomans. Given this long-term goal of papal foreign policy in the 1670s and 1680s, French and papal diplomacy generally operated at cross-purposes. On the other hand, the Austrian rulers could count on appreciable financial support from Rome.[42]

Less is known about the political tensions within Ottoman ruling circles that pushed Sultan Mehmed IV into embarking upon renewed war with the Habsburgs. Some stress has been laid upon the insecurity of Merzifonlu Kara Mustafa's position at court, which supposedly resulted in his undertaking the siege of Vienna even though Mehmed IV had not given his prior consent. The impact of the sultan's preacher, Vani Efendi, who played an active part during the siege of Vienna in 1683, also must be taken into account. Moreover, French diplomacy after the arrival of Louis XIV's new ambassador, Guilleragues, in 1680 continued to urge Ottoman intervention against the Habsburgs, while the still fairly-strong position of Tokoly in Hungary and Transylvania seemed to provide an opportunity for successful intervention.[43]

Due to the intervention of a relief army commanded by the Polish king Sobieski, the 1683 siege of Vienna ended in failure. During the years that followed, a war was fought over the possession of Hungary; Habsburg forces reached Belgrade in 1688. However the city was retaken soon afterwards by Grand Vizier Köprülüzade Mustafa Pasha. Venice entered the anti-Ottoman alliance in 1684 and briefly held the Morea and Athens. Moreover, in 1697 Czar Peter of Russia joined the league which had been concluded by the Austrian Habsburgs with Venice and Poland, with the aim of expanding his conquests on the north shore of the Black Sea. He arrived too late to gain substantially from this adhesion.[44] The failure of the Vienna campaign and the Hungarian war contributed to the deposition of Mehmed IV in 1687. However, only his son Mustafa II, who succeeded to the throne in 1695 after the brief reigns of two of his uncles, could take an active part in the Balkan wars. He himself led an Ottoman army in 1697, which was however completely routed in the battle of Zenta. The Ottoman chronicler Raşid blamed this defeat on bad relations between the grand vizier, a palace appointee, and other officials involved in the campaign.[45] From this time onward, negotiations for a peace were adumbrated. From the Ottoman point of view, there must have been considerable motivation to end the war before the Austrian Habsburgs, whose hands had recently been freed in Western Europe by the conclusion of the Peace of Ryswick, again turned their armies toward the Balkans. On the other hand, the impending War of the Spanish Succession, which followed the childless death of the Spanish king Charles II, made the Emperor Leopold wish for a disengagement in the Balkans.[46]

Negotiations which preceded the conclusion of peace in Karlowitz (Karlofça) embodied a concern for diplomatic equality between the powers involved; a special hall was even constructed with four symmetrical entrance gates, in order to minimize questions of precedence.[47] On the other hand, Ottoman officials of the time did not regard the peace negotiations of Karlowitz as constituting a diplomatic novelty. Admittedly, the peace was concluded upon the principle of *uti possidetis* and thus involved the loss of Hungary and of suzerainty over Transylvania. But care was taken to safeguard what, in Ottoman official parlance, was regarded as the sultan's honor. Thus Ottoman diplomats always assumed that the evacuation and/or destruction of fortresses close to the border was a device that could be used only to favor the sultan, and never to his disadvantage, and all appearances of a "dictated" peace were scrupulously avoided. Territorial losses were made palatable by reiterating the assumption inherent in Muslim religious law, namely that all peaceful understandings with unbelievers were strictly temporary, and revision of a disadvantageous treaty therefore could be expected in the immediate future. Even so, the legitimacy of Mustafa II, as the ruler who had concluded the Karlowitz treaty, was apparently undermined by the concessions which his negotiators had made to the infidel, and he was deposed in 1703.[48]

CONCLUSION

If in fact there existed a connection between Mustafa II's diplomatic concessions and the rebellion which cost him the throne, and if his father Mehmed IV was deposed due to the failure of Ottoman armies before Vienna, events on the post-1650 Rumelian frontier possessed considerable relevance in the political struggles which determined the fate of the highest Ottoman dignitaries. In the 1730s a costly war in Iran likewise precipitated the fall of Sultan Ahmed III and his grand vizier. Connections of this kind seem inherently reasonable to the modern researcher. But it is worth keeping in mind that the ageing Louis XIV of France during these same years survived a long period of military (and climatic) disasters, and that nineteenth-century Ottoman rulers maintained themselves in power even though the frontiers of the empire were constantly shrinking. It is thus worth investigating what made the Ottoman political structure of the seventeenth and early eighteenth century particularly sensitive to military reverses. Given the limited number of secondary studies at our disposal, it is not possible at present to supply satisfactory answers to this and similar questions. But by posing such problems, which may be considered as falling into the realm of political anthropology, the connection between social and political history becomes visible, and this, rather than any lingering assumptions about "the primacy of politics," is the rationale for including political history in a discussion of Ottoman social and economic life.

NOTES

1 Fleischer (1986), pp. 153ff.
2 Fleischer (1986); Pierce (1988).
3 Articles "Murad IV" in *İA* by Cavit Baysun; "Hüsrev Paşa" in *İA* by Halil İnalcık, Hammer (1827–35), V. pp. 543–48.
4 Eickhoff (1970), p. 118.
5 Abou-El-Haj (1984), pp. 22–29; 44–45.
6 Akdağ (1963), pp. 85–108.
7 Akdağ (1963), pp. 107–8.
8 *Ibid.*, pp. 190–201.
9 Griswold (1983), pp. 132–46.
10 *Ibid.*, pp.78ff.
11 Article "Fakhr al-Din" in *EI²* by Kamal Salibi; Abu Husayn (1985), pp. 67–128; Eickhoff (1970), pp. 142ff.
12 İnalcık (1980), pp. 290–98.
13 Article "Abaza" in *EI²* by Cl. Huart; de Groot (1978), pp. 74–80; article "Hüsrev Pasha" in *İA* by Halil İnalcık.
14 Aktepe (1970).
15 Article "Abaza" in *EI²* by Cl. Huart.
16 İnalcık (1980), pp. 299–300.
17 Compare the article "Köprülü" in *İA* by Tayyip Gökbilgin; Hüseyin Pasha ("Amudja-Zade") in *EI²* by Orhan Köprülü and "Karlofça" in *EI²* by Colin Heywood.
18 Savory (1970), pp. 418–19.
19 Bellan (1932), pp. 123ff.
20 Griswold (1983), pp. 104–9.
21 Bellan (1932), pp. 187–211, 241.
22 *Ibid.*, p. 280.
23 *Ibid.*
24 *Ibid.*, p. 288.

25 Article "Murad IV" in *İA* by Cavid Baysun.

26 Akdağ (1963), p. 214.

27 Parry (1976), pp. 118–20.

28 Nehring (1984).

29 Bayerle (1980); Nehring (1983).

30 Eickhoff (1970).

31 Heinisch (1974, 1975).

32 Heinisch (1974, 1975), part 2, pp. 99–100.

33 *Ibid.*, pp. 106–13.

34 Eickhoff (1970), pp. 196–227.

35 *Ibid.*, pp. 208–21.

36 Eickhoff (1970), pp. 366ff, 391–416; Barker (1982), pp. 110–40; Cenner-Wilhelmb (1983).

37 Stökl (1953), pp. 147–77; Gordon (1983), pp. 181ff.

38 Eickhoff (1970), pp. 265–72.

39 *Ibid.*, pp. 270–81.

40 Forst de Battaglia, 2nd ed. (1982), pp. 81ff; Eickhoff (1970), pp. 288–301.

41 Eickhoff (1970), p. 303.

42 Forst de Battaglia, 2nd ed. (1982), pp. 122–31; Eickhoff (1970), pp. 355ff.

43 Eickhoff (1970), p. 363.

44 Vaughan (1954), pp. 273–76.

45 Abou-El-Haj (1984), p. 54.

46 Vaughan (1954), pp. 277–78.

47 *Ibid.*, p. 278.

48 Abou-El-Haj (1984), p. 22.

16

MAKING A LIVING: ECONOMIC CRISIS AND PARTIAL RECOVERY

Fernand Braudel once commented upon the fact that where precapitalist economies and societies are concerned we know much more about the commercial sector than about agricultural or industrial production.[1] Certainly the Ottoman Empire is no exception to this rule. In fact, the production sector remains even more enigmatic than in other societies of a comparable degree of technical achievement, since the surviving documentation is to a large extent official in character. "Official" however means "connected with tax collection." But tax records are certainly not the most faithful mirror of any society, and least of all of its productive activities. Thus it is probable that the primacy of political conditions in determining economic conjuncture, which seems such an obvious fact of life to the historian of the Ottoman seventeenth century, is to a certain extent an optical illusion generated by the official character of the documentation at hand. But determining the extent of this distortion involves a fair amount of informed guesswork, and what is valid for one sector of the economy does not automatically apply to all others.

THE CELALİ REVOLTS AND THEIR SOCIO-ECONOMIC BACKGROUND

The last two decades of the sixteenth century were a period of financial, political, economic and demographic difficulties for the Ottoman Empire. As a symptom of financial crisis, there was the dramatic devaluation of the *akçe* (asper) in 1584–86, after the silver content of this coin had remained more or less stable throughout the long reign of Kanuni Süleyman (1520–66). This devaluation moreover had considerable political repercussions. In 1589, the Janissaries revolted when they found that they were to be paid in the new debased currency; they demanded and obtained the execution of the chief treasurer and other officials they regarded as responsible for the new policy. This was neither the first nor the last military rebellion; such events are known to have occurred even in the time of Mehmed the Conqueror (1451–81) and continued to recur throughout Ottoman history. But toward the end of the sixteenth and the early years of the seventeenth century, military rebellions became very frequent, and Ottoman high-level officials were obliged to take the possibility of rebellion into account in their day-to-day decision making.[2]

Military rebellion had yet another dimension. Ottoman rulers of the period engaged in a series of long wars, both on the Iranian and Habsburg frontiers. Moreover the cavalry of the *timar*-holders, who had formed the backbone of the Ottoman army in earlier centuries, was increasingly made obsolete by the ever more widespread use of firearms. Thus a major reorganization of the army became necessary, and the limited conquests that were still possible in the seventeenth century were no longer sufficient to make warfare profitable. Quite to the contrary, wars increasingly constituted a drain upon Ottoman state finances.

Under these circumstances, the Ottoman treasury tried to reduce expenditure on armed forces stationed in the provinces and more and more governors were expected to provide and pay for their own military retinues. These mercenaries were liable to lose their jobs whenever their employers were deposed, and provincial governors often stayed in office for only a short period.[3] As a result, a sizable number of armed bands roamed the Anatolian countryside in search of employment, meanwhile living off the peasants. At the same time, governors were forced to fill their purses during their tenure of office, so as to pay the mercenaries, without whom they could not hope to maintain themselves in power. This aim was usually achieved by touring the countryside and demanding a variety of *ad hoc* taxes from the peasantry. These practices, though widespread, possessed no official sanction, and in fact were vigorously condemned by the sultans of the time. Murad III, in a desperate attempt to secure the treasury's tax base, even permitted the peasants to refuse the governors and their men entry into the villages.[4] However, since these prohibitions did not abolish the governors' need for money, sultanic edicts concerning the protection of peasants generally proved difficult to enforce.

In addition, the existence of an armed retinue which they paid out of their own purses made it possible for provincial governors to rebel. This option had been much less in evidence when they only commanded the *timar*-holding cavalry, for over the latters' appointments provincial governors possessed only a limited degree of control. In some instances, the initiative to rebel might even come from the governor's mercenaries, who feared the prospect of fending for themselves on the roads. Most of these rebellions were aimed at having a deposed governor reinstated in office, or resulted from the latter's demand to be promoted to a more prestigious post. However, at least Canbuladoğlu Ali Pasha, whose 1607 rebellion was centered upon northern Syria, went much further, as the latter actually planned to set up a state of his own.[5] In Canbuladoğlu's case, his ambitions are revealed by documents in Florentine archives, since Ali Pasha had planned to grant the Florentines extensive commercial privileges in return for their political support. It is not impossible that certain other rebels of this period had similar ambitions, but our information on this issue is limited indeed.

The mercenaries (*levent*) serving Ottoman governors were generally former villagers. It has been suggested in the past that population pressure drove peasants from their holdings and into mercenary bands, but most recent researchers disagree with this hypothesis.[6] On balance it seems unlikely that Anatolia as a whole was sufficiently populated to make explanations based on population pressure seem credible, even though the situation may have been different in certain limited areas.[7] Overall Anatolian population, in spite of a substantial increase in the course of the sixteenth century, was probably not yet dense enough for the symptoms of agricultural over-population to emerge on a major scale.[8] Thus it now seems that the "pull" of outside employment opportunities, both as mercenaries and as urban producers, was more significant in promoting emigration from the village than the "push" of rural congestion. However, once villages were being over-taxed by the exactions of provincial administrators, the insecurity of the countryside must have constituted a considerable push factor in its own right.

To a certain extent unrest in the Anatolian countryside took on the form of a conflict between the overwhelmingly Muslim tax-paying peasants (or *reaya*, as both they and their Christian counterparts were called in the sources of the time) and the tax-exempt military establishment. Soldiers and their commanders, considered slaves of the sultan, were known as the *kul*, and formed part of the *askeri*, the servitors of the Ottoman central administration. In the sixteenth and seventeenth centuries, Ottoman officials considered a rigid division between the *reaya* and all military and civilian members of the administration indispensable for the proper functioning of the state apparatus. Ideally, though not necessarily in actual fact, the *reaya* were to be disarmed, and denied any possibility of turning into soldiers. From the sixteenth century onward, the Ottoman central administration moreover "phased out" military corps made up of peasant or even nomadic warriors, which had been of considerable importance in the conquest of Rumeli, or else relegated these corps to auxiliary branches of the army. Admittedly these policies were not always rigidly enforced. But in as far as they were applied, they left the Muslim peasants of the empire very little chance of ever rising into the *askeri*. On the other hand, the military and paramilitary bands (*sekban*, *sarıca*) recruited by the central government during the Ottoman–Habsburg War and later by provincial governors consisted largely of Muslim villagers, in this manner gained access to a military career. Thus one might regard the Celali rebellions as a struggle by which soldiers of Anatolian Muslim *reaya* attempted to gain some of the privileges hitherto reserved for the *kul*.[9] To a certain extent, the "new-style" soldiers succeeded, as military bands made up of former peasants became a recognized feature of the seventeenth-century political set-up. At the same time, the prestige and pay of these soldiers of *reaya* background were always much lower than those of the older army corps; moreover these men were dismissed whenever their employer no longer needed their services. The demand of these non-elite soldiers for job security and higher pay ultimately caused a considerable number of seventeenth-century rebellions.[10]

From the above it becomes apparent that the so-called Celali rebellions of the later sixteenth and early seventeenth century should not be regarded as peasant uprisings, of the kind that we encounter in China, Russia or Western Europe during the early modern period. This absence of peasant rebellion is worthy of closer examination, since the frequency of complaints against rapacious provincial officials shows us that Anatolian peasants of the years before and after 1600 had no reason to be particularly satisfied with their fate. It has sometimes been assumed that the overwhelming prestige of the sultan prevented peasant rebellions. However, it seems more probable that the mobility of Anatolian peasants played a significant role. At first glance this seems strange, since sixteenth-century tax regulations always emphasize that peasants were not allowed to leave their villages without the permission of the *timar*-holder, and the latter was authorized to demand the return of peasants who had settled in town without such permission. As a result, the sixteenth-century Ottoman peasant by the letter of the law was effectively tied to his village and to the land he tilled.[11] However, even by the second half of the sixteenth century, these rules became rather difficult to apply in practice. In most parts of the empire, the last coherent series of tax registers had been compiled in the 1570s or 1580s. Once they were out of date, it became very difficult to prove that a given peasant did in fact come from a certain village, and courts often decided in favor of migrating peasants. It must have been even easier for the mercenary to escape the attentions of a *timar*-holder demanding his return to the village. That *timar*-holders often were absent on campaign, and lacked an effective bureaucratic apparatus to enforce their orders during a long absence, must have constituted an additional factor working in favor of peasant mobility.

Christian *reaya* took little active part in the uprisings. This fact strengthens the interpretation of the Celali rebellions as an attempt on the part of Anatolian Muslim *reaya* to share in the privilege of the *kul*.[12] If population pressure within the village had been the principal reason for the unrest, non-Muslims should have participated more readily than they did. Many Christian *reaya*, and also Muslim peasants and townsmen not directly involved in the rebellions, responded to the unsettled conditions in places like Trabzon or Şebin-Karahisar simply by fleeing the area. Groups of migrants from eastern Anatolia settled as far as Varna, İstanbul or even the Crimea.[13] Moreover, the Turkish and Muslim population of the Balkans (for instance Thrace or the southern part of Bulgaria) did not participate in the rebellions to nearly the same extent as their Anatolian counterparts, although brigandage was not rare in the Balkans either. In search of an explanation, one might point to the specific political traditions of Ottoman Anatolia; after all, in central Anatolia the memory of pre-Ottoman local principalities was still alive, since some of these had continued to exist down to the 1520s. Thus one may assume that pre-conquest local elites retained a degree of influence, and that challenges to the political privileges of the *kul* could be formulated more effectively with local leaders readily available. Moreover, the tax load which the Ottoman administration placed upon Anatolian nomads caused widespread discontent and probably induced some of them to join the Celalis. On the other hand, due to the more drastic changes experienced by the political elites of the Balkans, pre-conquest political traditions did not retain any particular relevance in Ottoman Rumelia. However, this explanation is hypothetical, and better interpretations may emerge in the future.

The Balkan *hayduk* movements of the seventeenth and later centuries have been equally interpreted as a series of military rebellions.[14] In this case, the key factor was the receding frontier. Pastoral people, who previously had fought as irregular warriors and were accustomed to a life of booty, were now pushed back into the core territories of the empire and embarked upon a life of brigandage, punctuated by occasional rebellions. This situation is somewhat different from that in which the Celali revolts occurred; at the end of the sixteenth century, the Ottoman frontiers were still expanding, albeit somewhat spasmodically. But the *hayduk* who reacted against the devaluation of their military role, and who had no intention of becoming tax-paying peasants, acted out the same *askeri–reaya* conflict which constituted the base of the Celali rebellions. Yet there are important differences: Anatolian rebel leaders such as Kara Yazıcı or Kalenderoğlu attained major military stature and at least for a short time seemed capable of establishing regional power centers of their own. No such thing seems to have occurred in seventeenth-century Rumeli. Moreover, the interpretation of the Balkan *hayduk* movement as a series of military rebellions does not explain why Rumelian Muslim villagers apparently showed less desire to achieve *kul* status than did their Anatolian counterparts. The problem is certainly in need of further examination.

To sum up the present discussion, dissatisfied Anatolian villagers found it comparatively easy to rid themselves of their peasant status, and become either townsmen or mercenaries, a state of affairs also noted by the seventeenth-century memorialist Koci Bey. This might explain why the tensions between peasants and low-level administrators, so frequently cited in late sixteenth- and early seventeenth-century sources, did not lead to peasant uprisings.[15] On the other hand, mercenary soldiers of *reaya* background did not easily achieve a secure status, let alone equality with the more prestigious *kul*, and this state of affairs lay behind the frequent military rebellions of the late sixteenth and seventeenth centuries.

POPULATION MOVEMENTS AND THE DECLINE IN POPULATION: URBAN LIFE

One of the best-documented consequences of widespread unrest during the years before and after 1600 were the frequent interruptions of inter-regional trade. After all, certain major leaders of Celali bands, such as Kalenderoğlu or Tavil ("the tall one") established themselves in fortresses, assembled small armies, wintered in towns of considerable importance such as Urfa, laid siege to a commercial center such as Ankara, and even briefly occupied Bursa.[16] Under these conditions large towns such as Ankara sought to protect themselves by constructing a city wall of the type familiar from European medieval cities, since the customary citadel type of fortification was no longer considered adequate. However, many smaller towns suffered considerable damage: Tosya had its covered market attacked and plundered, while the covered market of Konya was even allowed to fall in ruins. But business still could be done in many Anatolian towns: even a small place such as Tosya was visited by foreign traders, and in 1613 food in Sivas was abundant and foreign trade was brisk.[17] Thus it seems that many Anatolian towns, in spite of population losses and Celali destruction, were able to weather the crisis of the years around 1600.

Yet, despite official attempts to resettle refugees in their former places of residence, many Anatolian towns were still in very serious difficulties by the middle of the seventeenth century. In the 1640s, a certain number of towns were covered by a census of urban taxpayers. The results were discouraging: compared to the 1570s and 1580s, Kayseri and Amasya had lost about one half of their taxpayers. Samsun had declined to the status of a fortified village. At first glance Tokat seemed to have held its own, but a closer examination reveals that the mid-seventeenth century tax register contains an appreciable number of female householders, a category absent from the earlier Tokat registers. Thus even this important center of the caravan trade with Iran had lost an appreciable share of its taxpaying population.[18] On the other hand, it would be a mistake to view the seventeenth century as a period of unmitigated urban decline. During this period İzmir developed into a major port city. This settlement held fewer than 3,000 inhabitants during the closing years of Kanuni Süleyman's reign, while in the mid-seventeenth century it contained about 90,000 persons.[19] Certainly İzmir might be considered an exception. Not only was the city an entrepôt for the growing trade with Europe, but it also had been able to take over the role of other Aegean ports recently silted up, such as Balat (Palatia-Milet) and Ayasoluk (Altoluogo-Ephesus). Towns in other parts of Anatolia also were thriving. The gardens and vineyards outside of late seventeenth-century Kayseri and Ankara were well cultivated and fetched a good price whenever they changed owners. Moreover, even though Ankara was severely damaged by an earthquake in 1668, many people rebuilt their houses in several stories according to the İstanbul fashion, a more elaborate and expensive style than the single-story buildings with flat roofs which dominated in the mid-sixteenth century. The impressions of Evliya Çelebi, who visited many Anatolian towns in the years between 1650 and 1670, certainly do not reflect an urban life in decay, even if one makes allowances for the traveller's inclination toward exaggeration. Provisionally, one might assume that in many Anatolian towns the early years of the century were extremely difficult, but that a trend toward recovery was visible between about 1650 and 1680.[20]

Studies of seventeenth-century Syria and Palestine are much more abundant. Both Aleppo and Damascus lost considerable numbers of people right down to 1597, the date of the last Ottoman tax register. But while indirect indicators show that Aleppo recovered during the seventeenth century, Damascus appears to have stagnated throughout this period, only experiencing a spurt of growth after 1700.[21] Among the smaller Syrian towns, the population of Hama in 1581 has been estimated at 12–14,000 inhabitants, but the town lost population in the seventeenth century.[22] Thus it is not improbable that minor Syrian towns conformed to the overall Mediterranean pattern outlined by Braudel: growth in the sixteenth century, stagnation or decline in the seventeenth, and a new spurt of growth after 1700.[23]

Much less is known about Cairo, the regional capital of Egypt and second city of the Ottoman Empire. The city, about 1660, should have held an economically active population of about 147,000 individuals, practically all of them adult males. This would point to a total population of over 400,000, since women and young children were not included in this count.[24] In the closing years of the seventeenth century, Cairo's population probably declined, at least temporarily; between 1694 and 1697, the city experienced a famine the like of which had not been encountered since the Fatimid period.[25]

In the Arabic-speaking provinces, the Ottoman conquest did not cause major changes in the ethnic composition of the towns. The situation was somewhat different in the Balkans. In the border province of Hungary, the towns, particularly the provincial capital of Buda, were progressively settled by Muslim Bosnians, Turks and Orthodox Serbs, while Hungarians moved away. This process had begun in the sixteenth century, but continued throughout the seventeenth. At the end of the seventeenth century only a single Hungarian family remained in Buda.[26] Balkan towns increasingly became Ottoman towns, not only in their architectural appearance but also in their economic life. Trade in artifacts from the Ottoman core lands increased. Balkan trade appears to have been lively enough to permit the recuperation of towns in Transylvania, Moldavia and Wallachia due to immigration, even after warfare had resulted in serious destruction. But the majority of city-bound migrants doubtless moved not to the provincial Balkan towns, but to the capital city of İstanbul.

PLAGUES, FAMINES AND EARTHQUAKES

Explaining this pattern of urban development and stagnation is not an easy matter. However, one of the major impediments to urban growth, namely the plague, has now been studied in detail with respect to the eighteenth century, and since the propagation of plague has not changed greatly over the centuries, many findings are valid for our period as well.[27] In İstanbul, epidemics usually began in late April or early May, reached their culmination point in August and did not subside until October. Plague epidemics in Alexandria might begin as early as January, ravaged the city during April, while the hot summer weather ended the epidemic by June. In Egypt, contamination by sea was the most frequent cause of plague epidemics. On the other hand, İzmir most often received the epidemic from caravans which had traversed the border region between the Ottoman Empire and Iran. Due to its central position in the Ottoman communication system, İstanbul also served as a relay in the propagation of plague; and quite a few epidemics in Egypt and the Balkans can be traced to ships or caravans arriving from the Ottoman capital.

Other natural calamities, such as local and regional harvest failures, have been less systematically investigated.[28] While in the middle of the sixteenth century the Venetians were able to legally import Macedonian and other Ottoman grains, the permissions upon which this trade depended were no longer obtainable in the last quarter of the century. Apart from population increase and internal unrest in the Ottoman Empire, bad harvests may also have been the reason for the prohibition to export grain, particularly since the 1590s are known to have been calamitous throughout the Mediterranean. Considerations of this kind, and the evidence concerning a "Little Ice Age" in late sixteenth- and seventeenth-century Europe have led scholars to pose the problem of the climatic history of the eastern Mediterranean during this period. At present no tree ring or polinological data have as yet been published, at least not in a form accessible to the non-specialist. Therefore the time has not yet come for a study of the possible social consequences of (presumed) climatic changes.[29] But the question remains as a challenge for the future.

The incidence of earthquakes in Ottoman territories is somewhat better known. Famous disasters include the earthquake which completely destroyed İzmir in 1688, but the series of earthquakes which made itself felt between Bolu and Erzincan in the summer of 1668 is less well known.[30] Studies concerning earthquakes are of considerable relevance for the economic and social historian, not so much because of the events themselves, but because of the recuperation period that followed. In general, localities with noteworthy commercial potential were reconstructed within a short time, while the decline of localities already "on the way down" was hastened by such a catastrophe. In an environment which produced few written records from which economic conjunctures can be reconstructed, such indirect evidence, already quoted in the case of Ankara, is too valuable to be treated with the contempt that historians often reserve for the " *faits divers.*"

POPULATION MOVEMENTS AND THE DECLINE IN POPULATION: THE COUNTRYSIDE

While evidence concerning the fate of Ottoman towns in the seventeenth century sometimes is ambiguous, population decline in the countryside is fairly well documented. Most of the evidence is indirect, since the Ottoman administration of the seventeenth century very rarely produced counts of its Muslim taxpayers. Only Christians and Jews were counted, since they were liable to a poll-tax, but records made before the 1691 reform of collection are of very limited value as demographic evidence. But fiscal records of the early and middle seventeenth century often show a dramatic decline in the amount of taxes collected, and the officials responsible explained this state of affairs with the flight of peasants.

The most detailed information of this kind can be found in the yearly accounts of certain pious foundations, such as those of Celaleddin Rumi, Seyyid Gazi, or Mehmed the Conqueror's grand vizier, Mehmed Pasha. Some taxpaying villages totally disappeared from the accounts, while the revenues of others by 1640–50 constituted a fraction of their late sixteenth-century levels. How much of this decline was attributable to the death of taxpayers, and how much to their flight, cannot be determined. It must be assumed that many peasants fled their villages to escape provincial governors and their bands of mercenaries and settled in towns, where epidemics and malnutrition took their toll. Thus we must reckon not only with a redistribution of population, but with its decline as well, even if the latter is impossible to quantify.

Another kind of evidence concerning population decline has been located by geographers dealing with historic settlement patterns. In the

Table II:1. Decline in expendable income: foundations of Mevlana
Celaleddin and Seyyid Gazi

Year	Mevlana Celaleddin	Seyyid Gazi
1596–97	296,475	—
1597–98	450,185	—
1598–99	267,122	—
1599–1600	403,484	249,317
1601–2	371,272	356,306
1618–19	—	92,690
1631–32	—	138,425
1649–50	199,626	—
1651–52	188,801	—
1652–53	—	98,300
1701–2	—	128,800

Source: Faroqhi (1988), p. 119.

Konya area of modern days, many sixteenth-century village names are still attached to uninhabited sites; thus these villages really were given up and did not simply change their names.[31]

The configuration of the terrain had considerable impact: in hilly country, villages survived much better than in the open plain, so that it becomes obvious that the latter settlements were abandoned due to insecurity. On the other hand, a comparison of Ottoman Palestine between 1595–96 and the early nineteenth century shows that many late sixteenth-century settlements close to the fringe of the desert equally were given up. The parallel to the Konya area is clearly visible; only in this case, Bedouins take the place of roving Celali bands. However, in the long run, the loss of settled land on the fringes of the desert partly was balanced by the settlement of the coastal strip, which had been only very thinly populated during the Mamluk and early Ottoman periods.[32]

For northwestern Anatolia and for the mining district of Şebin-Karahisar, more direct evidence is available. Between 1547 and 1615, the northwestern districts of İznik, Gebze and Üsküdar lost some of their population, but losses were more obvious in the Şebin-Karahisar district. In both cases population decline was not too dramatic, and given frequent epidemics and a highly mobile rural population, can be considered as a more or less "normal" fluctuation. But at least parts of western Anatolia (the province of Anadolu) also fared badly in the later years of the seventeenth century. Between 1677 and 1698, the number of units liable to the payment of *avarız* taxes ("*avarız* houses") declined from 51,292 to 34,700. Even if the "*avarız* houses" correspond to a varying number of real households and therefore constitute poor measures of population, an obvious decrease in the number of taxable units indicates population loss or impoverishment, and probably a combination of both.[33]

In central Anatolia, during the seventeenth century, nomadic and semi-nomadic forms of land use became increasingly widespread. This in itself might be taken as an indicator of population decline: during the sixteenth-century expansion, a considerable number of tribesmen under pressure had settled down as peasants. By contrast, between 1600 and 1700, tribes belonging to the great tribal confederations of eastern Anatolia entered the central and western sections of the peninsula. By 1673 a section of the Boz-Ulus had moved as far as Akşehir; they even crossed the narrow arm of the Aegean Sea which separates the island of Chios from the Anatolian mainland.[34]

In the early stages of the process, nomads probably moved into territory abandoned by settled peasants. But at a later stage, nomads and semi-nomads successfully opposed peasants wishing to reclaim their former lands, so that the area in question continued to be very thinly populated. In the absence of a very strong increase in population, reclamation of land for settled agriculture was only possible with the active support of the Ottoman state. Such support was rare before the end of the seventeenth century.

Table II:2. Total population estimates based on taxpayers (selected multipliers): Şebin-Karahisar and Kocaeli

Area–Date	Taxpayers	Multipliers	Total estimated population
Karahisar			
1547–48	5,197[a]	5[a]	25,985
	6,661	4.31	28,709
	6,661	2.72	18,118
1569	10,396	5	51,980
	13,679	4.31	58,956
	13,679	3.32	45,414
1613	5,972	5	29,860
	7,755	3.28	25,436
	7,755	2.47	21,094
Kocaeli			
1547–48	4,324	5	21,620
	5,439	4.31	23,442
	5,439	3.08	16,752
Ahmed I (1615)	3,595	5	17,975
	4,730	3.28	15,514
	4,730	2.72	12,866

[a] Only adult married males are included when using the *"hane"* multiplier of five.
Source: Erder and Faroqhi (1979), p. 335.

Table II:3. Provisions for the imperial larder, 1620 (in *kantars*)

Commodity	İzmir	Ayasoluk	Gördes	Manisa	Mendehorya	Menemen	Nif	Foça	Marmara	Total
Raisins	700					400	500	100		1,700
Beeswax	30									30
Olive oil	40		100					5		145
Dried beans	100									100
Figs	200					150				350
Honey	200[a]									200
Almonds	40					10	10			60
Sultanas		100		1,000					500	1,600
Wild apricots					100	20				120
Meviz kelter								200		200

[a] Calculated in boxes.

Source: Goffman (1990), p. 35.

An attempt at forcing the settlement of nomads and semi-nomads through administrative pressure was undertaken between 1691 and 1696.[35] Through forced settlement, the Ottoman central administration sought to end the depredations of tribesmen against the settled villagers, who were by far better taxpayers. But at the same time, the government hoped that the former nomads, even though settled, would retain enough military potential to protect southeastern Anatolia from the incursion of tribesmen from the Syrian desert. It seems likely that the two aims could not be reconciled, and that settlement sites were often selected for their strategic rather than their agricultural value. In addition, while the Ottoman government had made arrangements to win the more influential tribesmen over to the scheme, no material aid had been arranged for to tide the former herdsmen over the first difficult years. Such aid was sorely needed, for during this period the settlers lost many of their animals but were unable to make a living from agriculture. As a result, the 1691–96 project ended in disaster; the hungry tribesmen when faced with harvest failure left the sites assigned to them and took up a life of brigandage. The venture is memorable because it constituted the first effort of its kind to be extensively documented. In the nineteenth century, in an environment characterized by sustained population growth, projects of this type were to be repeated with greater success, though still at the price of serious conflicts.

Another attempt at reclamation after the collapse of rural settlement during the early years of the seventeenth century was Murad IV's policy of forcing refugees who had settled in towns, especially İstanbul, to return to their areas of origin.[36] This measure resulted in long treks of townsmen and villagers moving toward an uncertain future in eastern Anatolia. Many peasants had sold their lands, sometimes for a nominal sum, before fleeing to the safety of walled towns, or else their lands had been usurped by locally powerful men who refused to give them up in spite of pressure from the administration. Other peasants were unable to return because of debt. In yet other cases, locally influential people, dervish sheikhs among others, contracted with the Ottoman central administration to resettle a given village. Generally the arrangement involved a more or less prolonged period during which the new settlers were to pay reduced taxes. But once the settlement seemed well-established, potential tax-farmers would suggest to the treasury that the taxes due from the village in question might well be raised. Once this happened, peasants frequently abandoned their farmsteads, and the newly established settlement disappeared from the map. This fact in itself can be taken to indicate that population was sparse, and that other ways of making a living, such as settling in remote forest areas, were readily available to former peasants.

RURAL LIFE AND THE PROBLEM OF COMMERCIALIZATION IN AGRICULTURE

Due to the lack of data, we are unable to trace how peasants as producers reacted to the decline in rural population. It can be assumed that extensive breeding of sheep and, in the Christian regions of the Balkans, of pigs, became more common than it had been in the more densely settled countryside of the sixteenth century. This transition should have been easy since many settled villagers always had migrated to summer pastures in the uplands.

At the same time, low population densities encouraged men who possessed political influence with the Ottoman central administration to extend their landholdings. This process particularly was obvious in the immediate vicinity of İstanbul. In the district of İznik at the beginning of the seventeenth century, quite a few Janissaries and other wealthy outsiders were recorded as landholders.[37] Their presence also is attested indirectly for, around 1600, a few complaints refer to the Albanian seasonal workers employed by Janissaries and other landholders in northwestern Anatolia. It can be assumed that Janissaries and candidate Janissaries (*acemi oğlan*) formed connections in northwestern Anatolia when sent out, as was customary, to transport timber and firewood to the arsenal or the palace. The intruders' relative closeness to the centers of political power must have made it difficult for the villagers to resist their encroachments; although we know that resistance was sometimes attempted. This villager assertiveness is all the more remarkable since the Ottoman central administration then was engaged in a sustained campaign to remove all firearms from the possession of the subject population.[38] It is difficult to tell if most Janissary landholdings were genuine attempts at production for the market, or devices for extracting extra-economic rent from the surrounding peasantry, and occasionally from the İstanbul consumer. For complaints indicate that Janissary rackets simultaneously were driving up the price of firewood and hindering the marketing efforts of gardeners.[39]

In spite of these reservations, the areas supplying İstanbul were also those in which market-oriented production developed at an early date. In the early seventeenth century, only on the western Black Sea coast were sizable landholdings (*çiftliks*) producing for the market in significant numbers. Since seventeenth-century legitimate or contraband European traders were scarcely represented in the Black Sea area, the demand for foodstuffs in İstanbul must have constituted an incentive for the formation of *çiftliks*. In the later seventeenth and early eighteenth centuries, the western coast of the Black Sea and Macedonia–Thessaly were to become significant centers of *çiftlik* agriculture. The *çiftliks* of Macedonia–Thessaly may have been largely producing for export; but since the Black Sea even in this later period was still closed to non-Ottoman traders, supplying the capital may have been more lucrative than is generally assumed.

Under these circumstances, the existence of *çiftliks* should have deprived peasants of the profits which the existence of an urban market would otherwise have allowed them, as peasants paid to the *çiftlik*-holder whatever surpluses remained after satisfying the central government. In other words, one may assume that politically powerful men were able to appropriate a sizable share of the peasants' marketable surpluses.[40] This state of affairs probably explains why the expropriation of peasant land was not more common; for even though in the eighteenth and nineteenth centuries the exportation of agricultural commodities grew apace, peasant landholding continued as the dominant form of land tenure both in Anatolia and most parts of Rumelia.[41] After all, with the profits of commercialization lost to the peasants, the motivation for taking their land should have been much reduced.

On the other hand, usurpation of peasant land by locally powerful men could occur even in the absence of commercial incentive. Since the taxation system of the classical Ottoman period had left the peasants a certain minimum beyond subsistence, they might constitute a tempting prey for people sufficiently powerful to appropriate a share of peasant production. It often was sufficient to abolish peasant security of tenure through various kinds of legal or physical dispossession. Thereafter, everything the peasants produced beyond minimum subsistence requirements could be "creamed off" by the *çiftlik*-holder.[42] But the refusal of the Ottoman central administration to promote or legalize peasant dispossession, combined with limited commercial opportunities in the empire, made it unattractive for local power-holders to acquire landholdings in their own name, that is, carry peasant dispossession to its logical extreme. As a result, legal, semi-legal and illegal forms of rent payable by peasant smallholders remained the typical manner in which agricultural products were appropriated by the politically dominant group. Thus,

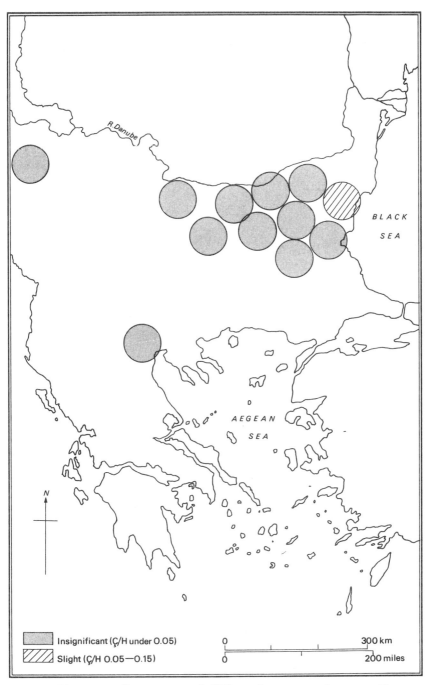

R. Danube

BLACK
SEA

AEGEAN
SEA

N

Insignificant (Ç/H under 0.05)

Slight (Ç/H 0.05—0.15)

0   300 km

0   200 miles

13 Evidence regarding presence of *çiftliks*, early seventeenth-century Ottoman Europe (Ç = *çiftlik*, H = *hane*, household).
Source: McGowan (1981), p. 76.

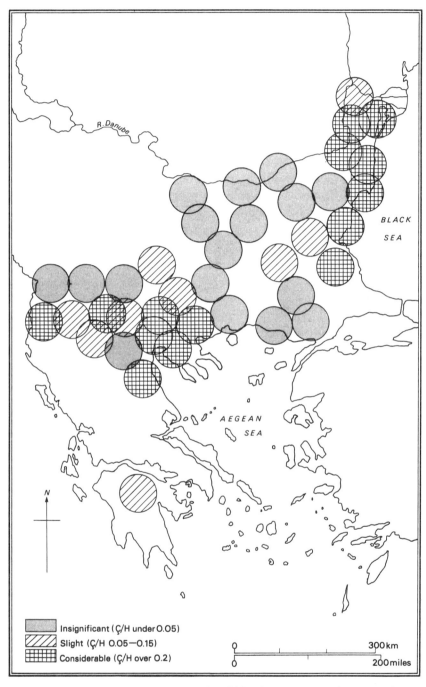

14 Evidence regarding presence of *çiftliks*, late seventeenth- to mid-eighteenth century Ottoman Europe (Ç = *çiftlik*, H = *hane*).
Source: McGowan (1981), p. 77.

local power-holders only rarely made the transition to agricultural entrepreneurship.

Obviously the spread of stock-raising ranches affected peasants in a more dramatic way than the extension of *çiftliks*. Field agriculture demanded at least a seasonal labor force, while cattle or sheep most easily bred in empty spaces. Probably because of their disruptive effect on the peasant economy, ranches were singled out for special attention in the late sixteenth- and early seventeenth-century rescripts attempting to protect the "classical" Ottoman land system.[43] The usurpation of land usually began in sparsely inhabited areas or, to put it differently, in the interstices of peasant settlement. Once a powerful man had achieved such a foothold, which might be recorded in the tax registers under the innocuous-sounding title of mill or sheep pen, his servitors took control of surrounding land by harassing the villagers until they left their farmsteads. Given the semi-arid character of many parts of Thrace and Anatolia, this often could be achieved by denying the peasants access to water sources. On the one hand, techniques of this kind were effective only in sparsely settled environments; apparently there remained quite a few areas in which population pressure was not a major problem.

On the other hand, more intensive forms of cultivation were not altogether unknown. A belt of gardens and vineyards usually owned as freehold property by the townsmen surrounded towns and cities. In many parts of Anatolia, the gardens and vineyards contained summer-houses for the townsmen. Many of these garden lands were cultivated with family labor, and the produce must have been largely consumed by the owners themselves. In the Aegean coastlands, however, the cultivation of olives, beans, almonds, figs and, above all, raisins clearly was undertaken for commercial purposes as well. The Imperial Larder supplied itself from this region, and it would not have made sense to assemble large quantities of produce from a multitude of subsistence producers. But fruit cultivation for sale was practiced in more outlying regions as well: the geographer and historian Katib Çelebi and his fellow scholars report sophisticated techniques for producing attractive-looking fruit in the vicinity of Malatya.[44] These techniques were quite labor-intensive, and the owners probably would not have taken so much trouble without the expectation of profit. Moreover, vineyards and gardens on the Aegean seaboard often supplied the market of İstanbul with raisins, vinegar, and in the case of non-Muslim consumers, wine. In addition, even where gardens and vineyards were cultivated primarily for direct consumption, these land parcels often changed hands at reasonably high prices. Thus we can surmise that gardens and vineyards produced a substantial share of the overall agricultural output, at least in western and central Anatolia.

CRAFT PRODUCTION: CRISIS AND RESILIENCE

As textile production constituted the leading "industry" in most pre-industrial economies (and is the best documented sector as well), much of the following discussion will deal with silk, woolens, mohair and cotton. Among Ottoman textile industries, silk manufacture has been studied most intensively. Down to the seventeenth century, most of the raw material was imported from Azerbaijan and Gilan, although silk also was grown in the eastern Mediterranean region, particularly in the Morea. Dependence upon imports made the industry vulnerable: supplies might not be forthcoming when the Ottoman Empire and Iran were at war. On the other hand, control over Azeri silk supplies was sometimes mentioned as one of the advantages that could be gained from war against Iran.

By the closing years of the sixteenth century, the silk manufacturers of Bursa confronted rising prices for raw silk.[45] In part, the difficulties of raising silkworms as Azerbaijan was being ravaged by war must have been responsible for this increase. But growing purchases by European merchants, particularly Englishmen and Italians, also played a significant and probably more important role in driving up prices. Increasing mechanization of silk-reeling in northern Italy stimulated demand for Levantine, that is Iranian, silk, which was used for the weft on fabrics whose warp consisted of mechanically reeled Italian silk. On the other hand, Bursa manufacturers were unable to pass on their increased raw material costs to customers, probably because silks were a luxury, and substitutes readily available. Moreover, as is apparent from the reports of Venetian merchants, the purchasing power of many well-to-do Ottoman customers had much declined at the end of the sixteenth century.[46]

Devaluation of the currency and the empire's financial difficulties may well have left their mark upon the incomes of many Ottoman officials, who normally would have purchased silk fabrics. Certain producers responded to a contracting market by manufacturing cheaper and lighter fabrics. Mixtures of silk and cotton became particularly popular. However, the production of cheaper fabrics was made very difficult not only by the resistance of more traditionally minded craftsmen, but also by the

Table II:4. Composite index of prices of the main
types of raw silk

Years	Composite index of a *lodra*[a] (in *akçe*[b])
1548	59.00
1557	83.78
1559	80.83
1566	94.40
1569	68.44
1570	41.89
1571	74.93
1572	81.42
1573	67.85
1575	71.98
1576	83.19
1577	80.24
1578	99.71
1579	84.37
1580	84.37
1581	136.29
1582	151.63
1583	144.55
1584	250.16
1585	158.71
1587	178.18
1588	182.90
1589	192.93
1594	207.09
1595	197.06
1597	224.79
1603	351.05
1607	233.05
1608	224.79
1614	189.98
1617	174.64
1622	338.07
1627	306.80
1629	294.41
1630	99.71
1634	240.72
1635	373.47
1636	315.65
1637	394.12
1639	250.75
1646	199.42
1647	216.53
1648	129.80
1650	100.89
1651	143.96
1652	93.81
1653	175.23

[a] *Lodra* was a weight unit, the exact metric equivalent of which
is subject to dispute.
[b] *Akçe* was the basic Ottoman coin, which included varying
amounts of pure silver over time.
Source: Çizakça (1980, reprinted 1987), p. 249.

Table II:5. Prices of Ottoman silk cloth (in *akçes*)

Years	1 *zira tafta*	Years	1 *zira vale*	Years	1 *zira kutni*	Years	1 *zira kemha*
1548	15	1545	14	1548	44	1545	29
1559	15	1557	7	1565	81	1548	35
1572	12	1559	14	1596	113	1553	40
1576	17	1571	13	1614	75	1567	59
1577	7.5	1572	9	1637	75	1571	59
1588	22	1580	8			1583	53
1596	55	1582	16			1595	45
1614	60	1588	18			1636	67
1617	32	1594	27			1646	74
1636	30	1597	35				
1647	25	1599	60				
1652	20	1600	40				
		1610	25				
		1637	35				

Source: Çizakça (1980, reprinted 1987), p. 252.

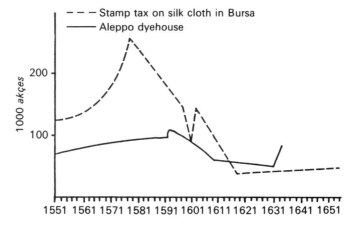

Fig. II:1 Cloth production in Bursa-Aleppo, 1551–1561. *Source*: Çizakça (1985), p. 364.

presence of the palace as the most important purchaser of luxury fabrics, and its insistence upon the maintenance of traditional standards. In addition, imported Italian fabrics competed with the domestic product. As a result, producers confronted a serious profit squeeze, that drove the industry into decline in the later sixteenth and in the seventeenth century. The crisis was exacerbated by the reliance of many manufacturers on slave labor, which was profitable only when profit margins were high. In certain years, producers were therefore confronted with both a contracting market and a scarcity of labor.

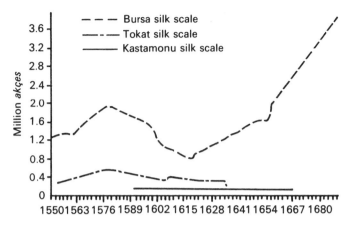

Fig. II:2 Silk production in Anatolia, 1550–1685. *Source*: Çizakça (1985), p. 360.

Salonica cloth manufacturers were confronted with a similar pressure on raw material supplies and profit margins. This industry was in the hands of Spanish Jews, who had immigrated into the Ottoman Empire after their expulsion from Spain in 1492. They produced the uniform cloth for the Janissaries, either as a tax or against payment of a price fixed by the Ottoman government. In addition, they supplied the Ottoman market with woolen cloth of medium quality, while the more luxurious types were imported from Europe. Throughout the sixteenth century and the first half of the seventeenth, sales of woolen cloth in the open market ensured the industry's prosperity. But difficulties began to manifest themselves. On the one hand, the Venetian woolen cloth industry, that peaked around 1600, depended considerably on Balkan wool supplies. Even though the Salonica manufacturers had legal rights to purchase their supplies of raw wool before other merchants, this increased Venetian demand must have raised prices.[47] One might object to this explanation that the Salonica industry was still fairly flourishing around 1600, when Venetian demand was at its height, and foundered around 1650, when Venetian industry had lost most of its significance. However, its seems that particularly French merchants imported wool from the Balkans in order to supply the rapidly developing manufactures of Languedoc, and their purchases made up for the decline of Venetian demand.

On the other hand, Salonica textile manufacturers confronted a profit squeeze no less serious than that of Bursa silk weavers and equally were unable to increase their sale prices in line with increasing raw material costs. But in their case, the profit squeeze derived from competition with English woolens, that had found markets in the eastern Mediterranean ever since the later fifteenth century.[48] With the founding of the English Levant Company in 1581, English merchants were able to sell woolens at drastically reduced prices. This was due to the fact that the Levant Company made most of its profits by importing Iranian raw silk to Europe; on the outgoing voyage any cargo that made even a moderate profit was preferable to sending ships out in ballast. Thereby English merchants captured a considerable share of the (limited) market in medium-priced woolen cloth, and the Salonica manufacturers inevitably felt the consequences.

The fate of the Bursa industry in particular has caused scholars to think about the broader outlines of Ottoman industrial history. It sometimes has been assumed that, as early as 1600, Ottoman crafts lost their capacity for dynamic expansion and that stagnation or even decline was due to the entry of Western European merchants into the Mediterranean. However, Fernand Braudel's work on the "industries" of Europe during the pre-industrial period shows that typically these manufactures did not flourish

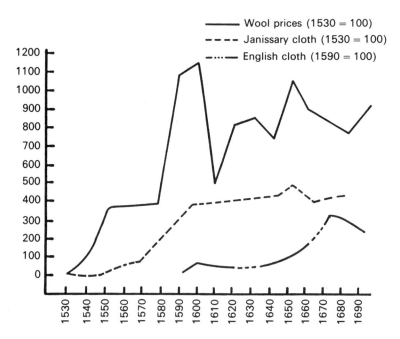

Fig. II:3. Indices of wool prices, Janissary cloth requirements, and English exports to the Levant, 1530–1690. *Source*: Braude (1979), p. 446.

for long in any other given place either.[49] Problems connected with the supply of raw material, wars, changing trade routes and competition with rival centers all led to the relatively rapid extinction of manufactures after brief periods of florescence. Thus it does not seem valid to judge the economic performance of a whole region by the history of one or two centers.

Ottoman textile industries in the seventeenth and eighteenth centuries certainly were not experiencing unrelieved decline. To name one (relatively well-studied) example, in the Plovdiv (Filibe) area, the manufacture of rough woolen cloth (*aba*) was practiced from the second half of the sixteenth century if not earlier, while the present-day Bulgarian town of Yanbol was a center of felt making. The cloth produced by these manufacturers, quite a few of them villagers, was marketed in small towns and country fairs, or carried to villages by peddlers, circuits that imported European fabrics were unable to enter before the nineteenth century. Filibe manufacturers probably flourished in the eighteenth and early nineteenth centuries, when their wares not only reached remote villages in Anatolia, but were marketed as far as India. The seventeenth century must have been the period in which Filibe woolens grew from a purely local specialty into a merchandise traded on an inter-regional level.[50]

If the woolen cloths of Filibe and the braid needed to convert them into coats were a novelty in inter-regional trade, the mohair manufacture of Ankara was an old industry that experienced both decline and revival during the late sixteenth and early seventeenth centuries. The manufacture of mohair cloth, that in the sixteenth century was something of a luxury, had been practiced in Ankara since at least the previous century. Moreover down to the nineteenth century, Ankara possessed a monopoly in this craft. With the possible exception of southeastern Anatolia, the mohair goat had not been successfully acclimatized in any other place.

At the height of the Celali rebellion, c. 1600, the fortunes of the Ankara mohair industry were at a low ebb.[51] But already by about 1615, local merchants were actively trying to put the industry back on its feet again. A count of mohair workshops in Ankara houses at the beginning and at the end of the seventeenth century suggests that the industry held its own fairly well. Thus we can assume that the downturn during the worst years of the Celali rebellions was followed by a fairly rapid recovery.[52]

There may have been special reasons for the recovery of the Ankara mohair industry. Among these, one might single out state protection, an advantage accorded to few other Ottoman industries. A tax on finished mohair cloth going through a special press constituted one of the principal revenue items collected in Ankara, and the tax-farmer was able to impede the sale of first-quality mohair yarn outside of the Ankara region. In addition, European demand for mohair yarn after all was limited.

In the seventeenth century, mohair yarn in Europe was used mainly for the manufacture of buttons; after 1700, even this demand weakened, as metal buttons came into fashion. Moreover limited quantities of finished mohair cloth were imported into sixteenth and early seventeenth-century Italy. As far as France was concerned, this trade continued until the beginning of the eighteenth century; but after 1730 imitations of Ankara mohair cloth manufactured in Amiens eliminated the demand for the Ottoman fabrics.[53] Thus the revival of the industry was probably aided by a measure of foreign demand. The history of the seventeenth-century Ottoman cotton industry is much less clear.[54] In the last quarter of the sixteenth century, raw cotton was mainly produced in the Adana area, on Cyprus, in northern Syria, in the Aegean coastlands of Anatolia and in the "lake district" around Isparta and Uluborlu as well as on the Rumelian side of the Aegean, in Thessaly. During this period, cotton export was prohibited, presumably to safeguard the Arsenal's supply of sailcloth.

The prohibition was enforced only sporadically while special permissions to export occasionally were granted. By 1623, however, the Ottoman administration had reversed its policy and permitted the export of cotton on a general basis. In fact Venetian exporters active in the hinterland of İzmir obtained special privileges. They not only could buy from the cotton growers directly, but they also paid their *pro rata* duties on the basis not of İzmir prices, but the lower prices offered in the countryside.[55]

Several reasons might be suggested for this reversal of policy. First of all, the decline of naval activity in the Mediterranean after the Ottoman–Spanish truce of 1580 lessened military demand for cotton. In addition, since cotton was in demand in Europe, tax-farmers of customs wishing to increase the yield of their farms probably put pressure on the Ottoman central administration to have the prohibition repealed. Probably tax-farmers' petitions occasioned many of the special permits issued before 1623. But, at the same time, it is likely that cotton production also was increasing. Contraband was frequent before 1623 and good prices certainly induced peasants to produce more. An exact assessment is not possible but the impression is that by the mid-eighteenth century the İzmir countryside had come to specialize in the production of grain, raisins and cotton.[56]

We know very little about the processes of cotton cloth manufacturing during this period, or about the commercial arrangements involved in the marketing of raw cotton and cotton cloth. Raw cotton sometimes was marketed, and presumably woven, at a considerable distance from its place of origin. Thus districts of the province of Hamid (Isparta), where cotton was probably not grown locally, already were weaving cotton cloth in the sixteenth century. Similarly towards the end of the century, merchants from Kayseri were engaged in the purchase of raw cotton, whether to have it worked up or for resale is impossible to determine. In the Aegean region, weaving was spread out over a great many localities, while dyeing for a while was concentrated in a limited number of towns. At least that was the claim of the Tire dyers, who in 1678–79 stated that the coarse cottons of Hamid, Denizli, Buldan and Manisa in the past had been processed in Tire. Complaining of competition on the part of newly opened dyers' workshops in Buldan and elsewhere, weavers in these cotton-manufacturing Aegean towns either worked on behalf of merchants, or else sold their output to traders, for it was the latter who brought the undyed cotton cloths to the dyers of Tire.[57] This pattern closely corresponds to putting-out arrangements observed in the Bursa region even in the sixteenth century.[58] But whether "putting-out" activities existed in sixteenth-century Aegean as well, or whether they spread to this area only in the seventeenth century, cannot be determined.[59]

Some seventeenth-century centers of cotton weaving can be located indirectly. The Ottoman central administration's demands for cotton cloth, which was used mainly for the undergarments of the Janissaries, can serve as an indicator of production. One such center was located in the Aydın–Manisa–Bergama area where, in 1622–23 and 1627–28, the weavers were expected to deliver 44,000 pieces of cotton cloth a year, each piece probably sufficient for one man's uniform.[60] Bergama was particularly important among the textile-producing towns of the Anatolian seaboard. At the beginning of the seventeenth century, its yearly quota amounted to 28,000 pieces. On the Rumelian side, the Thessalian towns of Yenişehir-i Fener (Larisa) and Tirhala owed the fisc 40,000 pieces in 1036/1626–27.[61]

Two decades later, the obligations of Yenişehir-i Fener alone amounted to 37,775 pieces. Since the Ottoman central administration generally paid very low prices for the goods it purchased, it is probable that the weavers could not subsist on what they were paid by the treasury. They must either have sold to private customers as well, or else made their basic living from agriculture.

Apart from the textile crafts, the manufacture of leather – boots, shoes and other leather items – was a major industry. Since carts and wagons were in frequent use both in Rumeli and in certain parts of western and central Anatolia, their manufacture also must have been significant. In addition, the different crafts connected with mining, smelting and the manufacture of copper cauldrons and vessels occupied appreciable numbers of people. But very little research has been done on these branches of Ottoman industry, so that a detailed discussion is not possible at present.[62]

PUBLIC CONSTRUCTION

Public construction remained a major activity after 1600. Two large İstanbul mosques were begun and completed during this period, namely that of Sultan Ahmed I and the Yeni Valide Camii.[63] Within the palace compound, the Baghdad and Revan kiosks were built to commemorate victories in the Ottoman–Iranian wars. Moreover, most İstanbul khans date from the seventeenth century. In Mecca, the Kaʿaba was rebuilt after it had collapsed during a rainstorm, and for this pious act a panegyrist placed the sultan in the illustrious line of prophets who previously had labored on Kaʿaba restoration. In Aleppo, the construction of the business district, though begun in the sixteenth century, continued apace after 1600. One of the most important structures, the Khan al-Wazir, was constructed between 1678 and 1682.[64] Moreover the frequent wars of this period necessitated a considerable amount of fortress construction and repair, quite apart from a sizable number of roadside khans meant to ensure safe communications. In addition, there must have been a vast amount of private building, as fires in the capital periodically destroyed entire city wards.

Methods of organizing a large public construction site did not change substantially between 1550 and 1610. The men employed as chief architects generally had gained experience in other professions before the ruler entrusted them with a large building project. Thus Mehmed Ağa, architect of the Sultan Ahmed mosque, had trained to be a court musician, switched to fine furniture-making and later served as a local administrator and military commander in Syria. This varied experience parallels that of the great sixteenth-century builder Sinan, who had been a Janissary and constructed bridges for the Ottoman army. Moreover, the fairly detailed biographies of the two architects (in Mehmed Ağa's case, the tone is almost hagiographic) indicated that Ottoman society of the sixteenth and seventeenth centuries did not regard architects as anonymous craftsmen.[65]

Quite to the contrary, such people achieved a reputation as possessors of superior skill.

Building stone for the Sultan Ahmed mosque was quarried in the immediate vicinity of the Sea of Marmara and brought to İstanbul by boat to avoid the prohibitive cost of transporting heavy materials overland. Rooftiles for the foundation complex also were manufactured in the immediate vicinity of the city. Some of the workshops apparently were operated by the state directly, but in addition work was given out to a large number of private entrepreneurs, both Muslims and Christians. Among marbles, a local variety was preferred and was quarried by slaves on the island of Marmara. It does not appear as if any effort was made to bring in structural elements from remote corners of the empire for the Sultan Ahmed Mosque. This type of conspicuous expenditure had not been uncommon in Kanuni Süleyman's time, but in the more stringent conditions of the early seventeenth century, the expense involved must have seemed prohibitive.[66]

Both trained master craftsmen and candidate Janissaries (*acemi oğlan*) worked on the Sultan Ahmed construction site. However, we do not know if the division of labor between the two groups was the same as it had been in the case of the Süleymaniye, where almost one half of all man-hours – largely unskilled labor – had been contributed by future Janissaries. It is, however, likely that the role of the *acemi oğlan* on the construction site of the Sultan Ahmed mosque was less prominent than it had been in the middle of the sixteenth century.

THE ARSENAL

Among the large-scale enterprises sponsored by the Ottoman central administration, the Arsenal is perhaps the most remarkable. Construction sites after all were active only for short periods of time, while the Arsenal was a permanent institution, even though the number of craftsmen employed varied with the number of ships being built.[67] Flexibility was ensured by maintaining only a limited number of men permanently on the payroll, while in years of peak activity, such as 1660–61, thousands of craftsmen might be employed on a short-term basis. Recruitment procedures resembled those described in the building of the Süleymaniye:[68] most temporarily employed artisans had been drafted, in some cases craftsmen working for private shipowners were required to present themselves at the Arsenal.[69] More usually, certain regions were assigned to the Arsenal as *ocaklık*, that is a permanent source of manpower and/or goods.

In such cases the district furnished a certain number of craftsmen whenever the activity of the shipyards increased beyond the capacity of the
permanently employed staff.[70] In addition, candidate Janissaries also
worked in the Arsenal, while Rumelian nomads, who by virtue of their
special status had to provide services to the Ottoman central administration, also occasionally were employed. All these features very much
resemble those observed on the construction site of the Süleymaniye
during the 1550s; thus, there were certain long-term patterns of labor
recruitment, with a very noticeable emphasis upon coerced labor. While
in all likelihood few of the workers on the construction site of the Süleymaniye freely elected to work on the project, the number of labor days
provided by actual slaves was strictly limited.[71] On the other hand, a
sizable number of slaves worked at the Arsenal, and, as a result, quite a
few military men were employed in guarding the premises.[72]

The study of the Ottoman Arsenal provides a welcome opportunity
to trace the interaction of seventeenth-century political and economic
conjunctures. On the one hand the demands of war and solvency of the
treasury, rather than purely economic considerations, determined the
level of its activity. This predominance of political factors was made
even more extreme by the fact that the Ottoman administration was a
notoriously bad paymaster. For example, oar cutters working for the
Arsenal complained, in 1660, that they had not received their pay, to
which the Ottoman administration responded simply by lowering their
wages from 1,000 to 500 *akçe*, and thereby canceling one-half of the
outstanding debt.[73]

Workers in the Arsenal received differential pay, possibly because
more skilled craftsmen worked on the more important ships, or because
certain vessels demanded more labor than others. By the middle of the
seventeenth century, Greek craftsmen did most of the Arsenal work
demanding special qualifications, and accordingly receiving higher pay,
while in the early sixteenth century most of the qualified workers had
been Muslims. Nothing is known about the manner in which this change
came about.[74]

Much of the preparatory work was not undertaken in the Arsenal.
Villagers were required to fell timber and saw it up, either for pay or in
lieu of taxes. Even though limited amounts of cash were thus expended,
economic constraints operated: when villagers were hard-pressed for
ready cash, illegal cutting of timber in the forests reserved for the Arsenal
increased. Moreover, impoverished villagers might band together and

impede the officials' collection of raw materials on behalf of the Arsenal. On a higher level of the political and economic hierarchy, tax-farmers instructed to pay the Arsenal's bills for raw materials out of their own funds might procrastinate or abscond. This in turn could lead to the flight of villagers unwilling to perform unpaid services and make the collection of further prestations increasingly problematic. Thus the Arsenal's level of activity was determined by the ability and willingness of the sultan's subjects to pay their taxes and deliver the prestations demanded.

This tension between the villagers and the representatives of the Ottoman state was particularly acute in the case of timber, the most essential of all raw materials. The replacement of galleys by sailing ships, which occurred largely during the second half of the seventeenth century, dramatically increased the demand for timber.[75] But this increased demand was not translated into larger amounts of timber demanded in lieu of taxes, although there might be "irregular" demands that do not show up in the yearly accounts.[76]

On the other hand, the price which the state paid for obligatory timber deliveries originally demanded in lieu of *avarız* taxes, that always had been much lower than the regular market price, was not increased throughout the seventeenth century, although the devaluation of the *akçe* continued unabated.[77] As a result, payments under this heading became increasingly symbolic; in 1682 the price paid by the state for obligatory deliveries amounted to one-fifth of the regular market price.[78] Moreover kadis and other officials involved in the collection of timber on behalf of the state often demanded additional payment for themselves, a practice that probably was very difficult to repress.[79] Thus, Arsenal demands for timber caused considerable dissatisfaction among the villagers. Occasionally the latter complained, but never were able to obtain satisfaction.[80] The only way to recoup their losses was to illegally sell timber to private traders. Only in 1675, when over-exploitation of forests had led to a decrease of usable timber, the villagers received the coveted privilege of paying a fixed sum of money in lieu of timber deliveries.[81]

Most of the Arsenal's demands for timber concern northeastern Anatolia, that is the area bordered to the north by the Sea of Marmara and to the west by the Aegean Sea. In addition, the western Black Sea coast of Anatolia, between Şile and Amasra, as well as the Bulgarian and Thracian Black Sea coasts, possessed appreciable timber resources. When the Arsenal began major-scale operations in the second half of the fifteenth

Table II:6. Carpenters, augerers and caulkers employed in the İstanbul Arsenal, 1648–49

Type of ship	Carpenters			Augerers			Caulkers			Total number of workers	Total wage payment
	Number	Wage	Wage per person	Number	Wage	Wage per person	Number	Wage	Wage per person		
Bastarda of Bedek Kapudan	159	77,616	488	155	39,180	252	44	8,964	203	358	12,756
Mavna of Mustafa Kaptan	346	120,404	348	168	40,245	239	84	16,261	193	598	176,910
Mavna of Hüseyin	341	89,300	261	151	32,114	212	82	15,320	186	574	136,734
Mavna of Murad	355	97,499	274	154	36,917	239	69	14,065	204	578	148,481
Mavna of omer	361	112,604	312	248	53,161	214	61	15,692	257	670	181,457
Mavna of Ali	376	110,617	294	184	44,985	244	67	13,921	208	627	169,523
Mavna of Mustafa	446	132,878	298	157	33,535	214	55	14,402	262	658	180,815
Kadırga of Ibrahim	168	56,281	335	93	22,397	240	31	7,212	233	292	85,890
Kadırga of Mustafa	185	60,185	325	80	24,320	304	34	6,925	204	299	91,430
Kadırga of Hüseyin	173	57,359	332	80	20,413	255	29	6,321	218	282	84,093
Kadırga of Hüseyin	166	55,633	335	91	22,204	244	30	6,435	215	287	84,272

Source: Çizakça (1981b), p. 781.

century, forests in the immediate vicinity of the coast probably provided all that was needed. But by the seventeenth century it had become necessary to tap resources much further inland, such as for instance the hills surrounding Bolu. This required the construction of roads usable for heavy cart traffic. Also, since the labor for such projects had to be provided by the villagers, the tensions generated by the Arsenal's demands were further increased.

The population inhabiting a short stretch of the Anatolian Black Sea coast, between Bafra and Fatsa, was obliged to provide the hemp indispensable for the manufacture of ropes. Raw hemp was collected from the villagers, who in this manner paid their *avarız* taxes. The area apparently lost some population in the course of the seventeenth century, declining from 5,612 *avarız* units in 1644 to 5,504 units in 1677. (In this particular instance, each *avarızhane* coincided with an ordinary household.) During the 1670s, the Ottoman administration made no attempt to adjust its demands in accordance with the decreasing number of producers. But by the 1690s, the central government recognized that the villagers were incapable of delivering the quantities of hemp which had been demanded in the past, and scaled down the amount by 33 percent.[82]

WAR AND THE ECONOMY

Apart from the Arsenal, we do not have a great deal of information on the manufacture of arms in the seventeenth-century Ottoman Empire; we know particularly little about the manufacture of handguns. The latter seems to have been quite widespread all over the provinces, in spite of strict prohibitions against use of firearms by ordinary peasants and townsmen. Young peasants wishing to join a governor's retinue as irregular soldiers easily procured the necessary firearms.[83] By the end of the century, a respectable inhabitant of a provincial Anatolian town frequently owned a musket or pistol.

Manufacturers of firearms left few traces of their activities. By contrast, there exists a large and almost untapped documentation concerning the Ottoman administration's methods of supplying itself with saltpeter for the manufacture of gunpowder. Water power was occasionally used in gunpowder manufacture even in the second half of the sixteenth century. Thus the superior results produced by this method were known; gunpowder produced by water power was not a complete novelty when reintroduced by European experts in the time of Selim III (1789–1807).

However, it seems that competition from flour mills for the limited water resources of Anatolia prevented the spread of the technique, so that most seventeenth-century gunpowder was of the inferior variety produced by horse-drawn mills.[84]

Iron for the manufacture of cannon balls came from the smaller mines of Anatolia. Iron for civilian purposes came mainly from Samakov in modern Bulgaria. Among the Anatolian mines, those associated with the town of Kıgı south of Erzurum were of particular importance due to their closeness to the Iranian front. Coerced labor was common. Certain villages were obliged to work the mines, while others compulsorily transported the finished cannon balls to the front. At least some laborers were remunerated, although the wages apparently were insufficient for subsistence; others may have served in the mines in order to work off tax obligations, particularly those arising from irregular taxes (*avarız*).[85]

Most of the people working in war-related sectors of the economy probably were employed in transportation. In the later sixteenth or early seventeenth century, districts located far from the route which the army was to follow paid a sum of money instead of delivering grain to the military. In such cases, the payments were several times the amount that this grain would have cost if it had been paid for at the price which the Ottoman administration had itself determined as applicable to "ordinary" market transactions (*narh*). People who paid in money were thus clearly penalized. Moreover the chronic lack of camels made these services extremely burdensome to the peasants. Since it was difficult to procure enough animals for transportation, the central administration attempted to keep its own camels. But the latter needed feeding and care and this was another expense that peasants and townsmen might be called upon to shoulder.[86]

Another war-related service that involved large numbers of people was the provisioning of army camps. In order to minimize discipline problems, Ottoman troops rarely were allowed to enter the empire's cities. A large number of artisans, who accompanied the army corps, were expected to set up shop whenever the army remained in one place for any length of time. One of the main functions of Ottoman guilds was to supply craftsmen in the number deemed necessary by army commanders. This service was doubly burdensome: the artisans selected were required to leave their homes and families for the duration of a campaign, and the guildsmen remaining at home had to provide the working capital to operate the shops of their colleagues serving the soldiers. In consequence many disputes concerning the distribution of these responsibilities were brought before the kadis of Ottoman towns, and have been preserved for posterity in their registers.

Apart from these more specific problems, what impact did warfare have on the complex of activities which, perhaps somewhat anachronistically, we call the Ottoman economy?[87] It now seems clear that warfare had no stimulating effects on economic activity either in the sixteenth or in the eighteenth century. Therefore, presumably, war was not an economic stimulant in the seventeenth century either. Given the scarcity of money and the high cost of transportation, the Ottoman state regularly had demanded many war-related goods and services from the direct producers, against a low or non-existent remuneration. From the administration's point of view this solution seemed so practical that its appropriateness was never questioned. But such an arrangement involved penalizing the larger and more efficient producers, to whom the state preferably addressed its demands. As a result, a long war led to a contraction of all economic activity, not just of those branches working for civilian customers. Moreover this economic contraction must have resulted in military defeats, as it became more and more difficult to supply the armies at the front. It thus seems tempting to explain the very limited success of the so-called "Long War" (1593–1606) and the disasters of the 1683–99 period to similar factors. After all, there is evidence of economic exhaustion and demographic decline, both for the beginning and the closing years of the seventeenth century.[88]

But if this analysis is correct, we need to explain why the equally long wars in, for example, the reign of Kanuni Süleyman did not produce the same disastrous effects. The answer might be in the following conjecture: *timar*-holders as individuals did not possess the right to requisition supplies, but had to pay for whatever they needed beyond the grains and other foodstuffs delivered to them by "their" peasants. As a result, the burden that they placed upon the economy may have been less than that caused by a centrally financed army, even though "a gun is cheaper than a horse."[89] Thus, if this analysis is valid, lamentations of sixteenth- and seventeenth-century officials about the decline of the *timar* system may make more sense than hitherto has been assumed.

CONCLUSION

While there is ample evidence for serious economic difficulties throughout the "long" seventeenth century, the interpretation of this evidence is more complicated than might appear at first glance. Progress in certain industries and regions occurred simultaneously with contraction in others. Even though no one would claim a balance between sectors in progress and those in crisis, the unilinear "decline" model so often associated with the Ottoman seventeenth century is being questioned. This period has not exactly been the favorite of twentieth-century researchers. Even so, it is possible to draw out certain lines along which future research will presumably move. To begin with, there is the debate concerning the influence of even minor climatic changes (the "Little Ice Age" of the seventeenth century) upon agriculture and the food supply of a society depending upon a preindustrial technology.[90] Calamitous harvests and Celali rebellions have been related to one another.[91] Relative neglect of this question by historians and archeometrists may not be entirely due to chance. Where Ottoman history is concerned, historians on both the left and the right of the political spectrum are reluctant for different reasons to consider the possibility of "extra-social" factors impinging on human society. To those with a generally left-wing outlook, a discussion of climatic factors may seem an almost culpable diversion from the major problems of European imperialism and underdevelopment. For those with a right-wing orientation, the acceptance of a common destiny that affects large sections of humanity at one and the same time and without any regard for national traditions may not come easily. That the determination of climatic change through the examination of pollen layers and tree-ring data is expensive, and cannot be conducted by historians in person, may have limited further the appeal of these techniques. On the other hand archeologists and archeometrists, as their name indicates, are often exclusively concerned with antiquity. Thus, it would seem, styles of thinking will have to change, at least in a minor way, before the possible repercussions of the Little Ice Age will get the attention they deserve.

Our received views concerning the general history of the Ottoman Empire have limited our perceptions in yet other ways. We have come to assume that, at least in the Ottoman case, "centralism" and "florescence" are practically one and the same thing. On the other hand, "decentralization" and "decline" also are considered all but synonymous. Obviously if one happens to be looking at Ottoman history from the point of view of a particular nation state in quest of its history, ambivalence toward the decentralization issue is likely to occur. While still regarded as a decline of the dominant power, decentralization is considered a precondition for the emergence of the nation state under discussion and thereby invested with positive values. As a result, the impact of early decentralization often is magnified beyond all measure, and the resilience of the Ottoman state apparatus studiously ignored.[92] This concern with the antecedents of the modern nation state to all intents and purposes makes it impossible for Ottoman historians to properly understand the different trajectories of regional development. For, instead of looking at regions as they existed in the seventeenth century, we impose upon our data the framework of nineteenth- and twentieth-century nation-states. We must now move out of this rather limiting framework, in order to reconstruct and then compare the histories of various regions as they existed in the seventeenth century, a task which has to date been undertaken only for a very few places, Syria–Palestine among them. Only after this task has been completed will we be able to decide where and to what extent there was economic decline in the seventeenth-century Ottoman Empire. Before that task has been completed, assertions of global decline should be taken for what they are, unproven assumptions.

The integration of crafts and agricultural production into the economic circuits of Ottoman society is another matter about which we know very little. Ottoman craft guilds and their activities certainly are less well documented than the sector in which the Ottoman state directly intervened to organize production. But even so, craftsmen organized in guilds are still much better known than the sector which might be called "putting-out" manufacturing. By this latter term we designate the activities of merchants financing and organizing production on the part of usually rural, non-guild producers. This lack of information has led certain observers to conclude that putting-out was absent from Ottoman society, or that the Ottoman state apparatus consciously prevented this kind of activity from evolving. This view is certainly inaccurate. However, at least where the seventeenth century is concerned, we can only enumerate examples of such activities, but presently cannot measure their importance in the economy as a whole.

Another unresolved problem is connected with the interrelation of economic and political conjunctures. We may suppose that the manner of financing wars ultimately "ran down" the economy to the point that the producers' capacity to reproduce themselves was impaired.[93] Or we may assume that internal tensions within Ottoman state and society had very little to do with the economic crises that occurred, and that everything can ultimately be derived from the impact of capitalist and mercantilist Europe.[94] Or else we may think about possible applications of the model drawn from European societies; namely that the various centralized state apparatuses and their wars were more than the low productivity of a pre-industrial economy could support.[95] If this model is adopted, the Ottoman crisis appears as just one more example of a world-wide "seventeenth-century crisis," and the next item on the agenda would be to compare the difficulties experienced by Ottoman society with those in other parts of the world.

If some modifications are introduced, it would doubtless be possible to combine the various approaches, especially the Genç and Steensgaard models. Other models will no doubt be devised. The Genç–Steensgaard models place considerable emphasis upon the internal dynamics of the social system involved and, at the present stage of our research, we need to articulate these internal dynamics with the impact of external economic pressures. It does not seem very convincing to view a major world empire, with the most modern arms at its disposal, as merely the helpless victim of circumstances beyond its control. Even less attractive are "stage theories," which assume that at a given point in time the Ottoman Empire, its economy included, passed from the stage of "florescence" into that of "decay." Given the fact that Ottoman political thinkers always considered expansion by war as a major *raison d'être* for the Ottoman state, it seems only reasonable to assume that the costs of war played a crucial role in the genesis of Ottoman economic crisis. But whether that is more than a somewhat naive conception of "poetic justice" only future researchers will be able to tell.

NOTES

1 Braudel (1979), II, p. 12.
2 Cemal Kafadar, unpublished Ph.D. dissertation, McGill University, Montreal, 1986. I am grateful to the author for allowing me to consult his work in manuscript.
3 Akdağ (1963), pp. 81–82; Kunt (1983), p. 75.
4 Akdağ (1963), p. 151.
5 Griswold (1983), pp. 110–56.
6 Cezar (1965), p. 83.
7 Cook (1972), pp. 10–11.
8 See also Jennings, forthcoming. I thank the author for allowing me to see his work in manuscript.
9 İnalcık (1980), p. 284.
10 İnalcık (1980), p. 303 and elsewhere.
11 İnalcık (1973), pp. 110–11.
12 İnalcık (1980), p. 287.
13 Faroqhi (1984), p. 276.
14 Adanır (1982).
15 Koçi Bey (1885–86), p. 61; İnalcık (1980).

16 Akdağ (1963), *passim*; Griswold (1983), pp. 157–209.

17 Andreasyan (1964), ed., pp. 84–87.

18 Jennings (1976), p. 41; Faroqhi (1978), pp. 46–47.

19 Faroqhi (1984), p. 120; Goffman (1990), pp. 13ff. The seventeenth-century figure is an estimate by the French merchant and traveler Jean Baptiste Tavernier.

20 Faroqhi (1987), p. 236.

21 It is possible that further monographs will modify these preliminary results.

22 Abdel Nour (1982), p. 74.

23 See Braudel (1949, 2nd edn 1966), pp. 298–325 for the factors influencing urban development. The second edition has been used throughout.

24 Raymond (1973–74), I, pp. 204–5; Raymond relays the figures given by Evliya Çelebi, assuming that they may be somewhat on the optimistic side, but that the order of magnitude given is probably the correct one. We possess no further counts of the population before 1798, when French scholars in the service of Napoleon arrived at a figure of 263,000. Raymond assumes that in 1517, the year in which the Ottomans conquered Cairo, the city had a population of 150,000, so that during the three centuries of Ottoman domination, the population grew by 60%.

25 Raymond (1973–74), I, pp. 86, 205.

26 Perenyi (1970).

27 Panzac (1985b), pp. 224–25. Panzac suggests that during the period he investigated there existed several areas in which mice, gerbils and other wild creatures of the fields were infected with plague and in which human beings might catch the disease without any infection from the outside. One long-term and major focus of infection was the border area between the Ottoman Empire and Iran, another the Albanian and Epirus mountains. While both these areas were sparsely settled and epidemics among mice, hamsters, gerbils and other wild animals did therefore not necessarily affect human beings, other less permanent foci of infection can be discerned in and around major cities of the eighteenth century.

28 Griswold (1983), pp. 238ff.

29 *Ibid.*

30 Ülker (1974), pp. 42ff; Ambraseys and Finkel (1987).

31 Hütteroth (1968), *passim*.

32 Hütteroth and Abdulfattah (1977), pp. 48–56; Abdel Nour (1982), pp. 80–87.

33 McGowan (1981), p. 119.

34 de Planhol (1968), pp. 235–36.

35 Orhonlu (1967), pp. 27–52.

36 Faroqhi (1984), pp. 284–85.

37 Erder and Faroqhi (1979), pp. 330ff.

38 İnalcık (1975); Ilgürel (1979); Jennings (1980).

39 Faroqhi (1984), p. 78; McGowan (1987).

40 İslamoğlu-İnan (1987b), pp. 123–25.

41 İslamoğlu-İnan (1985–86), p. 206; McGowan (1981), pp. 78–79.

42 McGowan (1981), p. 65.

43 İnalcık (1965).

44 Goffman (1990), p. 35; Katib Çelebi (1732), p. 900.
45 Çizakça (1987).
46 Sella (1968), p. 118.
47 Braude (1979).
48 Ashtor (1984).
49 Braudel (1979), II, p. 268.
50 Todorov (1967–68), p. 5.
51 Çizakça (1985), p. 367.
52 Faroqhi (1987), p. 211.
53 Kafadar (1986); Masson (1911), p. 457.
54 No comprehensive study is as yet available on the Ottoman cotton industry before the nineteenth century.
55 Goffman (1986), p. 230; Faroqhi (1986a), p. 373.
56 In the sixteenth century, a much more diversified agriculture had been practiced, therefore the hypothesis of increasing cotton production in the course of the seventeenth century appears probable. See Veinstein (1976), *passim*.
57 BBA, MD 96, no. 639.
58 İnalcık (1969), p. 118.
59 No quantitative data have been located concerning the amount of cloth woven on behalf of merchants.
60 BBA, MM 3457, pp. 3, 31.
61 BBA, MM 3457, p. 14.
62 Compare however Faroqhi (1984), pp. 156, 188.
63 Goodwin, (1975); Nayır (1975), *passim*.
64 Gaube and Wirth (1984), p. 366.
65 Gökyay (1975); Cafer Efendi, tr. and ed. by Crane (1987).
66 Barkan (1972–79), I, pp. 336–44.
67 I am greatly obliged to Dr. İdris Bostan for allowing me to consult the manuscript of his thesis on the seventeenth-century Arsenal, upon which the present section is based, and which, at the time of consultation, was unpublished. It has now been published as Bostan (1992).
68 Barkan (1972–79), I, pp. 93–137.
69 Bostan (1992), p. 71.
70 Bostan (1992), p. 138.
71 Barkan (1972–79), I, pp. 132–37.
72 Bostan (1992), pp. 5Iff.
73 *Ibid.* p. 74.
74 Çizakça (1981b).
75 Bostan (1992), p. 101 and elsewhere.
76 Bostan (1992), pp. 105ff. Possibly concern that the forest villagers employed as woodcutters might flee, if confronted with further demands for underpaid services, caused the Ottoman administration to purchase the extra timber required from merchants, at the – administratively determined – price payable also by ordinary customers.
77 Mantran (1962), pp. 284ff.
78 Bostan (1992), p. 109.
79 *Ibid.*, p. 115.

80 *Ibid.*, pp. 111.
81 *Ibid.*, p. 111.
82 *Ibid.*, pp. 221-22. Unfortunately the document recording this lowered tax demand does not tell us whether the decline in *avarızhane* had by this time reached the same alarming proportions.
83 İnalcık (1980), p. 294.
84 BBA, MD 34, p. 242 (1578-79).
85 Faroqhi (1984), pp. 184-87.
86 Güçer (1964), pp. 28-32; Faroqhi (1982), pp. 527ff.
87 Genç (1984); Finkel (1991).
88 Akdağ (1963), pp. 250-57; McGowan (1981), pp. 85ff.
89 Finkel (1991).
90 Braudel (1979), I, pp. 31-33.
91 Griswold (1983), pp. 238-39.
92 Compare Barbir (1980), pp. 6ff for a discussion of this matter with respect to Ottoman Syria.
93 Genç (1984).
94 Barkan (1975); Çizakça (1987) and (1985).
95 Steensgaard (1978), pp. 26-57.

17

॰

TRADE: REGIONAL, INTER-REGIONAL
AND INTERNATIONAL

GENERAL CONDITIONS

The debate on the status and role of trade and traders in the seventeenth-century Ottoman Empire has continued spasmodically over the last twenty or twenty-five years, and is as yet by no means resolved.[1] Until about 1960, Ottoman trade was viewed largely as a business carried out by foreign merchants and members of the minorities, with the exception of the İstanbul supply trade. However, the latter scarcely was regarded as authentic trade since it was subject to rigorous state controls; the involved merchants were seen almost as subordinates of the Ottoman central administration. While certain authors admitted that some merchants might find ways of profiting even from this trade, it was not presumed to hold any dynamic possibilities. By the seventeenth century, it was assumed, the Ottoman ruling group had lost all initiative *vis-à-vis* the merchants of mercantilist Europe.

This perspective, however, has changed to some extent during recent years. It has become clear that even in the sixteenth century, and certainly later on, peasants were involved in the marketing process, if only to pay their taxes. Internal trade in seventeenth-century Ankara or Bursa as well as in the Balkan towns of the eighteenth century led to a significant amount of social differentiation and capital accumulation. Thus it is generally recognized today that trade constituted an element essential to the cohesion of Ottoman state and society. By no means was it an activity that merely impinged upon state and society from the outside. One of the main problems confronting the Ottoman state administration c. 1600 was how to control merchant activities without hampering the commercial activity that was seen as essential for the normal course of tax collection.[2]

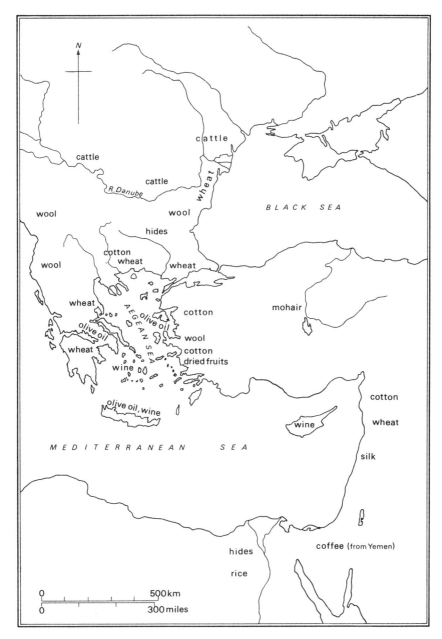

15 Indigenous exports of the eastern Mediterranean, later seventeenth century. *Source*: McGowan (1981), p. 33.

But significant gaps in our understanding still remain. No overall explanation has been developed for the fact that, despite considerable involvement in trade by members of the ruling class and professional merchants, no capitalism was generated.[3] Factors endogenous to the Ottoman system were important. Due to the prevailing distribution of political power, capital formation, though not insignificant, never progressed to the point of self-sustaining expansion of enterprises. On the other hand factors external to the Ottoman economy and society include European competition for markets and raw materials, which destroyed the dynamism of the Ottoman craft industry (see also Ch.16).[4]

The Ottoman textile industry, particularly its very dynamic cotton sector, was from the seventeenth century onward threatened not only by the West but also by the low wages of Indian artisans, and efficient networks of distribution which allowed imported Indian products to compete with those of Anatolian and Rumelian weavers.[5] Thus, in explaining the Ottoman Empire's long-term economic difficulties, we can observe a certain convergence between endogenous factors and those external to the Ottoman system. But no systematic attempt has been made to weigh the relative importance of the different factors, and this must be considered as one of the major gaps in our understanding of Ottoman socio-economic history.

When assessing the role of endogenous factors in preventing the emergence of capitalism, we need to discuss the status, role and limitations of Ottoman merchants, both Muslim and non-Muslim. Since little work has been done on this issue, it may be of some utility to review recent debates about the status, in pre-colonial times, of Middle Eastern, Indian and Malayan merchants, for this may clarify the terms in which the problem should be viewed. One school of thought holds that Middle Eastern merchants were essentially peddler, even when the volume of goods which they bought and sold was considerable.[6] Middle Eastern merchants, it is assumed, might travel in person or have their wares accompanied by an associate. They possessed little advance information concerning their targeted market. Since markets were isolated from one another, price differentials were often extraordinarily high, even between commercial centers located at moderate distances from one another. Given these circumstances, few merchants dared to convey large quantities of goods to any given market, and refused to trade if they could not expect a profit of at least 25–30 percent. In fact, "peddling" merchants were caught in a vicious circle. Because most did only a limited amount of business in any one locality, it scarcely paid to employ year-round resident buyers to take advantage of seasonally low prices. For a similar reason, few merchants were willing to invest in the construction of storage space. Moreover, individual merchants rarely were strong enough to put political pressure on rulers.[7] Therefore the latter freely increased tolls and duties ("protection costs") until merchants no longer found the trade worth their while and located alternative routes.[8] These organizational weaknesses are said to have disarmed the Middle Eastern merchant *vis-à-vis* his European competitors, and so, in the long run, European merchants captured Middle Eastern and Asian trade.

This view recently has been challenged. No one denies that a large share of Asian trade was in fact conducted by peddlers. On the other hand, there also existed, particularly in India, veritable "merchant princes," comparable to the Fuggers or Medicis.[9] In the pre-industrial world, whether in Europe or in Asia, all markets were characterized both by small size and violent price fluctuations. Thus the contrast between European and Asian or Middle Eastern conditions was less dramatic than had been assumed. The putative isolation of Asian markets also is being questioned: in the major trading centers of the time, a separate wholesaling market existed where merchants could buy either against immediate payment of cash or else contract for future delivery. Thus the major entrepôts of Asian trade might serve to integrate a number of distant markets, and the more important merchants at least were reasonably well provided with advance market information.

Very few researchers involved in Ottoman history have to this date taken up the challenge implicit in this controversy. However, it would be of great interest to know if the observations of Indian economic historians concerning the business practices of merchants on the Indian subcontinent have any parallel in Ottoman territory. To give a concrete example, we do need to find out whether the great pilgrimage fair at Muzayrib near Damascus was merely a place where a multitude of small transactions was effected, or whether this was also a wholesaling market for merchants supplying the Hejaz. It would appear that, at least in the eighteenth century, the coffee merchants of Cairo did not operate in the style of peddlers, even though their commercial techniques seem to have been quite simple.[10] At this time, it would certainly be premature to make general statements about the characteristic business methods of different types of Ottoman traders. But we can point to the importance of the problem and hope that it will be taken up in the future.

Braudel approaches the role of Asian and Middle Eastern merchants and the problem of pre-industrial market integration from quite a different angle.[11] Using the concept of "world economy" he differentiates between a number of European and non-European economic regions with more or less fixed boundaries, each variously integrated by lively internal trade. Each world economy is dominated by a single city, although this city may yield its place to a more fortunate rival without any change to the borders of the relevant world economy. Moreover, the space encompassed by a world economy is hierarchically organized: the countryside surrounding the dominant city often benefits from the latter's privileged position, and wealthy regions in close proximity to the central city gradually shade off into the "periphery." The countryside on the other hand is sparsely inhabited, economically undeveloped and easily exploited by the central city, a low level of prices serving as a fairly sure indication of a sluggish economic life.

Such a view of economic organization de-emphasizes the mutual isolation of markets, and implicitly contradicts the assumption that all Eastern or Asian trade was a kind of peddling. It is thus not by accident that Braudel dwells at length upon the merchant networks integrating local and regional markets. From his account, one rather gains the impression that the "capitalism" developed by Indian, Chinese or Armenian merchants permitted these traders a considerable degree of control over local economies. This view contradicts one of the more cherished assumptions of older European economic historiography. Without ever formally discussing the question, it long was assumed that the Ottoman ruling group had little or no interest in trade, therefore the Ottoman realm was open to European economic penetration whenever a strong state backed up its traders by naval power.[12] Braudel, on the other hand, regards the Ottoman Empire as a world economy in its own right. Ottoman traders controlled the vital land routes linking the different parts of the empire. In this sense, Braudel compares the Ottoman economic region to the Russian world economy, which by the seventeenth century also possessed very few links to a European-dominated world market.[13]

This use of the term "world economy" does not exclude a situation where a given region may have been integrated by military force, not by the action of merchants. Even if this broader definition of the term is adopted, there are some observations which make it seem problematic whether the seventeenth-century Ottoman Empire should be regarded as a "world economy" according to Braudel's definition. First of all, it is assumed that all fully developed world economies have only one economic center, polycentrism being regarded as the sign either of an immature world economy or else of a decaying one. But the Ottoman economic region, at its apogée in the sixteenth and seventeenth centuries, possessed not one but three centers, namely İstanbul, Aleppo and Cairo. Moreover, while Aleppo declined in the later seventeenth and early eighteenth centuries, İstanbul and Cairo retained roughly comparable economic levels. In the same way, the hierarchization of the entire region was not nearly as well developed as one might expect.[14] Around İstanbul there certainly existed "Thünen" rings of market gardening, grain growing and sheep breeding, although this pattern was distorted by the availability of waterways. But the countryside surrounding İstanbul does not conform to Braudel's model. Early seventeenth-century Ottoman documents do not indicate a particularly prosperous agriculture in northwestern Anatolia or eastern Thrace. If anything, the contrary is true. Only in Syria and Egypt do we find expanding agriculture and a well-cultivated countryside.[15] Given polycentrism, and the lack of a large-scale prosperous zone surrounding İstanbul, it does not seem appropriate to call the Ottoman realm a world economy in the sense intended by Braudel.

The concept of "world empire" used by Immanuel Wallerstein for socio-political entities resembling the Ottoman Empire is more serviceable. In the "world economy" merchants are capable of making the state act in conformity with their interests, in the "world empire" the state apparatus dominates the scene and merchants play second fiddle.[16] This seems a reasonable description of seventeenth-century Ottoman reality. Moreover a typical world economy consists of several states which may at certain times be at war with one another.[17] Obviously such a constellation has little in common with sixteenth- or even seventeenth-century Ottoman realities. Under the circumstances, the Ottoman Empire best is seen as a "world empire" in Wallerstein's sense of the term.

Whether the reader shares this view or prefers the Braudelian categorization, the main problem remains. Scholars generally agree that in the early sixteenth century the Ottoman Empire was not the economic satellite of an expanding European economy. There is an equally general agreement that the opposite was true by 1840.[18] But once we are dealing with the seventeenth century, the relationship of the Ottoman socio-political system to the expanding European world economy constitutes a problem. Large-scale destruction of Ottoman handicrafts seems to have taken place mainly in the late eighteenth and early nineteenth centuries and not earlier. Does this mean that the seventeenth-century Ottoman economy possessed no close links to Europe, except for the exchange of a few luxuries? That is obviously not true either. So we have to assume that throughout the seventeenth century certain areas of the Ottoman Empire exported agricultural produce and (to a limited extent) manufactured goods while importing European cloth. But these exchanges, while important on a regional level, were not so large as to make the Ottoman Empire as a whole dependent upon the European world economy. Marked discrepancies between maritime and landlocked regions characterize this "intermediate" period.

If we assume that Ottoman manufactures resisted European competition for an appreciable period of time, we need to explain the conditions of industrial survival. During much of the seventeenth century, European economic impact was limited, as quite a few regions and industries of Western and Central Europe then were passing through a depression phase. On the Ottoman side the military strength of the Ottoman state in the seventeenth century was sufficient to prevent limitless European penetration. Ottoman merchants succeeded in organizing craft industries and setting up efficient networks for distribution, and European traders attempting to break into Ottoman markets often found them tough competitors.

Since Ottoman merchants did set up their own networks and competed with European traders, it is difficult to regard the Ottoman socio-political system as passive and inert, an arena in which European merchants were completely free to act. At the same time, the historian's perception of Ottoman merchants is likely to be distorted, for while both European merchants and the Ottoman state have produced abundant records, Ottoman merchants have not. Occasional records of the latters' activities can be found in the kadi registers, but these are no substitute for account books and business correspondence, which, where the seventeenth century is concerned, either were not written or have not yet been found. However, an analogy with Indian merchants may be worth noting, where it has been suggested that some merchants avoided keeping records as they wished to "keep a low profile."[19] Even though few records concerning Ottoman and Middle Eastern traders have survived, this does not mean that all these traders operated as mere peddlers, with primitive commercial techniques and limited mutual communication. Such peddlers certainly existed, but the commercial world probably contained a variety of different types.

THE OTTOMAN STATE AND FOREIGN TRADERS

We know very little about the views of Muslim and non-Muslim Ottoman merchants about their European competitors. But a number of sultanic rescripts reflect official perceptions of French, English or Venetian traders.[20] These allow us to determine the context in which to interpret the privileges granted to various European nations, better known as the capitulations. Since the interpretations of the capitulations provided by European diplomats and lawyers have dominated our interpretation of these texts, and these do not coincide with Ottoman views at all, it is necessary to sketch the web of political relations within which foreign merchants and Ottoman officials conducted their daily business.

The Ottoman central administration viewed the affairs of foreign merchants as matters which should be handled by subordinate officials as much as possible. Thus foreign merchants very often dealt with mere temporary employees (*emin*) or tax-farmers (*mültezim*). In smaller centers of trade, many problems needed to be solved by *ad hoc* negotiation; in the more important ones, previous decisions were sometimes collected in a special record book and submitted to each new sultan for confirmation. These local regulations contained most of the material directly related to trade, while quite a few seventeenth-century capitulations, the Venetian ones in particular, dealt mainly with interstate relations and only secondarily with trade.[21]

İzmir, the booming port town of this period, was intentionally left a simple district center and not promoted to the rank of a *sancak* capital, so that the involvement of high-level officials was avoided as far as possible. From the foreign merchants' point of view, there were also certain advantages involved in this arrangement. Day-to-day affairs could be arranged according to mutual convenience, which would not have been possible if higher-ranking officials had been involved. A modern account of the often not unpleasant life of European merchants in seventeenth- and eighteenth-century İzmir specifically refers to "*la bienveillance des puissances.*"[22]

On the other hand, capitulations were not infrequently honored more in the breach than in the application. Certain items in the capitulations ran counter to the deeply held convictions of provincial and local officials. Muslim religious law (the Sharia) assumed that Holy War (*gaza*) against infidels was permanent, only to be interrupted, at the very most, by brief truces. The granting of capitulations, however, was based upon the assumption that peace was a more or less permanent state of affairs, even though seventeenth-century sultans remained free to revoke these privileges at will.

Given this tension, it is not surprising that commanders of, for instance, fortresses on the Adriatic coast continued to give shelter to

North African corsairs who had plundered Venetian or other ships in contravention of the capitulations. Occurrences of this kind become more comprehensible when one remembers that they had their counterparts on the Venetian side of the frontier. Thus certain Venetian commanders were notorious for their leniency in treating Christian pirates masquerading as "crusaders." Under these circumstances, it is a misleading over-simplification to assume that by the seventeenth century Muslim corsairs continued their expeditions because the central government could not enforce its orders in Albania or Cyprus. Rather, Ottoman administrators and military men had their own code which determined proper behavior for the positions they occupied. Obedience to the sultan certainly formed part of these officials' value system, but only a part and not the whole.

At the same time, one may assume that a ruling group able to function according to a well-established system of values was an element of strength, not weakness, for the state. Possibly this tendency toward an informal, well-established code of official behavior was strengthened by the formalization and bureaucratization of Ottoman government procedures beginning with the reign of Mehmed the Conqueror, gathering momentum under Kanuni Süleyman and continuing through the seventeenth century. We have not as yet fully explored the consequences of this increasing bureaucratization of Ottoman government.[23] But the problem of how the capitulations were applied may well constitute a useful starting point for investigations of this kind.[24]

In the late sixteenth century, foreign trade in the Ottoman realm changed dramatically. English traders entered the Mediterranean in large numbers, eclipsing the Venetians and importing large supplies of woolen cloth. Rapid change continued in the seventeenth century as well: the transit trade in spices declined while the importation of coffee increased, raw silk from Iran was now sold less frequently in Bursa but more frequently in İzmir. Indian merchants were active on both the Red Sea and Basra routes. However, it is difficult to determine whether Indian textiles and rice really became so much more important in the seventeenth century than they had been in the sixteenth, or whether we notice them more because documentation has improved. Ottoman officialdom responded to these changes by keeping more accurate track of foreign merchants; special registers were opened so that the responsible officials could easily determine how relations with a given merchant community had evolved, and whether taxpayers and tax-farmers had to be protected against scarcities due to exportation.

TRANSPORTATION NETWORKS: RIVER TRAFFIC

In Ottoman trade, land routes played a considerable role, even though transportation on camels or in ox-drawn carts was more expensive than by ship. The small number of navigable waterways explains this situation at least in part: in all of Anatolia, Syria and Iraq, only the Euphrates–Tigris system was navigable on a regular basis, although much less suitable waterways such as the Menderes were occasionally usable. However, since the water level even on the Euphrates changed dramatically according to the season, navigation was very difficult. Moreover, the Ottoman state of the seventeenth century had trouble policing this waterway; among others the Abū Rish Bedouins, centered around Ana on the Euphrates, threatened river shipping.[25] Perhaps even more dangerous were the people that Ottoman sources call the *Cezayir arapları*, who lived on a multitude of small islands in the Shatt al-Arab and about whom there are virtually no written records.[26]

At the end of the seventeenth century, however, this area abruptly was catapulted into history. In 1694 Mani, head of the Muntafik tribe, benefited from Ottoman involvement in a war with Austria and captured Basra. This led to a major Ottoman reaction, remarkable both as a campaign and a feat of civil engineering. In 1699 a war fleet was built in the Birecik arsenal on the Upper Euphrates. In 1701–2 a new branch of the Euphrates, which recently had formed and was preventing river navigation, was forced back into the main river bed; about 4,000 men were employed on this project. As a result, Indian traders who previously had deserted Basra for Iranian ports returned, particularly since the Ottoman official in charge of Iraqi river communications (the so-called *Şat kaptanı*) actively promoted trade. Seventeenth-century river transportation from Birecik to Baghdad was not a matter that would take care of itself; this route could only be kept open by constant state intervention.

The first *Şat kaptanı* after the campaign of 1699–1702 had been appointed to this post due to his experience on the Danube. Ottoman authorities thus acknowledged that navigation in these widely separated regions had certain problems in common. The Danube of the seventeenth century, however, was no major commercial artery connecting Central Europe with the Black Sea.[27] A natural obstacle, namely the Iron Gates, permitted the passage only of small boats and bottled up the river. From an Ottoman point of view, the Danube was commercially viable only below the Iron Gates for the transportation of grain to İstanbul. Thus the Lower Danube formed a kind of extension to the Black Sea, while the middle reaches of the river were mainly utilized for military purposes. At the same time, the agriculture of Sirem and the other Ottoman provinces along the Middle Danube was hurt by the lack of a convenient outlet to distant markets. A sparse population practiced extensive agriculture and animal husbandry, with pig breeding in the forests a major occupation. More intensive land use only became feasible after the construction of railways.

The only other major navigable river in the empire was the Nile. This river was the main commercial artery of Egypt, preferred not only due to its relative cheapness but also because of insecure desert routes. Agricultural goods from all over Egypt were brought to Cairo by way of the Nile, and the second city of the Ottoman Empire constituted Egypt's major market. From the fifteenth century onward, Bulaq was Cairo's main river port, where the trade in grain, rice and flax was located, and an impressive number of khans had been constructed. On the other hand, Mısr (Old Cairo), decaying since the later Middle Ages, handled a limited volume of trade with Upper Egypt. Boats on the Nile, without decks and bearing two or three masts, generally carried about 200 tons. Those used in the Delta were constructed solidly enough that they could equally be employed for short trips on the Mediterranean. By contrast, boats plying the Upper Nile were different from those used in the lower reaches of the river, and goods traveling from the Delta toward Upper Egypt generally were reloaded in Mısr or Bulaq. It seems that boat traffic on the Nile throughout the seventeenth century followed well-established patterns, with no major changes intervening in the course of the seventeenth century.[28]

TRANSPORTATION NETWORKS: CARAVAN ROUTES

Caravans were more important than river traffic for linking together different regions of the empire. Throughout the seventeenth century caravan routes were under the close control of the Ottoman state, and principally used by Ottoman merchants. The network of caravan routes is best discussed by starting from the four main nodes, namely İstanbul, Edirne, Aleppo and Cairo (see Map 11). İstanbul was linked to Belgrade and Buda by a route that followed the course of the Roman Via Egnatia by way of Edirne, Filibe (Plovdiv), Sofia and Niş. This was the route most commonly used by European travelers entering the empire, and for this reason it probably constitutes the best-known of all Ottoman routes.[29]

Three major routes linked İstanbul with the caravan cities of Anatolia. The most famous was the road connecting İstanbul to Aleppo and Damascus, which was traveled by most İstanbul and Anatolian Muslims undertaking the pilgrimage to Mecca. The road skirted the central Anatolian dry steppe, with Akşehir and Konya as major stops. Then the Taurus mountains were traversed, and the road entered the hot plain of the Çukurova, where a stop was made in Adana. From there onwards, caravans passed in close proximity of the Mediterranean, through the pass of Karanlık Kapu, and then headed due east to reach Aleppo, one of the empire's most important commercial centers. From there, pilgrims and merchants traveled directly to Damascus.[30]

For trade with Iran, Erzurum and Diyarbekir were the major entrepôts close to the border. Diyarbekir was connected to İstanbul only by rather circuitous routes.[31] On the other hand, the connection between İstanbul and Erzurum constituted one of the main arteries of Anatolian commercial traffic. If a merchant or traveller from İstanbul set out in the direction of western Iran, he had a choice of two routes: across the steppe to Ankara by way of Eskişehir, continuing through an area devoid of major settlements until he reached Tokat. The alternative was to travel through the hill chains of northern Anatolia, cross the Kızılırmak over a handsome bridge in Osmancık and then reach Amasya. Amasya had been an entrepôt of the silk trade and an occasional residence of sultans in the sixteenth century; but by the mid-seventeenth, the town was going through some very difficult times and its population fell by half.[32] From there it was but a short distance to Tokat, the main commercial center along this route, famous for its textiles and copperwork. By contrast, the next commercially significant stop, namely Erzincan, was a relatively modest town.[33] The border entrepôt of Erzurum at one time in the sixteenth century was all but deserted as people fled from continuous warfare along the Ottoman–Iranian frontier.[34] By the later sixteenth century the town was recovering, and this continued throughout the seventeenth century, in spite of probable fluctuations due to renewed warfare.

As a node of the Ottoman system of caravan routes, Edirne was at least as important as İstanbul; for here the traveller arriving from the capital and Bursa (by way of Gelibolu) could make a choice between connections to Moldavia and Wallachia by way of Sliven to Belgrade or

Sarajevo, and to Durres (Durazzo) on the Adriatic coast by way of Salonica. These routes linked the Rumelian provinces with Central Europe and Italy: Durres was frequently visited by Venetian ships and by boats from Spanish-controlled southern Italy.[35] From Sarajevo, a somewhat circuitous route led to Dubrovnik; a city-state that paid tribute to the Ottoman Empire and benefited substantially from the connection. The routes to Wallachia and Moldavia also linked the Ottoman Empire to Central Europe. Closest to the border, the vassal principality of Transylvania was connected to the Ottoman Empire by routes leading from Sibiu to Niğbolu, from Brašov to Giurgiu on the northern bank of the Danube and from there to Ruse, a district center in the province of Rumeli. Along these routes, Rumelian traders carried Ankara mohair cloths and various silks and spices and sold the English woolens they had purchased in the Rumanian principalities.[36]

Beyond Transylvania, trade routes led to Buda and to the Austrian border. This route would flourish in the eighteenth century, when the Levant Company had reduced its activity in the Mediterranean, and English goods began arriving by way of Vienna. Another important route linked the three Rumanian principalities to Lwow, at that time a Polish city. Great caravans of wagons traveled back and forth between Poland and İstanbul, and the Armenian merchants resident in Lwow who organized this traffic were known for their opulence.[37]

In Aleppo, four major long-distance routes came together: first of all, the connection to İstanbul, previously discussed, continued to Damascus and on to Medina and Mecca. As far as Damascus, this route led through the steppe; only then did it turn into a desert route properly speaking, which meant that the availability of water became the primary criterion in determining where the caravan was to spend the night. Beyond Damascus, not many towns were encountered until Medina. Settlements here were mostly fortifications manned by a small number of permanent inhabitants, not towns or villages. Even the great fair of Muzayrib, where many pilgrims purchased their provisions, did not develop into a permanent settlement.

In addition, Aleppo was linked to Baghdad by a well-traveled caravan route, which followed the course of the Euphrates. The traveler might elect to traverse the fairly well urbanized southeastern section of Anatolia, and by way of Birecik and Urfa, reach Diyarbekir and Tabriz. In addition, Aleppo was connected with Mediterranean sea routes by way of İskenderun and Payas. Payas never developed into a major port, even though the sixteenth-century Ottoman administration had constructed fortifications, a covered market and a number of shops. During the Iranian wars, this port gained an ephemeral importance as a point of transshipment for war material. In the seventeenth century, İskenderun was more active than Payas, even though a serious malaria problem prevented the development of a permanent settlement. In addition, there was a less important route from Aleppo to Tripoli, used by European merchants purchasing Syrian silk.[38]

As a last node of the Ottoman route system, the city of Cairo must be mentioned. Due to the importance of river and sea traffic, however, caravans played a subsidiary role. One of the most important was the Morocco caravan. Under the leadership of an official appointed by the sultan of Morocco, pilgrims and traders reached Cairo after traversing the desert as far as Gabes, and then traveling along the coast to Egypt. In addition, a pilgrimage caravan linked Cairo to Mecca and Medina. This caravan, like its Damascene counterpart, was protected by tribesmen who received grants-in-aid from the Ottoman central administration, and used specially fortified stopping points. In addition, many pilgrims traveled across the desert to Suez or one of the other Red Sea ports, and there boarded a vessel, often overloaded and dangerous, that took them to Jidda. Merchants engaged in the Red Sea trade, particularly coffee importers, used the same land–sea routes as the pilgrims. In addition, a caravan route linked Cairo to Damascus by way of Palestine; this passed through Al-Aris and Gaza with its covered market and from there continued to the pilgrimage center of Halilürrahman (Hebron). Most of these routes predated the seventeenth century and were used in subsequent centuries as well. But we have long since learned to visualize the "medium-speed" changes that become visible in the course of a century against the background of much more stable structures.

THE SEA ROUTES: A DECLINE IN OTTOMAN CONTROL

Cairo's fortunes in the seventeenth century depended on Mediterranean and Red Sea trade. Commerce with the Yemen and, through the latter, the Indian Ocean, was particularly significant from the late sixteenth century. At this time coffee imports supplemented and then replaced the transit trade in fine spices to Europe, that had been ruined by the occupation of the spice-producing islands by the Dutch c.1600. Egyptian merchants rarely traveled beyond Jidda, which, in addition, was an active center for the import of Indian textiles. These generally arrived in Indian ships, which used the monsoon winds blowing in the Indian Ocean. In addition, Yemeni and Jidda merchants also traded with India; by 1635, however, the Yemen had slipped out of Ottoman control.

In the seventeenth century, the Indian Ocean remained an open sea that no major state controlled. The Mediterranean and West European pattern of trading from fortified points, and the association of trade with naval control, had not yet been established in the Indian Ocean.[39] In the sixteenth century it had seemed this pattern was about to be instituted: the Portuguese in Goa and other Indian Ocean ports had attempted to ruin all Indian and Arab shippers that were unwilling to purchase their letters of safe-conduct. In response, Kanuni Süleyman had sent war fleets into the Indian Ocean in an attempt to dislodge the Portuguese. However, this attempt failed even though Ottoman naval activity did prevent Portuguese penetration into the Red Sea. Thus the Ottoman navy withdrew from the Indian Ocean, and to mention but one consequence, the Sumatran state of Atjeh was left without Ottoman support.[40] In the same vein, the Persian Gulf was the scene of intense rivalry between the Portuguese and the English, particularly between 1615 and 1635: but the Ottoman presence made itself felt only when Shah Abbas threatened Basra in 1623.[41] The shah benefited from the English–Portuguese conflict when English military support facilitated his reconquest of Hormuz in 1622.[42] Even though Basra's trade revived when the Portuguese rerouted their trade through Muscat and Basra, this did not lead to the Ottoman Empire's taking on a major role in Gulf politics.[43]

Merchants and ship owners from the Arabic-speaking provinces of the empire, however, continued to trade in the Red Sea and the Indian Ocean despite the Ottoman Empire's political withdrawal. On the other hand, even though the sultans maintained a formidable naval presence in the Mediterranean, a great deal of coastal trade between ports of the empire was lost by Ottoman shippers to European competitors. This was due not to a lack of tonnage, but to political factors. Throughout the period, the so-called "Regencies" of Algiers, Tunis and Tripoli used all available ships for corsair activity and chartered French or English vessels for trade and even for the transportation of pilgrims to Egypt. Such use of European ships in Ottoman coastal trade, known as the "caravane," recommended itself because the ruling groups that controlled Algiers, Tunis and Tripoli, even though paying allegiance to the Ottoman sultan, retained the right to attack vessels from all countries that had not come to a specific agreement with their own local governments. The ruling groups of Algiers, Tunis and Tripoli were not alone in applying such a policy; it was also common enough in the Christian world of the seventeenth century. Thus shippers from countries that had agreements with the Ottoman Empire, and more specifically with Algiers, Tunis and Tripolis, often successfully competed with ship captains from states which did not possess this advantage. Merchants from southern Italy, for instance, also used the services of the French caravane.[44] The Habsburg–Ottoman conflict thus provided commercial opportunities for shippers from neutral countries. However, this use of European ships in the internal coastal trade of the Ottoman Empire limited opportunities for locally owned shipping and increased dependence on imported semi-manufactured goods. Apart from the political choices of the Algerian or Tunisian ruling groups, the strong position of French, Dutch and English shipping also discouraged any inclination to build up a rival commercial fleet.

ORGANIZING INTERNAL TRADE: MARKETS, FAIRS AND CREDIT

In the aggregate a considerable volume of trade took place at village markets. In the Ottoman Empire before the middle of the sixteenth century, we often find but one market per district (*kaza*), which latter institution must have been indispensable for the smooth functioning of the tax-collection system. After all, peasants were required to pay certain taxes in money, and many *timar*-holders presumably needed to sell off some of the grain which they collected in order to procure horses and weapons. But from the 1560s onwards village markets proliferated particularly in settlements located on the more important trade routes, but often also in provinces where integration within systems of inter-regional exchange was comparatively slight. On the other hand, the investments of pious foundations in the shops and storage spaces of such village markets indicated the liveliness of local trade.[45]

The disturbances and population movements of the early seventeenth century probably led to the temporary or permanent disappearance of many such rural markets. However, in certain areas they persisted or were reestablished. After Evliya Çelebi in 1671 had traveled through the coastal plain between Antalya and Alanya, he claimed that the locals were so ignorant that they did not know the standard names for the seven days of the week. Instead they designated these days by referring to "the market day of the village of NN," which should mean that the inhabitants of a very remote area know of seven markets being held in their immediate vicinity.[46] These rural and semi-rural markets were attended by itinerant traders. In Thrace, they often transported their wares in wagons and assembled in special markets, probably located on the outskirts of settlements. Itinerant traders bought not only agricultural products, but also the products of rural industry, such as cotton thread. It is probable that traders sometimes worked for more important merchants in cities such as Bursa, who organized production within a putting-out system. More dramatic was the sixteenth- and seventeenth-century development of the fairs in today's northern Greece and southern Bulgaria. Many already existed in the later sixteenth century, sometimes as modest gatherings associated with the feast of the local church's patron saint. However, around 1600, patrons of major pious foundations, such as the Grand Vizier Rüstem Pasha and Sultan Ahmed I himself, frequently annexed these fairs to their foundations as revenue-producing items. This indicates that some of these fairs, particularly the famous gathering held in the Thessalian settlement of Maşkolur, already must have been prosperous. The construction of sometimes elaborate fair-grounds with a surrounding wall and fixed booths probably helped to increase the number of traders attending these events.

Many fairs formed part of inter-regional trade networks. In the 1560s and 1570s, rugs and *kilims* from Anatolia are recorded among the goods traded in Maşkolur.[47] Whether these exchanges continued in the unsettled conditions of the late sixteenth and early seventeenth centuries is uncertain; and after 1650, it becomes increasingly difficult to locate sources on the Balkan fairs.[48] At some time during the seventeenth century, the fairs possibly declined as nodes of internal trade, and when they were "resurrected" in the course of the eighteenth century, it was largely as a network for the distribution of imported manufactured goods.

Credit for both resident and itinerant traders was secured from pious foundations as well as from individuals.[49] In the middle of the sixteenth century, money-lending foundations were numerous in the major cities, particularly in İstanbul. However, the inflation of the late sixteenth and early seventeenth centuries eroded the capital of many foundations. Yet new donations were made, and money-lending pious foundations were common in the seventeenth century as well. Certain ulema regarded them as illegitimate, because they considered that only goods of permanent value, such as real estate, might constitute the base of a pious foundation, and because money-lending foundations contravened the religious prohibition of interest.[50] In the seventeenth century, a new type of

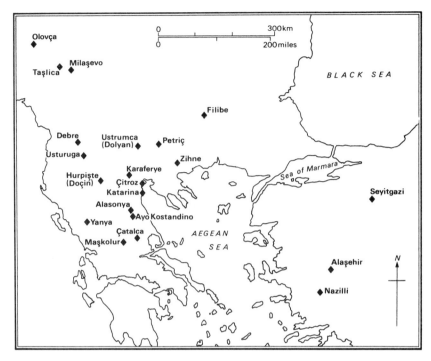

16 Fairs of the Balkans and Anatolia in the sixteenth and seventeenth centuries. *Source*: Faroqhi (1978), p. 68.

money-lending foundation gained popularity, in which the charity consisted of aid to a town quarter in defraying the burdensome *avarız* taxes. Pious foundations demanded collateral; and from the seventeenth-century examples of places such as Ankara or Kayseri, it becomes apparent that borrowers frequently surrendered their houses to the foundation. Thus at least certain foundations made loans to people of substance, and probably constituted a source of commercial credit.

Private lenders constituted another source of credit, that was widespread and decentralized.[51] Table II:7 indicates the distribution of loans in seventeenth-century Aleppo. In the Anatolian cities which have been investigated, there were no full-time money-lenders, although widows may have invested most of their capital in this fashion. Neither were there banks, even though c.1570 there was a short-lived attempt to establish a state-sponsored foundation that functioned as a source of investment credit for merchants.[52] The foundation's capital was derived from taxes paid mainly by merchants and craftsmen. Since only the wealthier can have been eligible for credit, the arrangement appears as an institution

Table II:7. Summary of court cases involving loans, Aleppo court registers, 1630–33 and 1635–37

Borrowers	Number of cases	% of total	Average amount (*kuruş*)	No. With multiple
Military to villagers	239	34	318	123
Muslims to villagers	164	23	113	65
Military to Muslims	62	9	90	13
Muslims to Muslims	122	17	50	11
Women borrowers	9	1	75	–
Women lenders	19	3	56	6
Military to *zimmis*	11	2	145	1
Muslims to *zimmis*	31	4	64	3
Zimmis to Muslims	9	1	134	–
Zimmis to *zimmis*	13	2	63	–
Guardian as lender	8	1	45	1
Vakf as lender	11	2	145	–
Muslims to military	2	–	–	–
Military to military	7	1	77	–
Total	707			

Source: Masters (1988), p. 154.

for transferring purchasing power from small craftsmen and traders to the more important merchants. The resistance of these disadvantaged petty entrepreneurs probably led to the phasing out of this loan fund in the 1590s.

In most credit transactions of the period, no secret was made of the fact that interest was demanded and paid. Informally established rules determined a "fair" rate of interest, namely between 10 and 20 percent, while pious foundations frequently demanded 15 percent. Feeling against usury and usurers was strong, certainly among members of the Ottoman administration and presumably among members of the "silent majority" as well. But this apparently applied to high rates of interest rather than to the taking of interest *per se*.[53] Interest-taking by pious foundations must have contributed toward legitimizing the practice. In the reign of Süleyman the Magnificent, Ebusuud Efendi defended the practice from a purely practical point of view; abolition of interest-taking would lead to the collapse of many pious foundations, a situation that would harm the Muslim community.[54]

In seventeenth-century Aleppo, however, lending by pious foundations constituted only a very minor part of all credit transactions. In this respect the Aleppines behaved like other Arab townsmen, among whom the money-lending pious foundation rarely took root. Aleppo money-lending was largely in the hands of military men; 46 percent of all cases in Table II:7 involved lenders in this category. In most cases military money-lenders must have belonged to the powerful Aleppo militias. Non-Muslim money-lenders were a negligible minority; neither in Aleppo nor in the towns of Anatolia was there any indication that non-Muslims might soon gain control over the money market.[55]

VARIETIES OF TRADE AND THE PRINCIPAL COMMERCIAL CENTERS: SUPPLYING İSTANBUL

We do not possess any reliable estimates for the seventeenth-century İstanbul population: a figure in the vicinity of 600,000–750,000 may be a reasonable assumption. To support these inhabitants the capital drew on the coastal areas of Rumelia and Anatolia, and also was supplied by boat traffic on the Marmara and Black Seas.[56] Agricultural production in the İstanbul region in many respects conformed to the model which economic geographers regard as standard: market gardening took place not only in the immediate vicinity of İstanbul, but even within the walls themselves.[57] But İstanbul's consumption of fruits and vegetables surpassed what could be produced in the immediate neighborhood, and villages along the Sea of Marmara were called upon to supply pomegranates and other fresh fruits. Olives came from Edremit and Ayvalık on the Aegean coast of Anatolia. Fresh grapes arrived from the vineyards which were taking the place of the fields and meadows surrounding Üsküdar by the last quarter of the sixteenth century. Raisins traveled a great distance, and were produced in the region of Aydın. Due to the difficulty of transporting timber and firewood, the latter normally were grown in a zone immediately beyond the market gardens and dairies. İstanbul neatly conforms to this general pattern, since the townsmen and the shipyards of the Arsenal received timber from northwestern Anatolia. In the early seventeenth century, certain sections of this area, which had been set aside for the exclusive use of the Arsenal, were inhabited by a floating population of legitimate and contraband woodcutters, often illegal immigrants from Rumeli.[58] Timber-smuggling was profitable because of high demand in Cairo, and Janissaries organized this trade to the detriment of the İstanbul consumer. More extensive than the forests of northwestern Anatolia were the grain-producing areas supplying İstanbul.[59] Apart from the western coastlands of the Black Sea, Thrace, as well as western Anatolia, Dobruja, Thessaly and Macedonia were at the disposal of the İstanbul consumer. The Nile and the Mediterranean afforded easy transport of Egyptian grain and rice, the latter particularly esteemed by wealthy consumers and the foundation-sponsored guest-houses which had adopted the consumption standards of wealthier Otto-man families.[60] In areas of Anatolia and the Balkans remote from the coast, only sheep breeding was oriented toward the İstanbul market. The exact limits between areas required to deliver grain to İstanbul and their exempt neighbors remain generally unknown to the twentieth-century researcher. But the peasants and townsmen of the time were perfectly conscious of these limits. Thus, in 1575–76, when a buyer demanded to purchase grain for İstanbul at Çorum, the local market overseer (*muhtesib*) refused, claiming that such deliveries were without preced-ent.[61] In the inland regions of the Balkans, wealthy men who did not necessarily own flocks were charged with the delivery of a given number of sheep to the capital.[62] In Anatolia, on the other hand, nomadic tribes-men brought sheep all the way from Erzurum and Diyarbekir, often resting them for a while on the pastures of Mount Erciyas in the heart of Anatolia. Not infrequently, a sizable number of sheep supposedly en route to İstanbul found their way to Bursa and even Rhodes, as prices there were higher than in the closely controlled market of the capital.

Manufactured goods sold in the markets and ships of the capital came from all areas of the empire. Anatolia was the most important source for a wide variety of textiles.[63] Silk fabrics from Bursa and Bilecik, cotton thread from Bolu and Çağa and cotton fabrics from the Aegean, particu-larly were prominent. In addition rugs and carpets of the rug-making centers at Uşak, Selendi, Kula and Gördes were produced not only for the palace and the principal mosques, but also for wealthy private buyers. One might add to this brief list the copper vessels of Kastamonu. From the Rumelian side of the Sea of Marmara, woolen fabrics were conveyed to the İstanbul consumer; the variety of woolen textiles from Salonica and its immediate vicinity shows that, as late as 1640, the weavers of Salonica were still producing for private customers, although they were to concentrate upon military supplies in future years. Ironware and leather constituted the only other industrial products of the Balkans which were at all prominent in İstanbul. Of Syrian and Egyptian manufactures, only textiles were important enough to merit inclusion in official price lists.

İstanbul thus exercised a very considerable impact upon Ottoman regional organization. After all, in the seventeenth century İstanbul was the largest city of both the Mediterranean lands and of Europe, and as Braudel has remarked more than once, large cities all over the world can command the services of smaller towns.[64] İstanbul was no exception; thus for instance, Ahyolu on the Black Sea and Tekirdağ-Rodosçuk on the

Table II:8. Wealthy persons proposed as butchers for İstanbul, 1570–94

No. of persons	Home town	Estimated fortune	Remarks
1	Eğridir	3,000 *filori*	Usurer, associate of former kadi
2	Ankara		Yürük
1	Beypazarı		
1	Kastamonu		
1	Bursa		*Kasaplar kethüdası* in Bursa
2	Ankara		Butchers in Ankara
1	Mudurnu	40–50,000 *filori*	Usurer
1	Siroz (Serrai)		Usurer, *naip*
1	Bender-Akkerman		
1	Mizistra		Non-Muslim
1	İstanbul		Grocer
2	Görice		Non-Muslim, usurer
1	Avlonya (Valona)		Usurer
2	Albanian *kaza*		Non-Muslim, usurer
1	Kasımpaşa (İstanbul)		Butcher
2	İstanbul		One *başçı*, one merchant and tavern keeper (at least one non-Muslim)
1	İstanbul		Slave trader
2	Atina (Athens)		
1	Manisa		One *kasapbaşı* in Manisa
1	Ruha (Urfa)		
1	Kalavorta (Kalavrita)	30–40,000 *filori*	Non-Muslim
1	Aydın	1,000,000 *akçe*	Speculator in raisins
1	Gelibolu	2,000,000 *akçe*	Non-Muslim
1	Ankara		Non-Muslim merchant
17	İstanbul		Non-Muslims, to be appointed auxiliary *kasap* (yamak)
15	Atina (Athens)	altogether 4,300,000 *akçe*	Non-Muslims
8	Bursa		
10	Galata (İstanbul)		Non-Muslims
9	Edirne		
1	Ahyolu (Ahtopol)		Non-Muslim
9	Süzebolu (Sozobol)		Non-Muslims
Totals			
100		at least 11,680,000 *akçe*	61 non-Muslims 9 usurers

Note: While an attempt has been made to locate as many instances as possible, the present list cannot claim to be exhaustive.
Source: Faroqhi (1984), p. 330.

Sea of Marmara functioned as subsidiary ports for the Ottoman capital. In Tekirdağ, special storehouses were constructed to keep supplies of Thracian grain and Egyptian rice in readiness for transport to the capital at short notice. Bursa served as a "workshop" for İstanbul, and to a lesser degree, Salonica's economy also was oriented toward İstanbul. Moreover it is probable that the capital's demands not only promoted but also inhibited urban development: İstanbul merchants controlled the trade in supplies to the capital, and sometimes intervened to limit provincial merchants who might become serious competitors. The weak development of seventeenth-century Anatolian port towns probably derived, at least in part, from the pressures generated by İstanbul merchants. İzmir constituted the great exception, but then the rise of this city largely was due to foreign trade.[65]

All deliveries to İstanbul were strictly controlled by the Ottoman state, through control mechanisms that remained unchanged from the sixteenth through the eighteenth centuries.[66] The keystone of official control was the legislated price (*narh*) which the İstanbul kadi determined after consultation with merchants and shipmasters. A controlled price in İstanbul, however, could be enforced only if sale prices in the producing areas also were regulated. Administratively established prices might vary according to seasons, particularly where foodstuffs were involved. But a major change in the silver content of the currency tended to upset the entire system, and made it necessary to establish entirely new price lists.

Control of prices did not necessarily prevent substantial profits for wholesalers. Wholesale grain dealers of İstanbul popularly were seen as disreputable persons who enriched themselves by other people's misery. In addition, there were appreciable profits in transporting grain. Thus a wealthy group of shipowners, mostly non-Muslim and owning on average three ships each, lived in Yeniköy on the Bosporus; they imparted so much commercial vitality to this little fishing village that the rates of exchange as practiced in this locality were considered worthy of a separate record. Viziers and other high-level Ottoman officials not infrequently invested in the İstanbul food trade.

Where the trade in live animals is concerned, by 1650 the position of wholesalers and butchers had improved considerably since the closing years of the sixteenth century. In the period before 1600, the retail price for meat frequently had been set so low that merchants were unable to stay in business, and appointment to the position of butcher in İstanbul was a much-feared penalty for usurers. But by the middle of the seventeenth century, the wholesalers supplying meat were prospering. There

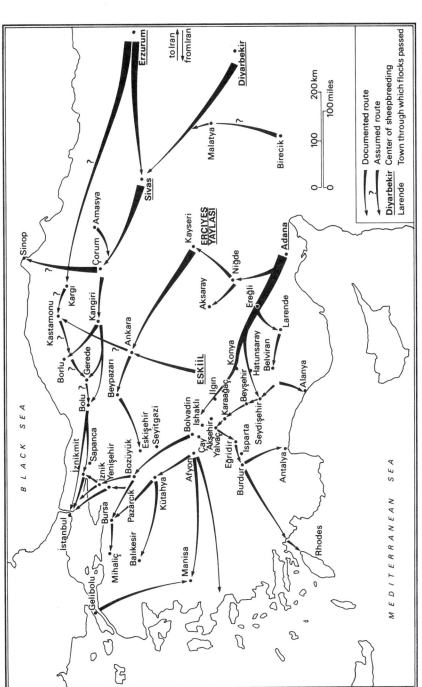

17 Trade in Anatolian sheep, sixteenth to seventeenth centuries. *Source:* Faroqhi (1984), p. 226.

Map labels:

Erzurum
to Iran
from Iran
Diyarbekir
Malatya
Birecik
Sivas
Amasya
Kayseri
ERCIYES YAYLASI
Çorum
Sinop
Nigde
Adana
Kargi
Kastamonu
Kangiri
Aksaray
Ereğli
Larende
Borlu
Gerede
Ankara
Konya
Hatunsaray
Belviran
Bolu
Beypazarı
ESKIIL
Ilgin
Beyşehir
Alanya
Iznikmit
Sapanca
Eskişehir
Seyitgazi
Bolvadin
Ishakli
Karaağaç
Seydişehir
Istanbul
Iznik
Yenişehir
Bozüyük
Çay
Akşehir
Yalvaç
Isparta
Antalya
Bursa
Pazarcik
Kütahya
Afyon
Eğridir
Burdur
Mihaliç
Balikesir
Manisa
Rhodes
Gelibolu

BLACK SEA
MEDITERRANEAN SEA

Legend:

Documented route
Assumed route
?
Diyarbekir Center of sheepbreeding
Larende Town through which flocks passed

200 km
100 miles
0   100   200

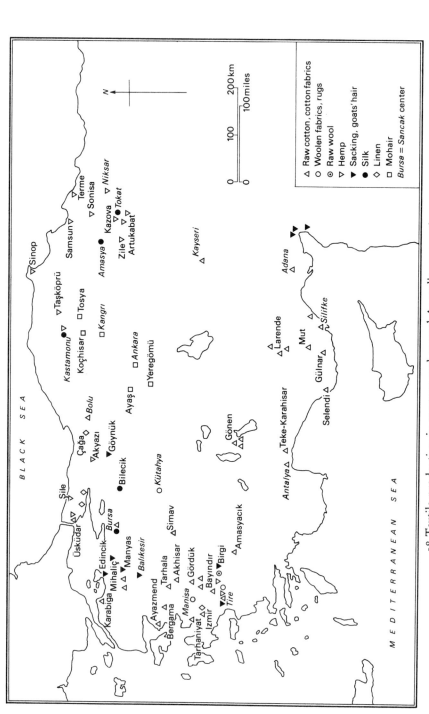

18 Textile production in western and central Anatolia, 1500–1650.

Source: Faroqhi (1984) p. 134.

is little doubt that a change in official policies was behind this notable turnaround in the wholesalers' fortunes. But at present we do not know anything about the political conflicts which must have been the cause for this reorientation of policy.

The İstanbul kadi played a key role in supervising the provisioning of the capital, for though he officially acted under the supervision of the grand vizier, he actually ran the day-to-day affairs of the city. He determined officially fixed prices for a host of goods, was responsible for the enforcement of these prices and adjudicated resulting disputes. In these duties he relied on his colleagues officiating in Galata, Eyüp and Üsküdar, and particularly upon his adjunct the *muhtesib* or market inspector.[67] The market inspector with his men physically patrolled the markets, and possessed the right to punish minor offenses on the spot; for more important ones, he reported to the kadi. In addition, the tax-farmers of the customs house, as well as a host of officials in charge of procuring goods for the palace also were concerned with the İstanbul food supply. In certain instances, the same might apply to the Janissary officers in charge of policing the city. Officials in charge of water conduits (*su yolcuları*), a chief of police (*subaşı*) and the chief architect (who was in charge of building regulations) mainly were concerned with problems of the capital. Some of these officials were employed and paid by the palace or the Janissary corps. Moreover by the seventeenth century, customs officers and market inspectors generally farmed their offices and recouped their expenses by specially instituted taxes. In other instances fees and fines might constitute the relevant officials' main sources of income.

ALEPPO: INTERNATIONAL VERSUS LOCAL TRADE

The closing years of the sixteenth and the beginning years of the seventeenth century constituted an apogée of Aleppo's caravan trade to Basra, Iran and the Hejaz. At the same time, caravan trade in the eastern Mediterranean had entered upon its last brief period of fluorescence. Prosperous until 1602, Venetian trade thereafter suffered from the attempts of the Venetian Senate to protect the city's merchant marine.[68] A decree placing major obstacles in the path of Dutch and English shippers wishing to acquire cargoes in Venice resulted in a serious slump, bankruptcies, and a reduction, probably, in the number of Venetian traders visiting Aleppo in the early years of the seventeenth century. More seriously, the Dutch occupation of the Moluccas drastically reduced the quantity of spices available in Aleppo for resale to Europe. However, for most of

Table II:9. Distribution of Aleppo quarters and housing units in 1683

| | Quarters | | Housing units | | Average housing |
	No.	%	No.	%	Units per quarter
Intramural town	24	33.3	5,111	36.9	213
Suburbs (total)	48	66.7	8,743	63.1	182
north	21	29.2	3,689	26.6	176
east	20	27.8	3,446	24.9	172
south	2	2.8	656	4.7	328
west	5	6.9	952	6.9	190
Total	72	100.0	13,854	100.0	192

Source: Raymond (1984), p. 457.

the seventeenth century Iranian silk continued to arrive in the city and, if the number of Venetians decreased, this loss was balanced for Aleppine merchants by a growing number of English traders.[69] Thus investment in the infrastructure of trade continued throughout the seventeenth century at almost the same level as in the previous fifty years: of eleven major khans in the inner city of Aleppo, five were built in the sixteenth and four in the seventeenth century, and numerous minor structures were evenly divided between the two centuries.

Aleppo's sixteenth- and seventeenth-century prosperity has been described "a façade behind which there was nothing but ruins," and the eighteenth-century decline of the city attributed to the collapse of its foreign commerce after the fall of the Safavid dynasty with its attendant civil wars had put a stop to the movement of silk caravans.[70] A contrary view has it that Aleppo's prosperity did not depend on transit trade, which involved only a few European and Iranian traders and did not even provide employment to large numbers of camel drivers and muleteers. If anything, the decline of international commerce benefited the regional economy of Aleppo as resources which had previously been exported were placed at the disposal of the local economy.[71] Such an assumption is only meaningful if increased demand did not lead to a commensurate increase in production; given the limitations of seventeenth-century agriculture, and the absence of quantitative data, it is probably wise to keep an open mind on this issue. Moreover, scholars discounting international trade link the decline of Aleppo in the eighteenth century to an agricultural crisis that befell its hinterland. Harvest failures and abandoned villages, not the Iranian civil wars or the withdrawal of English merchants, were perhaps the major cause of crisis in the Aleppo economy.

Table II:10. Distribution of Aleppo quarters in 1537, 1584 and 1683

	1537		1584		1683	
	No	%	No.	%	No.	%
Intramural town	22	34.9	23	33.8	24	33.3
Suburbs	41	65.1	45	66.1	48	66.7
Total located quarters	63		68		72	
Total quarters	72		73		74	

Source: Raymond (1984), p. 457.

If agricultural prosperity really constituted the key to Aleppo's success as a city, then we would expect that the closing years of the sixteenth century were characterized by an agricultural boom in northern Syria. The hinterland of Aleppo apparently was flourishing in the sixteenth and seventeenth centuries, and a real crisis did not ensue until the eighteenth. However, some evidence suggests that until c.1550, the agriculture of the Aleppo region went through a period of difficulties.[72] Agricultural tithes as collected in this region showed a consistently downward trend until 1551–52, and only stabilized between 1552 and 1570. Moreover, during the later sixteenth century there was a series of bad harvests, a catastrophe that affected the entire Mediterranean basin. Administrative peculiarities, rather than an actual decline in production, may have been responsible for decreasing tithes down to 1552. Probably the decline and stagnation of Aleppine tithes at least in part measured the intensity of political control rather than merely the size of the harvest. It thus is possible to explain how an apparently flourishing trade in rural products might be accompanied by stagnating or declining revenue from tithes.

Aleppo's hinterland was not purely agricultural, but contained industry as well. Certain small towns in the vicinity of the north Syrian metropolis, such as Ma'arrat al-Nu'man, produced silk and olive-oil. These goods were purchased not only by local customers, but by Aleppine traders as well. Sarmin, still a prosperous town in the 1650s, was surrounded by olive groves; when the town was ruined in the eighteenth century, local people attributed this catastrophe to the destruction of their trees. In İdlib, olive production gave rise to flourishing soap manufactures; under the name of Tripolis soap, the soap of northern Syria was available in seventeenth-century İstanbul. İdlib was equally noted for its cotton fabrics, as was the large village of Darit Izza. These products of

Aleppo's hinterland gave rise to a considerable amount of local, regional and inter-regional trade. As a result Aleppo may have been shielded from the vicissitudes of international commerce.[73]

THE DISTRIBUTION OF IRANIAN RAW SILK

Whatever the role of international trade in Aleppo's overall development, the city was the major entrepôt in the marketing of Iranian silk, brought into the city largely by Armenian merchants. Raw silk was bought from the shah himself, who took on a much more active role in international trade than the Ottoman sultan had; the merchants of New Julfa acted as his agents. Some of this silk was marketed in İstanbul, Bursa and İzmir, where it generally arrived by way of Erzurum and Tokat, and a substantial share of the raw silk brought into the empire was reexported to Europe by way of İzmir. After about 1620 the Armenian merchants of Iran also attempted to market their silk directly in Marseilles. But these attempts met with violent opposition from the local merchants, who pressured the French king for the exclusion of their competitors. The complaints of the Marseilles merchants finally resulted in special taxation being imposed upon the Armenians, which crippled their trade in France. But other Armenian merchants managed to market both raw silk and Iranian silk fabrics in Russia.[74] Yet others established themselves in Holland, importing silk and exporting the products of Dutch manufactures, particularly woolen cloth and furniture. Dutch laws for the protection of native trade and shipping were not infrequently circumvented by naturalization, and several seventeenth-century ships owned by Armenian merchants traded with the Levant under the Dutch flag. Thus the deliveries of Iranian silk to Aleppo, İstanbul and Bursa formed but a share, albeit an important one, of a vast network distributing the precious material all over Europe and the Middle East.

In the 1620s the value of all goods purchased by Europeans in Aleppo amounted to an estimated £E1,465,002.[75] Forty-one percent was raw silk, so that the shares of raw silk and pepper in the purchases of European merchants were exactly equal. This silk was then shared between English, French, Venetian and Dutch merchants. Competition was intense, and French purchases declined until in 1669 only a few hundred bales were bought, while the English imported increasing quantities. But then after 1700 English purchases declined and those of the French correspondingly grew.

Table II:11. English purchases of "Levantine" (i.e. Iranian) silk per
year (in kg)

c. 1590	1620s	1630s	1660–1700
13,000–14,000	65,000–70,000	130,000	170,000

Source: Stoianovich (1974), p. 69.

In 1621–22 Marseilles imported 137,000 kg of raw silk, most of it
Iranian, although some ships must have carried Syrian-raised silk as well.
This quantity was about equal to the amount which the Venetians had
been importing at the end of the sixteenth century. Thereafter, the Venetians lost most of their previous market share, and in the end imported
only a few hundred bales per annum (equivalent to about 27,000 kg).
English imports have been variously estimated during this period at
between 38,000 and 65,000–70,000 kg. European consumption of Asian
silk amounted to about 200,000–230,000 kg per year, and some 86 percent
of all silk imported into Europe ultimately came from Iran. If we assume
that all of this silk reached European merchants either by way of Aleppo
or by the Tokat route, an estimated 198,000 kg of raw silk passed through
the Ottoman Empire in transit every year.[76] Thus, the overall gain to the
Ottoman exchequer from customs and sales duties, as well as the money
earned by cameleers and victuallers – that is, the gain to the Ottoman
economy as a whole – must have been quite substantial.

This is reflected in what might be called the "politics" of the silk
trade. From 1619 onwards Shah Abbas of Iran made a determined
attempt to monopolize the exportation of silk. Since the principal silk
mart, namely Aleppo, was located on Ottoman territory, and Ottoman–Iranian warfare was frequent prior to 1639, the export of Iranian
raw silk was highly sensitive to political factors.[77] The matter became
even more complicated once English shippers began to trade in India
and the Persian Gulf. Shah Abbas attempted to reroute the silk trade
by cutting off deliveries to the Ottoman Empire and having British
merchants transport the silk to Europe around the Cape of Good
Hope. These plans were not very successful. When the East India
Company was interested, the project had low priority with Shah
Abbas because he was momentarily at peace with the sultan. When
renewed warfare stimulated Shah Abbas' interest, the East India Company was hesitant about the commercial possibilities, and after Shah
Abbas' death in 1629 the royal monopoly in the export of silk was
progressively dismantled. Even so, in certain peak years (for example in

1627–28, 1628–29, 1631–32, 1634–35) the Dutch and English companies carried between 10,000 and 12,000 kg of silk.[78]

Other projects to divert the silk trade also were political in character. A treaty thus was concluded, in 1667, between Czar Alexis Mihajlovich of Russia and two representatives of an Armenian commercial company located in New Julfa.[79] This treaty permitted Armenian merchants to use the route connecting Astrakhan with Archangel in the far north of Russia by way of Moscow, against payment of a 5 percent duty. Given the close involvement of the New Julfans with Iranian silk export, the route from the Caspian to the White Sea probably was meant to divert Iranian silk from the traditional Ottoman trade routes. But whether the motives were primarily commercial, or whether the negotiations were meant as a political move directed against the Ottoman Empire, is uncertain.

A project initiated at the end of the seventeenth century only makes sense in the climate of a bitter commercial rivalry between the East India Company and its competitor the Levant Company. The former was then under heavy criticism for its export of bullion to India, and the British government demanded that part of company imports must be balanced by the export of English cloth. Given the limited market for English woolens in India, the company attempted to develop its Iranian sales. This was possible only at the expense of the Levant Company. Throughout the seventeenth century the latter had been selling sizable amounts of woolen cloth in Aleppo, some of which was then reexported by Armenian merchants to Iran. For the Armenians of New Julfa, disposing of Iranian silk in Aleppo had the advantage that French and Venetian merchants were present and competed with the English and Dutch traders, who alone visited Isfahan. The merchants of New Julfa therefore had little interest in giving up their Aleppo trade. To the contrary, because of the combined resistance of the Levant Company and its Armenian trading partners, repeated East India Company attempts to divert the exchange of Iranian raw silk came to nothing. In the eighteenth century, the Levant Company in turn was forced to curtail its Aleppo trade: then, however, it was not the East India Company, but French merchants from Marseilles, that moved in to fill the gap.[80]

The many (unsuccessful) attempts to divert the silk trade from Ottoman territory suggest the value of this commerce. Quantitative data, however, are very scarce. One estimate suggests that in 1702, 2,000 bales of Iranian silk were brought to İzmir every year. But in addition, silk was delivered to İstanbul and Bursa as well, even though the difficulties of Bursa silk manufacturers and the increasing cultivation of raw silk in the vicinity of Bursa limited demand for the Iranian product.[81] In spite of these difficulties, supplies of Iranian raw silk continued to enter the region of Bursa in the mid-seventeenth century. Trade was still valuable enough to merit careful state supervision, but we can also conclude that in the 1640s Bursa was not a major manufacturing center, and many of its looms were no longer in operation. Data on taxes collected from Bursa silk sales indicate that the very worst years for Bursa silk weavers were 1617–18, while some recovery had taken place by 1649.[82] If this is true, the flow of Iranian silk to Bursa may also have increased after 1640.

THE RISE OF İZMİR: SILK EXPORT VERSUS THE TRADE IN LOCALLY PRODUCED GOODS

The debate over the role of international transit trade as opposed to local exchanges is also reflected in the story of İzmir's trade. In the period between 1570 and 1650, İzmir developed from a port of purely local importance into a major center visited by European traders active in the Ottoman Empire.[83] By the early years of the seventeenth century, İzmir first rivaled the former Genoese entrepôt of Chios and then surpassed it. In these early stages of the port's history, the exportation of Iranian silk, that played a significant role in İzmir's eighteenth-century prosperity, was of no major importance. İzmir first exported cotton, gallnuts and contraband grains, and only later on attracted the caravans of Iranian silk that were to make it famous. The city's foreign trade attracted migrants who left less prosperous places in order to make a living from international exchanges. Thus we find Jewish migrants trying to escape the difficult conditions created by the decay of the cloth industry in Salonica and taking up roles as translators and commercial middlemen. In rather different ways, tax-farmers and smugglers also were dependent upon the prosperity of international exchanges. Brigands and pirates preying on "legitimate" trade equally were attracted by the area's commercial opportunities; in fact, certain persons managed to combine the roles of pirates and traders. Thus a fair number of persons in the İzmir region do seem to have made a living directly or indirectly from foreign trade. But in the late sixteenth and early seventeenth centuries, İzmir was not yet one of the great international transit nodes, rather the city's prosperity depended upon the effective penetration of a regional economy by foreign traders in search for exportable goods.

After the great earthquake which destroyed İzmir in 1688, the city was rebuilt, but its commercial role changed rapidly. Among the late

Table II:12. Customs revenue in central-western Anatolia (in akçe)

Port	3 May 1604– 3 May 1605	3 May 1605– 3 May 1606	3 May 1606– 3 May 1607
Chios/Çeşme	1,064,025	859,005	600,192
İzmir	981,854	1,171,958	1,332,733
Urla	112,523	105,500	103,423
Kuşadası	33,402	55,458	48,012
Balat	6,000	5,200	6,000
Foça	135,434	155,378	158,434
Sığacık/Seferihisar	34,575	33,300	9,102
Sat	12,500	17,500	17,500
Mirdoğan	4,000	4,000	4,000
İpsara[a]	35,000	30,000	60,000
Musabey[a]	102	102	102
Koyun[a]	1,200	1,200	1,200
Köşedere	4,000	4,000	4,000
Haydarlı	canceled	canceled	canceled
Total	2,424,615	2,442,601	2,344,698

[a] These towns or islands were registered as single mukataas or resims. The customs revenue was not tabulated separately.
Source: Goffman (1990), p. 58.

seventeenth-century city's branches of commerce, pride of place went to the exportation of Iranian silk and the trade in angora wool and yarn, conveyed to İzmir from the mohair-producing center of Ankara.[84] Local products from the İzmir area seem to have played a much less important role after 1688 than c.1650. İzmir could take over the functions of Aleppo after warfare in Iran made the desert routes increasingly unsafe. The solid position which the city acquired as an export center for regionally produced goods formed an important asset when it came to attracting more far-flung and exotic transit trade.

THE SILK TRADE OF SOUTHERN SYRIA

On the role of silk raising and silkworms in mid-seventeenth century Syria, we possess some first-hand information, provided by an experienced silk-buyer who lived in Aleppo between 1656 and 1663 and traveled about purchasing silk on behalf of a Venetian merchant. In the vicinity of Tripolis there were entire woods consisting solely of mulberry trees, and between April and June, while the silkworms matured, huts were specially set up in the middle of the woods to facilitate the feeding of the worms.

An estimated 4,000 "centner" of raw silk were being produced in the area of Tripoli alone.[85] Silk could be purchased even more cheaply in

Beirut and its hinterland, however, and in the Mount Lebanon district of Kisrawan, the buyer negotiated with both Maronite dealers and Druze villagers for the purchase of the local crop. Between 1675 and 1750 French trade in Syria was constantly increasing, and raw silk played a significant role among the goods exported from Sayda, the region's principal harbor.[86] Thus in 1700–2, when the total of goods exported valued 1,446,000 *livres*, 52 percent consisted of cotton thread and 30 percent of raw silk. In exchange, Marseilles merchants sold mainly woolen cloth, sugar and dyestuffs. Thus, apart from export-oriented cultivation of raw fibers, the local textile industry retained a certain vitality.

CAIRO AS A CENTER OF INTER-REGIONAL AND INTERNATIONAL TRADE

European observers of the sixteenth century, but also twentieth-century researchers until the time of Frederic Lane and Fernand Braudel, had assumed that Cairo's role as an international entrepôt came to an end with the Portuguese opening-up of the ocean route to India. Braudel argued that the transit trade in Indian and Indonesian spices revived after the 1530s and continued until the end of the century.[87] Thus, Cairo's role as an emporium of international trade also should have continued until that time. But we now know that the trade in coffee, drugs, dyestuffs and Indian textiles flourished throughout the seventeenth century.[88] Only after 1750 did the competition of Antilles coffee and the unstable political situation significantly weaken the role of the city in international exchanges. Cairo's international trade continued over a period of several centuries, and outlasted that of its trade partner Venice.

The over-hasty inclination to proclaim the demise of Cairo as a center of international trade shows the persistence of a Eurocentric bias, which renders economic activities not responding to European needs or demands all but invisible. For example, even in the second half of the eighteenth century, which is the only period for which we possess comprehensive figures, Cairo's commerce with Anatolia, the Balkans and the Maghrib far outweighed trade with Europe.[89] In addition the city dominated the Red Sea trade, which involved both the importation of coffee and the supplying of pilgrims and townsmen in the Hejaz. The preponderance of commercial exchange within the empire in the balance of Cairo's trade must have been even more marked in the seventeenth century.

Seventeenth-century Cairo was mainly famous as a center for the transit trade in coffee. By the closing decades of the sixteenth century,

Table II:13. Middle Eastern non-Egyptian merchants in the "rich trades" of Cairo (coffee and textiles), 1679–1700

	No. of estate inventories	Value of estates (in *para*, adjusted for inflation)[a]
Total traders	169	50,589,237
Non-Egyptian Middle Easterners	64	20,550,046
% of total	37.8	40.6

[a] *Para* have been adjusted to eliminate the effects of inflation not only for the two decades covered by this table, but also for the entire eighteenth century.
Source: Raymond (1973–74), I, p. 283.

consumption of this stimulant had become common enough that even remote Anatolian towns possessed coffee houses. On the other hand, it was still not unusual for seventeenth-century coffee houses to be shut down, notably by order of Sultan Murad IV, and this situation made it necessary for coffee merchants to possess a substantial amount of capital.[90] Small traders might be hard hit by a temporary interruption of their business, but the wealthier merchants probably found ways of making a profit on the black market. However, during the years in which the trade in coffee was permitted, the Ottoman state profited by farming out the right of coffee-roasting to the highest bidder.[91] We possess few figures concerning the amounts of Yemen coffee imported into the Ottoman Empire of the seventeenth century, but in 1697, 32,000–40,000 *ferde* (4,096 – 5,120 tons) of coffee were imported into Egypt. Of this amount, 15,000 to 20,000 *ferde* were expedited to İstanbul and other provinces of the empire.[92] In addition, European traders purchased Yemeni coffee in Cairo. This trade was at its most prosperous in the late seventeenth and early eighteenth centuries, although even between 1624 and 1630 there were some very wealthy Cairo wholesalers dealing in coffee.

Cairo merchants were also prominent in the trade of the Hejaz, although they shared control of the desert routes with Damascenes. Mecca and Medina possessed few agricultural resources, and ever since the Mamluk period had depended on deliveries of Egyptian grain. Public foundations established by Mamluk sultans and augmented by Süleyman the Lawgiver and his successors delivered quantities of wheat free of charge. But the shortfall was made up by commercial deliveries which allowed speculative gains; when supplies did not arrive in time for the annual pilgrimage caravan, prices increased dramatically. Artificial scarcities were not unknown; these could easily be brought about by having

Table II:14. The "rich trades" (coffee, textiles) compared to total
commercial activity in Cairo, 1679–1700

	No. traders	%	Total value of estate (in para)[a]	%	Average value of estate
Traders in the "rich trades"	169	56.1	50,589,237	89.2	229,344
Other traders	132	43.9	6,168,850	10.8	46,734
Total	301	100	56,758,087	100	188,565

[a] *Para* have been adjusted to eliminate the effects of inflation not only for the two decades covered by this table, but for the entire eighteenth century.
Source: Raymond (1973–74), I, p. 290.

the port administration of Suez delay departures or by preempting the limited amount of Red Sea shipping. The Ottoman central administration reacted to complaints by declaring that donated grains should be transported before trade goods, a rule often difficult to enforce.[93]

In none of these trades did Cairene merchants compete with those of İstanbul, or act as the latters' subordinate partners. They controlled a major economic region in their own right, with little interference even from officials of the central administration. Moreover, this state of affairs went back to the sixteenth century, so that even in its "classical" period the Ottoman Empire seems to have possessed more than one economic center.

MEDITERRANEAN PRODUCE AND FOREIGN TRADE: TUNISIA AND THE WESTERN MEDITERRANEAN

Among the outlying provinces of the Ottoman Empire, Tunisia developed close commercial ties to Marseilles and Livorno, scarcely impeded by the slave-raiding of locally established corsairs. In the northwestern part of the province, wheat was grown for export to Provence, which imported large quantities in times of scarcity, such as the calamitous last decade of the century. But the Spanish province of Majorca and at times even Portugal relied on Tunisian grain, and overall exports grew dramatically in the course of the seventeenth century. By the 1690s olive oil had also become a profitable export item; olive plantations in the Sahel region were extended and the value of land planted with olive trees increased. For the beys of Tunis grain and olives turned into a major source of revenue, as they authorized exportation against payment of dues and themselves entered the market, even paying off debts through

Table II:15. Wheat exported from Tunisia to Marseilles, Toulon and Livorno (in kg)

Years	Livorno	Marseilles	Toulon	Total
1609	265,000			265,500
1651	867,000			867,000
1652	119,090			119,090
1653	1,545,300			1,545,300
1654	587,100			587,100
1655	1,422,100			1,422,100
1656	234,000			234,000
1657	470,850			470,850
1692	11,700	82,875	1,564,560	1,659,135
1693		33,600	666,750	700,350
1694		1,050	632,610	633,660
1695	52,800	1,026,912	1,393,500	2,473,322
1696		174,205	40,500	214,705
1697	54,000	2,375,799	492,120	2,921,919
1698	60,000	1,876,553	764,610	2,701,163
1700	798,000		1,079,610	1,877,610
1701	96,300		131,550	227,850
1702				
1703	12,300			12,300
1704	40,500		5,400	45,900

Source: Derived from Sadok (1987), p. 111.

Table II:16. Olive oil exported from Tunisia to Marseilles (in kg)

	1692	1693	1697	1698	1699
Tunis			14,400		
Sousse	12,348	48,353	3,876	86,240	
Sfax			11,358	9,288	540
Djerba					1,080
Bizerta				3,910	24,525
Total	12,348	48,353	29,683	99,438	26,145

Source: Sadok (1987), p. 117.

the delivery of olive oil. In the seventeenth century these ties to European Mediterranean economies were not yet close enough to endanger Tunisia's integration into the Ottoman economic orbit, where the woolen caps manufactured by Tunisian artisans found a ready market. But strong links to France had been established, which two centuries later could be turned into a colonial dependency.[94]

BOTH OUTSIDE THE EMPIRE AND WITHIN: THE CASE OF DUBROVNIK

As a tributary state, this Adriatic city with its Catholic, Italian-speaking merchant aristocracy of Slav background enjoyed substantial trade

Table II:17. Exports from the Ottoman Empire to Dubrovnik, early seventeenth century

Year	Place	Wares
From Kanuni Süleyman's reign to 1622–23	Çatalca	Limited quantities of grain
1621–22	Draç	Limited quantities of grain
1622–23	Egypt	Saltpeter
1622–23	Herzegovina	Saffian leather, leather, oxhides, grain
1623–24	Bosnia	Sheep, cattle
1623–24	Sofia, Samakov	Wool

Source: Faroqhi (1983), p. 218.

privileges within Ottoman territory. Dubrovnik merchants could enter the Black Sea, otherwise closed to non-Ottoman shipping. They paid less in customs duties than other foreign merchants, even though this advantage probably was offset by the lump sum tribute which Dubrovnik annually sent to the sultan. Of greater significance were the indirect benefits, such as diplomatic support from the Ottoman administration in trade disputes with the Venetians. Dubrovnik, also thanks to its tributary status, established a regular presence in the principal centers of Balkan overland trade. Grain, saltpeter, skins and hides, wool, leather, sheep and cattle were traded by merchants from Dubrovnik. While other European merchants doubtless visited these inland centers upon occasion, the political "harmlessness" of Dubrovnik allowed its merchants to build up a network unequaled by any other Christian state.

At the same time, late sixteenth-century Dubrovnik placed its considerable merchant marine at the disposal of the Ottomans' old opponent, the Spanish Empire. These services even included participation in Spanish military ventures – provided these did not directly affect the interest of the Ottoman Empire. Thus a substantial share of the Invincible Armada sent against England consisted of ships from Dubrovnik.[95] However, while such participation brought profits in certain instances, it led to very grave losses as well. Dubrovnik was probably pushed into this close association with Spain by the nature of its trade, which consisted essentially in exporting goods from the Balkans to Italy and importing textiles from Italy into the Balkans. For this trade, the good will of the Spanish kings and their viceroys in Italy was essential. The Ottoman government tolerated this state of affairs probably because the trade of Dubrovnik permitted the importation of goods from states with which the empire was technically at war.

The annual revenues drawn from import duties reflect the long-term prosperity and ultimate decline of Dubrovnik's trade. For the years which concern us here, we observe a long period of near stagnation at a fairly low level between about 1578 and 1645. This long period of mediocre business conditions was flanked by two extraordinarily prosperous periods. The first one coincided with the Cyprus War of 1570–73; after 1573 receipts continued to boom for some years before they again found their previous modest level. But the long Candian War (1645–69) induced an even more remarkable prosperity. Customs receipts rose steeply until 1660, but then diminished sharply. By the end of 1669, receipts already had declined from their previous boom level to about twice the amount collected in the immediate pre-war years. Revenues subsequently stabilized and fourteen years later, when the Austro-Ottoman War began, receipts resumed their upward course from a considerably higher level than in 1645. Once again this prosperity was war-induced, and receipts rapidly fell away as the war ended.

The import trade of Dubrovnik was in difficulties from 1530 onward, and all later improvements were caused purely by the fortuitous elimination of competitors due to war.[96] "The decline . . . of Venice and the end of Turkish expansion in the Mediterranean" dramatically decreased the benefits of neutrality to Dubrovnik. That the Candian War brought greater benefits to Dubrovnik than the Cyprus War probably can be explained by the fact that the Cyprus War was very short, so that rerouting of goods remained limited. After all, it had been for the sake of a still flourishing Mediterranean commerce that Venice had resigned herself to the loss of Cyprus and concluded a separate peace with the Ottoman Empire. As to the prosperity induced by the Candian War, one might remember the situation of Dubrovnik's potential and actual competitors. For France, this was the time of the depression that accompanied the Spanish War (until 1659), the civil wars of the Fronde and the calamitous first years of Louis XIV's personal rule. England and Holland were at war between 1652 and 1654, and again between 1665 and 1667. Thus it can be concluded that Dubrovnik's ships not only had taken over trade from Venetian vessels, but also profited from the wars in which the principal Western European states were involved during this period.

There is remarkable correspondence in trend between Dubrovnik's customs revenues from imports and those of the wool prices paid by the city's merchants in Sofia (see Figs. II:4, 5).[97] The correlation begins shortly after 1600, just after a steep rise in wool prices that commonly has been attributed to demand generated by the Venetian woolen industry.[98] Until the beginning of the Candian War, prices remained comparatively stable; obviously the decline of the Venetian industry was compensated by other demand factors. Then we encounter the same meteoric increase in wool prices that characterized import-based revenues during the Candian War. More surprisingly, prices did not increase nearly as much during the Austro-Ottoman War of 1683–99, although one would assume that in such a land war, Ottoman demand for woolen cloth should have been higher than for a series of campaigns in the warm waters of the Mediterranean. But due to a serious economic crisis in Italy after 1660, competition for Balkan wool probably was less keen than during the early years of the Candian War. Possibly the expanding manufacture of rough woolen cloth in the Filibe (Plovdiv) region (see Ch. 16) also helps to account for a rise in wool prices during the later seventeenth century, for they began to increase before the war actually broke out, and reached their peak well before 1690. The parallel development of import customs and wool prices clearly demonstrates the extreme dependence of Dubrovnik's trade upon wars and other political events beyond the control of its ruling group. This dependence was deepened by the fact that Dubrovnik never developed a flourishing woolen industry of its own, so that the city was not able to absorb any significant share of the raw wool which it imported. The only "cushion" that protected Dubrovnik from the shocks generated by the city's political environment was the activity of a significant merchant marine.[99] Ragusan sea captains were notably prosperous, not only in the closing years of the sixteenth century, but even down to 1620; these men, often of modest origins, were particularly important among the owners of liquid capital.

However, the competition of Venetian-held Split constituted a serious danger for Dubrovnik shipping, for apart from Venetian traders Split could count upon the patronage of Balkan merchants, especially the Bosnian Muslims who visited Venice in large numbers and were eager to establish direct relations with Italy without passing through Dubrovnik.[100] Moreover the Venetian government, given the threat to the city's Mediterranean trade by Dutch and English competition particularly, were anxious to stifle Ragusan trading in the Adriatic. In the long run, the competition from Dutch, English and French shipping caused as many difficulties for Dubrovnik as for its rival Venice. Already by 1643, complaints were heard about the decline of the Dubrovnik merchant marine. These long-term weaknesses in the Dubrovnik shipping sector explain why, particularly after 1700, the city lost its earlier importance as a center of commerce and shipping.

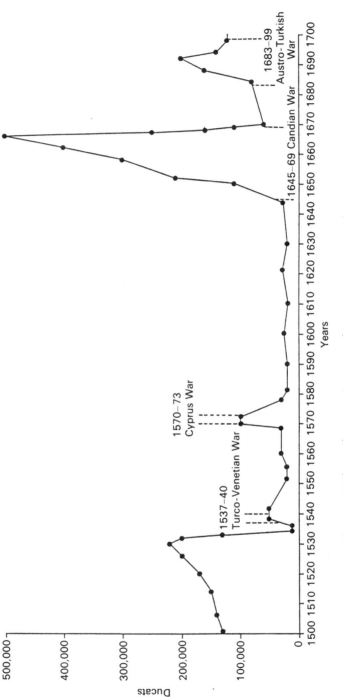

Fig. II:4. Dubrovnik's annual revenue from import customs duty, 1500–1700. *Source:* Carter (1972), p. 397.

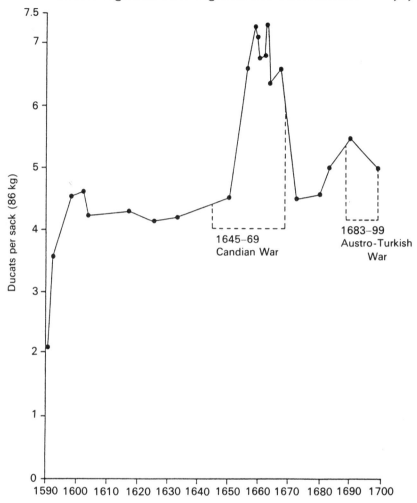

Fig. II:5. Price of wool, paid by Dubrovnik merchants in Sofia, 1590–1700.
Source: Carter (1972), p. 386.

MERCHANT NETWORKS: MUSLIMS

Many researchers view the seventeenth century, if not as a period dominated by conquering Orthodox merchants, then at least as a time of
decreasing participation of Muslim merchants in long-distance trade.[101]
Muslim participation in fact probably did decline, although no systematic
study has been made, and recent studies of eighteenth-century trade suggest that Muslim traders were eclipsed much less rapidly than has been
assumed in the past.[102] As a first step, it seems necessary to describe the

Muslim trading networks that functioned during the seventeenth century, and try to discern how these networks may have evolved over time.

The most detailed information concerns the seventeenth-century wholesalers of Cairo, who usually dealt in coffee and Indian textiles. While these merchants ran their businesses from the Egyptian capital, many were not native Egyptians.[103] The wealthiest of these foreign-born traders were from the Maghrib, but "Rumis," that is Muslim merchants from Anatolia and Rumelia, also were well represented among the rich traders of Cairo. However, since these Muslim traders were not considered as "foreign," the peculiarities of their networks are only discernible after close and intensive study. Their lifestyle resembled that of local merchants, with luxurious dwellings located in the quiet side streets in the vicinity of the Khan Khalili, Cairo's principal center of commercial activity. However, both the Maghribis and the Anatolian or Rumelian merchants maintained the solidarities derived from common origins, and thus formed one of the "minorities" whose social cohesion places them in an advantageous starting position with respect to other traders.[104]

Cairene merchants of the seventeenth and eighteenth centuries rarely traded beyond Jidda, their point of encounter with Indian and Yemeni traders. This must have limited the number of options open to the Cairenes, particularly since only limited amounts of Egyptian manufactured goods were sent to the Hejaz to pay for the imported coffee and fabrics. As a result, there were few opportunities for Cairene merchants to organize textile manufacture on a large scale, at a time when their Indian counterparts were active in the putting-out business.[105] Moreover, Cairene merchants were hampered by the lack of ship-building materials in all countries bordering on the Red Sea, which again placed them in a disadvantageous position *vis-à-vis* merchants from the Malabar coast of India and its active shipyards.[106] However, we hear of Rumi merchants active in India, and it is possible that many of these originally belonged to the Anatolian or Rumelian merchant community of Cairo.[107] Muslim traders also supplied the Hejaz with Egyptian foodstuffs. Others accompanied the pilgrimage caravan from Damascus to Mecca, presumably to do business at the famous fair in Muna, which followed completion of the pilgrimage ceremonies. This fair was protected by the Sharifs of Mecca, and exempt from dues. Merchants from Bahrain exhibited pearls, while precious fabrics and aromatics also changed hands, a typical example of a "rich trade," furthered by the large number of Indian traders *cum* pilgrims. A good deal of business was also done in Mecca itself during the pilgrimage season, and merchant customs indicate a close relationship to the western coast of India, where emigrants from the Arabian peninsula often settled. Other merchants financed pilgrimage caravans by lending money to their commanders; the pilgrimage thus constituted a unique opportunity to link up different merchant networks.[108]

In Anatolia and Rumelia as well, Muslim merchants and investors in commerce are well attested even for the seventeenth century. In the towns of Anatolia, foundations and private persons, many hundreds in number, lent out money, often openly taking interest.[109] Even though some of these loans may have been destined for the borrowers' consumption, investment in commerce must have been of considerable importance. Muslim traders from Kayseri or Ankara conveyed their wares to İstanbul through the services of their partners, and even more importantly, acted as wholesalers organizing the activities of dispersed urban or rural craftsmen. Chance has preserved the 1592 shop inventory of a Muslim dealer in shoes, active in Ankara, who seems to have operated as a putter-out.[110] There were traders who brought white cotton cloths, produced in Denizli and the "lake district" of Isparta, to the Aegean town of Tire for dyeing.[111] As Tire did not possess a large non-Muslim population, these putters-out were probably also Muslims. Thus putting-out systems organized by merchants, even though not a dominant feature of the seventeenth-century economy, were by no means absent, and commercial networks organized by Muslims had a share in these crucial activities.

NON-MUSLIM COMMERCIAL NETWORKS

Even so, the seventeenth century was characterized by increasing non-Muslim commercial activity. The "conquering Balkan Orthodox merchant" had early predecessors, who were non-Muslim though not Orthodox, and who did not limit their activities to the Balkans. Even in the fifteenth century, Armenians from Iran had traded in Bursa along with their Muslim merchants from the same country.[112] However, by the seventeenth century, the *Acem tüccarı* (Iranian traders) mentioned in the *Mühimme* registers were nearly all non-Muslims.

Armenian merchants active in the seventeenth-century Ottoman Empire distinguished themselves by their association with an international trade network centered around a suburb of Isfahan named New Julfa. Merchants from this town took an active role in the Iranian silk trade, at certain times a monopoly in the hands of the shah himself. Merchants of New Julfa also used the rivalry between the Ottoman

Empire and Russia in order to establish new trade routes for themselves, but most of their East–West trade probably continued to cross Ottoman territory. Even in the early eighteenth century, the customs revenues of Erzurum were stable, and did not decline until the middle of the century, largely the result of customs duties paid by Iranian–Armenian merchants.[113] Moreover, the same stability can be observed for the second half of the seventeenth century. Customs revenues of 92,250 *esedi guruş* per year in 1643–56, rose to 96,094 *guruş* per year in 1666–7, and in 1683–9 even to 100,094 *esedi guruş*, after which there was a decline to 95,094 *esedi*.[114] All this seems to indicate that the arrangement with the Csar did not draw off a great deal from the established Ottoman trade routes.

Other centers of Armenian trade in the Ottoman zone of influence were southern Poland and Transylvania, a network controlled by locally resident traders, and quite distinct from the activities of the New Julfa merchants.[115] While the Lwow and Transylvanian traders extended their activities as far as Venice and Central Europe, the goods they traded were often of Ottoman manufacture or had transited through the Ottoman Empire. Thus while the Armenian trading networks of the seventeenth century transcended the Ottoman borders, and the commercial centers of these merchants were for the most part located outside of the Ottoman state, commerce on Ottoman territory was crucial for the maintenance of these networks.

The principal Armenian merchants active in the seventeenth-century Ottoman Empire thus were participating in a major network of international commerce. Greek merchants of this period for their part were mainly active in Ottoman inter-regional trade. The growth of Greek trading activities dates from about 1650: in the Ottoman capital, Greeks were particularly active as traders and sea captains, carrying grain from the Balkan coastal regions adjacent to the Black Sea.[116] Some managed to become wealthy, in spite of the close control which the Ottoman central administration exercised over the provisioning of İstanbul. But most Greeks in the capital lived the narrow and circumscribed lives of small traders and artisans.[117]

Opportunities for enrichment seem to have been greater in the provinces. Many of the so-called Phanariote families of the eighteenth century, who exercised a degree of political power administering the Rumanian provinces on behalf of the Ottoman government, originally made their fortunes in places such as İzmir, Chios, Janina or Kastoria.[118] The merchants of Chios particularly were able to benefit from the rise of İzmir during the second half of the seventeenth century. Moreover, the silk manufacturers on Chios were prospering, and many local merchants made substantial profits either through their control of the production process, or by importing raw silks from Morea, Rumelia and Bursa, and selling them to manufacturers on the island.

In addition Greeks, along with Jewish merchants, in seventeenth and eighteenth-century İzmir found an economic niche for themselves as intermediaries for European merchants. Europeans bought and sold goods in İzmir, often through mechanisms that included "credit in kind."[119] Thus the European merchant might do a considerable amount of business by bartering woolen cloth against cotton or mohair yarn. The İzmir Greek, Jewish or Armenian merchant provided him, on credit, with a return cargo at the time when a suitable ship was ready to sail, thereby making himself indispensable to the European trader. In the eighteenth century, the capital and commercial experience accumulated by certain Greek traders were to allow them to enter European trade as independent merchants. But during the period under investigation, their principal role seems to have been as auxiliaries.

Jewish merchants active in İzmir at the end of the seventeenth century were considered the most serious competitors of English and French traders, selling woolens from Holland and England, Italian silkstuffs and other goods also traded by merchants from Europe.[120] But on the whole, Jewish merchants, at least after 1650, were less active on Ottoman territory than during the second half of the sixteenth century. Westward Jewish migration may have been involved. Amsterdam, the booming center of the seventeenth-century European world economy, and also London attracted merchants, while the commercial role of Jews in seventeenth-century İstanbul was insignificant.[121] In many important Balkan towns, the percentage of Jewish inhabitants increased substantially between about 1560 and 1660, only to decline thereafter.[122] Conjunctural factors perhaps were paramount in prompting out-migration: for example, the curtailment of Salonica trade during the long war over Crete (1645–69) and the decline of Dubrovnik's commerce. But, on the other hand, the prosperity of Balkan trade in the eighteenth century did not lead to a significant return of migrants; quite to the contrary, emigration continued. Perhaps it was the combination of contracting business opportunities, and the expanding activities of Greek and other Balkan merchants, that forced many Jewish merchants out of Balkan trade.[123]

FOREIGN MERCHANTS

European merchants operating in the seventeenth-century Ottoman Empire constitute by far the best researched sector of Ottoman commercial history. Yet care must be taken not to accord them too large an amount of space, since the reader may easily conclude that local economic life was too weakly developed to merit discussion.[124] Or one might even conclude that by the seventeenth century the Ottoman economy had embarked upon a long process of incorporation in the European-dominated world economy, and that therefore its development can only be understood within the context of European economic history. However, recent work on the seventeenth century shows that Ottoman economic life of the time was more dynamic than previously assumed and that many local crafts had surmounted the crisis of the early 1600s. The incorporation process into the European-dominated world economy, which had begun in the later sixteenth century, in fact was halted during the seventeenth, at least partly because Atlantic and Indian commerce occupied the attention of the principal European trading nations.[125] In addition it is also likely that the European economic depression of the seventeenth century limited opportunities for commercial penetration of the Ottoman Empire. Given this freedom of action, albeit limited, for Ottoman producers, it seems important to avoid giving excessive weight to the activities of European traders. In consequence, the following sections have been kept as brief as possible.

The Venetians

In spite of the serious crisis of Venetian trade visible at the beginning of the seventeenth century, the Venetian presence in Ottoman ports around 1620–30 was still far from negligible.[126] It is therefore important not to telescope the decline of Venetian trade in the eastern Mediterranean. While difficulties began early, their effects upon the Venetian presence in the Ottoman Empire were not too dramatic during the first quarter of the century. However, the decline accelerated during the Candian War.

The principal causes and aspects of the Venetian trade crisis have been analyzed in depth and only need to be briefly recapitulated. While the Portuguese circumnavigation of Africa led only to a temporary decline in the spice trade, the Dutch entry into the Moluccas after 1600 largely ended the importation of spices via the Red Sea route into the eastern

Mediterranean. Venice was unable to draw any benefit from the newly developing importation of coffee. While Cairo weathered the shock thanks to the simultaneous growth of the coffee trade, coffee entered Europe late and, what is more, by a route bypassing Venice. In addition, English competition was selectively aimed at Venetian shipping, not only by regular commercial means, but by piracy as well. Venetian ship building already was in difficulties due to the scarcity of raw materials.[127] Moreover, the woolen industry developed in the sixteenth century as a response to the contraction of commercial opportunities, reached its peak by 1600 and then rapidly declined due to the competition of cheaper English woolens.[128]

The unsettled financial situation in the Ottoman Empire, which diminished the purchasing power of wealthier Ottomans who previously had been good customers of the Venetians, also must have played a role. After about 1620, the destruction caused by the Thirty Years' War naturally had repercussions upon Venice, since this area had previously accounted for a good share of Venetian commercial activity. Ship building suffered due to the scarcity of timber. Last but not least, one must add Venice's political problems, particularly the struggle against Spanish hegemony on the Italian peninsula. Against these powerful odds, only a very solid organization of commercial activities enabled Venetian merchants to put up as long a resistance as they actually did.[129]

One of the principal elements of this organization was the network of consuls, which assured Venetians regular representation in almost any town where they might trade. The early professionalization of the Venetian consular service meant regularly paid fixed salaries, so that the consuls did not need to demand direct contributions from Venetian merchants. Salaries and the code of honor current among Venetian officials furthered high standards of performance.[130] Even so, the efficiency of the Venetian consular service could only delay and not prevent the decline of Venetian trade.

The French

On account of a formal privilege granted by the French king, all French merchants trading with the Levant had to operate through Marseilles, with the local Chamber of Commerce as a controlling body. This body was entrusted not only with the enforcement of quarantine and shipping regulations, but also with the licensing of French merchants wishing to depart for the eastern Mediterranean. But since French consuls farmed their office, the Marseilles Chamber of Commerce had relatively little control over the official representatives of the trading community.[131] Moreover, the French ambassador, to whom consular officials were answerable, was a royal appointee without direct links to trade. This situation explains why conflicts between French merchants and their consul, and of consuls with the ambassador, were comparatively frequent. In the seventeenth century, such disputes sometimes were submitted to the Ottoman administration for adjudication.[132]

After 1661, French Levant trade became subject to stringent royal regulation. Louis XIV's minister Colbert attempted to make Marseilles merchants more competitive by adopting the Dutch custom of sailing in convoy, which greatly reduced freight costs. To facilitate control, repeated attempts were made to establish a French Levant Company along the lines earlier adopted by Dutch and English merchants. The French companies were a failure, but the small ships of Marseilles, while more expensive than Dutch vessels, had long since found an "economic niche" by transporting small quantities of goods on behalf of merchants operating from Mediterranean ports. The carrying trade or "caravane" between Ottoman port towns constituted but one example of such services rendered on a small scale to individual customers. As a result, French ship owners of the seventeenth century showed little inclination to change their ways. Some may also have wished to keep a low profile in order to avoid reprisals when the French kings supported the Venetians during the Cretan War. Moreover, the long-term economic difficulties of the French economy during the second half of the seventeenth century discouraged investments. Yet the French commercial boom of the eighteenth century, when Marseilles merchants became the leading European traders active on Ottoman territory, at least partly was prepared by commercial and institutional reforms during the second half of the seventeenth century.

The Dutch

Seen from the Ottoman point of view, the beginnings of Dutch trade and diplomacy in the eastern Mediterranean were mainly an affair of high politics: ever since the 1560s, rebellions in the Netherlands prevented full deployment of Spanish resources in the Mediterranean.[133] Therefore the vizier and *kapudan* Halil Pasha assumed that political relations with the Netherlands might step up Dutch military activity against Spain. It is in this context that we must view the granting of a capitulation (*ahidname*) to the Netherlands in 1612.[134] However, the beginning of Ottoman-Dutch diplomatic relations coincided with the so-called Twelve Years' Truce (1609–21) between Spain and the Netherlands, so that a political alliance was not viewed as an urgent matter in The Hague. From the Dutch point of view, the ambassador was a liaison person, watching over the application of the capitulations and fostering a favorable atmosphere for his countrymen's trade. The first Dutch ambassador was politically active as long as his protector Halil Pasha held office. But since Ottoman government circles soon realized that the possible Dutch contribution to any common war effort against Spain would be strictly limited, the role of the Dutch ambassador remained circumscribed. Within the Dutch trading network, the Levant played a minor role: Dutch merchants visited both Aleppo and İzmir, but their share of the trade in silk, cotton, grain or gallnuts was small. To Ottoman wealthy customers, they brought pepper and fine spices from southeast Asia. But since pepper could be secured over the Basra and Red Sea routes as well, Dutch merchants were granted capitulations more for political than for economic reasons.

The English

English trade in the eastern Mediterranean increased in the second half of the sixteenth century, as English merchants and shippers aimed at eliminating their Venetian rivals. From the political point of view, they were in an advantageous position because, unlike Venice, seventeenth-century England was never at war with the Ottoman Empire. Moreover, English traders provided Ottoman rulers with valuable war materials, such as tin.[135] In addition the structure of their trade gave late sixteenth- and early seventeenth-century English merchants a distinct advantage. Since profits from the resale of Levant (principally Iranian) silk in Europe were high, the Levant Company's merchants were able to dump their woolen cloth and thereby eliminate Venetian competition.[136] As an added advantage, the institutional trading arrangements were favorable to English merchants. The Levant Company consisted of wealthy persons engaged in trade and reasonably successful in warding off royal interference. Moreover, the English ambassador in İstanbul and the consuls were appointed and paid by the Levant Company, not the English crown. Efficient support from official representatives increased the opportunities for profitable trade, while the rivalries between French merchants and ambassadors (and/or consuls) caused political embarrassment and financial loss.[137]

Throughout the seventeenth century, English trade in the Ottoman Empire far out-distanced its European rivals. In Aleppo around 1680, for example, the English "nation" and its consul occupied the largest khan.[138] After about 1717, however, war and civil war disrupted the Iranian silk trade, while Indian and Chinese silks competed advantageously with the Iranian and Syrian products. With return cargoes increasingly unavailable, English merchants importing woolen cloth during the mid-eighteenth century were forced one by one to wind up operations, particularly since competition from French-manufactured woolen cloth was becoming more pronounced.[139] After more than a hundred years of prosperity, the English Levant trade entered upon a period of sharp if temporary decline.

The Indians

Of all the major groups of merchants trading in the Ottoman Empire, least of all is known about the Indians.[140] Indians imported cotton cloth into the Ottoman Empire, where it was popular for high-priced turbans. Because of the low wages paid to Indian craftsmen, prices were competitive. In 1640 Indian cotton yarn was cheaper on the İstanbul market than some of the more expensive threads spun in Anatolia. From Basra customs regulations dated 1689–90, a long list of Indian fabrics imported into the Ottoman Empire can be compiled. Moreover, since these regulations accord preferential treatment to Muslim merchants and shipmasters, we can conclude that both Muslims and non-Muslims participated in the trade between India and Basra. Some of these non-Muslims probably were English or Portuguese. But it is likely that Hindu merchants were also represented, although most Indians operating on Ottoman territory seem to have been Muslims.

Indian traders active in Jidda during the late sixteenth century paid customs duties that constituted a significant revenue item both for the Sharif of Mecca and the Ottoman central administration. These Indian merchants deserted Jidda for Suez and other Red Sea ports, when the Sharif's men began mistreating merchants and expropriating their goods, as many merchants deserted trade routes when protection costs rose to intolerable levels.[141] In the early seventeenth century Muslim Indians were trading not only in İstanbul, Aleppo and Bursa, but also in provincial towns such as Manisa.[142] Moreover, these traders were organized and defended themselves as a group against Ottoman competitors, who, according to the Indians, hampered their trade with false accusations. The Indian traders received a rescript of protection addressed, not to the kadi or governor of a specific locality, but "to the kadis of all places where the Indians may go in the course of their trade." Thus there clearly existed a far-flung network of Indian traders, about which future research will hopefully provide information.

CONCLUSION

In the course of this chapter, reference has been made repeatedly to controversies surrounding Ottoman trade. A previous focus on European commerce, during the last thirty years or so, has been supplemented and in part replaced by emphasis on intra-Ottoman trade. The more "glamorous" long-distance transit trades increasingly have lost significance in the eyes of historians, and researchers dealing with such long-distance trading centers as Aleppo or İzmir have come to emphasize the commercial links of these two cities with their immediate hinterlands. This shift in emphasis closely parallels what happened in European economic history, only at a slightly earlier date; for grain, salt, building stones and other goods of everyday consumption have long since captured the attention of European historians of the medieval and early modern periods. The study of Ottoman regional and local trade has generated a new-style provincial history, with Syria and Tunisia as favored areas of research. Today we know much more about regional economies than we did forty years ago, even though it is often difficult to accommodate this information within broad concepts of economic history. Regional history for most Ottoman historians is still a fairly new area of interest; therefore it probably will be some time before we can assess the relative importance of intra-Ottoman and international trade, a process of reassessment which has been going on for some time among European economic historians.

Another basic issue is the nature of Ottoman economic relations with the European world economy of the time. After the later sixteenth- and early seventeenth-century crisis, certain Ottoman crafts recovered, and others, like the cheap woolens of Filibe (Plovdiv) were newly created and thrived. Thus it seems overly hasty to assume that around 1600 the Ottoman economy was transformed, once and for all, into an appendage of the European world economy. Rather it would seem there was a period of "economic disengagement," lasting from the early seventeenth to the mid-eighteenth century.[143] Among the reasons for this respite, the involvement of European merchants with India and China doubtless was important, but we also must take into account the Ottoman side of the matter. To put it differently, the Ottoman economy possessed potential of its own, and was not inert and defenseless. Even in the eighteenth century, English traders in Aleppo confronted Ottoman colleagues who were wealthy, commercially sophisticated and accustomed to doing business on a large scale.[144] Thus it would seem that Fernand Braudel was quite right in concluding that Ottoman mastery of the caravan routes permitted Ottoman merchants to build and control their own trading networks.[145] Away from the coastal areas, European imports before the second half of the eighteenth century were unable to compete with locally produced wares. Certain luxury goods constituted the exception that proves the rule. By the same token, the present chapter has emphasized the role of merchant networks in preserving the Ottoman realm from rapid absorption into the European-dominated world economy.

NOTES

1 Todorov (1970); İnalcık (1969), pp. 10ff.
2 İslamoğlu and Keyder (1977), pp. 46–7.
3 İnalcık (1969), pp. 135–6.
4 Barkan (1975).
5 İnalcık, (1979–80).
6 Van Leur (1955); Steensgaard (1974), pp. 22ff. Compare also Braudel (1979), II, p. 545.
7 Steensgaard (1978), pp. 61–2.
8 Lane (1966), pp. 373–428.
9 Chaudhuri (1978), pp. 138–39; Chaudhuri (1985), pp. 198ff; Braudel (1979), II, pp. 98ff.
10 Raymond (1973–74), II, pp. 292ff.
11 Braudel (1979), III, pp. 11–70.
12 Masson (1896), p. 8; Rambert and Paris, (1957), p. 80.
13 Braudel (1979), III, p. 402.
14 Von Thünen, ed. Lehmann and Werner (1990), pp. 16ff, 129ff, 161ff.
15 Aigen, ed. Tietze (1980), pp. 59–60; Shaw (1962), p. 68 states that the expansion of agriculture and settlement in Egypt continued well into the seventeenth century.
16 Wallerstein (1980), pp. 117ff.
17 Braudel (1979), III, pp. 74ff. The first part of this proposition remains true even though scholars like E. Ashtor (1978), pp. 681ff, insist on the decay of Middle Eastern textile manufacturing as early as the fifteenth century, and ascribe this decline to technological backwardness *vis-à-vis* an "industriali-

zing" Europe. Ashtor's arguments have on the whole not made much of an impression upon Ottoman historians, particularly since the work of Halil İnalcık has shown the existence of numerous prosperous textile manufactures in the fifteenth- and sixteenth-century Ottoman Empire: İnalcık (1960, 1969, 1979–80).

18 Wallerstein (1980), p. 121.

19 Chaudhuri (1985), p. 204.

20 These rescripts, generally made out at the request of European consuls and merchants, by the seventeenth century were generally collected in special registers devoted to the affairs of a particular state (*Ecnebi Defterleri*).

21 Faroqhi (1986).

22 Rambert and Paris (1957), p. 443.

23 Abou-El-Haj (1991).

24 It would have been desirable at this juncture to discuss the ideas that Ottoman administrators held with respect to internal trade as well. However at present no primary sources have been located that indicate any major changes in this matter between the fifteenth and sixteenth centuries on the one hand, and the seventeenth century on the other. Possibly a more detailed analysis of the sources will later show us that at least a change in nuances did after all occur, but given the lack of secondary studies it is impossible at present to be more specific.

25 Orhonlu and Işıksal (1962–63).

26 So little is known about them that Orhonlu suggests collating the scattered information about their frequent uprisings, to map the places in which different sub-groups of the *Cezayir araplan* must have lived.

27 McGowan (1987).

28 Or at least that is the impression one gains upon perusing the work of Nelly Hanna (1983) and André Raymond (1973–74), I, pp. 246–7. In the sixteenth century the expansion of Bulaq points to a change in trade routes, and probably to growth in the volume of Nile traffic as well. But after that, no further transformations are mentioned until the end of the eighteenth century.

29 Among the many seventeenth-century authors that have left descriptions, one might mention, as a recently published example, the account of the Habsburg embassy sent to İstanbul in 1606 to negotiate the peace of Zsitva-Török: Nehring (1983).

30 Taeschner (1924–26), I, *passim*.

31 *Ibid.*, appended map.

32 Jennings (1976), p. 4.

33 1,777 taxpayers if indeed the tax register prepared in 1591–92 gives some idea of the towns' size in the seventeenth century as well.

34 Jennings (1976), p. 47.

35 Compare map in İnalcık (1973), pp. 122–23.

36 Cernovodeanu (1969), p. 652.

37 Braudel (1979), II, p. 133.

38 Aigen, ed. Tietze (1980) pp. 114ff.

39 Chaudhuri (1985), p. 14.

40 Reid (1969).
41 Steensgaard (1974), p. 355.
42 *Ibid., passim.*
43 Compare also Boxer (1935) and Khoury (1991).
44 Masson (1911), p. 401; Sadok (1987), pp. 92ff.
45 Faroqhi (1979a).
46 Evliya (1896–97 to 1938), IX, p. 291. Official documents occasionally refer to village markets continuing in operation, sometimes to the detriment of urban-based trade (for example compare MD 80, p. 458, 1024/1615). However, in other instances villagers petitioned for the abolition of markets, complaining that they attracted robbers and other undesirables, quite apart from giving rise to supplementary exactions on the part of local administrators.
47 Faroqhi (1978), p. 60.
48 This may be in part due to the changing character of Ottoman archival documentation. After all in Evliya's imagery, even by the 1670s the Maşkolur fair was still the epitome of a large gathering of buyers and sellers, and thus should have retained something of its former importance.
49 Barkan and Ayverdi (1970), pp. xxxvff; Barkan (1975).
50 Mandaville (1979).
51 Jennings (1973).
52 Çağatay (1971); Faroqhi (1984), pp. 233ff.
53 Compare Barkan (1966), pp. 38–39.
54 Mandaville (1979).
55 Masters (1988), pp. 154ff.
56 Mantran (1962), pp. 179–213.
57 Von Thünen, ed. Lehmann and Werner (1990), p. 16.
58 Faroqhi (1984), p. 79.
59 Mantran (1962), pp. 187ff.
60 Barkan (1962–63), pp. 276–77.
61 MD 27, p. 390 (1575–76).
62 Cvetkova (1976).
63 Kütükoğlu (1983).
64 Braudel (1979), I, p. 494.
65 Goffman (1990).
66 Güçer (1949–50), Güçer (1951–52), Mantran (1962), pp. 186–92.
67 Kütükoğlu (1983), pp. 34ff. So far the most detailed example of a seventeenth-century price list is the 1640 document published by Kütükoğlu, but shorter lists were compiled much more frequently, and have sometimes been preserved in the kadi's registers. For an example, compare Kütükoğlu (1978).
68 Sella (1968), pp. 88–105.
69 Davis (1967), *passim*; Abdel Nour (1982).
70 Sauvaget (1941).
71 Both Steensgaard and Abdel Nour take a stance almost reminiscent of Frank (1969), pp. 10–12; Steensgaard (1973), pp. 175–93; Abdel Nour (1982), pp. 276–77. For a recent study of Aleppo's economy, see Masters (1988).
72 Venzke (1984), pp. 255ff.

73 Abdel Nour (1982), p. 273.
74 Rambert and Bergasse (1954), pp. 64ff; Kévonian (1975), p. 205.
75 Stoianovich (1974), p. 69.
76 Stoianovich (1974), p. 73; Steensgaard (1974), p. 161.
77 Steensgaard (1974), pp. 377ff. On the political complications connected with the sixteenth-century trade in Iranian raw silk, compare İnalcık (1960a and b).
78 Steensgaard (1974), pp. 367–68, 395.
79 Kevonian (1975), p. 213.
80 Ferrier (1973).
81 Ülker (1974), p. 82; Çizakça (1985, 1987).
82 Çizakça (1987), pp. 140–41.
83 Goffman (1990), pp. 50ff.
84 Ülker (1974).
85 Aigen, ed. Tietze (1980), pp. 15–26.
86 Rambert and Paris (1957), p. 407.
87 Braudel (1949, 2nd edn 1966); Lane (1941, repr. 1966).
88 Raymond (1973–74), I, pp. 129–56.
89 *Ibid.*, p. 193.
90 Kissling (1957); Mantran (1962), p. 430.
91 Mantran (1962), p. 431.
92 Raymond reports Thévenot's record of 30,000 loads of coffee being imported about 1660: Raymond (1973–74), I, p. 147. See also Mantran (1962), p. 209.
93 Faroqhi (1990), pp. 200–22.
94 Sadok (1987), pp. 111, 117.
95 Carter (1972), p. 404.
96 *Ibid.*, p. 396.
97 *Ibid.*, p. 386.
98 *Ibid.*, p. 385.
99 Tadić (1961), p. 254.
100 Kafadar (1986).
101 Stoianovich (1960).
102 Panzac (1985), p. 186.
103 Raymond (1973–74), II, pp. 464ff.
104 Braudel (1979), II, pp. 139ff.
105 Chaudhuri (1978), pp. 253ff.
106 Chaudhuri (1985), pp. 157–58.
107 For sixteenth-century evidence, see Özbaran (1977), pp. 111, 137, 140.
108 Faroqhi (1990), pp. 216–17.
109 Jennings (1973).
110 Faroqhi (1984), p. 165.
111 BBA, MD 96, p. 127 (1678–79).
112 İnalcık (1960b), p. 52.
113 Erim (1984), p. 177.
114 *Ibid.*, p. 21.
115 Kévonian (1975), p. 213.
116 Stoianovich (1960), p. 269.

117 Mantran (1962), p. 451.
118 Stoianovich (1960), pp. 270–71.
119 Frangakis (1985), pp. 33–34.
120 *Ibid.*, p. 33; Goffman (1990), pp. 78ff.
121 Stoianovich (1960), pp. 270–1.
122 *Ibid.*, pp. 245–6.
123 *Ibid.*, pp. 261–62.
124 Anderson (1989) is a good example of a Europe-centered study dealing with seventeenth-century İzmir.
125 Çizakça (1985), p. 371.
126 Goffman (1990), *passim*; Faroqhi (1986a).
127 Tenenti (1967), pp. 58ff.
128 Sella (1968), p. 118.
129 Sella (1968); Lane (1973), pp. 418ff.
130 Steensgaard (1967), pp. 25–26.
131 *Ibid.*, pp. 28–31.
132 Goffman (1990), p. 123.
133 Braudel (1949, 2nd edn 1966), II, pp. 340–43.
134 De Groot (1978), pp. 231–65.
135 McNeill (1974), p. 285.
136 Braude (1979).
137 Skilliter (1977); Steensgaard (1967); Goffman (1986).
138 Davis (1967), p. 5.
139 *Ibid.*, p. 125.
140 İnalcık (1979–80), p. 30–37.
141 BBA, MD 53, p. 66 (1584); Steensgaard (1973), p. 66.
142 BBA, MD 78, p. 555.
143 Çizakça (1985), pp. 370–74.
144 Davis (1967), p. 39.
145 Braudel (1979), III, pp. 410–15.

18

৯

FINANCES

It is impossible to determine what percentage of Ottoman "gross national product" was handled by the state, if only because the vast realm of peasant autoconsumption cannot be even approximately measured. But minimally, the tithe (*öşür*) accounted for one-tenth, and in many regions for one-eighth to one-third of the peasant harvest. In addition, irregular taxes, which in principle were to be collected in wartime only, but which in the seventeenth century had a tendency to become perpetual, brought the total to far higher levels. Thus any discussion of Ottoman economic activity would be misleading without an overview of state finances.[1]

THE CASH SECTOR

One of the more far-reaching transformations of Ottoman state finance was the progressive changeover from services and deliveries in kind to taxes collected in cash. This development was by no means unique to the seventeenth century: in the centuries when the Ottoman political system came into being, several services (*kulluk*) had been converted into money taxes, and some of the most characteristic peasant taxes recorded in the sixteenth-century tax registers consisted of converted services.[2] However, this process of conversion into cash accelerated in the later sixteenth and seventeenth centuries. Until the later sixteenth century, the holders of small tax assignments or prebends (*timar*) generally had lived in or near the villages where the assigned revenues were generated and had consumed a certain proportion on the spot. On the other hand, the tax-farmers, who accounted for a growing share of seventeenth-century Ottoman taxes, converted almost all the grains they collected into ready cash. The central administration also more commonly demanded cash instead of deliveries in kind. As an example one may mention the *nüzul*, which originally had consisted of grains that Ottoman taxpayers conveyed to fixed stopping points for the army on its march to the front.[3] Taxpayers did not necessarily regard this conversion as an advantage, although presumably transportation services were a heavy load.[4] In quite a few cases, the difficulty of obtaining access to a market and seasonal price variations seem to have been regarded as major liabilities of the new arrangement.

Among the cash taxes, the oldest was the *cizye*, the head-tax payable by non-Muslim subjects of an Islamic state ever since the earliest years of Islam. This tax in principle was collected by the Ottoman central treasury directly. Until 1691, the tax frequently was demanded from households rather than from individuals, women, children, the old and the disabled generally being exempt. Certain villages also contracted for payment as a lump sum, an arrangement that worked to the taxpayers' advantage as long as population increased, but resulted in the abandoning of depleted villages as peasants found it impossible to pay the dues of their departed fellow villagers.[5] The reform of 1691, when war with the Habsburgs and their allies made it necessary to increase revenues, reinstituted the arrangement originally contained in Islamic religious law (*şeriat*), namely that every taxable individual was to pay separately. Collection thereafter seems to have proceeded in a reasonably regular fashion.[6]

While the *cizye* had been a money tax ever since its institution, some of the taxes collected from sheep raisers, which also accrued to the central treasury, originally had been collected in kind. In the closing years of the seventeenth century, this tax, along with payments demanded from the men who supplied sheep to İstanbul slaughterhouses, constituted 1–2 percent of the central treasury's revenues.[7] A further source of cash was the *nüzul bedeli*, which after 1683 was turned into an annual tax.[8]

Apparently the *nüzul* taxes throughout their existence were associated with the *avarız*, another irregular wartime tax in kind which had been converted into money in the course of the sixteenth century. At an early stage, *avarız* and *nüzul* seemingly constituted alternatives, that is, in a given year a village might be confronted with either a demand for cash (*avarız*), or else a demand for deliveries in kind (*nüzul*). However, the wars and inflationary pressures of the seventeenth century resulted in the conversion of the *nüzul* into a money payment that might be collected in the same year as the *avarız*.

The *avarız*, which became an annual tax during the first half of the seventeenth century, was collected on the basis of a unit especially instituted for this purpose.[9] In principle, though not always in practice, taxpayers were to be taxed according to their ability to pay, and therefore officially recorded as "wealthy," "middling" or "poor." In addition, taxpayers were grouped into units known as *avarızhane* (tax house), all of which were assessed the same amount of money. A 'tax house' consisted of 2–15 households, and was kept small if the component households were considered wealthy, while in the case of poor people, the number of households was augmented. In case of agricultural crisis, villages might be granted relief by increasing the number of households recorded in an *avarızhane*.[10]

In the 1660s and 70s, the *avarız* tax constituted about 20 percent of the total cash revenue collected by the Ottoman central administration. However, this share could easily be expanded, since the state also demanded services, such as the provision of rowers for the imperial navy. These services could be converted into money and thereby dramatically raise the share of the *avarız* in the central administration's budget.[11]

DELIVERIES IN KIND

Aside from the unpaid services that had formed part of the *avarız-nüzul* complex, goods and services might be demanded against payment, even though in certain instances remuneration was more or less symbolic. These demands affected a large share of the taxpaying population. While a sizable number of people were exempted from payment of the *avarız* because they tended bridges, served as miners, caught falcons for the sultan's hunt, or performed a multitude of other services, such exemptions were not valid if the deliveries were even minimally renumerated.[12] Moreover (real or fictitious) payment for such deliveries, known in Ottoman terminology as *sürsat*, served to justify the demand for *nüzul* and *sürsat* taxes during the same year (see Tables II:18 and 19).

Concerning the relationship between prices paid to the villagers delivering flour or barley as *sürsat*, and prices demanded in other contexts, a few figures dating from Murad IV's Iranian campaigns provide an indicator: in 1637–38, villagers were paid 12 *akçe* for a *kile* of barley, while in the case of districts unable to fulfill their quotas, the money equivalents demanded ranged between 20 and 60 *akçe* per *kile*.[13] In the case of flour, villagers were paid 20 *akçe* per *kile*, while whenever the central administration demanded cash instead of goods, 60 to 100 *akçe* were due for every *kile* of flour. In İstanbul after the currency reform of 1640, the price for a *kile* of barley in the market was fixed at 23 *akçe*,

Table II:18. Assessment and collection of the *nüzul* (Caucasus campaign of Ferhad Pasha, 1590)

Province	Number of districts	Avarız "tax house"	flour barley	Delivered in kind	Money payments	Arrears
		Assessed		Collected		
Anadolu	144	82,983	55,312	46,119	27,515	6,441
Karaman	43	37,356	24,904	22,129	845	1,929
Maraş	15	21,678	14,452	10,269	436	3,749
Rum	57	35,654	23,770	18,507	1,025	4,277
Halep	19	15,829	10,552	6,899	98	3,466
Total		193,500	128,990	103,923	29,919	19,862

Source: Derived from Güçer (1964), p. 83.

Table II:19. Grain deliveries (*sürsat*) demanded from a number of Anatolian districts (unit of measurement not specified)

Avarız "tax house"	Sub-province: district	1623–24	1633–34	1623–24	1633–34
		Flour		Barley	
10	Sivas: Karahisar	100	100	200	200
10	Konya: Kureyş	100	100	400	400
10	Maraş: Samantı	100	100	300	300
20	Canik: Satılmış	100	100	300	300
30	Sivas: Sivasabat	200	200	500	500
30	Canik: Kavak	100	100	400	400
30	Canik: Devrekni	100	100	400	400
30	Canik: Ceviz Deresi	100	150	400	450
30	Bozok: Bozok	50	50	100	200
30	İçili: Gülnar	100	100	200	200
30	Malatya: Taşeli	150	30	400	300
30	Adana: Kınık	150	150	400	400
30	Adana: Tarsus	200	200	1,000	1,000
40	Amasya: Artikâbat	–	150	–	500
40	Divriği: Darende	100	100	1,000	500
40	Niğde: Anduğu	150	200	500	400
40	Kırşehir: Keskin	200	200	300	350
40	Adana: Karaisalı	200	50	400	400
40	Diyarbekir: Siirt	–	100	–	300
40	Erzurum: Kuruçay	200	50	1,000	300
40	Erzurum: Tercan	200	50	1,000	400
40	Erzurum: Kelkit	200	100	1,000	350
40	Karahisar-ı Şarki: Ebülhayır	150	80	200	400

Source: Güçer (1964), p. 94.

that is, twice the price paid to the villagers, while the price for flour in İstanbul varied between 50 and 65 *akçe*.[14] Thus the villagers suffered appreciable losses; moreover, the very fact that the *sürsat* could be converted into money payments emphasizes its character as a tax.[15]

In addition, grain for Ottoman armies on the march also was secured by the so-called *iştira*, a device used particularly to fill state granaries in the rear of the fighting armies. In the early seventeenth century, the *iştira* differed from the *sürsat* in that the sellers were to receive the same price they would have obtained if selling to civilian consumers (*narh-ı ruzi*). However, transportation costs again placed an appreciable load upon the villagers, since we find that the producers of a single district were sent to supply a whole series of stopping points on a given army route.[16]

In addition to these war-oriented and, in their early stages, intermittent prestations, there was the *öşür* (tithe), from the earliest days of the empire one of the major taxes collected from agriculture. Tithes were due from all agricultural products; only where deliveries in kind were impracticable, as in the case of fresh fruit and vegetables, was money demanded. Thus this tax could not be eroded by inflation, as happened to taxes permanently converted into money. On the other hand, the *öşür* often formed the major source of income assigned to receivers of prebends owing military service (*timar*) or to pious foundations. Therefore the *öşür* was available to the Ottoman central administration only if the lands in question were taxed directly by the central treasury.[17]

SERVICES

Services were demanded from villagers and townsmen mainly for fortifications and other construction projects, in the mines and for the transportation of foodstuffs and fodder to the army (for remunerated services of craftsmen in the building trades, see Ch. 16). Certain nomads of Rumelia (yürük) formed part of the Ottoman army, and their obligations often were converted into transportation services. The yürük were exempt from taxes such as the *avarız* and were expected to bring their own animals to work. They served on a rotational basis, and those nomads not currently on active service provided for the expenses of their fellows. In the course of the seventeenth century, this ancient organization was in full disarray as many nomads had settled down and were no longer available for military service. Therefore in 1691, at the height of the Ottoman–Habsburg War, a new register of nomads owing service was compiled and the organization given the name of Evlad-ı Fatihan ("Descendants of the Conquerors"). In this new guise the nomads of Rumelia continued to perform service until the Tanzimat period.[18]

Miners also served the central government against exemption from taxes, particularly the *avarız*, although wage labor in the mines was not unknown. A corpus of tax regulations from the province of Erzurum refers to the rationale for mining services from the central government's point of view: peasants living in infertile and mountainous areas, who because of their poverty were unable to carry a full tax load, yet could be made useful to the treasury by employing them as miners.[19] Problems might arise from the fact that it was not always clearly spelled out which services were to be performed in lieu of taxes and which were to be remunerated. Moreover even when wages were paid, they sometimes were too low for the mine workers' subsistence. It was assumed that miners would earn their living in agriculture, a not always realistic assumption.[20]

We do not possess any studies that allow us to estimate the value of peasant or nomad services in money, and thus we have no way of determining the direct and indirect benefits to the Ottoman state. However, it is misleading to regard the income of the seventeenth-century state as consisting exclusively of cash, even though our vision of the modern state predisposes us in this direction. From the taxpayers' point of view, transportation services particularly might constitute a heavy load: peasants and animals were removed from productive activities at times which were not necessarily attuned to the agricultural cycle. Viewed from the Ottoman army's angle, it was the existence of services which accounted for the often praised efficiency of its supply system. Ottoman state finances thus need to be regarded as part of a broader and more encompassing setup, and not as an analogy to the finances of a modern state.

THE FINANCIAL BUREAUCRACY

Recent research has shown that the Ottoman financial bureaucracy became increasingly elaborate between 1510 and 1560, when substitute *defterdars* (finance directors) were created and a new bureaucratic structure designed. Between 1560 and 1660 there was a period of relative stability, but the finance department went through another period of structural change in the later seventeenth and eighteenth centuries. The finance directors of the late sixteenth century had been responsible for the empire's major regions, that is, Rumelia, Anatolia and the Arab provinces. This division of labor by region was given up some time after 1660, and replaced by a division along functional lines, so that individual taxes or groups of taxes were handled by a greatly increased number of bureaus.

In the seventeenth century, we observe changes in the number and composition of the corps of scribes staffing the finance offices. Before 1600 the typical scribe was designated in the salary registers as a *katib*, assisted by apprentices (*şakird*). Scribes occasionally had religious training, but recruitment of the sons of scribes became increasingly significant. Most importantly the number of scribes grew, and the department's limited funding did not permit the payment of full salaries to all of them. High-level scribes were given *timar*s, while the salaries of less fortunate officials were slashed by inflation. Now only the bureau chiefs had a right to the prestigious title of *katib*, while all other scribes, regardless of experience, were known as *şakird*. The prestige of the office probably declined.

Contemporary authors of advice literature frequently complain about corruption in office, but apparently these strictures did not apply to the financial bureaucracy before 1660, although they may have been more justified after this date. Between 1560 and 1660, scribes of the finance bureaus needed to cope with vast amounts of paperwork, particularly after the *avarız* had been turned into an annual tax. This task they handled with considerable competence, and increased efficiency was reflected particularly in the manner of tax assessment and responses to taxpayers' complaints.[21]

FORMS OF TAX COLLECTION

Even though the military importance of the prebend (*timar*) holders was waning by the seventeenth century, the latter continued to collect a significant share of taxes directly from the peasants. However the money which reached the central treasury was usually collected either by salaried officials (*emin*) or by tax-farmers (*mültezim*). Salaried officials were employed whenever the central treasury intended to maintain direct control over a source of revenue. Moreover, certain sources of revenue did not attract satisfactory bids from tax-farmers, because collection was known to be unprofitable. In such cases a salaried official was appointed until such time as the productivity of the revenue source regained satisfactory levels.

Tax-farmers, who normally contracted for a three-year period, were responsible for the payment of the sum fixed in their contract and for a variety of additional dues. The central administration was not obliged to leave the tax-farm in the hands of any contractor for the duration of the farm. Whenever a better bid was made, the tax-farmer either paid the difference or lost his right to collect. When the central administration was not under excessive financial pressure, concern about securing the services of reliable tax-farmers over a long period of time limited the turnover. But in wartime, particularly during the Ottoman–Habsburg War of 1683–99, attempts to maximize revenues in the short run led to rapid appointments and dismissals of tax-farmers. This policy resulted in serious losses to contractors, particularly to those in charge of dues based upon agricultural activities, which normally could be collected only once a year. Tax-farmers were often deposed before they had made any profit to balance their expenditures. In 1691, there was an attempt to remedy the situation by allowing tax-farmers possession, for at least a full year, of the revenue source for which they had contracted. By this measure the central treasury attempted to protect the taxpayers, who were subjected to all sorts of pressures from tax-farmers anxious to recoup as much of their outlay in as short a time as possible. Moreover, constant uncertainty had led to a decline in the number of bidders and to low bids, which meant loss of revenue.[22] The institution of the long-term tax-farms known as *malikâne* equally constituted an attempt to cope with the late seventeenth-century crisis of tax-farming.

THE TAX LOADS OF INDIVIDUAL PROVINCES

With the establishment of provincial treasurers in many parts of the Ottoman Empire during the second half of the sixteenth century, annual records of provincial incomes and expenditures were drawn up in increasing numbers.[23] A few samples are available in print, concerning Egypt and the Yemen.[24] Although for the sake of brevity these accounts are often described as budgets, they were not intended as a schedule for future spending. On the contrary, these "budgets" differed from their twentieth-century counterparts in that they record revenues already collected and expenditures already undertaken, often encompassing a full solar or else lunar year.

The budget of Yemen in 1599–1600 shows that in this remote province a very considerable share (35 percent) of Ottoman revenues came from the ports. This was due both to the fact that these were more accessible than the hinterland, and also to the lively trade with India and Egypt which took place in these towns, particularly Muha and Hudeyde. Even so, more than half of all revenues originated in the agricultural pursuits of the hinterland, collected in the shape of a tax on agricultural land.[25]

Yemen-based revenues constituted about one-quarter of the sum of money which the Ottoman administration derived from Egypt in the year 1596–97 (65,902,000 *para* without the arrears from previous years). Given the country's agricultural wealth, the relative weight of customs dues was much less than in Yemen (8.2 percent). However, revenues drawn from Cairo, that is from merchants and artisans, made up 6.6 percent of total revenues. Thus non-agricultural dues amounted to at least 16.8 percent of the total. Moreover, some of the miscellaneous revenues which totaled 10.9 million *para* (16.5 percent) must also have been non-agricultural in origin. But land taxes and the sale of treasury-owned grains constituted by far the most important sources of the central administration's income. Taken together, these two items amounted to 43.8 million *para*, or 66.3 percent of all Egyptian revenues.[26]

While taxes from the Arab provinces were calculated in *para* and Ottoman gold coins (*sikke-i hasene*), Anatolian provincial budgets of the later sixteenth and early seventeenth centuries were expressed in *akçe*.[27]

The fiscal yield of Anatolia was quite modest: Karaman province, which encompassed most of southern central Anatolia with the sizable towns of Kayseri, Konya and Niğde, produced only about 4 percent of the revenues which the administration had gained from the Yemen in 1599–1600.[28] Even if we admit that the Karaman figures were temporarily depressed due to the destruction caused by the Celali rebellions, the crucial importance of Yemen and Egypt in the cash income of the empire clearly stands out.

Among the more significant revenue items recorded for Karaman were grain deliveries from the town of Niğde, the monetary value of which amounted to 18 percent of total revenues. The *cizye* (non-Muslim head-tax) and a number of unspecified sources of revenue accounted for most of the central administration's remaining income. Other provincial budgets from different parts of the seventeenth-century empire are needed before we can evaluate how "typical" were these three provinces, and determine the principal sources of the empire's financial strength.

(NOT) BALANCING THE BUDGET

Although a number of budgets documenting the revenues and expenditures of the central treasury during the seventeenth century have been published, they do not provide a satisfactory picture of the geographical distribution of revenue sources.[29] While sixteenth-century budgets normally had listed revenues according to their geographical origin, seventeenth-century Ottoman accountants acquired the habit of recording revenues by the treasury office in charge of their administration. Although many offices were concerned with revenues from a particular area, the geographical origin of certain revenues remains masked from everyone except the most expert historians of Ottoman finances.[30]

The "expenditures" sections of both central and provincial budgets reflect the high cost of administration relative to total income. Thus, at the turn of the seventeenth century, the grand vizier, along with provincial governors and officials on duty in Egypt, all received yearly salaries based on Yemeni revenues, as did soldiers stationed both in Egypt and in Yemen. Administrative expenditures within Yemen itself were so large that a deficit ensued, which amounted to over 6.5 million *para*.[31]

By contrast Egyptian revenues in 1596–97 by far surpassed provincial expenditures.[32] About one-third of all Egyptian revenues (32 percent) left the country, for the most part remitted to İstanbul. But Egyptian revenues also fed pilgrims and permanent residents of the Holy Cities of the Hejaz, and a smaller sum was set aside for the needs of Jerusalem. Provincial expenditures amounted to 44.7 million *para*. Salaries (*salyane*), for the most part to high-ranking officials, accounted for 15 percent of this figure, while others on the state payroll, for the most part military men, received 26.6 million *para* (59 percent of all expenditures). Thus the 1596–97 budget confirms the image of Egypt as a major source of financial strength, and it becomes apparent that the retention of Egyptian revenues by the Mamluk elite during certain years of the seventeenth century constituted a cause for major financial embarrassment.

Given the modest resources of the province of Karaman (expenditures surpassed revenues by the small sum of 1,030 *akçe*), salaries to high-ranking officials again occupied an important place. The governor of Karaman received the largest salary, followed by the treasurer of the province. Much smaller sums went to two dervish lodges of Konya, the celebrated convent of Mevlana Celaleddin Rumi among them. Scribes in the financial administration and employees of certain pious foundations received smaller sums. The garrisons of towns such as Konya or Kayseri do not appear in the budget. The largest share of provincial revenues, however, was appropriated by the central treasury in İstanbul (38 percent). Even in the mid-sixteenth century, the day-to-day business of the Ottoman government largely had been financed by revenues obtained from western and central Anatolia on the one hand, and eastern Rumelia on the other.[33] Apparently the upheavals of the Celali rebellions, and the ensuing financial weakness of Karaman province, did not significantly disrupt this pattern.

In the 1669–70 budget, the central administration's expenditures are recorded in a much less ambiguous fashion than its revenues. Thus we can determine how in this year, when warfare was limited to the Ukraine, and all was quiet on the Polish and Habsburg fronts, the Ottoman budget showed a deficit of 44.7 million *akçe* (7.3 percent). Almost two-thirds of expenditures were military in character: apart from the pay for an army of 98,342 men, which accounted for 35.5 percent of all expenditures, considerable sums were spent on food, uniforms made of Salonica woolen cloth, the manufacture of gunpowder in Karaman and Salonica, and other military needs. Given the comparatively minor importance of the navy during the years which followed the end of the Cretan War, the Arsenal was less well provided for than the armies; but even so, the latter received 41.3 million *akçe* (6.5 percent).

For the sultan's person and the upkeep of his palaces, 189.2 million *akçe* were set aside, which amounted to 29.5 percent of all expenditures. Under this heading, the budget includes the sums of money which the sultan reserved for his private disposal, and also the funds spent on stables and kitchens, on the pages being trained in Galatasaray, on the wages of artisans working for the ruler, and on payments to the officials and servants who kept the palaces running. Manufacture of robes of honor also proved costly, particularly since constant warfare in the Ukraine must have disrupted the supply of furs. Compared to the palace, the *divan* and the offices subordinate to it did not cost the Ottoman taxpayer very much, their expenditures amounting to less than one percent of the total.

Among expenditures less easily categorized, one might mention construction projects and gifts. The former were not very significant: even with repairs and other miscellaneous items included, they amounted to no more than 2 percent of all expenditures. More important were the salary payments through which sultans and viziers took charge of a sizable number of mosques and mausolea. Moreover ambassadors, the Tatar Khan and certain Circassian lords also received gratifications, and 3.5 million *akçe* (0.5 percent) were spent upon the *hajj* and the inhabitants of Medina.[34]

CONCLUSION

At the present stage of our knowledge, the late sixteenth- and seventeenth-century Ottoman financial administration appears as a body of specialists, trained for the arduous task of supplying the resources needed by an ever-more demanding governmental apparatus. War was by far the greatest source of expenditure. Twentieth-century researchers frequently have dwelt upon the reasons why war became increasingly expensive: confrontation with comparatively large and well-organized states such as the Austrian Habsburg and Safavid Iran, an increasing use of money throughout the economy as a whole, a growing demand for musketeers who needed to be paid in cash. However, more recently it has become apparent that war-related demands had weighed heavily upon the Ottoman peasantry even in the fifteenth century. Thus it seems wrong to assume that ordinary taxpayers began to feel the impact of war only from the later years of the sixteenth century onward, even though the load probably became much heavier from this time on.[35]

We have accustomed ourselves to seeing the Ottoman Empire as a state particularly geared toward the pursuit of war, and at first glance the budget of 1669–70, with 62.5 percent of all expenditures related to warfare, seems to confirm this impression. But to place matters in their proper perspective, we may glance briefly at the "first and last" overall budget of *ancien régime* France, summarizing revenues and expenditures of the year 1788.[36] More than half of all expenditures were interest payments, and the debts which had occasioned them had to a considerable extent been contracted in order to finance war. In addition, current military expenditures amounted to 26 percent; if expenditures apart from interest payments are taken as a base value, the proportion rises to 53 percent. The expenses of king and court amounted to almost 6 percent of total expenditure, and to 12 percent of expenses apart from debt servicing. The major difference between the two budgets lay in the sums of money set aside for the civilian administration, rather than in military and palace expenditures.

While expenses connected with civilian administration were negligible in the budget of the Ottoman central government, in 1780s France, 23 percent of all expenditures (debt servicing included) were recorded under this heading. But it is probable that a French budget of the 1670s, if such a thing had existed, also would show lower expenditures on civilian administration. At the same time, the political power of the Ottoman palace in the second half of the seventeenth century was such that certain palace expenses probably could be considered as expenditures for civilian administration as well. Both budgets show that the governments of the time placed a low priority upon education and welfare, which were left to the initiative of private donors. The highest priority in both instances was financing past, present and future wars, and, in this respect, the Ottoman Empire is probably less unique than it has been made out to be.

NOTES

1 An important source is the unpublished dissertation by Linda Darling (1990), in addition Genç (1975, 1987); Tabakoğlu (1985a, b); Cezar (1986). I thank Linda Darling for showing me her manuscript.

2 İnalcık (1959).

3 Güçer (1964), pp. 67–92; Tabakoğlu (1985a), pp. 157–58.

4 Güçer (1964), p. 29.

5 Compare the article "Djizya" in *EI*,[2] by Halil İnalcık.

6 McGowan (1981), pp. 80–81.

7 Tabakoğlu (1985a), pp. 165–67.

8 *Ibid.*, p. 158; McGowan (1981), p. 109 suggests that this happened between 1585 and 1625.

9 Darling (1990), pp. 328–29.

10 Compare the article "Avarız" in *İA* by Ö.L. Barkan; Linda Darling, unpublished communication at the MESA Convention of 1986.

11 Barkan (1955–56a), p. 213; McGowan (1981), p. 205.

12 Tabakoğlu (1985a), p. 158.

13 Güçer (1964), pp. 104–6, 113.

14 Kütükoğlu (1983), pp. 92–97.

15 Güçer (1964), p. 97.

16 *Ibid.*, pp. 115–18.

17 *Ibid.*, pp. 44–66.

18 Gökbilgin (1957), pp. 255–56.

19 Barkan (1943), p. 72.

20 Faroqhi (1984), p. 186.

21 Darling (1990).

22 Tabakoğlu (1985a), p. 124.

23 Fleischer (1986), pp. 311–14.

24 Shaw (1968); Sahillioğlu (1985).

25 Sahillioğlu (1985), pp. 302–3.

26 Shaw (1968), p. 21.

27 An account concerning the province of Karaman in 1020–21/Dec. 1611 – Jan. 1613 records revenues totaling 1,649,098 *akçe* for a timespan of one lunar year, two months and eight days (MM 5285, p. 6). The fluctuating rate of exchange between *akçe* and *para* makes it difficult to compare this figure with the Egyptian and Yemeni data. No figures are available for 1612, but since both in 1014/1605–6 and in 1027/1617–18 the *para* was equivalent to 3 *akçe*, Karaman-based revenues should have corresponded to 549,669 *paras*: Sahillioğlu (1964), p. 229.

28 Karaman figures refer to a period slightly longer than a solar year.

29 Barkan (1955–56a, b).

30 Tabakoğlu (1985a), p. 168; (1985b), p. 393.
31 Sahillioğlu (1985), pp. 310–19.
32 Shaw (1968), p. 21; *Idem* (1962), pp. 284, 295.
33 Barkan (1953–54), p. 273.
34 Barkan (1955–56a), pp. 214–24; for revenues and expenditures during the closing years of the seventeenth century, see also Sahillioğlu (1981).
35 Lowry (1986).
36 Soboul (1970), p. 470.

19

ॐ

THE RULING ELITE BETWEEN POLITICS AND "THE ECONOMY"

While Chapters 16, 17 and 18 deal with the more or less long-term changes in economic life made visible by customs duties, foundation revenues, or provincial budgets, the two chapters that follow concentrate upon the people active in bringing about these changes. It would have been desirable to add a third chapter dealing with the lives of peasants and nomads, but since the latter have been little studied, what is known about them already has been summarized in Chapter 16. In a survey of social and economic life, the more distinctly political and military activities of the elite cannot be discussed in any detail. But, particularly in a non-capitalist or pre-capitalist context, it is impossible to neatly separate the economic from the political. Just as a discussion of economic life in sixteenth- and seventeenth-century France will devote a great deal of time and space to the policies of the state, so an account of Ottoman economic life will discuss the role of the political elite where it impinges on the economic activities of the subject population. This matter already has been touched upon when dealing with the elite's attitude to foreign trade (see Ch. 17), but far transcends that particular issue. Therefore, after discussing the Ottoman elite's views on matters which nowadays we would call economic, we need to take a closer look at the concrete activities by which individual members of the political class sought riches and power. Moreover, changes in the composition and life-styles of the elite led to new forms of taxation practices, and the latter transformed the economic impact of the Ottoman state apparatus upon the society it dominated.

ATTEMPTS AT REGULATING ECONOMIC LIFE

The Ottoman ruling elite was by no means hostile or even indifferent to trade; quite to the contrary, large-scale wholesaling traders were allowed to enrich themselves.[1] However, even the largest merchants could not rival a middle-level member of the political class such as a junior governor (*sancakbeyi*) in terms of wealth, to say nothing of officials higher up in the administrative hierarchy.[2] Moreover it is true that merchants, in so far as they refrained from tax-farming and other activities through which they might become debtors of the treasury, were able to pass on their estates to their heirs. But this principle notwithstanding, policies followed by the late sixteenth-century Ottoman state quite often were inimical to the accumulation of commercial capital, particularly when there was a suspicion of speculative gains or interest-taking. Thus merchants might be drafted to serve as butchers in İstanbul or in the trade which supplied the Hejaz caravans with camels, activities in which the risk of substantial losses was very high. Throughout the sixteenth and seventeenth centuries, even wealthy merchants remained under the control of the political class.

This control was secured by the administratively imposed price (*narh*). However this institution, in spite of its crucial importance for the functioning of the Ottoman system of government, was challenged by certain members of the elite. Since early Hanafite scholars had opposed administrative control of prices and favored a *laissez-faire* policy *vis-à-vis* the market, certain Ottoman ulema continued to have hesitations with respect to the legality of administratively imposed prices. Fazıl Mustafa Pasha, one of the grand viziers from the Köprülü family, who distinguished himself by his training in religious law, also was notable for his reluctance to enforce administered prices.[3] However, the dominant current of opinion, even among ulema, accommodated legal opinions to government practice. It was frequently claimed that the moral fiber of mankind had deteriorated since the time of the Prophet and the early legists, so that measures of control unnecessary and even blameworthy in those times now had become allowed and necessary. Thus we find kadis acting as the key officials, determining and enforcing officially administered prices, consulting with merchants and craftsmen and deciding complaints concerning the application of these measures.

The manner in which prices were administratively enforced favored long-distance traders over craftsmen.[4] Craftsmen were only allowed a profit margin of 10 to 20 percent, which left little room for capital accumulation, while long-distance traders often enough were allowed to determine their own prices. Even if the prices were decided by the kadi, the latter usually had to rely on merchants for information concerning purchase prices in distant places, a situation which allowed traders ample room for maneuver. Apparently one of the main reasons for price-fixing was to ensure that the Ottoman government could purchase goods at predetermined low prices. Actual sales prices as applied to private persons often may have diverged from the official price to quite a considerable extent.[5] While general consumer protection was part of Ottoman elite ideology, the system of administered prices above all served to protect the interests of the political class and the more important merchants. This situation also explains why official prices were promulgated for all kinds of goods in İstanbul, while provincial price registers usually limit themselves to necessities.

The other principal mechanism by which the Ottoman elite influenced the economic life of its subjects was the ruler's control over the currency. As this constituted one of the main symbols of the ruler's power, devaluation was often regarded as a symptom of the decline of the state.[6] Janissaries' uprisings against devaluation of the currency, while directed against the erosion of their own purchasing power, also were caused by a perception that corrupt officials were luring an inexperienced sultan into destroying the state.

Currency manipulations had an immediate impact on prices, and gave rise to serious disruption as prices often increased more than a given devaluation might warrant, while merchants hesitated to lower prices following a revaluation. At all times there were vast numbers of substandard coins in circulation, and this fact could easily be used as a pretext by traders wishing to justify their own profiteering.[7] Major mutations in the currency made it necessary to publish very full lists of newly determined official prices.[8] Control of prices and control of the coinage thus were closely connected, and could be used to increase the Ottoman administration's revenues and to augment the purchasing power of taxes already collected.

"OTTOMAN ESTATES" AND THE ENTREPRENEURIAL ACTIVITIES OF A GRAND VIZIER

To understand more clearly the economic views and activities of the seventeenth-century Ottoman elite, there follows a discussion of a particularly well-researched example. Derviş Mehmed Pasha, who died in 1655 after having held the office of grand vizier in 1653 and 1654, was considered by contemporary Ottoman historians to have been remarkable mainly for his wealth. This wealth was acquired largely by using the opportunities of high office to engage in trade, agriculture and money-lending.[9] In this manner, Derviş Mehmed Pasha preempted certain opportunities for making money, which under less enterprising governors had accrued to provincial elites in Damascus and Baghdad, where Derviş Mehmed Pasha held office for considerable periods of time. This explains why he was execrated by most provincial chroniclers, while authors close to the Ottoman center, such as Naima and Evliya Çelebi, expressed a neutral or even positive opinion. Among Derviş Mehmed Pasha's many business activities, Naima reports the sending of agents to India, Basra and Aleppo. Of the goods these people brought back, the governor kept what he needed for himself and his household, and resold the remainder to merchants in the city. Derviş Mehmed Pasha particularly specialized in the luxury trades, but also invested money in the extension of agricultural production in Iraq. Furthermore, his agents travelled in the north of Iraq, where they bought sheep from the local nomadic tribes. These sheep fed his own troops and household without endangering the food supply of Baghdad, and also were sold to the inhabitants of the city. Naima claims that even though Derviş Mehmed Pasha made an appreciable profit on these operations, the people of Baghdad were satisfied because he charged moderate prices. Unfortunately we possess no means of checking that claim.[10]

In a certain sense, Derviş Mehmed Pasha revived practices that were common enough in the domains of the Mamluk sultans, where the rulers and their lieutenants frequently engaged in commerce and even monopolized certain branches of the luxury trade.[11] A few earlier Ottoman viziers had also acted in a similar fashion. Süleyman the Lawgiver's grand vizier Rüstem Pasha, for instance, was most successful as a businessman. On the other hand, Ibn Khaldun, the influential political theoretician of the fourteenth century, opposed the rulers' participation in commerce and agriculture and stated forcefully that only in the last stages of political decadence did the ruler thus engage in unfair competition with his subjects. The seventeenth-century memorialist Koçi Bey also felt that the sultan's servitors should avoid *reaya* occupations.[12] Moreover, according to Ibn Khaldun, such competition was in the long run disadvantageous to the ruler himself, since he thereby deprived himself of much needed tax revenues. This latter view had become dominant among Ottoman political thinkers of the sixteenth century, whose thinking seems to have reflected the standard political practice of the time.[13] After all, Ottoman sultans rarely engaged in major commercial operations, and apart from Hungarian wine at certain times of the year (*monopolya*), mining products and a few dyestuffs, did not attempt to establish large-scale monopolies. However, quite a few viziers of the sixteenth century engaged in trade on their own behalf, so that Derviş Mehmed Pasha's business activities cannot be regarded as something without precedent. Had the opposite been true, it is unlikely that, given the conservative stance of the Ottoman ruling group, he would have found approval among authors such as Evliya Çelebi or Naima.

Yet at least Naima was aware that Derviş Mehmed Pasha's commercial and agricultural activities, and the arguments with which he defended them, were at variance with the socially approved division of labor. Naima expressed the governor's position in Ibn Khaldunian terms, and at the same time subverted the latter's teachings by a statement diametrically opposed to Ibn Khaldun's intentions. According to Naima, Derviş Mehmed Pasha claimed that a ruler who did *not* engage in business activities must carry the blame for imposing excessive burdens on his people.[14]

This debate leads us to the broader question of divisions within seventeenth-century Ottoman society. Political thinkers of the time, such as for instance Mustafa Ali and the anonymous author of the *Kitab-ı müstetab*, never tired of asserting that the taxpaying population (*reaya*) must be barred from entering the political class.[15] This was not a purely literary topos; in the second half of the sixteenth century, concerted efforts were made to remove officials of known *reaya* descent from the bureaucracy. But such a principle could not be applied consistently in practice. As a first exception, one might mention the *devşirme*, that is the recruitment of Christian peasant boys from within the Ottoman Empire as the sultan's servitors (*kul*), to be employed in the army, the palace, and the administration; however, in the course of the seventeenth century the *devşirme* was declining in importance. Moreover, it remained necessary to reward frontier warriors in the "Long War" between the Ottomans and the Habsburg Empire (1593–1607) by assigning them prebends out of tax revenue (*timars*).[16] The privileges granted to the more important tax-farmers often included their subordinates' appointment to *timars*, which should have provided the latter with a means of entering the Ottoman ruling group. Admittedly, this arrangement was assumed to be temporary, but ambitious members of the subject population must have used it as a stepping-stone to a more permanent change of status. Last but not least, in the 1590s impecunious *timar*-holders quite frequently alienated the revenues of their prebends.[17] While this arrangement did not make the new holders into members of the Ottoman ruling group, it is easy to envisage that some of the people involved used their temporary position to gain a more permanent social and political advantage. Moreover, craftsmen working for the Ottoman administration on a full-time basis were often counted as *askeri*, and some of their sons must have satisfied recruiting authorities concerning their non-*reaya* background (Table II: 20).

But even if in practice the boundaries between the *reaya* and the political class were not as firmly drawn as in the political treatises of the time, the distinction formed the basis for Ottoman political thinking in the years before and after 1600. This fact can be illustrated by a practical example: over the centuries, the estates of members of the political class were recorded in separate registers by an official appointed for this very purpose, the *askeri kassam*.[18] Since the estates of members of the political class, with the exception of the ulema, were liable to confiscation by the sultan, while those of the *reaya* devolved upon the heirs of the deceased, the distinction between the two groups was not easily forgotten.

But apart from the distinction between the *reaya* and the political class, we need to discuss the problem whether in Ottoman society there existed an institution comparable to the "estates" of early modern Europe. At first glance, the answer seems to be a clear negative. The Ottoman Empire did not possess a hereditary nobility apart from the descendants of the Prophet, whose political importance was comparatively limited. Moreover a mid-sixteenth century observer, the shrewd Habsburg ambassador Oghier Ghiselin de Busbecq, commented that all members of the political class regarded themselves as nothing more than the servitors of the sultan. Since the latter might elevate or punish anyone at will, members of the Ottoman political class supposedly placed scant emphasis upon descent or family connections. Given these circumstances, there should have been little opportunity for members of the political class to acquire an "established position," which could be passed on for at least a few generations, and which seems the minimal precondition for even an informally recognized estate system.

And yet after the death of Süleyman the Magnificent (1566) matters came to be less clear-cut. Even in the sixteenth century there had been power-holders whose position was more secure than that of the typical *devşirme* recruit who had achieved a high rank. Foundation administrators or the sons of governors and rich *timar*-holders fell into this category. Their wealth and power was less exalted than that of viziers or provincial governors, but it could be transmitted to heirs. One may even claim that by the second half of the sixteenth century, the number of people who could transmit wealth and power to their sons increased. Features developed which remind us of the estate system of early modern Europe, albeit with the important difference that early modern estates

Table II:20. *Askeri* 1545–1659: occupation, place of residence and possible non-Muslim origins

| | Place of Residence | | | | | | total | | "Abdullah oğlu" (probable converts) | |
| | town | | country | | unknown | | | | | |
	No.	%	No.	%	No.	%	No.	%	No.	%
Janissaries	258	78.8	58	17.7	11	3.5	327	21.3	127	38.8
Sipahi	509	77.4	129	19.6	19	3.0	657	43.9	158	24.0
Ulema	327	93.1	19	5.4	5	1.5	351	23.4	33	9.4
Palace officials	50	87.1	6	10.5	1	1.8	57	3.7	23	40.3
Craftsmen	93	83.7	16	14.4	2	1.9	111	7.6	30	27.0
Total	1,237	82.1	228	15.4	38	2.5	1,503	100	371	24.6

Note: The table concerns the 1,503 persons whose estates were divided by the *askeri kassam* and whose occupation could be determined.
Source: Barkan (1966), p. 17.

in Europe had privileges sanctioned by law, while Ottoman "estates" functioned in a purely non-official manner. In part this transformation of Ottoman social structure can be explained by changes in landholding patterns. In certain Arabic-speaking provinces and in parts of Anatolia and the Balkans, local notables seized former state-owned lands and attempted, sometimes successfully, to transfer them to their heirs. Even though this transformation in the seventeenth century was not as widespread as previous researchers have assumed, even in its initial stages local power-holders stabilized their positions *vis-à-vis* the Ottoman administration. Material underpinnings that approximated private property contributed to the establishment of "political families or households" which were able to hold on to political power at least for the space of a few generations. In the same way, patronage relations, and the ties between Janissaries and craftsmen, which will be discussed in the following chapter, resulted in the formation of recognized political bodies.[19]

Thus we can summarize the dominant attitudes of the Ottoman elite toward economic activity in the following manner: on the one hand, trade and crafts were regarded as the proper sphere of the subject population, whose members were to be strictly excluded from government and political activity. At the same time, practical mobility was greater than these frequently repeated principles might lead us to believe. Moreover, while the dominant groups within the Ottoman political class subscribed to the notion that trade and agriculture were not the proper province of the ruler or his officials, and should be reserved to the taxpaying subjects, an active minority made substantial profits from trade and acquired land, using political position to gain economic advantage. Moreover, while the ideology that all servitors of the sultan rose and fell according to the latter's will alone should have inhibited the development of "constituted bodies," such bodies showed increasing coherence on the provincial level. This feature constitutes one of the more important transformations to be observed in the course of the seventeenth century.

BUREAUCRATIC ROUTINIZATION AND THE DEBATE ON "OTTOMAN DECLINE"

Another aspect of seventeenth century Ottoman transformation can be described as the establishment of a developed political bureaucracy. This institution was able to function even if, as frequently was the case in the seventeenth century, the reigning sultan was unconcerned with politics, was a minor or a madman. In the past fifty years, scholars have frequently tended to view this decreasing participation of the sultan in political life as evidence for "Ottoman decadence," which supposedly began at some time during the second half of the sixteenth century. But recently, more note has been taken of the fact that the Ottoman Empire was still a formidable military and political power throughout the seventeenth century, and that noticeable though limited economic recovery followed the crisis of the years around 1600; after the crisis of the 1683–99 war, there followed a longer and more decisive economic upswing. Major evidence of decline was not visible before the second half of the eighteenth century.[20] These observations have caused quite a few researchers to question the assumption that centralized rule was always equivalent with economic, political and cultural florescence, and that the absence of a strong sultan necessarily resulted in the decay of crafts and trade.

A closer study of certain Ottoman authors of the sixteenth and seventeenth centuries, who may be regarded as the real origins of the "decline" paradigm, has confirmed the scepticism of modern economic historians. In particular, recent work on Mustafa Ali has led to the understanding that sixteenth-century Ottoman authors, in this respect no different from writers of other times and places, responded both to literary traditions and to the tensions and frustrations in their own professional lives.[21] This realization has allowed us to evaluate Ali's remarks about Ottoman decline in a more critical fashion. After all, the decline topos is found in many literatures all over the world, and was for instance employed by Sultan Bayezid II's son Korkud in the political treatise which he wrote in the early 1500s.[22] Ali was of the opinion that his career had been much less successful than his merits deserved, and, subjectively speaking, thus had every reason to emphasize the motif of declining standards in an elite that had slighted him. Given these considerations, we adopt the more neutral term "transformation" for what happened in the political life of the seventeenth-century Ottoman Empire. This term allows for a variety of divergent trends, and does not imply that any deviation from the standards of an idealized "Süleymanic age" is equivalent to deterioration.

The organization of Ottoman governmental service and particularly the nature of the divisions of which it consisted, have given rise to considerable debate among twentieth-century scholars. Older accounts assume a fairly rigid division between the ulema on the one hand and all other public officials on the other.[23] The authors contrast a "ruling institution" and a "religious institution," each recruiting its junior members from distinct sections of the Ottoman population. This interpretation has been challenged by researchers assuming a much more flexible organization according to career lines, principally the military-administrative, bureaucratic-scribal and ulema.[24] According to this model, a certain amount of changeover between careers remained possible even after the system had assumed its fully developed form in the seventeenth and eighteenth centuries.

On the other hand, a recent work on the late eighteenth and nineteenth centuries has returned to the notion of an Ottoman bureaucracy consisting of two separate branches, namely the soldier-administrators and the ulema. Moreover, it is assumed that administrative change occurring after 1600 should be viewed as an aspect of Ottoman decline. The two main branches of Ottoman government in "classical" times, namely the military-administrative and the ulema, supposedly declined in power as they became more and more incapable of living up to the professional and moral standards of the past. But at the same time, the palace service, which in classical times had been little more than an offshoot of the military-administrative branch, gained in political prominence, particularly during the eighteenth century, and became increasingly bureaucratized in the process.[25]

The history of the scribal service, which in the sixteenth century had been comparatively small in scale, forming part of the palace organization or working under the grand vizier, is regarded as further evidence for increasing bureaucratization. But this process, which historians of early modern Europe regard as evidence for the development of a modern state, and value accordingly, is here viewed as a negative phenomenon. The growth of a scribal service, culturally distinct from the ulema and organizationally independent of the military-administrative complex, is seen as characteristic of the "period of decline," and more particularly of the second half of the seventeenth century.[26]

The idea that the Ottoman administration of the "classical period" consisted of only two major components has tempted scholars due to its neatness and clarity, but there is a serious empirical difficulty. Before the empire developed a specialized financial bureaucracy, taxes were largely administered by temporary state servitors, the *emin*, and these officials did not disappear even after finance departments became part and parcel of most provincial administrations. Temporary officials were paid a salary, and unlike tax-farmers were not supposed to make a profit from their offices; employing *emin*s gave the state administration flexibility, as an *emin* did not need to be part of the political class, and was often a non-Muslim. The office must have served to bind wealthy *reaya* to the state by allowing them to exercise power and influence, albeit on a temporary basis, and a model of the Ottoman administration which disregards the *emin*s is unsatisfactory.

Moreover, observations concerning administrative change should be detached from the model of "Ottoman decline," with which they do not possess any necessary connection. Professionalization of the scribal bureaucracy, particularly the financial bureaucracy, was well on its way by the mid-sixteenth century.[27] Thus if one does not wish to make the decline of the empire begin about 1550, there is no reason to describe the professionalization and specialization of the Ottoman administrative services as a decline phenomenon, unless of course one chooses to see professionalization and specialization as indicators of decadence *per se*, an attitude which makes it necessary to rewrite large sections of early modern European history.

Certain twentieth-century scholars have in fact proposed a date in the middle of the sixteenth century as the starting point of "Ottoman decline."[28] In defense of this interpretation, these authors have dwelt upon growth of European commercial capitalism on the one hand, and the civil wars accompanying the struggle for Kanuni Süleyman's succession on the other. But it would be difficult to claim that European commercial penetration of the eastern Mediterranean was especially intense in the 1550s, while long and dramatic struggles among princes for the succession of an ageing sultan were certainly not an unprecedented phenomenon either.[29] Moreover, endemic unrest, at least in Anatolia, during the closing years of Selim I and the beginning of Süleyman Kanuni's reign makes it appear unlikely that the struggle for the latter's succession constituted a peculiar turning point.

There is a further reason for insisting on this matter. Recently our attention has been drawn to the fact that, while seventeenth-century Ottoman finance officials may have used paper of a worse quality than did their mid-sixteenth century predecessors, by contrast the quality of their work tended to get better. Accounts were kept more regularly, and the number of mechanical errors decreased.[30] This is, in itself, not surprising; after all one would expect that with more formalized training of scribes and accountants, the quality of their work would improve. The same phenomenon can be observed in the kadi registers of major provincial cities such as Ankara and Kayseri. Late seventeenth-century documents emanating from the kadis' offices are longer and more overloaded with bureaucratic formulas than during the later sixteenth century.

But, at the same time, poor spelling and incomplete information were encountered more rarely. By and large, the growth of a professionalized bureaucracy seems to have improved the quality of certain aspects of Ottoman administration, and it is difficult to see why greater technical competence should indicate decline.

THE SCRIBAL BUREAUCRACY: RECRUITMENT, CULTURE AND CAREER

Given the rapid expansion of the Ottoman bureaucracy during the second half of the sixteenth century, the question of recruitment is of particular significance. Mustafa Ali and other authors of his time never denied that an education in the theological-legal colleges known as *medrese* was open to every young man intelligent and persevering enough to succeed in this long course of study. Thus entry into the ulema hierarchy in principle was open to all. Yet Ali seems to have assumed that the sons of established state servitors were the most desirable recruits into the financial and administrative bureaucracy. Certainly he did not advocate that this career be thrown wide open to the sons of ordinary taxpaying peasants and townsmen, a sentiment in tune with the actual practice of his time. While recruitment into the scribal career was more open than, for instance, appointment to a *timar* (which in principle was limited to the sons of *timar*-holders), it often did seem to require some prior family association with service to the Ottoman state.[31]

Down to at least the middle of the sixteenth century, the *medrese* provided the only thorough course of intellectual training. For this reason, an official who had gone through a full course of *medrese* study and training might regard himself as specially qualified to obtain high office, particularly if he had concentrated on grammar, rhetoric and the art of letter-writing.[32] Thus it is worth noting that the relatively open character of the theological colleges did not devalue the education obtained there, even though the sons of officials rubbed shoulders with young men from the subject population. But, at the same time, from the second half of the sixteenth century onward, in-service training for aspiring young scribes became increasingly common. The training of these young bureaucrats has been compared with the apprenticeship of craftsmen, and the organization of scribes in active service with that of guildsmen.[33] In the course of time, the culture of the scribal corps also became quite distinct from that of the ulema. In scribal circles, it was certainly considered necessary to be a Muslim, but on the whole religious concerns were of secondary importance. *Belles-lettres* constituted a major part of a young scribe's education, and many of the books and epistles on Ottoman political problems written during the seventeenth century were a product of this particular sub-culture.

For advancement in his profession, the ambitious young scribe depended on the favors of a patron, and in this respect his position resembled that of recent recruits into the military-administrative and ulema careers. The ideal patron of course was the sultan himself, but only a very few had the opportunity to catch the sultan's eye. Some people relied on influential relatives, as apparent from the career of Evliya Çelebi (about 1610 to 1683); Evliya, whose social talents made him a favored companion of high-level officials, used his relationship to the Grand Vizier Melek Ahmed Pasha and other prominent court figures, not for appointment to well-paid positions, but rather to obtain opportunities for travel.[34] In other cases relationships with potential advantages for a political career might be formed at the meetings held by an influential dervish sheikh. Literary salons, which seem to have abounded in late sixteenth-century İstanbul, were another meeting ground where such relationships might be established.[35] But a scribe who was unable to form such relationships, or whose sources of patronage failed him, could look forward only to a modest career.

THE ULEMA

Ulema careers are easier to follow than those in the military-administrative, scribal or palace sections of the Ottoman central administration, for the medieval Islamic tradition of compiling biographical dictionaries concerning such personages continued throughout the Ottoman period as well. As a result, the ulema have been extensively studied, even though the history of seventeenth-century scholar-bureaucrats is still difficult to place within the context of an overall history of the Ottoman scholarly establishment.[36]

Ulema possessed a special privilege in that they could transfer estates to their heirs, while high officials in other branches of the Ottoman administration had to reckon with the possibility of confiscation of their property after death. Moreover, the control that ulema exercised over pious foundations, either as administrators or else as overseers, equally allowed them to consolidate their holdings, for, unlike private property, pious foundations could not be divided among heirs. It is presumably due to this double privilege that ulema families were able to maintain themselves on the pinnacle of wealth and power much longer than either members of the administrative-military establishment or rich merchants. There are some remarkable cases of ulema families in the Arab provinces, who remained in positions of eminence for three hundred years.[37]

Even though families located closer to the Ottoman center were not able to duplicate this performance, there are examples of high-level ulema families retaining a prominent position over several generations. An example are the descendants of Sadeddin Efendi, the historian and teacher of Sultan Murad III (1574–95). Two of Sadeddin's sons successively became Sheyhülislam that is head of the ulema hierarchy, while a granddaughter was married to Sultan Osman II. In some ways the case of Feyzullah Efendi, the descendant of a family of Iranian ulema settled in Erzurum, is even more remarkable. Feyzullah enjoyed the patronage of Sheikh Mehmed Vani, the sultan's preacher, who wielded considerable influence at court and introduced his protégé into palace circles. Feyzullah became teacher to the prince who ascended the throne as Mustafa II, and retained considerable influence over the ruler in his adult years. Feyzullah himself rose to be the head of the official ulema hierarchy; his son Fethullah was appointed syndic of the descendants of the Prophet (*nakibüleşraf*). However, it was partly Feyzullah's nepotism, considered excessive even by the standards of the time, which led to his downfall and death in the rebellion of 1703.[38]

Immediately after the rebellion, with both Feyzullah and Fethullah dead, it seemed as if the "house of Feyzullah" had disappeared from the stage of Ottoman history. However, during the events which led to the overthrow of Ahmed III in 1730, descendants of the deceased Sheyhülislam again were able to play a political role, even though at the time the surviving members of the family had been banished to Bursa and thus were removed from their potential power bases in both İstanbul and Erzurum.[39] Even the confiscation of Feyzullah's property (he had acted so much like a vizier that his descendants were unable to retain more than a small share of his estate) did not in the long run prevent the survival of the family as a focus of political power.

Feyzullah Efendi also is remarkable for the openness with which he flaunted the new self-confidence of the head of a major "political household." He even documented his feelings in writing, for he has left a history of his ancestors and another of his personal career, the latter composed about 1702.[40] Very noticeable is Feyzullah's regard for his patrons Sheikh Vani and Sultan Mustafa II. But even stronger is the emphasis on his own family, the careers of whose more prominent members he describes in detail. It is obvious that Feyzullah took pride in their achievements, and he also made it clear that it was through his own influence that his numerous sons reached prominent positions when still quite young. Moreover, even though Sheikh Vani had affected an ascetic posture, Sheyhülislam Feyzullah did not believe that wealth was something to be ashamed of: he recounts with evident satisfaction how he had a mansion built in Erzurum. In Feyzullah's eyes, and probably those of most people who headed a "political household," any lingering stigma connected with great wealth was effaced by the fact that it had been granted by the sultan. In fact, to follow as closely as possible the model provided by the sultan and his household became the hallmark of the grandees of the empire, and obviously one could not adopt this kind of lifestyle and still maintain a reserved attitude *vis-à-vis* the riches of this world.[41] However, when the political power of an Ottoman grandee was challenged, his great wealth might be counted against him, as happened to Sheyhülislam Feyzullah during the rebellion of 1703.

Moving from these top-level members of the Ottoman scholarly and judicial hierarchy to less exalted but still influential people, we may use as an example a monograph concerning the family of the historian and biographer Uşakizade.[42] Uşakizade (1664–65 to 1725) was a descendant of the Prophet and in more recent generations of the prominent dervish sheikh Hasan Uşaki from Buhara. Born into a family where scholarly and judicial careers had become normal on both the paternal and maternal sides, Uşakizade made a respectable career for himself, in which the high points were the times when he officiated as a judge, first in Medina and later in İzmir. However, the really successful member of the family was his elder brother, who twice reached the *kadi-asker*ship of Rumeli, the second-highest position in the Ottoman scholarly-judicial hierarchy. Uşakizade's career shows the advantages and the risks involved in attaching a career to that of a more prominent patron. Both Uşakizades were known as protégés of Sheyhülislam Feyzullah, and after his death were penalized by being downgraded from the positions they already had obtained. In the long run however, the family, just as Feyzullah's own, managed to survive. In the generation following the historian Uşakizade there was a kadi of Damascus, while another family of ulema, descended from the fifteenth-century commander Gazi Evrenos, continued to launch its sons into high-level careers until the beginning the nineteenth century (cf. Fig. II:6).[43]

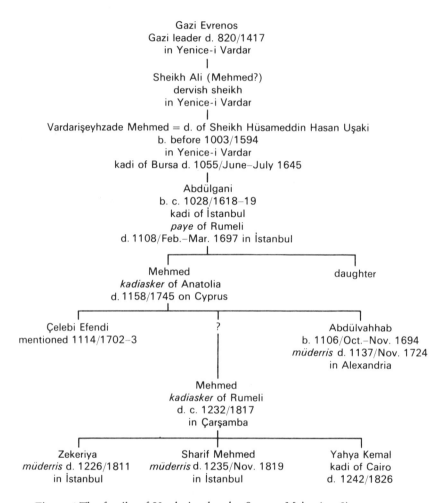

Fig. II:6 The family of Vardarişeyhzade. *Source*: Majer (1978), p. 132.

Ulema belonging to the middle-to-upper levels of the judicial-professorial hierarchy were by no means inactive, nor were their positions sinecures. Quite to the contrary, the biographies of the people in Uşakizade's circle make it apparent that at least adult appointees carried out their duties in person, and did not generally rely on the services of substitutes.[44] Moreover, even the high-level dignitaries close to the Ottoman central administration by no means constituted a closed caste. Access to the charmed circle in the capital was possible for young scholars from the provinces. Sons of merchant families, and, on occasion, even ulema from outside the empire, within a few generations could aspire to top-level positions in the scholarly-judicial hierarchy.[45] Being a descendant of the Prophet might be helpful, especially if one could claim association with a syndic of the corporation in which the latter were organized (*nakibüleşraf*). But the meritocratic element had not disappeared from seventeenth-century ulema careers, and the dignitaries at least of Uşakizade's circle took their scholarly and religious obligations very seriously.

On the other hand, certain seventeenth-century İstanbul ulema developed links to a "grassroots" movement, which gave them political leverage of quite a different kind from that enjoyed by Feyzullah and members of the Uşakizade family. From the second half of the sixteenth century, Birgevi Mehmed Efendi had challenged the compromises that high-level Ottoman ulema were willing to make with practices not sanctioned by religious law (*şeriat*). Birgevi particularly denounced the practice of interest-taking, which by the sixteenth century had become so widespread that even pious foundations commonly lent out money to finance their charities (see Ch. 17).[46] After Birgevi's death, his concerns were taken up by his student Kadızade and his adherents, the so-called Kadızadeliler, who preached a return to modes of behaviour as they presumedly had existed in Arabia at the time of the Prophet. They particularly directed their ire against the religious music and dances of the Mevlevis.[47] The Kadızadeliler found adherents among highly placed members of the Ottoman ruling class, particularly during the reign of Murad IV (1623–1640).[48] However, the alliance between the Kadızadeliler and Ottoman ruling circles broke down in 1661, when Köprülü Mehmed Pasha had certain leaders of the movement exiled from the capital.[49] Under the grand vizierate of Köprülü Fazıl Ahmed Pasha, some of the ideas of the Kadızadeliler once more found an influential exponent in the sultan's preacher Sheikh Mehmed Vani; but the latter's involvement in the Vienna campaign of 1683 led to his banishment from court and to the decline of the movement.[50]

THE PALACE CIRCLE

Research currently in progress promises to profoundly change our understanding of Ottoman palace life.[51] This revision particularly concerns the political influence of the Harem, a matter which to date more often has been mentioned in disparaging asides than seriously studied. In the later sixteenth century, changes in the system of accession to the throne were probably associated with a change in the position of royal consorts. Down to the middle of the sixteenth century, that is, prior to the special status achieved by Kanuni's wife Hürrem Sultan (in European sources, Roxelana), a royal consort customarily bore but a single son.[52] When the latter, at a fairly young age, was sent to the provinces to learn the art of governing, his mother accompanied him, as her political connections might be valuable assets to the young prince in his struggle for the throne. With Hürrem Sultan's ascendancy, most of the contending princes were the sons of one and the same mother, namely herself. Under the circumstances, the mother's co-residence was deemed too great an advantage to be allowed any single contender, and even after Hürrem Sultan's and Kanuni Süleyman's deaths, royal consorts ceased to leave the capital. To what extent this change in living arrangements furthered the growth of a political power node in the seventeenth-century Harem as yet remains to be examined.

Parallel to developments in medieval Europe, offices in the administration of the Ottoman state often evolved out of what had originally been palace functions.[53] Young boys recruited into top-level military-administrative careers usually served their apprenticeships as pages in the palace (see Fig. II:7).[54] Contacts established with the ruler while performing personal services constituted the foundation of many an administrative career, even though an author like Mustafa Ali might vehemently deplore the practice.[55] In a more direct fashion, the process can be observed in the development of the office of the Chief Black Eunuch (*Darüsseade Ağası, Kızlar Ağası*). It had been this functionary's original function to guard the Harem. But from 1598 we find him acting as supervisor of the pious foundations established by the sultans and, later on, by members of their families as well.[56] Given the extension of foundations by rulers such as Mehmed the Conqueror (1451–81), Kanuni Süleyman (1520–66) or Ahmed I (1604–17), this office involved considerable political power. Thus all the non-Muslims of İstanbul paid their head-taxes to the foundation of the Conqueror, while one of the more important Balkan fairs served to finance the foundation of Ahmed I. Foundations established by private persons also could be placed under the control of the Chief Black Eunuch. This control over a not-inconsiderable sector of Ottoman public finances surely formed the material basis for the political power that certain Chief Black Eunuchs were able to exercise.

THE MILITARY-ADMINISTRATIVE SECTOR

Even though this sector was, in a sense, the main focus of power within the Ottoman governmental system, we are only partially informed about

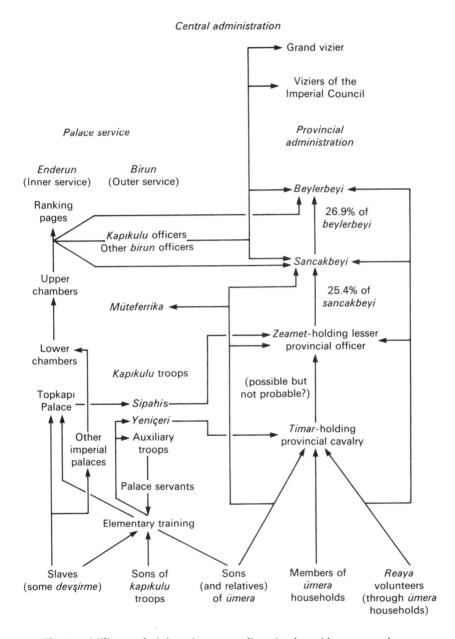

Fig. II:7 Military-administrative career lines in the mid-seventeenth century. *Source*: Kunt (1983), p. 68.

its functioning. As has been mentioned, by the seventeenth century the number of young men recruited through the levy of boys was declining. On the other hand, it was now more common for young men to enter the sultan's service through the mediation of a patron. By the middle of the sixteenth century, certain servitors (*kul*) of the sultan were raising servitors of their own in their separate households.[57] These people were apparently trained in more or less the same skills as the sultan's pages. After the death of the household head, a high-ranking palace official, some of these servitors of servitors' might seek and find employment in the palace.

Training given in the palace seems to have been flexible and geared to the individual talents of a given page. Schooling included poetry, *belles-lettres* as well as military exercises aside from religious studies, while those with a special interest might pursue painting or music. Thus Mimar Mehmed Ağa, later the architect of the Sultan Ahmed Mosque (completed 1616), when studying music in the palace school, decided, upon his own initiative, to exchange this career for the craft of fine furniture making. He was permitted to do this and remain in the palace. Upon completion of his training, he was appointed not to service positions involving craft skills, but to posts of military command in the provinces, while his career ultimately culminated in the office of chief architect.[58]

Pages leaving the palace for state service were launched upon a variety of careers (see Fig. II:7). Some were sent to the provinces as administrative officials and later as governors. The share of former pages appointed directly to the post of provincial governor (either as *sancakbeyi* or even as the higher-ranking *beylerbeyi*) increased from the mid-sixteenth to the early years of the seventeenth century (cf. Table II:21).[59] However, it is not easy to determine what this change may have meant from a political point of view. Possibly it indicates a devaluation of the *timar* system and equally of the *sancakbeyi*s in command of provincial *timar*-holders.[60] Lower-level governors also lost prestige, as *sancak*s were increasingly granted simply to supply revenue to absentee functionaries, and administered by relatively low-ranking representatives.[61] Given the level of unrest and rebellion in many seventeenth-century Ottoman provinces, one may argue that the central administration attempted to maintain control by appointing more governors directly from the palace school.[62] But whether these measures were successful in practice is of course a different matter.

Table II:21. Career backgrounds of new *sancakbeyi,* 1570–1640 (% in brackets)

	1568–74	1578–88	1632–41
Central administration	19 (32.2)	25 (44.6)	31 (49.2)
Kapıkulu officers	7	3	6
Müteferrika	3	7	11
Other *birûn* officers	4	9	11
Imperial captains	4	4	–
Enderûn	–	–	2
Others	1	2	1
Provincial administration	40 (67.8)	28 (50.0 %)	16 (25.4)
Alaybeyi	7	2	8
Zâim	6	5	5
Timar kethüdası	11	7	–
Timar defterdârı	–	2	–
Captain	3	3	–
Hazine defterdarı	4	2	–
Tribal chief	–	–	1
Others	9	7	2
Ümera-related	–	2 (3.6 %)	10 (15.9)
Ümera son	–	1	3
Household officers	–	1	7
Outside the realm	–	1 (1.8 %)	6 (9.5)
Total	59 (100)	56 (100)	63 (100)
(a) Ümera son or relative	8	11	9
(b) Ümera household officer	–	3	8
Total (a) + (b)	8 (13.6)	14 (25.0)	17 (26.9)

Source: Adapted from Kunt (1983), p. 64.

THE PROVINCIAL ADMINISTRATION AND THE ROLE OF THE "AYAN"

An older view of center–periphery relations in the Ottoman Empire implies that participation by local notables (*ayan*) in the business of governing constitutes evidence for "Ottoman decline." Some authors even go further and regard seventeenth-century administrative decentralization as evidence for what one might call "proto-nationalism." However, in more recent years, a different interpretation has gained currency, which takes more account of variation from province to province and at the same time of flexible policies on the part of the Ottoman central administration. Thus a recent study stresses the very special trajectory of Syria, with its "country gentlemen" firmly ensconced in their ancestral mountain villages.[63] Throughout the sixteenth century, these rural dignitaries were allowed to participate extensively in local administration. Only in the 1630s, after the defeat of the Druze magnate Ma'noğlu Fahreddin, was rural Syria more directly administered by the Ottoman center, a development which runs counter to the assumption of an overall seventeenth-century decentralization.

Different meanings and values can be attached to the term "decentralization."[64] On the one hand, the appointment of locally prominent men, with a following among the Bedouins, to the position of governor in charge of a sub-province or commander of the pilgrimage can be regarded as evidence for administrative decentralization. This type of appointment was common practice at least in southern Syria at the end of the sixteenth century.[65] By this token, Syria during this period was administered in an indirect fashion through the mediation of local notables. On the other hand, it has been argued that the Ottoman government was flexible enough to accommodate itself to the participation of local men whenever that seemed advisable, without any loss of ultimate control. Viewed from this angle, the central administration's flexibility was a source of strength and not of weakness, of endurance and not of decline.[66]

Other researchers have tackled seventeenth-century decentralization from quite a different angle, namely by examining the problem of finances.[67] The later sixteenth and the entire seventeenth century were a period of increasing financial demands upon the Ottoman central administration.[68] As a result, the center tended to unload more responsibilities upon provincial administrators, who therefore were in greater need of revenues and reacted by levying special taxes upon the inhabitants of "their" provinces. At the same time, particularly during the early seventeenth century, population decline in many parts of the empire and incessant migration must have strongly affected the tax base in certain areas, even though the number of people involved in each individual case was not necessarily very high. As a result constant readjustments were needed to make the taxes demanded more or less correspond to the size of the population involved. Notables were able to control this adjustment procedure, thereby gaining financial advantages both for themselves and for their clients.[69]

In addition, administrative reorganization at the Ottoman center led to the frequent assignment of revenues to nominal governors who rarely visited "their" provinces. Such governors, constantly on campaign or else retained in the capital, were represented by substitutes (*mütesellim*) who collected taxes. Such deputy governors often were selected for their ability to secure payment of dues, and as a result were men with connections in the provinces which they administered. Men with a local power base might also enter the provincial administration through tax-farming. In Syria, even toward the end of the sixteenth century it was not uncommon for a provincial governor to be the principal tax-farmer in that province. In the Turkish-speaking parts of the empire during this same period, this custom also was spreading, but had not gained the same currency as in the Syrian provinces. Mustafa Ali, for one, was vocal in expressing his indignation at the irregular career patterns which ensued.[70] Moreover, tax-farmers in charge of large units of revenue farmed out villages to sub-contractors, and pious foundations also often employed small-scale, village-based tax-farmers. As a result, there existed opportunities for capital investment even by persons possessing but a modest supply of ready cash, and those successful on the local level might pass on to higher things. Thus the Karaosmanoğulları, who in the eighteenth century were to dominate the region of Aydın, İzmir and Manisa, had risen to prominence as tax-farmers and tax collectors.[71]

While tax-farming thus offered opportunities for advancement to a limited number of local notables, the damages suffered by peasants and craftsmen often were very high. To remedy this situation, an experimental form of tax-farming was instituted in 1695, which combined certain features of the nearly defunct system of assigning taxes in exchange for service (*timar*) with tax-farming proper.[72] Such new-style tax-farms (called *malikâne*) were assigned for life, and while a large sum was required upon entering possession, the yearly payments due from the incumbent were both low and fixed for the duration of the farm (for example, see Table II:22). At the same time the arrangement probably reflects a power struggle between "ordinary" tax-farmers, who often were members of the subject population, and people who claimed to be servitors of the Ottoman administration. The party of the "servitors" was victorious, and it was decreed that a member of the subject population could not bid for a lifetime tax-farm, for it was deemed that only people with the proper governmental background could be trusted to "protect" Ottoman subjects during the process of tax collection.[73]

But from our point of view, the *malikâne* is important because even in the years immediately after its inception it must have permitted certain people with governmental connections to build themselves a political base in the countryside. At the same time, the fact that many of the grantees continued to live in the capital and employed short-term

Table II:22. From short-term to life-long tax-farm (*malikâne*): the
stamp tax of the Amasya dye-house

	Payment to treasury			Value of tax-farm	Down payment (*muaccele*)
	Tax	Supplementary dues	Total		
1688				305	
1690				400	
1695				720	
1701	800	80	880		2,500
1731	1,136.5	113.5	1,250		
1735	1,836.5	183.5	2,020		1,950

Source: Genç (1975), p. 280.

sub-contractors frequently nullified the positive effects of the principal
beneficiaries' lifetime tenure.

Throughout the seventeenth century the number of *timar*s continuously decreased. Moreover as the Ottoman central government proved
unwilling to tie down much-needed cash in provincial administration,
provincial governors, their substitutes, and simple tax-farmers came to
depend upon mercenaries for the exercise of their power. An analysis of
the income and expenses of Silahtar Hacı Ömer Pasha, in 1670–71 governor of the province of Diyarbekir, shows that he employed twenty-
three mercenary captains.[74] These captains, along with their troops and
additional military men in the pasha's employ, received 12.7 percent of
the governor's total budget as salaries (Table II:23). Moreover, expenditures for feeding the pasha's household, which mainly consisted of these
mercenaries, increased this figure to 14.5 percent.[75] Turnover among mercenary captains was very high, making the roads more unsafe, as mercenaries in search of employment turned to brigandage and extortion.[76]

"ORDINARY TAXPAYERS" AND THE POLITICAL PROCESS

This brings us back to the tensions between taxpaying subjects, mercenaries of peasant background and regular soldiers enjoying the privileges
normally granted to servitors of the sultan (cf. Ch. 16). The underlying
reason for recurrent mercenary rebellions was a demand by Anatolian
Muslim taxpayers for admission into the political class.[77] These tensions
can only be properly understood if studied in a much broader context
than their role in fomenting rebellion. Even in a society in which the

Table II:23. Income and expenditure of an Ottoman governor (Ömer
Pasha of Diyarbekir), 1670–71

	Amount	%
Catagories of income		
Related to judical and peace-keeping functions	28,354	22.9
Appointment fees	8,052	6.5
Monthly dues and office fees	36,885	29.8
From the official estates	11,114	9.0
Customs	1,765	1.4
Province-wide collections	6,881	5.6
Urban revenues	13,849	11.2
Sales	7,539	6.1
Debt collection	5,400	4.4
Miscellaneous	3,758	3.0
Total	123,597	99.9
Categories of expenditure		
To the central government	46,350	36.0
Related to the pasha's agent in İstanbul	11,054	8.6
Personal expenses of the pasha	4,000	3.1
Commissary steward's expenses	21,560	16.7
Household expenses	13,385	10.4
Expenses on household personnel	2,316	1.8
Salaries	16,362	12.7
Loan payments	6,918	5.4
Largesse	4,498	3.5
Miscellaneous	2,293	1.8
Total	128,736	100.0

Source: Kunt (1981), p. 48.

monopoly of political activity theoretically was vested in the sultan and
his servitors, channels were needed by which taxpaying subjects could
voice complaints. Moreover the system needed to allow for negotiations
by which individuals and communities might obtain redress of their
grievances. Only when these channels turned out to be inoperative did
peasants respond by fleeing their villages, artisans by closing their shops,
and mercenaries by rebellion.[78]

Petitioning the sultan directly, on his way to Friday prayers or when
he was out hunting, was a custom sanctioned by both Ottoman and
pre-Ottoman political ideologies; for in overriding the injustices committed by his officials, the ruler, according to a tradition going back to the
Sassanian kings, was legitimized as just.[79] In practice this meant that
complaints were submitted to the sultan's bureaucracy and answered in
official rescripts. The process of decision-making could take a long time,
since complaints frequently were recorded by the *Mühimme* and *Beylikçi*

chanceries and then sent back to the local kadi with an order to report on the situation prior to a decision in the sultan's council (*Divan-ı hümayûn*).[80] Even after a formal decision by the sultan had been issued, one of the parties might refuse to comply, making yet another round of correspondence necessary.

Villages, guilds and other groups of organized petitioners often hired a man to take their complaints to İstanbul. In the eighteenth century the Ottoman bureaucracy tended to regard such visits as so many pretexts for unauthorized immigration into the capital and therefore strove to limit the number of petition-carriers.[81] It is not known whether similar restrictions were enforced during the seventeenth century as well. Instead of presenting their plea directly, certain petitioners preferred to use people with influence at court or in the capital as mediators. Thus the Sheikh Mahmud Üsküdari's (died 1628) intercession was solicited by the Dutch when they attempted to secure capitulations.[82] Even after the sheikh's death, the inhabitants of his native village invoked his name when defending themselves against the vexations of a local governor. In the same vein, the sheikh of the Halveti *tekke* of Koca Mustafa Pasha (İstanbul) and his dervishes occasionally were solicited to protect peasants from excesses committed by local tax collectors.

PATRONAGE, THE "GREAT HOUSEHOLD," AND THE DECLINE OF THE *DEVŞİRME*

Interventions of the type outlined above indicate the importance of patron–client relationships in seventeenth-century Ottoman society.[83] From an "established" official's point of view, furthering the careers of young men closely associated with himself had certain obvious advantages. After all, the career and often the life of a palace official depended upon factional struggles in which all parties attempted to gain influence over other high palace officials, the sultan's Mother and ultimately the sultan himself. A well-placed protégé might inform his patron about intrigues which threatened the latter's position, or even exercise his influence on the patron's behalf.[84] On the other hand, while association with a powerful patron might further a young official's career, this association also forced him to take sides in whatever factional struggles the patron happened to be involved. Loyalty to one's teacher, mentor or protector constituted one of the principal values of an Ottoman gentleman and involvement in the patron's factional struggles might have far-reaching consequences, sometimes well beyond the death of the patron himself. Mustafa Ali claimed that his career was blighted by the negative influence of Koca Sinan Pasha, Murad III's influential grand vizier (died 1596), known as the sworn enemy of Ali's former patron Lala Mustafa Pasha.[85]

Patron–protégé relationships had been important even in the second half of the sixteenth century. But they became even more vital during the seventeenth, due to the decline of the *devşirme*, the recruitment of non-Muslim boys into state service that had been characteristic of the Ottoman political establishment during the fifteenth and sixteenth centuries. As to the reasons for this decline, at the present state of our knowledge we can only make informed guesses. Once there was a sizable number of educated people with one or more ancestors who had served the Ottoman state, pressure probably built up against the recruitment of "outsiders."[86] In Ottoman state service, even of the sixteenth century, there was some opprobrium attached to the recruitment of "outsiders" (*ecnebi, ecanib*); thus the *devşirme* always had constituted something of an uncomfortable exception to the principles of Ottoman statecraft. In addition the factional struggles among *devşirme*-recruited officials themselves, who often associated on the basis of common ethnicity, must have contributed toward undermining the system.[87] Moreover the Iranian wars of the late sixteenth century brought a large influx of Muslim-born Azeris and other Iranians into the Ottoman state service, a novelty vehemently deplored by some intellectuals such as Mustafa Ali.[88] The often very considerable influence of this group, some of whose members reached high positions, must have contributed further to the gradual abandoning of the *devşirme*. In a sense it may be claimed that the disappearance of the levy of boys allowed the heads of vizier, pasha and high-level ulema households to build up organizations which more closely resembled the sultan's household. After all, even though high-ranking officials occasionally had raised young servitors whose qualifications closely resembled those of pages educated in the imperial household, systematic recruitment of future officials by means of the *devşirme* remained a prerogative of the sultan. On the other hand, to recruit the sons of clients or young slaves was a procedure which both the ruler and his higher-ranking officials could adopt. Now we may assume that in the seventeenth century the heads of the more important "political households" had gained an unprecedented measure of political power, self-confidence and prestige. In these circumstances, it is in a sense not surprising that the grandees of the Ottoman realm not only attempted to make their own establishments resemble that of the sultan, but also, within certain limits, made the sultan's household resemble the organizations which they themselves had built.

Given the interest which the political households of the seventeenth to nineteenth centuries have been attracting during the last twenty years, it is remarkable that we know so little about the financial bases of their power. The formalized structures of the households headed by the more important members of the Ottoman political class made them more effective in appropriating revenue, while at the same time the demands of household members for daily sustenance made a financial base more necessary than ever. But only detailed investigations of some of the more important political households' material bases will allow us to understand how the latter acquired (and lost) property. At the present date, however, such investigations simply do not exist.

CONCLUSION

"Ottoman observers of Ottoman decline" frequently have dwelt upon the post-1550 changes of the later sixteenth and seventeenth century that made the Ottoman administration into something very different from what it had been in the age of Kanuni Süleyman.[89] Researchers at work during the last twenty or thirty years would generally agree with the statement that important changes did in fact occur, but would describe these changes in rather a different manner. Particularly the value judgement that labels these changes as "decline" has been called into question. Not all researchers necessarily believe any more that because a number of writers active during the years before and after 1600 described certain administrative changes as decline, twentieth-century researchers must necessarily share this point of view. It is difficult to deny that authors such as Mustafa Ali and Koçi Bey wrote in order to promote both public policies and personal careers. Once this statement is taken seriously, it becomes impossible to accept their claims at face value, and their writings must be studied according to the same principles of historical criticism that have been established for writers of other times and places.

At the same time, research into Ottoman administrative history has allowed us to draw a more differentiated picture of structural change than had been possible in the past. From the early sixteenth century onward, Ottoman officials apparently followed career lines that allowed for change and flexibility. Even so, frequent changes from one career line to another might be detrimental to the career of the official in question. With increasing specialization, a process that can be observed clearly from about 1550, more and more career lines were established, such as the scribal services, finance administration or the palace hierarchy. One might link this tendency toward administrative specialization, and the increasing efficiency which at least the first stages of this process entailed, with the growing difficulty of maintaining central control over the empire's periphery. If decentralization in the seventeenth century did not result in losses of Ottoman power in the provinces, this was due in part to such gains in efficiency at the center.

On the other hand, the last years of the sixteenth and the first half of the seventeenth century witnessed a growing need for revenue. The proliferation of firearms, along with longer-lasting wars, certainly increased the central administration's need for money. At the same time, it must be pointed out that a similar crisis could be observed in most major European states of the period, and that the constant demand for increasing revenues constituted a problem that the Ottoman Empire shared with its neighbors. Moreover, given a technological level which in the seventeenth century was still roughly comparable, responses to the increasing expense of administration were often comparable as well. Thus the proliferation of mercenaries and their excesses have been described for seventeenth-century Italy, and the flight of Ottoman peasants due to war and over-taxation has parallels all over Europe. If indeed we can assume the existence of conjunctures not only in the field of economics but of politics as well, the Ottoman Empire and much of Europe during the seventeenth century still shared a common fate, even though in their culture and self-images they may have been worlds apart.[90]

NOTES

1 İnalcık (1969, 1970).
2 İnalcık (1953–54), pp. 60–61.
3 Compare the article "Köprülüler" in *EI²* by Tayyip Gökbilgin and Richard Repp.
4 İnalcık (1969), p. 106.
5 Kafadar (1986), p. 128.
6 *Ibid.*, pp. 85ff.
7 Mantran (1962), pp. 248ff.
8 For a particularly elaborate example, compare Kütükoğlu (1983).
9 Kunt (1977).
10 *Ibid.*, p. 203.
11 Lapidus (1967), pp. 44–78.
12 Koçi Bey (1885–86), p. 115.
13 Kunt (1977), p. 210.

14 *Ibid.*, pp. 206–7.
15 Fleischer (1986), p. 156.
16 Finkel (1988), p. 30.
17 Faroqhi (1986b), pp. 68–69.
18 For seventeenth-century examples, see Barkan (1966).
19 Abou-El-Haj (1991); Bodman (1963); Schatkowski-Schilcher (1985).
20 İnalcık (1980); Barbir (1980), p. 8; Raymond (1985), pp. 39, 58, 271; Genç (1984); Panzac (1985), pp. 186ff.
21 Fleischer (1986).
22 Fleischer (1986).
23 Lybyer (repr. 1966); Gibb and Bowen, I (1950), *passim.*
24 Itzkowitz (1962).
25 Findley, (1980), pp. 46–47. Findley's classification ignores the *nişancı* and his scribes, who were neither ulema nor military men. Officials such as the *nişancı* were few in number, but their high prestige suggests that they should not be excluded from a model of Ottoman administration.
26 Findley (1980), pp. 48–51.
27 Fleischer (1986), pp. 311–14.
28 As an example compare Akdağ (1959, 1971), I, pp. 331–442.
29 The struggle for the succession of Bayezid II, in the early sixteenth century, had been equally protracted.
30 Darling (unpublished communication at the MESA meeting of 1986).
31 Fleischer (1986), pp. 19–20.
32 *Ibid.*, p. 36.
33 Findley (1980), pp. 26–30.
34 Article "Evliya Çelebi" in *İA* by Cavit Baysun.
35 Fleischer (1986), p. 23.
36 Compare İpşirli (1983–87) for a recent example.
37 Raymond (1985), pp. 84–85.
38 Türek and Derin (1969–70); Abou-El-Haj (1984), p. 57.
39 Aktepe (1958b), pp. 111–12.
40 Türek (1959); Türek and Derin (1969–70).
41 Findley (1980), pp. 33–40.
42 Majer (1978).
43 *Ibid.*, pp. 132ff.
44 *Ibid.*, pp. 174–80.
45 *Ibid.*, pp. 123ff.
46 Cf. Ch. 17.
47 Gölpınarlı (1953), pp. 165–66.
48 İnalcık (1973), pp. 184–5; Zilfi (1986).
49 Zilfi (1986).
50 Gölpınarlı (1953), pp. 167–68.
51 Necipoğlu-Kafadar (1991); Leslie Peirce is working on a study of Ottoman royal women, and I have benefited from an oral presentation of hers (not yet published, January 1994).
52 Peirce (1988).
53 Findley (1980), p. 48.

54 Uzunçarşılı (1945), pp. 300ff.
55 Fleischer (1986), p. 159.
56 Uzunçarşılı (1945), pp. 177–78.
57 Kunt (1975).
58 Gökyay (1975); Cafer Efendi, ed. Crane (1987).
59 Kunt (1983), p. 95.
60 *Ibid.*, p. 88.
61 *Ibid.*, p. 87.
62 *Ibid.*, p. 90.
63 Abu Husayn (1985), p. 21 and elsewhere.
64 Barbir (1980), p. 4; Rafeq (1981–82), pp. 149–50; Raymond (1985), pp. 30–31.
65 Rafeq (1966), pp. 52–57.
66 Barbir (1980), pp. 4–8.
67 İnalcık (1980); McGowan (1981), pp. 46ff.
68 İnalcık (1980).
69 *Ibid.*, p. 335; McGowan (1981), p. 156.
70 Fleischer (1986), p. 98.
71 Uluçay (1948), p. 246.
72 Genç (1975).
73 *Ibid.*, p. 239. The further history of the *malikane* concerns the eighteenth century: compare Cezar (1986), pp. 43ff, 128ff.
74 Kunt (1981), pp. 23–26.
75 *Ibid.*, p. 17.
76 *Ibid.*, p. 25.
77 İnalcık (1980), p. 284.
78 İnalcık (1988).
79 İnalcık (1965), pp. 49–51.
80 Temelkuran (1975); Majer (1984), pp. 17ff.
81 Aktepe (1958), p. 11.
82 de Groot (1978), p. 112.
83 Abou-El-Haj (1974); Findley (1980).
84 Findley (1980), p. 39.
85 Fleischer (1986), pp. 88–108.
86 Kunt (1983), p. 76.
87 Kunt (1974).
88 Fleischer (1986), p. 159.
89 Lewis (1962).
90 On this issue, compare Hess (1978), pp. 210–11.

20

SOCIAL LIFE IN CITIES

Only where the largest cities of the empire are concerned do we know very much about the changing relationships between urban social groups, barely enough to roughly sketch out historical processes. Our information is much scantier for towns of the second order, and largely is limited to present-day Bulgaria and Syria, and to the Anatolian trading centers of Bursa, İzmir, Ankara and Kayseri.[1] The smallest towns largely remain *terra incognita*, and the bias of primary documentation and secondary research in favor of the largest cities must never be lost from view. However, considerable progress has been made in the field of urban studies during the last twenty years or so, and the overall picture is broader and more nuanced than it used to be.

URBAN POLITICS

Ottoman towns (with a very few exceptions) possessed no charters, and therefore it has often been assumed that they were directly administered by the central government. This is true only of İstanbul. In provincial cities an urban elite of ulema, tax-farmers, and Janissary commanders gained considerable room for maneuver. Lower-level kadis often came from families domiciled in the region, while the commanders of Janissaries and other military (or later, paramilitary) corps were involved in trade, or related to merchants or craftsmen. These activities provided them with an economic base for political activity. Tax-farmers sometimes also were involved in local politics. To protect their revenue, the tax-farmers of the Ankara mohair presses even procured a sultanic command prohibiting the exportation of first-grade mohair thread. This measure protected the raw material supplies of local weavers, and must have gained the tax farmers a degree of political support.[2] The most serious challenge to town and district administrators was the protection of local food and raw material supplies, since at the same time they were obliged to comply with the incessant demands of the central administration. There existed customary rules concerning the demands made on a given town or region, but after bad harvests or during campaigns there often were unexpected increases. A local market inspector or other well-connected official might attempt to ward them off. The grain demanded by the central administration was not always delivered in full, a proof of the bargaining skills of local notables and officials.[3]

Given widespread evidence of political initiatives by local elites, it does not seem reasonable to regard Anatolian and Balkan towns of the seventeenth century as closely dependent upon the central government. In a spectrum running from "autonomous" to "dependent," Ottoman provincial cities occupied middle ground and may be described as "semidependent." In a system of categories which includes the ancient Mediterranean city, the autonomous city of the European Middle Ages, and the "subject city" incorporated into the realm of a modern territorial ruler, Ottoman cities fall into the third category. Even after subjection, however, cities of early modern Europe retained some room for political maneuver, and the same applies to Ottoman cities.[4]

MAIN ELEMENTS OF THE OTTOMAN CITYSCAPE: MOSQUES, CITADELS, MARKETS AND QUARTERS

Towns clustered around the main mosque(s), the citadel and the business district. Medium and smaller towns contained only one Friday mosque, singled out by one or two minarets and a preacher's pulpit. New foundations established in the late sixteenth or seventeenth century were often located at some distance from the old town, where there was sufficient space for the walled and planted courtyards which surrounded monumental Ottoman mosques. The citadel was often a pre-Ottoman construction, but the Celali rebellions prompted the restoration of citadels in many Anatolian towns. Citadels encompassed a whole town quarter, and often the most valuable houses were located here; in addition the citadel possessed a garrison and a jail. Governors and kadis resided and officiated in the same buildings, which in some places acquired the character of official residences; the kadis' archives probably were kept in the courthouse, which accounts for their frequent preservation.

A town of some importance possessed a covered market (*bedestan*), most of which in old established towns had been founded in the fifteenth and early sixteenth centuries; later foundations indicate a town which had but recently become significant, such as Üsküdar. *Bedestan*s served the traders in valuable goods, such as jewelry, textiles and slaves.[5] When the Celali rebels and other brigands interrupted the trade routes, many merchants preferred to conduct a diminished volume of business in less expensive locales, and seventeenth-century disputes concerning *bedestan*s often involved administrators trying to counter this trend. Many shops belonged to pious foundations, and in some cases tenants acquired a hereditary right to the property by the payment of an important sum of money upon entering possession.[6] Even in small towns markets might possess large numbers of booths, which tenants could rent from a pious foundation. For Rumeli, where goods were mostly transported by wagon, special markets were made accessible to wheeled traffic (*araba pazarı*).

Residential districts were divided into quarters, which contained between ten and a few hundred families each. Possession of a house made an individual liable to the payment of *avarız* taxes, and this constituted a manner of establishing official residency. Inhabitants of a town quarter paid damages if those responsible for an accident or a crime could not be located. Therefore the presence of strangers in residential areas was not appreciated, and few streets were designed for through traffic. A person's reputation in his or her town quarter might become essential for continued residence in the city, for in tense moments, such as an imminent Celali attack, only those people were allowed to remain who could find a neighbor to vouch for them. In court cases, a person's reputation among his or her neighbors might also be taken into consideration.

Houses were built of whatever material was most easily available, and even the dwellings of wealthy families were seldom built of stone. Therefore seventeenth-century housing only survives in a few rare instances. İstanbul housing styles affected the larger cities of Anatolia and the Balkans: by the seventeenth century Ankara's one-story houses were being replaced by buildings with an upper floor and decorated with numerous balconies.[7] From the East, the influence of Syrian building styles made itself felt, and the border between the two stylistic regions ran through central Anatolia.

THE CITYSCAPE AS AN INDICATOR OF SOCIAL LIFE

The French school in urban studies, which has influenced greatly much of the work concerning the Ottoman realm, emphasizes the character of the town or city as an entity in space. The latter is perceived as possessing a definite spatial layout, which is characteristic enough to form the basis of a typology. This school links the city to its hinterland and to more remote cities by a web of caravan routes and, in certain cases, by sea lanes. Thus cities are perceived as nodes of a network covering the empire as a whole, and urban history links up with historical geography. In this context, certain researchers have concerned themselves with the spatial location of trade, crafts and the activities of the ruling group in cities such as Cairo, Mosul or Algiers.[8] Others have studied the configuration of a city's rural hinterland; such work has been particularly intensive with respect to Damascus, Tripolis and Aleppo.[9]

Urban patterns are of interest not for their own sake but as the result of human activity; moreover they often provide information about the functioning of urban society that would be difficult to obtain in any other fashion. The construction of certain types of buildings, for example, may serve as an indicator of urban growth or contraction. Thus public baths were built whenever a large enough population had accumulated on a given site to create a demand. While baths were by no means an exclusively urban phenomenon, the construction of public baths in the vicinity of a given city usually indicates that the area surrounding the new baths was gaining in population and being incorporated into the city. In the same fashion the location of tanneries may be regarded as an indicator of urban growth: because of the pollution caused, tanneries usually moved to a more distant site when the city expanded, while the "Old Tanneries" quarter in many Syrian and Anatolian towns became a residential area like any other.[10] If we possessed reliable population counts, observations of this kind would be only of limited interest. But given the almost total absence of such data for the seventeenth century, indirect information concerning the size of urban populations becomes very precious.[11]

In the business sections of the larger towns, a sizable share of real estate was held by pious foundations. To foundation administrators, the struggle against deterioration of the buildings entrusted to their care was a permanent concern: fires destroyed valuable buildings which foundations were not able to reconstruct from their own resources. Such properties were then let out at low rents to whoever undertook the rebuilding, and often enough passed out of the foundation's possession entirely. Khans and covered markets were particularly vulnerable once the trade of a town declined; thus in the troubled years around 1600, the covered market of Konya was permitted to deteriorate to such an extent that it could not be restored to its former purpose without extensive rebuilding.[12] Due to this situation, documents concerning deterioration and reconstruction of foundation-owned buildings, as well as records concerning the changing tenants of these structures, are valuable indicators for the fortunes of a city.

The configuration of residential areas also constitutes both a spatial feature and an indicator of social relations. While shops, workshops and living quarters in European cities of the medieval or early modern period often formed part of one building, sixteenth-, seventeenth- and eighteenth-century Ottoman cities exhibited a different pattern. In a manner almost reminiscent of twentieth-century arrangements, the business district with its khans, shops and covered or open markets emptied at night, except for a limited number of transients residing in khans. Residential quarters contained only a few shops selling everyday needs, such as grocers or bakeries, and were served by a multitude of peddlers.

Strict separation of business and residential quarters has been linked to the value placed upon family privacy in an Islamic context, although in the more recent literature this view is no longer defended without qualification.[13] Family privacy certainly was valued, but this emphasis did not preclude considerable regional variation in residential construction patterns. In Syria, southeastern Anatolia or North Africa, courtyard houses that were all but invisible from the street, closed off by high windowless walls, predominated. By contrast, in İstanbul or western Anatolia, windows overlooking the street were common, and privacy was protected by using first and second floors as living space, while the ground floor was mostly employed as a service area. In Cairo, structures containing multiple residences were not unusual. In these apartment buildings, privacy was protected in a different way, by assigning each household a separate space on the roof which neighbours could not easily overlook. Moreover in Syria and Egypt, poor dwellings often were grouped around a central courtyard shared by all residents, so that privacy was available only within the built-up area. Similarly, not all Ottoman townsmen were equally concerned about removing the house from the main thoroughfare, and the popularity of the cul-de-sac seems to have varied according to time and place. Thus it appears that, while privacy was a major consideration, one should not assume that this concern was the only significant factor in determining urban form.

While in the business quarter, members of different ethnic and religious communities often worked side by side, residential quarters generally were inhabited by people of the same ethnic or religious group. However, while the Ottoman central administration assumed that Muslim and non-Muslim quarters were to remain separate, and occasionally enforced this view through legislation, real-life arrangements were much more flexible. In seventeenth-century Ankara and Kayseri, Muslims and non-Muslims sold real estate to one another without much concern for the location of the property. In certain cases, mixed Muslim/non-Muslim occupancy of a given town quarter might indicate that the quarter in question was passing from the hands of one group into that of another. Thus the traveller Evliya Çelebi recounts that, after the construction of the Selimiye mosque in Edirne, Muslim traders left the cramped quarters of the old walled town and built a more spacious business district near the new foundation, abandoning the old town to the non-Muslims.[14] But in other cases mixed occupancy was a permanent feature: for example in nineteenth-century Ankara, certain quarters had been inhabited by both Muslims and non-Muslims for more than two centuries. It would be worth investigating whether the eighteenth- and nineteenth-century confessionalization of urban politics, which has been observed in Syria, also led to a more rigidly segregated pattern of urban residence on an empire-wide level.[15]

Urban residence patterns indicate social structure in a different way: it has often been suggested that segregation by wealth was unknown in Ottoman town quarters of the sixteenth to eighteenth centuries, and rich and poor members of one and the same religious or ethnic community lived in the same town quarter. Recent research shows that this statement needs qualification: wealthy officials in İstanbul resided in the vicinity of the palace, while in seventeenth- and eighteenth-century Cairo there were quarters inhabited mainly by Mamluks and other rich families.[16] In a much more modest town such as Ankara, there also was a tendency for wealthy households to cluster in certain areas, but much more noticeable is the existence of quarters inhabited mainly by poor people. In part, the varying profiles of different town quarters may have been due to the fact that the members of certain communities were on the whole wealthier than others. Thus, in the course of the seventeenth century, the Christian population of cities like Ankara and Kayseri seems to have increased in wealth and acquired some of the more expensive houses in these localities. In the same way, an area inhabited largely by Mamluks should have been wealthier than a quarter inhabited by any other group of Cairenes. But even if residential segregation according to wealth occurred only as a consequence of other more primary phenomena, it was not in itself an unknown feature.

PIOUS FOUNDATIONS AS A FOCUS OF URBAN LIFE

Since seventeenth-century construction activity was much less extensive than the public building which had taken place earlier, it is easy to ignore the continuing impact of seventeenth-century pious foundations upon urban life. To begin with the most mundane aspect, in certain provincial cities the construction of khans and shops continued throughout the seventeenth century; in this period, a number of minor Anatolian towns, usually due to their location on the main highways, were endowed with fairly important structures (see also Ch. 16). In Malatya, for example, a large khan was built in 1637, and in the vicinity, the roadside stopping point of Hekimhan developed into a town after a complex of pious foundations had been established in this locality.[17] Moreover the Grand Vizier Merzifonlu Kara Mustafa Pasha in 1666 had endowed his home town of Merzifon with an impressive mosque, which dominates the centre of this town to the present.[18]

In addition to these fairly "official" establishments, dervish lodges and their patron saints had an impact on the way that seventeenth-century townsmen perceived their settlements. Thus a legend of the dervish saint Piri Baba of Merzifon, who probably flourished in the fifteenth century but whose two vitas date from the seventeenth, makes the saint enter into a contest with one of the ulema from neighboring Amasya. The triumph of the untrained former peasant boy and shoemaker's apprentice over the learned scholar certainly was meant to convey the superior status of mystical knowledge over mere religious scholarship. But, at the same time, it would seem that the story-tellers who fashioned the legend of Piri Baba were trying to define Merzifon as the home of a saint, *vis-à-vis* Amasya as the seat of learned men. Moreover, Piri Baba's saintly prowess was associated with public buildings of the town, particularly the bath, since the lodge (*zaviye*) generally considered a saint's official residence was only built after Piri Baba's death, a fact the authors of the legend freely admitted. In this context, it is revealing that when Evliya Çelebi described Merzifon in his travelog, he included one of the two versions of Piri Baba's legend which have survived to the present day.[19]

The *zaviye* of Mevlana Celaleddin Rumi in Konya also played a major role in urban life, along with the associated foundation bearing the name of Mevlana's mother, located in the nearby town of Larende-Karaman. The head of the family of Mevlana Celaleddin controlled a large lodge, which also functioned as the center of the order, in the middle of the most populous quarter of Konya. The Mevlevi order of dervishes was popular enough in the seventeenth century that a dervish of this period (Sakıp Dede, died in 1735) wrote a collection of biographies of famous Mevlevis in which he devoted considerable space to his contemporaries. However, relations between the çelebi ("gentleman"), the head of the order, and the townsmen and peasants whose dues paid for the upkeep of the foundation, were anything but cordial. The collapse of rural settlement in early seventeenth-century central Anatolia had greatly decreased the revenues of the lodge. About 1650, money was so scarce that the famous orchestra indispensable to the·order's ceremonies had been reduced to a skeleton of its former self.[20] Under these circumstances the Çelebi increased the pressure upon his dues-paying flock, at a time when the latter were barely able to survive. An unsavory scandal ensued, in which Sultan Murad IV sided against the Çelebi. This decision must have been made easier by the sultan's sporadic alliance with the literalist and Sharia-minded Kadızadeliler, for whom dervishes and dervish ceremonies were anathema anyway.[21] Thus the existence of a major dervish lodge in seventeenth-century Konya did not necessarily focus the townsmen's loyalties, but may have become a divisive element.[22]

It would seem, however, that the case of Konya constituted something of an exception. If the attitude of Evliya Çelebi is indicative of seventeenth-century educated opinion, it appears that dervish lodges were regarded, along with mosques and *medrese*s, as the principal ornament of every city.[23] Moreover, saints' tombs and dervish lodges were associated not only with the world of work and official piety, which was embodied in the city center. They were also located on the picnic grounds where the townsmen sought relaxation after work, which to Evliya were no less worthy of mention than the towns' most distinguished buildings. Thus the saints may have been viewed as presiding over the festive times that punctuated the yearly cycle, and in this manner, played a role as conciliators among the townsmen visiting them.

CONTROL, DECISION-MAKING AND POWER STRUGGLES WITHIN THE URBAN ELITE

In spite of the overwhelmingly official nature of the documentation at hand, the decision-making groups of many Anatolian towns are not easily identified. It is apparent that functionaries of the central administration, such as the kadi or the governor of Ankara sub-province, had a key role to play.[24] But, at the same time, these figures and their official retinues did not dominate the scene as fully as their counterparts officiating in İstanbul. Local notables, the sources of whose influence are unclear, were quite capable of making decisions: thus when the business district of late sixteenth-century Ankara was considered unsafe, these people took it upon themselves to hire and pay guards. Men of artisanal background could rise to rank among a town's most influential residents; but there is no way of finding out how many generations intervened between a modest ancestor and his influential descendants. Nor are we as yet able to determine to what extent commerce prompted a seventeenth-century Ankara, Kayseri or İzmir family's rise to influence, and to what extent these families' fortunes were political in origin. Tax-farming and deputizing for absent governors constituted the basis for the fortunes of most provincial notables known as *ayan*, and quite a few *ayan* lived in towns, where they doubtless were active in urban affairs (cf. Ch. 18).

A crucial political role was played by the Janissaries and other soldiers stationed in large and medium-level Anatolian cities. This military presence was a comparatively new phenomenon; before the heyday of the Celali rebellions, 1596–1607, many Anatolian towns possessed only minor garrisons. Once Janissaries were installed, they managed to obtain positions of esteem: among all the people mentioned in the kadi registers of a good-sized town, they figure among the few distinguished by the honorific title of *bey* ("lord, master"). In many places Janissaries gained control of lucrative tax-farms, which allowed them to participate in urban politics and gain a certain freedom of maneuver even *vis-à-vis* their own commanders in İstanbul.[25] Rivalries between the Janissaries and members of other military units, such as the *sipahi*s of the Porte, must have been quite frequent, given the importance of the revenues at stake in the wealthier cities. But at the same time Janissaries and other military men also came to represent local interests against those of the central administration, although we lack urban monographs to show us the concrete shapes of these tensions.

We are better informed about late seventeenth-century Arab cities. In Cairo, the chiefs of the major Mamluk households constituted the most powerful group and dominated political life through their control of rural tax-farms. Moreover, Mamluk control extended into the city, since Cairenes were dependent on the Egyptian countryside for essential food supplies. But apart from the ruling group, the major traders in coffee and Indian textiles also amassed very considerable fortunes, which implies that they were at least able to protect themselves against day-to-day intervention on the part of the Mamluks. In addition, even though the militiamen associated with the paramilitary corps known as the *ocak* did not, as individuals, form part of the ruling class, the corps as a whole wielded considerable influence. Politics in seventeenth-century Cairo consisted of the struggles between these three groups.

In the Syrian provinces, the paramilitary corps in Damascus and Aleppo also wielded appreciable political power that often had a decisive impact upon the fortunes of provincial governors.[26] On the other hand, there were no Mamluk houses competing for power on the provincial level in Syria, and factionalism among different types of paramilitary corps (the "regularly constituted" *ocak* and their locally recruited auxiliaries, the so-called *yerliyya*) often played a decisive role. The situation in Aleppo was somewhat special: by the eighteenth century, the descendants of the Prophet had constituted themselves as a counterweight to the power of the militias and as a major force in city politics. This state of affairs probably also obtained during the later years of the seventeenth century.[27]

In southeastern Europe during the later seventeenth century, association with the Ottoman ruling group was frequently the source of local power. Only in the eighteenth century did increasing trade with Europe lead to a broader range of opportunities by which "ordinary" townsmen might acquire wealth, and thereby challenge the predominance of the administrators and military men who had previously controlled many cities of Rumeli.[28] In the seventeenth century, by contrast, firm control by the center inhibited the development of major disparities of wealth among the craftsmen of Sofia and other towns of present-day Bulgaria. However, these modest craftsmen invoked and received the protection of the central government against local officials attempting to extract more in taxes than had been legally conceded. This alliance between the central government and ordinary taxpayers against provincial administrators, while inherent in the Ottoman system of state and society throughout its existence, was particularly apparent during the civil wars of the later sixteenth and early seventeenth centuries.

At present we have more information on urban centers in Syria and Egypt than on most other parts of the empire. It is probably due to this greater knowledge that we can identify, in the cities of this region, power struggles which transcended mere short-term military rebellions and factional quarrels. Thus in the last quarter of the seventeenth century, the Cairene Janissary officer Küçük Muhammad tried to aid small shopkeepers and artisans by eliminating certain levies which the Janissaries and other paramilitary corps used to demand as "protection money." A number of years later, this same officer attempted to prevent the inordinate rise of grain prices after an unsatisfactory flooding of the Nile delta by engaging in a political struggle with boat owners and grain traders, many of whom were allied with the same Janissaries who formed Küçük Muhammad's own power base.[29] Here we can discern a struggle between affluent and less well-to-do inhabitants of the city, which the poor lost after the assassination of Küçük Muhammad. In other instances a struggle might ensue between a centrally appointed governor and locally based paramilitary corps, in which the governor attempted to increase İstanbul's share of taxes and the corps tried to keep it down.[30] As the central government's control over Egyptian resources was at issue in this dispute, the significance of the conflict by far transcended the day-to-day matters immediately at stake. Other struggles of more or less long-term significance certainly also occurred in Anatolian towns. Thus a closer study of seventeenth-century Ottoman cities shows these to have been much less immobile than appears at first glance, and further processes of long-term significance will probably come to light as our knowledge advances.

THE GUILDS AS A FOCUS OF HISTORIOGRAPHICAL DEBATE

Researchers dealing with this topic have proposed two divergent perceptions. According to one point of view, Ottoman guilds should be regarded as reasonably autonomous organizations of the guild masters, which defended their interests against members of other guilds, workmen outside the guild and merchants.[31] Thus representatives of one guild might take members of another guild to court, often because the product of one guild served as input for the work process of the other, and previously concluded agreements about the delivery of inputs had been allegedly violated. Or else new products might appear on the market that members of more than one guild wished to produce. In addition, there were disputes which arose from the requirement that guilds send a certain number of craftsmen to accompany the Ottoman armies on campaign, and individual guilds were eager to shift the burden onto their competitors.[32]

Guild masters' relations with their workmen were quite often tense, even though journeymen never set up separate organizations as they did in parts of Europe.[33] In certain larger cities, workmen unable to establish themselves as master craftsmen might find a niche by opening shops on the outskirts of the city, where a subsidiary business area might establish itself with time. Obviously, the more established masters resented this kind of competition and they were vocal in complaining about the technical incompetence of the newcomers.[34] Other disputes might concern conditions at the workplace, or even the status of the workmen involved. Apprentices were not remunerated throughout the duration of their apprenticeship, which lasted at least three years; therefore it might pay the master to allege that a given workman had no claim to any wages at all, since he was still in the process of learning his trade.

If guildsmen organized to resist pressures originating from people who were their inferiors in the social hierarchy, we also encounter cases in which the guild tried to exert pressures against craftsmen trying to raise themselves over their fellows. In extreme cases, guildsmen are known to have declared that one of their fellow artisans had lost all claim to guild membership, since he had turned into a merchant.[35] Tensions between guildsmen and merchants were particularly apparent in localities where a rudimentary putting-out system operated, and certain craftsmen, though formally still independent producers, were falling under the control of merchant entrepreneurs. Particularly revealing in this context is a complaint from the poorer dyers of Bursa, who resented the fact that some of their wealthier fellow guildsmen were attracting customers by offering easy terms of credit (1571–72). It seems that the wealthier Bursa dyers were trying to capture the custom of putting-out merchants engaged in the business of organizing textile production.[36] In cases of this kind, Ottoman guilds should be regarded as organizations serving the interests of the "middling" master craftsmen.

On the other hand, it has been suggested that defending craftsmen was only a minor function of the guilds. In this perspective, Ottoman guilds appear essentially as organizations established by the central government to supervise and tax craftsmen. Otherwise, given the weakness of urban organization, the latter would have all but escaped central control.[37] Among other evidence in support of this view, one may point to the fact that leading guild officials occasionally were selected by the Ottoman central administration.[38] Moreover since the Ottoman army needed the services of large numbers of artisans, organization by craft facilitated recruitment. This model deemphasizes autonomous activities on the part of craft organizations, and the guilds are viewed as yet another arm of the central government.

A model which defines Ottoman guilds as basically government-sponsored also downplays the religious aspects of guild organization. Certain seventeenth-century guilds, in İstanbul and elsewhere, were headed by a religious elder or sheikh. The latter was responsible for the initiation ceremonies by which new masters were inducted into the guild, and otherwise symbolized the links of latter-day guilds with the *fütüvvet*, that is the religious and moral principles of the fourteenth-century urban organizations known as the *ahis*. The professional ethics of Ottoman guildsmen were recorded in treatises concerning *fütüvvet*. However, by the seventeenth century, the sheikh had lost most of his practical role in the leadership of the guild to the *kethüda*, whose religious functions were nil.[39] While earlier treatments of Ottoman guilds had emphasized the putative links between craftsmen's guilds and dervish orders, particularly the Bektashis, the existence of these links has not been proven.[40]

Implicit in the debate about Ottoman guilds is a comparison with European guilds of the medieval and early modern periods, even though this concern is not always spelled out directly. When emphasizing the "government-determined" features of Ottoman guilds, researchers often dwell on the greater autonomy enjoyed by their European counterparts.[41] But other differences have also been established: if conditions in seventeenth-century Bursa are not completely atypical, Ottoman guilds should have been much easier to enter than those in most places of early modern Europe. In Bursa, it was often sufficient for a craftsman to practice a trade and pay taxes along with his colleagues from the relevant guild, to be recognized as a member of the organization in question.[42] Moreover it was not uncommon, particularly in occupations in which the mercantile outweighed the manufacturing aspect, for people to change occupations and therefore guilds at least once in the course of their career, and such changes do not seem to have created major problems from the guild administration's point of view. As far as can be concluded from the available documentation, no Bursa guild ever kept lists of its members, which made it difficult to prove that a given taxpaying practitioner of a craft was not a member of the requisite guild. In the same vein, the fact that most arrangements involving craftsmen were oral, and were only put into writing when there was cause for complaint, must have made for a certain flexibility in applying guild regulations.

However, given the limited number of urban histories available, it is hard to determine the typicality of the situation in Bursa. Thus in Cairo during the eighteenth century, and possibly in earlier periods as well, guild elders did keep membership lists for "their" guilds.[43] Moreover in the course of the seventeenth and eighteenth centuries, craftsmen in İstanbul, who previously had owned only their tools and raw materials, evolved a new form of property, namely the right to set up shop in a given locality (*gedik*).[44] Occasional references to *gedik* can also be found in late-seventeenth century Cairo; the fact that property of this kind usually was known by the same Turkish term as in İstanbul indicates that developments in the two cities were connected.[45] Once this form of property had become widespread, movement from one guild to another should have become much more difficult than previously; and since the *gedik* could be inherited, its existence should have strengthened the already powerful tendency for sons to enter their fathers' crafts. At present we do not know very much about the social pressures that favored the adoption of the *gedik*. One might associate this arrangement with a closing of economic horizons, with crafts that had lost their markets outside of the towns in which they were being practiced. But while many craftsmen in eighteenth-century İstanbul may well have been in this position, the silk manufacturers of seventeenth-century Bursa at least went through a period of difficulties, and yet did not develop *gediks*. We are not able to explain fully why the guild system in Bursa should have been as flexible as it appears to have been.

THE GUILDS: PRINCIPLES OF ORGANIZATION

The principle underlying the formation of craft organizations was a division of labor among producers. Most craftsmen were responsible for a long sequence of stages in the productive process, whether they manufactured goods for sale to the final consumer, or semi-finished products that needed to be worked up by domestic labor or other guildsmen. The range of goods each craftsman manufactured was quite limited, so that a diversification of, for example, hoes or tobacco pipes led to the proliferation of guilds producing these articles. On the other hand, such a division of labor did not allow for any great increase in productivity, nor would there have been a market for a greater quantity of goods. Investment in tools and other means of production was limited, and most seventeenth-century Ottoman towns marketed only few goods over major distances.[46]

There was no centrally imposed pattern of guild organization, and thus local arrangements diverged considerably. Due to the availability of extensive monographs on Cairo and İstanbul, we will concentrate upon these two major urban centers of the empire.[47] In both cases, the main primary source is an enumeration provided by Evliya Çelebi, who probably based himself upon archival materials now lost. The number of guilds in Cairo remained more or less constant from the 1660s down to the French occupation of 1798. However, certain luxury crafts contracted and the number of guilds concerned with this type of production declined. At the same time, we observe a tendency among guildsmen practicing their craft in one and the same street to "hive off" and form separate organizations, a process already observed in fifteenth- and sixteenth-century Bursa.[48] Thus even in the seventeenth century and later, organizational arrangements among Cairene guildsmen changed in response to social and economic needs, and were by no means rigidly fixed. We do not know whether long-term changes in İstanbul paralleled those observed in Cairo, for as yet there exists no full-length study of the Ottoman capital in the eighteenth and early nineteenth centuries.[49]

As to the number of men organized in the seventeenth-century İstanbul and Cairo guilds, our main source is Evliya Çelebi (see Table II:24). Cross-checking with seventeenth-century archival documents in the case of İstanbul, and with late eighteenth-century French records in the case of Cairo, shows that his figures are probably reliable at least with respect to the orders of magnitude involved. In mid-seventeenth century İstanbul, 126,400 – 260,000 artisans were organized in 1,109 guilds. This involves an average size of 114–234 craftsmen per guild, although individual cases varied widely.[50] In Cairo during the 1680s, 119,140 artisans were members of about 260 guilds, which results in an average of 455 members.[51] Apparently there were no organizations that brought together the craftsmen working in related industries, even though Evliya Çelebi's order of enumeration indicates that Ottoman officials possessed a system of guild classification.[52] From the administration's point of view, the key criterion was the official to whom the guildsmen paid their taxes.[53] Whatever cooperation between guilds may have occurred must have been on an *ad hoc* basis and without involving any overall coordinating bodies.

Both İstanbul and Cairo guilds grouped craftsmen and shopkeepers practicing the same trade in the same locality, irrespective of religion. This meant that a considerable number of guilds had both Muslim and non-Muslim members in varying proportions. It also happened that a craft was practiced exclusively either by Muslims or else by non-Muslims. Certain trades, such as tavern-keeping, were closed to Muslims due to the prescriptions of Islamic religious law, but other crafts might be limited to non-Muslims for much more fortuitous reasons. Thus in Cairo many goldsmiths and jewellers were Copts.[54] In the case of "mixed" guilds the principal guild officials were always

Table II:24. Distribution of Cairo's active population about 1660, according to Evliya Çelebi

| | Crafts | | | Individuals | |
	No.	%	Shops and workshops	No.	%
Artisans	136	51.9	13,149	59,214	49.7
Traders	103	39.3	12,013	38,513	32.4
Services	23	8.8	375	21,413	17.9
Total	262	100.0	25,537	119,140	100.0
Various	11		307	13,871	
"Disreputable trades"	16		40	14,355	
Total	289		25,884	147,366	

Source: Raymond (1973–74), I, p. 204.

Muslims. In İstanbul there seem to have been few misgivings about allowing non-Muslims to organize a guild, which was run by non-Muslim officials.[55] On the other hand, such hesitations appear to have existed in Cairo. It has been surmised that the merchants of Hamzavi Khan were the only group of traders established in a separate business district who did not possess their own guild, because this would have involved an organization encompassing non-Muslims only.[56]

Seventeenth-century public opinion differentiated between respected and more or less disreputable kinds of work, and therefore between reputable and disreputable guilds. Among the most disreputable were the organizations whose members were engaged in criminal pursuits. Twentieth-century authors generally doubt the very existence of thieves' guilds and the like, although Evliya claims that they sometimes participated in public processions.[57] Among legitimate trades, several considerations determined the status that a guild might enjoy. *Fütüvvet* manuals generally consider "dirty" kinds of work, such as tanning or oil-pressing, as leading to a loss of status. Other activities such as goldsmithery were regarded as dubious from a religious point of view. It was also of some importance whether the craftsmen involved were rich or poor. In an indirect way, this consideration is reflected even in the *fütüvvet* manuals, for certain guilds were downgraded due to the ignorance of their guild elders, which state of affairs in turn was connected with the poverty of the craftsmen involved. Moreover most of the "rich" trades, particularly the buying and selling of textiles, were considered honorable both by the authors of *fütüvvet* manuals and by chroniclers.

While the term "guilds" evokes the image of craftsmen selling the products of their own workshops, merchants' guilds were also well represented in the major Ottoman cities. In İstanbul, individual activities probably were more important than those of the guild as a whole.[58] In seventeenth- and eighteenth-century Cairo, merchants' and artisans' guilds seem to have shared certain basic characteristics: they participated in public ceremonies, were led by guild elders, and paid taxes as a group.[59] However, while artisans' guilds often bought their raw materials in common and shared them according to pre-established criteria, there is no evidence that merchant guilds acted in this fashion.

The organizational structure of guilds in Cairo differed from those in İstanbul: in Cairo the key figure was the sheikh, whose powers were much wider than those of his İstanbul namesake. His office in principle was elective but often passed from father to son. Although the sheikh was assisted by a council of experienced masters, the latter had a very limited degree of influence and the sheikh himself made most important decisions. He adjudicated disputes between guildsmen, and in some cases found employment for members of "his" guild; in such cases, he assumed responsibility for their good conduct. Moreover the sheikh was responsible for distributing taxes demanded from the guild as a whole among individual members; this function for certain sheikhs may have constituted a source of considerable power. However it was not impossible for guildsmen to remove their sheikh from office. In craftsmen's, though not in merchants' guilds, it was by no means essential that the sheikh be one of the wealthier members of the group; and many sheikhs lived and died as poor men.[60]

In seventeenth-century İstanbul, by contrast, *kethüda* and *yiğitbaşı* were the real heads of the guild.[61] Generally, the *kethüda* was elected by the masters, but apparently needed to be confirmed in office by the kadi. The İstanbul *kethüda* possessed most of the rights and discharged the duties which had been assigned to the sheikhs in Cairo, including the adjudication of disputes. But while the Cairene sheikhs often ran "their" guilds more or less single-handedly, this was not true of the İstanbul *kethüda*s. The latter needed to consult with one or more *yiğitbaşı*s who were elected by the guild members, and shared the *kethüda*s' rights and responsibilities. Moreover, since in guilds of mixed Muslim/non-Muslim membership the *yiğitbaşı*s acted as representatives of their respective constituencies, the element of formalized negotiation seems to have been more apparent in İstanbul than in Cairo.

CRAFTSMEN, MERCHANTS AND THE PROBLEM OF PROTECTION

In eighteenth-century İstanbul, Cairo and many Rumelian cities, a large number of artisans were members of one or the other paramilitary corps. This was a comparatively new development. In the sixteenth century, individual military men certainly had established close ties with the population of the localities in which they were stationed, but incorporation of craftsmen into military units then was fairly rare. The change largely occurred in the seventeenth century, and to date has been well studied only in the case of Cairo. Where İstanbul is concerned, we know very little. It has been assumed that Janissary officers, particularly those in charge of police duties, were the first to acquire shops and/or the right to exercise a craft (*gedik*). Probably the fees demanded were so high that investments of this kind remained closed to ordinary soldiers.[62]

On the other hand, the process by which merchants and craftsmen were incorporated into the military and later paramilitary units of Cairo, especially the Janissaries and the *azab* (irregulars) can be followed in considerable detail (see Table II:25).[63] Apparently the officers of the paramilitary corps wished to control the guilds through their most influential members, and therefore furthered the incorporation of the guild elders, while the richest merchants, with a position and wealth to lose, were probably the most assiduous in seeking the protection of the corps. Accordingly the elders of guilds were first to join, and the wealthiest merchants in coffee and spices became members of the paramilitary corps with greater frequency than their more modest competitors. By 1700, the process of incorporation was virtually completed, and by this time non-Muslim merchants and artisans remained the only major sector of the economically independent Cairene population not organized in one or another of the paramilitary corps.

Merchants and craftsmen joined the Janissaries or *azab* to protect themselves from legal and illegal taxes. Since the corps farmed a considerable number of urban dues, which were collected from the same craftsmen and merchants, the chiefs of the corps possessed a means of pressuring the more recalcitrant Cairenes to comply. In exchange for this protection, merchants and artisans paid a fee to the corps. In addition,

Table II:25. Major Cairo merchants affiliated to the paramilitary corps, 1681–1710

Period	Major merchants		Major merchants affiliated to the Janissaries			Major merchants affiliated to the azab		
	No.	Estate value	No.	% of total	Estate value	No.	% of total	Estate value
1681–90	41	18,513,964	24	58	11,744,211	9	22	3,407,761
1691–1700	35	24,529,067	23	66	17,156,059	7	20	6,513,344
1701–10	12	6,893,981	7	58	5,359,738	2	17	471,831

There is no adjustment for devaluation of the currency.
Source: Raymond (1973–74), II, p. 669, based upon the Cairo kadı registers.

about one-tenth of the estate of every protected "member" of the corps was turned over to the organization after his death. By and large, the corps provided effective protection against the exactions of Mamluk beys and Ottoman governors and the later years of the seventeenth century, when the power of the corps reached its apogee, were also a time of prosperity for merchants and artisans.

The community of interests between merchants and artisans on the one hand, and the Cairene paramilitary corps on the other, was further reinforced by the tendency of many military men stationed in Cairo to enter into partnerships with traders and craftsmen. In many cases this was simply a repetition, on an individual level, of the "fleecing" already described on the group level. But in certain instances the relationship might lead to genuine business investment. Moreover family ties between members of the paramilitary units and the economically active population of Cairo reinforced business connections, particularly since not only the sisters and daughters, but also the freedwomen of a powerful officer might make desirable marriage partners for merchants and craftsmen.

In addition certain wealthy inhabitants of seventeenth-century Cairo also used Janissary pay tickets as a form of investment, paying over a given sum of money and receiving a perpetual rent in exchange. This type of relationship disappeared in the early eighteenth century, when the treasury stopped honoring pay tickets of corps members not on active duty. Certain wealthy merchant families gained, through their connections with the ruling groups, more long-term advantages in tax-farming. Seen in a broader context, the membership of many non-combatant merchants and craftsmen doubtlessly weakened the corps from a military point of view. But the close connection between merchants and craftsmen on the one hand, and the corps on the other, provided an avenue for social mobility, as certain members of the taxpaying subject population entered the ruling class. From this point of view, the transformation of the military into a paramilitary corps may well be regarded as one of the factors stabilizing Ottoman rule in the provinces.

NON-GUILD WORKERS: PEDDLERS, WOMEN AND SLAVES

Although it was once assumed that the entire active population of seventeenth-century Ottoman towns was enrolled in guilds, that claim is an exaggeration. Guilds did exist even in very small towns, places whose urban character was doubtful. But non-guild laborers could be found

even in the largest cities. Ambulant vendors, for example, were not generally part of any guild.[64] Frequent complaints that these people competed
with established shopkeepers and yet paid no taxes makes it seem likely
that itinerant traders and craftsmen were outside of the established guild
system. Moreover, in many places domestic servants lacked any organization to protect their interests. For instance in Ankara shortly before and
after 1600, young girls and boys were handed over by their parents to
serve in their masters' homes without any reference to guild regulations
appearing in the contract. However in Cairo, a guild of domestic servants
did exist.[65]

Women usually were not guild members, even though they did work
for wages, particularly as spinners. Female employment was apparently
most frequent in large and active commercial centers such as Bursa, while
in inland market towns such as, for instance, Kayseri, opportunities were
much more limited.[66] Bursa women worked for merchants bleaching and
spinning silk; in 1678, 150 out of the 300 silk-spinning implements in
the city were owned and/or operated by women. In the absence of a
guild organization, these women must have established links with the
market through the mediation of merchants. In addition, certain Bursa
women worked in their homes and sold the product of their labor in the
streets and even on a special market, without being members of a guild
and without paying guild taxes.[67]

In addition to these artisanal activities, women provided services for
other women. Thus tradeswomen supplied the harems of the wealthy
with cloth and jewelry. Services of this kind constituted the basis for the
influence of a Jewish businesswoman active in the palace at the end of
the sixteenth century.[68] We also find occasional references to female slave
traders and brokers. Moreover women with more modest resources must
have been active as bath attendants and entertainers in wealthy
households.

On the other end of the social scale one encounters rich women who
took an active role in administering their own property. Thus a resident
of Bursa who died in 1682, leaving an estate of almost a million *akçe*,
had invested more than a quarter of this fortune in loans, but at the same
time she had borrowed money to engage in further business dealings.
Women also entrusted money to merchants in order to import merchandise such as Iranian silk, and at least one seventeenth-century Bursa textile trader was a female.[69]

Slaves constituted another part of the labor force not enrolled in any
guild. A considerable number of slaves entered the territory of the empire

as war captives, and if one allows for the time lag, representatives of the principal opponents of Ottoman armies were found among the slaves in a large Anatolian city such as Bursa.[70] In the later sixteenth and in the seventeenth century, Hungarians and Russians most frequently were recorded among the Anatolian servile population. Slaves also were recruited closer to home: the population of border provinces sometimes complained of unprovoked Janissary slave raids. The courts of even inland cities such as Ankara occasionally needed to decide the claims of slaves who complained about illegal enslavement. In addition to captives, there were slaves imported by traders; such traders were active in what is today southern Russia, buying captives from the Tatars or from slave-raiders such as the Abaza. Importation through Anatolian Black Sea ports continued throughout the seventeenth century.

Circassian and Georgian male slaves were still sold to Egypt, where the Mamluk oligarchy continued to perpetuate itself through the purchase, training and later manumission of young military slaves, as had been the custom in pre-Ottoman times.[71] Since a Mamluk, whether military leader and head of a large establishment or simple soldier, could not be succeeded by his son (who had no option but to join the Egyptian subject population), supplying Egypt with military slaves continued to be a profitable venture. New recruits were trained in the house of a military leader (*bey*), to whom they owed loyalty even after manumission; in addition a Mamluk soldier was bound to his comrades in training who had shared with him slavery in the house of the bey. In pre-Ottoman times only high-ranking members of the military establishment had been permitted to own Mamluks. However by the seventeenth century this rule was not always applied, and wealthy merchants might purchase Mamluks, provide for their training and secure for them entry into the political class. This practice was part of the search for protection from arbitrary exactions described above; in this manner, a rich merchant might lay claim to the loyalty of a member of the dominant class.[72]

In addition to slaves from Hungary, southern Russia and the Caucasus, African slaves were imported into the Ottoman Empire, generally by way of Egypt. Already by the last quarter of the sixteenth century, slaves and freedmen of African descent were visible enough in the Aegean province of Aydın that a rescript was sent out from İstanbul prohibiting assemblies of these people. Even though the text is not very explicit, it is probable that some of the customs involved were regarded as dubious from a religious point of view.[73] On the island of Cyprus both black slaves and free blacks have left a record in the kadi registers, the proximity of Egypt explaining the frequency of their mention.[74] But the destination of the most valuable black slaves was the sultan's harem; the ascendancy of the *Kızlar Ağası* (Chief Black Eunuch) in the palace bureaucracy of the time must have had an impact upon recruitment practices.

Somewhat more is known about slaves employed in commerce and manufacturing. In fifteenth- and sixteenth-century Bursa, silk merchants and manufacturers commonly acquired slaves, and after they had worked for a given time, manumitted them and provided them with the means of setting up in business on their own.[75] However the decline of Bursa silk manufacture during the late sixteenth and early seventeenth centuries probably led to the gradual disappearance of slaves and manumitted slaves from this branch of production. In Cairo, by contrast, the practice still was current in the seventeenth century; this may be linked to the fact that the merchants and artisans of this city experienced a period of prosperity in the second half of the seventeenth century.[76]

But most slaves in the Ottoman Empire probably were in domestic service; the "great households" of the time could not have functioned without male and female slaves. Documents concerning pious foundations often preserve a record of these men and especially women, for a wealthy former owner might, if other heirs were lacking, make the descendants of his/her slaves administrators of his/her foundations. More immediately, foundations might be instituted to give old retainers a house to live in. In other cases a manumitted slave was married by her former owner; such freedwomen can be distinguished in the estate inventories of the time by the patronymic "b. Abdullah."[77]

WOMEN AND THE FAMILY

Few systematic studies of this subject exist.[78] Apart from female members of the elite, for whom a wider range of sources is available, a study of women and the family must rely almost exclusively upon entries in the kadi registers and occasional estate inventories. Family arrangements in the provincial towns of Anatolia show certain special features, which remained fairly constant from the seventeenth to the nineteenth century. Marriage to more than one woman at a time was very rare and, by contrast, divorce comparatively frequent. While divorces pronounced unilaterally by the husband and not complicated by unusual property transactions were not normally recorded in the registers, divorces in which the wife "purchased" a dissolution of the marriage for a pecuniary consideration can be found in the registers even of small towns. A woman desiring a divorce, at the very least, renounced her claim to support for the waiting period during which a divorcee could not remarry. Usually she also renounced the sum of money which her spouse had settled upon her at marriage, to be paid out in case he died or unilaterally divorced her. In many cases, the wife might offer an additional sum of money. Other divorces might result from the fact that the husband was absent for long periods of time, as a trader, or else because he sought employment in foreign parts. In such instances, both the husband's and wife's interests might be served by a divorce: the husband might wish to avoid paying over most of his capital as support money during his absence, while the wife must often have wished to end a situation in which she had all the responsibilities of a married woman and few of the advantages. Therefore contracts of "conditional divorce" can occasionally be found: in such cases the husband stated that his wife was divorced if he did not return by a certain date, or else he appointed a representative to pronounce the divorce in his stead.

Women had the right to own both personal and real property, and according to Muslim religious law a husband could not touch the property of his spouse during her lifetime. He remained responsible for her support even if she possessed property of her own. Apart from the cases of women earning money, discussed in the previous section, the obvious manner in which a woman could obtain property was through inheritance. For this potential control of property to become a reality, it was necessary that women obtain protection against male relatives wishing to deprive them of their inheritance. In seventeenth-century Anatolian towns, the kadis' courts were active in securing women's rights, and particularly inheritance rights according to the Muslim religious law or Sharia. No stigma seems to have attached to a woman's attending court in person, and quite a few women took care of their affairs in this manner, without the mediation of a male representative.

In Anatolian provincial cities women appear to have received their share of an inheritance as cash, cloth or jewelry. Any shares in a house or shop which they received typically were sold (Tables II:26 and 27). On the other hand, women's ownership of real estate seems to have been much more common in Aleppo, probably because in this affluent milieu more families considered that they could afford to leave valuable property in female hands. Wealthy families may also have assigned property to women in order to protect the family wealth in case of business failures. In Aleppo we also find husband and wife owning their dwelling in

Table II:26. Male and female sellers of houses, Ankara and Kayseri

Location	Information not usable	Sellers all male	Sellers all female	Mixed	Total usable descriptions	Grand total (cases)
Ankara, 1600	124	139 (63.8)[a]	56 (25.7)	23 (10.6)	218	342
Kayseri, 1600	61	122 (69.7)	31 (17.7)	22 (12.6)	175	236
Ankara, 1690	60	135 (59.0)	68 (29.7)	26 (11.4)	229	289
Kayseri, 1690	58	138 (61.3)	53 (23.6)	34 (15.1)	225	283

[a] Percentages (in brackets) are based not upon the grand total, but upon the total of usable descriptions.
Source: Faroqhi (1987), p. 159.

Table II:27. Male and female buyers of houses, Ankara and Kayseri

Location	Information not usable	Buyers all male	Buyers all female	Mixed	Total usable descriptions	Grand total (cases)
Ankara, 1600	124	192 (88.1)[a]	23 (10.6)	3 (1.4)	218	342
Kayseri, 1600	61	156 (89.1)	16 (9.1)	3 (1.7)	175	236
Ankara, 1690	61	197 (86.4)	30 (13.2)	1 (0.4)	228	289
Kayseri, 1690	58	180 (80.0)	38 (16.9)	7 (3.1)	225	283

[a] Percentages (in brackets) are based not upon the grand total, but upon the total of usable descriptions.
Source: Faroqhi (1987), p. 159.

common, a feature that was all but absent from seventeenth-century Anatolian towns such as Ankara or Kayseri.[79]

Quite different were the arrangements where women's ownership of rural property was involved. Gardens and vineyards were freehold and therefore could be inherited in the same manner as urban real estate. However, while in eighteenth-century Aleppo, gardens and vineyards rarely were allowed to pass into female hands, in seventeenth-century Anatolian towns women did own such property.[80] Furthermore in the kadi registers of late sixteenth-century Ankara, we find evidence of women receiving the usufruct of state-owned lands through the mediation of a *timar*-holder or administrator of crown lands, even though regulations promulgated before 1590 usually had disallowed this type of acquisition.

Provisions for women in widowhood and old age are not recorded in the kadi registers with any frequency; among the few such devices that we know of, one might mention husbands donating a house or some other substantial item of property during their own lifetimes. Such a donation was meant to supplement the wife's modest share in her deceased husband's estate, or provide for her in case she was a non-Muslim and could not inherit from her Muslim spouse. Another device, used by women as well as men, was the donation of a house or other real property to a member of the younger generation. In exchange, the beneficiary undertook to care for the donor until death, and the donation could be revoked in case of non-fulfillment. The percentage of households headed by widows could be quite substantial. But at least where urban widows are concerned, we know very little about their means of support, apart from the money-lending of some of the more substantial property-holders.[81]

Families of the İstanbul elite differed considerably from those formed by ordinary Anatolian or Aleppine townsmen. Thus elite households were enlarged by the presence of male and female slaves, who were much less frequent in non-elite households. Polygyny was common, and sometimes one of the wives might be given special status. Sheyhülislam Feyzullah recounts that while all of his numerous children had different mothers, he had always felt a particular regard for the daughter of his patron Sheikh Vani.[82] In these households, just as in the sultan's palace, female children were important, for their marriages served to cement alliances; one of Sheyhülislam Feyzullah's daughters married a man who later himself obtained the office of Sheyhülislam and thus became the head of the ulema hierarchy.[83]

As a result of these arrangements, elite families quite often possessed more than one branch. The memoirs of Sheyhülislam Feyzullah make it clear that while his immediate family resided in İstanbul (and was banished to Bursa after his death) quite a few family members remained in his home town of Erzurum. In the milieu of sheikhs and ulema to which the chronicler Uşakızade belonged, large families with many branches, often established in different localities, also were frequent.[84] Extended families of this type provided an insurance against the early death of the father, an event which might prove very detrimental to the careers of young sons.[85] Uncles and other male relatives might be expected to arrange for the education of an orphan and later use their own patronage networks in order to find the young man a position.

Non-Muslim family life is more difficult to study, due to the rarity of documentation. However it is probable that the influence of the majority Muslim family arrangements was often quite strong. Thus the priest Grigor of Kemah in eastern Anatolia, when describing the disorder of his flock during the difficult years of the Celali uprisings, mentions that several prominent members of the local Armenian community had taken more than one wife. One of his first actions as a parish priest was to dissolve these irregular unions.[86]

Apart from informal channels of influence, the tendency of many non-Muslims to record their family matters in the kadis' registers must have increased Muslim influence upon non-Muslim family arrangements; for cases judged in the kadis' court could only be decided according to the Sharia. Thus the seventeenth-century register of the Morean town of Balyabadra (Paleopatras) contains records of weddings in which both partners were Greek Orthodox. It has been suggested that by this device the partners were creating a situation which would in the future allow them to avail themselves of Sharia rules governing marriage.[87] In Anatolia, non-Muslims most frequently turned to the Sharia court when dividing the estate of a deceased person. The sanction of the court presumably was sought to make sure that the division, once agreed upon, could not be contested; but if such contestation occurred, the matter again had to be decided according to the Sharia.

The kadi records also provide information on the negotiations which preceded a non-Muslim marriage. In the non-Muslim communities of central Anatolia, it was often the mothers of the bride and groom who negotiated the marriage. They were also the persons to decide when an engagement should be broken off. In such cases, the two women returned the engagement gifts, which consisted of textiles and jewelry, as was common also among Muslims of nineteenth- and twentieth-century Anatolia. Ethnographical studies of twentieth-century Anatolia also stress the strong, if less formalized, roles of the mothers of bride and groom in marriage negotiations. Thus the kadi registers probably reflect standard practice among both Muslims and non-Muslims.[88]

NON-MUSLIMS AS URBAN DWELLERS

In the sixteenth century, most of the larger Balkan towns had been inhabited largely by Muslims.[89] In middle-level and smaller urban centers, the non-Muslim share was much more important, but even among these there were almost completely Muslim settlements, such as Yenice-i Karasu, Yenice-i Vardar and Yenişehir (Triccala). By the eighteenth century the non-Muslim population of Balkan towns increased both in size and in wealth,[90] but it is hard to determine to what extent this process had begun in the seventeenth century. On the other hand, population movements associated with the Habsburg–Ottoman war of 1682–99 certainly changed

Table II:28. The religion of people selling houses, Ankara and Kayseri

Location	Information not usable	Sellers all Muslim	Sellers all non-Muslim	Mixed	Total usable descriptions	Grand total (cases)
Ankara, c. 1600	124	169 (77.5)[a]	47 (21.6)	2 (0.9)	218	342
Kayseri, c. 1600	61	125 (72.6)	48 (27.4)	0	175	236
Ankara, c. 1690	60	176 (76.9)	53 (23.1)	0	229	289
Kayseri, c. 1690	58	181 (80.4)	42 (18.7)	2 (0.9)	225	283

[a] Percentages (in brackets) are based not upon the grand total, but upon the total of usable descriptions.
Source: Faroqhi (1987), p. 159.

pre-existing population balances, as at first Muslims fled from the advancing Habsburg armies, while at a later stage non-Muslims who had thrown in their lot with the occupying forces followed the retreat of the imperial armies.[91] As a result of these migrations, a counter-trend to the settlement of Balkan towns by the non-Muslim element surely ensued, as the Muslim population increasingly preferred to live in the larger cities.

In central Anatolia, non-Muslims by the end of the seventeenth century were buying more houses than they sold (see Tables II:28 and 29), and their houses were more valuable even than those acquired by members of the Ottoman administration. This indicates growing wealth and relative security, which permitted a degree of ostentation. But on the whole little is known about social relations between Muslim and non-Muslim townsmen. In Sofia, Muslim and non-Muslim craftsmen such as tanners, furriers or cap makers worked under very similar conditions, and from court cases and other complaints it would seem that their daily concerns were very much the same: both complained about competition from newly established masters or about increasing prices of raw materials.[92] Similar conditions prevailed in Anatolian Kayseri, where the Greek, Karamanlı and Armenian minorities largely had been assimilated on a cultural level, since most of the Kayseri Christians were turcophone and knew no other language.[93] The kadi's court was vigilant in defending the rights that non-Muslims possessed according to the Muslim religious law, and this institution seems to have contributed toward the maintenance of peaceful relations.

Balkan historians have often defended the view that non-Muslim communities declined culturally during the Ottoman period. Several factors supposedly played a role in this process; for example, there no longer existed a native ruling class to patronize literature and the arts.[94] Secondly, while the ban on building new churches often was circumvented

Table II:29. The religion of people buying houses, Ankara and Kayseri

Location	Information not usable	Buyers all Muslim	Buyers all non-Muslim	Mixed	Total usable descriptions	Grand total (cases)
Ankara, c. 1600	124	165 (75.7)[a]	51 (23.4)	2 (0.9)	218	342
Kayseri, c. 1600	61	125 (71.4)	49 (28.0)	1 (0.6)	175	236
Ankara, c. 1690	61	161 (70.6)	67 (29.4)	0	228	289
Kayseri, c. 1690	59	142 (63.4)	82 (36.6)	0	224	283

[a] Percentages are based not upon the grand total, but upon the total of usable descriptions.
Source: Faroqhi (1987), p. 159.

in practice, the obligation to keep these new structures low and not too visible to the public eye is assumed to have limited opportunities for artistic creativity. However, in recent years this view has been challenged. There is a renewed interest in the so-called neo-Byzantine art which flourished particularly in Greece and Serbia during the sixteenth and seventeenth centuries. Thus it has been suggested that the relatively modest level of such creativity in certain areas of Rumeli, such as present-day Bulgaria, had little to do with overall Ottoman prohibitions and much more with local constraints.[95]

Concerning the Jewish minority, research has concentrated upon the textile-producing Sephardim of Salonica (see Ch. 16), the port city of İzmir, and upon the Jewish presence in Palestine, particularly Jerusalem.[96] In many respects, the situation of Jews in late sixteenth-century Jerusalem was comparable to that of Christians residing in seventeenth-century Kayseri. Thus even though both Jews and Christians in Jerusalem tended to live close to one another, there were no ghettos, and the Jewish people maintained multiple ties with their Muslim co-residents. While there existed an officially recognized head of the Jewish community, who needed the support of local Jewish notables to maintain his position, this personage was in no way the only channel through which the Jews of Jerusalem contacted the outside world. Thus it has been concluded that the model of more or less autonomous communities (*millet*), concerned mainly with their own internal affairs and engaged only in minimal contact with the outside world, is inapplicable to Jerusalem during the sixteenth and seventeenth centuries.

This conclusion has a wider relevance. Due to a considerable body of research on Ottoman minority affairs, previously accepted doctrines concerning a fixed and well-established organization of Greeks, Armenians or Jews under an officially recognized head of the community are no longer accepted as valid.[97] Thus what is conventionally understood by a *millet* organization did not exist during the fifteenth and sixteenth centuries, and probably not in the seventeenth century either. Research on non-Muslim communities is now directed more toward local and regional than empire-wide horizons. But much research upon minorities still shows a tendency to contrast the situation in the "classical" period of the fifteenth and six-teenth centuries with the "modern age" of the post-Tanzimat years, with all intervening transformations excluded from the picture. In Ottoman social and economic history as a whole, this limited perspective is slowly being superseded, as more evidence on seventeenth and eighteenth-century history becomes available. Thus it seems most promising to treat the his-tory of Ottoman non-Muslim minorities as an integral part of Ottoman history, and not as a development that can be studied more or less in isola-tion. Only when that is achieved will we be able to escape the anachronistic projection of nineteenth-century institutions onto earlier periods, that has justly been criticized by recent researchers.[98]

CONCLUSION

If one were to draw an overall conclusion from the studies on Ottoman urban society which have appeared in the last thirty years or so, it seems that researchers have moved away from seeing social relations as gov-erned by rigid and unchangeable patterns. To use a visual image, one might speak of *décloisonnement*, or say that in the view of scholars now working from a broader evidential base, barriers previously regarded as watertight and impassible are now considered lower and more permeable. Town quarters and ethno-religious groups, for example, are now under-stood to have interacted more intensively than would have been conceded in the past. Guilds sometimes could be entered by "outsiders" and thus were less rigidly closed off than originally had been assumed. Migration from the countryside now appears to have been easier than had been suggested by the study of normative evidence alone, an observation made independently by researchers working on both the Balkans and Anato-lia.[99] Anatolian women who in the past had been regarded as cut off from interaction with people outside their own families have emerged as artisans, money-lenders and even landholders. Last but not least, even the highway robbers of those years punctuated by Celali rebellions were often part of networks spread out over wide areas, and goods stolen from a traveler might surface in towns scores of miles away from the locality where the attack had taken place.

At the same time, researchers have paid more attention to urban conflict, and many of the disputes analyzed, which at first glance had seemed of minor importance, later turned out to be major indicators of social structure and social change. As long as it was assumed that social conflicts in Ottoman cities were sufficiently explained by a reference to, for example, factionalism among members of different paramilitary corps, these conflicts did not seem to merit closer analysis. But it has become apparent that certain disputes which involve competing factions contain an element of economic rivalry as well.[100] The role of factionalism itself demands closer investigation: we must inquire under what kinds of conditions factionalism evolved, and what types of needs it responded to. In this perspective, it is probable that social historians will be able to learn from anthropological studies concerning the modern Middle East, where patronage and the closely allied issue of factionalism have become the subject of detailed studies.[101] To sum it all up, social historians dealing with the Ottoman seventeenth century have been most successful where they partly have overcome the dismissive attitude toward social phenomena which characterized so many older studies of the Ottoman realm.

NOTES

1 Raymond (1973–74, 1984a and b, 1985) on Cairo and other Arab cities; Abdel Nour (1982) on Syria; Masters (1988) on Aleppo; Mantran (1962) on İstanbul; Todorov (1980) on the towns of present-day Bulgaria; Frangakis (1985) and Goffman (1990) on İzmir; Jennings (1972), Ergenç (1973), Yavuz and Uğurel (1984) and Faroqhi (1987) on Ankara and Kayseri.
2 Faroqhi (1982–83).
3 Faroqhi (1986b).
4 Stoianovich (1970); Braudel (1979), I, pp. 453ff; Ergenç (1981).
5 Faroqhi (1984), pp. 26ff.
6 Kreiser (1986).
7 A research team from the Architectural Faculty of Middle East Technical University, Ankara, recently discovered a seventeenth-century wooden dwelling in Mudanya.
8 Raymond (1985).
9 Abdel Nour (1982), pp. 257–398.
10 Raymond (1973–74), II, p. 327.
11 Compare, however, Raymond (1984a) on the population of Aleppo.
12 Faroqhi (1984), p. 27.
13 Raymond (1984b), pp. 78–90; Marcus (1986).
14 Darkot (1965), p. 7.
15 Çadırcı (1980); Faroqhi (1987), p. 158; Thieck (1985).
16 Raymond (1984b), p. 63; Behrens-Abouseif (1985).

17 Göyünç (1970).
18 *Türkiye Vakıf Abideleri* (1972), I, p. 293.
19 Faroqhi (1979b).
20 Faroqhi (1988b).
21 Zilfi (1986).
22 Gölpınarlı (1953), pp. 163–64.
23 For an example compare Evliya Çelebi (1896–97 to 1938), IX, pp. 80 ff. on Manisa.
24 For detailed work on Ankara compare Ergenç (1973, 1981).
25 İnalcık (1980), pp. 290–91.
26 Compare Pascual (1984) on members of paramilitary corps acquiring a hold over the Damascene countryside.
27 Bodman (1963), p. 97.
28 Todorov (1970); (1964 repr. 1977), pp. 2–9.
29 Raymond (1973–74), II, pp. 741–48.
30 *Ibid.*, pp. 745–47.
31 Mantran (1962), pp. 368ff.
32 Faroqhi (1986b), p. 79; Veinstein (1988).
33 İnalcık (1969), p. 117.
34 *Ibid.*
35 *Ibid.*, p. 105.
36 BBA, MD 10, p. 157; İnalcık (1969), p. 118.
37 Baer (1970a, 1970b, 1970c).
38 Mantran (1962), p. 373.
39 *Ibid.*, p. 364.
40 Baer (1970b), p. 48.
41 Todorov (1964 repr. 1977), pp. 6–7.
42 Gerber (1976), p. 64.
43 Raymond (1973–74), II, p. 561.
44 Akarlı (1986). However other scholars assume that *gedik* existed in earlier periods as well.
45 Raymond (1973–74), II, pp. 549–50.
46 İnalcık (1973), pp. 156ff.
47 Raymond (1973–74), II, pp. 503ff; Mantran (1962), pp. 349–95.
48 İnalcık (1969), p. 117.
49 Such a study will be based upon the kadi registers of the different sections of İstanbul (İstanbul *intra muros*, Galata, Üsküdar, Haslar in addition to Yeniköy which covers the Bosphorus villages). At present consult Aktepe (1958b).
50 Mantran (1962), p. 355.
51 Raymond (1973–74), II, pp. 511–14.
52 Mantran (1962), p. 355.
53 Raymond (1973–74), II, pp. 519–20.
54 Raymond (1973–74), II.
55 Mantran (1962), p. 352.
56 Raymond (1973–74), II, p. 526.
57 *Ibid.*, p. 527.
58 Mantran (1962), p. 427.
59 Raymond (1973–74), II, p. 521.

60 *Ibid.*, pp. 562–82.
61 Mantran (1962), pp. 373ff.
62 *Ibid.*, p. 370
63 Raymond (1973–74), II, pp. 659ff.
64 Mantran (1962), p. 439.
65 Raymond (1973–74), II, p. 567.
66 Compare the findings of Jennings (1975) with those of Gerber (1980).
67 Gerber (1980), p. 238.
68 Mordtmann (1929).
69 Gerber (1980), p. 235.
70 İnalcık (1979); Sahillioğlu (1979–80), pp. 87ff.
71 Ayalon (1977).
72 Raymond (1973–74), II. pp. 67ff
73 BBA, MD 27, p. 306.
74 Jennings (1987).
75 Sahillioğlu (1979–80), p. 122.
76 Raymond (1973–74), I, pp. 84–85.
77 Barkan and Ayverdi (1970), index.
78 Compare Jennings (1975); Gerber (1980); Ortaylı (1980); Marcus (1983) and Kafadar (1991).
79 Marcus (1983), p. 154. The Aleppo observations concern the eighteenth century, but in the absence of studies on the seventeenth, they have been included for purposes of comparison.
80 Marcus (1983), p. 151.
81 Jennings (1975), pp. 101–2.
82 Türek and Derin (1969–70), p. 71.
83 Majer (1978), p. 204.
84 Majer (1978), pp. 125–67.
85 *Ibid.*, p. 180.
86 Andreasyan (1976), p. 49.
87 Alexander (1985).
88 On modern ways of arranging a peasant marriage, compare Sırman (1988). I thank the author for allowing me to see her work in manuscript.
89 Todorov (1972, repr. 1977) interprets the sixteenth-century figures in such a manner as to stress the continuing importance of the non-Muslim element.
90 Stoianovich (1960), pp. 248ff.
91 Sugar (1977), p. 222.
92 Faroqhi (1987), pp. 148, 156ff; Todorov (1964, repr. 1977).
93 Jennings (1987).
94 Sugar (1977), pp. 251ff.
95 Kiel (1985).
96 Cohen (1982, 1984, 1989).
97 Braude (1982).
98 *Ibid.*, p. 69.
99 Todorov (1972, repr. 1977), II, p. 217; Faroqhi (1984), p. 271.
100 For an analysis of eighteenth- and nineteenth-century urban conflict from this point of view, see Shatkowski-Schilcher, (1985), pp. 27–50.
101 Compare Waterbury (1977).

21

ه

SYMBOLS OF POWER AND
LEGITIMATION

A study of Ottoman social life would be incomplete without a closer
look at the sultans, and the manner in which they were presented to their
subjects as well as to outsiders. During the last few decades, with Ottoman documentation becoming increasingly accessible, researchers have
attempted to break free from the assumption that legal norms, including
the Sharia and the more accessible *kanun* collections, provide an adequate
and sufficient description of the functioning of the Ottoman state apparatus. However, once we try to pass beyond purely normative aspects,
we find that many questions cannot be satisfactorily answered on the
basis of texts alone. Thus the symbolism of buildings, miniatures, or
courtly ceremonies must be interpreted. Most of the limited research
available to date concerns the sixteenth century and especially the reign
of Kanuni Süleyman. The present section therefore is intended to indicate
future directions of research, and hopefully will soon be superseded by
more sophisticated studies.

The study of Ottoman festivities, a crucial source for understanding
Ottoman imperial symbolism, has been inspired by the work on European public celebrations of the Renaissance and Baroque periods. Seen
from one point of view this makes good sense: obviously Ottoman festivities were so impressive that they attracted the attention of many French,
Flemish and English travelers. Quite a few features were common to
Ottoman and European festivities of the time: thus people in Renaissance
Europe decorated their houses with colorful draperies during the passage
of a procession, while Ottoman townsmen put up brightly colored textiles in front of their houses to mark the streets traversed by a victorious
sultan. In addition, the presence of acrobats, jugglers and other public
performers at such festivities was common to Ottomans, Europeans and
other inhabitants of the Old World. However, while Ottoman and

European festivities had certain features in common, twentieth-century researchers are still having great difficulty in interpreting the meaning of Ottoman celebrations and other commemorative activities. Symbolism connected with the ruler constitutes a comparatively accessible aspect of these festivities, and it may therefore be useful to recapitulate some of the more salient features.

THE SULTAN AS A PROTECTOR OF THE *HAJJ* AND OF THE HOLY CITIES

Among the most important images which the sultans were concerned to project was the role of the ruler as a protector of the pilgrimage (*hajj*) and of the Holy Cities. Aside from the texts of inscriptions commemorating major construction projects in Mecca and Medina, there are narrative sources that reveal how different sultans acted as benefactors to pilgrims and permanent residents of the Hejaz. In addition, a considerable number of archival documents survive.

The impact of inscriptions was clearly appreciated and the latter were used as a means of policy. Thus when in 1576 an inscription was ordered to commemorate recent construction in the Holy City of Mecca, the text was drafted in İstanbul and the kadi of Mecca commanded to insure that the inscription was made as visible as possible. Evliya Çelebi, who visited Mecca in 1671–72, comments on the many inscriptions bearing the name of the reigning Sultan Mehmed IV, although this ruler was not particularly renowned as a sponsor of public buildings.

By prominently displaying their names all over Mecca, the sultans may have been intent upon documenting a political victory over the sharifs, who, after 1517, continued to govern the Hejaz, but under Ottoman suzerainty. After all in the twelfth century, and later as well, whoever wished to establish a pious foundation in the Hejaz had to purchase the privilege by paying very substantial fees to the sharifs.[1] More immediately, prominently visible construction activity in Mecca and Medina showed the Ottoman rulers as successful competitors of the Mamluks, and particularly of the munificent Sultan Kayıtbay. Ottoman high-level officials probably had not forgotten that Mehmed the Conqueror had been refused permission to undertake public construction in the Hejaz, so as not to infringe the privileges of Mamluk rulers.[2] On the other hand, Ottoman sultans did occasionally permit foreign Islamic rulers to establish pious foundations in the Holy Cities. Indian pilgrims of the seventeenth century found accommodation in the hospice founded by the Moghul ruler Akbar.[3] However, foundations established by foreign potentates were exceptional and the privileged role of Ottoman rulers as benefactors of the Hejaz therefore was maintained.

Apart from buildings located in the Holy Cities themselves, the sultans manifested their concern for pilgrims by financing the upkeep of cisterns and fortified stopping points on the desert routes from Cairo and Damascus to the Hejaz. But it seems that during the 1683–99 war these installations, and security on the desert routes in general, deteriorated. Therefore, the early eighteenth-century Ottoman administration, in a concerted move, sought to reestablish control over the desert routes, accompanied by a program to restore and rebuild the khans and other installations facilitating the use of the pilgrimage route.[4] Apart from direct intervention on the part of Ottoman rulers, women of the imperial dynasty frequently donated khans, cisterns and other facilities along pilgrimage routes.

More visible, on a day-to-day level, were the sultans' deliveries of foodstuffs and money to many inhabitants of Mecca and Medina, from public foundations located primarily in Egypt. The importance of these donations is emphasized by the large number of account books documenting the amounts of grain to be distributed, and the number of recipients benefiting from the sultans' largesse. Here again the Ottoman sultans of the later sixteenth and of the seventeenth century continued a Mamluk tradition and, in a sense, competed in munificence with their Mamluk predecessors. It is in this sense that we must interpret remarks of a late sixteenth-century Meccan chronicler who stresses the deterioration of previously established foundations during the sixteenth century. Statements of this kind probably were intended to shame the ruler into greater generosity.[5] On the other hand, a sultan such as Murad III (1574–95) carried on the tradition established by Süleyman the Lawgiver and substantially increased the resources of Egyptian foundations benefiting the inhabitants of the Holy Cities.

The propaganda effect of Ottoman donations was less than it might have been, since the expectations of the Hejaz population were so high. Evliya Çelebi, a worldly-wise and shrewd observer, once commented that the inhabitants of the Hejaz regarded all aid given to them not as alms but simply as their due.[6] But then the legitimizing effects of donations to the Hejaz were not limited to the inhabitants of this province. The intended audience also included the people of İstanbul, Cairo or Damascus. It is worth noting that, particularly in these cities, the departure of the sultans' pious gifts to Mecca was celebrated by a round of processions and parades. At present, we do not possess a good synthetic study of the evolution of these ceremonies. Great importance was given to the procession by which the departing caravan was conducted out of the city along with the imperial gifts which it bore.[7] These festivities in part celebrated the departing and returning pilgrims; inhabitants of Cairo and Damascus expressed their solidarity with those who were fulfilling an arduous religious duty. But at the same time the multiple processions of Cairo also intended to emphasize the activities by which members of the Cairene ruling group assumed responsibility for the pilgrims' well-being. All this activity by local people ultimately was undertaken in the name and on behalf of the Ottoman ruler, whom these festivities therefore further legitimized. The role of the Ottoman sultan was recalled particularly when parading the *mahmal*, an empty palanquin which accompanied both the Egyptian and the Syrian *hajj* caravans all the way to Mecca and Arafat. That the *mahmal* was viewed as a symbol of Ottoman state power becomes apparent from the reaction of the Wahhabis in the early nineteenth century, who refused passage to the palanquin for exactly that reason. The Cairo and Damascus palanquins also were viewed as regional symbols and became the objects of intense rivalry, particularly on the part of the Janissaries sent out to guard the pilgrim caravans.[8] The guards of the two *mahmal*s often quarreled over precedence; apparently the sultan's order that the two *mahmal*s were to leave Arafat at the same time proved difficult to enforce.

Thus it appears that the sultans established themselves as protectors of the pilgrimage and of the Holy Cities through building activity, largesse and ceremonies. At the same time, members of the provincial elite, and the soldiers associated with them, were able to share in the ruler's prestige. But the political impact of Ottoman munificence was weakened because the sultans were competing against their Mamluk predecessors. Since nobody knew exactly what Kayıtbay or other Mamluk rulers had spent on the Hejaz, it was always easy to claim that Ottoman rulers fell short of the standard set by their predecessors. The festivities surrounding departure and arrival of the pilgrim caravans were intended, at least in part, to give increased visibility to the donations made by the sultans for the benefit of the Holy Cities.

THE OTTOMAN DYNASTY AS SEEN THROUGH ITS FESTIVITIES

Public construction in İstanbul during the seventeenth century was at a lower level than it had been during the sixteenth (see Ch. 16). However, public festivities and the accompanying decorations could be used almost as effectively to emphasize the central position of the sultan in the life of the state. Thus, life-cycle ceremonies related to the life of the ruler and his immediate family constituted the principal occasion for public festivities. The birth of a prince or princess was celebrated by public rejoicing; even when the ruler ordered only a modest celebration, this included the firing of cannon salutes. Festivities surrounding the birth of royal children were meant to mark the continuity of the dynasty; the birth dates of the eldest children were celebrated with greater éclat than those of the younger ones. The births of female children equally might be the occasion for lavish celebrations. After all, Ottoman princesses might be affianced at a very young age, often while still in the cradle, and thereby cement alliances of the dynasty with high-level officials.[9] Moreover the latter might be counted upon to offer handsome gifts in order to show their gratitude, so that, from a dynastic point of view, princesses constituted an asset and by no means a liability.

The principal festivity in the life of an Ottoman prince was associated not with his birth but rather his circumcision. The circumcision of a prince and the wedding of a princess have been viewed as closely parallel events. Circumcision perhaps may have been accorded the status of a principal life-cycle ceremony after Ottoman rulers consorted only with slave women and ceased to contract formal marriages.[10] Circumcision ceremonies very often involved large numbers of children; it was considered a charity to have boys from poor families circumcised at the same time as members of the royal family, thereby providing the children of the poor with lavish festivities at no expense to their parents. Princely circumcision festivities constituted the occasions for the most elaborate feasts ever recorded in Ottoman history, such as the feast given upon the orders of Murad III for his heir, the later Mehmed III (1582), and the famous celebrations of 1675 which Mehmed IV organized in Edirne.[11] Sometimes marriages of princesses and circumcisions of princes were combined in a single round of festivities; a practice encouraged by the fact that the entertainments offered were essentially the same.

Ottoman princes were entrusted to a tutor at the age of seven, and the beginning of their formal education was marked by special celebrations. Relevant documentation begins in the year 1680.[12] Perhaps not coincidentally, the closing decades of the seventeenth century marked the apogee of the power of Sheikh Feyzullah, who had risen to his eminent position as Sheyülislam due to the fact that he was the former tutor of Mustafa II.[13] In celebrations inaugurating a young prince's formal education, the boy publicly memorized the first letters of the alphabet and/or a section of the Quran. He often appeared on horseback, and thereby was shown to have entered the world of adults. As in the case of other festivities, several princes of approximately the same age might be fêted on one and the same occasion.

The last major ceremony in the life of certain – particularly fortunate – Ottoman princes was their accession to the throne. On the other hand the funeral of a dead ruler was usually an unostentatious affair.[14] The principle *"le roi est mort, vive le roi"* applied to the Ottoman dynasty even more than to European dynasties of the seventeenth century. Apart perhaps from the funeral of Murad III (1595), there was scarcely a parallel with the pomp and ceremony that accompanied baroque funerals in Europe. All major rites of passage publicly celebrated by the Ottoman dynasty, apart from accession to the throne, were centered around young children, and as many seventeenth-century Ottoman rulers were enthroned as mere boys, even the accession often involved a young person. The particular attention paid to the youngest members of the dynasty probably was connected with the high mortality of young children in all preindustrial societies. Celebrations marking the birth and very rapid passage of Ottoman princes and princesses into adult society thus were meant to ensure stability of the dynasty and cement the latter's ties to the upper levels of the political class in the empire.

Ottoman victories were particularly prominent occasions for public rejoicings. But lack of success on the battlefield also might be downplayed by the organization of lavish festivities, often of events in the life-cycle of the dynasty.[15] In addition, the arrivals of ambassadors, particularly from Muslim countries, often were marked by brilliant celebrations. This happened particularly when ambassadors from Iran appeared in the capital; given the rarity of direct contact with the Moghul rulers of India, the shah of Iran was the only ruler who might be regarded as being on the same level as the Ottoman sultans. Ottoman palace culture largely was Iranian in inspiration, and through the exhibition of artifacts, the composition of poetry and other "cultural events," the Ottoman ruling group attempted to demonstrate that local artists, artisans and the educated public in general were fully in control of the language of Iranian-style courtly culture.[16] Ottoman attempts to compete by means of cultural artifacts were not limited to the visits of Iranian ambassadors: in the later sixteenth century, the decoration of the sanctuaries of Kerbela and Nechef in modern-day Iraq was also the occasion for lively competition by means of rugs and other items of artistic value which had been donated by the Ottoman and Safavi dynasties respectively.[17]

Very few Ottoman festivities of the seventeenth century were in any way connected with the annual cycle. This perhaps was due to the fact that the two principal Muslim feasts, namely the Feast of Sacrifices and the Ramadan Bayramı which marks the conclusion of the fast month of Ramadan, are both determined by the lunar calendar.[18] On the other hand, only the solar year had any significance for the harvest and therefore for the everyday lives of the ordinary population. Certainly both Muslim feasts were celebrated by visits of congratulation and good wishes, in palace circles as well as among less exalted inhabitants of the empire. But festivities organized upon these occasions never competed in brilliance with the celebrations connected with the dynastic life-cycle. Thus in spite of the role of religion in public life, Ottoman festivities of the seventeenth century were much more secular than those celebrated in Europe during the same period.[19]

Ottoman festivities have captured the attention of twentieth-century researchers mainly because of the opportunities they provided for the performing arts. Performances were public in character; they generally were held in the open air, and there was no equivalent to the theatre or opera house, open only to invited or ticket-purchasing visitors. For the duration of the festivities, restrictions on the appearance of women in public were considerably relaxed. Performers included acrobats, jugglers and sword dancers; plays, either pantomimic or dramatic in character, also were shown. Other literary activities included the recitation of poetry.

Public festivities in the Ottoman Empire resembled those of sixteenth- and seventeenth-century Europe: much time, money and effort was spent upon various types of non-permanent decoration, which imitated nature or else architecture. In the Ottoman case, cones or pyramids decorated with fruit often adorned wedding or circumcision festivities.[20] Architectural representations included the famous three-dimensional model of the Süleymaniye paraded during the circumcision festivities of Mehmed III, more than twenty-five years after the completion of the building. This model must have been remarkable because of its scale and lavishness, particularly as three-dimensional models were still something of a rarity.[21]

In addition to displaying a young prince(ss) and thereby the rejuvenation and permanence of the dynasty, Ottoman festivities provided an opportunity to establish and renew the bonds between the sultan and the population of the capital. Since important festivities were replicated in Aleppo or Cairo, ties with the inhabitants of the more important provincial cities were cemented as well. The parade of guildsmen, who either carried along the symbols of their craft or else had prepared floats which showed them actually exercising their special skills, were a marked feature of sixteenth- and seventeenth-century festivals. Such a parade formed part of the 1582 festivities in honour of the young Mehmed III, and has been illustrated in a series of famous miniatures. Another parade of İstanbul craftsmen took place in 1657, during the war over Crete, while the circumcision festivities of 1675 also featured a procession of guildsmen.[22] In all these instances, the craftsmen were ordered to expend sums of money which, relative to their rather meager incomes, must have constituted very considerable sacrifices. On the other hand, the sultan showed his appreciation by gifts of money. While we cannot determine whether the exchange was approximately equal, the ruler and the İstanbul craftsmen thus were linked by a reciprocal exchange of gifts. The significance of the sultan's tie to the craftsmen of the empire is apparent from the custom of having young princes trained in a craft. No special studies as yet have been made regarding the craftsmanship of sultans during the late sixteenth and seventeenth centuries, yet this linkage of the ruler to the world of the craftsman certainly was not considered trivial.[23]

THE OTTOMAN PALACE AS AN IMAGE OF THE RULER'S POWER

Ottoman palace architecture and its meaning will only be touched upon very briefly here.[24] The *pars pro toto* which symbolized an Ottoman palace or mansion was its gate (*kapı, bab*). In fact the monumental gate was of crucial importance both because of the number of guards quartered there and because it was the place at which the ruler emerged from the secluded confines of his residence and contacted the outside world. At the end of the sixteenth century, the throne where Murad III received ambassadors and other dignitaries was located immediately behind the gate that separates the second from the third courtyard of Topkapı Sarayı. Ceremonies of the palace emphasized this feature of royal seclusion, which became more and more marked between the fifteenth and seventeenth centuries. Mehmed the Conqueror is usually credited with inventing the ceremonial that raised the sultan above even his most prominent subjects by isolating him. But the ulema of the Conqueror's times publicly conversed and joked with the ruler in a manner difficult to envisage for later periods.[25] The seclusion of the ruler was further intensified in the course of the sixteenth century. Given this course of affairs, the role of the gateway as the proper frame for the appearance of the ruler must have increased.

The other key element of Ottoman palace and well-to-do residential architecture was the *köşk* (kiosk), a small structure with many windows providing a view of gardens and the landscape in general. In our modern view of the Topkapı Palace, this type of structure is particularly associated with the seventeenth century since, apart from the Conqueror's own Çinili Köşk, we possess practically no examples of pre-seventeenth century royal kiosk architecture. On the other hand, Murad IV's (1623–40) successes in the Iranian wars were commemorated by the construction of the Revan and Baghdad kiosks, while İbrahim I was responsible for the seaside kiosk known as the Sepetçiler Köşkü.[26] In this environment, stress was laid upon closeness to nature, in the shape of arbors, ponds and a view of the nearby Golden Horn. As a concession to monumentality these kiosks were built in stone and not wood, as was common enough in less formal settings and even in the palace grounds themselves. But otherwise the scale of these buildings was in no way imposing, and the effect intended was that of elegance rather than of power.

Kiosks, gates and most larger buildings were assigned their place in the hierarchically organized whole which made up the palace, by being located adjacent to or in the vicinity of one of the major courts. Taken together, the four main courts and their appendages constituted the core of the palace's built-up area. This setup predated the seventeenth century and was to remain a permanent feature of the Topkapı Palace. Judging from the buildings still in existence, it would seem that seventeenth-century rulers concentrated their attentions upon the Harem and the third court. Throughout the history of the palace, this area had been assigned to the sultan himself, as opposed to the second court given over to the Imperial Council and court officials. As most seventeenth-century rulers tended to leave government business to viziers and the now fully developed Ottoman bureaucracy, this concentration upon the residential sphere of the sultan appears understandable.

On the other hand, new forms of making the ruler visible to the public were devised in the seventeenth century, so that one may guess at a counter-trend against the increasing withdrawal of the sultan from public life. Hunting as a royal pastime, to which Mehmed IV particularly was devoted, was sometimes justified on the grounds that it permitted the ruler to meet people who otherwise would never have access to the court. Moreover while it once had been possible for non-courtiers to present petitions to the sultan when the latter left the palace for Friday prayers, after 1650 it was deemed necessary to provide a more elaborate setting for these meetings. Beginning with the Yeni Cami (completed in 1664), mosques founded by members of the ruling family often included a pavilion directly connected to the mosque. Such a pavilion was often lavishly decorated and its upper floor made accessible to coaches and horses by means of a ramp.[27] Ahmed III, who ascended the throne in 1703, was noted for his interest in kiosks and summer palaces outside the confines of the palace, and for his frequent entertainments in these locations.[28]

Thus it would seem that the representation of seventeenth-century Ottoman sultans through palace construction, festivities and ceremonial evolved in two different directions. At the most public and official state occasions, the ruler's hieratic dignity, and the role of the high officials authorized to speak in his name, was emphasized by having him appear for only a brief instant and speak but a few words. At the same time, however, the ruler was publicly shown to enjoy the pleasures and amenities which his quality as sultan afforded him. The tendency to represent the ruler in this fashion by far predates the Ottoman Empire: the hunt, drinking and dancing girls constituted a frequently represented feature of kingship even in Sassanian and Umayyad times.[29] Thus, the ruler was legitimized by publicly enjoying what was inaccessible to most mortals and, in the case of wine, even prohibited. However, in Ottoman politics of the later seventeenth and early eighteenth centuries, there seems to have been a definite limit beyond which the ruler's public enjoyment of pleasure ceased to be legitimizing and turned into its opposite. Mehmed IV was deposed, at least in part, due to his excessive involvement with the hunt.[30] In the early eighteenth century, the pleasure abodes of Ahmed III and his courtiers were to arouse the violent opposition of certain sections of the İstanbul population; so much so that the rebels demolished Sadabad after Ahmed III's deposition in 1730. A parallel from eighteenth-century French history easily comes to mind. While in the previous century Louis XIV had built Versailles by using an appreciable degree of force and violence, it was not Versailles but the more modest pleasure abodes of Trianon which materially contributed toward discrediting the French dynasty in the second half of the eighteenth century.

Perhaps the pietistic currents so strong in İstanbul during the second half of the seventeenth century were in part responsible for lowering the level of tolerance toward royal enjoyment of pleasure. When Sheikh Mehmed Vani was influential at court, a wide audience was ensured for the latter's Sharia-minded preaching. The fact may be worth considering even though people like Patrona Halil, the leader of the rebellion which finally overturned Ahmed III, were not apparently much involved with religious concerns. [31]

The decreasing emphasis on the sultan's role in government functions, and the growing stress upon imperial enjoyment of pleasure may reflect not so much the "Ottoman decline" so frequently argued by previous generations of historians, but rather the ascendency of an institutionalized bureaucracy. This shift probably played some role in discrediting individual rulers, and thus facilitating their removal. Such "delegitimization" and the fragility of imperial tenure of office in turn served the interests of higher-level Ottoman officials, who thereby ensured a sultan amenable to their wishes would be placed upon the throne.

THE IMAGE OF A WARRIOR SULTAN

The counter-image to the ruler as an all-but inert symbol of the state and an addict to worldly pleasures is that of the warrior sultan who takes the field in person and conquers extensive provinces from the infidel. This image was still powerful in the minds of seventeenth-century Ottoman audiences, and several rulers attempted to live up to it. Thus Mehmed III was present at the battle of Mezsokerestes (1593), while Osman II participated in person in campaigns against Poland, and Murad IV led Ottoman armies to the reconquest of Baghdad. Toward the end of the century, we find Mustafa II, along with his mentor Feyzullah, taking an active part in a campaign against the Habsburgs.[32] In a context where a fairly developed bureaucracy controlled many aspects of the empire's administration, the sultan's personal participation in a campaign conferred considerable status and legitimacy. On the other hand, both Osman II and Mustafa II were deposed, and Osman II was even killed in a Janissary rebellion. The legitimizing role of campaigning was easily offset by other factors.

Under these circumstances it became important to emphasize the participation of the sultan in victorious campaigns through appropriate ceremonies and celebrations. For only in this manner could feats of arms that had taken place in remote provinces be made immediately visible to the Janissaries and craftsmen of the capital. In the case of Mehmed III's Eğri campaign, the parade of the victorious sultan into his capital (1596) was commemorated in a miniature. Along the route taken by the ruler, the inhabitants of İstanbul lined the road, holding up decorated fabrics so that the parade passed in front of a colorful backdrop. In addition the extraordinary character of a victory parade was further stressed by the presence of women, who were not only tolerated but actually required.[33] The image of the victorious ruler was also evoked in festivities of a more peaceful character, such as circumcisions and weddings, where the burning of a model of an enemy fortress constituted a favorite entertainment.[34] Thus, even though in the later sixteenth and in the seventeenth century actual campaigning on the part of Ottoman rulers was not a frequent occurrence, festivities and ceremonial made it possible to keep the model of the warrior sultan alive.

CONCLUSION

At present, political historians have not concerned themselves much with the meaning of Ottoman court festivities and ceremonial; and historians of the performing arts, who have expressed an interest in these matters, are still mainly engaged in the collection and sifting of raw material. While certain art historians have recently become involved with the symbolic representation of the sultan's power, anthropologists dealing with the Middle East, unlike some of their colleagues concerned with Africa, have rarely approached these issues. As a result we are still very far removed from a full understanding of Ottoman ceremonies and festivities, but at least it has become clear that this is due to a lack of interest on the part of twentieth-century researchers and not to lack of source material.

At the same time, our comprehension of festivities is not always facilitated by the detailed European descriptions of Ottoman ceremonial: these outsiders were likely to misunderstand what they saw. In this respect Ottoman archival records may become available as a corrective once the necessary spadework has been done.[35] However, the outside observer may at times have the advantage of naiveté. Thus contemporary travelers recorded the presence of Kanuni Süleyman at the festive shows of his reign, but the seventeenth-century historian Peçevi thought it necessary to stress Kanuni's gravity and seriousness by claiming that the ruler did not attend these performances.[36] As this example shows, an investigation of Ottoman festivities and their meaning encompasses a study of the attitudes with which various kinds of witnesses and seventeenth-century historians regarded the events in question. We are dealing with the mentalities of sultans, high-level officials, European diplomats or casual observers. Novel and fruitful studies can be expected in this field.

NOTES

1 Faroqhi (1990), pp. 142ff; Evliya Çelebi (1896–97 to 1938), IX, pp. 752–54; Ibn Djubayr, tr. Gaudrefroy-Desmombynes, II, p. 149.

2 Faroqhi (1990), p. 40.

3 Evliya Çelebi (1896–97 to 1938), IX, pp. 772–73.

4 Sauvaget (1937); Barbir (1980), pp. 133ff.

5 Wustenfeld, (repr. 1964), p. 302.

6 Evliya Çelebi (1896–97 to 1938), X, pp. 433–34.

7 *Ibid.*, IX, p. 566; Maundrell (repr. 1963), pp. 171ff. Uzunçarşılı's remarks on İstanbul ceremonies concern mainly the eighteenth century. Jacques Jomier has used a book by the organizer of many sixteenth-century pilgrimages, Abdu'l-Kadir al Djazari, to document the continuity of Cairene customs between the Mamluk period and the reign of Süleyman the Lawgiver. However, both Uzunçarşılı and Jomier ignore the vast treasury of information that Evliya Çelebi has accumulated, especially with respect to the *hajj*-related festivities of Cairo: Uzunçarşılı (1945), pp. 181–83; Jomier (1953), pp. 74ff.

8 Ali, ed. Tietze (1975), pp. 55–56.

9 And (1982), pp. 12–13.

10 *Ibid.*, p. 13.

11 Nutku (1972).

12 And (1982), pp. 22ff.

13 Appointed in 1671. Türek and Derin (1969–70), pt. 1, p. 217.

14 For a description see Reyhanlı (1983), pp. 62–63.

15 And (1982), p. 3.

16 *Ibid.*, p. 26.

17 BBA, MD 24, p. 44, no 124 (1573–74).

18 And (1982), p. 1.

19 *Ibid.*, p. 6.

20 Nutku (1972), pp. 67–71.

21 Necipoğlu-Kafadar (1986a), p. 239.

22 Mantran (1962), p. 353; Nutku (1972), pp. 73–76.

23 Lowry, oral communication (Chicago, 1986).

24 Necipoğlu (1991) throws new light on the workings of the Ottoman palace. The present chapter is greatly indebted to her work.

25 Taşköprüzade tr. Rescher (1927), pp. 75–76.

26 Nayır (1975), p. 239; see also Goodwin (1971).

27 Nayır (1975), p. 157.

28 Aktepe (1958b), pp. 46–53.

29 Grabar (1973), p. 157.

30 On the actual course of events, compare Abou-El-Haj (1983), pp. 46–47.

31 Aktepe (1958b), *passim*.

32 Abou-El-Haj (1983), pp. 53–54.

33 Reyhanlı (1983), p. 66.
34 Reyhanlı (1983), p. 57; Nutku (1972), p. 115.
35 Filiz Çalışlar is currently preparing a dissertation on Ottoman records of court ceremonial under the direction of Prof. Mübahat Kütükoğlu.
36 Nutku (1972), p. 2.

॑

BIBLIOGRAPHY

Abdel Nour, Antoine (1982). *Introduction à l'histoire urbaine de la Syrie ottomane (XVI–XVIII siècles)*, Beirut.

Abou-El-Haj, Rifa'at, A. (1974). "The Ottoman vezir and pasha households 1683–1703: a preliminary report," *JAOS*, XCIV, 438–47.

(1984). *The 1703 rebellion and the structure of Ottoman politics*, Leiden.

(1991). *Formation of the modern state: the Ottoman Empire, sixteenth to eighteenth centuries*, Albany.

Abu-Husayn, Abdul-Rahim (1985). *Provincial leaderships in Syria, 1575–1650*, Beirut.

Adanır, Fikret (1982). "Heiduckentum und osmanische Herrschaft, sozialgeschichtliche Aspekte der Diskussion um das frühneuzeitliche Räuberwesen in Südosteuropa," *SF*, XLI, 43–83.

Aigen, Wolffgang (1980). *Sieben Jahre in Aleppo (1656–63). Ein Abschnitt aus den Reiss-Beschreibungen des Wolffgang Aigen*, Andreas Tietze, ed., Vienna.

Akarlı, Engin (1986). "Gedik: implements, mastership, shop usufruct and monopoly among İstanbul artisans, 1750–1850," *Wissenschaftskolleg Berlin Jahrbuch*, 223–231.

Akdağ, Mustafa (1959, 1971). *Türkiye Iktisadi ve Içtimai Tarihi*, 2 vols., Ankara.

(1963) *Celali İsyanları (1550–1603)*, Ankara.

Aktepe, Münir. (1958a) "İstanbul'un Nüfus Meselesine Dair Bazı Vesikalar," *TD*, IX (13), 1–30.

(1958b). *Patrona İsyanı (1730)*. İstanbul.

(1970). "İpşir Mustafa Paşa ve kendisi ile ilgili bazı belgeler," *TD*, XXIV, 45–58.

Alexander, John (1985). "Law of the conqueror (the Ottoman state) and law of the conquered (the Orthodox Church): the case of marriage and divorce," *XVI Congrès international des sciences historiques, Rapports*, 2 vols., Stuttgart, II, pp. 369–70.

Ali, Mustafa (1975). *Mustafa Ali's description of Cairo of 1599*, trans. and ed. by Andreas Tietze, Vienna.

Ambraseys, N. N. and Caroline Finkel (1987). "The Anatolian earthquake of 17 August 1669," in V. Lee, ed., *Proceedings of the symposium on historical seismographs and earthquakes*, Tokyo, pp. 400–7.

And, Metin (1982). *Osmanlı Şenliklerinde Türk Sanatları*, Ankara.

Anderson, Sonia P. (1989). *An English consul in Turkey, Paul Rycaut at Smyrna (1667–78)*, Oxford.

Andreasyan, D. Hrand (1964). ed., *Polonyalı Simeon'un Seyahatnamesi, 1608–19*, İstanbul.

(1976). "Celalilerden Kaçan Anadolu Halkının Geri Gönderilmesi", in *Ord. Prof. İsmail Hakkı Uzunçarşılı'ya Armağan*, Ankara, pp. 45–54.

Ashtor, Eliyahu (1978). "Les lainages dans l'Orient médiéval," reprint in: Eliyahu Ashtor, *Studies on the Levantine Trade in the Middle Ages*, London.

(1984). "Die Verbreitung des englischen Wolltuches in den Mittelmeerländern in Spätmittelalter," *Vierteljahrsschrift für Sozial- und Wirtschaftsgeschichte*, 71, 1–29.

Ayalon, David (1977). *Studies on the Mamluks of Egypt (1250–1517)*, London.

Aymard, Maurice (1966). *Venise, Raguse et le commerce du blé pendant la seconde moitié du XVIe siècle*, Paris.

Bachrouch, Tauofik (1977). *Formation sociale barbaresque et pouvoir à Tunis au XVIIe siècle*, Tunis.

Baer, Gabriel (1970a). "The structure of Turkish guilds and its significance for Ottoman social history," *Proceedings of the Israel Academy of Sciences and Humanities*, IV (10), 176–96.

(1970b). "The administrative, economic and social functions of Turkish guilds," *IJMES*, I, 28–50.

(1970c). "Guilds in Middle Eastern history," in M. A Cook, ed., *Studies in the economic history of the Middle East*, London, pp. 11–30.

Barbir, Karl K. (1980). *Ottoman rule in Damascus 1708–58*, Princeton Studies on the Near East, Princeton.

Barkan, Ömer Lütfi (1943). *XV. ve XVI. Asırlarda Osmanlı İmparatorluğunda Zirai Ekonominin Hukuki ve Mali Esasları, I: Kanunlar*, İstanbul.

(1953–54). "H 933–934 (1527–28) Mali Yılına ait bir Bütçe Örneği," *İFM*, XV, (1–4), 251–77.

(1955–56a). "Osmanlı İmparatorluğu Bütçelerine Dair Notlar," *İFM*, XVII (1–4), 193–224.

(1955–56b). "1070–1071 (1660–61) Tarihli Osmanlı Bütçesi ve bir Mukayese," *İFM*, XVII (1–4), 304–47.

(1962–63). "Şehirlerin Teşekkül ve İnkişafı Tarihi Bakımından Osmanlı İmparatorluğunda İmaret Sitelerinin Kuruluş ve İşleyiş Tarzına ait Araştırmalar", *İFM*, XXIII (1–2), 239–96.

(1966). "Edirne Askeri Kassamına Ait Tereke Defterleri (1545–1659)," *Bl*, III (5–6), 1–479.

(1972–79). *Süleymaniye Cami ve İmareti İnşaatı (1550–57)*, 2 vols., Ankara.

(1975). "The price revolution of the sixteenth century: a turning point in the economic history of the Near East," *IJMES*, VI, 3–28.

Barkan, Ömer Lütfi and Ekrem Hakkı Ayverdi (1970). *İstanbul Vakıfları Tahrir Defteri 953 (1546) Tarihli*, İstanbul.

Barker, Thomas M. (1982). *Doppeladler und Halbmond, Entscheidungsjahr 1683*, transl. and ed. by Peter and Getraud Broucek, Graz, Vienna, Cologne.

Bayerle, Gustav (1980). "The compromise at Zsitvatorok," *AO*, VI, 5–53.

Behrens-Abouseif, Doris (1985). *Azbakiyya and its environs from Azbak to Ismail, 1476–1879*, Cairo.

Bellan, Lucien-Louis (1932). *Chah ʿAbbas I, Sa vie, son histoire*, Paris.

Bodman, Herbert L. (1963). *Political factions in Aleppo, 1760–1826*, Chapel Hill, N.C.

Bostan, Idris (1992). *Osmanlı Bahriye Teşkilâtı: XVII. Yüzyılda Tersâne-i Âmire.* Ankara.

Boxer, C. R. (1935). "Anglo-Portuguese rivalry in the Persian Gulf, 1615–35," in Edgar Prestage, ed., *Chapters in Anglo-Portuguese relations*, Watford, pp. 46–129.

Braude, Benjamin (1979). "International competition and domestic cloth in the Ottoman Empire, 1500–1650: a study in undevelopment," *R*, II(3), 437–451.

(1982). "Foundation myths of the *millet* system," in Benjamin Braude and Bernard Lewis, eds., *Christians and Jews in the Ottoman Empire*, 2 vols., New York and London, I, pp. 69–88.

Braudel, Fernand (1949, 2nd edn. 1966). *La Méditerranée et le monde méditerranéen à l'époque de Philippe II*, 1st ed., Paris; 2nd ed., 2 vols., Paris.

(1979). *Civilisation matérielle, économie et capitalisme, XV–XVIIIe siècle*, 3 vols., Paris: I: *Le possible et l'impossible*, II; *Les jeux de l'échange*, III: *Le temps du monde.*

Busbecq, Ogier Ghiselin von (1926). *Vier Briefe aus der Türkei*, trans. by Wolfram von den Steinen, Erlangen.

Caʿfer Efendi (1987). *Risale-i miʿmariyye, an early seventeenth century Ottoman treatise on architecture*, trans. and ed. by Howard Crane, Leiden and New York.

Carter, Francis W. (1972). *Dubrovnik (Ragusa): a classic city-state*, London and New York.

Cenner-Wilhelmb, Gisela (1983). "Feind oder zukünftiger Verbündeter? Zur Beurteilung der politischen Rolle des Emerikus Thököly in den grafischen Blättern seiner Zeit," in Gernot Heiss and Grete Klingenstein, eds., *Das Osmanische Reich und Europa 1683 bis 1789: Konflikt, Entspannung und Austausch*, Vienna.

Cernovodeanu, Paul (1969). "Les marchands balkaniques, intermédiaires du commerce entre l'Angleterre, la Valachie et la Transylvanie durant les années 1660–1714," *Actes du Premier Congrès International des Études Balkaniques et Sud-est Européennes*, III, Sofia, pp. 650–71.

Cezar, Mustafa (1965). *Osmanlı Tarihinde Levendler*, İstanbul.

Cezar, Yavuz (1986). *Osmanlı Maliyesinde Bunalım ve Değişim Dönemi (XVIII. yy.dan Tanzimat'a Mali Tarih)*, İstanbul.

Chaudhuri, K. N. (1978). *The trading world of Asia and the English East India Company*, Cambridge.

(1985) *Trade and civilization in the Indian Ocean, an economic history from the rise of Islam to 1750*, Cambridge.

Cohen, Amnon (1982). "On the realities of the *millet* system: Jerusalem in the sixteenth century," in Benjamin Braude and Bernard Lewis, eds., *Christians and Jews in the Ottoman Empire*, 2 vols., New York and London, II, pp. 7–18.

(1984). *Jewish life under Islam, Jerusalem in the sixteenth century*, Cambridge, Mass. and London.

(1989). *Economic life in Ottoman Jerusalem*, Cambridge.

Cook, M.A. (1972). *Population pressure in rural Anatolia 1450–1600*, London.

Cvetkova, Bistra (1976). "Les registres des *celepkeşan* en tant que sources pour l'histoire de la Bulgarie et des pays balkaniques," *Hungaro-Turcica, Studies in Honour of Julius Nemeth*, Budapest, pp. 325–35.

Çadırcı, Musa (1980). "1830 Genel Sayımına Göre Ankara Şehir Merkezi Nüfusu Üzerinde bir Araştırma," *JOS*, I, 109–132.

Çağatay, Neşet (1971). "Osmanlı İmparatorluğunda Riba-Faiz Konusu, Para Vakıfları ve Bankacılık", *VD*, IX, 39–56.

Çizakça, Murat (1981a). "Sixteenth–seventeenth century inflation and the Bursa silk industry. A pattern for Ottoman industrial decline?" Ph.D. dissertation, University of Pennsylvania.

(1981b). "Ottomans and the Mediterranean: an analysis of the Ottoman ship-building industry as reflected by the arsenal registers of İstanbul 1520–1650," in Rosalba Ragosta and Luigi de Rosa, eds., *Le gente del mare mediterraneo*, Naples, II, pp. 773–87.

(1985). "Incorporation of the Middle East into the European world economy," *R*, VIII (3), 353–77.

(1987). "Price history and the Bursa silk industry: a study in Ottoman industrial decline," *JEH*, XL(3), 533–50; reprinted in Huri İslamoğlu-İnan, ed., pp. 247–61.

Dan, Mihail and Samuel Golderberg (1969). "Marchands balkaniques et levantins dans le commerce de la Transylvanie aux XVIe et XVIIe siècles," in Association Internationale d'Études du Sud-est Européen, *Actes du Premier Congrès Inter-national des Études Balkaniques et Sud-est Européennes*, III, Sofia, pp. 641–49.

Darkot, Besim (1965). "Edirne, Coğrafi Giriş," in *Edirne, Edirne'nin 600. Fetih Yıldönümü Armağan Kitabı*, Ankara, pp. 1–12.

Darling, Linda (1985). " *Avarız Tahriri*: seventeenth and eighteenth century Ottoman survey registers," unpublished paper given at the MESA convention.

(1986). "The Ottoman *maliye* in an era of change," unpublished paper given at the MESA convention.

(1990). "The Ottoman finance department and the assessment and collection of the *cizye* and *avarız* taxes, 1560–1660," unpublished Ph.D. thesis, University of Chicago.

Davis, Ralph (1967). *Aleppo and Devonshire Square: English traders in the Levant in the eighteenth century*, London, Melbourne and Toronto.

Derin, Fahri (1959). "Şeyhülislam Feyzullah Efendi'nin Nesebi Hakkında Bir Risale," *TD*, X, 14, 97–103.

Eickhoff, Ekkehard (1970). *Venedig, Wein und die Osmanen, Umbruch in Südost-europa 1645–1700*, Munich.

Erder, Leila and Suraiya Faroqhi (1979). "Population rise and fall in Anatolia, 1550–1620," *MES*, XV, 322–45.

Ergenç, Özer (1973). "1580–1596 Yılları Arasında Ankara ve Konya Şehirlerinin Mukayeseli İncelenmesi Yoluyla Osmanlı Şehirlerinin Kurumları ve Sosyo-ekonomik Yapısı Üzerine bir Deneme," unpublished Ph.D. thesis, A. Ü. Dil Tarih ve Coğrafya Fakültesi, Ankara.

Ergenç, Özer (1981). "Osmanlı Şehirlerindeki Yönetim Kurumlarının Niteliği Üzerinde Bazı Düşünceler," in *VIII. Türk Tarih Kongresi, Ankara, 4–15 Ekim 1976, Kongreye Sunulan Bildiriler*, 3 vols., Ankara: II, pp. 1265–74.

Erim, Neşe (1984). "Onsekizinci Yüzyılda Erzurum Gümrüğü," unpublished Ph.D. dissertation, İstanbul University.

Evliya Çelebi (1314/1896–97 to 1938). *Seyahatname*, İstanbul.

Faroqhi, Suraiya (1978). "The early history of the Balkan fairs," *SF*, XXXVII, 50–68.

(1979a). "Sixteenth century periodic markets in various Anatolian *sancaks*: I, İçel, Hamid, Karahisar-Sahib, Kütahya, Aydın, and Menteşe," *JESHO*, XXII (1), 32–80.

(1979b). "The life story of an urban saint in the Ottoman Empire," *TD*, XXXII, 655–78, 1009–18.

(1981). "Seyyid Gazi revisited: the foundation as seen through sixteenth and seventeenth century documents," *Turcica*, XIII, 90–122.

(1982). "Camels, wagons and the Ottoman State in the sixteenth and seventeenth centuries," *IJMES*, XIV 523–39.

(1982–83). "Mohair manufacture and mohair workshops in seventeenth-century Ankara," *İFM*, 41: *Ord. Prof. Ömer Lütfi Barkan'a Armağan*, 211–36.

(1983). "Die osmanische Handelspolitik des frühen 17. Jahrhunderts zwischen Dubrovnik und Venedig" in Gernot Heitz and Grete Klingenstein, eds., *Das Osmanische Reich und Europa, 1683–1789: Konflikt, Entspannung und Austausch*, Vienna, pp. 207–22.

(1984). *Towns and townsmen of Ottoman Anatolia, trade, crafts and food production in an urban setting 1520–50*, Cambridge.

(1986a). "The Venetian presence in the Ottoman Empire 1600–30", *JEEH*, XV(2), 345–84.

(1986b). "Town officials, *timar*-holders and taxation: the late sixteenth-century crisis as seen from Çorum," *Turcica*, XVIII, 53–82.

(1987). *Men of modest substance, house owners and house property in seventeenth-century Ankara and Kayseri*, Cambridge.

(1988a). "A great foundation in difficulties: or some evidence on economic contraction in the Ottoman Empire of the mid-seventeenth century," in *Mélanges Professeur Robert Mantran*, ed. by Abdelgelil Temimi, Zaghouan, pp. 109–21.

(1988b). "Seventeenth-century agricultural crisis and the art of flute playing," *Turcica*, XX, 43–70.

(1990). *Herrscher über Mekka. Die Geschichte der Pilgerfahrt*, Munich and Zurich.

Ferrier, R. W. (1973). "The Armenians and the East India Company in Persia in the seventeenth and early eighteenth centuries," *EcHR*, XXVI, 38–62.

Findley, Carter V. (1980). *Bureaucratic reform in the Ottoman Empire: the Sublime Porte 1789–1922*, Princeton.

Finkel, Caroline (1988). *The administration of warfare: the Ottoman military campaigns in Hungary 1593–1606*, Vienna.

(1991). "The costs of Ottoman warfare and defence", *BF*, XVI, 91–104.

Fleischer, Cornell H. (1983). "From Şehzade Korkud to Mustafa Ali, cultural origins of the Ottoman *nasihatname*," unpublished paper presented at the Third International Congress on the Social and Economic History of Turkey.

(1986). *Bureaucrat and intellectual in the Ottoman Empire: the historian Mustafa Ali (1541–1600)*, Princeton.

Forst de Battaglia, Otto (1982). *Jan Sobieski*, Graz, Vienna and Cologne.

Frangakis, Elena (1985). "The raya communities of Smyrna in the 18th century (1690–1820), demography and economic activities," *Praktika tou Diethnous Symposiou Istorias Neoellenike Pole*, Athens, pp. 27–42.

Frank, André Gunder (1969). *Capitalism and underdevelopment in Latin America, historical studies of Chile and Brazil*, New York and London.

Gaube, Heinz and Eugen Wirth (1984). *Aleppo, historische und geographische Beitrage zur baulichen Gestaltung, zur sozialen Organisation und zur wirtschaftlichen Dynamik einer vorderasiatischen Fernhandelsmetropole*, Wiesbaden.

Genç, Mehmet (1975). "Osmanlı Maliyesinde Malikane sistemi," in Osman Okyar and Ünal Nalbantoğlu, eds., *Türkiye İktisat Tarihi Semineri, Metinler Tartışmalar 8–10 Haziran 1973*, Ankara.

(1984). "XVIII. Yüzyılda Osmanlı Ekonomisi ve Savaş," *Yapıt, Toplumsal Araştırmalar Dergisi*, 49(4), 51–61; 50(5), 86–93.

(1987). "A study of the feasibility of using eighteenth-century Ottoman financial records as an indicator of economic activity," in İslamoğlu-İnan, ed., pp. 345–73.

Gerber, Haim (1976). "Guilds in seventeenth-century Anatolian Bursa," *AAS*, XI (1), 59–86.

(1980). "Social and economic position of women in an Ottoman city, Bursa, 1600–1700, " *IJMES*, XII, 231–44.

(1988). *Economy and society in an Ottoman city: Bursa 1600–1700*, Jerusalem.

Gibb, H.A.R. and Harold Bowen (1950–57). *Islamic society and the West, a study of the impact of Western civilization on Moslem culture in the Near East*, 1 vol. in 2 parts, London, New York and Toronto.

Goffman, Daniel (1986). "The capitulations and the question of authority in Levantine trade 1600–1650," *RRJTS*.

(1990). *İzmir and the Levantine world, 1550–1650*, Seattle and London.

Goodwin, Godfrey (1971). *A history of Ottoman architecture*, London.

Gökbilgin, Tayyip (1957). *Rumeli'de Yürükler, Tatarlar ve Evlad-ı Fatihan*, İstanbul.

Gökyay, Orhan Şaik (1975). "Risale-i Mimariyye-Mimar Mehmet Ağa-Eserleri," in *İsmail Hakkı Uzunçarşılı'ya Armağan*, Ankara, pp. 113–215.

Gölpınarlı, Abdülbaki (1953). *Mevlana'dan Sonra Mevlevilik*, İstanbul.

Gordon, Linda (1983). *Cossack rebellions, social turmoil in the sixteenth century Ukraine*, Albany.

Göyünç, Nejat (1970). "Eski Malatya'da Silahdar Mustafa Paşa Hanı," *Tarih Enstitüsü Dergisi*, I, 63–92.

Grabar, Oleg (1973). *The formation of Islamic art*, New Haven and London.

Griswold, William J. (1983). *The great Anatolian rebellion 1000–1020/1591–1611*, Berlin.

Groot, A.H. de (1978). *The Ottoman Empire and the Dutch Republic, a history of the earliest diplomatic relations*, 1610–1630, Leiden.

Güçer, Lütfi (1949–50). "XVIII. Yüzyıl Ortalarında İstanbul'un İaşesi İçin Lüzumlu Hububatın Temini Meselesi", *İFM*, XI (1–4), 397–416.

———(1951–52). "Osmanlı İmparatorluğu Dahilinde Hububat Ticaretinin Tabi Olduğu Kayıtlar", *İFM*, XIII (1–4), 79–98.

———(1964). *XVI.–XVII. Asırlarda Osmanlı İmparatorluğunda Hububat Meselesi ve Hububattan Alınan Vergiler*, İstanbul.

Hanna, Nelly (1983). *An urban history of Bulaq in the Mamluk and Ottoman periods*, Cairo.

Heinisch, Reinhard (1974, 1975). "Habsburg, die Porte und der böhmische Aufstand (1618–1620)" *SF*, XXIV, 125–65; XXIV, 79–124.

Hess, Andrew (1978). *The forgotten frontier*, Chicago.

Hütteroth, Wolf-Dieter (1968). *Ländliche Siedlungen im südlichen Inneranatolien in den letzten vierhundert Jahren*, Göttingen.

Hütteroth, Wolf-Dieter and Kamal Abdulfattah (1977). *Historical geography of Palestine, Transjordan and southern Syria in the late 16th century*, Erlangen.

Ibn Jobair (1949). *Voyages*, ed. and tr. by Maurice Gaudefroy-Demombynes, Paris.

İlgürel, Müderris (1979). "Osmanlı İmparatorluğunda Ateşli Silahların Yayılışı," *TD*, XXXII, 301–18.

İnalcık, Halil (1953–54). "15. Asır Türkiye İktisadi ve İçtimai Tarihi Kaynakları," *İFM*, XV (1–4), 51–57.

———(1959). "Osmanlılar'da Raiyyet Rüsumu," *B*, XXII, 575–610.

———(1960a). "Bursa and the commerce of the Levant," *JESHO*, III, 131–47.

———(1960b). "Bursa XV. Asır Sanayi ve Ticaret Tarihine Dair Vesikalar," *B*, XXIV (93), 45–99.

———(1965). "Adâletnâmeler," *Bl*, II (3–4), 49–145.

———(1969). "Capital formation in the Ottoman Empire," *JEH*, XXIX, 97–140.

———(1970). "The Ottoman economic mind and aspects of the Ottoman economy," in M.A. Cook, ed., *Studies in the economic history of the Middle East*, London, pp. 207–18.

———(1973). *The Ottoman Empire, the classical age 1300–1600*, trans. by Norman Itzkowitz and Colin Imber, London.

———(1975). "The socio-political effects of the diffusion of fire-arms in the Middle East," in V.J. Parry and M.E. Yapp, eds., *War, technology and society in the Middle East*, London, pp. 195–217.

———(1979). "Servile labour in the Ottoman Empire," in A. Archer *et al.*, *The mutual effects of the Islamic and Judeo-Christian worlds: the East European pattern*, Brooklyn, N.Y., pp. 25–52.

———(1979–80) "Osmanlı Pamuklu Pazarı, Hindistan ve İngiltere: Pazar Rekabetinde Emek Maliyetinin Rolü," *TITA*, II, 1–66.

———(1980). "Military and fiscal transformation in the Ottoman Empire, 1600–1700," *AO*, VI, 283–337.

———(1988). "Şikayet Hakkı: Arz-ı Hal ve Arz-ı Mahzar'lar," *JOS*, VII–VIII, 33–54.

İpşirli, Mehmet (1983–87). "Şeyhülislam Sunullah Efendi," *Tarih Enstitüsü Dergisi*, XIII, 209–56.

İslamoğlu-İnan, Huri (1985–86). "Die Osmanische Landwirtschaft im Anatolien des 16. Jahrhunderts: Stagnation oder regionale Entwicklung," *Jahrbuch zur Geschichte und Gesellschaft des Vorderen und Mitteleren Orients*, 165–214.

(1987a). "Introduction," in *idem*, ed., *The Ottoman Empire and the world-economy*, Cambridge and Paris, pp. 1–26.

(1987b), "State and peasants in the Ottoman Empire: a study of peasant economy in north-central Anatolia during the sixteenth century," in *idem*, ed., *The Ottoman Empire and the world-economy*, Cambridge and Paris, pp. 101–59.

İslamoğlu, Huri and Çağlar Keyder (1977). "Agenda for Ottoman History", *R*, I (1), 31–55.

Itzkowitz, Norman (1962). "Eighteenth-century Ottoman realities," *SI*, XVI, 73–94.

Jennings, Ronald (1972). "The judicial registers (*Şer'i mahkeme sicilleri*) of Kayseri (1590–1630) as a source for Ottoman history," Ph.D. thesis, UCLA.

(1973). "Loan and credit in early 17th century Ottoman judicial records: the Sharia court of Anatolian Kayseri," *JESHO*, XVI (2–3), 168–216.

(1975). "Women in early 17th century Ottoman judicial records – the Sharia court of Ottoman Kayseri," *JESHO*, XVIII (1), 53–114.

(1976). "Urban population in Anatolia in the sixteenth century: a study of Kayseri, Karaman, Amasya, Trabzon and Erzurum," *IJMES*, VII, 21–57.

(1980). "Firearms, bandits, and gun-control: some evidence on Ottoman policy towards firearms in the possession of *reaya*, from judicial records of Kayseri, 1600–1627," *AO*, VI, 339–58.

(1987). "Black slaves and free blacks in Ottoman Cyprus, 1590–1640," *JESHO*, XXX, 286–302.

(1993). *Christians and Muslims in Ottoman Cyprus and the Mediterranean world, 1571–1640*, New York.

Jireček, Constantin (1877). *Die Heerstrasse von Belgrad nach Constantinopel und die Balkanpässe, Eine historisch-geographische Studie*, Prague.

Jomier, Jacques, O.P. (1953). *Le mahmal et la caravane égyptienne des pélerins de la Mecque (XIIIe–XXe siècles)*, Cairo.

Kafadar, Cemal (1986a). "A death in Venice (1575): Anatolian Muslim merchants trading in the Serenissima," *RRJTS*, X, 191–218.

(1986b). "When coins turned into drops of dew and bankers became robbers of shadows: the boundaries of Ottoman economic imagination at the end of the sixteenth century," unpublished Ph.D. dissertation, McGill University.

(1991). "Mütereddit bir Mutasavif Üsküplü Asiye Hatunun Rüya Defteri 1641–43," *Topkapı Sarayı Yıllığı*, V, 168–222.

Katib Çelebi, 1145/1732. *Cihan-nüma*, İstanbul.

Kévonian, Keram (1975). "Marchands arméniens au XVIIIe siècle, À propos d'un livre arménien publié à Amsterdam en 1699," *CMRS*, XVI (2), 199–244.

Khoury, Dina Rizk (1991). "Merchants and trade in early modern Iraq," *New Perspectives on Turkey*, 5–6, 53–87.

Kiel, Machiel (1985). *Art and society of Bulgaria in the Turkish period*, Assen and Maastricht.

Kissling, Hans Joachim (1957). "Zur Geschichte der Rausch- und Genussgifte im Osmanischen Reiche," *SF*, XVI, 342–55.

Koçi Bey (1885–86). *Risalesi, Nizam-ı Devlete Müteallik Göriceli Koçi Begin Rabı Sultan Murad Han Gaziye Takdim Eylediği Risaledir*, İstanbul.

Kreiser, Klaus (1986). "Icareteyn: zur 'Doppelten Miete' im Osmanischen Stiftungswesen," *RRJTS*, X, 219–26.

Kunt, Metin (1974). "Ethnic-regional (*cins*) solidarity in the seventeenth century Ottoman establishment," *IJMES*, V, 233–39.

    (1975). "Kulların Kulları," *Boğaziçi Üniversitesi Dergisi, Hümaniter Bilimler*, III, 27–42.

    (1977). "Derviş Mehmed Paşa, *Vezir* and entrepreneur: a study in Ottoman political-economic theory and practice", *Turcica*, IX (1), 197–214.

    (1981). *Bir Osmanlı Valisinin Gelir-Gideri, Diyarbekir 1670–71*, İstanbul.

    (1983). *The Sultan's servants, the transformation of Ottoman provincial government, 1550–1650*, New York.

Kütükoğlu, Mübahat S. (1978). "1009 (1600) Tarihli Narh Defterine göre İstanbul'da Çeşidli Eşya ve Hizmet Fiatları", *Tarih Enstitüsü Dergisi*, IX, 1–86.

    (1983). *Osmanlılarda Narh Müessesesi ve 1640 Tarihli Narh Defteri*, İstanbul.

Lane, Frederic C. (1966). *Venice and history, the collected papers of Frederic C. Lane*, Baltimore.

    (1973). *Venice, a maritime republic*, Baltimore.

Lapidus, Ira Marvin (1967). *Muslim cities in the later Middle Ages*, Cambridge, Mass.

Van Leur, J.C. (1955). *Essays in Asian social and economic history, Indonesian trade and society*, The Hague.

Lewis, Bernard (1962). "Ottoman observers of Ottoman decline," *Islamic Studies*, I, 71–87.

Lowry, Heath (1986). "Changes in fifteenth century peasant taxation: the case study of Radilofo (Radolibos)", in Anthony Bryer and Heath Lowry, eds., *Continuity and change in late Byzantine and early Ottoman society*, Birmingham, Washington, DC, pp. 23–38.

Lybyer, Albert Howe (1966). *The government of the Ottoman Empire in the time of Suleiman the Magnificent*, New York.

Majer, Hans Georg (1978). *Vorstudien zur Geschichte der Ilmiye im Osmanischen Reich*. I: *Zu Uşakizade, seiner Familie und seinem Zeyl-i Şakayik*, Munich.

    (1984), ed. *Das osmanische "Registerbuch der Beschwerden" "(Şikayet defteri) vom Jahre" 1675*, Vienna.

Mandaville, Jon E. (1979). "Usurious Piety: The Cash Waqf Controversy in the Ottoman Empire," *IJMES*, X, 289–308.

Mantran, Robert (1962). *İstanbul dans la seconde moitié du XVIIe siècle, Essai d'histoire institutionelle, économique et sociale*, Paris.

Marcus, Abraham (1983). "Men, women and property: dealers in real estate in 18th century Aleppo," *JESHO*, XXVI (2), 137–63.

    (1986). "Privacy in eighteenth century Aleppo: the limits of cultural ideals," *IJMES*, XVIII, 1–13.

Masson, Paul (1896). *Histoire du commerce français dans le Levant au XVIIe siècle*, Paris.

    (1911). *Histoire du commerce français dans le Levant au XVIIIe siècle*, Paris.

Masters, Bruce (1988). *The origins of Western economic dominance in the Middle*

East. Mercantilism and the Islamic economy in Aleppo 1600–1750, New York.

Maundrell, Henry (1963). *A journal from Aleppo to Jerusalem in 1697*, intr. by David Howell, reprint, Beirut.

McGowan, Bruce (1981). *Economic life in Ottoman Europe, taxation, trade and the struggle for land 1600–1800*, Cambridge and Paris.

(1987). "The middle Danube *cul-de-sac*," in İslamoğlu-İnan, ed., pp. 170–77.

McNeill, William (1974). *Venice, the hinge of Europe 1081–1797*, Chicago and London.

Mordtmann, J. H. (1929). "Die judische Kira in Serail der Sultane," *Mitteilungen des Seminars fur Orientalische Sprachen*, XXXII, 1–38.

Morineau, Michel (1970). "Flottes de commerce et trafics français en Méditerranée au XVIIᵉ siècle (jusqu'en 1669)", *Le XVII siècle*, 86–87, 135–72.

Nayır, Zeynep (1975). *Osmanlı Mimarlığı'nda Sultan Ahmet Külliyesi ve Sonrası.* İstanbul.

Necipoğlu-Kafadar, Gülru (1986a). "Plans and models in 15th and 16th century Ottoman practice", *Journal of the Society of Architectural Historians*, XLV (3), 224–43.

(1988b). "The Süleymaniye complex in İstanbul: an interpretation," *Muqarnas*, III, 92–117.

(1991). *Architecture, ceremonial and power: the Topkapı Palace in the fifteenth and sixteenth centuries*, Cambridge, Mass.

Nehring, Karl (1983). *Adam Freiherrn zu Herbersteins Gesandtschaftsreise nach Konstantinopel, Ein Beitrag zum Frieden von Zsitvatorok (1606)*, Munich.

(1984). "Die Bocskai-Krone als Objekt des *patrimoine intellectuel*," *SF*, XLIII, 123–33.

Nutku, Özdemir (1972). *IV. Mehmet'in Edirne Şenliği (1675)*, Ankara.

Orhonlu, Cengiz (1963). *Osmanlı İmparatorluğunda Aşiretleri İskan Teşebbüsü (1691–96).* İstanbul.

(1976). *Osmanlı İmparatorluğunda Derbend Teşkilatı*, İstanbul.

Orhonlu, Cengiz and Turgut Işıksal (1962–63). "Osmanlı Devrinde Nehir Nakliyatı Hakkında Araştırmalar: Dicle ve Fırat Nehirlerinde Nakliyat," *TD*, XIII (17–18), 79–102.

Ortaylı, İlber (1980). "Anadolu'da XVI. Yüzyılda Evlilik İlişkileri Üzerine Bazı Gözlemler," *JOS*, I, 33–40.

Özbaran, Salih (1977). "Osmanlı Imparatorluğu ve Hindistan Yolu, Onaltıncı Yüzyılda Ticaret Yolları Üzerinde Türk-Portekiz Rekabet ve İlişkileri," *TD*, XXXI, 66–146.

Panzac, Daniel (1985a). "Les échanges maritimes dans l'Empire ottoman au XVIIIe siècle", *ROMM*, 39(1), 177–88.

(1985b). *La peste dans l'Empire ottoman 1700–1850*, Louvain.

Parry, V.J. (1976). "The successors of Sulaiman, 1566–1617," in M.A. Cook, ed., *A History of the Ottoman Empire to 1730*, Cambridge.

Pascual, Jean-Paul (1984). "The Janissaries and the Damascus countryside at the beginning of the seventeenth century according to the archives of the city's military tribunal," in Tarif Khalidi, ed., *Land tenure and social transformation in the Middle East*, Beirut, pp. 357–70.

Perenyi J. (1970). "Villes hongroises sous la domination ottomane aux XVIe–XVIIe siècles, les chefs-lieux de l'administration ottomane," in Nikolai Todorov, ed., *La ville balkanique, XV–XIX siècles, SB*, 3, 25–32.

Pierce, Leslie (1988). "Shifting boundaries: images of Ottoman royal women in the 16th and 17th centuries," *Critical Matrix*, 4, 43–82.

de Planhol, Xavier (1968). *Les fondements géographiques de l'histoire de l'Islam*, Paris.

Rafeq, Abdul Karim (1966). *The province of Damascus 1723–1783*, Beirut.

(1981–82). "Review of Karl Barbir, *Ottoman Rule in Damascus 1708–1758*," *IJTS*, II (2), 149–52.

Rambert, Gaston (1954), ed. *Histoire du commerce de Marseille*, IV: *De 1599 à 1660*, ed. by Louis Bergasse and Gaston Rambert, Paris.

(1957), ed. *Histoire du commerce de Marseille*, V: *De 1660 à 1789*, ed. by Robert Paris, Paris.

Raymond, André (1973–74). *Artisans et commerçants au Caire au XVIIIe siècle*, 2 vols., Damascus.

(1984a). "The population of Aleppo in the sixteenth and seventeenth centuries according to Ottoman census documents," *IJMES*, XVI, 447–60.

(1984b). *The great Arab cities in the 16th–18th centuries, An introduction*, New York and London.

(1985). *Grandes villes arabes à l'époque ottomane*, Paris: Sindbad.

Reid, Anthony (1969). "Sixteenth-century Turkish influence in western Indonesia," *JSAH*, X (3), 395–414.

Reyhanlı, Tülay (1983). *İngiliz Gezginlerine Göre* XVI. *Yüzyılda İstanbul'da Hayat (1582–99)*, Ankara.

Sadok, Boubaker (1987). *La Regence de Tunis au XVIIe siècle: ses relations commerciales avec les ports de l'Europe méditerranéenne, Marseille et Livourne*, Zaghouan.

Sahillioğlu, Halil (1964). "XVII. Asrın İlk Yarısında İstanbul'da Tedavüldeki Sikkelerin Raici," *Bl*, I (2), 228–33.

(1979–80). "15. Yüzyılın Sonu ile 16. Yüzyılın Başında Bursa'da Kölelerin Sosyal ve Ekonomik Hayattaki Yeri," *TITA*, 67–138.

(1981). "1683–1740 Yıllarında Osmanlı İmparatorluğu Hazine Gelir ve Giderleri," *VII. Türk Tarih Kongresi, Kongreye Sunulan Tebliğler*, Ankara, pp. 1389–406.

(1985a). "Slaves in the social and economic life of Bursa in the late 15th and early 16th centuries," *Turcica*, XVII, 43–112.

(1985b). "Yemen'in 1599–1600 Yılı Bütçesi," in *Yusuf Hikmet Bayur Armağanı*, Ankara, pp. 287–319.

Sauvaget, Jean (1937). "Les caravansérails syriens du hadjj de Constantinople," *Ars Islamica*, IV, 98–121.

(1941). *Alep, essai sur le développement d'une grande ville syrienne des origines au milieu du XIXe siècle*, Paris.

Savory, R.M. (1986). "The Safavid administrative system," in Peter Jackson and

Laurence Lockhart, eds., *The Cambridge History of Iran*, VI: *The Timurid and Safavid periods*, Cambridge, pp. 351–72.

Sayar, Ahmet Güner (1986). *Osmanlı İktisat Düşüncesinin Çağdaşlaşması*, İstanbul.

Schatkowski-Schilcher, Linda (1985). *Families in politics: Damascene factions and estates of the 18th and 19th centuries*, Wiesbaden and Stuttgart.

Sella, Domenico. (1968). "The rise and fall of the Venetian woolen industry," in Brian Pullan, ed., *Crisis and change in the Venetian economy in the sixteenth and seventeenth centuries*, London, pp. 106–26.

Serban, C. (1970). "Le role économique des villes roumaines aux XVIIe et XVIIIe ss. dans le contexte de leurs relations avec l'Europe du Sud-est," in Nikolai Todorov, ed., *La ville balkanique XV–XIX siècles*, *SB*, III, 139–54.

Shaw, Stanford, J. (1962). *The financial and administrative organization and development of Ottoman Egypt, 1517–1798*, Princeton, N.J.

(1968). *The budget of Ottoman Egypt. 1005–1006/1596–1597*, The Hague and Paris.

(1971). *Between old and new; the Ottoman Empire under Sultan Selim III, 1789–1807*, Cambridge, Mass.

Sırman, Nükhet (1988). "Peasants and family farms: the position of households in cotton production in a village of western Turkey," Ph.D. dissertation, University College, London.

Skilliter, Susan (1977). *William Harborne and the trade with Turkey, 1578–1582. A documentary study of the first Anglo-Ottoman relations*, Oxford.

Soboul, Albert (1970). *La civilization et la Révolution Française*, 4 vols.; I: *La crise de l'Ancien Régime*, Paris.

Steensgaard, Niels (1967). "Consuls and nations in the Levant from 1570–1650," *Scandinavian History Review*, XV, 13–55.

(1974). *The Asian trade revolution of the seventeenth century: the East India Companies and the decline of the caravan trade*, Chicago and London.

(1978). "The seventeenth-century crisis," in Geoffrey Parker and Lesley M. Smith, eds., *The general crisis of the seventeenth century*, London and Boston, pp. 26–57.

Stoianovich, Traian (1960). "The conquering Balkan orthodox merchant," *JEH*, XX, 234–313.

(1970). "Model and mirror of the pre-modern Balkan city," *SB*, III, 83–110.

(1974). "Pour un modèle du commerce du Levant: économie concurrentielle et économie du bazar, 1500–1800," in *İstanbul à la jonction des cultures balkaniques, méditerranéennes, slaves et orientales, AIESEE Bulletin*, XII(1), 61–120.

Stökl, Gunter (1953). *Die Entstehung des Kosakentums*, Munich.

Sugar, Peter (1977). *Southeastern Europe under Ottoman rule, 1354–1804*, Seattle and London.

Tabakoğlu, Ahmet (1985a). *Gerileme Dönemine Girerken Osmanlı Maliyesi*, İstanbul.

(1985b). "XVII. ve XVIII. Yüzyıl Osmanlı Bütçeleri," *İFM*, XCI (1–4), 389–414.

Tadić, Jorjo (1961). "Le commerce en Dalmatie et à Raguse et la décadence économique de Venise au XVIIe siècle," in *Aspetti e cause della decadenza economica veneziana nel secole XVII*, Venice and Rome, pp. 237–74.

Taeschner, Franz (1924–26). *Das anatolische Wegenetz nach osmanischen Quellen*, 2 vols., Leipzig.

Taşköprüzade (1927). *Es-saqaiq en-nomanijje*, ed. and trans. by O. Rescher, Istanbul.

Temelkuran, Tevfik (1975). "Divan-ı Hümayun Mühimme Kalemi," *Tarih Enstitüsü Dergisi*, VI, 129–76.

Tenenti, Alberto (1967). *Piracy and the decline of Venice, 1580–1615* trans. by Brian and Janet Pullan, Berkeley, Los Angeles.

Thieck, Jean Pierre (1985). "Décentralisation ottomane et affirmation urbaine à Alep à la fin du XVIIème siècle," in Mona Zakaria et al., *Mouvements communautaires et éspaces urbains au Machreq*, Beirut, pp. 117–68.

Todorov, Nikolai (1964, repr 1977). "The socio-economic life of Sofia in the 16th and 17th centuries," *Izvestija na Instituta za istoria*, 14–15, Sofia, 1964; repr. in *La ville balkanique sous les Ottomans XV–XIXe s.*, London.

(1967–68). "19. Yüzyılın İlk Yarısında Bulgaristan Esnaf Teşkilatında Bazı Karakter Değişmeleri," *İFM*, XXVII (1–2), 1–36.

(1970). "La différenciation de la population urbaine au XVIII s., d'après des registres de cadis de Vidin, Sofia et Ruse," in *idem*, ed., *La ville balkanique XV–XIX siècles*, *SB*, III, 45–62.

(1977). "Quelques aspects de la ville balkanique aux XVe et XVIe siècles. Nombre et population," *Actes de IIe Congrès international des études du sud-est européen*, III: *Histoire*, Athens, 1972; repr. in *La ville balkanique sous les Ottomans (XVe–XIXe siècles)*, London.

(1980). *La ville balkanique aux XVe–XIXe siècles*, Bucharest.

Türek, Ahmed and F. Çetin Derin (1969–70). "Feyzullah Efendi'nin Kendi Kaleminden Hal Tercümesi," *TD*, XXIII, 205–18; XXVI, 60–92.

Türkiye Vakıf Abideleri (1972–). 5 vols to date, Ankara.

Uluçay, Çağatay (1948). "Karaosmanoğullarına ait Düşünceler," in *III. Türk Tarih Kongresi*, Ankara, pp. 241–59.

Uzunçarşılı, İsmail Hakkı (1945). *Osmanlı Devletinin Saray Teşkilatı*, Ankara.

Ülgener, Sabri (1981). *İktisadi Çözülmenin Ahlak ve Zihniyet Dünyası*, İstanbul.

Ülker, Necmi (1975). "The rise of İzmir, 1688–1740," Ph.D. dissertation, University of Michigan, Ann Arbor.

Vaughan, Dorothy M. (1954). *Europe and the Turk, a pattern of alliances*, Liverpool.

Veinstein, Gilles (1976). " 'Ayan' de la région d'İzmir et le commerce du Levant (deuxième moitié du XVIII siècle)", *EB*, XII (3), 71–83.

(1988). "Du marché urbain au marché du camp: l'institution ottomane des *orducu*", in Abdeljelil Temimi, ed., *Mélanges Professeur Robert Mantran*, Zaghouan, pp. 299–327.

Venzke, Margaret L. (1984). "The question of declining cereals' production in the sixteenth century: a sounding on the problem-solving capacity of the Ottoman cadastres," *Turks, Hungarians and Kipchaks, a Festschrift in honor of Tibor Halasi-Kun*, *JTS*, VIII, 251–65.

von Thünen, Johann Heinrich (1990). *Der isolierte Staat in Beziehung auf Land-*

wirtschaft und Nationalökonomie, ed. by Hermann Lehmann and Lutz Werner, Berlin.

Wallerstein, Immanuel (1980). "The Ottoman Empire and the capitalist world-economy: some questions for research," in Osman Okyar and Halil İnalcık, eds., *Türkiye'nin Sosyal ve Ekonomik Tarihi (1071–1920)*, Ankara, pp. 117–25.

Waterbury, John (1977). "An attempt to put patrons and clients in their place," in Ernest Gellner and John Waterbury, eds., *Patrons and clients in Mediterranean societies*, London, pp. 329–41.

Wustenfeld, Ferdinand (1964, repr.). *Geschichte der Stadt Mekka*, 4 vols., Beirut.

Yavuz, Erdal and Uğurel, Nevzat (1984), eds. *Tarih İçinde Ankara, Eylül 1981 Seminer Bildirileri*, Ankara.

Zilfi, Madeline (1986). "The Kadızadelis: discordant revivalism in seventeenth-century İstanbul," *Journal of Near Eastern Studies*, XCV (4), 251–69.

(1988). *The politics of piety: the Ottoman ulema in the postclassical age (1600–1800)*, Minneapolis.

Part III

ċ

THE AGE OF THE *AYANS*, 1699–1812

BRUCE McGOWAN,
U.S. CONSULATE, ST. PETERSBURG

22

☾

A PERSPECTIVE ON THE EIGHTEENTH CENTURY

The precarious international reputation of the Ottoman state successfully was guarded during the better part of the eighteenth century, but then went into swift decline. Fiscal reorganization, caution, and a ration of good luck brought the Ottoman enterprise to the eve of its first war with Catherine (1768–74) with a semblance of success. But Russia's population had doubled in the eighteenth century and Russia shared, though at a distance, European improvements in technology and techniques of government. The formidable adverse shift of power which this produced could be corrected only after the destruction of the Janissary corps in 1826.

If we divide the long century 1699–1812 into two parts, the seam between the two is formed by Catherine's first war. Coincidentally the economic history of the Ottoman eighteenth century also divides, though less distinctly, around the same time. The first sixty years saw credible if unspectacular beginnings in a number of new technologies: glass, soap, sugar, gunpowder and paper. After the 1760s these efforts seem to falter, and in some cases to decline. Though foreign trade expanded somewhat until the 1760s, the value and content of the trade remained unprogressive, since the Ottomans supplied Europe with raw goods, particularly cotton, while receiving finished goods in return.

The unprecedented program of fortress building during the first decades of the century gave perfect architectural expression to a more defensive outlook upon the world. The fact that few great mosques were built in the eighteenth century reflects not so much a lack of means as a lack of confidence. It is arguable whether the Ottoman elites became more or less worldly. But their expectation of worldly success, as defined by their forefathers, was in decline. The architectural expression of this shift in attitude can also be seen in the characteristic civic structures of the century: libraries, schools, baths, fountains, and shoreline pavilions – embellishments to ease life in a transient and unsteady world.

Even after the peace of 1699, reform meant a search for the old forms which had been the underpinning of earlier Ottoman centuries. After a second round of punishment, ending with the Treaty of Passarowitz (1718), we see the first evidence, at the very top of society, of experimentation with Western models. But before this flickering interest could be translated into tentative reform programs, a crucial change was needed inside the palace itself. Ever since the time of Sultan İbrahim, who had crept from the cage to the throne in 1640, the harem mostly had held the upper hand in the palace. For a century thereafter, sultans were unfitted, unwilling or unable to take full responsibility for their theoretically awesome powers. And with the exception of the first three Köprülü viziers in the latter half of the seventeenth century, a long line of grand viziers found it impossible to shake off the influence of the harem and its favorites. Oddly, one of the turning points of the century was 1757, when a determined grand vizier, Mehmet Koca Ragıp Pasha, eliminated the Chief Eunuch, thereby putting an end to a century of harem influence upon the viziers and also, in effect, to the cage system as well.

While the harem influenced political life from above, popular opinion, especially at İstanbul, exerted pressure from below. At several crucial moments in the eighteenth century popular unrest exercised a decisive influence. Usually if the grand vizier was relatively strong and backed by the sultan, the influences of the harem and of the crowd could be resisted. But when the grand vizier was weak, the ulema would join with the Janissary agha in blocking him, almost always in a conservative anti-reformist mode, opposed to any alteration of the inherited constitution of government. Power in the bazaar and in the street was exactly what the classic constitution of Ottoman society had been designed to prevent. But once the Janissary corps had evolved into a kind of militia, melting into a population with whom it married and whom it fathered, it was impossible to prevent the participation of the İstanbul crowd in matters of war and peace and in other questions affecting the fortunes of the state. These uprisings were not intended as revolutions: there was little conflict between classes in the modern sense, and Ottoman society remained too segmented to support uprisings which transcended local concerns.

This unintended union of the military with the populace, a political problem with a long past, accompanied an unintended rift between Muslims and non-Muslims. Ottoman defeats at the hands of European powers and the experience of occupation by foreign armies sharpened the awareness of several Ottoman peoples – the Serbs, Rumanians, and Greeks first of all – regarding their destinies as conquered nations. There were other sources of disaffection near the center. The commercial partnership of the Ottoman minorities with European merchants brought knowledge of a world superior to that of the Muslim majority and, often, the possibility of changing status and even loyalty. The success of these mercantile partnerships, seen against a background of Ottoman suspicion of all wealth not associated with the palace, made alternative investment in industrial activities an unpromising business. Thus, unintentionally, three bills fell due because of relative Ottoman liberality towards foreign merchants: first, the development of a colonial (or peripheralized) pattern of trade, secondly, the partial alienation of minority merchants and agents, and thirdly, the diversion of energy and capital into trade and away from industry.

It helps to understand the Ottomans of this period if we set them against the background of the European "absolutist" states of the age. Neither cameralists nor physiocrats, the Ottomans were free traders by default. Like the physiocrats, they placed great importance on agriculture, which directly supplied the great bulk of their revenues. They might almost be called precocious had they been more aware of what they were doing. But in fact they were trading on terms which they later would have cause to regret.

As fiscalists, rather than economists, the Ottomans were somewhat similar to the "absolutist" states of Europe but at an earlier stage. Their tax system as reformed at the beginning of the eighteenth century was demonstrably less burdensome and more progressive than in neighboring states. Despite their difficulties in maintaining centralized control, their fiscal practices, upon close inspection, may turn out to have been one of their best cards, enabling them to accumulate significant reserves during the first half of the century, "bright coins for dark days," as the Turkish saying goes. However, they did not participate in the new world of credit operations and central banking invented by the Dutch and English, with the result that prolonged war found them dangerously short of staying power.

The increasingly rational bureaucracy evolving in eighteenth-century absolutist states like France and Prussia partly were anticipated by the Ottoman Empire during its classical age. The nation-army which the Prussians adopted was a neater, modernized version of an ideal largely realized by the Ottoman absolutists of the sixteenth century on a

sprawling imperial scale. The crux of the difference between these Western and Ottoman bureaucracies in the eighteenth century lies in their
relative competence. Though we have not proven it carefully, we know
that Ottoman education, even in the elite career lines, failed to advance
and regenerate in step with the times. Like Europe's absolutist states, the
Ottomans had their bureaucracy, but one which was unreformed and
increasingly unable to meet the challenges of the later decades of the
eighteenth century.

The Ottomans, by contrast, made no bargain with an aristocracy as
did other absolutist states. They gave less and, in exchange, received less.
Even their religious aristocracy, if we can call it that, was bound by
Muslim inheritance rules which made it difficult to leave wealth intact
from one generation to the next. And because the sultans had no permanent baronies whose wealth and power were dependent upon their own,
the dynasty and its advisors chose to rely on official cadres who were
rotated in provincial offices. As these cadres declined in effectiveness,
it is no wonder that the center became dependent upon a stratum of
intermediaries in the provinces, men who knew the territory because
they lived there. Indeed the rise of that provincial stratum, with ambivalent powers which could be used either in the dynasty's interests or their
own, was so characteristic of the eighteenth century, and so intimately
intertwined with its problems, that we have chosen to call this their era –
the age of the *ayan*s.

AN OVERVIEW OF POLITICAL CHANGE

Extreme centralization of state power, which in the sixteenth century
had meant decisive military advantages, was becoming dysfunctional by
the eighteenth century. In the two centuries intervening, Western states
drew on new sources of power generated by parts of society which were
allowed to keep a part of their wealth and to enjoy the protections of
developing codes of law. Under the Ottoman system, neither the towns
nor anyone in them could expect the kind of security from interference
which would encourage the technical experimentation, and study of
nature which were among springs of growing power in the West. Instead
the Ottoman ruling clique and the palace collaborated on short-sighted
policies which brought in revenues but stifled technical progress, and
even the maintenance of the indispensable military and bureaucratic
cadres. Paradoxically, this extreme recentralization of resources set the
stage for the most serious decentralization of power in Ottoman history.

The Ottomans' extreme want of money during the long war over Hungary left them with an excessive respect for its power. By this time, their armies depended on huge levies of peasants and others who had to be paid with cash. One price for this policy was very uneven success in the field; another was wrenching disorder in the provinces following each demobilization. To forestall these difficulties, the ruling clique turned to hoarding, as though that were the whole art of government. For the first seven decades of the century, the regime usually was well in the black, but without sufficient resources for a long war.

The weakness of the army also was costly politically. Two serious rebellions, which ended with the unseating of sultans (Mustafa II in 1703 and Ahmet in 1730), took place in the shadow of failure on the battlefield. But there were other causes. Both these sultans, deprived of an education befitting a ruler, relied too heavily on a single advisor, and thus isolated could not measure the discontent of the capital. The nepotism of Mustafa's religious advisor Feyzullah was later rivaled by the luxury of Ahmet's son-in-law İbrahim. In both cases a rebellion blew up which could have been stopped by alert counter action.

The four wars of the first half of this century gave mixed results. Successes were due as much to luck as to competence; during the peaceful middle decades of the century the rulers thus enjoyed a false sense of security. The first of these four wars, fought against Peter of Russia, largely owed its fortunate outcome to the Russians' difficulties with supply. Peter was ambushed (1709) and extracted himself only at the price of giving up Azov, the first Russian foothold near the Black Sea. The second war of the century, against the Venetian–Austrian Alliance, brought success in regaining all that had been lost to the Venetians in the long war, but failure against the Austrians, who grabbed half of Serbia and a piece of Wallachia, ending with the Peace of Passarowitz (1718).

The third war was of a dubious kind, since it attempted to match Russian efforts to capitalize on crumbling Safavid rule in Persia. Traditionally the Ottomans had fought the Persians only when they had to, perhaps because they were fellow Muslims, or perhaps for fear of two-front warfare. The indecisive campaigns in the east brought no lasting gain and instead set the stage for the humiliating Patrona Halil uprising of 1730, in which the luxuriant Ahmed III was replaced by Mahmud I.

In the fourth war, this time against the increasingly suspicious allies Russia and Austria, the Ottomans took back from Austria all that they had lost in the preceding conflict. Russian performance again was hampered by poor supply, and the war ended with extreme good luck at the negotiating table at Belgrade, which was dominated by the French ambassador Villeneuve. Once again France, eclipsed for many decades owing to its ambiguous policies and to the activities of the Dutch and English, reemerged in its traditional role as the Ottomans' best friend in Christendom.

A deceptive period of peace lasting three decades ensued upon the outcome at Belgrade (1739). Beneath the exterior, the costs of the Ottoman policy of parsimonious status quo were accumulating. The first experiment with military reform, overseen by the renegade Comte de Bonneval, drifted away with his death. Wise policies of provincial discipline and international peace, championed by the mid-century grand vizier Ragıp Mehmet, were not matched by efforts to improve the professionalism of the military. The desuetude of the *timarlı* corps was not a great problem since the usefulness of cavalry generally was becoming marginal. However, the Europeans, by advances in artillery, discipline, supply and maneuver, now seriously outclassed the tradition-bound Ottomans without their realizing it.

Neglect of the military was matched by a short-sighted approach to provincial government that aimed only at keeping the imperial coffers filled without enough regard for long-term consequences. Fiscal expedients (explained below) subverted the land regime. Office-holders, such as governors and judges, were squeezed and rotated as quickly as possible. No wonder that provincial and district governments became increasingly dependent upon the advice of locals and that in the more distant provinces, such as Iraq and Egypt, upstarts were losing their fear of İstanbul. The parsimony of the palace aimed at having the money to purchase security in wartime substituted for all other policies which might have improved security – that is, improvement of the military and the bureaucracy, nurturing prosperity, cultivating education and the natural sciences.

The price paid for this neglect became clear through defeats in the ensuing wars. Three wars against Russia (ending in 1774, 1792, and 1812) deprived the Ottomans of the northern shores of the Black Sea, including the Crimea, home of their erstwhile Tatar allies. The Rumanian principalities, which experienced long and increasingly lenient occupations, were edging towards independence. The Serbs, schooled by collaboration with the Austrians in the second of these wars, likewise began to see themselves differently. And since the Black Sea monopoly enjoyed by the Ottomans was finally breached in 1783, the Greeks, plying the new trade with Russia, extended their commercial diaspora and rekindled memories of their history as a nation.

In each of these later wars, the Ottomans also were attacked from within by provincial warlords arisen from the ranks of the tax-farming elite. Whole provinces defected until peace was restored. A climax of provincial horrors, unmatched since the Celali rebellions of the early seventeenth century, tormented the Rumelian provinces, especially in the decade 1797–1807. Arabia was lost to a Wahhabi religious sect, led by the Saudi family. Egypt, impoverished by Mamluk abuses and an invasion of the French (1798–1802), fell into the lap of a talented Albanian mercenary, the famous Mehmed Ali of Kavala (1811).

Defeats spurred piecemeal military reform programs in the 1780s, sponsored by the Grand Vizier Halil Hamid, and the heroic admiral Algerian Hasan. But a systematic European-style reform found its champion in Selim III and a palace clique of like-minded favorites. Selim was the harbinger of a new line of sultans raised to govern outside the cage system. He had early contact with Europeans and was ready to employ them as advisors on a large scale to advise a new-style army (the *Nizam-ı cedid*), and a new-style navy. But this reforming sultan did not have a firm commitment to reform and could not crush the inevitable resistance of the Janissary corps and its numerous allies. Undone (1807), then killed (1808), he left to his great successor Mahmud II the task of outwaiting and outwitting the Janissaries, which took until 1826.

Meanwhile the dependence of the Ottomans upon European good will increasingly became apparent. The French, English, Prussians, Swedes and Russians alternated as allies. By the end of the eighteenth century neither war-making nor peace-making were possible without them. Conversely, and ironically, the European competitors needed the Ottomans for tasks in addition to supplying them with materials and to buying their manufactures. It became safer to allow the Ottomans to continue to occupy real estate too valuable to let fall into the hands of rival governments.

23

͡

POPULATION AND MIGRATION

Contemporary estimates of total Ottoman population around 1800 vary between 25 and 32 millions.[1] Taken as a whole, the Ottoman Empire did not participate in the often dramatic gains registered in Western and especially Eastern Europe after the middle of the eighteenth century.[2] In southeastern Europe some uneven gains, especially in Serbia and Bosnia, represent a partial recovery from the general Mediterranean trough of the seventeenth century.

Any eighteenth-century gains in Anatolia seem debatable, except at İzmir. Tax records suggest that, while the population of Rumelia out-weighed that of Anatolia in the seventeenth century, in the eighteenth century they more nearly were equal.[3] The Arab lands generally, with the possible exception of the Arabian peninsula, were still trending down-ward at the time of Napoleon's expedition to Egypt. It is certain that both Syria and Egypt experienced great losses during the last third of the eighteenth century, owing to the combined scourges of war, fiscal rapa-city and insecurity.[4]

It may seem a paradox that the Ottoman territories were strikingly urbanized, when compared with Europe. The observer Beaujour was amazed to find that only two persons lived on the land in Macedonia and Thessaly for every one person in town.[5] But flight from the land to the towns and cities was one of the main responses to the insecurity and misgovernment of the times. The others were migration into the hills where herding seemed safer than farming, or migration northward into the Habsburg or Russian territories, or an escape into banditry when civilized life had become a travesty. No general measurement can ever be arrived at which will express the great variety of tax burdens and other insecurities borne by the Ottoman peasantries in this century. But the frequent flight of peasants in all parts of the empire and their frequent resort to brigandage speak eloquently of conditions unfavorable to population growth.

MIGRATIONS

Whereas wartime and its after-effects broke loose waves of migration, in peacetime there was a constant trickle. Of the two processes, the latter was the more important but harder to measure. Throughout large parts of the Ottoman Empire, and especially in southeastern Europe, newly established habits of transhumance emerged, not simply shepherds looking for pasture, but men in search of work, cyclically returning to families left behind in poorer but safer places of refuge.[6] At the time of the Patrona Halil rebellion of 1730, İstanbul sheltered perhaps 12,000 Albanian immigrants, who provided the tinder for the rebellion.[7] Similarly, Albanian mercenaries revolted at Tripoli in 1745.[8]

At the end of the century Cairo contained 15–20,000 Moroccans, many of whom had come there with pilgrimage trains bound for the Holy Cities and then stayed on.[9] In bad times the pilgrimage from Syria might swell from a normal assembly of 20,000 to 60,000 or more.[10] In all Ottoman towns there were bachelors' quarters which were locked at night to improve the security of the common people.[11] Migrant and seasonal labor was thus an ever-present phenomenon, more observable in towns only because of the greater numbers concentrated there. Perhaps the Ottoman bachelors can be compared to the wandering poor of Europe, except that in the Ottoman case it was mostly men who wandered, with the expectation of returning to families far away sooner or later.[12]

Waves of migration already were moving as the eighteenth century opened. Muslim Bosnian garrisons driven from Hungary returned to settle in Bosnia, or wherever they could, crossing paths with a north-bound flow of Orthodox Christian Serbs into Hungary, and Bosnian Catholics into Slavonia.[13]

Simultaneously, to the east, the Ottoman government was pushing Turkoman and Kurdish nomads to the edge of the Syrian desert, where it was hoped that they would act as a counterweight to the pressure of Bedouin tribes encroaching upon the towns of Syria and the pilgrimage route.[14] This program soon failed as the displaced Turkomans drifted back to the better pastures from which they had been driven, though recorded attempts to enforce the program occurred as late as 1745.[15]

The challenge to Ottoman authority by the Bedouin tribes of the desert was a secular factor in Ottoman history. This challenge had increased in the seventeenth century with the movement northward of the Anazeh tribes into the Syrian periphery. These were followed by the Shammar tribes in the early eighteenth century, increasing the pressure on Syrian villagers, especially in the south, and upon the pilgrimage caravans which set out yearly from Damascus. East of the Tigris, Kurdish tribes, with a predatory reputation far surpassing that of the Turkomans, drifted southward from Anatolia.[16] Following the battle of Ayn Dara (1711), political realignments on Mount Lebanon drove the Druze faction to Hawran, east of Lake Tiberias, while Christian peasants moved south-ward across Mount Lebanon under the protection of the now-dominant Shihabi princes.[17]

The intermittent northward migration of the Serbs, which had begun again during the long war over the fate of Hungary (1683–99), swelled to great waves set off by each eighteenth-century war, and fell to a steady trickle in between. Famine and epidemic accompanied wholesale loss of life by Bosnia's Muslim defenders during this long war, and the first three wars against the northern powers in the eighteenth century (ending 1711, 1718 and 1739) were accompanied by much famine and epidemic. In eastern Bosnia the formerly predominant Muslim population gradually was replaced by northward-bound Serbian Orthodox peasants, some of whom accepted the harsh conditions of Bosnia and some of whom moved on into the reconstituted *pashalık* of Belgrade after 1739.[18] Many Serbs also crossed the Sava river into Habsburg territory during the 1736–39 war, never to return.[19]

In the Rumanian provinces, the harsh Russian occupation during the war of 1736–39 and fear of servitude drove many peasants into Habsburg territory.[20] This trend continued after the war as up to 77,000 Rumanian peasants fled from renewed Phanariote rule into the Banat and into Transylvania, causing a crisis in government in two Ottoman provinces.[21] These provinces, and the empire generally, enjoyed relatively greater security during the subsequent three decades of peace at mid-century. But İstanbul allowed many thousands of Moldavians to be carried off in 1758 by the Tatars, as punishment for a rebellion against the intensified state effort to channel grain to İstanbul by forced sales in the two Ruman-ian principalities.[22]

With the resumption of war against Russia in 1768, new waves of migration broke loose, followed by others still later, caused by the pro-vincial chaos which prevailed in the final two decades of the period (1792–1812). These late eighteenth-century migrations immediately affected the

Serbs, the Albanians, the Bulgarians, the Greeks, the Tatars and the Arab villagers of the Syrian periphery.

The Habsburg authorities wisely permitted Serbian refugees to settle in their southernmost provinces during the disturbed years of the eighteenth and early nineteenth centuries. These emigrés often enlisted in the longstanding Habsburg border (*Grenzer*) militia under a special regime.[23]

The movement north across the Habsburg frontier marked the furthest stage of the centuries-long southwest-to-northwest advance of the Serbian people from the Kossovo, and from Montenegro, across Bosnia, into what is today Serbia, and beyond into the trans-Danubian zone known as the Voyvodina, including the wedge between the Sava and the Danube known as Srem. Not all those who crossed over stayed, since Habsburg taxes were heavy. During the 1770s and the 1780s, there was much spontaneous northbound migration across the Sava and the Danube, in part responding to the attraction of the new towns of Zemun and Novi Sad.[24] The crossings were especially heavy during the war of 1787–92, when many Serbs were organized into Austrian *Freikorps*, and also during the Serbian war of independence in 1804, 1806, 1809, and 1813, when pressure from the Ottoman ripostes made life dangerous for the Serbs.[25] But the Serbian state to be also was receiving large numbers of immigrants from both north and south, many of them returnees from the Habsburg lands.[26] Bosnia continued to lose as many Serbs across its northern border as it attracted from still harsher provinces to the south.[27]

Albanian tribesmen and mercenaries, migrating from a region that relatively was densely populated at the time, found a place in most of the great retinues of Ottoman Europe during the eighteenth century, and often went much further afield, to Syria, North Africa and Egypt. Alongside the Muslims of Bosnia, they became the leading fighters on the European side. However, they could be difficult to control because of their powerful kinship relations. Used in Greece during the war of 1768–74, they then settled down as predators and usurers, and had to be rooted out long after the war had ended. The havoc they created in defeated Morea caused a great portion of the Greeks there to migrate in the 1770s, some into the Pindus mountains as far as they could go, to Italy, to Austria, to Russia, but above all to the Sporades Islands and the Anatolian shore opposite Greece.[28] Many Moreotes were also sold as slaves during the nine-year Albanian occupation.[29] The flight of Greeks sometimes was answered by a movement of Turkish peasants to take their place, as in this account from Larissa about 1806:

> The Greeks are continually migrating, chiefly to the districts of Ionia gov-
> erned by the family of Karaosmanoğlu; in return Turkish peasants from
> Asia Minor have settled on some of the Larissaean Farms, and have been
> able to live better than the Greeks, because they are exempt from the
> Kharatj [head tax], and some impositions to which the Greeks alone are
> liable.[30]

The Tatars, who until then had been the predators, became the victims
after 1770. Between 1770 and 1784, in what may have been the single
greatest surge of migration during the eighteenth century, up to 200,000
Tatars emigrated out of the reach of the Russians, many ending up in
the Dobruja province on the western shore of the Black Sea.[31] Also, in
connection with the loss of the Crimea, a "deluge" of Christians
(probably mostly Greeks and Slavs) were driven by the Russians towards
Azov beginning in 1778.[32] Once a grave threat to Moscow, the Tatar
nation finally survived only as a diaspora.

Russian occupations of the Rumanian provinces were more orderly
beginning with Catherine's reign. Bucharest began to recover from a
mid-century nadir and also to attract Bulgarian refugees. Each of the
three Russo-Turkish Wars between 1768 and 1812 caused waves of Bulgarian refugees, totaling as many as 200,000, to cross over into the Rumanian provinces, many, perhaps most of them continuing into the newly
conquered Russian territories where they crossed paths with the
retreating Tatars.[33] The second of these three wars also drove many Bulgarians into Thrace and Macedonia.[34] Their fate could not have been
happy since this was also the beginning of a climatic period of two decades in which the newly risen warlords of Ottoman Europe (the *ayans*)
were locked in a struggle for dominance. Between 1797 and 1800, in
particular, there occurred a large-scale flight of Bulgarian refugees into
İstanbul.[35] These movements, like those of the Greeks, brought many
Bulgarians into touch with foreign cultures and stimulated their emergence as a modern nation.

The same wars had further devastating effects because they loosened
Ottoman control over the Arab provinces. The Shammar tribes came
into conflict with the expanding Saudi confederation in the 1780s and
were pushed into northern Iraq. In the Syrian desert the Anazeh were
ever stronger, especially after the arrival of their Amarat kinsmen from
eastern Arabia, 1800–8.[36] The raiding of these decades, the Saudi takeover
of the pilgrimage route, and the loss of Ottoman control over their Syrian
tax-farmers combined to complete the devastation of the villages around
Aleppo.[37]

NATURAL DISASTERS

Virtually all the great cities of the empire experienced natural catastrophes during the eighteenth century. İstanbul was especially vulnerable to fire and suffered tremendous loss of property and life in the great conflagrations of 1718, 1750 (when perhaps 80,000 houses burned), 1756, 1782, and 1787 (when two-thirds of the city outside the walls burned, with a loss of perhaps 40,000 lives).[38] Though İstanbul suffered a great earthquake in 1756, the more usual enemy was epidemic, reflecting the human traffic to which it was exposed. According to the saying of the times, "Pera has three things to curse: plague, fire and interpreters."[39] The capital often traded epidemics with Cairo, as in 1719 and 1720.[40] Especially virulent epidemics, in which up to 150,000 persons died, hit İstanbul in 1719 and in 1770; in 1786 a third of the city may have been lost.[41] The capital experienced many food shortages but, because of the étatist regime which worked to guarantee its food supply, not actual famine.

The most unlucky cities of the empire with respect to epidemic disease were those which functioned as ports and as caravan terminals, especially Aleppo and İzmir. İzmir seems to have suffered from one epidemic or another in more than half of the years of the eighteenth century.[42] Aleppo, likewise exposed to both the traffic of ships nearby and caravans, experienced at least a dozen years of epidemic during the century[43] but underwent its worst catastrophe with the wholesale destruction of its villages by Bedouin raiding in the later years of the century, creating a long-running famine which by 1798 killed half of its inhabitants.[44] Salonica also experienced a dozen years of epidemic during the century, the most serious being in 1781, when 25,000 died.[45]

The cities of North Africa not only dealt with much human traffic but occasionally were decimated owing to crop failures which they did not have the resources to recoup. Cairo experienced several years of hunger in the first decades of the century, then seven severe years of deprivation owing to Mamluk misrule in the period 1780–1800. In 1784, famine drove Egyptians onto the streets of every town in the Levant, as far as Diyarbekir.[46] Trablus and Tunis were hard-hit by famine in 1784 and 1785 respectively.[47]

More isolated cities often were spared for decades, then smitten lethally. Diyarbekir suffered a terrific famine in 1757 in the aftermath of a locust invasion.[48] Famine killed most inhabitants in the siege of Baghdad in 1733; in 1773 an epidemic carried off two-thirds of Baghdad's people, while the same year also decimated Basra.[49]

Albania and the Rumanian provinces frequently were hit by epidemic in the eighteenth century. Bosnia experienced severe epidemics in 1762 and 1783–84,[50] and Belgrade suffered major losses from epidemic in 1794.[51] Epidemics in the towns of the Balkans often had the result of affecting the ethnic balance, as when deceased Muslims were replaced by Orthodox Christians in the towns of northern Bulgaria in the years 1716–18.[52]

POPULATION ESTIMATES

Contemporary estimates vary widely. Though some, like those of the French in Egypt, were based on objective criteria, no census of any part of the empire took place before 1831. (One day mathematical models, applied to scattered and fragmentary documentary evidence, may correct this unsatisfactory situation.) Old İstanbul, within the walls, may have held about 300–350,000 inhabitants when not devastated by fire or epidemic.[53] The total population, including suburbs, amounted to about 600,000 in the late eighteenth century.[54] One Jesuit's estimate early in the century includes among the total about 200,000 Greeks and 80,000 Armenians. Western residents numbered 3,000, not counting 20,000 galley slaves and 4–5,000 domestic slaves of Western origin.[55]

Presumably every loss through catastrophe was quickly made up, since İstanbul was a favorite destination for fugitives and migrants in search of work, as is proven by the oft-repeated decrees of the eighteenth century forbidding further in-migration from the countryside. The Ottoman authorities could not have known what we now suspect: İstanbul, like other pre-modern cities of Europe, could not sustain its population through natural increase alone, but depended upon a flow of newcomers from the outside for its equilibrium.

The population of the Balkans, according to one estimate, fell from a high of eight millions in the late sixteenth century to a mid-eighteenth century low of three millions (Fig. III:1).[56] This estimate is in harmony with the first findings based on Ottoman documentary evidence.[57] Serbia grew swiftly during the eighteenth century, from about 60,000 in 1739 to about 200–230,000 by 1800, much of it owing to immigration from the southwest.[58] Belgrade still had a relatively modest population of about 25–30,000 in 1816.[59]

Rumania's population fell from about a million in 1700 to half that at mid-century,[60] and the population of Bucharest declined along with it from about 60,000 to a mid-century low of 30,000.[61] Much of these losses was owing to flight.[62] Considerable immigration, as well as better

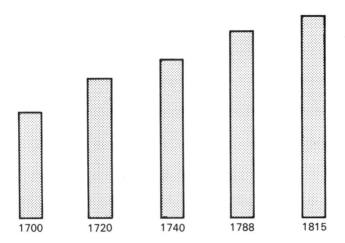

Fig. III:1 Head-tax receipts from the Balkans, inferring population increase in the eighteenth century (Belgrade and Morean blocs omitted). *Source*: McGowan (1981), p. 84.

administration, increased the population to an estimated one million in Wallachia during the first decade of the nineteenth century, and in Moldavia to one-half million. Bucharest then numbered about 80,000, Jassy about 40,000 persons.[63]

Edirne had an estimated 20,000 houses in the early eighteenth century, which may mean a population of about 100,000, the same figure offered a century later.[64] Bulgarian towns are given impressive, perhaps inflated estimates for the second half of the century: Sofia 70,000, Plovdiv (Filibe) 50,000, Ruse (Rusçuk) 30,000, Sümen 30,000, Vidin 20,000, Nicopolis 20,000, Svistov (Zistovi) 20,000, and Varna 15,000.[65]

Sarajevo (Bosnasaray) had an estimated 40–45,000 around 1800 and estimates of population for Bosnia as a whole vary at around one million in this period.[66] The Tsintsar center of Moscopolje, which may have reached 40,000 before being sacked for the first time in 1769, was almost as large as Sarajevo.[67]

Trade boosted the population of several Albanian towns during the eighteenth century. Shkoder (Shkodra) had about 30,000 inhabitants in 1739 but reportedly doubled to 60,000 by 1793.[68] Other Albanian towns at the end of the century: Arta held 10,000 persons, and Preveza 10–12,000. Elbasan already had 6,000 families, and Berat 5,000 families in the seventeenth century, implying populations of 30,000 and 25,000 respectively, though these seventeenth-century figures do seem high.[69]

The population of Greece as a whole was an estimated half-million on the eve of the rebellion of 1821.[70] This represents a comeback from the dark days of reprisal, the 1770s, when the Morea seems to have lost 30–60,000 residents, who either had died or fled to more hospitable places on the Aegean periphery and elsewhere.[71] The port of Salonica (Selanik) was the largest town of Greece, growing spectacularly in the eighteenth century, with a population of 60–70,000 by its end.[72] Other towns of Greece around 1800: Seres 30,000; Larissa (Yenişehir) 20,000; Vodina 12,000; Patras 10,000; and Athens 12,000. Yanina, which was also a Greek town, may have numbered 16,000 in population.[73]

No estimate of Anatolia's population can be offered with confidence, though fiscal records suggest parity with Rumelia in the eighteenth century.[74] Eighteenth-century estimates for İzmir, the premier port of empire, vary between 65,000 and 102,000.[75] Bursa around 1802 is estimated at about 60,000.[76] Ankara was probably equally populous.[77]

The cities of Iraq are thought to have lost much or most of their population during the eighteenth century, largely because of epidemic disease.[78] Baghdad at the end of the century numbered perhaps 80,000, Mosul about 65,000.[79] Basra, which survived a long Persian siege in 1775, was reduced to a fraction of its former populace of 40,000 – perhaps as few as 4,000 persons.[80]

Before the raiding and famine of the 1780s and 1790s, Aleppo's population may have exceeded 100,000, a considerable drop from its seventeenth-century peak, but still impressive.[81] By the end of the century Aleppo may have been close to parity with Damascus although both cities' populations had fallen dramatically.[82] Raiding and predation by the Bedouins and Kurds, already a major problem early in the eighteenth century, had reduced much of the coastal plain to marsh, thus condemning the coastal towns of Tripoli, Sidon, and Latakia (Antakya) to relative insignificance.[83] Yet at the end of the century the towns of Palestine were still considerable: Jerusalem 9–12,000; Acre 8,000; Gaza 8,000; Nablus 7,500; Safed and Hebron 5,000 each.[84] And in the hills and mountains, out of reach of desert raiders, there lived a population which included fugitives from the plains.

The population of Egypt in 1800 is estimated at 4 or 4.5 millions; Cairo held 210–260,000 persons and Alexandria another 10–15,000.[85] These figures represent the low end of a downward slide owing to increasingly chaotic political conditions and accompanying peasant flight, especially characteristic of the late eighteenth century.[86]

Algiers in the eighteenth century was mid-way on a continuum between the 100,000 estimated as its seventeenth-century peak, and the 40–50,000 who remained at the time of the French expedition of 1830.[87] By that time Constantine had about 25,000, Tlemcen about 20,000. Algeria's total population in the early nineteenth century was an estimated 2.5 to 3 millions.[88] In the same period Tunisia had a population of one million.[89] Tunisia was on a growth trajectory in the eighteenth century, at least between 1760 and 1784, after which it seems to have declined.[90] In 1800 the city of Tunis had an estimated population of 100,000,[91] and was recovering from the epidemic losses of 1784–85. Tripoli also was hard hit by a combination of famine and epidemic in 1784–85, losing about a quarter of its population of 14,000.

NOTES

1 Issawi (1980), p. 18; Panzac (1985), p. 516; Issawi (1982), p. 94.

2 Panzac (1985), p. 516; Grigg (1980), p. 59; Abel (1966), p. 276.

3 McGowan (1981), pp. 88–89; Sućeska (1965b), p. 48.

4 A bibliography on Ottoman demography appears in Panzac (1981), pp. 119–37.

5 Beaujour (1800), p. 85.

6 Lampe and Jackson (1982), p. 38; Faroqhi (1984), p. 271; Cvijić (1918), pp. 156–57.

7 Aktepe (1958), p. 170.

8 Dumont (1972), IV, p. 85.

9 Raymond (1973–74), II, p. 471.

10 Rafeq (1966), p. 61.

11 Barkan (1955), p. 304; Todorov (1983), p. 462; Faroqhi (1984), p. 271.

12 Grenville (1965), p. 74; Olivier (1801), II, p. 307.

13 q.v. "Bosna" in *EI²*; Hoffman (1977), pp. 476–78; Jelavich (1983), I, p. 88; ISN (1986), vol. 4, pt. 1, p. 329; Sućeska (1965b), p. 42.

14 Kassimy *et al.* (1980), p. 248.

15 Altınay (1931), pp. 202–6; Barbir (1980), p. 104; Orhonlu (1963), pp. 88–89, 96.

16 Hourani (1957), pp. 94–95; Holt (1966), p. 102.

17 Hourani (1957), p. 95; Holt (1966), p. 121.

18 Sućeska (1980), p. 152; ISN (1986), vol. 4, pt. 1; Vucinich, ed. (1982), p. 17.

19 Lampe and Jackson (1982), p. 45.

20 Jelavich (1983), I, p. 125; Lampe and Jackson (1982), p. 85.

21 McNeill (1964), p. 199; Jewsbury (1976), pp. 66–73; Sugar (1977), p. 137.

22 Eton (1798), p. 301 (based on Peysonnel); Alexandru-Dersca (1957), p. 19.

23 Gavrilović (1969), p. 242.

24 Gavrilović (1969), p. 243; Lampe and Jackson (1982), p. 44.

25 Gavrilović (1969), pp. 242–44; ISN (1986), vol. 4, pt. 1, pp. 377–400.

26 Gavrilović (1969), p. 244; Djordjević and Fisher-Galati (1981), p. 28.

27 ISN (1986), vol. 4, pt. 1, p. 479; Sućeska (1978b), pp. 218–19; Eren (1965), p. 42.

28 Clogg (1976), p. 3; Lampe and Jackson (1982), p. 43; Vacalopoulos (1973), pp. 460–61.

29 Alexander (1985), p. 52.

30 Leake (1967), I, p. 441.

31 Fisher (1970), p. 146.

32 Fisher (1976), p. 65; Eton (1798), pp. 327–28.

33 Kassimy *et al.* (1980), pp. 248, 557; Jewsbury (1976), pp. 66–73; Lampe and Jackson (1982), p. 44.

34 Kassimy *et al.* (1980), p. 557.

35 ISN, Vol. 5, p. 167; Eton (1798), p. 255.

36 Nieuwenhuis (1982), pp. 119, 125.

37 Thieck (1985), p. 134; Bodman (1963), p. 16.

38 q.v. "İstanbul" in *EI²*; Inciciyan (1976), p. 85.

39 Italian version found in Shay (1944), p. 38: "In Pera sono tre malanni: peste, fuoco, dragomanni."

40 Eton (1798), p. 255.

41 Masson (1911), p. 315; q.v. "İstanbul" in *EI²*; Panzac (1985), pp. 46, 60–73.

42 Panzac (1985), p. 46; Nieuwenhuis (1982), p. 64.

43 Bodman (1963), p. 16.

44 Volney (1788), II, pp. 145, 152; Eton (1798), p. 267.

45 Svoronos (1956), p. 135; Vacalopoulos (1963), p. 108; Panzac (1985), p. 77.

46 Raymond (1973–74), I, pp. 100, 106; Volney (1788), I, 193.

47 Stoianovich (1983), p. 339; q.v. "Trablus" in *EI²*.

48 Eton (1798), p. 276.

49 Longrigg (1925), p. 134; Masson (1911), p. 315; Nieuwenhuis (1982), p. 64.

50 Panzac (1985), pp. 77, 109, 116; ISN (1986), vol. 5, pt. 1, p. 477.

51 Popović (1964), p. 309.

52 Lampe and Jackson (1982), p. 38.

53 q.v. "İstanbul" in *EI²*.

54 Issawi (1977), p. 152.

55 Letter of Father Tavillon cited in Frazee (1983), pp. 156–57.

56 Lampe and Jackson (1982), p. 38.

57 McGowan (1981), pp. 80–103.

58 ISN (1986), vol. 1, pt. 1, p. 321, relying on estimates by Cubrilović, "About 40,000 'Turks' are included in this estimate": Vucinich, ed. (1982), p. 25.

59 Popović (1964), p. 347.

60 Peysonnel (1787), p. 194.

61 Lampe and Jackson (1982), pp. 82, 86.

62 Stefanescu (1969), p. 7.

63 Wilkinson (1971), pp. 60–61.

64 Cf. Özkaya (1985), p. 148 (based on a French report) with Issawi (1980), p. 34.

65 Paskaleva (1968a), p. 134.

66 Šamić (1961a), p. 133; Eren (1965), p. 19.
67 Lampe and Jackson (1982), p. 45.
68 Naci (1966), p. 133.
69 Cf. Ars (1963), p. 125; Naci (1970), p. 40, and Pollo and Arben (1981), p. 91.
70 Andreades (1910), p. 171.
71 Camariano-Cioran (1965), p. 537; Dakin (1972), p. 17.
72 Beaujour (1800), pp. 30, 53; Vacalopoulos (1963), p. 98; Svoronos (1956), p. 7.
73 Beaujour (1800), p. 85; Clogg (1976), p. 4; McGrew (1977), p. 113; Vacalopoulos (1973), p. 497.
74 McGowan (1981), p. 113.
75 Panzac (1985), p. 233; Özkaya (1985), p. 143; Masson (1911), p. 552.
76 Walpole, ed. (1820), p. 111.
77 Özdemir (1986), p. 114.
78 Issawi (1982), p. 162.
79 Olivier (1801), II, pp. 357, 388, 400.
80 Cf. *ibid.* with Issawi (1982), p. 101; Volney (1788), II, p. 145; Baer (1981), p. 628.
81 Raymond (1985), pp. 5, 7; Gaube and Wirth (1984), p. 248.
82 Masters (1988), pp. 38–41; cf. Schatkowski-Schilcher (1985), p. 3.
83 Cf. Rafeq (1977), p. 62 with Gaube and Wirth (1984), p. 248; Eton (1798), p. 268.
84 Ben Arieh (1975), pp. 51–53, 68.
85 Cf. Raymond (1973–74), I, p. 166 and II, p. 452; Issawi (1982), p. 101; and Raymond (1981), p. 687.
86 Baer (1982), pp. 57–58; Abdul-Rahman and Nagata (1977), p. 178; Raymond (1980), pp. 170–75.
87 q.v. "Algiers" in *EI²*; Valensi (1977a), p. 34; Julien (1970), p. 290.
88 Valensi (1977b), p. 1; Lacoste *et al.* (1960), pp. 217–18.
89 Valensi (1977b), p. 1.
90 Valensi (1977a), pp. 140, 316; Cherif (1982), p. 74.
91 Issawi (1982), p. 101.

24

۩

THE ELITES AND THEIR RETINUES

The most important changes in Ottoman society and government since the sixteenth century had been gradual, unintended, usually unrecorded and therefore poorly understood. The eighteenth-century Ottoman leadership was unable either to defend effectively what was left of the empire, or to reform the system in a manner which took account of the changing world order. The various expedients of the eighteenth century did not add up to reform. The weakness at the center suddenly became very obvious to the provincial elites after the first of Catherine's wars (1768–74). Ironically the climax of confusion and misrule in this century coincides with the reign of the first real reformer, Sultan Selim III (1789–1807). This well-meaning but irresolute sultan proved unable to master the spiral of violence and disorder in his most important provinces and instead allowed rising provincial warlords and Mamluk elites to find their own solutions.

Important Ottoman institutions, tissues in an ageing body, no longer functioned as intended in the eighteenth century. In a century when the Habsburgs were gaining strength by building a bureaucracy separate from society, the Ottoman bureaucracy lost more of its ethic of service, and some of its separateness from society. Because of the widespread use of personal agents and elite alliances, power washed back and forth between center and provinces in the service of private interests. In the center provinces, an experiment in delegating tax collection and the levying of troops to provincial elites, which was the characteristic development of the century, ended with an unintended reversal in power relations almost fatal to state and dynasty. Meanwhile, in the Arab provinces, never so tightly bound to İstanbul, other elites fought to shake off all controls.

Following are some of the main changes in institutions, then sketches of power shifts in the major provinces. Among institutions which began or continued their transformation in the eighteenth century were the Janissaries, the provincial cavalry, the governors, the judges and, beneath all, the system of state ownership of land (*miri*) on which the empire had risen.

From being a standing army corps, the Janissaries during the eighteenth century evolved into an almost unpaid militia, made up of small tradesmen whose main rewards were judicial and tax immunities, which they increasingly were unable to justify on the battlefield. The second great component of the classic Ottoman army, the *timarlı* cavalry stationed in the provinces, already was moribund by the beginning of the century. Their incomes had declined dramatically in the seventeenth century, and along with their incomes, their numbers. Because they had been part of the reason for the successes of the golden age, the Porte remained ambivalent about them, allowing their decline yet defending their remnant.[1] In some provinces, such as Serbia, their continued existence can be attributed to their employment as a counterweight against the pretensions of local militia. Although only a few thousand *timarlı* cavalry were available to fight in the war of 1768–74,[2] decrees aimed at reforming this ghostly corps continued to be issued, to little avail.[3]

The newly improvised appanages left to provincial governors usually were not sufficient to support the large retinues which had buttressed their power in the seventeenth century.[4] This led in the early eighteenth century to a crisis in incomes and to a plethora of temporary and illegal levies by which this besieged stratum of officials struggled to maintain itself and its dwindling retinues.[5]

Governors and their deputies now were frequently individuals with a scribal, rather than a military background. A European observer at Aleppo, writing at mid-century, remarked this trend, adding that the practice "greatly raised the value of manuscripts for the Sheikhs, who used formerly to have been the only bidders at auctions, and who are unable to contend with rich competitors."[6]

Whether or not the subversion of their incomes deliberately had been intended,[7] a new set of provincial taxes had to be devised to support the governors by legal means, to obviate the need for illegal levies. Since governors now were moved frequently, the new provincial taxes, in order to be effective, required the mediation of local committees of notables (*ayans*), usually themselves prominent landholders, who knew their localities intimately, and who were able to adjust taxes to fit local realities.[8]

The rise of the local committees, whose power in effect replaced the power inherent in the dying *timar* system, signaled a shift of gravity towards the towns, which increasingly contained all the instruments needed for regional control.

Ottoman judges (kadis) also had passed their peak of prestige and effectiveness by the eighteenth century. The Porte shortened their terms in office, starting in the reign of Ahmed III. To counteract the tendency to find jobs for the increasing number of candidates who had completed their training, the itinerant judges were forced into close alliance with standing committees of provincial notables, whose cooperation they increasingly needed in all matters of administration, especially since the old record systems had been allowed to decline, and could be updated only with the help of these district residents.[9]

Official indifference, poor administration, and actual collusion by the courts permitted Ottoman elite figures of all descriptions to alienate estates from the great reservoir of state-owned land (*miri*). Tax-farmers with life-leases and military status were especially well-placed to bring this about. Thus, by the early nineteenth century, some foreign observers believed that a half to two-thirds of Ottoman land was held as family mortmain (*vakıf*) outside state control, though this is open to question. The vast majority of these alienations had been achieved in the course of the eighteenth century. At its end, Selim III sought to recover some of these estates by converting them into state-controlled revenues. Meanwhile the massive alienation of state land had reduced the tax base, while guaranteeing security for many elite families.[10] Abuse of the mortmain institution also deprived many Islamic schools of their material base, thus deepening the educational crises of the learned stratum (the ulema).[11]

Yet another fundamental state concept, the military/non-military dichotomy on which Ottoman society was constructed, changed in the eighteenth century, at least in the European provinces. By joining the various militias raised during the century, or by buying their way into the Janissary corps, Muslim peasants near the European frontiers often were able to take their place in towns alongside the heretofore tax-exempt military class. These pseudo-Janissaries were joined by all those Muslims who participated in tax gathering, and who thereby changed their status, assimilating to the governing class.[12] According to a European who was in Crete at mid-century: "All the Turks belong to some military body. The harach and customs pay all the soldiers except the Janissaries, whose money is brought from abroad."[13]

In contrast, a breakdown of population figures at Ankara for the period after 1785 shows a ratio of tax-liable to tax-exempt persons of about 19:1, a ratio similar to that of the sixteenth century: thus the overflow of the military stratum seems not to have taken place everywhere. It may come as a surprise that in the 1790s the majority in the small garrison at Ankara were non-Muslim.[14]

The state's land reserve (*miri*) system, and the privileged military (*askeri*) status, were thus profoundly changed during the eighteenth century. Many individuals profited directly from the subversion of these two institutions, securing their position among the Muslim elite, or at least among the military class. Nor was there any road to reform without basic restructuring, a process which took place only in the following century.

Against this background of institutional decay, two rising groups stand in dramatic profile: the tax gatherers, and the local committees (*ayan*s) – at first as separate groups with distinct functions, but, with the passage of time, as a single merged class with roots both in the country and in İstanbul. The delivery of provinces, sub-provinces, and districts into the hands of fiscal agents on a temporary basis was already a common practice in the seventeenth century.[15] Governors often were absent either by choice, or on campaign, or between appointments, but the business of tax collecting could not wait and was carried on by deputies armed with full powers. Meanwhile treasury holdings in the same provinces were auctioned off as tax-farms by the central government, and then often renegotiated by the contracting tax-farmers for collection by lesser tax-farmers. These two systems, deputization and tax-farming, merged early in the eighteenth century to form a single tax-farming system, in which the appanages formerly assigned to military officers were counted among the tax-farms pertaining to the treasury, and some portion of these (but never enough) assigned to the provincial governors. Also there appeared a system of life-term tax-farm leases, which raised ready money for the hard-pressed treasury and also were intended to ease the lives of the peasantry, and to preserve their revenue potential. The institutional price was the alienation from the tax-farm reservoir of numerous grants of varying size which then might never revert to the public domain owing to falsified evidence, or to collusion by the life-term lessee with some official. All those involved in tax gathering seem to have aspired to joining the rising class of these life-lessees (*malikaneci*s).

On the rise, with the tax-farmers and life lessees, were the bankers who financed the tax-farming system and who were indispensable to its operation. About a thousand large-scale bidders, backed by their bankers, dominated tax-farming auctions at İstanbul throughout the eighteenth century. The ulema, whose list of abuses in this century continued to include sale of office, usury, and creation of family mortmain, also were involved in the tax-farming system.[16] With the elaboration of the tax-farming system in the course of the century, on the large as well as the small scale, the tax-gathering structure at the sub-provincial or provincial level actually replaced the former structure of government in many places, thus revealing tax gathering as the chief, if not the only, business of government besides defense.[17]

The recruitment of agents for the tax-gathering system helped maintain the Ottoman tradition of upward mobility into the dominant stratum. According to one English merchant at the capital:

> dragomans ... are uncommonly generous to the meanest, and the most indigent Turk, treating them with deference and politeness: when the reason is asked, they tell you, they have seen so many, from the very lowest, rise to the highest stations, that it is necessary to guard against their revenge.[18]

Because of the decline of local record-keeping, the customary brevity of official appointments, and changes in local conditions wrought by time and chance (e.g. depopulation through flight) it became indispensable for provincial tax gatherers, even before the end of the seventeenth century, to have the support and counsel of provincial and district notables (*ayans*). These local figures, who might be merchants, money-lenders, military officers, or landholders, sought to have a hand in the allocation of various taxes. Holders of life-leases had a good chance of taking part in such committees. Conversely members of the *ayan* committees increasingly were appointed as state tax collectors and participated in the imperial tax-farming system in other ways. Supported by the judge of their district, they enjoyed a large degree of illegal immunity, and thus became increasingly influential in the course of the century.[19] To their position as landholders many were well placed to add new functions as money-lenders to villagers in need of help, and ultimately perhaps even as tax intermediaries (*deruhdecis*) able to shelter whole strings of villages from the fisc in return for near total control over village finances.

From the ranks of these local notables, there in time emerged a second, more select group, also misleadingly known as *ayans*. In fact, since they often seized power by force and formed quasi-feudal networks, they were closer to being warlords. The crucial period for their emergence was the war of 1768–74, even though some, like the Buşatlı family of

Albania, already were carving out fiefdoms for themselves years earlier. Muhsinzade Mehmed Pasha, an Ottoman vizier charged with retaking Morea from the rebelling Greeks, quickly discovered that he could do this most readily by calling on the nearby *ayan*s of Macedonia and Thessaly for help in rounding up troops. Militarily, these levies were successful, but often they were Albanian mountaineers, whose rampages would go on in the Morea until rooted out almost a decade later by the famous Algerian Hasan Pasha.[20] Elsewhere behind the Rumelian battle lines, *ayan* grandees called upon to raise and lead militia during this war were discovering that İstanbul's viziers did not have the respect of the army. This discovery led to their dealing directly with the central government, forming a new habit which they did not quickly lose.[21] Using the war as a cover, *ayan* warlords of various origins also appeared in Anatolia, Syria and Egypt, and, like the *ayan*s of Rumelia, these moved a long way towards an unintended decentralization of political power.

Having taken the first draught of *ayan* assistance in the war of 1768–74, the Porte took a near-fatal dose in 1788–92. By this time the Porte's advisors had learned that they could not prohibit the process of decentralization by mere fiat, having issued decrees on the subject which largely were ignored.[22] But some alternative had to be found to the nearly useless Janissary militia. Therefore the Porte relied still more heavily on general levies raised by *ayan*s in Rumelia and in Anatolia, often led by *ayan* chiefs themselves.

Following this war came the greatest crises of the government in this long century: the wide ranging Kırcalı bandit raids of 1797–1807, complicated by Napoleon's invasion of Egypt in 1798 and the rising of the Serbs in 1804. Under Sultan Selim's unsteady leadership, the *ayan* warlords of Rumelia and Anatolia alternately were threatened and flattered, sometimes awarded high offices in İstanbul, sometimes charged with rooting out the very bandits they were fomenting against their rivals.[23] The new century opened with feudal rivals to central power in Greece, Albania, Bulgaria, Syria, Iraq and Egypt. Seen against this context, the Serbs stand out as different because of the national character of their uprising.

THE BELGRADE *PASHALIK* (SERBIA)

When Ottoman rule was restored in Serbia after the Treaty of Belgrade (1739), the Ottoman authorities stationed a large Janissary garrison in the newly rebuilt fortress, and inscribed a sizable territorial cavalry onto the provincial rolls, a force which tended to reside in Belgrade but had its living in the countryside. For perhaps a decade these *sipahi*s were accepted as the senior partners in the military setup. But from the moment of reconquest the Janissary chiefs scouted the Serbian landscape for villages to take under their protection. A decade of competition between cavalry and militia reached a climax in 1762 when the commandant at Belgrade ordered all the Janissary inns destroyed on the road between Belgrade and Niş. But the Janissaries soon emerged from this scuffle as the winners, and thereafter until 1792, when they were ousted from the *pashalık* by a decree of the sultan, Janissary chiefs ran Serbia much as they pleased.

More numerous than the *sipahi*s, Janissaries were able to dispossess or at least dominate the weaker of them, and establish numerous "farms" (*çiftliks*) of their own, on which they took the place of the hapless Serbian peasants in the sense of being formally entitled to the land, thus adding a layer of rents to those due to the *sipahi*s. These were mixed rather than intensively cultivated estates and Belgrade continued to receive its grain cheaply from the Habsburg side. But a variety of dues and services were demanded and obtained from the peasants. After 1792, while the ousted Janissaries sheltered with Pazvantoğlu at Vidin, plotting their return, Serbian peasants knew several good years living under their own headmen in a kind of home rule. This ended when a hard-pressed sultan felt obliged to grant the Janissaries the right to return to Belgrade. The Serbs by then had accumulated some military experience and had tasted a freer life without the Janissaries. The returnees were insolent and violent and the stage thus was set for the popular explosion which came in 1804.[24]

BOSNIA

In the first two decades of the eighteenth century, Bosnia was refashioned by the Ottomans as the main bulwark of the northern border facing Austria. The province was given four times as many *sipahi*s as Serbia, and a defense in depth based on forty fortresses, many of them new. The commanders of these fortresses, the famous *kapetan*s of Bosnia, held virtually full powers over their districts and lived like feudal lords. They and their garrisons shared with the tradition-bound *sipahi* class the privilege of bequeathing their livings to their heirs, a fact which gave to Bosnian society somewhat the character of a corporation with interests to protect. A powerful council of *ayan*s at Sarajevo, and the presence there of a proud and turbulent populace of Janissary-craftsmen, obliged the

Bosnian vizier to move his residence to Travnik. There too, however, the yearly assemblies of *kapetans*, *beys* and *ayans* obeyed the vizier only when he agreed with them, or was particularly skilled and energetic.

In the countryside the traditional holdings of the *sipahis* and their officers were evolving into a system of landholding which was far more demanding of peasants than before. The depopulation of parts of Bosnia forced some *sipahis* to work their own land. More typically, however, the estates of *sipahis*, *kapetans* and *ayans* of the towns were growing in the eighteenth century on the basis of dispossessions, and the resettlement of pastoralists and immigrants from the south. Loosened control by the center permitted conditions of labor which were particularly harsh, ameliorated only by the fact that Bosnia was geographically ill-suited to large-scale agriculture and was characterized, as it is now, by a mixed economy in which orchards and animal raising were of equal importance.

Muslim peasants regularly were called on in wartime to risk their lives on the frontier. As peasants they not only bore the customary burdens, but were required, from about 1720, to help Christian peasants shoulder a newly introduced system of provincial taxation known as the *taksit*. This led to a stubborn rebellion by the Muslims, lasting from 1748 to 1756, which was worsened by the participation of the Janissaries of Sarajevo. The introduction of the hated *taksit* into Sarajevo later in the century aroused the people to close the *çarşija* (central market). An accommodation with the new tax system was reached when the authorities conceded that all Bosnia's Muslims were indeed members of the military class. This compromise of the classic system was the most dramatic demonstration of the widespread aspiration of Muslims in Rumelia to elevate their status, and thus lighten their liability to taxation.[25]

BULGARIA AND MACEDONIA

The forty years before the enthronement of Mahmud II in 1808 were years of great insecurity for the Bulgarian and Macedonian peoples. Bulgaria was, of course, the causeway for each war fought against northern neighbors. In this period it also became the arena for the empire's fiercest feudal struggles. Already by the mid-1760s competition began for domination among the *ayans* of Seres in Macedonia, and at Vidin on the Danube. The war of 1768–74 worsened these struggles, since the involvement of the *ayan* committees of the region in the war effort offered them new opportunities to advance their families' interest while imperial forces were engaged at the front. Demobilization after the war released many thousands of Albanian irregulars, who then enlisted as the retainers of ambitious would-be warlords. Thus the 1770s and 1780s were filled with sharp struggles between such retinues aimed at establishing a hierarchy of power in an emerging refeudalized order.

A comparison of the two most famous *ayan*-warlords of the region, İsmail Pasha of Seres and Osman Pazvantoğlu of Vidin, offers an insight into the formula for establishing regional power. Both had large retinues. Both held hundreds of "farms," not estates organized by them for agriculture so much as fiscal estates on which they had prior claims to all rents and on which they were well placed to hold back all or most taxes formally owed to the central government. Finally, both were on good terms with the merchants and tradesmen of their respective towns, to whom they offered the best chance for security and peace. This was somewhat easier at Vidin, for at Seres, as at Sarajevo and Belgrade, tension between Janissaries and *sipahi*s was endemic.

The second war with Catherine, 1787–92, left the *ayan*-warlords along the Danube in charge of most of the fighting, while lesser *ayan*s to their rear once again engaged in an accelerated sorting-out of power. The demobilization was so dangerous that the peasants of Bulgaria, like those of Serbia, were permitted to keep their arms. Bandits appeared in ever greater numbers, many of them Muslim smallholders from the Haskovo region. While during much of the 1770s banditry had centered on central and eastern Macedonia, during the 1790s it was much closer to İstanbul, and centered on eastern Thrace. The connection between *ayan* conflicts, which raged for ten years (1797–1807) in eastern Thrace, is shown by the fact that they halted suddenly when the leading warlord of the moment, Mustafa Bayraktar of Silistre, took power as grand vizier at İstanbul in 1808.

Sultan Selim himself and the advisors around him clearly had contributed to widespread disorder in the Rumelian provinces, that worsened with Selim's enthronement during wartime. The state used a whole bag of tricks, all save determination, to deal with the warlords of the time. An *ayan* chief might be appointed to put down bandits, as was İsmail of Seres in 1793–94, or forgiven, as was Osman Pazvantoğlu in 1796, or besieged in vain (1797), or made into a vizier (1799–1801). But while the Porte and its advisors might gain some momentary advantage by a change of tactics, they were up against individuals more resolute than themselves, and who rarely if ever visited İstanbul. These were all but final products of that age of the *ayan*s, no longer simply servants of the empire, but instead quite ready to take a role in deciding its fate.[26]

GREECE AND ALBANIA

In the western Balkans, the careers of the Buşatlıs overlapped that of Ali Tepedelenli without major confrontation, as though a baton had passed between them. Mehmed Buşatlı built the power of this first family among the Balkan warlords upon a foundation of *çiftliks*, both real farms and tax-farms. In the Albanian coastal plain, specialized agriculture aimed at export already had made its appearance in the 1750s and with the sponsorship of the Buşatlıs, continued to develop. Taking advantage of their distance from the capital, the Buşatlıs formed a unique coalition with the merchants and tradesmen of fast-growing Shkoder, whose interests they championed, and with Albanian, and even Montenegrin and Bosnian tribes to their north. The family used both of Catherine's wars as a screen for expansion even into the Kossovo plain. The hero of the line, Kara Mahmud Buşatlı, successfully survived two sieges (1787, 1793) and an unlucky flirtation with the Austrians, but came to an end during an adventure in Montenegro (1796). After his demise, the surviving Buşatlı line seems to have preferred a policy of cooperation with the Porte, always an option to be tried sooner or later.

By this time a great rival for power in the western Balkans already was installed at the Albanian-Greek town of Yanina. Ali Tepedelenli, soon to be known as the "Lion of Yanina," along with another Albanian, Mehmed Ali of Egypt, was one of the two most famous warlords of the era. The main basis for Ali's power both early and late, was his intimate knowledge of and influence over the police (*derbentci*) system of the western Balkans, which had been set up by the Ottomans in the 1760s in the hope of stopping the endemic banditry there. The police (*derbentcis*, or *armatoli*) were drawn from the ranks of the bandits (*klephts*) they were supposed to suppress and it thus required deft handling and strict discipline to keep them honest.

Such police were seldom above suspicion.

> The greater part of the *armotoli* employed against the thieves ... have themselves followed the same trade. If they voluntarily make their submission, they are always favorably received at the time, although perhaps marked out for future destruction. As many of them have brothers or cousins among the thieves there is generally a secret correspondence between the two parties, and the best mode of attacking a village is often pointed out to the robbers by one of their opponents.[27]

Named a commander in the police system in 1787, Ali showed himself to be an expert player in this ambiguous role, failing to be helpful during wartime but remembering obedience just in time for peace. He gave the Porte reason to be grateful when twice charged with the top responsibility (*başbuğ*) in the police system (1793–94, 1803–04) and was present at one of the sieges against the Buşatlıs. The Porte's gratitude was tangible, finally leaving Ali and his sons as the rulers of a mini-empire of perhaps 1.5 million souls, reaching from the Tosk plain of Albania to the Gulf of Corinth.

Like other warlords, Ali had a numerous Albanian retinue, and manipulated the native elites under his control, exploiting their influence over their people. He held at least a thousand fiscal estates under his control and conducted a foreign policy of his own, flirting alternately with the French and English, and using the war years 1806–12 to advance his own borders southward. Like all great *ayans*, he had little money to spare for İstanbul, and jealously suppressed, or eliminated, or manipulated the lesser chiefs within his zone of influence. He also assiduously preserved the security of roads, which endeared him to the merchants of his region. Here is an eyewitness description of Ali's justice, which probably is valid in some degree for all the larger warlords of the time:

> the woods and hills of every part of his government were . . . in possession of large bands of robbers, who were recruited and protected by the villages; and who lay large tracts under contribution; burning and plundering those districts under the Pasha's protection. Against these he proceeded with great severity: they were burned, hanged, beheaded, and impaled, and have disappeared from many parts, especially upper Albania, which before were quite subject to those outlaws.
>
> It is by such vigorous measures that the Vizier has rendered many parts of Albania . . . perfectly accessible . . . and consequently by opening the country to merchants . . . has not only increased his own revenues, but bettered the condition of his subjects.[28]

NON-MUSLIM ELITES OF OTTOMAN EUROPE

Virtually all the villages of southeastern Europe were represented to some degree by headmen, and where the villagers were non-Muslims, so were the headmen. Ottoman rule encouraged this degree of organization, especially when the head-tax was taken from villages as a lump sum, a common practice in the eighteenth century. But the need to deal with villages as collectivities would have been inevitable anyway since other government requirements, such as irregular tax levies, corvée, and debt collections involving whole villages required collective representation. These headmen were known by different terms among each of the subject peoples but their general powers were similar: in addition to organizing tax payment (often in return for personal tax exemption), they settled minor disputes such as those involving land, and enforced customary law.

Besides the ubiquitous headmen, there was a second, more consequential elite which was the by-product of increased regional and foreign trade in the eighteenth century. These native men of influence frequently appeared in more than one guise – as merchants, as money-lenders, and sometimes as tax collectors, and landholders. In many parts of the Balkans quite impressive houses were erected for their families, and their style of life differed only somewhat from the Muslim elite who were their neighbors. This was particularly true of the Bulgarian native elite, who prospered as animal traders, as middlemen for village products, and as itinerant merchants at the great fairs, and even at İstanbul. At many places, as at Larissa and Salonica, it was common practice for such prosperous families to buy protection from some powerful Muslim.[29]

Alongside the secular elites were those of the clergy. The Greek and Armenian patriarchs at İstanbul regularly dispatched their own tax collectors to call upon monasteries as well as bishops to collect sums accumulated from occasional fees and contributions paid by parishioners.

> In the larger sees . . . where the clergy are more numerous, and there are Greek families of opulence, the bishop demands a portion of the profits derived by the former from the confessions, domestic services, and . . . daily prayers, which are read in many families by a priest.[30]

The clergy in turn passed on to their flocks the contributions for which the Church as a whole was liable. Greek monasteries and bishoprics of the late eighteenth century commonly labored under a burden of public debt, upon which they paid a yearly interest of 12 percent.[31] According to one interpretation, the suppression of the Slavic patriarchates at Peč and Ohrid in 1766–67 was really intended to relieve their acute financial embarrassment.[32]

In İstanbul itself the merchant princes of the Greek quarter of Fener lent money to advance their interest in Church affairs, especially after 1763, when the patriarchate introduced the practice of requiring candidates for the office of patriarch to pay the succession tax from their private funds.[33] On their own behalf these merchant princes also bribed and intrigued to obtain the governments of the Rumanian principalities, offices which during the century before the Greek war broke out in 1821 were reserved for this circle alone. Eight families dominated the two

Rumanian appointments, and two of them, the Mavricordatos and the Ghicas, held either one or the other for 89 of 191 years (a combined total for both provinces).

Sent out for an average term of office of two and a half years, the temporary ruler of Bucharest and Jassy took with him a numerous entourage. These underlings, who were needed for the work of governing, mingled with the Rumanian boyar class. Thirty-six boyar families even intermarried with them, offering the Greek spouses opportunities to invest, since investments in Rumania were not subject to confiscation and were therefore attractive to the İstanbul Greeks. A few of the higher offices under Phanariote rule were reserved to the Rumanian boyars. But mostly they were content with the care of their estates, trading livestock, wine and brandy, collecting cash commutations from their peasants, and in the later part of the century building seignorial reserves of land, as if anticipating the approaching boom in Rumanian grain.

At the other end of the peninsula, another class of Greek primate dominated the Morea. These formed a shadow government alongside the Muslims, usually were both large landholders and traders, and often had a hand in contraband and piracy, which prospered especially during the Napoleonic years between 1793 and 1815. As at İstanbul and in Rumania, the clerical and non-clerical elites were intimately intertwined. Many Greeks donated land as religious foundations. Thus a large portion of Morean land, perhaps a third, was under the formal protection of the Orthodox Church. The Greek primates of Morea, Chios, and Crete lived much like the pashas of their vicinities and justify the historians' inclination to think in terms of a shared Ottoman culture, particularly in the far less literate eighteenth century.[34]

ANATOLIA

The rise of the *ayan* class in its Anatolian variants already was well advanced in the Tulip Period (1718–30) on the basis of widespread purchase of life-lease tax-farms. By 1760 all remaining *timar* land in Anatolia had been usurped by the rising class of fiscal entrepreneurs, probably because *timar*s had been deemed less useful on the Anatolian side. The effort by the Grand Vizier Muhsinzade Mehmed Pasha to centralize official appointments in İstanbul (1765) made little difference to their progress, since the real basis of their power was their landholding via the auction system, not the appointment system. The high offices awarded many Anatolian *ayan*s were just one of the tricks by which the center sought to maintain balance between competing families in Anatolia, as in Rumelia.

The career of the Çapanoğlu family in central Anatolia reveals significant details. This family repeatedly was rewarded with desirable offices, beginning in 1755, because of services which they rendered the Porte, in this earliest instance because Ahmed Çapanoğlu had helped to alleviate the shortage of meat at İstanbul. He was rewarded with official recognition as the tax-farmer (*voyvoda*) of Bozok, which was to become the family's home. This was followed in 1761 by his appointment to Sivas as governor (*vali*) for two years. It is interesting to note the alternation of a large scale tax-farming appointment with full governorship – in theory these were offices with different powers but one can see how the distinction between them was breaking down in this period. The appointment in Sivas was intended to prevent another family, the Zaralızades, from becoming too entrenched there. Next Ahmed Agha was given Çorum as appanage, *arpalık*, suggesting that the tax-farms of the sub-province which were not alienated already from the treasury instead went to him as salary. In 1764 he gained the Niğde sub-province as well (again as *arpalık*), because of his success against bandits. But because of his excesses, or his disturbing success in three such sub-provinces, the Porte arranged for his execution by rival families in 1765, perhaps as part of its current "centralization" program.

Only three years later, the Çapanoğlu family was back in favor, though part of their earlier holdings had been confiscated. The family had been disciplined but not destroyed. For his services in rooting out bandits at Hacıbektaş and Avanos, Mustafa Bey Çapanoğlu was awarded a high central post (*kapıcıbaşı*) which tended to be reserved in this period for just such occasions. During the war of 1768–74, though the governorship (*mutasarrıflık*) of Bozok changed hands frequently, actual control over the tax-farms of the sub-province remained in the hands of Mustafa Bey (as *mütesellim*).

There then followed a period of intense rivalry, partly manipulated from İstanbul, with the Canikli family to the north. The holdings of both families fluctuated dramatically around their respective home territories. Süleyman Çapanoğlu, along with his son, took the route of serving the sultan loyally; they appeared at the head of their own troops on the Danube front in 1790. For their wartime services they received a mixture of honorific offices at the center (*mirahorluk*, *kapıcıbaşılık*) and real power as tax-farmers at Ankara (*mütesellimlik*) and at Amasya (*muhassıllık*). In the reform period of Sultan Selim III, the Çapanoğlus

remained mostly obedient, so that even though the next sultan, Mahmud
II, pursued a general policy of disciplining the *ayans*, there was still an
occasion to reward the Çapanoğlus with the governorship of Aleppo in
1813.[35]

Significant and little researched is the fact that in Anatolia, as in Rumelia, a quasi-feudal hierarchization of larger and smaller *ayan* families took
place in the later decades of the century, with half a dozen great families
at the top. In this process bandits played a role, first to test the power
of rivals, and then, by their suppression, to establish and demonstrate
power. Even without bandits the retinues of the great lords, often 4–
5,000 men, created havoc in their surrounding districts. However important they became as tax-farmers or as landholders, the Anatolian *ayans*
did little to organize agriculture, preferring usury as the better, more
predictable road to wealth. Nonetheless a European merchant like Peysonnel might prefer the protection of an *ayan* family (in this case the
Karaosmanoğlu), whatever the cost, since they actually were in a position
to impose discipline on their neighborhood, in contrast to many of the
officials sent from İstanbul.[36]

SYRIA

In Syria, as in the central provinces, tendencies toward local autonomy, a
response to looser control, became increasingly obvious in the last three
decades of the century. Whereas before the 1770s the governors of Aleppo
and Damascus (or their surrogates) contended with local elites to maintain
a balance of power, after 1770 the coastal town of Acre emerged to challenge them as the third center of power in Syria, based on a lion's share of
the tax-farms and the largest military retinues of the province.

Both Aleppo and Damascus had competing local factions, with alliances which brought them support either from imperial Janissaries
(Damascus) or from some tradesmen of their cities in their guise as local
Janissaries (both Damascus and Aleppo). At Damascus the Azm family,
allied with imperial Janissaries, championed regional trade, while a
second local faction was allied with the pilgrimage trade.[37] In each city,
one of the competing factions controlled the countryside outside the city,
not only holding tax-farms, but also controlling the affairs of villagers as
their creditors and middlemen, often buying up crops in advance of harvest.[38] This last practice (in theory prohibited by Islam) easily led to

engrossment of food supplies. Without the protective food regime practiced at İstanbul, the two Syrian cities frequently were hostage to engrossment schemes practiced upon them by their own *ayan* elites, who used their power of supply in the countryside to withhold grain from their own city until prices rose to advantageous levels. Even governors might collude in these schemes. Thus, in the last decades of the century, when internal affairs in the two cities were dominated by struggles between local factions, the faction in power invariably would try to enrich itself by engrossment of food supplies.

Retinues also played a large role in Syrian life and politics throughout the century. Even the Azms of Damascus, a popular local dynasty, felt the need for them. Taxes on the desert periphery had to be collected by means of an annual expedition (*dawra*) similar to those of North Africa. And the ever-present tribes (Kurds and Turkomans near Aleppo, Bedouins near Damascus) had to be overawed with military force when not bought off with privileges. The arrangement by which the leading tribes profited from the annual pilgrimages broke down in 1768 and could not be reconstructed once the Wahhabis became the masters of the pilgrimage route.

Mount Lebanon, with its Christian, Shiite and Druze minorities, was structured communally, with power centered upon the elders of each confessional community, confirmed in their roles by kinship and alliance hierarchies. Naturally the local tax-farms were in the hands of these communal oligarchs.

The situation in southern Syria on or near the coast was quite different. While Aleppo and Damascus lost some relative importance during the century with the drying up of the Iranian silk trade, the Palestine area gained in importance as the home of cotton raising and cottage craft based on cotton, supplemented by grain, olives and tobacco. This explains why the local tax-farmer Zahir fortified Acre on the coast, and used it as his base of operations. This relocation was so successful that his Bosnian successor Cezzar accepted the whole arrangement, and when he was named governor of Syria, ruled from Acre. Though he often pretended to be the loyal servant of the Porte, Cezzar sought to maintain the maximum possible autonomy. To protect his grip on the province, he maintained large ethnically balanced retinues in which the North African element took its place alongside Albanians, Bosnians, and Syrians. Cezzar took a tax-farmer's approach to trade at the seaside, where the leading figures were the minority merchants, and where the items traded included grain which he had transferred from the hinterland.[39]

IRAQ

The towns of Iraq – Mosul, Baghdad and Basra – resembled those of
Syria in certain essentials. In Iraq also, *ayan* elites of composite origin –
military, ulema, merchant – controlled a large part of the surrounding
countryside through various mechanisms. Sometimes they had their own
rural holdings, which they increasingly regarded as outright property
(*mülk*), or equally secure family foundations (*vakıf*). Or, as money-
lenders, tax-farmers and middlemen, they collected taxes and protected
villagers from demands in excess of their ability to pay. This fiscal and
fiduciary domination of the country by the nearby town was in varying
degrees characteristic of all Ottoman provinces in the eighteenth century.
In irrigated areas near the river in lower Iraq, it was displaced by the
interference of Bedouin chiefs, who, as an alternate elite, also took tribute
from trade caravans coming from all directions.

Baghdad and Mosul each had complicated politics which involved
internal alliances between the elite and the Janissary-tradesmen, and outward alliances with some of the surrounding tribes. The Iraqi towns also
had Mamluks, like those of Egypt and Tunis. These were retinues of a
special kind, not only ethnically separate from the surrounding populace,
but as a rule purchased and nurtured as slave soldiers, with loyalty and
courage as their primary ethics. Bolstered by their Mamluk backers, the
Iraqi governors – the Jalili family in Mosul and a dynasty of former
Mamluks at Baghdad – were able to dominate their turbulent environments with surprising success and continuity. The Mamluk retinue at
Baghdad, an estimated 800 in 1765, reached its peak of 3,000 persons
under Süleyman the Great, a Mamluk dynast, at the end of the century.
As in Egypt, a majority of these Mamluks were Georgians, and while
they were not on the economic level of the local *ayan*s, they partook of
the revenues of the provincial governors, with little or nothing left over
for İstanbul. Iraq therefore stood in an intermediate position between
Syria and Egypt, sharing with Syria the problem of the tribes, sharing
with Egypt the Mamluk retinues.[40]

EGYPT

This Ottoman province began the eighteenth century under a tax-farming
system dominated by Mamluks, and ended it with a landowning system
in which the Mamluks played a much-diminished role. Roughly
speaking, the Mamluk class moved into Cairo around mid-century.

There, it found a new economic base by seizing city tax-farms formerly pertaining to the Egyptian treasury and ultimately to İstanbul, meanwhile abandoning the tax-farms of rural Egypt to a composite class of land-owners in which wealthy merchants and ulema predominated. In the city, the Janissaries and their tradesmen allies, who until then had domin-ated the urban tax-farms, thus lost out, as did the Ottoman treasury, which received steeply diminished tribute from Egypt after mid-century. In the countryside the new landowning class drove the villagers into debt and often into flight during the last decades before Napoleon's arrival.

Egyptian history throughout the eighteenth century was dominated by the Mamluk class, an elite of slave-soldiers which differed organi-cally from the Mamluks of the thirteenth to sixteenth centuries. The earlier Mamluks had remained an isolated elite retinue; the mostly-Georgian Mamluks of the eighteenth century by contrast actually intermarried with the descendants of earlier Mamluks, forming together an arrogant half-Egyptianized class which was organized into warring households (*bayats*) led by Mamluk patriarchs. At their peak they may have numbered 10,000, but attrition through violence was continu-ous, and a British observer in 1789 put their numbers at 4,000.[41]

At Cairo, the Mamluks also formed alliances outside their households with some of the imperial military corps permanently stationed there, and with members of the ulema and merchant classes, with whom they shared material interests. Like politics in the cities of Syria, Cairene political life was organized, then reorganized into giant factions, with Mamluk coali-tions as the principal parties. Since the Mamluks were more powerful than the Ottoman governors, inevitably one or more strongmen would arise from their ranks in an attempt to dominate the government of Egypt. The most remarkable of these was Ali el-Kebir, not an *ayan* upstart like his con-temporaries of the 1760s, the Buşatlıs and Çapanoğlus, but rather a Mamluk officer bent on wresting Egypt from the weakening Ottoman grasp. Yet Ali's methods were not very different from those of the warlord *ayan*s of the central provinces. He too kept a large retinue of mercenaries (not Mamluks) and attempted to monopolize large areas of economic life to pay them (especially the urban tax-farms of Cairo and the customs system). He too gave guarantees of internal security favorable to trade, and had a program of territorial expansion – into upper Egypt, the Hejaz and, when the war of 1768–74 provided an opportunity, into Syria.

Distance, wars and internal disorder prevented the Ottomans from reasserting their claim to their customary share of Egypt's wealth except briefly in 1786 and, with help from English allies, in 1801. Meanwhile the traditional tribute became the prize of the warring Mamluk households, which did not hesitate to supplement their extravagant lifestyle with various extortions aimed at the people of Cairo.

Like other fertile regions of the Ottoman Empire, riverine Egypt gradually escaped the tax regime proposed by the central government. In its place arose a mixture of life-leases, foundations (*vakıfs*) and the personal estates of a composite class of Mamluk allies and city dwellers – among them merchants, ulema and women. These left actual supervision of their estates to local agents in the countryside, while in some more distant places villagers lived under the close control of Bedouin sheikhs.

Downward demographic trends in city and country attest to the severe costs of Mamluk predation during the last decades of the century. Mamluk resistance to the French invasion, since it was without popular support, therefore collapsed. The invaders relieved the losers of their urban tax-farms. Although still a force to contend with, the Mamluks were far weaker both numerically and institutionally when the French withdrew and were out-maneuvered rather easily by the new strongman of the age, an Albanian usurper. Mehmed Ali, when the accounts were settled in 1811, adopted most of the program of his Mamluk forebear Ali el-Kebir, and maintained a Mamluk household of his own, indeed the only one to survive in the now-autonomous province.[42]

NORTH AFRICA

In the first decade of the eighteenth century, all three North African city-states shook off most vestiges of political control from İstanbul. Yet each remained in some degree the captive of the social system bequeathed by Ottoman rule and each accepted Ottoman culture as a model. Nor was the breach quite complete, since as late as 1795 Tunis honored İstanbul's request for assistance against Tripoli, and in 1810 assisted the Ottomans in a campaign aimed at Crete.

Having cut most ties with the Ottomans, the three city-states were on their own in confronting the European maritime powers, above all France, England and the Netherlands. The free-wheeling piracy and slaving of the seventeenth century ended, now replaced by a combination of trade, supervised by the consuls of the major powers, and piracy aimed only at minor trading states, among them the Italians, Hanseatics and Scandinavians. Tunis sponsored the most trade and piracy throughout the century, but all three states enjoyed a last burst of pirate zeal after the French suppressed the Maltese, Papal and Viennese fleets in 1793 and before the European powers, led by the Americans, ended piracy after Napoleon's final defeat.

Throughout the period, Algiers was in the hands of its Janissary garrison, periodically recruited from the Anatolian shores (a main reason for the continued ascendance of the Ottoman cultural model). Their chief, the *dey*, was the creature of the Janissary council (*divan*) and seldom died naturally. The limited amount of piracy permitted under eighteenth-century conditions was a state-run activity whose revenues went to the ministers. Algeria, like the other two desert states, was mostly tribal. Therefore tax gathering was done by means of twice-yearly expeditions (*mahalles*), which were meant not only to fill the coffers, but to discipline the unruly, and to show the flag. The system, with variations, was the same at Tunis and Tripoli.

Unlike Algiers, the other two city-states were ruled by true dynasties, the Karamanlıs at Tripoli, and the Husainids at Tunis. Both were the masters of their largely Turkish retinues. At Tunis, the most complex of the North African city-states, there also were Mamluks. Relatively few in number (between 100 and 200), these held most, perhaps all, of the high offices. Power in the provinces was shared with tribal sheikhs. It is instructive of the nature of government that only twenty of the sixty Tunisian sub-governments (of the early nineteenth century) were territorial, while the other forty were tribal. To control these nomadic and warlike peoples, the state enfranchised certain tribes (the *mahzen* tribes) as tax-exempt, and used them to control the others. This practice, like the twice-yearly expeditions, was a feature of all three governments.

While, in strict political terms, the three pirate states were independent entities during the eighteenth century (or nearly so, since Tunis was under tribute to Algiers), social and cultural ties to the Ottomans remained intact so long as the retinues were Turkish. By contrast, the corsair fleets were manned mostly by Greeks and Albanians. These social ties were broken first at Tunis in 1811 when the Turkish retinue revolted and was replaced by Berbers (Zouaves), but remained intact at Algiers until the coming of the French in 1830.[43]

NOTES

1 Anderson (1979), p. 321.
2 Nagata (1976b), p. 65.

3 Dimitrov (1962b), *passim*; Özkaya (1985), p. 46.

4 Özkaya (1985), p. 59; İnalcık (1977), p. 29.

5 1717 is offered as the date for the formal abolition of *hass* estates belonging to *beylerbeys*: Uzunçarşılı (1945), p. 203.

6 Russell (1794), II, p. 91.

7 Thieck (1985), p. 118.

8 Radusev (1980), p. 88; Özkaya (1985), pp. 93, 182, 187, 193.

9 Abdul Rahman and Nagata (1977), p. 192; İnalcık (1977), p. 44; Özkaya (1985), pp. 210–15.

10 Cf. Yediyıldız (1982c), pp. 151–61; Barnes (1986), p. 42; İnalcık (1978), pp. 87–88; *idem* (1983), p. 111; *idem* (1955), p. 225.

11 Zilfi (1983), p. 326.

12 Abdul Rahman and Nagata (1977), p. 185.

13 Pococke (1745), II, p. 267.

14 Özdemir (1986), pp. 114, 156.

15 Kunt (1983), *passim*.

16 Berkes (1964), p. 53; Özkaya (1985), p. 209.

17 Abdul Rahman and Nagata (1977), pp. 188, 192; cf. İnalcık (1977), p. 31; *idem* (1980), pp. 316, 334; Özkaya (1985), p. 93.

18 Porter (1771), p. 6.

19 Sućeska (1965a), p. 229; Mutafčieva (1965), p. 244; Dimitrov (1962a), pp. 129ff.

20 Nagata (1976b), p. 103.

21 Özkaya (1983), pp. 14–15.

22 In 1765, 1784, and 1786: İnalcık (1977), pp. 47–49; Nagata (1976a), p. 33; Sućeska (1965a), p. 229; Mutafčieva (1965), pp. 241–42.

23 İnalcık (1977), p. 45; Nagata (1976b), p. 97; Shaw (1971), p. 213; Mutafčieva (1965), p. 235.

24 ISN (1986), vol. 4, pt. 1, pp. 328–29; Sućeska (1965c), p. 322; Tričković (1970), pp. 525–49.

25 Sućeska (1969), p. 206; Nagata (1979), pp. 12–32; Kreševljaković (1954), p. 68; *idem* (1951), p. 126; Sućeska (1965a), pp. 227–29; *idem* (1980), pp. 144–56; Eren (1965), pp. 25–40; q. v. "Bosna" in *EI²*.

26 Mutafčieva (1965), p. 245; *idem* (1962), pp. 179, 212; Mutafčieva and Dimitrov (1968), p. 50; Kosev (1970), p. 69; Lampe and Jackson (1982), p. 36; Lascaris (1938), p. 384; Özkaya (1983), pp. 16, 103–5; Sadat (1973), pp. 208–17; Dimitrov (1962a), pp. 129–65; BAN (1985) vol. 5, pp. 39–47, 163–68; Nagata (1976a), p. 35; Gökçe (1967), pp. 108–9; Gandev (1960), p. 211.

27 Leake (1967), IV, pp. 353–54.

28 Hobhouse (1813), I, pp. 117–18; cf. Mutafčieva (1965), p. 245; Pollo and Arben (1981), pp. 94–98; Shaw (1971), pp. 228–98, 317; Frasheri (1964), pp. 109–17; Ars (1963), p. 124; Naci (1966), p. 133; BAN (1985), vol. 5, p. 163; Skiotis (1971), pp. 221–43.

29 Leake (1967), IV, p. 295.

30 *Ibid.*, I, p. 240.

31 *Ibid.*, IV, pp. 487, 540; III, p. 355.

32 Papadopoulos (1952), pp. 89–90.

33 *Ibid.*, p. 132.
34 İnciciyan (1976), p. 22; Nagata (1976b), p. 44; Skiotis (1975), pp. 312–15; Paskaleva (1962), p. 128; Runciman (1968), pp. 362–74; Oteţea (1960), pp. 306–10; İnalcık (1978), pp. 87–88; Berindei (1984), pp. 318–25; Cernovodeanu (1986), pp. 251–52; Chirot (1976), p. 79; Petrovich (1976), 1, p. 18; Orhonlu (1967), pp. 119–35; Grozdanova (1974), pp. 147–59; BAN (1985), vol. 5, pp. 76–7; Clogg (1976), pp. 3–7; Dakin (1972), pp. 12–20; Hobhouse (1813), II, p. 597; Wagstaff (1965), p. 301.
35 Further details on this family's career in Mert (1980), pp. 28–64.
36 Sakaoğlu (1984), pp. 10–61; Veinstein (1975), pp. 131–42; Özkaya (1985), pp. 17–59; Nagata (1976b), pp. 14–32; İnalcık (1977), p. 33; Shaw (1971), p. 215.
37 Schatkowski-Schilcher (1985), p. 35.
38 Meriwether (1987), pp. 58–72.
39 Cohen (1973), pp. 312–27; *idem* (1971), pp. 47–53; Nour (1982), p. 365; Baer (1982), p. 629; Barbir (1980), pp. 68–89, 312; Harik (1969), pp. 48–68; Hourani (1957), pp. 98–99; Thieck (1985), pp. 120–30, 135–37; Bodman (1963), pp. 24–32, 98–118; Rafeq (1975), pp. 285–87; Hourani (1968), pp. 48–54; Rafeq (1966), p. 35; *idem* (1981), p. 674; Shaw (1971), p. 219.
40 Nieuwenhuis (1982), pp. 35–110; Raymond (1985), p. 77; Shaw (1971), p. 221; Hourani (1968), p. 52; *idem* (1957), p. 100.
41 Ayalon (1960), p. 151; for accounts of their traditional training and subsequent careers, cf. Shaw (1962), pp. 2–3; and Brown (1974), pp. 41–64.
42 Abdul Rahman and Nagata (1977), pp. 171–72; Baer (1982), pp. 53–59, 609–10; Ayalon (1960), pp. 151–62, 285–91; Colombe (1951), pp. 6–15; Raymond (1973–74), II, pp. 418–31, 673; Shaw (1962), pp. 7–9; *idem* (1971), p. 217; Baer (1980b), pp. 12–17; Marsot (1984), pp. 5–18, 70–74; Raymond (1985), p. 77; Staffa (1977), pp. 277–311.
43 Abun-Nasr (1971), pp. 175–85, 194–98; Dumont (1972), pp. 64–85; Field (1969), p. 29; Hess (1970), pp. 75–83; Brown (1974), pp. 55, 66, 92, 102–13; 121; Julien (1970), pp. 284–332; Valensi (1977b), pp. 8–74; Wolf (1979), pp. 287–325.

25

##

PEASANTS AND PASTORALISTS

The majority of Ottoman revenues still derived more or less directly from rural sources in the eighteenth century. It was peasants above all who paid the bill, both literally and figuratively, for the decay of imperial norms, for the subversion of the land regime, and for the introduction of new expedients to cover defects which appeared in the fiscal system. Dependence on out-of-date records often led to intolerable injustices at the village level around the end of the seventeenth century, since the system was not yet sufficiently flexible to take into account the natural and man-made variations in rural production. The resolution of this problem of reallocating rural tax burdens is a main feature of Ottoman governance in the eighteenth century.

LIFE IN THE VILLAGES

The flight of peasants is the best guide we have to actual economic conditions prevailing in the various areas during the eighteenth century. Attempts to measure output and taxation will remain unsatisfactory for all but limited areas and cannot form the basis for generalizations about so vast and various an empire. Even under the prescriptions of the classic period of Ottoman history, the amount of the religiously sanctioned "tithe" (*öşür*) varied from place to place between one-eighth and one-fifth.[1] Measurements based on such documentation in any case remain difficult since the available evidence almost always pertains to the community, rather than the individual producer, and cannot be assumed to be complete. But there is no doubting the frequency of peasant flight in one or another Ottoman province during the eighteenth century, nor is it difficult to interpret its significance. Peasants do not decamp readily since this means leaving behind houses, walls, gardens, and other forms of labor investment. When they do flee, it means that life has become so intolerably burdensome or dangerous as to justify both the sacrifice and the risks of leaving everything behind.

Does flight necessarily mean over-taxation? There was probably a general trend towards heavier rural taxation which began in the seventeenth century and continued into the eighteenth. As a rule of thumb we may say that total rural taxation under the classical prescriptions varied between 20 and 25 percent of output. At the other extremity, Ottoman sharecropping of the eighteenth century and later took as much as 50 percent in unirrigated zones. And this might be tolerated if the landholders protected the peasant from other taxation, as frequently as they could. But wars, brigandage, tax-farming based on out-of-date records, along with bad weather and other natural vicissitudes sometimes resulted in tremendous variations. When insecurity of life thus is added to economic insecurity, the result is flight. A good demonstration of this took place on the Danubian frontier with occupied Rumania in the later wars of the century. There, Bulgarian and Macedonian peasants quit their hard-pressed villages and crossed the river in the direction of the newly opened tracts in the Ukraine. Insecurity on the roads, and the poor quality of the roads, probably explains why Balkan freight rates were twice those prevailing in Western Europe as of 1787. Balkan prices for wheat and livestock were also more volatile, even though generally lower.[2]

The literature on late Ottoman times often mentions the *çiftlik* as though this were a well understood term. In fact the term is as general as the English term "farm." It originally did mean a farming unit which could be plowed with a single pair of draft animals. But the term soon evolved to mean also a unit of indeterminate size whereby the essential thing implied was ownership (or at least entitlement) by one party and actual production by others. In the eighteenth century, the vast majority of agricultural units were very small by modern standards. Even in limited zones where monocultures such as cotton were characteristic, a larger unit might only be an agglomeration of smaller ones, without implying any change in land use or in technique.

There was virtually no "high farming" on the Ottoman scene and a three-field, or fallow system of farming remained the rule almost everywhere in Ottoman territories. Indeed recorded land values are so variable as to suggest that there was no value of land for itself, no Ricardian rents. Valuations instead expressed prior investments of labor in preparing land for cultivation, or improving it by roads, fences or other structures. Land was always worth controlling, regardless of price, so that the superior party could determine the terms of the agreement with persons who actually worked on it. But finding and keeping the labor was more difficult in this century of relative land abundance and labor scarcity.

As one might expect, great variations in conditions were found in the provinces of this still vast empire.

WALLACHIA AND MOLDAVIA

The Rumanian Principalities under Phanariote rule were among the less densely populated regions of the empire. Taken as a whole these provinces probably continued a long downward demographic trend with its nadir at mid-century, whereas by the end of the eighteenth century the trend was again upwards. Yet as late as 1820, a British observer thought that only one-sixth of the Wallachian countryside was under cultivation.[3] Even then the two provinces were predominantly pastoral. Peasants lived in a transhumant pattern, some of them farming the lowlands in the summer while others herded in the highlands. For protection, most homesteads were located in the hills, where the products of their crafts were exchanged, along with livestock. Cultivation techniques were rather primitive, reflecting land abundance, having advanced from slash and burn only in the seventeenth century.[4] Grain was stored in cistern-like repositories underground, a system also known among the South Slavs,[5] and grain served as a kind of currency.

An English consul of the Napoleonic period describes peasants' dwellings as follows:

> In winter they retire to cells underground, easily kept warm by means of a little fire made of dried dung and some branches of trees. Each family, however numerous, sleeps in one of these subterraneous habitations, men, women, and children, all heaped together; and their respective beds consist of one piece of coarse woolen cloth, which serves in the double capacity of mattress and covering . . . Their ordinary food is composed of mammalinga [a mash made from maize][6]

The mid-century demographic nadir largely derived from peasant flight, first as the result of a harsh Russian occupation in the late 1730s, then as a response to newly opened lands in the Ukraine and the Banat in the 1740s. This brought on a crisis of government revenues. The Phanariote ruler Constantine Mavricordato offered a solution in a series of similar decrees issued in Wallachia and Moldavia between 1746 and 1749. He abolished the now-unenforceable serfdom which had been on the books since the age of Michael the Brave, and he set uniform limits on the taxes and labor dues which could be required of peasants. The intention was in line with earlier Ottoman practice: to provide conditions attractive enough to prevent flight and to leave peasants strong enough to sustain direct state taxation. Besides the tithe, landlords annually could demand no more than twelve days of labor, far less than contemporary Habsburg or Russian landholders.[7] Rumanian peasants, nominally free under the law, in fact were bound by certain obligations attached to the land they worked, to which they were thus bound by circumstance, like peons.

Until well into the nineteenth century, Wallachian landholders had only limited use for the days of labor which were their right. Moldavian landholders were somewhat more interested in cultivating their seignorial reserves, and thus were more demanding.[8] In the first decades after the mid-century reforms, most landholders, in common with landholders in Bohemia and parts of France, drew the bulk of their revenues from various monopoly rights they enjoyed, such as rights on mills, stills and markets. Then, with the better international markets of the Napoleonic years, they became more interested in farming seignorial reserves, often threatening village common lands, or making new demands on woodlands.[9] Though the Ottoman grain purchase system was not finally dissolved until 1830, the early nineteenth-century opportunity to participate in an international grain market heightened Rumanian landlords' interest in taking full advantage of the prescribed days of labor, which until then had usually been commuted to cash payments.

Not until the late nineteenth century did Rumanian labor dues equal those already common under the Russian and Habsburg systems. By then maize, which had become important as animal food in the late eighteenth century, was the staple of human diet as well.[10]

The Rumanian peasantry was not completely defenseless, but always had the option of flight, which they chose again during the Pazvantoğlu raids at the beginning of the nineteenth century. Moreover, they might resist encroachment upon customary village rights such as the use of common lands. Like other villages of the Balkans, the Rumanian villagers had their tax-exempt headmen who often functioned as agents of the regime in collecting taxes and organizing the corvée. These surely also served as the representatives of villages organized as corporations when these bargained with their local landholders for better terms within the prevailing regime.[11]

SERBIA

Owing to natural increase and immigration, the population of the Belgrade *pashalık*, which was largely reconquered in 1739, grew steadily until the 1804 rebellion. Yet, on the eve of the rebellion, land was still so abundant that livestock raising predominated, while Belgrade depended for its grain upon the Habsburg provinces across the Danube and the Sava. The Serbs meanwhile sold cattle to the Bosnians, who resold them in Dalmatia, sheeps and goats to the Muslims among them, and pigs to the growing populations across the Habsburg border.[12]

The Serbs often lived in large extended families (*zadrugas*), housed in wood and stone, usually in upland villages that either were widely scattered, or linear in form.[13] Village headmen acted as judges in lesser cases settled by customary law. The villages of the *pashalık* were organized into 45 districts, represented at Belgrade by *oborknezes*, a system introduced during the Austrian occupation of 1717–39.[14]

Serbian agriculture used a light plow with several sub-types, drawn by oxen, which at 250 kg scarcely could be compared with those in Western Europe. They plowed the land twice before sowing, reaped with a sickle, and threshed with a hand flail. Grains were sown in both autumn and spring. Vegetable gardens, very important to the household economy, contained cabbages, onions, turnips, radishes, gourds, cucumbers, melons, leeks and garlic. Vineyards were widespread, while orchards often were associated with monasteries and churches. Manuring is documented in vineyards, one method being to move the fenced night stands of cattle. Otherwise the three-field system was used, with the fallow this implies, and with rotation of wheat, millet and oats. Maize appeared in the latter half of the eighteenth century and quickly became important for humans and animals alike.[15] The diet of the rebel leader Karageorge is recorded: black bread, sour cabbage, bacon, hard cheese, mush (from maize), onions, and plum brandy.[16]

In the eighteenth century, the Serbs of the *pashalık* confronted mixed conditions – improved trade with their kinfolk across the northern border but with security threatened by continuous battle between authorities and the Janissary recruits of the Belgrade garrison. That the actual material conditions in which they lived possibly were better than in the Habsburg lands is shown by the large number of returned emigrants, especially after the end of the war in 1792 and during the years of the rebellion after 1806. Indeed the consensus of Serbian historians is that during the exceptionally favorable years, 1792–96, when the Janissary recruits had been banished from the *pashalık*, the Serbs were not dissatisfied with their lot.[17] Ottoman taxes were not always collected rationally but at the same time were not in their totality as heavy as those of the northern empires.

When Ottoman rule had been restored in Serbia following the Treaty of Belgrade (1739), a large garrison of 2,400 Janissaries was established along with 900 *sipahis*, more than ever before.[18] Because their pay was a pittance, the Janissary recruits quickly became a chronic problem for the provincial government. Operating through their *dahi* leaders (thus fashioned after the Janissary *deys* of North Africa), the Janissaries and *sipahis* competed for control of the Serbian villages. By a variety of means, often by imposing loans upon the populace, the Janissaries succeeded in establishing *çiftliks* ("farms"), and ultimately *çiftlik* villages. They then acted as tax collectors and "protectors" either in competition with local *sipahis* or in connivance with them.[19] The outcome was not necessarily so much intolerable taxation as intolerable insecurity. Vuk Karadžić, a young official during the Serbian rebellion, has left a vivid sketch of the *çiftlik* of those times.

> In Serbia they call *chitluk* that village which has a landlord in addition to the sipahi ... The [landlord] took a ninth of the grain ... fruit, and hay. Trsicani (where I was born) gave him five okkas of peas per tax liable person (about 15 pounds), and one skin of butter per house. Aside from that they labored for him in the summer in the fields, at first usually on Sundays, and later when injustices mounted up also on other days, not only in summer but in winter, whenever he needed something, for instance to cut and carry wood ... In places [landlords] had houses in their villages where they went with their families on excursions in summer or in winter to hunt and in places where they did not have houses they might visit the village frequently and everywhere villagers would have to feed them. ... [Landlords] protected their tenants and so far as they could defended them from the other Turks ... The *chitluk* landlords of Serbia were worse and harder on the people not only than *sipahis* but than all of the other Turks, but compared to the Bosnian *chitluk* landlords they were milder. There villagers didn't even have their own houses but occupied as renters the houses of their aga.[20]

A few good years without those self-imposed Janissary landlords (1792–96) had been followed by several harsh years after their return from Pazvantoğlu territory. The results were incendiary, since the Serbs permitted to carry arms in those troubled times had grown accustomed to using them in their own defense. Thus a taste of progress sufficient to leave behind new barns and inns, the taunts of Serbs across the river, and the arbitrary demands of the Muslim occupiers, made up the discordant elements in a revolutionary situation.[21]

BOSNIA

Karadžić's remark about the *çiftlik* tenants of Bosnia not even owning their own houses shows us that the Bosnian agricultural unit indeed was unusual, closer in spirit perhaps to the *çiftlik* of late Ottoman times since the tenant was allowed to own very little and to retain perhaps only half the crops produced. These tenancies were typically on the converted estates of *sipahis*, *kapetans* and other military persons.[22] The misery of the Bosnian Christian tenants led many to flee west to Dalmatia, or north into Serbia. Alongside the Christians were Muslim peasants, also Slavs, who tolerated conditions almost as harsh, sometimes even paying taxes typically levied on non-Muslims, such as the tithe (*öşür*), and even the head-tax.[23] Heavy taxes and military service combined to set the stage for a long mid-century rebellion of these Bosnian Muslim peasants against the imposition of a new system of additional taxes (the *taksit*). Eventually very many Muslim peasants tried to strengthen their position in society by acquiring Janissary pay tickets and the tax exemptions that went with them. But the *taksit* system of additional taxes did not disappear and in the war of 1768–74 was applied in Sarajevo and in the countryside.

BULGARIA AND MACEDONIA

Bulgarian historians concede that the eighteenth century was a period of population growth and expansion into unused lands.[24] Although most of the agriculture of Bulgaria and Macedonia remained on a traditional small-scale basis,[25] certain limited zones saw the development of specialized agriculture in response to rising demand from urban and international markets. Near Vidin, Ruse and Sofia, where agricultural products found a ready sale, there appeared farms (*çiftliks*) of a latter-day type, employing contract labor on a large scale from nearby villages. Such farms might first organize around a limited operation such as a mill, then expand by purchasing land from the treasury (as at Vidin), or by seizing the commons of nearby villages.

Once a village lost the common pasture and woodlot, it also lost viability as an economic collectivity and was obliged henceforth to supply laborers to man the expanding farms nearby who were now underemployed at home. Such villages became known as *agha* villages since, in addition to their customary obligations to the treasury, they also paid rent to their *agha* (landlord) for the use of their former commons.[26] Elsewhere some peasants took loans from a prominent neighbor to pay their taxes and ended by providing corvée labor on his reserve in lieu of interest. It was never difficult to arrange such relationships since the Ottoman courts, though lax in defending villagers' rights to their customary commons, zealously enforced loans contracted at high interest.[27]

Bulgarian and Macedonian agriculture was practiced on a three-field basis, using a light plow similar to that of the Serbs.[28] Social inequality among the villages was on the increase since, in addition to the Turkish landholders, there appeared more merchants, tax-farmers, and money-lenders of native origin. Some began as peddlers, others as suppliers to the capital or in connection with one of the great annual fairs, such as at Uzuncaova. At these fairs they sold the products of specialized villages, such as those near Samakov, which produced ironware,[29] or in Rhodope producing shepherds' cloaks, which found markets as far away as Syria.

Further south, and open to the Mediterranean, some Bulgarian and Macedonian river valleys were well sited for specialized commercial agriculture, which developed rapidly, especially after 1750. Great stands of mulberry trees appeared at Haskovo, Kazanluk, Tirnovo, Vracan, Monastır and Ohrid. The first traffic in rose oil developed at this time. Rice was grown by irrigation at Skopje, Peč, Pristina and Plovdiv (Filibe). Tobacco cultivation increased in many areas and in the Mritsa, Struma, and Vardar valleys. Especially near Seres, cotton raising found a ready vent for sale either by sea to France, or overland to Germany.[30] At some locations, specialist agriculture stimulated the formation of larger farms (*çiftliks*) of a latter-day type on which the labor force were tenants. But sharecropping was far more widespread.

Because of harsh tenancies and heavy tax burdens, peasant flight seems to have been more common in Macedonia than in Bulgaria.[31] But both zones participated in the migratory waves to the Ukraine and Bessarabia in 1774 and 1792, and both were affected deeply by the profound disorder of the period of Kırcalı raiding, especially between 1797 and 1807, when palisades and towers were erected in many places, and when villagers were permitted to go about armed.[32]

ALBANIA AND EPIRUS

Because of their position opposite Italy, the Albanian and Epirote shores had long familiarity with the effects of sea-borne trade in commodities.

Some kind of commercial production for the international market may have begun in the seventeenth century, presumably in grains. By 1735–40 export-oriented agricultural estates were widespread on these shores, though it remains to be answered what style of organization was characteristic. Violent usurpation of land is thought to have been common, after which the obligations incumbent upon the peasant increased from one-eighth to one-third.[33] The Buşatlı family introduced both rice and cotton raising on their estates in the 1760s.[34] Maize took its place in the peasant diet, which also included olives, cheese, yogurt, onions and garlic.[35] The province was relatively heavily populated and, like Montenegro, still primarily organized in tribes in the upland areas, a great source of strength in chaotic times. As in Bulgaria, cloak-making was an important village industry, aimed partly at exports.

GREECE

In Greece, as elsewhere, Muslim landholders, who were the successors of the defunct *sipahi* system, controlled almost all the land. In most places agriculture was small-scale and even marginal, so that *çiftliks*, when they formed, were not necessarily aimed at reorganizing agriculture but rather at some form of fiscal mediation. William Leake, a British agent who was personally in touch with the warlord Ali Pasha of Janina, has left a very suggestive sketch of how such an estate might be formed (Ali had many of them):

> Matzuki has become a tjiftlik of the Vezir [Ali] since my last visit to these mountains. Unable to pay the impositions, the poor villagers were obliged to borrow money at Ionnina or elsewhere, at an interest of 20 percent; or even at 2 percent per mensem. Their difficulties having been of course increased by this measure, some of the inhabitants fled to Agrafa, the rest presented themselves to the Vezir with an offer to sell the whole village and its territory. The price demanded was 12 purses and the public debt. His Highness had no difficulty in declaring the place his tjiftlik; but instead of 12 purses he gave only 2, and instead of paying the debts, referred the creditors to the Matzukiotes who had fled to Agrafa.

This example shows how commonly villagers dealt with the authorities as a collectivity, paying or failing to pay their debts as a community, and also how easy it was, in Greece and elsewhere, for the powerful to exploit village indebtedness to take villagers under their control.[36]

Greek villagers typically sharecropped and surrendered one-third to two-thirds of their product to Turkish landlords, depending upon the quality of the land[37] and the portion of the stock of equipment which the latter supplied. They also had to contribute to the increasingly regular additional taxes (*imdat, taksit*) which supported the local administration. Muslim peasants (*reayas*) also were expected to share these burdens and, as in Bosnia, rebelled over the collection of the province-level contributions in the 1750s and 1760s as well as over demands for corvée labor to help build fortresses (1748–58).[38]

As in the other parts of the Balkans, Greek peasants often sought relief by practicing a second trade, sometimes smuggling or piracy, which were widespread in the Morea. Here is Colonel Leake reporting on conditions in the early nineteenth century:

> The villagers which are least favored in respect of soil have resources in the manufacture of cotton and wool, such as coarse cloth shawls for the head and girdle, and towels. It is reckoned that one third of the inhabitants of Agrafa gain a living by weaving. There are also many workers in gold and silver; and at Skatina is a fabric [factory] of swords-blades, gun barrels, and locks of pistols . . . A large portion of the Agrifiotes, like the other mountaineers of Greece, gain a livelihood abroad as shopkeepers or artisans, or as carriers in the neighboring districts.[39]

Uneven weather contributed to other factors subverting security; hence life in Greece sometimes struck Europeans as especially vulnerable. Following is the same writer's description of the village of Khalike:

> Once the most important village of Pindus . . . is on the point of being deserted on account of the excessive burthen of the taxes, and of a debt of 100 purses. When the village was in its prosperity, the inhabitants abandoned their corn for sheep, and have now very little of either, their property consisting almost entirely of horses and mules, with which they gain a livelihood as carriers. Yet the annual contribution is still 400 to 700 piastres from the head of a family.[40]

Even diet was affected by insecurity:

> To botanize in search of esculent wild herbs in the spring and early summer is a common occupation of the women of Greece, those herbs forming an important part of the food of the poor during the fasts of that season. In the summer they have no such resource. . . . The summer productions, of the garden . . . which depend on irrigation . . . are too dear for the poor, or rather not be had as gardening . . . can never flourish in a country where property is as insecure as in Turkey. The chief food of the lower classes, therefore, in the summer fast is salted star-fish [octopus?], olives, goats, cheese, and bread of maize, seasoned with a garlic or onion, and washed down perhaps with sour wine.[41]

ANATOLIA

Far more than the provinces of Europe, Anatolia in the eighteenth century was still home to numerous nomadic (or transhumant) Turkomans. Its population was stagnant at best and, though statistical evidence is lacking, still may not have recovered from the tremendous social upheaval of the early seventeenth century.

As in Europe, land valuations varied enormously, reflecting relative abundance. Thus the Anatolian version of the three-field system allowed fields to rest for two years out of three.[42] Following a Middle Eastern pattern, grain crops were planted in fall. Houses of wood and stone in the west gave way in the unwooded eastern regions to structures of adobe and stone. Where nomads wintered, they might erect huts of cane, then set them ablaze upon leaving for summer pasture.[43]

Villages were not near main roads, since marauding vagabonds were endemic at all times and were especially bad following wars. The number of tax-liable peasants (reayas) continually fell, since Muslim villagers who visited İstanbul would take the opportunity, especially later in the century, to purchase Janissary pay tickets. Although these were worthless in terms of pay, they were very valuable in conferring tax immunity if honored in their villages.[44] Villagers typically no longer paid taxes or rents to a sipahi, but to a tax-farmer, who often held a life lease (malikane), or to his agent.[45]

Certain limited zones, such as those near the great port of İzmir, contained large estates held by one of the powerful provincial families. But it remains moot how production was actually organized on these estates, since some relied on sharecroppers and others on hired labor, with wide variation in size of units. In all likelihood the landholding families were more tax gatherers and usurers than agricultural managers.[46] Since cotton was prominent in İzmir's exports, we can infer cotton production in its hinterland, as well as wheat and grapes, though the latter were less traded.

IRAQ

The rivers of Iraq flooded each spring, endangering the winter crops and requiring much corvée labor and annual redistribution of holdings, in order to cope with the changes brought by the flooding. Along the rivers, the tribes competed to control the cultivators who, in irrigated areas, surrendered up to two-thirds of their output to their protectors, the Shammar federation in northern Iraq and the Muntafik in the south.

Nearer to Baghdad and Mosul, cultivators were under the control of the town elites – merchants, money-changers, or the administrators of religious or family foundations (*vakıf*), or officials of the province. In the latter half of the century the urban elites were challenged so little that they treated the holdings they controlled as their own property, keeping tenants in permanent debt and sometimes pushing so hard for tax arrears as to cause flight. Staples included rice as well as other grains, fruits, and dates grown near the Gulf.[47]

SYRIA

Aleppo and Damascus lived in uneasy symbiosis with the nearby Turkoman and Kurdish tribes, which supplied them with sheep, wool, butter and cheese, carpets, camels, beeswax, tobacco and gallnuts for dyeing.[48] The tribes took with them to their summer pastures on the Anatolian plateau the goods they received in return: fabrics, dyes, weapons, jewelry, coffee, sugar, and other sweets.[49]

Villagers living near the main towns of Syria were invariably the tenants of the town elites, who treated their holdings as possessions, and might even buy and sell them. The townsmen held the villagers collectively responsible for taxes, and the debts associated with them,[50] frequently buying up their crops in advance of harvest by way of payment.

In the densely settled valleys of Mount Lebanon, so much land was devoted to mulberry stands that the zone needed food from the outside to sustain itself.[51]

In southern Syria and Palestine, the gradual infiltration of the Anazeh Bedouins boxed the villagers behind high walls, leaving the plains largely depopulated except for the summering tribes.[52] Despite this pressure from the tribes, cotton cultivation in the south accounts for a major north-to-south shift in population during the course of the century and a corresponding change in the relative importance of the ports on the coast.[53] Cotton was two to three times more profitable than wheat, and, as in İzmir and Salonica, caused a major alteration in the economy during the course of the century.[54]

EGYPT

Egypt's peasants lived in one-story houses of mud and dung (adobe).[55] Like villagers on the riverbanks of Iraq, they surrendered up two-thirds of their product to the village tax-farmer (*mültezim*), a townsman who would resell the grain at Cairo. The tax-farmer not only ruled the village, insofar as one could who did not live there, he also held there a reserve of his own. This reserve he came to treat as his outright property, and worked it with the corvée labor of his villagers, who were always in debt to him.[56] There was much flight by villagers in the second half of the century. It is noteworthy that they usually fled not to a city but to other villages, perhaps because a disappearing population was freeing up land. Some villagers paradoxically managed to accumulate land, apparently profiting from the carelessness of Mamluk administration. Runaways could be returned by force.[57] This close control over labor and the production process resembles in spirit the stereotypical *çiftlik* village of late Ottoman times, save that the peasants may have owned their homes. In 1785, the observer Volney offered a rich description of Egyptian peasant life:

> The rice and corn they gathered are carried to the table of their masters, and nothing is left for them but dourra or Indian millet, of which they make bread without leaven ... This bread is eaten with water and raw onions, their only food throughout the year; and they esteem themselves happy if they can sometimes procure a little honey, cheese, sour milk, and dates. Flesh, meat, and fat, which they are passionately fond of make their appearance only at the great festivals ... Their clothing consists of coarse blue linen, and in a clumsy black cloak.[58]

Except for the inevitable transactions with the tax-farmer or his agent, Egyptian villagers lived quite self-contained lives, the masters of many crafts at a time when urban crafts were on the decline because of over-taxation. Disputes between villagers were settled by local referees, guided by custom. Religious life was much influenced by the brotherhoods, but in village versions distinct from those of the city.[59]

NORTH AFRICA

The Maghrib generally was the most rural of the Arab lands and more in the hands of the tribes. Around the towns, there were the characteristic rings of gardens and these, together with farms located in the most favored plains, were in the hands of townsmen – merchants, military men, or high officials who treated them like property. In some tribal areas there were also farms held by the sheikhs. Any of these might be worked by migrants, men away from their families.[60]

The extremely uneven grain harvests of North Africa were due to rainfall variation and may help explain the region's unsteady demographic record. Pastoralism predominated, with each tribe practicing its own particular mixture of herding, extensive and intensive farming. Within tribes great inequalities existed, and subject (*reaya*) tribes were bound to pay tribute to the official (*mahzen*) tribes. Customary law prevailed, especially among the Berbers of Algeria. But abject tenantry was exceptional and most Maghribians owned their own houses, and went about armed down to the time of the French conquest.[61] Most textiles of the region were made in the countryside, the work of women.[62]

NOTES

1 İnalcık (1955), p. 225.
2 Berov (1976), pp. 147, 319.
3 Mellor (1975), p. 177.
4 Neamtu (1975), p. 239.
5 *Ibid.*, pp. 258–63.
6 Wilkinson (1971), p. 157.
7 Chirot (1976), pp. 76–79; Alexandrescu-Dersca (1957), p. 35; Oteţea (1960), pp. 302–4.
8 Jewsbury (1976), p. 14; Jelavich (1983), I, pp. 107–9.
9 Oteţea (1960), pp. 310–11.
10 Stoianovich and Haupt (1962), p. 85.
11 Radutiu (1981), p. 506.
12 Cvijić (1918), p. 148; ISN (1986) vol. 4, pt. 1, p. 421; Warriner (1965), p. 315.
13 Mellor (1975), pp. 167–68.
14 Petrovich (1976), I, pp. 18, 23.
15 Blagojević (1973), pp. 418–26.
16 Vucinich, ed. (1982), p. 27.
17 ISN (1986), vol. 4, pt. 1, pp. 411, 327–8.
18 Tričković (1970), p. 531.
19 ISN (1986), vol. 4, pt. 1, p. 421; Tričković (1970), pp. 531–43.
20 Karadžić (1852), 'Citluk'.
21 Stojančević (1984), p. 142.
22 Eren (1965), p. 27; Sućeska (1965b), pp. 53–55.
23 Sućeska (1980), p. 145.
24 BAN (1985), vol. 5, p. 32.
25 Todorov (1983), p. 41.
26 Gandev (1960), pp. 208–17; Grozdanova (1974), pp. 44–45.
27 Grozdanova (1974), pp. 42–44.
28 BAN (1985), vol. 5, p. 32.
29 *Ibid.*, pp. 75–77.
30 *Ibid.*, pp. 33–45.
31 Matkovski (1978), pp. 241–42; BAN (1985), vol. 5, pp. 163–64.
32 BAN (1985), vol. 5, pp. 164–69.

33 Naci (1966), p. 133; *idem* (1970), p. 38; Ars (1963), p. 124.
34 Naci (1966), p. 133.
35 Mile (1977), p. 145.
36 Leake is quoted in Clogg (1976), p. 11.
37 Leake (1968), I, p. 11; II p. 144; *idem* (1967), III, p. 545.
38 McGrew (1977), pp. 151–53; 118.
39 Leake cited in Clogg (1976), p. 13.
40 Leake (1968), I, p. 258; cf. Wagstaff (1965), pp. 296–98.
41 *Ibid.*, p. 11.
42 Owen (1981), p. 40.
43 Orhonlu (1963), pp. 87–88.
44 Özkaya (1985), pp. 30–57.
45 İnalcık (1978), pp. 87–88.
46 Nagata (1976a), pp. 5–11, 24–28, 30–36; and İnalcık's comments (1983), pp. 117–19.
47 Nieuwenhuis (1982), pp. 6–12.
48 Bodman (1963), p. 5.
49 Owen (1981), p. 44.
50 Rafeq (1981), p. 672.
51 Harik (1969), p. 45.
52 Cohen (1973), p. 22; Owen (1981), p. 38.
53 Rafeq (1977), p. 72.
54 Barbir (1980), p. 180; Issawi (1982), p. 120.
55 Baer (1981), p. 597.
56 Staffa (1977), p. 314; Baer (1982), pp. 54–59.
57 *Ibid.*, p. 57.
58 Volney (1788), I, pp. 176–77.
59 Baer (1982), p. 57.
60 Valensi (1977a), pp. 30–36; Lacoste *et al.* (1960), pp. 174–78.
61 Cherif (1982), pp. 77–79; *idem* (1976), p. 113; Valensi (1977b), pp. 350, 308–13; Valensi (1977a), pp. 18, 26–27, 33.
62 Valensi (1977b), p. 209.

26

⌣̇

MERCHANTS AND CRAFTSMEN

Ottoman craft associations confronted conditions that changed particularly quickly after 1750 and led to fierce competition with Western manufactures at the beginning of the next century. The Ottoman merchant class, for its part, changed in several ways during the eighteenth century owing to its increasing contact with the West. Rising European interest in certain Ottoman commodities, above all cotton, gave opportunities to Ottoman merchants of all confessions and educated some of them, especially the Orthodox Christian merchants of southeastern Europe, to play a leading role in preparing their peoples for independence.

European demand for cotton cloth gave a boost to weaving at Edirne, Salonica and Shkoder as well as a number of smaller Balkan towns such as Verria, Elassona and Trnovo (in Thessaly) and to the east at Ankara, Bursa, Tokat, Antakya, Diyarbekir, Aleppo, and Baghdad. Until the 1760s one has the impression of Ottoman manufactures successfully participating in international trade. But with the stiffening of mercantilist policies in the Habsburg domains in the 1770s, followed by the internal disorder of the last two decades of the eighteenth century, this appearance fades. Raw materials began to play an ever larger part in Ottoman exports. Meanwhile crafts at home continued to use traditional methods and therefore were vulnerable to the onslaught of foreign wares which the nineteenth century would bring.

Of the various abuses of the century, two especially affected the Ottoman merchant class. Pashas in every important Ottoman port extorted the illegal (but tolerated) levies (*avanias*) from the colonies of foreign merchants living in their jurisdictions. Since members of the Ottoman minorities acted as the agents of Europeans in all Levantine ports, they too were affected by the *avanias*, which constricted but did not kill off the trade.

After 1740, a second abuse became prominent. Inaugurated to defend against the first abuse, foreign embassies began to extend their protection (including tax exemptions and other privileges) over a growing legion of patent-bearing protégés, drawn from the Ottoman minorities. Some of the patent holders were involved in trade, but not all. Orders issued to Aleppo in 1759, 1766, and 1786 indicate that protégés also were involved in crafts, tax-farming and money-lending.[1] At the end of the eighteenth century, it is believed that the Austrians alone were protecting 200,000 individuals. By 1805, however, the Ottoman government was selling its own patents of protection to Ottoman merchants, offering at a price the same advantages enjoyed by the European protégés. And, by 1812, all the European trading nations had been forced to accept new restrictions on their authority to extend protection.[2]

The craft associations continued to live a traditional life, apparently unresponsive to technical innovation elsewhere. In the eighteenth century the tendency for Ottoman craftsmen to work side by side in the same streets became stronger. The government encouraged this tendency because this made it easier to collect taxes and to demand requisitions when needed. The craftsmen themselves found it easier when concentrated in this way to band together to defend their monopoly rights, which were backed by the state, and to police prices and quality. Living and working near to one another also tended to strengthen their other social ties.

Such tight control over price and quality usually also meant that the craft could not raise enough capital unaided in order to erect a common building for industrial purposes. The factory-warehouse buildings, known as *han*s, which became characteristic in this century were usually established by some government figure, or by the government as a whole, and were financed by *vakıf* bequests. In these buildings craftsmen could band together and rent space from the *vakıf* administrator.

The tendency for craftsmen to congregate, for the government to seek control, and for warehouses to be built under government auspices were interlocking trends which developed together in this century.[3]

The social life of craftsmen wove together multiple identities: association with other craftsmen working in the same market-place, membership in a militia, religious fraternity or parish, residence in a particular quarter along with relatives of the same ethnic background. Income differentiation was limited. In the same sector the ratio between the incomes of the poorest and richest craftsmen seldom exceeded one to seven. Workshops almost always employed fewer than twenty journeymen and usually far less. Even state-run workshops were small scale and involved little division of labor, except for those producing gunpowder and armaments, where 50–100 workers might be employed.[4]

Migration into towns placed continuous pressure upon the associations for permission to enter: their most common complaint to the courts during the eighteenth century. As in the past, the courts continued to defend the views of the craft association councils (*loncas*) regarding limits to be set upon new shops, etc. Two associations, the tanners and the tailors, played an important role in the politics of several towns during the eighteenth century, especially in Albania and Syria. Otherwise their traditions insulated craftsmen from rapid change, just as distance insulated them from the actions of their fellow craftsmen in other cities. Purely commercial shops remained exceptional. Most products continued to be sold by their makers, the members of traditional associations; therefore, they did not participate in the important trends in inter-regional and international trade which were taking place in the eighteenth century and which would threaten them later.

In some remote villages, and out-of-the-way neighborhoods of the capital city, there were occasional attempts to hide new workshops, so as to escape the controls of the state and some craft association. Thus not all migration was towards the cities. The disincentives of agriculture under Ottoman rules pushed some villagers, especially in hilly regions, to develop products, such as yarn, dyestuffs, and olive oil, which they might process and either sell locally or to agents of a wider trade. Our knowledge of the locations of such villages is very incomplete. At present we can point to villages near Seres (cotton), Samakov (ironwork), and Tokat (silk, or copperwork) as examples. But the fact that we are able to name these areas indicates that these were all too well known to escape government control.

Just as Ottoman governments favored and supported concentration of production under craft association controls, by the same token they discouraged production outside older production centers. Penalties could be steep. Whereas normal cases of tax evasion could involve a 100 percent fine, "renegade" production could result in a fine of 200 percent, or confiscation or destruction of equipment, or even banishment to the galleys. But such harsh penalties were aimed at international trade, not local trade. Given such attitudes on the part of the Ottoman government, and the associations themselves, it is hard to see how the Ottoman economy could have kept up with contemporary technological innovations, even if its communications had been better.[5]

A list of the craft associations found at Ankara in 1827 suggests the material culture (and the importance of textiles) of the preceding century: tanners, catgut makers, cobblers, sandal makers, perfumers, goathair spinners, quilt fluffers, tailors, goldsmiths, grocers, silk spinners, cloth merchants (a very important group), weavers, goathair sellers, goathair dyers, cloth dyers, blacksmiths, musket makers, sword makers, blacksmiths, butchers, bakers, spinning-wheel makers, tobacconists, axle makers, saddlers, tinners, copperware makers, cleat makers, candle makers, pastry cooks, rice sellers, helva makers, fruiterers, barbers, felt makers, coffee sellers, coffee roasters, pot makers, millers, porters, weighers, chick-pea peddlers, fish and olive sellers, metal workers, fringe makers, furriers, *kalpak* makers, skullcap makers, quilt makers, linseed oil sellers, trough makers, leather workers, goathair spinners, rag sellers, knife grinders, cloak makers, merchandise brokers, carpenters, whitewashers, plasterers, stonemasons, pipe makers, (rush) mat makers, gardeners, horseshoers, bullet makers, henna sellers, pastrami sellers, snuff sellers, vegetable peddlers. The above list preserves the order of the original. Ankara was at that time a town of approximately 60,000–100,000 inhabitants.[6]

OTTOMAN EUROPE (RUMELIA)

In this century, town–country integration in various parts of the Ottoman Empire was on the increase, partly because either the *ayan*s or the Janissaries of most towns took an active role in some form of domination over village life, such as tax-farming or money-lending. In Rumelia integration was also taking place because of increased merchant activity as intermediaries for village products sold in towns, regional fairs, and distant ports or markets which specialized in international trade. These might be livestock and animal by-products such as tallow, hides and wool, especially in Bulgaria and Macedonia; wheat from locations near the Aegean coast; or village craft products for which there was a regional, inter-regional or international demand. Most prominent among the craft products were the rough woolen cloaks called *aba*s made at various places in Bulgaria and Albania, ingots and ironwares coming from several locations in Bulgaria and Macedonia, and cotton cloth or yarn from several places in Bulgaria, Macedonia and Thessaly. Certain towns had other specialities – rifles at Sliven or Prizren, furs at Kastoria, leatherwork at Sarajevo and at certain Bulgarian towns.[7]

The observer Leake, in 1806, offered a detailed description of lead and silvermining, as practiced near Sidrekapsı in the Khalkidiki.

> The mines now wrought are . . . in a deep ravine, where a stream of water serves for the operations of washing, as well as to turn a wheel for working the bellows of the furnace. The whole is conducted in the rudest and most slovenly manner. The richest ore is pounded with stones upon a board by hand, then washed and burnt with charcoal; the inferior ore is broken into larger pieces, and burnt twice without washing. . . . The heaps of wrought ore . . . on the side of the mountain below the present works, show how very extensively these mines have once been wrought.[8]

Putting-out systems at the village level were widespread because of their relative flexibility and freedom from interference. In making these systems work, the merchant played the essential role, moving surpluses to market, and thereby increasing their value.[9]

In the early decades of the eighteenth century, the main centers for international commerce which rose in Ottoman Europe were Salonica, where the French and British established consulates, and Brašov, in Transylvania, where Habsburg authorities permitted the establishment of an "Ottoman" settlement. The Treaty of Belgrade (1739) and its liberal clauses gave a great stimulus to trade in southeastern Europe. For three decades Ottoman merchants – at first Serbs, then Bulgars, Orthodox Greeks, Macedonians and Hellenized Tsintsars – enjoyed exceptional opportunities in wholesale trading with the Habsburg lands, where they paid a lesser customs rate and were exempt from other taxes aimed at Habsburg subjects. A remarkable "Ottoman" diaspora ensued which saw tens of thousands of Orthodox Ottoman subjects, above all Greeks, resettled at Lwow, Leipzig, Vienna, and Trieste and most towns in Hungary. (By contrast Ottoman merchants resident at Ancona and Livorno in Italy tended to be Jews or Armenians.) By 1754 there were thirteen Ottoman (Orthodox) commercial companies established in Hungarian towns, and that number later doubled.[10] This trading bonanza flattened in the period 1766–72, when Maria Theresa's counselors changed the rules of the game, tightening the passport regime, forbidding the import of finished foods and the presence of foreign companies on Habsburg soil. Most of the Ottoman newcomers then chose to be naturalized and increasingly traded in native Habsburg goods such as wine.[11]

Like all town dwellers in the Ottoman Empire, the Orthodox merchants were taxed relatively lightly as individuals. Also the taxes these merchants paid at market were at relatively moderate rates which tended to lag behind inflation. Their disadvantages, as Ottoman merchants, were in the insecurity of the roads and their vulnerability to extortion, especially in towns like Salonica, Belgrade and Sarajevo, where Janissaries (or pseudo-Janissaries) held the upper hand. Nonetheless there is a body of evidence to show that from Nauplia to Jassy many merchants did prosper, especially in the middle decades of the century. In Bulgaria, the weight of scholarship in fifty monographs points to widespread town growth and increased commercial prosperity during the third quarter of the century. Elsewhere commercial centers also flourished, such as the Tsintsar emporium of Moskopolje in western Macedonia, Shkoder in Albania, and Ambelakia in Greece.[12]

Members of merchant families commonly were scattered abroad, as shown in this contemporary (c. 1802) description of a Vlah village of Thessaly:

> The wealthier inhabitants are merchants, who have resided abroad many years in Italy, Spain . . . Austria, or Russia; and who, after a long absence, return with the fruits of their industry to their native towns, which they thus enrich, and in some degree, civilize. But they seldom return for permanent residence till later in life, being satisfied in the interval with two or three short visits. The middle classes . . . return more frequently, and many of them spend a part of every summer in their native place. These are chiefly shopkeepers . . . or artisans.[13]

But the degree of foreign influence upon these merchants was uneven, as we see from Leake's 1806 report on Yanina:

> The domestic manners of the Greeks of Ionnina have in general been little affected by the long residence of many of the merchants in foreign countries. They are almost identical with those of the Turks . . . The Greek women are as uneducated as the Turks, and are held in subserviency . . . Little respect is paid to age, especially when the parents . . . are in part maintained by the children, and live in the same house . . . The common employment of the women . . . are the embroidery of coarse German muslins, in imitation of those of Constantinople.[14]

To provide the houses of this rising commercial class, builders' villages appeared, especially in western Macedonia, which sent out their craftsmen in all directions, as far as İstanbul and Bucharest. One symptom of the insecurity of life which plagued the eighteenth century was the favored design for great houses in many places – a high cubical fort-like structure that still can be seen in rural areas in the Balkans, such as Bosnia, and in western Macedonia.

Even when not designed for defense, merchants' houses were expensive.

Building is very costly in Greece, as well on account of the high price of
mechanical labor as because plank, glass, nails, every thing but the stone
and mortar, comes from Trieste and Fiume. ... The better houses of
Ionnina have an inner window frame behind the bars, containing small
panes of a very bad kind of glass brought from the Adriatic; this addition
which is seldom seen in Asiatic Turkey ... is here rendered necessary by
the long winter.[15]

The number of costly houses at Sofia doubled in the second half of this
century.[16]

Among the merchants a growing knowledge of the world, and a richer
associational life became characteristic. Partly this arose from their
involvement at home in the affairs of their parishes, which they increasingly organized and led; it also was a by-product of their cooperation
abroad in the numerous mercantile companies. Since banking facilities
were scant, commercial agreements usually were enacted by word alone.
Younger members of merchant families were stationed at river and border
crossings for long periods and entrusted with great responsibility.

Because Balkan commerce was growing in this century but was still
without the permanent facilities which commerce demands, the greatest
fairs of the Ottoman Empire appeared at this time. Most fairs traded in
local livestock, a means for transferring surpluses at the village level.
Others, especially the great annual fair at Uzuncaova in eastern Thrace,
were exchanges of inter-regional and international significance. At its
height Uzuncaova attracted 50,000 people, and was visited by merchants
from Russia as well as the West. This great fair also operated as a bourse/
borsa at which bills of exchange circulated. When the chaos of the 1780s
and 1790s closed down Uzuncaova, the new banking functions moved
north across the Danube to Bucharest, where Austrian and Russian consuls guaranteed protection after 1784. By the end of the eighteenth century, the Wallachian capital regularly handled not only the usual banking
functions but also large transfers of bullion and coin in and out of the
Ottoman Empire, an arbitrage trade necessitated by the swift currency
fluctuations of the Napoleonic era.[17]

The development most affecting the lives of artisans in the numerous
craft corporations during the eighteenth century was the infiltration of
these fraternities by putative Janissaries. There were at least 50,000 so-
called Janissaries garrisoned throughout the empire at mid-century, few
of whom could truly be called soldiers. Since Janissary pay by then was
merely nominal, most of these "Janissaries" actually were craftsmen who
wanted the traditional Janissary privileges of tax exemption and judicial

immunity. By the late eighteenth century, virtually all the Muslim guildsmen of Belgrade, Sarajevo, and Salonica called themselves "Janissaries," or at least "recruits" (*yamak*s). One effect was to sharpen the distinction between themselves and Christian and Jewish townsmen, who could not claim Janissary membership. Naturally it was extremely difficult for the local commander (*dizdar*), much less for İstanbul, to exercise authority over this self-nominated militia. As a result, several Balkan towns were virtually plebian republics, which a strong governor might fear, even if tradition demanded (as at Sarajevo) that he be greeted upon arrival with an evening parade of the assembled guildsmen, accompanied by a roar of cannons from the fortress.

Other traditions of the Ottoman craftsmen were preserved as well. At Sarajevo the youths of each new generation were handed over to the masters by their parents with the ancient formula, witnessed by all: "Strike: the bones are mine, but the flesh is yours." In practice, however, the abuse of apprentices and other transgressions against tradition could be brought before the assembly (*lonca*) of the association. An offender might lose the right to keep apprentices, or be forced to close his shop for a time, or in extreme cases be obliged to close permanently and be reduced to the status of a journeyman.[18]

Rarely did the associations of Bosnia resort to government courts for a decision. An assembly of masters and journeymen set prices; then the association informed the court of its decision. The masters as a group also kept tight control over the opening of new shops – one either had to be the son of a master, or have the permission of the chief (*kahya*) of the association's assembly. Powerful masters might be tempted to improve their position by buying out weaker shops in time of crises, then employing additional help and behaving like merchants. At the other end of the scale, hard-pressed journeymen might be found at mid-winter selling their goods at isolated locations and at sacrifice prices to buyers from another province.[19]

ANATOLIA

A lion's share of the international trade involving Anatolia concentrated at the great port of İzmir (Smyrna), already on the rise in the late seventeenth century and destined to become the leading port of the empire. To the Jewish and Armenian protégés who worked for European traders, the migration from Morea in the 1770s added more Greeks, giving to the port a polyglot character. By this time, a large part of the İzmir trade had reverted to the native "Levantine" minorities. The Dutch had

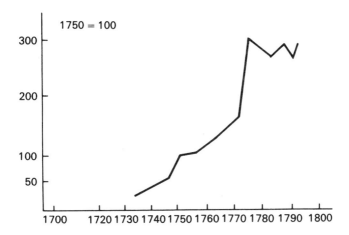

Fig. III:2 Duties collected on cotton and cotton cloth for export. *Source*: Genç (1976).

accorded them all the rights of their own merchants and since 1730 had tolerated the establishment at Amsterdam of merchants who were the relatives of the Jews, Armenians and Greeks of İzmir. Indeed the opportunities for trade in this century were so promising that the Ottomans lost a portion of their Jews and Armenians, who resettled at various European merchant capitals, leaving to the Greeks a leading role in Ottoman trade.

Raw cotton was the leading commodity at İzmir, losing ground only as American cotton began to enter world markets towards the end of the century. Cotton-cloth weaving at Ankara, Bursa, and Tokat thrived in the first sixty to seventy years of the eighteenth century, but thereafter tended to fall off. Between the 1760s and 1790s there was also a loss of as much as 30 percent of the cape-making production of Ankara and of silk production at Chios. Bursa's loss of revenues from silk and cotton-cloth production was even more dramatic, perhaps as much as 60 to 70 percent between 1769 and 1797. Figures from the dye works at Tokat show that peak years for production of cotton cloth and white and yellow silk were 1764–66. After this trade declined, Tokat developed instead into the main Anatolian center for copper manufactures, drawing on the mines at Ergani, Küre and Gümüşhane.[20] These trends are based on incomplete evidence and need further research, but they fit with a general impression of faltering commercial conditions in the last decades of the eighteenth century and the first decade of the subsequent century.

Anatolian towns nonetheless continued to supply specialties for regional and international markets – goat hair from Ankara, shoes and skins from Konya, tanned leather, saddles and dyed cloth from Kayseri, and tiles from Kütahya, where a fall in quality would seem to indicate that upper-class clients were increasingly buying European imports. Bursa held an annual fair each June, and there were other such fairs in Anatolia.[21]

ISTANBUL

The Ottoman metropolis was really three towns joined by water. Only two groups of workers – the boatmen and the porters – had associations which united İstanbul, Pera and Üsküdar, and only the tanners had ties with other cities. About forty building trades were grouped under the supervision of a state-appointed official, the chief architect, while the rest recognized a degree of unofficial coordination under the supervision of a jointly elected sheikh.[22]

As elsewhere, craft associations in İstanbul were under continuous pressure to admit newcomers in the eighteenth century: their petitions to the courts frequently requested protection from "strangers," or from undue contact between Muslims and non-Muslims, as for instance at the baths, possibly indicating growing tension between major sectors of society. İstanbul's 40,000 "Janissaries" were well-integrated into the craft associations, and manned its fire brigades as well.

The associations were self-policing in most respects: an elected elder headed each and was guided by a representative committee of masters (the *lonca*). This did not prevent eighteenth-century governments from assigning additional individuals from outside the association as intendants (*kahyas*). This amounted to a tax on the associations, of course, but in return offered the members access to government. Begun in the seventeenth century, this practice became widespread in the following century. Persons with military status would be encouraged to bequeath their salaries to the treasury, and in return would be assigned as intendant to one of the craft associations. From İstanbul the practice spread to other cities as well.[23]

Ultimate authority over quality and price at İstanbul was left to courts of the tripartite capital. Usually transgressions against the standards brought a mere warning. If the transgression was grave or repeated, a

Muslim offender might go to jail, or a non-Muslim to the galleys. Sometimes offenders were obliged to stop working, but only temporarily.

The incomes of İstanbul's craftsmen varied within a narrow range, possibly as a result of close court supervision. This meant that the associations had insufficient capital to build commercial inns (*hans*), bathhouses, or even shops. These were typically the endowments of foundations, to be rented by the craftsmen or merchants. Whereas the Ottoman commercial inn provided rents for such foundations, the Ottoman rural inn (caravanserai) instead typically was supported by the foundation, and provided space free of charge to travellers.[24]

Since İstanbul was more a center of consumption than production, its leading merchants frequently were those associated with the city's command economy, supplying staples for the people of the capital, and occasionally involved in engrossment schemes. The 5,000 plus shops concentrated in the old city on the palace side included many which dealt in luxury wares for a courtly clientele. Some of these, such as goldwork and jewelry, were of world-class quality. Remarks by one European contemporary regarding the quality of Ottoman products – textiles, arms and ships – are in general admiring, except with respect to technical innovation, where they lagged.

Muslim merchant families usually lacked generational continuity because of the Islamic requirement that inheritances be sub-divided with each generation. This was not true of the large and heterogeneous Orthodox community (Greek, Armenian, Bulgarian and Albanian) whose leading (Greek) families were rooted in the Fener (Phanar) district. These dominated the affairs of their Patriarchate, competing for the prestigious appointments to the Rumanian principalities, plums reserved (at a price) for this Phanariote elite.

Also very influential at the capital, but in a less ostentatious way, were the inner band of money-lenders and money-changers (*sarrafs*) who financed the empire's wholesale tax-farming system. Without the backing of a recognized and trusted lender, even prominent officials could not participate in this system, which far outpaced trade as a source of wealth and power in the Ottoman capital at this period.[25]

CAIRO

At the counter-capital of Cairo, interpenetration of the Janissaries into the numerous craft associations already was complete early in the century. But Janissary control of the corporations seems to have gone farther here than at İstanbul since craftsmen also were placed under "protection" by the Janissary *agha*, who extended immunity from the traditional market regime (*hisba*) under Islamic government. Thus when units from the Janissary regiments which invaded Egypt in 1801 threw their colors on the doors of stores they intended to "protect," they were simply renewing long-established practice. Little wonder that the average income of Cairo's craftsmen, who comprised half the city's population, declined drastically during the course of the century.

The richest merchants of Cairo were not those associated with the city's trade in provisions, since this was under the protection of the Janissary *agha*. Rather they were the merchants of the international trade network, especially the trade in coffee. Banking and insurance were little developed. Most merchant ventures were carried on by partnerships.

Several ethnic minorities coexisted at Cairo, each tending to dominate certain wards, each specializing in certain crafts or lines of business. The richest of these, surpassing the Maghribi, Coptic and Jewish merchants, was the Syrian Catholic (Melkite) community, who had gained a favored position under Mamluk rule since their arrival in Egypt in the 1730s. As aggressive and capable outsiders, the Syrians first were allowed to participate in the Mediterranean and Red Sea trades. After the Mamluks made their historic move into the city of Cairo at mid-century, they were permitted to displace the Jews as masters of the customs tax-farms. Almost everyone else suffered as the rapacity of the Mamluks was applied to Cairo's various commercial resources, increasing in tempo during the decades leading to the French invasion.[26]

THE ARAB PROVINCES

At all the ports of the Levant, the Jews, Greeks and Armenians, as partners and protégés of European traders, dominated international trade as well as the inter-regional waterborne trade. French shippers also played a leading part on the sea routes, until displaced by the Greeks. Thus the ports constituted a separate outward-facing trading world with their own peculiar composite social constitution. Inland towns, such as Aleppo, Damascus, Baghdad and Mecca, were ethnically different from the ports and also differently constituted in their economic life.

The alliance of local Janissaries with local craft corporations characterized the inland towns of Syria and Iraq, just as in other Ottoman provinces. At Baghdad, a Mamluk stratum provided the essential (though expensive) services of security and political leadership. But, at Aleppo and Damascus, the Janissary-guildsmen were involved in notorious long-running factional struggles. At Aleppo the factions, each with allies among the local Kurdish and Turkoman tribes, were organized around native Janissary-guildsmen on the one hand, and the *eşraf* (a religious fraternity) on the other. At Damascus the factions, each with its own local elite allies, opposed local Janissary-guildsmen against imperial Janissaries, charged with guarding the pilgrimage. The fact that the factions in both towns tended to be equal (like the factions of Cairo in the first half of the same century) is a clue to their meaning: the struggle between the parties was a struggle for control over economic life.

The distinction between guildsmen and merchants was less clear in the Arab provinces than in other Ottoman areas. Both shared control of the two great sources of economic life – the caravans and the countryside – and both engaged in trade.[27] Whereas merchants generally held the tax-farms of the villages surrounding Arab towns, guildsmen in their guise as Janissaries showed up in the tasks of tax collection, money-lending, and the supervision of religious foundations (*vakıf*). The merchants capitalized the caravans, while whole quarters of people made their livings from the other functions required for the caravan trade – provisions, camels, packing, security and storage. The faction which maintained superiority at Aleppo and Damascus also held the upper hand in obtaining tax-farms, organizing the caravans, and profiting from the engrossment of staples – a damaging practice which became increasingly frequent after c. 1750.

Like their counterparts in other Ottoman provinces, craftsmen in Aleppo lived under a self-imposed discipline, usually pooling their supplies and incomes and accepting other restrictions typical of association life. Although price controls relatively were freer at Aleppo than in other imperial cities, the craft associations frequently appeared before the court to record prices agreed among themselves. The court tended to favor the interests of the craft association, though these occasionally might conflict with Islamic norms such as the sanctity of contract and property.[28]

Merchants, especially those dealing in the caravan trade, were far freer of restrictions and were more accustomed to the radical price fluctuations of long-distance commodities such as indigo and coffee. To hedge their risks, merchants sometimes impinged on craft prerogatives by making putting-out agreements outside the craft associations. This tendency increased after 1758, when al-Ghazzi reports the beginning of a long depression in the textile crafts.[29]

Standing between the two extremes in terms of freedom were the retail associations which, though they accepted the authority of their sheikh, made no attempt to restrict the number of shops. Serving both Aleppo and the villages of the vicinity were the peddlers, who maintained networks to collect soap, gallnuts, wool, cotton cloth and thread for sale at Aleppo, much of it entering the inter-regional trade.[30]

NOTES

1 Bağış (1983), p. 44.
2 *Ibid.*, pp. 63–84.
3 Genç (1990), pp. 6–7.
4 *Ibid.*, p. 14.
5 *Ibid.*, pp. 8–12.
6 Özdemir (1986), p. 229.
7 Frasheri (1964), pp. 103–4; Naci (1970), pp. 40–42; Pollo and Arben (1981), p. 92; Naci (1966), p. 135; Paskaleva (1968a), pp. 134–35; Shkodra (1975), pp. 61–71; Sugar (1977), pp. 229–30; Todorov (1983), pp. 456–61, 211, 223; Vacalopoulos (1973), pp. 289, 386, 410, 454–78, 540; Kiel (1985), pp. 118–35; BAN (1985), vol. 5, pp. 53–8, 72–3, 75–81; Berov (1974), p. 176; Berov (1976), p. 147; Paskaleva (1978b), pp. 42–48; Leon (1972), pp. 27–32; Svoronos (1956), p. 193; Trianta (1975), p. 86; Vacalopoulos (1963), p. 99; Lascaris (1938), p. 267; Jonville (1939), p. 267; Beaujour (1800), pp. 30, 183, 350, 430.
8 Leake (1967), III, p. 164.
9 Todorov (1983), pp. 456–61.
10 Hering (1987), p. 83.
11 ISN (1986), vol. 4, pt. 1, pp. 418, 312–13, 350, 457, 465–68, 479; Popović (1964), p. 127; Šamić (1961b), p. 11; Spiesz (1968), pp. 390–416; Tričković (1970), p. 532; Bur-Markovska (1981), pp. 137–38; Stoianovich (1960), pp. 266–306; Runciman (1968), p. 360.
12 Popović (1937), p. 36.
13 Leake (1967), I, p. 275.
14 Quoted in Clogg (1976), pp. 5–7.
15 Leake (1967), I, p. 611; and IV, p. 144.
16 Todorov (1977), p. 61.
17 Limona (1974), pp. 386–94; Penelea (1973), pp. 23–24; Sousa (1933), pp. 33, 59, 88; Stefanescu (1969), pp. 9–10.
18 Kreševljaković (1949), pp. 203–6.
19 *Ibid.*, pp. 199–206; and *idem* (1957), pp. 11–31; Georgieva (1970), p. 323; Genç (1986), p. 114; Stojančević (1984), pp. 142–50; Baer (1980a), p. 96; Braudel (1982), pp. 64, 85–96; Clogg (1976), pp. 5–7; Genç (1984).
20 Genç (1987), pp. 146–57.
21 Kreševljaković (1949), pp. 54–55; Baer (1980a), p. 99; Carswell (1977), p. 355; Özkaya (1985), pp. 30, 62–69, 145–49; Stoianovich (1960), p. 271; Sahillioğlu (1968a), p. 62.
22 Genç (1986), p. 114.
23 Genç (1990), p. 5.
24 Genç (1986), pp. 115–22; and Kreševljaković (1957), pp. 28–31.

25 Baer (1980a), p. 100; *idem* (1970), p. 161; Barkan (1955), pp. 304–9; Baykal (1962), p. ix; Genç (1986), pp. 114–24; q.v. "İmtiyazat" in *EI²*; İnalcık (1969), pp. 105–7, 138; İnciciyan (1976), pp. 23, 35–37, 102; Issawi (1980), p. 57; *idem* (1977), p. 160; Çadırcı (1980), pp. 238–41; Özkaya (1985), pp. 69, 78, 81, 346; Runciman (1968), p. 362; q.v. "İstanbul" in *EI²*.

26 Baer (1982), p. 206; Raymond (1984), p. 109; *idem* (1985), p. 51; *idem* (1973–74), I, pp. 206–15, 243, 259, 298, 301–2; II, pp. 403, 418–25; 452–87, 508–11, 518, 549, 565–75, 598, 601, 663, 692, 698, 703; *idem* (1977), pp. 184, 200; Staffa (1977), p. 338; Shaw (1964), p. 26; Marsot (1984), pp. 11–16.

27 Masters (1988), p. 48.

28 *Ibid.*, pp. 204–9.

29 *Ibid.* pp. 206–10.

30 *Ibid.*, p. 53; Baer (1982), pp. 158, 180, 203–15; Baer (1980a), pp. 97–99; *idem* (1981), pp. 597–609, 629; Raymond (1984), pp. 92–106; *idem* (1985), pp. 28–51; Nieuwenhuis (1982), p. 72; Nour (1982), pp. 98–99, 129; Thieck (1985), p. 142; Hourani (1968), p. 53; Rafeq (1975), pp. 283, 302–5, 279; Rafeq (1966), pp. 29, 72; Abun-Nasr (1971), pp. 176, 183, 194; Brown (1974), pp. 188–90; Valensi (1977a), p. 209; *idem* (1977b), p. 36.

27

∴

THE STATE AND THE ECONOMY

The sheer volume of fiscal innovation implemented by the Ottoman government during the eighteenth century belies the myth of stagnation so popular among historians until recently. The weight of past practices, however, was heavy and these are examined first.

With the appearance of the first free trade clauses in the Treaty of Utrecht (1713), West European nations began their retreat from the protectionist mentality which formed much of the mercantilist agenda.[1] In several states the evolution towards outright property in land was near completion, as was the establishment of outright property in ideas imbedded in patent law.[2] By now the English had invented the funded national debt which was to prove so useful in wartime, while the Dutch and Italians mastered another new world of credit instruments.[3] By contrast the Ottomans, intellectually cut off from most of these innovators, had to cope as well as they could without examining the mostly unconscious economic attitudes which they had inherited from the past.

Far from being protectionist (except for war material), the Ottomans remained quite ready to import whatever appealed to them, including bullion or specie. Although they exported, they did so without any sense of overall national interest or purpose. Ottoman merchants (by now often non-Muslims) were tolerated rather than admired in their own society, and trade existed by sufferance rather than encouragement.[4] Although the confiscation of merchants' estates was not normal (as it was in the case of tax-farmers), this inhibition began to break down late in the century when the government's need became extreme.

Ottoman merchant families did not form dynasties. Ottoman credit facilities were little developed, and export duties continued in force.[5] Concepts such as "balance of trade" did not enter into the government's calculations.[6] Investments of all kinds were held down not only by the rapid degeneration of capital goods and market volatility characteristic of pre-modern life, but also by the insecure status of merchants and would-be entrepreneurs.[7]

Throughout the Ottoman world (except at Cairo after the Mamluks invaded the city at mid-century), the old tendency to tax the countryside and favor the town prevailed. (By contrast in Great Britain and Prussia a reverse trend was under way.)[8] Officially the traditional sources of revenue changed little. In the Rumanian provinces, for instance, cattle, horses, wine, and the new crop maize went untaxed.[9]

The tithe, which France's Physiocrats criticized as a brake on productivity (since it led to economizing on inputs) remained a bedrock of Ottoman fiscal practice, subsumed under the tax-farming system.[10] At the beginning of the century, the tithe provided 42.5 percent of central government revenues, while the head-tax on non-Muslims provided 45.5 percent. At mid-century (1740), the contribution of tax-farming to general state revenues was estimated at 50 percent, with the head-tax providing another 40 percent, a correlation which suggests little change in method.

Ottoman fiscal conservatism also meant reluctance to raise tax rates, even when justified by currency devaluation. For the first sixty years of the century the *guruş*, the basic coin of the realm, remained almost constant in value. In the following fifty years (1760–1812), the *guruş* devalued at an average annual rate of 3 to 3.5 percent, not a rate which could be called socially disruptive.[11] In the same period, tax rates officially changed little, so that merchants had the advantage of a vast interior market less encumbered by official taxes than contemporary Germany, though without comparable security.[12]

Another drag on governmental efficiency was caused by obsolete records. Already by the late seventeenth century outdated cadastral records and unjust tax quotas based on them caused widespread peasant flight, a situation with parallels in contemporary France.[13] *Timar* records were so neglected that by 1759 the government could count on only half the 12,000 *timarlı* cavalry which the European provinces were supposed to contain.[14]

Head-tax records became so stereotyped that the observer Beaujour, at the end of the eighteenth century, believed that the head-tax might vary in value from district to district by a ratio of one to five.[15] One example of how outdated some records had become can be inferred from the practice of the Jewish community of İstanbul, which allocated its perennial and unvarying 20,000 head-tax certificates among the butchers and grocers of the community, who were expected to factor the amount of the taxes into the prices they charged for food.[16]

Another form of atrophy, representing an enormous loss of revenue for the treasury, was caused by the proliferation of the tax-exempt family trust (*vakıf*). The eighteenth-century family trust was a perversion of the venerable Islamic institution by which a pious donor established a fund, usually in the form of income-producing property (a bath, a warehouse, etc.), in support of some religious or charitable purpose deemed to be of value for the community of believers. In its typical eighteenth-century version, representing 75 to 80 percent of all such trusts, the descendants of the donor, or even the donor himself, were the first beneficiaries of the trust (as prebendaries), while the charitable or religious purposes of the trust could be postponed indefinitely.[17]

An estimated 80 percent of urban land was in trust during the eighteenth century.[18] In an estimated 90 percent of such cases, the founder belonged to the ruling stratum, thus no one seems to have questioned the use of such trusts for family purposes.[19] Using this device, military families might share the immunities of the clericals, against whom confiscations were not permitted.

In the countryside, some portion of the arable land was also alienated from the treasury in trusts. However, according to one experienced scholar who has studied the question, evidence of such conversions is lacking in the eighteenth century. Her hypothesis is that the rise of the life-lease system made it unnecessary for would-be estate owners to resort to forming trusts. If this is correct, then it follows that trust formation as a large-scale phenomenon may have skipped a century, emerging again in the nineteenth century after the demise of the life lease. In such distant provinces as Syria and Iraq, land was easily usurped by townsmen and treated in Iraq, at least, as outright property.[20] Much of this alienation already had occurred in the eighteenth century owing to the neglect of tax-farming leases which officially were forgotten, and to the dispossession of peasants by influential members of the military stratum.[21] Moreover in distant provinces such as Syria and Iraq, numerous alienations of this sort owed much to their remoteness from the capital and were one expression of loosened political control.[22] At that distance it was just as easy to convert usurpations to outright private property, without converting it to trusts.

FISCAL INNOVATIONS AND THEIR SOCIAL EFFECTS

Conservatism and retention of existing practices, however, were only one side of the coin. It was also the eighteenth-century Ottoman style to improvise and implant new institutions alongside the old to somehow save a situation. In 1695, almost simultaneously with France, the Ottomans reformed their head-tax system, creating three levels of liability for all adult males of the non-Muslim communities. Their main motive apparently was to return to more strictly Islamic norms, the head tax now replacing the earlier household tax of the European provinces applied since the time of the conquest. This three-tier personal tax system was to endure, though the great majority of taxpayers ended up in the middle category.[23]

In the same year that it reformed the head-tax, the Ottoman treasury also experimented with its other main source of revenues – the tax-farms. The government now began to grant life leases in return for a down payment of ready cash, a short-term palliative to relieve pressure on the treasury. Applied first in Syria and in eastern Anatolia, the life lease has been interpreted as an antidote to over-exploitation by tax-farmers concerned only with short-run yields. Accordingly, the life lease gave the tax-farmer a motive for preserving the prosperity of the peasants under his charge.[24]

This is a good example of how the Ottomans operated. Instead of a wholesale reform of the tax-farming system based on auctions that they had lived with throughout the preceding century, they erected a new system alongside it which gradually replaced or merged with the first. Thus the new system was accepted fully only after a small-scale experiment that tested its merits.

As the century passed, every sort of revenue was converted to the new life-lease system. Each year 150 to 300 new leases went on sale for purchase on a lifetime basis. A stratum of one to two thousand individuals, a privileged rentier circle, usually residing at İstanbul, arose to purchase them. Whereas 65 percent of life-lease holders were living at İstanbul in 1734, the ratio had risen to 87 percent by 1789. The annual take from down payments on life leases (*muaccele*) by then amounted to 10 percent of central government revenues (not including the annual rents for which lessees were also liable).

Not all lessees were of the elite stratum and sometimes several individuals shared a lease. This last practice naturally complicated the question as to when a life lease actually ended. Not surprisingly, a great many leases went astray because of collusion or neglect and thus were lost to the system. Larger leases were more profitable than smaller ones, which consequently lost popularity among the bidders. But so lucrative was the system in general that in Bosnia, even in the twentieth century, the slang expression for "easy money" was *"malikane"* (life lease).[25]

There was a tremendous slippage in the life-lease system, since the ratio between the yearly yield to the lessee and to the treasury of annual rents (*mal*) varied greatly from one lease to another.[26] Moreover, since the great majority of primary lessees lived at İstanbul, the system created great opportunities for secondary lessees, the innumerable agents who actually lived in the provinces and collected the specified funds. These agents as a group overlapped with the *ayan* stratum, as that term was originally used.

Despite all the abuses, the life-lease system survived until the Tanzimat era of the following century, for two reasons. First, the convenience to the treasury was no less than under the preceding system of annual auctions, whatever the waste involved. Second, most highly placed officials favored life leases that offered handsome, convenient and reasonably secure incomes. Through these they were bound still more closely to the fortunes of the dynasty.

Foreigners were appalled by the apparent waste of revenues in the life-lease system. One found that the central government received less than 4 million of 20 million pounds sterling annually collected on behalf of the state.[27] And they estimated Ottoman annual state revenues in 1789 at a mere 2.25 million pounds,[28] compared with Great Britain's 16.8 millions and France's 24 millions.[29] According to Ottoman government documents, however, these estimates may be too low by as much as a third. Even if these foreign estimates are only roughly accurate, however, we must be impressed by the disparity between these modest revenues and the heavy responsibilities involved in governing so vast an empire.

Another innovation of the eighteenth century was in the allocation of tax burdens (other than head-tax) at the level of the district. The leading fiscal authorities of contemporary France – Terray, Turgot and Necker – stated that the use of locals to carry out the reallocations was the fairest and most effective means of reallocating rural tax burdens to reflect continually changing rural conditions.[30] The Ottomans employed precisely this method in the eighteenth century as a substitute for a centralized record system which they no longer had the cadre to maintain.

After experimenting with an "assistance" tax (*imdat*) in wartime, the treasury began to impose these taxes in peacetime as well, starting in 1718. The peacetime "assistance" tax was the instrument of the local committees just described, and financed the needs of provincial governors, or other visiting high officials, as well as other district or provincial expenditures, such as maintaining bridges or fortifications, etc. The local committees administered the reallocation of these surtaxes in their districts.[31]

This new "reallocation" (*tevzi*) system developed, not by decree but gradually, organically and unevenly. Under this system, the local committees maintained district-level registers that allowed the weight of any new surtax to be shifted around within a district in keeping with current realities relating to productive strength, just as the Physiocrats would have prescribed. Naturally members of the committees used their positions to personal advantage and fortified their claims to being the leaders (*ayans*) of their respective districts.[32]

Reliance on these local *ayan* committees obtained admirable short-run results. The committees overall offered an effective antidote to a heretofore insoluble problem – that of forestalling illegal levies by the state's own high officers, which, along with the depredations of wandering and demobilized soldiers, plagued the era. But, as already seen, this system of reallocation of taxes by local figures had in it the seeds for further problems.

The power of the local committees could be used in various ways to indebt villagers to usurers or tax-farmers, who typically were members of the committee. Later in the century strings of estates and even whole villages were removed by subterfuge from the competence of the reallocation committees, so that the burden of taxation was less equitably shared than before. Domination of such committees became the platform by which the leading tax-farmer of a district frequently began his rise towards becoming a warlord or the ally of a warlord.

The central government tried several times to centralize and control the appointment of committee chiefs, naming them in effect as the official *ayans* of their respective districts (in 1765, 1779 and 1784). But the government in these later decades was at a great disadvantage. Since it had allowed locals to gain effectual control over their districts, while itself remaining remote from the scene, the central government saw the attempts fail utterly. Exploiting their multiple powers – as landholders, as the lessees or sublessees of tax-farms, as the principals on local reallocation committees, and in time of war as recruitment agents – the *ayan* hierarchies by the end of the century challenged the government's control of increasingly large zones.[33]

Other innovations followed the head-tax reform, and the reallocation device. Notably Ottoman treasury officials succeeded in creating two forms of public securities which served to raise money for the government when the need was desperate. By the middle of the century, the treasury of Egypt had pointed the way towards a market in securities by issuing some 20 percent of military salaries as promissory notes, which then were sold and resold among money-changers.[34] For its part, the Ottoman central treasury had long before learned the trick of leaving pay in arrears as one way of easing the demands of war. Thus, when the foreign advisor De Tott was active at İstanbul during the war of 1768–74, he discovered Janissary pay to be nine quarters in arrears. He also noted that the Ottomans had begun issuing numerous pay tickets in lieu of money which were being traded between parties as a kind of public security. He estimated that there might be about 400,000 of these in circulation, about twice the number of effective troops which the government could hope to raise, even in wartime.[35] Later, in 1782, when the Grand Vizier Halil Hamid ordered a Janissary inspection, he found that only 10 percent of the names on these certificates belonged to real men who could present themselves for duty.[36]

The second of the new public securities came about as the result of the settlement at Küçük Kaynarca (1774). This treaty confronted the Ottoman government with reparation demands quite beyond its means. The treasury therefore introduced a class of public annuities which could be purchased by individuals whose means were far below those of the elite rentier holders of life leases. These annuities also came to be traded freely between parties and ended as a favorite form of investment for the public at large.[37]

Reform within the treasury itself also was attempted with some success. In 1757 the Grand Vizier Ragıp Pasha laid hands on vast trust properties (*harameyn*), until that time controlled by the harem.[38] This did not end the influence of the harem, which reappeared under the next sultan, but it did make the income of these trusts available to help the government in the second of Catherine's wars (1787–91), and thereafter to relieve pressure on the Mint.[39] In this way religious trusts again began to come under the control of the government, not the first time this had happened in the history of this empire. But their final reorganization under a regular government ministry did not take place until the reign of Mahmud II, who followed the example of Mehmed Ali in Egypt.[40]

Table III:1. Imperial revenues and expenditures, 1701–85, according to
Ottoman official figures (in piasters)

	Revenues	Expenditures
1701/02	9,852,728	10,094,824
1704/05	10,451,135	10,847,892.5
1710/11	10,840,971.5	8,339,041
1746	12,857,190	9,278,000
1748	13,741,281.5	14,255,470
1761/62	14,514,288.5	14,064,788.5
1784	14,488,382.5	15,808,250
1785	14,809,666.5	18,693,336.5

Source: Genç (1984), p. 86.

The program of the would-be reformer Selim III likewise called for
treasury reorganization, this time to pay for the new infantry corps being
planned. Thus in 1793 he formed an independent special-purpose treasury, separate from the main treasury, to fund the new military corps.
He founded another special-purpose treasury in 1795 to fund the newly
reorganized grain acquisition system, and a third new treasury in 1805
in order to fund an expansion of the shipyards. These innovations once
again were done in the style typical of the Ottomans: instead of replacing
an older structure outright they fostered a new one to grow up alongside
it. The special-purpose treasuries seem to have fulfilled their functions
well enough, but the military reforms they supported were doomed to
failure in the short run.[41]

ÉTATIST ENTERPRISES

The first priority of eighteenth-century Ottoman governments continued
to be provisioning for defense, or war. Goods regarded as strategic, and
long forbidden for export, were often the same goods which the government had produced under its own controls, or under other special
arrangements: strategic metals including specie, gunpowder, ships'
timber, cloth for uniforms, as well as grain and meat for the military, the
palace and the capital.

Usually a tax-farmer supervised these strategic industries, operating
within the framework of the general tax-farming system. Thus, for the
tax-farmer at least, they must have been profitable arrangements. But
concentration of production under state control had unintended effects.
Production remained locked into older patterns, shutting out the possibility of new efficiencies based on division of labor or new technique.
The traditionalist tendencies of the workmen were reinforced, making

them even more resistant to change. The rentier-leaseholder who oversaw the industry also resisted change; his attention was concentrated on preserving the short-run flow of revenues, not on improving efficiency of production. Thus it is no surprise that the productivity of state-controlled industries tended to decline over time.

Especially pernicious in their effect were the requisitions of Ottoman governments during wartime, when they typically tried to supply their sudden need for strategic goods (sailcloth, gunpowder, iron, copper, timber, pitch, hemp, etc.) at below-market prices. The result was that in wartime workshops which supplied the most lost the most, and emerged from the war in weakened condition.[42]

Remnants of the old system of service villages also were associated with strategic production enterprises. Villages near a mine, for example, might enjoy tax exemptions in return for supplying the mines with charcoal, firewood, food or labor. During wartime other villages might be called upon in the name of the old "tax house" (*avarız*) system to provide saltpeter for the advancing army. Still other villages lying near the line of advance might be forced to sell grain for the army at an administered price (*sürsat*).

Villages lying farther from the war zone also participated in the general war effort by providing peasant soldiers if there were a general levy, or by providing the wartime assistance tax (*imdat*, or *taksit*). The Jews of Salonica played a special role in supplying Janissary cloth,[43] at least until the 1730s.[44] We may surmise that the villages near Sinop, on the Black Sea,[45] and some of those on the isle of Thassos in the northern Aegean, similarly supplied ships' timber for the navy.

State-run enterprises did not always produce results of high quality, especially during wartime when the government was tempted to depend more frequently on the tax-house system.[46] One example of shortcomings of the étatist approach to supply is seen in a petition from the blacksmiths of İstanbul in 1804. The petitioners complained that the (fixed price) horseshoes they were receiving from the Samakov region were of poor quality; better quality horseshoes, they said, were being diverted to Sofia and exported through Rodosto.[47] Army cloth produced under state monopoly was of such poor quality that soldiers preferred to sell it to the truly poor and dress themselves in imported cloth.

To call these government industries mercantilist would not be appropriate because this implies a partnership that was not present, between the government and the merchant stratum, sharing a common strategy. Yet certain viziers of the eighteenth century did appreciate the contribution to the general welfare which new industries could make. It is less clear whether they related these to imports, exports or to any such notion as the "balance of trade".[48] Merchants from France, the main trading partners of the empire, watched each new étatist enterprise with the utmost concern. Throughout the century, when such occasions arose, the current French ambassador used his considerable influence at court to block government-sponsored initiatives, with apparent success.[49]

Most étatist enterprises that were not related to war dealt with textiles. In 1704 the Grand Vizier Rami Pasha attempted to establish new textile workshops at Bursa. This program continued in the following reign when the Grand Vizier Damad İbrahim authorized new woolen mills at Salonica (1712–14). To counteract their growing dependency on cloth imports from France, the Ottoman leadership found some Polish weavers in 1709 to help establish a new cotton print industry; this effort was short-lived, having been subverted by the French. Then, after the war with Venice and its allies, an effort was launched in 1716 to replace the Venetian silks formerly sold to palace circles with domestic silks, with the help of Chiote weavers.[50] After supplying palace circles, the state-sponsored silk industry was allowed to market its surplus in the İstanbul *bedestan*, where one could find them as late as 1760. After that the state-sponsored silks seem to have been displaced by the products of other weavers, both of İstanbul and of Chios.[51] In the 1780s the Grand Vizier Halil Hamid decreed that domestically produced textiles should be patronized; this followed an attempt a few years earlier to open a new textile factory at İstanbul.[52]

Besides textiles, there were other state-sponsored enterprises – in dyes, tobacco, china, bottle making, paper making, and sail making.[53] Sail making was a prototypical state-run industry. Ottoman governments perennially sought to purchase sails for the navy at 30 percent below market prices, driving down quality. Under these conditions the Ottoman sail-makers failed to expand production sufficiently, so that it was necessary to supplement the domestic product with sailcloth from abroad during the wars of the later eighteenth century.[54]

THE PROVISIONING OF ISTANBUL, THE GARRISON AND THE PALACE

Although the Ottomans traditionally had taken pains to keep the capital and the army well provisioned, their system of grain and sheep requisitions underwent further transformation in the eighteenth century, reflecting new circumstances.

In the sixteenth and seventeenth centuries the duty to supply sheep to the butchers of İstanbul was imposed upon the wealthiest of the city's food purveyors. The assignment involved risk since the judges tended to set meat prices too low to offset the real value of the animals, that mostly came from Bulgaria.[55] In the eighteenth century, however, sheep purveyors no longer risked much by participating in the system. Instead of actually rounding up the sheep from the Balkans, as they had formerly, they now farmed a tax to be collected from areas which had provided such sheep. They then used the funds to purchase other sheep voluntarily driven to market, presumably at prevailing market prices; thus sheep prices at İstanbul were considerably higher than in the provinces. These same agents also dealt in tallow, fat and other animal products at a profit.[56] Eggs and cheese in İstanbul usually cost two or three times what they did in the provinces.

In this century sheep also came from the Rumanian provinces as one form of tribute, along with other Rumanian products such as butter, tallow, farina and wheat.[57] The traveler Thornton claimed that in his time (1808) Rumania provided İstanbul with a half million sheep yearly; we can assume these were sold at market prices since by that time the relationship of the two principalities had evolved a long way in the direction of autonomy.[58]

In the eighteenth century, the organization of grain requisitions for the capital, the army, and the palace became tighter than ever before. Once the Phanariote Greeks drove out the native princes, the Rumanian provinces increasingly were defenseless to resist demands from the capital. By mid-century, the two provinces had become the focal point for an ever-more demanding grain supply network which also included, according to need, the shores of the Crimea, Bulgaria, northern Greece, and the Marmara Sea.

In 1748, the judges of İstanbul, who also were in charge of this system, began to assign ships to go to the most likely destinations. At this point, therefore, a greater degree of rationality entered the grain transport business. This further organization of the grain system may arise from the fact that Lazes who had been active in this trade had been driven from the Rumanian provinces in the years just preceding.[59] To replace them, the Porte began to depend more on the merchants of the Golden Horn, who supplied up to 90 percent of the capital involved in the trade.

According to a decree of 1756, the grain prices paid by İstanbul merchants were to be negotiated between these merchants and representatives of the producers, mediated by local judges.[60] A second bargaining process then ensued at İstanbul, which the government also mediated. Beaujour describes how grain was purchased at Salonica under this system. In effect a quota system prevailed, with Salonica and Volos responsible for fixed deliveries at administrative prices which probably were well under the market rate.[61] Because of these administered prices, grain bought at İstanbul generally cost less than in the provinces, despite transport costs.[62]

The government's direct participation in the grain system as a shipper on its own account probably did not exceed 10 percent of the total capitalization involved. The government's grain, already marked for the state, went directly to the Admiralty at Kasımpaşa on the northern side of the Golden Horn.[63]

In earlier times, the Ottoman government had taken some responsibility for provinces experiencing bad harvests, and in the eighteenth century this occasionally was still done. Volney describes how in 1784 the pasha of Damascus decreed that village storehouses be emptied to supply the city of Damascus.[64] And al-Jabarti, writing in the same year, recorded grain sent to Egypt from Syria and Anatolia, owing to a shortage caused by insufficient flooding of the Nile.[65] In general grain prices doubled during wartime.[66]

In the latter decades of the century, the semi-tributary grain-supply system underwent certain shocks which led to its evolution in the direction of free market processes. Because of changing local political conditions, by the 1760s Egypt was losing its role as a normal backup supplier. Later the settlement at Küçük Kaynarca (1774) had a moderating influence on the manner of purchase permissible in the Rumanian provinces. In 1783 the loss of the Crimea intensified İstanbul's need, so that old prohibitions on the export of grain, so often winked at in practice, were now published with great frequency.[67]

This evolution accelerated with the peace settlement of 1792, since grain purchases were henceforth to be made at market prices. This made it necessary for the Porte to organize a special grain-purchase treasury from dedicated sources of income. Purchases from the newly opened Russian ports of the Crimea then became normal, so that by 1800 some 700–800 ships visited these ports annually, most of them seeking to load grain. Many or most were manned by Ottoman Greeks, sailing under the Russian flag.[68]

NOTES

1 Schumpeter (1981), p. 370.
2 Anderson (1979), p. 429.

3 Braudel (1982).

4 İnalcık (1969), pp. 102, 107, 135.

5 İnalcık (1970), p. 217; *idem* (1969), p. 135.

6 İnalcık (1970).

7 Kuznets (1966); Braudel (1982).

8 Anderson (1979), pp. 243, 264.

9 Warriner (1965), pp. 139–41.

10 Ardant (1975), p. 210; Genç (1975), p. 248; Tabakoğlu (1985), p. 242.

11 Genç (1975), p. 283; cf. Svoronos (1956), p. 82.

12 BAN (1985), vol. 5, p. 78.

13 McGowan (1981), pp. 45–79; Ardant (1975), p. 185.

14 Özkaya (1985), p. 42.

15 Beaujour (1800), p. 82.

16 İnciciyan (1976), pp. 23–24.

17 Yediyıldız (1982b), p. 9.

18 Tankut (1975), p. 262.

19 Barnes (1986), p. 43.

20 Mutafčieva (1981), pp. 40–41.

21 Baer (1966).

22 Marsot (1984), p. 18; Nieuwenhuis (1982), p. 110; Fisher (1970), p. 9.

23 Tabakoğlu (1985), pp. 259–65; McGowan (1981), pp. 80–94; Ardant (1975), p. 185.

24 Genç (1975), p. 237; cf. Braudel (1982) for some earlier European experiments.

25 Genç (1975), pp. 238–58.

26 Genç (1975), p. 250.

27 De Tott (1973), p. 135.

28 Karpat, ed. (1974), p. 269.

29 Cited in Levy-Leboyer (1981), p. 238; cf. Grenville (1965), p. 34. According to government documents cited by Genç, these outside estimates may be too low by as much as a third: Genç (1975), p. 247.

30 Ardant (1975), p. 210.

31 A surtax might begin as a tax in kind, then be commuted to a tax in money transferrable to a distant province. An example of this is documented by Göyünç (1983), p. 331.

32 McGowan (1981), pp. 105–70; Cezar (1986), p. 54; Radusev (1980), p. 75; İnalcık (1980), pp. 313–16; and Özkaya (1985), p. 184.

33 Sućeska (1965b), *passim*; Tričković (1970), p. 536; Özkaya (1985), p. 100; McGowan (1981), pp. 45–79, 121–70; İnalcık (1977), p. 49; Mutafčieva (1965), p. 235; Thieck (1985), p. 129.

34 Shaw (1962), p. 219; *idem* (1964), p. 24.

35 De Tott (1973), II, pp. 133, 137.

36 Uzunçarşılı (1935), p. 232.

37 Cf. Genç (1975), p. 247; and Cezar (1986), pp. 79, 104.

38 Barnes (1986), pp. 62, 71.

39 Cezar (1986), p. 99.

40 Marsot (1984), p. 66; Barnes (1986), p. 69.

41 Cf. Cezar (1982–83), pp. 361–88; Shaw (1971), pp. 71–76.

42 Genç (1990), pp. 7, 13.
43 Stoianovich (1974), p. 111.
44 Lascaris (1938), p. 381.
45 Lists of mines and powder mills have been published by Özkaya (1985), pp. 299–302; for details on their administration: *ibid.*, pp. 305, 311; for mines on Thassos and Halkidiki, cf. Vacalopoulos (1973), pp. 541 and 549; for the gunpowder mill at Hama, cf. Nour (1982), p. 320.
46 Genç (1984), p. 59.
47 BAN (1985), vol. 5, p. 81.
48 Genç (1984).
49 Stoianovich (1974), p. 110; cf. Trianta-Fyllidou (1975), p. 75.
50 Genç (1984).
51 Özkaya (1985), p. 142; Tabakoğlu (1985), p. 295; Vacalopoulos (1973), p. 541.
52 Genç (1990), pp. 19–20.
53 Greenwood (1988).
54 BAN (1985), vol. 5, p. 76.
55 Cvetkova (1970), pp. 189–91.
56 Thornton (1809), pp. 2, 30.
57 Alexandrescu-Dersca (1957), p. 19; and (1983), p. 318.
58 Güçer (1980), p. 28.
59 Beaujour (1800), pp. 118–22; and Svoronos (1956), p. 49.
60 Berov (1974), p. 169.
61 Güçer (1980), p. 31.
62 Volney (1787), II, p. 416.
63 Colombe (1951), pp. 9–10.
64 Berov (1976), p. 147.
65 Chirot (1976), p. 64; Genç (1984), p. 55.
66 Güran (1984–85), pp. 29–30.
67 Eton (1805), p. 2.
68 Güran (1984–85).

28

○

TRADE

Perhaps the most important single fact about Ottoman trade with the world in this century was that it was still dwarfed by trade within the empire. Thus when the French ambassador Vergennes estimated France's textile exports to Ottoman territory at a time (1759) when that trade was near its peak, he added that textile imports would clothe no more than 800,000 people annually, a small fraction of the whole population.[1] Similarly, a ranking of Egypt's trade in the eighteenth century places that with other parts of the empire at the top, its trade with the Red Sea region in second place, and its trade with Europe last.[2] "Absolute Western predominance" in trade, to use Mantran's phrase,[3] simply meant leadership in trade within a vast and largely self-sufficient realm which though not very secure was basically friendly to trade.

Since Christian corsairs then outnumbered Muslim corsairs even in the eastern Mediterranean, much seaborne trade between Ottoman regions was carried in foreign, especially French ships. One contemporary account reminds us that much of the traffic between Ottoman ports also was a passenger service, from which we may infer that many Muslim traders accompanied their goods and preferred the safest passage available under the most convenient flag.[4] Recent research also shows that most of the merchant principals (not the shippers) involved in the intra-Ottoman caravan trade were Muslims. Thus, while the minorities gained ground in the external trade, the Muslim community held its own in trade within the region.[5]

Estimates and comparisons of the Levant trade are often problematic. The "piastre" to which trade accounts so often refer actually meant four different coins. Depending upon the period and the context, it either was: the Spanish "piece of eight" early in the century, then for the better part of the century the "lion dollar" of the Dutch, later in the century the Maria Theresa dollar of the Austrians, or in any period (depending on the context) the Ottoman *guruş*, influenced in its design by all the popular foreign coins in their turn.[6]

The value of the Ottoman *guruş*/piastre remained largely stable between 1700 and 1760 and thereafter lost about half its value by the end of the century. Coincidentally the general level of European prices doubled in those forty years.[7] Ottoman manufactures are thought to have faltered in the same forty years, while – at least until the French Revolution – imports climbed. It is tempting to relate all these trends to one another. But, very probably, Ottoman manufactures were hurt most of all by heightened insecurity, not by higher international prices, or a debased coinage.

Trade estimates for the late eighteenth century are difficult to compare because they are stated in several currencies. Overall, Ottoman trade in the late eighteenth century was worth 290 million grams of silver; this estimate is derived from Volney's measurement of total Ottoman seaborne trade in 1784[8] plus other parts of Ottoman external trade he did not count.[9]

This figure, when compared to Ottoman trade a century earlier, indicates that the external trade of the Ottomans scarcely changed as measured in silver. But, in the meantime, the value of total world trade had increased steadily; by the end of the century, the Levant trade counted for less as a percentage of total world trade than it had two centuries earlier.[10] Thus, Ottoman external trade remained fairly stable in value until the early decades of the nineteenth century, when the outpouring of Europe's new goods began in earnest. The Levant trade in the course of the eighteenth century evolved from reliance on the re-export of luxuries, chiefly silk, which crossed the Arab provinces by caravan, to a trade of very different character. The emerging export trade of the eighteenth century relied chiefly on largely unprocessed Ottoman surpluses, locally produced, of relatively lower value by weight.[11] This evolution was the culmination of a trend begun three centuries earlier when the Portuguese circumnavigated Africa, capturing some of the Levant trade in luxury goods, such as spices. While the eighteenth-century Levant trade was not colonial because it was neither large nor exclusive enough, it nonetheless fit in well with the mercantilist intentions of Western trading partners, above all the French.

After the 1740s the Ottoman shores, beginning to become involved in the international market for commodities, also became the destination for colonial goods coming from the New World – sugar, dyestuffs, and

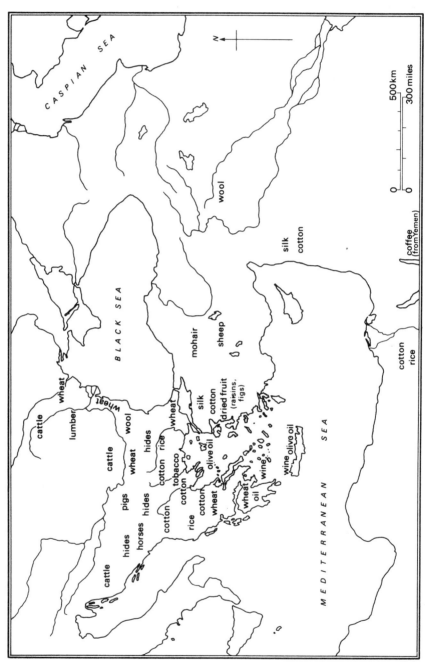

19 Indigenous exports of the eastern Mediterranean, later eighteenth century. *Source*: McGowan (1981), p. 33.

coffee of the Antilles, cheaper than the familiar Mocha.[12] Much of the newer imports embodied slave labor, thus making the Ottoman provinces involuntary participants in a wider world trading system, involving a new division of labor based on comparative advantages in costs.

To these imported colonial goods we add a list of European manufactures which perennially appealed to Ottoman tastes. The list differs from one province to another only in emphasis: woolen textiles (especially those of Languedoc and Lyons), hardware, glassware, porcelain, gunpowder of superior quality, paper, medicines, and luxuries or curiosities, especially timepieces.[13] The total value of imports never equaled exports. Silver coinage made up the difference, for which the Ottoman appetite was augmented by that of the lands further east, where the same coins bought more than in their lands of origin. Thus the Levant trade fed coins to all of south Asia, which needed specie.[14]

Three major trends can therefore be seen in the Ottoman external trade of the eighteenth century: a shift in the content of the export trade, a shift in its geographic distribution, and a shift in the relative rank of the trading partners. The waning of European, especially English interest in the silk of Persia opened a breach in the list of customary Ottoman re-exports. For the most part this gap was filled by cotton, which grew well in several provinces and was increasingly needed for the looms of France and Germany. Total exports in cotton wool, plus cotton thread, probably tripled in the course of the century, to be displaced by American cotton only after the Napoleonic period.[15]

Erratic price differentials caused by the weather kept alive a brisk trade in grain, which was ever forbidden but always practiced. Aside from this erratic international trade in grain, one Ottoman province might sell its grain to relieve another, as when Tunisia shipped grain to the coast of Syria in 1769, and 1771–73.[16] Ottoman wool, skins, furs, hides and tallow continued to be exported as in earlier times. Rising in importance as exports, along with cotton, were the tobacco of Macedonia and Latakia, as well as the olive oil of the Archipelago.

The increased importance of home-grown Ottoman products naturally affected the fortunes of the ports which supplied them. İzmir grew spectacularly and was the favorite port of the Dutch, helped by local agents. Salonica became the northern rival to İzmir, visited above all by the French, and, after the onset of the French Revolution, by sea traders from the new Habsburg port of Trieste. İstanbul, never the leading port in this century, continued to import far more than it exported. In Syria the gradual replacement of silk by cotton caused the northerly port of

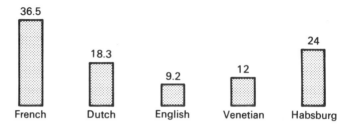

Fig. III:3 Shares in the Ottoman export trade, c. 1784 (percent).
Source: McGowan (1981), p. 18.

Alexandretta to be replaced in importance by southerly ports, especially
Saida, then Acre. Alexandria's importance as an entrepôt for Yemeni
coffee waned over the century, long before this port reawakened as an
outlet for Egypt's cotton in the age of Mehmed Ali.[17]

England ceased to be the Ottomans' leading trade partner in the 1720s,
after a determined and succesful trade campaign by the French, relying
on textiles better adapted to the Levant trade. From the 1720s to the
1760s, England's textile deliveries direct to the region dropped by half,
while France's quadrupled.[18] The English, who earlier had stopped regularly at Livorno and Malta, were hampered by the local introduction of
quarantine regulations.[19] In response, like the Dutch, the English relied
on trade intermediaries– Greeks, Jews and Armenians. The French, by
contrast, did not depend much on intermediary carriers, and even dominated regional trade between Ottoman ports, the cabotage trade.[20]

France's rise as the leading Ottoman trading partner also gained
impetus from the French–Ottoman commercial agreement of 1740, which
the Ottomans conceded to the French as a reward for their effective
diplomatic assistance in a recent war.[21] The 1740 agreement was the first
to extend "most favored nation" treatment to an Ottoman trading partner. By it, the French gained the right to a 3 percent customs rate, the
lowest rate applicable to foreigners. In fact, when other customary
charges were added to the negotiated rate, the actual rate (which varied
from one port to another) tended to be about 10 percent for all foreigners,
including the French.[22]

All foreign states sooner or later sought the protection of agreements
(called capitulations) such as those enjoyed by France, England and the
Netherlands. The reason, as one contemporary explained, was that the
Ottomans did not recognize reciprocity as a principle. Foreign merchants, in order to enjoy any special protection at all, needed the shelter

of such treaties.[23] On the other hand, the Ottomans were largely indifferent to the treatment of their own merchants abroad, so that the Marseilles Chamber of Commerce met no resistance in excluding Ottoman (as well as North African) traders from France in the eighteenth century.[24]

France's importance as a Levant trade partner grew until the 1780s, when their trade was greater than that of the Dutch and English combined. With the opening of the Black Sea in 1783 and the French Revolution in 1789, the trading situation changed in new directions. The Germans, now trading by sea as well as by land, took France's place in the Levant trade. Ottoman Greeks, flying every flag, including Russia's,[25] began to emerge as the usual carriers to ports in the eastern Mediterranean and to those newly opened in the Ukraine.[26]

Even at its eighteenth-century peak, the Levant trade amounted to only 7.5 percent of France's external trade, and less than 1 percent of England's.[27] Meanwhile, beyond the confines of the Mediterranean, a world-wide trade was growing in which Ottoman ships and merchants had almost no role.

Ottoman towns and fairs were at this time just beginning to be involved in international credit operations. A considerable traffic in bills of exchange circulated between French factors at İstanbul and their counterparts in other parts of the Levant. This traffic reflected the excess of İstanbul's imports over its exports, which had to be covered with a flow of credits.[28] Bills of exchange also flowed between the great fair at Uzuncaova, through the Greek and Armenian bankers of Edirne and İstanbul.[29] Starting in the 1760s, merchants trading in Ottoman waters participated in a widening financial network which involved banks at Venice, Vienna, Livorno, Genoa and Amsterdam.[30]

A slave trade continued throughout the century. The Tatars contributed to it until finally defeated by the Russians on whom they traditionally had preyed. Some prosperous households of every faith employed slaves, though field slaves were rare.[31] Greeks are said to have preferred Bulgars as slaves, while Turks preferred Africans.[32]

DOMESTIC TRADE

Trade within and between Ottoman provinces is far less well understood than the external, foreign, trade. There are two main reasons: first, foreign traders rarely traveled in the interior since they were at a disadvantage there relative to native merchants. Second, Ottoman governments' interest in trade was only in its fiscal outcome: thus, even where market data can be recovered, there is neither certainty about the quantities which the revenues represent, nor about the content of trade. Although it has been shown that market revenues declined after 1760 at İstanbul, Kavala, Varna, Tokat and the Danube, the significance of this trend for trade is not at all clear.[33] In any case, the number of internal customs' posts was fewer and their demands upon trade more moderate than in contemporary European settings such as Germany.[34]

There is little doubt that unusual insecurity on the roads was the main cause for the slowdown in Ottoman manufactures in the last decades of the century. There was then, probably, a retrenchment in rural population overall. About Syria and Egypt there can be no doubt. As for Europe (Rumeli), it is difficult to review the warring and banditry of these neo-feudal decades without concluding that there must have been a great loss of life. If manufactures slowed down, so did trade. Collapse of the great fair at Uzuncaova, the razing of the Vlah emporium of Moscopolje, and the increasing vulnerability of the pilgrimage to the Holy Cities, starting with the 1760s, all aptly symbolize the slowdown in trade.

Because of the fall-off in Egypt's trade with the West, its trade with the Ottomans was by the 1770s two to three times that with Europe.[35] Half of Egypt's coffee trade from Yemen went to the Ottoman provinces, supplemented by rice, sugar, beans, linen, flax, dates, safflower, ammonia, hides and wheat, though less of the last-named as the century passed.[36] In return, Egypt took from the other provinces goods such as fabrics, furs, tobacco, iron, arms, timber, firewood, soap, and dried fruits.[37] The coffee component of the trade, though relatively compact, was of high value.

Four great caravans annually continued to travel the Aleppo–İstanbul road, just as they had in the previous century, though perhaps smaller than before.[38] Caravans between Syria and Iraq, though partly undercut after mid-century by Western traders in the Gulf, continued to carry an important amount of internal trade.[39] Even after the ravages of the late eighteenth century, Aleppo, swollen with refugees, continued to produce for the intra-Ottoman trade. As in Bulgaria, a network of peddlers circulated in the countryside nearby.[40] Aleppo redistributed woven silks coming from Bursa, Tokat and Amasya to the Syrian hinterland, a quarter of it going on to Egypt.[41] To Egypt, Syria also sent tobacco, dyestuffs, fruits, raw silk and cotton, taking in return coffee, etc. (see above).[42] To Anatolia, Syria transshipped goods from other places,[43] receiving in return textiles, including woven silk, wood, furs and arms.[44] Wheat might travel in either direction, depending on the harvest.

The fall-off of Persian silk in the early part of the century stimulated silk weaving in many Anatolian locations (and also at Chios, Cyprus, Tripoli and Trnovo). Along with the silk cloth of Bursa, Tokat, Amasya, Giresun and other Anatolian places, traders carried skins from Konya, mohair from Ankara, the cloth and tanned leather of Kayseri, linen from Rize, copper from Tokat, hazelnuts and dried fruit. The ceramic tiles of Kütahya were still traded but were dropping in quality, probably because better-off families now preferred European tiles.[45]

Provinces nearest to the İstanbul–Edirne–Bursa triangle carried on a relatively close-knit regional trade. From Bulgaria via Edirne came rice, tobacco, raisins, wine, wool, furs, metals, horseshoes and other ironwork, raw silk, beeswax, and rough woolen clothing including cloaks, used as far away as Syria.[46]

An important voluntary branch of trade in agricultural products accompanied the state-controlled trade from the Rumanian provinces. Thus, Rumania's trade with Ottoman markets still accounted for about 60 percent of the external trade of those provinces at the end of the Napoleonic period.[47] Most Bulgarian products likewise continued to find regional buyers.[48]

The more distant provinces on the European side also sent their products to Ottoman markets in order to pay for the colonial goods which they received through Ottoman ports: muskets and other arms came from Prizren and Bosnia, as well as leather and ironwork. Shkoder supported many looms in excess of its own needs.

FOREIGN TRADE

Egypt

France was Egypt's main foreign trading partner throughout the century and, being also the main shipper, influenced the conditions of trade. The re-export of Mocha coffee via Egypt completely dominated their bilateral trade until the 1740s, when the French began to draw upon the Antilles as a new source. Nonetheless coffee still accounted for two-thirds of Egypt's imports from the Red Sea in the late eighteenth century, mostly re-exported either to other Ottoman provinces or abroad.[49] As with other commerce with the East, a good part of the Red Sea trade was paid for with silver coin. Besides coffee this trade still brought to Egypt the spices and medicaments of South Asia, according to an old pattern.

France's eighteenth-century export drive resulted in a seven-fold increase in French textile imports into Egypt between the 1740s and the 1780s. Yet barriers to imports erected at Marseilles caused France's intake of Egyptian textiles to fall. By 1783, the French–Egyptian trade balance began to tilt against Egypt, in contrast to other Ottoman provinces.[50] At this time, almost 60 percent of Egypt's exports to Europe were raw or semi-processed goods, while a like portion of its imports from Europe were manufactured goods, above all French textiles.[51]

Syrian Christians, whom the Mamluks had installed as the leading minority in finance, increasingly brokered Egypt's exports to Europe. Besides coffee, exports to Europe included rice (despite the official embargo on grain), wool and cotton thread, flax and linen, leather and pelts, and saffron. Egypt took from France textiles and the usual colonial goods, plus dyestuffs, and European luxuries.[52] In addition to inter-regional imports and imports from the West, Egypt also received several caravans a year from East Africa, carrying slaves, gold and ivory, as well as a caravan from the Maghrib, in connection with the annual pilgrimage to the Holy Cities.[53]

North Africa

France likewise dominated the trade of Tunis and Algiers. The older relationship, in which piracy played so large a part, was mostly replaced in this century by trade, dignified by agreements reached in 1741 and 1748.[54] Imports came mostly from France and in French ships, though sometimes transfers took place with other carriers who were not as protected from piracy as the French.[55] Smaller trading nations like the Dutch made their own arrangements with the North African city-states, creating a system of consular "gifts" and safe-conduct passes.[56]

Algeria's grain, oil, hides, vegetables, honey and wax were routed through the French outpost at Bastion de France on the coast.[57] Tunisia's exports – wool, skins, dates, wax and olive oil – mostly went to the free port of Livorno,[58] where they were awaited by the kinsmen of Tunisian Jews. In much the same fashion Tripoli also maintained its connections with Livorno.

In 1783 the Spanish bombarded Algiers, a maneuver which led to the establishment by treaty of a coastal bastion of their own, Mers el-Kebir (1791).[59]

Iraq and Syria

The Dutch and English had replaced the Portuguese in the Persian Gulf in the first half of the seventeenth century. After the Dutch finally quit the region in 1769,[60] the English stayed on, supplying the riverain markets with the usual mix of colonial goods from America, European manufactures, plus light cotton cloth and spices from their Indian trade. In return they carried away dates, gallnuts, wool, skins, tobacco, rice, salt, and silk and cotton textiles.[61]

To the neighboring shores of the Gulf, Iraq exported large quantities of dates. Most of Iraq's trade with the East was paid for with silver coin, at that time amounting to about ten million piastres via the Gulf, five million piastres to Persia, and one million to Anatolia.[62] Usually the trade of Iraq enjoyed (at a price) the protection of local tribes; this protection repeatedly was interrupted in the first years of the nineteenth century by the raids of Saudi/Wahhabi tribal cohorts.

England's seventeenth-century role as leader of the Levant trade on the Syrian coast gave way early in the next century to French domination. Perhaps because of long interruptions in the supply of silk on the English market, this component of the old Levant trade had dwindled to very little by the 1730s. Simultaneously, the French were re-establishing their trade on a new basis. The English Levant Company was forbidden to exchange coin for cloth for half a century after 1718, but the French could. Given the popularity of their own woolen textiles, and their appetite for cotton for looms at home, the French had little difficulty in regaining leadership during this century in the important Syrian branch of the Levant trade.[63]

Aleppo, formerly the main terminus for caravans from the East, had been the primary entrepôt for the Levant trade in the seventeenth century, along with its port of Alexandretta. In the eighteenth century, the French and their local agents concentrated on the southern ports of Syria which served Damascus. The chief of these was Saida, replaced later in the century by the fortified port of Acre, where Napoleon's expedition came to grief.

Fig. III:4 Ports handling Ottoman exports, c. 1784 (percent).
Source: McGowan (1981), p. 28.

Through these ports passed the usual list of Western goods, while exports included the white and yellow silk cloth woven in the south Syrian hinterland, especially Mount Lebanon, large quantities of locally produced cotton wool and cotton thread, olive oil, soda ash, and occasionally grain.[64] Taken together, the ports of Syria handled about one quarter of the empire's seaborne trade in the later decades of the century.[65]

Izmir

İzmir, outlet for western Anatolia, already was an important port when the century opened. It soon became the premier port of the empire, handling about one-third of the seaborne trade,[66] and remained the favorite port of the Dutch, who traded indirectly through their agents, drawn from among the minorities. Probably because they traded through others, the Dutch were outnumbered by the French. By 1756, about 60 percent of the ships stopping at İzmir were French, though some of this trade was cabotage.[67]

İzmir's relative popularity derived from its more moderate administration by Ottoman pashas earlier in the century and by local *ayan* dynasts later on. Although the merchant "nation" of İzmir had to pay arbitrary *avania*s to the pashas just as in Syria, these apparently were levied with less severity at İzmir, perhaps because of its greater proximity to the capital.[68]

The chief imports at İzmir conformed to the empire-wide pattern: cloth, especially French cloth, other European manufactures and a growing proportion of colonial goods. Anatolia's exports through İzmir abounded in animal fibres from deep in the interior: sheep's wool, camel's hair, and mohair.[69] By mid-century, cotton overshadowed the others and continued to rise in importance until after the Napoleonic years. Most of this cotton grew in the hinterland region of the port. Just as in Syria,

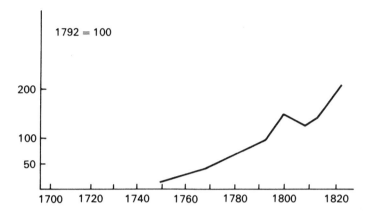

Fig. III:5 Duties collected by weight at İzmir. *Source*: Genç (1976).

the silk which had arrived by caravan in the seventeenth century gave way in this century to locally grown cotton.[70] After the Black Sea was opened to foreign trade, the merchants of Brašov began to cart such İzmir goods as cotton, olives, figs, etc. inland from the seaport at Galatz (Constanța).[71]

Despite the formal prohibition on the export of grain, wheat was regularly transferred to foreign ships, often through Hydra, which was first among the Greek islands in this trade. At mid-century an English traveler happened upon a scene on the shore of the Troad, just outside the Straits where such an exchange was apparently imminent:

> When we sat by the seaside, we had observed a fire blazing on an eminence before us ... We were told it was a signal for a boat designed to be laden clandestinely with corn [wheat], the exportation of which is prohibited under severe penalties ... At midnight the Aga of Chemali, who was concerned in this contraband business, had come prancing along the shore with two Turks, armed, on long tailed horses, to inquire who we were.[72]

The Greek and Albanian shores

The French trade campaign had especially important effects on the port of Salonica, which rose to become the second port of the empire after İzmir, meanwhile doubling its population.[73] Since they had established a network of consular agents throughout Greece and Albania before 1715,[74] the French were in a good position to profit from the discomfiture of

Table III:2. Evolution of external trade at Salonica, 1700–1800

	Ottoman piastres (thousands)	Index
1700–18	900	81.8
1722–37	1,100	100
1738–43	1,600	145.5
1744–49	1,450	131.8
1750–70	3,500	318.2
1771–77	6,000	545.5
1778–87	7,500	681.8
1786–1800	9,500	863.6

Sources: Genç (1976) and Svoronos (1956).

the English, who were hampered by the prohibition on the use of coin (1718) and by quarantines at Malta and Livorno.[75] Thereafter, until the French Revolution, the French were the leading traders at Salonica, drawing products from the entire region, and also loading clandestine cargoes of wheat from the Archipelago and the shores of the Aegean. At mid-century three-quarters of all ships stopping at Salonica were French.

Imports via Salonica resembled those at other Ottoman ports, and included Indian cottons and colonial goods, plus European luxuries such as medicines, watches, mirrors, windowglass and stationery.[76] Exports were more balanced than at other important ports. Although the new crops cotton and tobacco topped the list, older items such as wool, hides, raw silk, beeswax, and shepherds' cloaks continued in importance.[77] Whereas İstanbul absorbed half the imports brought by sea to the European provinces, Salonica handled half the seaborne exports.[78]

The Albanian shore was more closely tied to Italy by trade, especially to Venice, which still dominated the Adriatic shores through most of this century. Although Durres was the leading port when the century opened, with half a dozen consuls resident,[79] Shkoder soon took its place.[80] The list of exports through Shkoder to Italy resembled the list at Salonica, but also included rice, olive oil and maize.[81] The leading export at Shkoder was wool, until the Buşatlı family expanded the region's cotton production in the last decades of the century and doubled aggregate trade.[82]

After mid-century Greek and Albanian shippers, sailing under several flags, carried more and more of the cargoes of the region. About this time, the use of bills of exchange became common, linking Salonica with İstanbul, İzmir, Venice and Vienna.[83] The British allowed the use of their

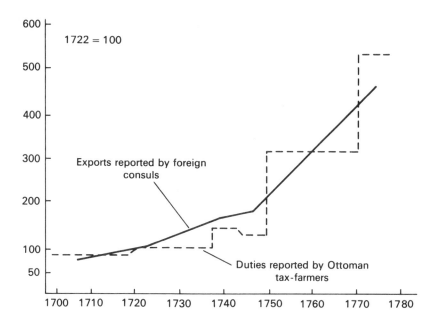

Fig. III:6 Relation between duties reported at Salonica, and export trade at Salonica.

flag to all who wished to exchange cargoes at Livorno, Malta, Majorca and Genoa.[84] The capitulation obtained by the duke of Tuscany in 1747 improved the position of Livorno and of the Jewish and Armenian merchants who traded there.[85]

Trieste had been proclaimed a free port in 1719. Its steady rise as a port, involving many Greek ships, began only after the Habsburg government built new roads to the coast, and defeated Venetian claims to supremacy on the Adriatic. By the end of the century Austrian flag commerce was as dominant at Salonica as French flag commerce had been previously, with about half the total handled through Greek intermediaries.[86] By that time Russia also had a significant share of the trade.[87]

The young Greek fleet, like the Ragusan, was stimulated by the Seven Year's War (1756–63) and by the succeeding two Russo-Ottoman Wars (1768–74, and 1787–92). Greek ships under various flags probably carried about three-quarters of the Levant trade during the Napoleonic period, while other Greeks vied with each other to prey on trade as pirates, regardless of flag.[88]

By land to the north and west

When European populations rose after their seventeenth-century trough, prices followed. After the mid-eighteenth century, European prices of all kinds began a long rise. In southeastern Europe (Ottoman Europe), however, prices did not rise but instead continued to exhibit the extreme volatility characteristic of premodern conditions, such as difficulty of transport and imperfectly organized markets. As a result of the widening contrast between population densities in Ottoman Europe and the lands to the north and west, a differential opened up in the prices of agricultural and pastoral products. This differential enhanced the advantages which southern provinces such as Thessaly and Macedonia already enjoyed in producing crops such as tobacco and cotton. Possibilities for trade were further improved by the advantages which Ottoman traders enjoyed under the peculiar Habsburg customs regime that characterized the middle decades of the century.[89]

Set against the generally lower Ottoman prices for grain and other agricultural products were transportation realities. Since the price of wheat doubled with each 100 km of distance it traveled overland, wheat and other grains were traded only by sea, unless temporary conditions created a very sharp differential, such as the anomalous demands of the Napoleonic period.[90] Therefore, Ottoman exports which went northward by land tended to be products which were relatively more valuable by weight than grain. Foremost among these was the cotton of Macedonia (especially the zone around Seres). About one-third went by sea through Salonica, and the balance went northward by land, crossing into Habsburg territory either at Zemun, opposite Belgrade, or by routes crossing the Danube at Ruse and Nicopolis, further east.[91]

Profiting from a combination of favorable trade conditions, Ottoman exports northward by land increased tenfold during the period 1743–67.[92] Whereas a large portion of the Ottoman rural surpluses – cotton, wool, tobacco and wax – continued north to other European markets via Lwow (Lemberg), Leipzig and Vienna, some manufactures such as leatherwork and textiles found buyers in Hungary.[93] Also important were semi-processed products such as cotton thread, silk, furs and pelts coming from a network of southerly towns such as Ambelakia and Yanina.[94] Even after the Habsburg authorities imposed protectionist measures in the 1770s, the value of Ottoman exports by land outweighed Ottoman imports by as much as five to one.[95]

In the period c. 1790–1810 new trade conditions created new patterns. Ottoman trade fairs were disrupted by provincial power struggles and the trade of the rising port of Trieste diverted Habsburg exports to the sea lanes. But while both these new factors worked to weaken the land routes, two other new factors worked in an opposite way. The quickly growing population on the Habsburg side of the Danube created markets for a regional trade of shorter range. After the Russo-Turkish War of 1787–92, Transylvanian merchants established agencies on the south side of the Danube at Silistre, Ruse and Svistov. Up to 10,000 Ottoman subjects participated in the periodic fairs at Leipzig. At Vienna, a large part of the 60,000 people involved in the cotton manufacturing industry at Schweichat were of Ottoman origin.[96]

Hungary's grain, wine and hardware now were traded into Serbia and Bosnia. Meanwhile the peak prices of the Napoleonic years stimulated exports of livestock, hides, timber, wax and honey, not only north across the Habsburg borders with Serbia and Moldavia, but even west across Bosnia to the Adriatic coast, a route that employed some 20,000 pack animals in 1812.[97]

Overland trade to Iran also survived, though diminished, reflecting the fact that Iran's towns had shrunk by two-thirds during the course of this troubled century. Most of the traffic to Iran on Ottoman routes (including the Trabzon route via the Black Sea) were transshipments from the West: the usual list of Western manufactures plus coin and specie. Iranian traders in return also often transshipped printed cotton and dyes from India, along with Iranian tobacco and lambskins.[98]

Demand fell off sharply at the end of the Napoleonic years. But before that happened, other indicators show that the empire was moving in the direction of further assimilation into a world-wide trading system, in which the Ottoman role was passive. The demise of the great fair of Uzuncaova prepared the way for a brisk new arbitrage trade in money and commercial paper concentrated on the erstwhile provincial center of Bucharest. In 1795 the money-changers of capital petitioned for a decree to legitimize the taking of interest, formally forbidden under Islamic norms. In 1801 a visitor to Ambelakia in Greece learned that the thread merchants there were feeling the effects of competition from cheaper English thread in the German markets.[99] A new era was opening.

NOTES

1 Stoianovich (1974), p. 89.
2 Marsot (1984), p. 2.

3 Grenville (1965), pp. 58–60; cf. Masters (1988), p. 101; Raymond (1973–74), I, p. 170.

4 Mantran (1977), p. 218.

5 Panzac (1985), pp. 183–88.

6 Ülker (1974), pp. 151–52.

7 Bairoch (1974), p. 42.

8 McGowan (1981), pp. 16–17; cf. estimates based on Beaujour in Stoianovich (1974), p. 95; Grenville (1965), pp. 58–60; Issawi (1974), p. 246.

9 Lampe and Jackson (1982), p. 59.

10 Stoianovich (1974), p. 96.

11 McGowan (1981), pp. 28–44.

12 Stoianovich (1974), p. 83.

13 *Ibid.*, p. 83.

14 Olivier (1801), p. 452; Özkaya (1985), p. 131.

15 Stoianovich (1974), pp. 108–9; McGowan (1981), pp. 28–44.

16 Valensi (1977b), p. 305.

17 McGowan (1981), pp. 27–32.

18 Stoianovich (1974), pp. 83, 86–89.

19 Porter (1771), p. 232.

20 *Ibid.*, p. 402.

21 Pelissie de Rausas (1911), pp. 82–88.

22 See Owen (1981).

23 Porter (1771), p. 232.

24 Mantran (1977), p. 229.

25 Dostjan (1974), p. 187.

26 Stoianovich (1974), p. 94; McGowan (1981), pp. 18–27.

27 Stoianovich (1974), p. 95.

28 Eldem (1986), p. 89.

29 Sahillioğlu (1986), p. 66.

30 Eldem (1986), p. 91.

31 Özdemir (1986), p. 128; ISN (1986), vol. 4, pt. 1, p. 465.

32 Vacalopoulos (1973), p. 310.

33 Genç (1976), pp. 13–14.

34 Paskaleva (1968b), p. 270; Vacalopoulos (1973), p. 385.

35 Raymond (1973–74), II, pp. 189, 193.

36 Cf. Marsot (1984), pp. 4, 18; Masters (1988), p. 64; Owen (1981), p. 52.

37 Raymond (1973–74), I, p. 188; Vacalopoulos (1973), pp. 301–2.

38 Gaube and Wirth (1984), p. 251.

39 *Ibid.*, pp. 247, 250; Masters (1988), pp. 13, 120.

40 Masters (1988), p. 53.

41 Gaube and Wirth (1984), p. 251.

42 Masters (1988), p. 102; Owen (1981), p. 52.

43 Owen (1981), p. 52.

44 *Ibid.*, p. 52.

45 Özkaya (1985), pp. 145–50; Carswell (1977), p. 355; Eton (1798), p. 246.

46 BAN (1985), vol. 5, pp. 5, 33, 58; Faroqhi (1984), p. 291; Paskaleva (1978b), pp. 42–48; Cernovodeanu (1976), p. 115.

47 Šamić (1961b), p. 12; Shkodra (1969), p. 764.
48 *Ibid.*, p. 765.
49 Meignen (1977), p. 110; Marsot (1984), pp. 3–4; Raymond (1973–74), I, pp. 185–86, 136.
50 Marsot (1984), p. 3; Raymond (1982), p. 227.
51 Raymond (1973–74), I, p. 174.
52 Colombe (1951), p. 19; Raymond (1973–74), pp. 174–75.
53 Colombe (1951), p. 19.
54 Valensi (1977b), pp. 65–67.
55 Grenville (1965), p. 60; Filippini (1977), p. 130.
56 de Groot (1978).
57 Julien (1970), p. 312; Lacoste *et al.* (1960), p. 171.
58 Abun-Nasr (1971), p. 194.
59 Wolf (1979), p. 305.
60 Sestini (1789), p. 207.
61 Nieuwenhuis (1982), p. 86.
62 Olivier (1801), II, p. 452; Masters (1988), p. 30; Issawi (1986), p. 168; Özkaya (1985), p. 131.
63 Davis (1967); *idem* (1970), p. 193.
64 Gaube and Wirth (1984), pp. 245–46; Masters (1988), p. 120; Thieck (1985), pp. 144–45; Nour (1982), p. 338.
65 Rafeq (1966), p. 76; McGowan (1981), p. 28.
66 McGowan (1981), pp. 28, 30.
67 Panzac (1980), p. 159.
68 Gaube and Wirth (1984), p. 245.
69 Masters (1988), pp. 87–88.
70 Holland (1815), p. 84; cf. Chandler (1971), p. 33; Grenville (1965), p. 4.
71 Bur-Markovska (1987), p. 53.
72 Chandler (1971), p. 73.
73 Stoianovich (1967), p. 251; Svoronos (1956), pp. 7–10.
74 Leon (1972), p. 27.
75 Davis (1967), p. 193; Chaudhuri (1978), p. 169.
76 BAN (1985), vol. 5, pp. 71–3.
77 *Ibid.*, p. 73; Holland (1815), pp. 324–25; Vacalopoulos (1963), pp. 97, 319; Beaujour (1800), p. 382; Jonville (1939), p. 23.
78 Lampe and Jackson (1982), pp. 39–42; Beaujour (1800), p. 382.
79 Shkodra (1969), p. 763.
80 Naci (1970), pp. 39, 41.
81 *Ibid.*, pp. 39, 41.
82 Paskaleva (1968b), p. 277; Naci (1970), p. 42.
83 Svoronos (1956), pp. 118–19.
84 Leon (1972), p. 27.
85 Mantran (1983), p. 292.
86 Paskaleva, ed. (1978a), pp. 231, 233.
87 Beaujour (1800), p. 163.
88 Svoronos (1956), pp. 193–97; Lampe and Jackson (1982), p. 41; Leon (1972), pp. 27–32.

89 Spiesz (1968), p. 10; Abel (1966), p. 43; Bairoch (1974), p. 42; Berov (1976), pp. 319, 147.

90 Berov (1974), p. 169.

91 Lascaris (1938), p. 384.

92 Bur-Makovska (1981), pp. 138–40; for a map of the trade routes northward, based largely on Vacalopoulos, see McGowan (1981), p. 24.

93 Paskaleva, ed. (1978a), p. 228.

94 Castellan (1974), pp. 75–76.

95 ISN (1986), vol. 4, pt. 1, p. 346; Leon (1972), p. 26; Mehlan (1938), p. 101; Paskaleva (1968b), p. 276; Peysonnel (1787), II, pp. 185, 197.

96 Paskaleva (1986), pp. 68, 97, 100.

97 ISN (1986), vol. 4, pt. 1, pp. 469, 343; Warriner (1965), p. 315; Šamić (1961a), pp. 112–13, 116; Lampe and Jackson (1982), p. 57.

98 Issawi (1971), p. 264; *idem* (1977), p. 162.

99 Stoianovich (1967), pp. 88, 303; Stefanescu (1969), p. 10.

BIBLIOGRAPHY

Abdul Rahman, Abdul Rahim and Yuzo Nagata (1977). "The iltizam system in Egypt and Turkey," *Journal of Asian and African Studies* (Tokyo), XIV, 169–94.

Abel, Wilhelm (1966). *Crises agraires en Europe (XIIIe–XXe siècle)*, 2nd. ed., Paris.

Abou el-Haj, Rifaat (1969). "The formal closure of the Ottoman frontier in Europe, 1699–1703," *JAOS*, LXXXIX, 467–75.

(1974). "The Ottoman vezir and pasha households, 1683–1703," *JAOS*, XCIV (4), 438–47.

(1984). *The 1703 rebellion and the structure of Ottoman politics*, Leiden.

Abun-Nasr, Jamil (1971). *A history of the Maghrib*, London.

Aktepe, M. Münir (1958). *Patrona İsyanı (1730)*, İstanbul.

Alexander, J. (1985). *Brigandage and public order in the Morea 1685–1806*, Athens.

Alexandrescu-Dersca, M. (1957). "Contribution à l'étude de l'approvisionnement en blé de Constantinople au XVIIIe siècle," *Studia et Acta Orientalia*, I, 13–37.

Alexandrescu-Dersca-Bulgaru, M.M. (1983). "Les rapports économiques de l'Empire ottoman avec les principautés roumaines et leur réglementation par les *khatt-i şerif* de privilèges (1774–1829)," in J.-L. Bacqué-Grammont and Paul Dumont, eds., *Économies et sociétés dans l'Empire ottoman (fin du XVIIIe – début du XXe siècle)*, Paris.

Altınay, Ahmet Refik (1930). *Anadolu'da Türk Aşiretleri, 966–1200 (A.D. 1558–1792)*, İstanbul.

(1931). *Eski İstanbul*, İstanbul.

Anderson, Matthew (1966). *The eastern question, 1774–1923*, New York.

Anderson, Perry (1979). *Lineages of the absolutist state*, London.

Andreades, A. (1910). *L'Administration financière de la Grèce sous l'administration turque*. Paris.

Ardant, Gabriel (1975). "Financial policy and economic infrastructure of modern states and nations" in Charles Tilly, ed., *The formation of national states in Western Europe*, Princeton.

Ars, G. (1963). *Albania i Epir v konce XVIII – nacale v.*, Moscow.

Association Internationale d'Études Sud-est Européennes (1975). *Structure sociale et développement culturel des villes sud-est européennes et adriatiques aux XVII et XVIII siècles*, Bucharest.

Ayalon, D. (1960). "Studies in al-Jabarti, I: Notes on the transformation of Mamluke society in Egypt under the Ottomans," *JESHO*, III, 148–74, 275–325.

Bacqué-Grammont, J.-L. and Paul Dumont (1983), eds. *Contributions à l'histoire économique et sociale de l'empire ottoman*, Paris.

Baer, Gabriel (1966). "The evolution of private ownership in Egypt and the Fertile Crescent," in Charles Issawi, ed., *The economic history of the Middle East, 1800–1914*, Chicago, pp. 80–90.

(1970). "Monopolies and restriction practices of Turkish guilds," *JESHO*, XIII, 145–65.

(1980a). "Ottoman guilds: a reassessment," in Osman Okyar and Halil İnalcık, eds., *Social and economic history of Turkey (1071–1920)*, Ankara, pp. 95–102.

(1980b). "Patrons and clients in Ottoman Cairo," in *Memorial Ömer Lütfi Barkan*, Paris.

(1981). "Village and city in Egypt and Syria, 1500–1914," in A.L. Udovitch, ed., *The Islamic Middle East, 700–1910. Studies in economic and social history*, Princeton.

(1982). *Fellah and townsman in the Middle East: studies in social history*, London.

Bağış, Ali İhsan (1983). *Osmanlı Ticaretinde Gayri Müslimler (1750–1839)*, Ankara.

Bairoch, Paul (1974). *Révolution industrielle et sous-développement*, Paris.

Barbir, Karl (1980). *Ottoman rule in Damascus, 1708–1758*, Princeton.

Barkan, Ömer Lütfi (1955). "Quelques observations sur l'organisation économique et sociale des villes ottomanes," *Recueil Société Jean Bodin*, VII, 289–312.

Barnes, J.R. (1986). *An introduction to religious foundations in the Ottoman Empire*, Leiden.

Barsoumian, Hagop (1982). "The dual role of the Armenian amira class within the Ottoman government and the Armenian millet (1750–1850)," in Braude and Lewis, eds., I, pp. 171–84.

Baykal, Bekir (1962). *Destari Salih Tarihi*, Ankara.

Beaujour, Felix de (1800). *Tableau du commerce de la Grèce*, Paris (English translation: *A view of the commerce of Greece*, London.)

Ben-Arieh, Yeshua (1975). "The population of the large towns in Palestine during the first eighty years of the nineteenth century, according to Western sources," in Moshe Maoz, ed., *Studies on Palestine during the Ottoman Period*, Jerusalem.

Berindei, Dan (1984). "Fanariotische herrscher und rumanischen Bojaren in den rumanischen Fürstentum (1711–1821)," *Revue Roumaine d'Histoire*, XXIII (4), 313–26.

Berkes, Niyazi (1964). *The development of secularism in Turkey*, Montreal.

Berov, Ljuben (1974). "Changes in price conditions in trade between Turkey and Europe in the 16th–19th centuries," *EB*, X (2–3), 168–78.

(1975). "Transport costs and their role in trade in the Balkan lands in the 16th–19th centuries," *Bulgarian Historical Review*, III–IV, 74–98.

(1976). *Dvizienieto na tsenite na Balkanite prez 16–19 v. i evropeiskata revolutsiia na tsenite*, Sofia.

(1984). "The material status of the freelance professions in southeastern Europe (18th–19th centuries)," *EB*, XX (1), 3–27.

Berque, J. and D. Chevalier (1976), eds., *Les arabes par leurs archives (xvi–xx siècles)*, Paris.

Beydilli, K. (1984). "Ignatius Mouradgea D'Ohsson," *TD*, XXXIV, 247–314.

Blagojević, Miloš (1973). *Zemljoradnja u srednjovekovnoj Srbiji*, Belgrade.

Bodman, Herbert (1963). *Political factions in Aleppo, 1760–1826*, Chapel Hill, N.C.

Braude, Benjamin and Bernard Lewis (1982), eds., *Christians and Jews in the Ottoman Empire*, 2 vols., New York.

Braudel, Fernand (1982). *Civilisation and capitalism, 15th–18th centuries*: II, *The wheels of commerce*, New York.

(1984). *Civilisation and capitalism, 15th–18th centuries*: III, *The perspective of the world*, New York.

Brown, Carl (1974). *The Tunisia of Ahmed Bey, 1837–55*, Princeton.

Bur-Markovska, Marta (1981). "Österreichs Handel mit Südosteuropa und die wirtschaftliche Bedeutung der Bulgarischen Länder bis Ende des 18 Jahrhunderts," *Mitteilungen des Bulgarischen Forschungsinstituts in Österreich*, IV (2).

(1987). "Die Stadt am Unterlauf der Donau im internationalen Handel (18.–19. Jh.)," *Bulgarian Historical Review*, XV (2), 49–55.

Çadırcı, Musa (1980). "II. Mahmut Döneminde (1808–39) Avrupa ve Hayriye Tüccarları," in Osman Okyar and Halil İnalcık, eds., *Social and economic history of Turkey (1071–1920)*, Ankara, pp. 237–41.

Camariano-Cioran, Ariadne (1965). "La guerre russo-turque de 1768–74 et les grecs," *RESEE*, III (3–4), 513–47.

Carswell, John (1977). "From the tulip to the rose" in Naff and Owen, eds., pp. 328–55.

Cassels, Lavender (1966). *The struggle for the Ottoman Empire, 1717–40*, London.

Castellan, Georges (1974). "L'influence de Constantinople sur la vie quotidienne des villes balkaniques (fin XVIII-début XIX siècles)," *Bulletin de l'Association Internationale des Études Sud-Est Européennes*, XXII (1), 91–106.

(1980). "Les fonctions culturelles de la ville du Sud-Est Européen, XVIII–XX ss.," *EB*, XVI (4), 27–39.

Cernovodeanu, Paul (1967). "The general condition of English trade in the second half of the 17th century and the 18th century," *RESEE*, V, 447–60.

(1976). "British economic interests in the Lower Danube and the Balkan shore of the Black Sea between 1803 and 1829," *JEEH*, V, 105–20.

(1986). "Mobility and traditionalism: the evolution of the boyar class in the Romanian principalities in the 18th century," *RESEE*, XXIV (3), 249–57.

Cezar, Mustafa (1965). *Osmanlı Tarihinde Levendler*, İstanbul.

Cezar, Yavuz (1982–83). "Osmanlı Devletinin Mali Kurumlarından Tersane-i Amire Hazinesi ve Defterdarlığının 1805 Tarihli Kuruluş Yasası ve Eki," *İFM*, XLI, 361–88.

(1986). *Osmanlı Maliyesinde Bunalım ve Değişim Dönemi (XVIII. yy.dan Tanzimat'a Mali Tarih)*, İstanbul.

Chandler, R. (1971). *Travels in Asia Minor, 1764–65*, London.

Charles-Roux, François (1928). *Les échelles de Syrie et de Palestine au XVIII siècle*, Paris.

Chaudhuri, K.N. (1978). *The trading world of Asia and the English East India Company, 1660–1760*, Cambridge.

Cherif, Mohamed (1982). "Document rélatif à des tribus tunisiennes dès débuts du XVIIIème siècle: enseignements démographiques et économiques," *ROMM*, XXXIII, 67–87.

Chirot, Daniel (1976). *Social change in a peripheral society: the creation of a Balkan colony*, New York.

Ciercerska-Chapowa, Teresa (1972–73). "Échanges commerciaux entre la Pologne et la Turquie au XVIII siècle," *Folia Orientalia* (Crakow), XIV, 261–87.

Ciobanu, Veniamin (1980). "Aspects du trafic commercial fluvial dans la zone de la Mer Noire dans la 2e moitié du XVIII siècle," *Revue Roumaine d'Histoire*, XIX (4), 733–39.

Clogg, Richard (1976). *The movement for Greek independence, 1770–1821: A collection of documents*, London.

 (1980). "Elite and popular culture under Turkish rule," in John Koumoulides, ed., *Hellenic perspectives: essays in the history of Greece*, Lanham, Md.

Cohen, Amnon (1971). "The army in Palestine in the eighteenth century: sources of its weakness and its strength," *BSOAS*, XXXIV (1), 47–53.

 (1973). *Palestine in the 18th century: patterns of government and administration*, Jerusalem.

Colombe, Marcel (1951). *La vie au Caire, XVIIIe siècle*, Cairo.

Constantinescu, Ioana (1981). "L'affermage des domaines aux paysans corvéables dans les Principautés Danubiennes sous le régime phanariote," *Revue Roumaine d'Histoire*, XX (3), 517–34.

Cook, Michael (1976). ed., *A history of the Ottoman Empire to 1730*, London.

Cvetkova, Bistra (1964). "Recherches sur le système d'affermage dans l'Empire ottoman au cours du XVIe–XVIIIe ss.," *Rocznik Orientalistyczny* (Warsaw), XXVII (2), 111–32.

 (1970). "Les Celep et leur role dans la vie économique à l'époque ottomane (XVI-XVIII s.)," in Michael Cook, ed., *Studies in the economic history of the Middle East from the rise of Islam to the present day*, London.

Cvijić, Jovan (1918). *La peninsule balkanique*, Paris.

Dakin, Douglas (1972). *The unification of Greece, 1770–1923*, London.

Davis, Ralph (1967). *Aleppo and Devonshire Square: English traders in the Levant in the eighteenth century*, London.

 (1970). "English imports from the Middle East, 1580–1780" in Michael Cook, ed., *Studies in the economic history of the Middle East*, London, pp. 193–206.

de Groot, A.H. (1978). *The Ottoman Empire and the Dutch Republic*. Leiden and Istanbul.

de Tott, Baron (1784). *Mémoires sur les Turcs et les Tartares*, 2 vols., Amsterdam.

de Tott, François (1973). *Memoirs of Baron de Tott*. New York.

Dimitrov, Strasimir (1962a). "Za agrarnite otnošeniià v Blgariià prez XVIII," in *Paisii Hilendarski i negovata epoha . . .* , Sofia, pp. 129–65.

 (1962b). "Politikata na upravliavstvata v'rhuska v Turtsia spriamo spahiistvooto prez vtorata polovina na XVIII v.," *Istoričeski Pregled*, XVIII (5), 32–60.

Djordjević, Dimitrije and Stephen Fischer-Galati (1981). *The Balkan revolutionary tradition*, New York.

Djurdjev, Branislav. "Bosna," *EI²*.

Dostjan, I. (1974). "Les échanges commerciaux par la Mer Noire et les Detroits pendant le XVIII et la première partie du XIX siècle," *Bulletin de l'Association Internationale des Études Sud-Est Européennes*, XII (2), 185–94.

Dumont, Jean (1972) ed., *L'histoire générale de l'Afrique*, V, Paris.

Eldem, Edhem (1986). "La circulation de la lettre de change entre la France et Constantinople au XVIII siècle," in Hamit Batu and Jean-Louis Bacqué-Grammont, eds., *L'empire ottoman, la république de Turquie et la France*, İstanbul.

Erdbrink, G. R. Bosscha (1975). *At the threshold of felicity: Ottoman–Dutch relations during the embassy of Cornelius Calkoen at the Sublime Porte, 1724–1726*, Ankara.

Eren, Ahmet Cevat (1965). *Mahmud II Zamanında Bosna-Hersek*, İstanbul.

Erginç, Özer (1986). "XVIII. Yüzyılda Osmanlı Taşra Yönetiminin Mali Nitelikleri," *JTS*, X, 87–96.

Eton, William (1798). *A survey of the Turkish Empire*, London.

  (1805). *A concise account of the commerce and navigation of the Black Sea*, London.

Faroqhi, Suraiya (1978). "The early history of the Balkan fairs," *SF*, XXXVII, 50–68.

  (1979). "Alum production and alum trade in the Ottoman Empire (about 1560–1830)," *WZKM*, LXXI, 153–75.

  (1984). *Towns and townsmen of Ottoman Anatolia, trade, crafts and food production in an urban setting, 1520–1650*, Cambridge.

Field, James (1969). *America and the Mediterranean world*, Princeton.

Filippini, J.P. (1977). "Livourne et l'Afrique du Nord au 18e siècle," *Revue d'Histoire Maghrebine*, XXVII–XXVIII, 125–49.

  (1983). "Les provinces arabes de l'Empire ottoman vués de Livourne au XVIII siècle," *Revue d'Histoire Maghrebine* (Tunis), XXXI–XXXII, 207–10.

Findley, Carter (1980). *Bureaucratic reform in the Ottoman Empire: the Sublime Porte, 1789–1922*, Princeton.

Fisher, Alan (1970). *The Russian annexation of the Crimea, 1772–1783*, Cambridge.

  (1976). *The Crimean Tatars*, Palo Alto.

  (1980). "Studies in Ottoman slavery and the slave trade, II: Manumission," *JTS*, IV, 47–56.

Frasheri, Kristo (1964). *Histoire d'Albanie*, Tirana.

Frazee, C.A. (1983). *Catholics and sultans: the Church and the Ottoman Empire, 1453–1923*, Cambridge.

Gandev, Hristo (1960). "L'apparition des rapports capitalistes dans l'économie rurale de la Bulgarie du nord-ouest au cours du XVIII siècle," *Études Historiques*, I, 207–20.

Gaube, Heinz and Eugen Wirth (1984). *Aleppo*, Wiesbaden.

Gavrilović, Slavko (1969). *Prilog istoriji trgovine i migracije Balkan-Podunavlje: XVIII i XIX stoljeca*, Belgrade.

Genç, Mehmet (1975). "Osmanlı Maliyesinde Malikane Sistemi," in Osman

Okyar and Ünal Nalbantoğlu, eds., *Türkiye Iktisat Tarihi Semineri*, Ankara.

(1976). "A comparative study of the life term tax farming data and the volume of commercial and industrial activities in the Ottoman Empire during the second half of the 18th century," Hamburg, March 1976, Association Internationale des Études Sud-Est Européennes Symposium.

(1984). "XVIII. Yüzyılda Osmanlı Ekonomisi ve Savaş," *Yapıt: Toplumsal Araştırmalar Dergisi*, 49 (4), 51–61.

(1986). "Osmanlı Esnafı ve Devletle İlişkileri," in İstanbul Esnaf ve Sanatkarlar Dernekleri Birliği, *Ahilik ve Esnaf*, pp. 113–24.

(1987). "17.–19. Yüzyıllarda Sanayi ve Ticaret Merkezi Olarak Tokat," in *Türk Tarihinde ve Kültüründe Tokat Sempozyumu*, Ankara, pp. 145–70.

(1990). "Manufacturing in the 18th century," paper presented at the Fourth Biennial Conference on the Ottoman Empire and the World-Economy on "Manufacturing in the Ottoman Empire and Turkey, 1500–1980" held in Binghamton, New York on November 16–17, 1990.

Georgieva, Cvetana (1970). "Organisations et fonctions du corps de Janissaires dans les terres bulgares du XVI jusqu'au milieu du XVIII siècles," *Études Historiques*, V, 319–36.

(1974). "Za proizhoda i socialnata sstnost na corbadziite prez XVIII siecle," *Godisnik na Sofijskija Universitet, Istoriceski Fakultet*, LXVIII, 171–86.

Gerber, Haim (1982). "The monetary system of the Ottoman Empire," *JESHO*, XXV (3), 308–24.

Gökçe, Cemal (1967). "Edirne Ayanı Dağdevirenoğlu Mehmed Ağa," *TD*, XVII (22), 97–110.

Göyünç, Nejat (1983). "The procurement of labor and materials in the Ottoman Empire (16th and 18th centuries)," in J.-L. Bacqué-Grammont and Paul Dumont, eds., *Économies et sociétés dans l'Empire ottoman (fin du XVIII – début du XX siècle)*, Paris.

Greenwood, A. (1988). "İstanbul's meat provisioning: a study of the *celepkeşan* system," Ph.d. dissertation, University of Chicago.

Grenville, Henry (1965). *Observations sur l'état actuel de l'Empire ottoman*, Ann Arbor.

Grigg, David (1980). *Population growth and agrarian change*, Cambridge.

Grozdanova, Elena (1974). "Les fondements économiques de la commune rurale dans les régions bulgares (xv-xviii siècles)," *EB*, X (1), pp. 30–45.

Güçer, Lütfi (1980). "Grain supply of İstanbul in the eighteenth century," in Issawi, pp. 26–31 (originally published in [1949–50]. "XVIII. Yüzyıl Ortalarında İstanbul'un İaşesi İçin Lüzumlu Hububatın Temini Meselesi," *İFM*, XI, 397–416).

Güran, Tevfik (1984–85). "The state role in the grain supply of İstanbul: the grain administration, 1793–1839," *IJTS*, III (1), 27–41.

Hadžijahić, M. (1961). "Die privilegierten Städte zur Zeit des osmanischen Feudalismus," *SF*, XX, 130–58.

Halaçoğlu, Yusuf (1981). "Osmanlı İmparatorluğunda Menzil Teşkilatı Hakkında Bazı Mülahazalar," *JOS*, II, 123–32.

Harik, Ilya (1969). *Politics and change in a traditional society: Lebanon, 1711–1845*, Princeton.

Heinz, W. (1967). "Die Kultur der Tulpenzeit des Osmanischen Reiches," *WZKM*, LXI, 62–116.

Heper, Metin (1985). *The state tradition in Turkey*, Hull.

Hering, Gunnar (1987). "Die griechische handelsgesellschaft in Tokaj. Ihre ordnung und ihre auflösung 1801," *SF*, XLVI, 79–93.

Hess, Andrew (1970). "The forgotten frontier: the Ottoman North African provinces during the eighteenth century," in Naff and Owen, eds., pp. 74–87.

Heyd, Uriel (1961). "The Ottoman 'ulema and westernization in the time of Selim III and Mahmud II," in Uriel Heyd, ed., *Studies in islamic history and civilization*, Jerusalem.

Heywood, Colin (1980). "The Ottoman menzilhane and ulak system in Rumeli in the eighteenth century," in Osman Okyar and Halil İnalcık, eds., *Social and economic history of Turkey (1071–1920)*, Ankara, pp. 179–86.

Hobhouse, J.C. (1813). *A journey through Albania and other provinces of Turkey in Europe and Asia to Constantinople during the years 1809 and 1810*, 2 vols., London (or Philadelphia, 1817).

Hoffman, George (1977). "The evolution of the ethnographic map of Yugoslavia: a historical geographic interpretation," in F. Carter, ed., *An historical geography of the Balkans*, London, pp. 437–99.

Holland, Henry (1815). *Travels in the Ionian Isles, Albania, Thessaly, Macedonia, etc. during the years 1812 and 1813*, London.

Holt, P.M. (1966). *Egypt and the Fertile Crescent, 1516–1922*, London.

Hourani, Albert (1957). "The changing face of the Fertile Crescent in the eighteenth century," *SI*, 89–122.

(1968). "Ottoman reform and the politics of the notables," in Polk and Chambers, eds., pp. 41–68.

İnalcık, Halil (1955). "Land problems in Turkish history," *The Moslem World*, 221–8.

(1960a). "İmtiyazat," *EI²*.

(1960b). "İstanbul," *EI²*.

(1969). "Capital formation in the Ottoman Empire," *JEH*, XXIX (1), 97–140.

(1970). "The Ottoman economic mind and aspects of the Ottoman economy," in Michael Cook, ed., *Studies in the economic history of the Middle East*, London, pp. 207–18.

(1977). "Centralization and decentralization in Ottoman administration," in Naff and Owen, eds., pp. 27–52.

(1978). "The Ottoman decline and its effects upon the reaya," in *IIe Congrès International des Études du Sud-est Européennes*, III, *Histoire et litterature*, Athens, pp. 73–90.

(1980). "Military and fiscal transformation in the Ottoman Empire, 1600–1700," *AO*, VI, 283–337.

(1983). "The emergence of big farms, *çiftliks*: state, landlord, and tenants," in Bacqué-Grammont and Dumont, eds., pp. 105–26.

İnciciyan, G. (1976). *XVIII. Asırda İstanbul*, İstanbul.

Issawi, Charles (1971). *The economic history of Iran, 1800–1914*, Chicago.

(1974). "The Ottoman Empire in the European economy, 1600–1914," in Karpat, ed.

(1977). "Population and resources in the Ottoman Empire and Iran," in Naff and Owen, eds., pp. 152–64.

(1980). *The economic history of Turkey, 1800–1914*, Chicago.

(1982). *An economic history of the Middle East and North Africa*, New York.

(1986). "Notes on the trade of Basra, 1800–1914," *IJTS*, X, 167–74.

Itzkowitz, Norman (1962). "Eighteenth-century Ottoman realities," *SI*, XVI, 73–94.

Jelavich, Barbara (1983). *History of the Balkans: eighteenth and nineteenth centuries*, 2 vols., Cambridge.

Jewsbury, George (1976). *The Russian annexation of Bessarabia: 1774–1828*, Boulder, Col.

Jonville, Thomas de (1939). *Le commerce de Salonique au milieu et à la fin du XVIII siècle d'après les consuls de France Thomas de Jonville et Felix Beaujour*, ed. by Michel Lascaris, Athens.

Julien, C. A. (1970). *A history of North Africa: Tunisia, Algeria, Morocco from the Arab conquest to 1830*, London.

Karadžić, Vuk (1852). *Srpski Rječnik*.

Karpat, Kemal (1972). "The transformation of the Ottoman state," *IJMES*, 243–81.

(1974), ed. *The Ottoman state and its place in world history*, Leiden.

Kassimy, Zafer *et al.* (1980). "Les mouvements migratoires au depart et à destination de la Syrie de la fin du XVIII siècle à nos jours," in *Les migrations internationale de la fin du XVIII siècle à nos jours*, Paris, 241–61.

Kevonian, Keram (1975). "Marchands arméniens au XVII siècle," *CMRS*, XVI (2), 199–244.

Kiel, Machiel (1985). *Art and society of Bulgaria in the Turkish period*, Assen, Netherlands.

Kireev, N.G. (1974). "On the history of Russian–Turkish trade relations via İstanbul in the middle of the 18th century," *Bulletin de l'Association Internationale des Études Sud-est Européennes*, XII (1), 12–31.

Kosev, D.K. (1970). "Les rapports agraires et le mouvement paysan en Bulgarie de la fin du XVIIIème siècle à nos jours," *Études Historiques*, 57–99.

Kosev, D., V. Paskaleva and S. Dojnov (1980). "Les migrations bulgares de la fin du XVIIIème siècle à la seconde guerre mondiale," in *Les migrations internationale de la fin du XVIII siècle à nos jours*, Paris, pp. 556–563.

Kreševljaković, Hamdija (1949). "Gradska privreda: esnafi u Bosni i Hercegovini," *Godišnjak Istoriskog Društva Bosne i Hercegovine*, I, 168–209.

(1951). "Prilozi povijesti bosanskih gradova pod turskom upravom: Contribution à l'histoire des villes de Bosnie sous l'administration turque," *Prilozi* (Sarajevo), II, 115–84.

(1954). *Kapetanije u Bosni i Hercegovini*, Sarajevo.

(1957). *Hanovi i Karavansaraji u Bosni i Hercegovini*, Sarajevo.

Kunt, Metin (1983). *The Sultan's servants. The transformation of Ottoman provincial government, 1550–1650*, New York.

Kuznets, S. (1966). *Modern economic growth*. New Haven, Conn.

Lacoste, Yves, André Nouschi and André Prenant (1960). *L'Algerie passé et present*, Paris.

Lampe, John and Marvin Jackson (1982). *Balkan economic history, 1550–1950*, Bloomington, Ind.

Lape, Ljuben (1959). *Odbrani Tekstovi za Istorijata na Makedonskiot Narod*, Skopje.

Lascaris, Michel (1938). "Salonique à la fin du XVIII siècle d'après le consul de France," *Les Balkans*, X, 371–98.

Leake, William (1967). *Travels in Northern Greece*, 4 vols., Amsterdam.

(1968). *Travels in the Morea*, 4 vols., Amsterdam.

Leon, George (1972). "The Greek merchant marine, 1453–1850," in S.A. Papado-poulos, ed., *The Greek merchant marine, 1453–1850*, Athens.

Levy-Leboyer, Maurice, (1981), ed. *Disparities in economic development since the industrial revolution*, New York.

Lewis, Bernard (1953). "The impact of the French Revolution on Turkey," *Journal of World History*, I, 105–25.

Limona, Dumitru (1974). "Les relations commerciales du sud-est de l'Europe à la fin du XVIII siècle et au debut du XIX siècle reflectées dans les documents archivistiques de Bucharest, Sibiu et Brasov," in *Symposium: L'époque phanariote*, Salonica, 385–99.

Longrigg, Stephen (1925). *Four centuries of modern Iraq*, Oxford.

Mantran, Robert (1974). "Civilisation administrative et financièere, problème du ravitaillement d'İstanbul aux XVII–XVIII siècles," *Bulletin de l'Association des Études Sud-est Européennes*, XII (1), 59–68.

(1977). "The transformation of trade in the Ottoman Empire in the eighteenth century," in Naff and Owen, eds., pp. 217–35.

(1983). "Commerce maritime et économie dans l'Empire ottoman au XVIII siècle," in J.-L. Bacqué-Grammont and Paul Dumont, eds., *Économie et sociétés dans l'Empire ottoman (fin du XVIII–début du XX siècle)*, Paris, pp. 289–96.

Mardin, Şerif (1969). "Power, civil society and culture in the Ottoman Empire," *Comparative Studies in Society and History*, XI, 258–81.

Marinescu, Florin (1981). "The trade of Wallachia with the Ottoman Empire between 1791 and 1821," *BSt*, XXII (2) 289–319.

Marsot, Afaf Lutfi al-Sayyid (1984). *Egypt in the reign of Muhammad Ali*, Cambridge.

Masson, Paul (1911). *Histoire du commerce français dans le Levant au XVIII siècle*, Paris.

Masters, Bruce (1988). *The origins of western economic dominance in the Middle East. Mercantilism and the Islamic economy in Aleppo 1600–1750*, New York.

Matkovski, Aleksander (1978). *Kreposništvoto vo Makedonija vo Vreme na Tur-skoto Vladeenje*, Skopje.

McGowan, Bruce (1981). *Economic life in Ottoman Europe*. Cambridge.

McGrew, N. D. M. (1977). "The land issue in the Greek war of independence," in N.D. Diamandouros, ed., *Hellenism and the Greek war of liberation*, Salonica.

McKay, Derek (1977). *Prince Eugene of Savoy*, London.

McNeill, William (1964). *Europe's steppe frontier, 1500–1800*, Chicago.

Mehlan, Arno (1938). "Mittel und Westeuropa und die Balkanjahresmarkte zur Türkenzeit," *SF*, III, 69–120.

Meignen, Louis (1977). "Esquisse sur le commerce français du café dans le Levant au XVIII siècle," in J.P. Filippini, ed., *Dossiers sur le commerce français en Méditerrannée orientale au XVIII siècle*, pp. 103–50.

Mellor, Roy (1975). *A geography of the Comecon countries*, New York.

Meriwether, Margaret (1987). "Urban notables and rural resources in Aleppo, 1770–1830," *IJTS*, IV (1), 55–73.

Mert, Özcan (1980). *XVIII. ve XIX. Yüzyıllarda Çapanoğulları*, Ankara.

Mihordea, V. (1970). "Les lignes du développement de la diplomatie roumaine au XVIII s.," *Revue Roumaine d'Histoire*, XIX (1), 43–62.

Mile, Ligor (1977). "Aspects du mode de vie du village albanais de la fin du XVIII s. aux années 70 du XIX s.," *Studia Albanica* (Tirana), XIV (2), 135–62.

Mitchell, B. R. (1975). *European historical statistics*, New York.

Morier, J. (1812). *A journey through Persia, Armenia and Asia Minor, to Constantinople in the years 1808 and 1809*, London.

Mutafčieva, Vera (1962). "Feodalnite razmirci v severna Trakija prez kraja na XVIII i nacaloto na XIX v.," in *Paisij Hilendarski i njegovata epoha*, Sofia, 167–212.

(1965). "L'Institution de l'ayanlik pendant les dernières décennies du XVIII siècle," *EB*, II–III, 233–47.

(1981). *Le vakif: un aspect de la structure socio-économique de l'empire ottoman (XVe–XVIIe s.)*, Sofia.

Mutafčieva, Vera and Strasimir Dimitrov (1968). *Sur l'état du système des timars des XVII–XVIII ss.*, Sofia.

Naci, Stavri (1966). "Le pachalik de Shkoder considéré dans son développement économique et sociale au XVIII s.," *Studia Albanica* (Tirana), III (1), 123–44.

(1970). "Le facteur Albanais dans le commerce Balkanique au XVIII siècle," *Studia Albanica*, VII (2), 37–42.

Naff, Thomas and Roger Owen (1977), eds. *Studies in eighteenth century Islamic history*, Carbondale, Ill.

Nagata, Yuzo (1976a). *Some documents on the big farms (çiftliks) of the notables in Western Anatolia*, Tokyo.

(1976b). *Muhsinzade Mehmed Pasha ve Ayanlık Müessesesi*, Tokyo.

(1979). *Materials on the Bosnian notables*, Tokyo.

Neamtu, V. (1975). *La technique de la production céréalière en Valachie et en Moldavie jusqu'au XVIII siècle*, Bucharest.

Nieuwenhuis, Tom (1982). *Politics and society in early modern Iraq: Mamluk pashas, tribal shayks and local rule between 1802 and 1831*, The Hague.

Nour, Antoine Abdel (1982). *Introduction à l'histoire urbaine de la Syrie ottomane (XVI–XVIII siècle)*, Beirut.

Olivier, G.A. (1801). *Voyage dans l'Empire ottoman, l'Egypte et la Perse*, 2 vols., Paris.

Olson, Robert (1975). *The siege of Mosul and Ottoman–Persian relations, 1718–43*, Bloomington, Ind.

Orhonlu, Cengiz (1963). *Osmanlı İmparatorluğunda Aşiretleri İskan Teşebbüsleri (1691–96)*, İstanbul.

(1967). *Osmanlı İmparatorluğunda Derbend Teşkilatı*, İstanbul.

(1984). *Osmanlı İmparatorluğunda Şehircilik ve Ulaşım Üzerine Araştırmalar*, İzmir.

Oteţea, Andrei (1960). "Le second asservissement des paysans roumains (1746–1821)," *Nouvelles Études d'Histoire* (Bucharest), 299–312.

Owen, Roger (1981). *The Middle East in the world economy, 1800–1914*, London.

Özdemir, Rifat (1986). *XIX. Yüzyılın İlk Yarısında Ankara*, Ankara.

Özkaya, Yücel (1979). "XVIII. Yüzyılın Sonlarında Tımar ve Zeametlerin Düzeni Konusunda Alınan Tedbirler ve Sonuçları," *TD*, XXXII, 219–54.

(1983). *Osmanlı İmparatorluğunda Derbend ve Dağlı İsyanları (1791–1808)*, Ankara.

(1985). *XVIII. Yüzyılda Osmanlı Kurumları ve Osmanlı Toplum Yaşantısı*, Ankara.

Panzac, Daniel (1980). "Activité et diversité d'un grand port ottoman: Smyrne dans la première moitié du XVIII siècle," in *Mémorial Ömer Lütfi Barkan*, Paris, pp. 159–64.

(1981). "La population de l'Empire ottoman et de ses marges du XVe au XIXe siècle: bibliographie (1941–80) et bilan provisoire," *ROMM*, XXXI, 119–37.

(1985). *La peste dans l'Empire ottoman, 1700–1850*, Louvain.

Papadopoulos, T.H. (1952). *The history of the Greek church and people under Turkish domination*, Brussels.

Paskaleva, Vera (1958). "Austro-b'lgarski trgovski vrzki v kraia na XVIII i načalato na XIX v.," *Istoričeski Pregled*, XIV (5), 83–92.

(1962). "Razvitie na gradskoto stopanstvo i genezisat na b'lgarskata burzoazija prez XVIII v.," in *Paisij Hilendarski i njegovata epoha*, Sofia, pp. 71–126.

(1968a). "Die bulgarische Stadt im XVIII und XIX Jh.," *Südosteuropa Jahrbuch* (Munich), VIII, 128–45.

(1968b). "Contribution aux relations commerciales des provinces balkaniques de l'Empire ottoman avec les états européens au cours du XVIII et la première motié du XIX s.," *Études Historiques*, III (3), 265–92.

(1978a), ed. *Iz istoriata na targovijata v b'lgarskite zemi prez XV-XIX v.*, Sofia.

(1978b). "La production marchande dans les terres bulgares au XVIII siècle," *Bulgarian Historical Review*, VI (4), 40–50.

(1986). *Sredna Europa i zemite po Dolnija Dunav prez XVIII–XIX v.* Sofia.

Pelissie du Rausas, G. (1911). *Le régime des Capitulations dans l'Empire ottoman*, 2 vols., Paris.

Penelea, Georgeta (1973). *Les foires de la Valachia pendant la periode 1774–1848*, Bucharest.

Petrovich, Michael (1976). *A history of modern Serbia, 1804–1918*, I, New York.

Peysonnel, Ch. (1787). *Traité du commerce dans la mer Noire*, II, Paris.

Philby, H. St. John (1955). *Sa'udi Arabia*, London.

Pococke, R. (1745). *A description of the East and some other countries*, II, London.

Polk, William and Richard Chambers (1968). *Beginnings of modernization in the Middle East: the nineteenth century*, Chicago.

Pollo, Stefanaq and Puto Arben (1981). *The history of Albania*, London.

Popović, Dušan (1937). *O cincarima*, Belgrade.

(1964). *Beograd kroz vekove*, Belgrade.

Porter, James (1771). *Observations on the religion, law, government and manners of the Turks*, London.

Pribram, Karl (1983). *A history of economic reasoning*, Baltimore.

Radusev, Evgenij (1980). "Les dépenses locales dans l'Empire ottoman au XVIII siècle (selon des données de registres de cadi de Ruse, Vidin, et Sofia)," *EB*, XVI (3), 74–94.

Radutiu, Aurel (1981). "Les institutions rurales dans les pays roumains au XVIII siècle," *Revue Roumaine d'Histoire*, XX (3), 503–15.

Rafeq, Abdul Karim (1966). *The province of Damascus, 1723–1783*, Beirut.

(1975). "The local forces in Syria in the seventeenth and eighteenth centuries," in V.J. Parry and M.E. Yapp, eds., *War, technology and society in the Middle East*, London, pp. 277–307.

(1977). "Changes in the relationship between the Ottoman central administration and the Syrian provinces from the sixteenth to the eighteenth centuries," in Naff and Owen, eds., pp. 53–73.

(1981). "Economic relations between Damascus and the dependent countryside," in A. L. Udovitch, ed., *The Islamic Middle East, 700–1900*, Princeton, pp. 653–86.

Raymond, André (1970). "North Africa in the pre-colonial period," in *The Cambridge History of Islam*, II, Cambridge, pp. 266–98.

(1973–74). *Artisans et commerçants au Caire au XVIIIe siècle*, 2 vols., Damascus.

(1977). "The sources of urban wealth in eighteenth century Cairo," in Naff and Owen, eds., pp. 184–204.

(1980). "La population du Caire et de l'Egypte à l'époque ottomane et sous Muhammed Ali," in *Mémorial Ömer Lütfi Barkan*, Paris, pp. 169–78.

(1981). "The economic crisis of Egypt in the eighteenth century," in A.L. Udovitch, ed., *The Islamic Middle East, 700–1900*, Princeton, pp. 687–707.

(1982). "L'impact de la pénétration européene sur l'économie de l'Égypte au XVIII siècle," *Annales Islamologiques* (Cairo), XVIII, 217–36.

(1984). *The great Arab cities in the 16th–18th centuries*, New York.

(1985). French edition of (1984). *Grand villes arabes à l'époque ottomane*, Paris.

Reed, Howard (1980). "Ottoman reform and the janissaries: the *eşkinci layihası* of 1826," in Osman Okyar and Halil İnalcık, eds., *Social and economic history of Turkey (1071–1920)*, Ankara, pp. 193–8.

Rothenberg, E. Gunther (1966). *The military border in Croatia, 1740–1881*, Chicago.

Runciman, Steven (1968). *The great church in captivity*, Cambridge.

Russell, Alexander (1794). *The natural history of Aleppo*, 2 vols., London.

Sadat, Deena (1973). "Ayan and aga: the transformation of the Bektashi corps in the 18th century," *Muslim World*, LXIII (3), 206–19.

Sahillioğlu, Halil (1965). "Bir Asırlık Osmanlı Para Tarihi, 1640–1740," unpublished Ph.D. dissertation, University of İstanbul.

(1968a). "XVIII. Yüzyılda Edirne'nin Ticari İmkanları," *BTTD*, III (13), 60–68.

(1968b). "XVIII. Yüzyıl Ortalarında Sanayi Bölgelerimiz ve Ticari İmkanları," *BTTD*, II (11), 61–66.

Sakaoğlu, Necdet (1984). *Anadolu Derebeyi Ocaklarından Köse Paşa Hanedanı*, Ankara.

Samardžić, Radovan (1976). "Stages of development of Balkan culture and education under the Ottomans in the eighteenth century," *East European Quarterly*, IX (4), 405–14.

Šamić, M. (1961a). "Ekonomski život Bosne i Sarajeva početkom XIX vijeka," *Godišnjak Istorijskog Društva Bosne i Hercegovine*, IX, 111–34.

(1961b). *Francuski izveštaj o Bosni pocetkom XIX vijeka (1806–13)*, Sarajevo.

Sanjian, Avedis (1965). *The Armenian communities in Syria under Ottoman domination*, Cambridge, Mass.

Sayar, Ahmer Güner (1986). *Osmanlı İktisat Düşüncesinin Çağdaşlaşması*, İstanbul.

Schatkowski-Schilcher, Linda (1985). *Families in politics: Damascene factions and estates of the 18th and 19th centuries*, Wiesbaden and Stuttgart.

Schumpeter, Joseph (1981). *History of economic analysis*, New York.

Serban, Constantin (1974). "Les préliminaires de l'époque Phanariote," in *Symposium: L'époque phanariote*, Salonica, 29–39.

Sestini, Dom (1798). *Voyage de Constantinople à Bassora en 1781*, Paris.

Shaw, Stanford (1962). *The financial and administrative organization and development of Ottoman Egypt, 1517–1798*, Princeton.

(1964). *Ottoman Egypt in the eighteenth century: the Nizamname-i Mısır of Cezzar Ahmed Pasha*, Cambridge, Mass.

(1971). *Between old and new: Ottoman Empire under Sultan Selim III, 1789–1807*, Cambridge, Mass.

Shay, Mary (1944), ed., *The Ottoman Empire from 1720 to 1734 as revealed in the dispatches of the Venetian Bailio*, Urbana, Ill.

Shinder, Joel (1973). "Career line formation in the Ottoman bureaucracy, 1648–1750: a new perspective," *JESHO*, XVI, 217–37.

(1979). "Mustafa Efendi: scribe, gentleman, pawnbroker," *IJMES*, X (3), 415–20.

Shkodra, Ziya (1966). "Le marché ´Albanais au XVIII siècle," *Studia Albanica* (Tirana), III (1), 159–72.

(1969). "Le marché albanais au XVIII siècle," *Actes* III (Sofia), 761–74.

(1975). "Les esnafs ou corporations dans la vie urbaine balkanique des XVII–XVIII siècles," *Studia Albanica* (Tirana), XII(2), 47–76.

Skiotis, Dennis (1971). "From bandit to pasha: first steps in the rise to power of Ali of Tepelen, 1750–84," *IJMES*, II, 219–44.

(1975). "Mountain warriors and the Greek revolution," in V.J. Parry and M.E. Yapp, eds., *War, technology and society in the Middle East*, London.

Sousa, Nasim (1933). *The capitulatory regime in Turkey*, Baltimore.

Spiesz, Anton (1968). "Die orthodoxen Handelsleute aus dem Balkan in der Slovakei," *BSt*, IX, 381–428.

Staffa, Susan (1977). *Conquest and fusion: the social evolution of Cairo*, A.D. 642–1850, Leiden.

Stanojević, G. (1966–67). "Miletačke i dubrovačke vijesti o austrijsko-turskim ratovima u XVIII v.," *Godišnjak Društva Istoričara Bosne i Hercegovine*, XVII, 209–30.

Stefanescu, L. (1969). "Les rapports économiques de la ville de Bucarest avec le sud-est européen pendant la deuxieme moitié du XVIII s.," *Actes du Premier Congres International des Études Balkaniques et Sud-est Européennes*, IV, pp. 7–11.

Stefanescu, S., D. Mioc and H. Chirca (1962). "L'évolution de la rente féodale en travail en Valachie et en Moldavie aux XIV–XVIII siècles," *Revue Roumaines d'Histoire*, I, 39–60.

Stoianovich, Traian (1960). "The conquering balkan orthodox merchant," *JEH*, XX, 243–313.

(1967). *A study in Balkan civilization*, New York.

(1974). "Pour un modèle du commerce du Levant: économie concurrentielle et économie de bazar, 1500–1800," *Bulletin d'AIESEE*, XII(2), 61–120.

(1983). "Commerce et industries ottomans et maghrebins: pôles de diffusion et aires d'expansion," in Paul Dumont and J.-L. Bacqué-Grammont, eds., *Contribution à l'histoire économique et sociale de l'Empire ottoman*, Leiden.

Stoianovich, Traian and G.C. Haupt (1962). "Le mäis arrive dans le Balkans," *Annales: ESC*, XVII, 84–93.

Stojančević, Vladimir (1984). "Gradovi, varoši, palanke i tržišta pred prvi Srpski ustanak 1804, godine: kulturno-istoriska problematika," in Radovan Samardžić, ed., *Gradska Kultura na Balkanu, XV-XIX vek*, Belgrade, pp. 141–68.

Sućeska, Avdo (1965a). "Ekonomske i društveno-političke posljedice pojačanog oporezivanja osmanskog carstva u XVII i XVIII stoljeću," *Godišnjak Pravog Fakulteta u Sarajeva*, XIII, 223–39.

(1965b). "O nastanku čifluka u našim zemljama," *Godišnjak Društva Istoričara Bosne i Hercegovine*, XVI, 37–57.

(1965c). *Ajani*, Sarajevo.

(1969), "Seljačke bune u Bosni u XVII i XVIII stoljeću," *Godišnjak Drustve Historičara Bosne i Hercegovine*, XVII, 163–207.

(1978a). "The position of Bosnian muslims in the Ottoman state," *IJTS*, I (2), 1–24.

(1978b). "The position of the raya in Bosnia in the 18th century," *Survey* (Sarajevo), III, 209–25.

(1980) "Postaveni bosenskych muslimu v osmanskem state," in *Ottoman rule in the Middle Europe and Balkans in the 16th and 17th centuries*, Prague, pp. 142–75.

Sugar, Peter (1977). *Southeastern Europe under Ottoman rule, 1354–1804*, Seattle.

Svoronos, Nicolas (1956). *Le commerce de Salonique au XVIIIe siècle*, Paris.

Tabakoğlu, Ahmet (1985). *Gerileme Dönemine Girerken Osmanlı Maliyesi*, İstanbul.

Tankut, Gönül (1975). "Urban transformation in the eighteenth century," *Mimarlık Fakültesi Dergisi*, I (2), 247–62.

Thieck, Jean-Pierre (1985). "Decentralisation ottomane et affirmation urbaine à Alep à la fin du XVIIIème siècle," in Mona Zakaria *et al.*, *Mouvements communautaires et éspaces urbains au Machreq*, Beirut.

Thornton, Thomas (1809). *The present state of Turkey,* 2 vols., London.

Todorov, Nikolai (1977). *La ville balkanique sous les Ottomans, XV-XIXe siècles,* London.

(1983). *The Balkan City, 1400–1900,* Seattle.

Topping, Peter (1977). "Premodern Peloponnesus: the land and the people under Venetian rule (1685–1715)," in *idem., Studies on Latin Greece,* A.D. 1205–1715, London.

Tournefort, Pitton de (1717). *Relation d'un voyage du Levant,* 2 vols., Paris.

Trianta-Fyllidou, Yolanda (1975). "L'industrie du savon en Crete au XVIII siècle: aspects économiques et sociaux," *EB,* XI (4), 75–87.

Tričković, Radmila (1970). "Čitlučenje u beogradskom pašaluku u XVIII veku," *Zbornik Filozofskog Fakulteta* (Belgrade), XI (1), 525–49.

Uluçay, M. Çağatay (1955). *18. ve 19. Yüzyıllarda Saruhanda Eşkiyalık ve Halk Haraketleri,* İstanbul.

Uzunçarşılı, İsmail Hakkı (1935). "Sadrazam Halil Hamid Paşa," *TM,* V, 213–67.

"Hasan Paşa" (Cezayirli Gazi), *İA.*

(1945). *Osmanlı Devleti'nin Saray Teşkilatı.* Ankara.

Ülker, Necmi (1974). "The rise of İzmir, 1688–1740," unpublished Ph.D. dissertation, University of Michigan, Ann Arbor.

Vacalopoulos, Apostolos (1963). *A history of Thessaloniki,* Salonica.

(1973). *A history of Macedonia, 1354–1833,* Salonica.

Valensi, Lucette (1977a). *Fellahs tunisiens: l'économie rurale et la vie des campagnes aux 18 et 19 siècles,* Leiden.

(1977b). *On the eve of colonization: North Africa before the French conquest,* New York.

Veinstein, Gilles (1975). " 'Ayan' de la région d'İzmir et le commerce du Levant (deuxième moitié du XVIII siècle)," *EB,* XII (3), 71–83.

Volney, C.F. (1966). "État du commerce du Levant en 1784, depuis les registres de la chambre de commerce de Marseilles," in Charles Issawi, ed., *The economic history of the Middle East, 1800–1914,* London.

(1787). *Travels through Syria and Egypt in the years 1783, 1784, and 1785,* 2 vols., London.

Vucinich, Wayne (1982) ed., *The first Serbian uprising, 1804–1813,* New York.

Wagstaff, J.M. (1965). "The economy of the Mani Peninsula (Greece), in the eighteenth century," *BSt,* VI, 293–304.

Walpole, Robert (1820) ed., *Travels in various countries of the East . . . ,* London.

Ware, Timothy (1964). *Eustratios Argenti: a study of the Greek church under Turkish rule,* Oxford.

Warriner, Doreen (1965) ed., *Contrasts in emerging societies: readings in the society and economic history of Southeastern Europe in the nineteenth century,* Bloomington.

Wilkinson, William (1971). *An account of the principalities of Wallachia and Moldavia,* New York (original published in London, 1820).

Wilson, Duncan (1970). *The life and times of Vuk Stefanovic Karadžić, 1787–1864,* Oxford.

Wolf, John (1979). *The Barbary Coast: Algeria under the Turks,* London.

Yediyıldız, Bahaeddin (1980). "Vakıf Müessesenin XVIII. Asırda Kültür

Üzerindeki Etkileri," in Osman Okyar and Halil İnalcık, eds., *Social and economic history of Turkey (1071–1920)*, Ankara, pp. 157–61.

(1982a). "Müessese-Toplum Çerçevesinde XVIII. Asır Türk Toplumu ve Vakıf Müessesesi," *VD*, XV, 23–53.

(1982b). "Vakıf Müessesesinin XVIII. Asır Türk Toplumundaki Rolü," *VD*, XIV, 1–27.

(1982c). "Türk Vakıf Kurucularının Sosyal Tabakalaşmadaki Yeri, 1700–1800," *JOS*.

Yenişehiroğlu, Filiz (1983). "Western influences on Ottoman architecture in the 18th century," in Gernot Heiss and G. Klingenstein, eds., *Das Osmanische Reich und Europa 1683 bis 1789: Konflikt, Entspannung und Austausch*, Vienna, pp. 153–78.

Zilfi, Madeline (1983). "Elite circulation in the Ottoman Empire: great mollas of the eighteenth century," *JESHO*, XXVI (3), 318–64.

Part IV

THE AGE OF REFORMS, 1812–1914

DONALD QUATAERT, STATE UNIVERSITY OF NEW
YORK AT BINGHAMTON

29

〰

OVERVIEW OF THE NINETEENTH CENTURY

Despite strong threads of continuity with previous eras, the nineteenth century was one of exceptional changes in Ottoman social, economic and political life. The relative international position and territorial possessions of the "Sick Man of Europe" steadily diminished. The Ottoman state structure, however, not only survived but flourished, thanks to a mutual accommodation between European political-economic interests and the needs and concerns of the Ottoman bureaucracy. (In assessing the factors that helped the Ottoman state to survive when its European neighbors possessed clear military and political advantage, we take for granted both Great Power rivalries and Ottoman diplomatic skills.) From the economic perspective, the Great Powers acquiesced in the continuation of the Ottoman state because this was not a threat to Western commercial and financial interests. European merchants and entrepreneurs usually had access to the Ottoman economy through a variety of mechanisms (discussed below). When disorders in the various Ottoman provinces – for instance, in the regions of Greece, Serbia, Moldavia and Wallachia – started becoming uncontrollable, access to these markets became uncertain. At this juncture, the Great Powers assisted Ottoman subjects in their break-away movements, a transition from Ottoman control to political independence that occasioned some risk to the commercial or financial interests of a particular European state. But, overall, Western access to the economies of these former provinces remained secure. In the areas remaining under Ottoman control, the economic policies of the İstanbul bureaucracy kept markets open, even though there were some efforts towards protection. Thus, the Powers had few economic reasons to seek Ottoman destruction. Indeed, the Western nations had cause to strengthen the Ottoman central state. It was easier and more profitable to dominate the empire's market through privileges and concessions from a single centralized Ottoman administration than it would have been through multiple provincial dynasts and notables whose fragmented polity had made commerce difficult during the eighteenth century. And so, the Powers allowed the Ottoman central state to continue and they encouraged the emerging bureaucracy to expand its scope of activity and spheres of responsibility.

During the nineteenth century, the central Ottoman state structure became more powerful, more rational, more specialized and more capable of imposing its will on society, in part because this was a shared goal of the bureaucrats and the Great Powers. And, in part, this greater strength may have derived from the reduced territory that the bureaucrats now managed. However terrible the financial blow suffered from the loss of wealthy provinces, once these rebellious units were gone, the bureaucracy more readily could focus on problems of state building to survive.

Sweeping global changes, that brought mounting European influence, triggered a major restructuring of Ottoman institutions. The outlines of the economic restructuring are distinctly visible in the post-1750 period. During this first phase, such diverse regions as Salonica, Aleppo and İzmir began to produce raw materials for export to Europe, while the export of manufactured goods diminished. Thus, by the beginning of the nineteenth century, the commercialization of Ottoman agriculture for international export was already under way. The next phase of economic restructuring involved industry and, after being hidden by the Napoleonic and Greek Independence wars, surfaced in the 1830s. The influx of European goods began in earnest – hand manufactures made in labor-intensive Western workshops as well as the more familiar machine-made cotton yarn and cloth. At about this time, that is, nearly a half century after the agrarian changes had begun, the İstanbul regime embarked on its famous course of political reordering (Tanzimat) with the support of the European powers. This process included the recentralization and Westernization of government structures and the formation of a more powerful and expanded central state apparatus. This reorganizing state eliminated or weakened its domestic rivals – urban guilds, tribes and provincial notables – while maintaining its place in the new world order. The central state apparatus paid the price for European support as Ottoman economic activities became more oriented towards furnishing the West with raw material exports and buying the products of its expanding industry.

From the perspective of Ottoman economic policy, the nineteenth century seems to divide into four periods. During the first, until 1826, restrictive economic policies dominated, emphasizing monopolies and the retention of raw materials for domestic use. The second, from c. 1826 to c. 1860, is characterized by accommodation, as the bureaucracy granted open access to Ottoman markets in exchange for relative domestic freedom of action. Free-trade liberalism in the Ottoman lands, as almost everywhere else in the international economy, prevailed without serious challenge. The next epoch, c. 1860 to 1908, began when Ottoman planners raised import duties and offered some protection to local manufacturers. Between 1867 and 1874, the state's Industrial Reform Commission attempted to partially restore the privileged, monopolistic position of some Ottoman guilds, contradicting the *laissez-faire* tendencies of the previous years. Neither initiative achieved much success. But these were the opening Ottoman salvos against the dominion of free trade. In its origins, this Ottoman challenge seems to have anticipated, by at least a decade, the international attacks on British free trade that marked the final quarter of the nineteenth century. Economic liberalism remained the dominant Ottoman practice but Ottoman protectionists sporadically fought against its Ottoman and European advocates. The fourth period begins with the 1908 Young Turk Revolution and continues into World War I. In this era, the battle was fully joined and the proponents of a protected "national economy" finally prevailed over the advocates of free trade.[1]

These century-long convolutions in economic policies mirror a prolonged transition occurring in Ottoman economic theory. Economic liberalism only partially was absorbed into Ottoman economic theory between the 1830s and 1860s. Its adoption was not wholesale but rather, in bits and pieces, a very gradual and prolonged process. Considerable confusion in economic thinking continued until the end of the empire. On the one hand, classical Ottoman economic theory eroded only very slowly. On the other, fashions among European theorists shifted over to a rising affection for protectionism.[2]

The landmark events of the nineteenth century include more than the Reform edicts of 1839 and 1856 or the Constitution of 1876. Such events are important for they publicly acknowledged, reaffirmed and maintained the new centralizing/westernizing course of the Ottoman state. These enactments specifically pledged the government to a policy of change, greater justice, a rule of law and equality of all subjects before the law. The Reform edicts confirmed a commitment to economic improvements as well. From the perspective of economic history, however, there are other and perhaps more crucial dates.

The vital political significance of the destruction of the Janissary corps in 1826, an act that removed military opposition to military reform, has long been noted. But it has an additional economic and social importance. In İstanbul and many other cities, the Janissaries had played a crucial role in the Ottoman urban economy. These one-time professional soldiers had become a group who first of all were artisans and guildsmen and only incidentally were on the military payroll. The sultan's actions in 1826 disarmed the urban guildsmen and eliminated the most powerful and best-organized advocates of protectionism. Thus, the 1826 event paved the way for the subsequent evolution of Ottoman economic liberalism.

The famed Anglo-Turkish Convention of 1838 was the next step. Signed under duress to gain British support for the struggle with Mehmed Ali, the treaty eliminated state monopolies and removed many of the barriers in the way of European merchants. While there is debate about the actual impact of the treaty, it was not a radical departure from existing economic policy.[3] Rather, the Convention continued along the already established path of economic liberalism set in 1826. These two decisions further integrated the Ottoman and European economies, just as the 1839 and 1856 Reform decrees and the 1876 Constitution more closely aligned Middle Eastern with Western political structures. The Commercial Treaty of 1861–62 and the Industrial Reform Commission of 1867–74, for their part, unsuccessfully sought to re-define Ottoman terms of participation in the international economy.

The intra-Ottoman struggle between protectionists and free traders continued while the basic commitment of the Ottoman polity to integration with the European economy remained intact. Two, superficially different, events reaffirmed this commitment late in the period. The first, Ottoman acceptance of the Public Debt Administration in 1881, provided assurances that integration would proceed without risk to Western investors. The Debt Administration emerged from negotiations following the Ottoman fiscal crisis of the 1870s, when Ottoman ability to repay its international loans was in doubt. The Ottoman leadership did not renege on these debts via state bankruptcy. Instead, it agreed to their rescheduling and to formation of the Debt Administration, that represented the European creditors, for their collection. The second, the 1908 Young Turk Revolution, provided a different kind of reassurance. It was more than simply a reaction to the absolutism of Sultan Abdülhamid and continuing territorial losses. Emerging bureaucratic and military cadres launched their coup against a background of mounting social unrest –

taxpayer revolts and numerous labor strikes and violence during the half-decade preceding the revolution. The new cadres seized power and prevented the spread of social revolution; thus, they circumscribed the kinds of changes that would occur. Despite this, extensive labor unrest persisted for the next six years and hundreds of strikes took place throughout the empire. These strikes might have led the Ottoman polity in new and uncharted directions. But the movement was derailed by the rapid succession of World War I, the collapse of the Ottoman Empire, the imposition of French and British mandates and Great Power support for the new Kemalist state in Turkey.[4]

SUMMARY OF DOMESTIC POLITICAL CHANGES

Ottoman reformers – Sultan Mahmud II, the Tanzimat statesmen, Abdül-hamid II and the Young Turks – sought to achieve a series of political and military goals that are well-known in Ottoman history and can be summarized here.[5] Learning from the failures of his predecessor, Mahmud II carefully built a coalition, bided his time, and after eliminating the Janissaries in 1826, energized his reform program of centralization and westernization. From his death until c. 1877–78, westernizing bureaucrats (Men of the Tanzimat) replaced sultans as the major force behind the reform program, that included the secularization of Ottoman life and ultimately touched upon every area of political, social, cultural and economic life. The changes ranged from the adoption of Western theater plays and music to full legal equality of Muslims and non-Muslims and, among a few of the elite, to calls for equality for women and for representative government. The state-imposed reforms slowly percolated from the top down. And, consistent with developments in most European countries, the scope, responsibility and sheer size of the government grew. By the century's end, the state employed at least half a million civil servants. They not only managed money but also assumed functions that we now associate with the normal duties of a modern state. State employees administered hospitals, quarantine centers, hundreds of secular schools, as well as model farms and fields and agricultural schools, not to mention the construction and maintenance of highways, telegraph lines and railroads.

The Ottoman state of 1914, in common with those in Western Europe, played an unparalleled role in the lives of its subjects. And, thanks to modern weaponry and communications technology, the state enforced its will more effectively than ever before in the 600-year history of the empire. Many of these trends came to fruition under Abdülhamid II, who restored power to the sultanate in the late 1870s and whose reign in many respects extended the programs of the Tanzimat era. His rule began with the profound crisis of 1876–78, a time of fiscal disaster and the catastrophic Russo-Turkish War. A Muslim reaction to the Tanzimat emerged and generated a resurgent Islamist-traditional consciousness that the sultan came to represent. He continued the technological reforms of his predecessors while, re-emphasizing Islamic values, seeking to reverse cultural Westernization. Also, Abdülhamid abandoned the minority stance of liberal political reformer and ruled as an autocrat until curbed and then deposed by the Young Turks. No sultan thereafter exercised real authority. The Young Turk leadership seized power and expanded still further the programs of their predecessors. If, for example, dozens of Ottoman students went abroad for agricultural training in the late nineteenth century, hundreds followed in their footsteps during the Young Turk era. Westernization, secularism, and centralization remained enshrined in the pantheon of Ottoman elitist values throughout most of the century. And, at the very end of the era, nationalism joined their ranks. For, after Ottomanist and Pan-Islamist appeals apparently had failed to unify the empire, the Young Turks adopted nationalism, thus raising it from an ideology of the subject peoples to that of the imperial elite.

MILITARY REFORMS: TERRITORIAL LOSSES AND DOMESTIC SUCCESSES

The reformers sought to create more powerful armed forces both to defend the empire against foreign enemies and to destroy or humble domestic rivals of the İstanbul government. To these ends, they imported Western military advisors, equipment, tactics and strategy and they founded military schools to perpetuate these importations. The effort acquired real momentum late in the second quarter of the century: Ottoman naval and land forces relied on Mehmed Ali to crush the Wahhabi forces and then the Greek revolutionaries and performed poorly against the Egyptian ruler's armies in the final showdown. After this debacle, the Ottoman military became better armed and trained and increasingly more effective.

On the international front, however, improved military performance stanched but could not halt the territorial hemorrhaging. Despite some

Table IV:1. Ottoman territorial losses
(approximate dates)

1811	Egypt
1812	Bessarabia
1817	Serbia
1828	Greece
1829	Abaza and Mingrelia
1856	Moldavia and Wallachia
1878	Bosnia, Herzegovina, Bulgaria, Kars, Ardahan and Cyprus
1908	Crete
1912	Cyrenaica and Tripoli
1913	Macedonia
1913	Albania

bright spots, such as the siege of Plevna in 1877 and the 1897 war with Greece, the loss of European provinces in fact accelerated during an era of growing Ottoman military strength. Relative to its own earlier record, Ottoman military capability in World War I was at a peak; but the strength of these armed forces remained disastrously inferior to those of the European powers.

Few territorial losses were temporary, Arabia and the Syrian provinces ultimately were reintegrated into the empire, despite their earlier conquest by the Wahhabi and Mehmed Ali. Most cessions of land were permanent and extremely costly as the state withdrew from its wealthiest, most fertile, advanced and populous provinces. Rich Cyprus fell to British control after 1878. In Africa, Algiers and Tunis (that were not economically significant) actually had fallen away in the eighteenth century and then formally in the nineteenth century. Libya remained Ottoman until 1912. Bonaparte and then Mehmed Ali and his heirs captured Egypt, that great millennial breadbasket of empires.

With the exception of the territories just mentioned, the lost provinces lay in Europe and had been the core of the empire. Before 1850, the European lands contained perhaps one-half of all Ottoman subjects; by 1906, this share had fallen to just one-fifth and was still smaller in 1914. Bessarabia and Serbia had slipped from effective Ottoman control by 1815 and Greece became independent some fifteen years later. The rich Rumanian provinces of Moldavia and Wallachia effectively were gone by 1856. Another war with Russia led to disastrous withdrawals from Bulgaria, Montenegro, Bosnia, Herzegovina and areas of the Caucasus in 1878.

Between 1911 and 1913, almost all the remaining European provinces fell away, including the great port-city of Salonica, but not Edirne and the plain stretching to İstanbul. In this final withdrawal, the empire lost over one-quarter of its remaining population and over 10 percent of its land. In common with earlier losses in Europe, these provinces possessed the most advanced agriculture, commerce and industry in the empire, with standards of living well above the Ottoman average.[6]

It is difficult to over-state the damage that these territorial losses inflicted on the Ottoman economy. The immediate losses in human, mineral, agricultural and industrial resources were just the beginning. Fewer people living on less well-endowed lands spelled a meager legacy; there was less to work with for each succeeding Ottoman generation. The body blows to the economic structure were devastating. Centuries-old ties – that had brought Anatolian shoe leather (from Kayseri) to Rumania, Bulgarian wool cloth to Kayseri and Tokat cottons to Abaza and the Crimea – were weakened and sometimes severed. The prosperity of whole regions faltered as the common Ottoman market on which they depended shrank steadily.

The new reformed military could not halt territorial losses. But it did serve the central government extremely well on the front of domestic policies. It reduced the spheres of independence won by guilds, tribes and local notables during the preceding decades of decentralization, and it regained for İstanbul a greater share of the economic surpluses from the urban and rural economies.

The beginning of the end for the guilds, as indicated above, came in 1826. The Janissaries not only had opposed military improvement and imposed the popular will on the sultan and governing authorities in various provincial centers, but they also had enforced the restrictive economic practices of the guilds. Their disappearance was a major event in the on-going struggle between the central state and the urban guilds that had won a host of monopolistic privileges between 1750 and 1815. The loss of their Janissary ally severely jeopardized the guilds' hard-won gains. Caught between an expanding central state and the nineteenth-century secular drop in the price of manufactured goods, the guilds struggled tenaciously. Their autonomy, together with their livelihoods, declined sharply. But some survived, aided by bureaucrats who either were unconvinced by economic liberalism or saw the guilds' value for domestic power struggles. The issue was not resolved until 1913 when the continuing expansionist state, in its Young Turk guise, finally abolished the guilds altogether.

Subjugation of the tribes similarly was a prolonged process in which the state scored visible and major successes. The armed forces of the

İstanbul government began reaching into the Syrian and Iraqi interior only around 1850. Thereafter, central state control expanded continuously and substantially. Tribes in some of the most mountainous districts, such as the Kurds of eastern Anatolia, often retained, as they do today, considerable freedom of movement, but lost their political autonomy. But everywhere the zone of tribal dominion shrank. A new security of life and property for agricultural producers became commonplace in many areas by the end of the century, bringing in its train truly remarkable changes. Defiantly nomadic tribes, for whom sedentary life was inconceivable, withdrew from the zone of state control, deeper into the desert regions. Vast lands once either marginally cultivated or held by pastoral nomads came to support numbers of new farming settlements that generated sharp increases in agricultural production. Thus, military improvements caused revolutionary changes in Ottoman land use and transformed the face of the countryside.

The central bureaucracy's conflict with local elites was the most prolonged and, in some respects, the least successful of its domestic struggles. Most local notables who had created autonomous spheres of power in the later eighteenth century certainly suffered losses, succumbing to threatened or real military action by the central state. In Anatolia, most notables had surrendered by the end of the 1810s. At the mid-century mark, almost all provincial dynasts throughout the empire overtly obeyed the will of the central state and ceased functioning as independent or autonomous decision-makers. Centrally appointed and İstanbul-trained officials increasingly assumed provincial posts and enforced the writ of the capital. Correspondingly, the provincial elites lost much of their previously undisputed access to locally generated revenues that now were seized for the centralizing regime. But the battle was hardly over. Centralization remained incomplete. The central state and the local elites worked out a historic compromise: İstanbul retained political supremacy and local notables kept substantial power and wealth. They continued to dominate provincial councils and they retained an important share of the local surplus. The İstanbul government failed, despite repeated efforts, to replace tax-farming with direct collection by its own agents. Until the end of the empire, tax-farmers collected the vast bulk of the main agricultural tax, the tithe (*öşr*). And, local notables formed the majority of the tax-farmers. Thus, provincial elites maintained control of important economic resources and, consequently, over the cultivators as well. Such control and their capacity as conduits channeling revenues to İstanbul gave these elites considerable clout in dealing with the central government. Thus, while the Ottoman state achieved an impressive ability to impose its authority, it continued to share power with provincial notables.

TRENDS IN THE INTERNATIONAL ECONOMY

The international economy increasingly shaped the nature and direction of Ottoman social and economic change during the nineteenth century. By no means does this imply that domestic factors were unimportant. To the contrary. The value of intra-Ottoman trade, for example (as seen below), was greater than that with Western states. But it does seem that the most powerful forces affecting economic change were external ones.

Led by Western Europe and the United States, the global economy expanded at an extraordinary rate during the course of the nineteenth century. Gross national product in Europe rose over six times and about threefold on a per capita basis. Moderate growth prevailed until c. 1840 and then soared through the late 1860s, the so-called mid-Victorian boom. During the price depression of 1873–96, European per capita income virtually stagnated but thereafter grew at a record rate.

European per capita income generally increased at about 0.9 percent per annum but there were major regional differences. In the Mediterranean and East European countries, the rate was half the general average, only 0.4 percent per year.[7] Another estimate suggests that per capita income in the advanced countries annually rose at about 1.1 percent between 1820 and 1870 and, thereafter, until 1913, at c. 1.4 percent.[8] The economic center of Europe continued to shift to the north, away from the Mediterranean basin, as it had been doing since the seventeenth century. This shift was due mainly to important improvements in industrial productivity. Throughout the nineteenth century, Great Britain maintained the highest per capita gross national product of any European

Table IV:2. Growth rates in per capita European income, 1800–1913 (percent)

1800–40	0.5
1841–70	1.2
1871–90	0.2
1891–1914	1.5

Source: Bairoch (1976), pp. 273–340.

country but was surpassed by the United States c. 1870–80. Other European states, moreover, were quickly catching up. Significantly, by the end of the period, the gap had widened between the rich nations of Europe and those of "Third World" countries, a category that included the Ottoman Empire. In fact, per capita income in this Third World probably had declined between 1800 and 1890 and then improved slightly until 1913.[9] This conclusion, debated by some economists, seems correct to this writer. Other data show that the average economic growth rate in countries such as Brazil, China, Mexico and India was well below that of the advanced countries between 1820 and 1913.[10]

Global trade expanded some fifty times in real terms, more than three times faster than during the eighteenth century.[11] These increases occurred in both the most and least developed groups of countries. During the mid-Victorian boom, world trade grew in a truly spectacular manner, at the incredible rate of 50 percent per decade. The global price depression of 1873–96 slowed the growth rate in world trade but it still averaged 30 percent per decade. When the depression ended, world trade grew at more than 45 percent per decade.

Regarding price trends, the nineteenth century overall was an era of deflation. Prices generally fell by some 50 percent between 1820 and 1913 but actually had started to rise after 1896. During the Crimean and American civil wars, however, prices for agricultural products rose sharply, to the benefit of primary producers such as the Ottoman Empire.

Great Britain led the industrializing nations until c. 1870 but thereafter, France, Germany and the United States increasingly challenged this hegemony. After 1870, the rate of British industrial growth was only one-half that of the United States and Germany and, c. 1890, Britain fell behind its major rivals in steel production. On a global scale – if we exclude Europe, the United States and Japan – the nineteenth century has been understood as a period of de-industrialization, a decline in the contribution of manufacturing to total output. Industrial exports from the less developed countries are said to have expanded only during and after the depression of 1873–96. In 1876–80, industrial exports from these countries constituted 1.5 percent of world trade, rising to 5 percent in 1896–1900. Significantly, this share increased again to nearly 8 percent in 1913. Thus, the less developed countries sharply increased industrial production for export after the end of the depression in 1896. Recent scholarship, moreover, demonstrates that much manufacturing was rural, household and non-mechanized in nature.[12]

The four great industrial powers – Great Britain, the United States, France and Germany – accounted for the vast bulk of global commerce. By contrast, all of Asia, Africa, Latin America and the East Indies contributed only one-quarter of total world trade during the period c. 1870–1913. Raw materials formed c. 77 percent of all exports from the lesser developed countries. The four industrial leaders imported 76 percent of all the food and raw material exported globally during the late 1870s, and 73 percent in 1913. In 1913, these four countries produced three-quarters of world industrial production.

Vast increases in industrial productivity steadily lowered the prices of manufactured goods and, in large measure, account for the price deflation of .the era. But, equally important for the Ottoman Empire, agricultural productivity also improved in many countries. By the 1860s, most of the basic principles of modern agricultural machinery had been patented. At about that date, the United States began to assume its role of global provider and, by 1914, it alone contained over 33,000 tractors, trucks and combines. These improvements in agricultural productivity limited the ability of many countries to compete in the world market. In 1831, for example, Britain obtained 86 percent of its wheat, the major import, from other European countries. By 1913, however, Europe's share was a mere 5 percent; the United States and Canada had become the primary suppliers. Some countries came to specialize in providing certain food products: e.g., Argentina shipped beef while Denmark exported wheat and dairy products. Other nations specialized in raw materials, e.g., Chilean nitrates and copper and Australian wool. The Ottomans, as we will see, usually exported a diversified mix of foodstuffs and raw materials.

During the 1830s, with the profits generated by industrialization, Europe began to export substantial amounts of capital. Near the mid-point of the century, financial developments, notably the joint stock investment bank, tapped previously unused savings and Europe became banker of the world.[13] The floating of loans became a vastly profitable enterprise. Britain led the way in foreign investment during the first half-century; in the 1840s, for example, it provided over half of the capital invested in French railways. Between the end of the price depression and World War I, British foreign investment rose an impressive sevenfold. But, c. 1850, truly massive amounts of French capital began flowing outward to most European countries and then beyond. French capital exports quadrupled between the Napoleonic and Crimean wars, doubled again from the 1850s through 1897, and doubled yet another time until

1913.[14] Although much of the considerable capital generated in Germany remained at home to finance industrialization, important sums began entering the international market towards the end of the century. By 1914, Great Britain, France and Germany together accounted for one-third of all foreign-owned capital in the world.

Until the 1870s, most of the invested capital remained within Europe. For example, just over one-half of British investment capital went to Europe and the United States between 1860 and 1870. But, by c. 1913, the non-industrial nations consumed an increasing proportion of British foreign investments and only 25 percent went to the U.S. and Europe. During the depression of 1873–96, however, capital exports from the industrial nations fell sharply. For several decades after 1873, most non-industrial nations could not count on outside funds to finance additional imports; the available export capital mainly went to white-settler states (with important effects on Ottoman manufacturers).

In the non-industrial countries, the combination of declining commodity prices, falling terms of trade, and interrupted capital flows from abroad caused grave fiscal instability. International financial controls of one sort or another were erected in Tunisia, Egypt and the Ottoman Empire by 1881, and in Serbia, Greece, Venezuela, Morocco and Saint-Dominique by 1905.

The pattern of foreign investment in the Ottoman public and private sectors followed the global pattern of capital flows. There was little direct European investment in the Ottoman lands until the 1880s. However, the İstanbul regime had accumulated debts through state borrowing that dated back to the 1850s. Rising international capital availability and an Ottoman need to finance the Crimean War produced the first international loan. In an era of sharply rising exports and prosperity in the Ottoman economy, loan followed loan until the Ottoman default of the 1870s. The funds, however, were lent at increasingly unfavorable terms, with an average effective interest rate of 10–12 percent. Between 1869 and 1875, the state borrowed more than its estimated revenues for the same period. But capital imports from Europe ceased with the depression of 1873, and the İstanbul government declared a debt payment moratorium. Debt rescheduling simultaneously occurred in eight Latin American countries, in Liberia and in Egypt. In the Ottoman Empire, this crisis led, in 1881, to the Public Debt Administration. The formation of this organization, as seen, guaranteed that the state would honor its obligations and had accepted its status as a debtor nation in the world financial system. International capital henceforth became available under better terms for the remainder of the period. France, Great Britain and Germany provided 80–90 percent of all Ottoman government loans and, in 1914, France furnished over one-half and Germany one-fifth of the total. The British share of 14 percent represented a two-thirds decline since 1881 while the German participation had tripled in importance.

Direct foreign investment in the Ottoman economy, as distinguished from loans to the government, remained at very low levels through the 1850s. It then climbed between the 1860s and 1880s, primarily due to British-financed railroad building. The vast bulk of direct foreign investment, however, came very late in the period. France, the most important single investor with over one-half of the total, placed 80 percent of its investments in the empire after 1893. Relatively, German financial commitments grew most impressively, from about 1 percent to 27 percent of the total between 1888 and 1914. The British share of investments, in common with its commercial interests and participation in Ottoman public obligations, declined sharply, from 56 to 15 percent of the total, between the 1880s and 1914. By the latter date, German direct investments exceeded those of Great Britain.

The overwhelming majority of the invested funds built enterprises that facilitated commercial exchange with the international economy. Railroad investments accounted for perhaps two-thirds of all foreign capital while ports and public utilities made up another 10 percent.[15]

The Ottoman Empire declined in relative global economic importance during the nineteenth century, particularly, it seems, after 1870. On the one hand, this was due to territorial shrinkage, to the just-mentioned loss of wealthy and populous provinces. On the other hand, the economies of other regions simply grew more rapidly or were the object of more intense Western economic interest.

French and British imports of Ottoman goods, for example, declined after c. 1870. Between 1840 and 1913, Ottoman per capita exports expanded at rates actually somewhat "lower than those of per capita world trade and per capita center–periphery trade."[16] Globally, after 1850, the rate of growth in Ottoman trade fell behind that of the industrial nations as well as of the so-called tropical countries.[17] The patterns of foreign investment abroad suggest a similar conclusion. In the period 1852–81, about one-quarter of all French funds invested abroad (in government securities and direct investments) were in the Ottoman Empire and Egypt. (This was a remarkable rise, since French investment in the Ottoman realms had amounted to only 5 percent in c. 1816.) In the 1881–1914 period, the absolute amount invested rose sharply. But the relative

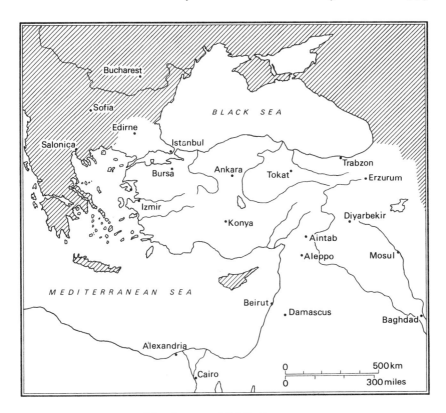

20 The Ottoman Middle East, c.1914.

importance of the empire to French investors fell sharply, to only 12 percent of all French funds invested abroad.[18]

Finally, it remains to be said that the Ottomans were poor, when compared to their neighbors in both Western and Central Europe. Their per capita income in 1913 was about one-twentieth that of British residents and one-tenth that of Europeans generally. Still worse, perhaps, per capita income levels in the lands remaining under the jurisdiction of İstanbul were only one-fifth those of the Ottoman successor states of Bulgaria, Serbia and Greece, and about one-seventh the per capita income of post-Ottoman Rumania.[19]

NOTES

1 Toprak (1982).
2 Sayar (1986).

3 Kurmuş (1980).
4 Quataert (1983); Beinin and Lockman (1988); Sencer (1969).
5 Readers not familiar with the flow of Ottoman political history are referred to Davison (1968); Lewis (1961); Shaw and Shaw (1977).
6 Pamuk (1987), p. 35.
7 The following section, except where otherwise noted, is based on Maddison (1964), Bairoch (1975, 1983), Pollard (1981), Crafts (1984) and Pamuk (1987).
8 Maddison (1964).
9 Bairoch (1976).
10 Maddison (1964), p. 28.
11 Issawi (1982), p. 23.
12 See Ch. 34, on industry, for a contribution to this debate.
13 Feis (1930).
14 Cameron (1961), p. 61.
15 The growth curves of Ottoman foreign trade and direct foreign investment are inversely related. Direct foreign investment in the Ottoman Empire stayed more or less constant from the 1860s to the 1880s but then tripled between 1890 and 1914. The growth in Ottoman trade primarily took place before 1870 and thereafter rose at a relatively slow rate.
16 Pamuk (1987), p. 38.
17 Issawi (1982), p. 25.
18 Cameron (1961), pp. 65, 67, 294.
19 Bairoch (1976) and compared with Eldem (1970), pp. 302–5 and Issawi (1982), p. 6.

30

☾

POPULATION

Population changes had a profound and positive impact on the nine-teenth-century Ottoman economy. Overall, the number of Ottoman sub-jects increased significantly, at an estimated rate of 0.8 percent per year. Before the 1830s, the population probably had declined. Thereafter, a complex combination of factors promoted important increases in popula-tion: these included reduction of disease and improvements in sanitation, security, transportation and communication, as well as a vast migration of peoples into the empire.

Positive demographic trends, however, were disguised by the steady territorial shrinkage of the Ottoman state during the nineteenth century.[1] Large regions that possessed the greatest population densities in the empire – Serbia, Greece, Wallachia, Moldavia, and Bulgaria – withdrew from the Ottoman system. In 1800, the Ottoman Empire embraced an estimated 3,000,000 sq. km. but, in 1914, it measured only about 1,300,000 sq. km. At this latter date, the Ottoman Empire possessed about the same number of subjects as it had c. 1800, approximately 26 million. Population densities, therefore, generally had doubled.

These increased densities provided a powerful engine for economic growth. There were more cultivators for the agrarian sector and larger markets for Ottoman industrial manufacturers. In addition, the enlarged labor pool facilitated execution and completion of massive transportation projects during the second half of the century, notably the vast railroad and telegraph networks. The more compact population, for its part, reduced the production costs of such transportation and communication enterprises.

But the Ottoman lands overall remained sparsely inhabited. Their thinly settled quality retarded industrial development and, as we will see, Ottoman industry tended to concentrate in the areas of comparatively dense settlement. Furthermore, these population patterns surely discouraged the emergence of intensive agriculture, even when favorable market conditions were present. Thus, extensive agriculture remained the norm. And, construction costs of infra-structural projects remained comparatively high (see the case of railroad building) because of the need to traverse nearly empty tracts that separated the various regions of the empire.

GENERAL CHARACTERISTICS

Overall, the distribution of the population followed certain patterns. First, thanks to the advantages of water transport, it had concentrated in coastal areas or along navigable rivers, while in the drier regions the inhabitants had clustered around water sources, such as oases. As trade with Europe mounted during the century, the relative concentration around water routes increased but later, with railroad building, refugee settlement and tribal sedentarization, the population of the interior regions rose. Population densities were greatest in the northwest, European, regions of the empire and decreased as one moved east and south through Anatolia, Syria and Iraq. Towards the end of the period, c. 1910, the number of residents per square kilometer in the remaining European holdings was about double that in Anatolia. In turn, the population density of Anatolia was two to three times greater than in Syria and Iraq and five times that in the Arabian peninsula.[2]

Varying population densities derived from, *inter alia*, regional differences in attitudes towards children, household structures, inheritance patterns, as well as disease, climate and soil fertility. For example, the Balkan lands were the best-watered and most fertile but large sections of Anatolia and Syria received marginal levels of rainfall. At the same time, overabundant water harbored malarial diseases in parts of Iraq and Anatolia. Political factors, notably security of life and property, similarly played a role.

There were many violations of this neat northwest-to-southeast regional pattern of population density. For example, the Lebanon district, one of the most densely populated areas of the empire, was embedded in the sparsely settled Syrian provinces. We cannot be very precise about densities and changes over time. Even the abundant and relatively accurate statistics of the later nineteenth century must be used with considerable caution. For example, an 1894 official Ottoman source claims that Salonica and Basra provinces contained the highest and lowest densities

Table IV:3. Ottoman population, 1820–1914 (in millions)

Date	Balkans	Anatolia	Total
1820–40	9.2		
1831	10.7		
1844–56	15.5	10.7	35.4
1867	18.5	12.8	40.0 w/Egypt
1870s	10.0		
1872–74	14.8	9.4	29.0 w/o Egypt
			40.0 w/Egypt
1884	4.8	9.8	19.0 w/o Egypt
1890s	6.3		
1894			27.0 w/o Egypt
1897	5.6	11.4	29.0 w/o Egypt
1906			21.0 w/o Egypt
1914	1.9	12.5	21.0 w/o Egypt

Source: Generally derived from Karpat (1985a), pp. 109–14. For 1884 and 1897 see Eldem (1970), pp. 52–53.

Table IV:4. Population of selected districts, 1831 (in thousands)

Province	Muslim	Others
Rumeli	337	724
Silistre	488	829
Anadolu	1,084	89
Karaman	229	35
Sivas	278	50
Adana	88	4
Cezayir-i Bahr-i Sefid	109	123
Trabzon	125	12
Çıldır	73	5
Kars	18	2

Source: Derived from Karpat (1985a), pp. 109–14.

in the empire, respectively 74.9 and 2.4 persons per square kilometer. But other Ottoman statistics dating from 1899 rank seven provinces with higher densities than Salonica and four provinces with lower densities than Basra.[3]

At the onset of the nineteenth century, the European provinces held the majority of the population, but their share thereafter shrank steadily (see Tables IV:3–6).[4] According to a defective survey in 1831, these provinces contained about one-third of the counted Ottoman population, surely an under-representation.[5] In the 1850s and 1860s, when there reportedly were some 18 million Ottoman subjects, the European provinces held some 45 percent of the total.[6] As territorial losses accelerated in the last quarter of the century, the Balkan share of the total Ottoman

Table IV:5. Population of selected districts, 1914 (in thousands)

District	Muslim	Others
Edirne	360	277
İstanbul	560	350
Çatalca	20	40
Erzurum	673	142
Adana	342	69
Ankara	877	77
Aydın	1,249	360
Bitlis	310	128
Hüdavendigar	475	141
Diyarbekir	492	128
Van	179	80
Beirut	648	177
Aleppo	576	92
Suriye	792	126
Total (all districts)	15,045	3,475

Source: Derived from Karpat (1985a), pp. 188–89.

Table IV:6. Population, 1884–1913 (in thousands)

Regions	1884	1897	1913
Rumeli and islands	5,014	5,594	642
İstanbul	895	1,052	1,160
Anatolia	10,388	11,430	13,522
Syria	2,700	3,001	3,075
Iraq	1,400	1,550	2,371

Source: Derived from Issawi (1980), p. 17.

population fell drastically. In what turned out to be its last census, the Ottoman government in 1906 found only 23 percent of its subjects residing in Europe, some 4.9 of a total 20.9 million persons.[7] Territorial losses shifted the demographic center of the empire steadily southeastward; in 1914, it probably rested somewhere between İstanbul and İzmir.

Another way of weighing the demographic impact of territorial shrinkage is to look at the population of some of the larger successor states in the Balkans. The population densities in independent Bulgaria, Serbia, Rumania and Greece were far greater than those in the remaining Ottoman lands: they were double and triple the densities in Anatolia and perhaps seven times greater than those in the Syrian and Iraqi regions.[8] In approximately 1914, Serbia contained 2.9 million persons, Bulgaria over 4 million, Rumania just over 7 million and Greece 2.6 million. If

Table IV:7. Population of selected towns, 1830–1912 (in thousands)

Town/city	1830s–40s	1890	1912
İstanbul	375	900	1,125
Edirne	100	87	83
Salonica	70	78	150
Seres	15	28	32
Pristina	10	–	21
İzmir	110	200	300
Bursa	70	76	80
Sivas	40	43	60
Trabzon	33	35	50
Erzurum	15	39	43
Diyarbekir	54	35	38
Eskişehir	4	19	42
Samsun	4	11	25
Erzincan	15	23	25

Source: Derived from Issawi (1980), pp. 34–35.

these lands had remained under the domination of İstanbul, the total Ottoman population in 1914 would have been 42.5 million and not 26 million persons.[9]

Most Ottomans lived in the countryside and rural dwellers accounted for about 80 percent of the total population. The relative urban–rural distribution shifted somewhat during the century. Between 1840 and 1913, the proportion of Ottoman urban dwellers rose from 17 to 22 percent.[10] Thus, the domestic market for Ottoman agricultural products increased commensurately and, to some extent, so did that of local manufacturers as well. On the eve of World War I, the cities of Damascus, Aleppo, Beirut and Jerusalem contained about one-quarter of the population of Greater Syria. In the Iraqi regions, the cities of Baghdad, Mosul, Hille and Basra accounted for 15 percent of the total while towns in Anatolia held about 18 percent of regional inhabitants (see Table IV:7). (In post-Ottoman Bulgaria, Rumania and Serbia, urban centers similarly contained less than 20 percent of the total while in Greece they held a greater share, c. 30 percent.)[11]

A number of cities and towns increased impressively in size, particularly ports that owed their emergence and/or growth to the European trade. The expansion of these port communities in turn helps explain the rising proportion of Ottomans living on the coasts. İzmir grew from 100,000 to c. 300,000 residents while those in Beirut soared from fewer than 10,000 in 1800 to an estimated 150,000 in 1914. İstanbul, for its part, at least doubled in population, in large measure thanks to the influx of immigrants (see below). By 1914, the capital contained over one million persons and easily remained, as it always had been, the largest city in the Ottoman world. Salonica had doubled in size to perhaps 150,000 persons by 1912. (Post-independence Bucharest topped the list of Balkan cities, with c. 350,000 inhabitants.) Baghdad, thanks to the economic boom brought by the Suez Canal, may have doubled in size to 150,000, in a half century[12] (see Table IV:7).

Some cities, however, fell or stagnated due to wars or secular shifts in trade routes. The number of residents at Edirne in Europe and Diyarbekir in Anatolia, for example, respectively fell some 20 and 25 percent over the period.[13]

As a direct result of the territorial losses, the Muslim proportion of the total Ottoman population increased over time. As the various provinces broke away, resident Muslims fled and/or were expelled. At the time of the 1831 enumeration, which certainly is not accurate, the state counted some two-thirds of its subjects as Muslim, fewer than 1 percent Jewish and the balance largely Christian of one denomination or another. More certain is an observation from the 1850s, probably based on a 1840s Ottoman survey, that Muslims comprised some 60 percent of the total Ottoman population. The first reliable registration, carried out between 1881 and 1893, after the great territorial losses of the Russo-Turkish War, noted a 72 percent Muslim majority, 12.6 million among the total of 17.4 million persons. Some 180,000 were Jews, 135,000 were foreigners, and almost the entire balance of 4 millions (23 percent) were Christians. The 1906 official registration revealed a very similar pattern: Muslims were about 74 percent while the Christian share amounted to about one-quarter of the total; the Jewish portion for its part relatively had risen to just over 1 percent.[14]

The relative share of the various religious communities varied considerably in the European, Anatolian and Arab regions. The Anatolian and Arab provinces throughout the century contained relatively more Muslims, usually above 80 percent, than the European regions. In 1831, the inhabitants of locales such as Kars and Trabzon were more than 90 percent Muslim while those of European Rumelia were more than two-thirds Christian. Another count, for the period 1820–40, suggests that about one-half of the population in the European provinces was Christian, 4.7 of 9.2 million persons. Looked at somewhat differently, only about 18 percent of all Ottoman Muslims resided in the European provinces, including İstanbul, during the first half of the century. In the capital city itself, at this time, Muslims formed some 44 percent of the total. The Muslim percentage in the remaining portions of Ottoman Rumelia climbed steadily from the 1820s, beginning at 32 percent and reaching 48 percent in the 1890s, thanks to the relocation of Muslim refugees and a slightly higher birth rate in the region.[15] Muslim preponderance also grew in the Arab provinces. At the 1831 count, Muslims were about 76 percent of the total Syrian population. By the time of the 1906 registration, they accounted for 84 percent of the Syrian population (and 87 percent of the residents in Aleppo province).

Within the specific provinces of a particular region, there were similar varieties in the relative concentrations of religious groups. For example, Muslims formed 87 percent of the population of Ankara province in 1911 but only 67 percent of the population in Bitlis province. Ottoman Christians formed a significant minority of the population in provinces such as Bitlis and Van where Armenians respectively formed 31 and 26 percent of all inhabitants but less than 15 percent of the population in Bursa/Hüdavendigar province. Greeks, for their part, respectively were 14 and 18 percent of all residents in Trabzon and Aydın provinces but, in Rumelian provinces such as Yanya and Salonica, 55 percent and 45 percent of the total (see Tables IV: 4, 5).[16]

The impact of these regional and provincial patterns of religious group distribution is unclear. But they certainly were not important. Neither agriculture nor industry were confined to areas of Christian, or for that matter, Muslim demographic predominance. Although nineteenth-century contemporaries were fond of reserving diligence to the Christians and aloof indifference to Muslims, these stereotypes do not bear close scrutiny. Instead, we find enterprising Muslim and Christian cultivators and manufacturers everywhere. Concentrations of market agriculture and industry were present in areas of Muslim, Christian and Jewish (in the unique case of Salonica) demographic majority. Christian centers such as Harput bustled with manufacturing activities and so did Muslim towns such as Uşak. We search in vain if we seek religion (or ethnicity) as the key to Ottoman economic activity.

Contemporary European observers unanimously agreed that Muslims' death rates were higher and the birth rates lower than among Ottoman Christians. This agreement, however, was founded on impressions, not statistics and was strongly colored by what the observers expected (and perhaps even hoped for). Overall, the non-Muslim population may have grown at an annual rate of 2 percent after the 1830s while death rates for Muslims equalled or slightly exceeded the birth rates. But this observation too lacks a firm statistical base; there are no dependable data until the final quarter of the century, and statements about birth and death rates in the early nineteenth century are "retro-projections" based on post-1878 data.[17] Fertility rates among Muslims may have begun to rise after 1878 but this has not been established with any certainty.[18] The relatively good data, presently available for the period 1878–1914, concern only Muslims in İstanbul and, to a much lesser extent, those in Anatolia. The data suggest fertility and death rates equivalent to those of an average preindustrial state, for example, eighteenth-century France. In fifteen provinces and autonomous districts in Anatolia, c. 1900, the best available estimates suggest a Muslim birth rate of 49 per thousand and a death rate of about 29–38 per thousand.[19] (Ottoman successor states in the Balkans – Serbia, Bulgaria and Hungary – had birth rates of c. 40 per thousand and death rates of c. 19 per thousand in the period 1900–10.) Anatolian women who survived their child-bearing years bore an average of six children, three of whom died before five years of age. Estimates of life expectancy ranged from a high of 35 years in Trabzon province to 27 years in the provinces of Sivas, Ankara, Bitlis and Harput. Those who survived to the age of five, however, generally lived to the age of 45–50 years. In rural Anatolia as a whole, approximately one-half of all children born never lived long enough to marry and have children in their turn.[20] If European contemporaries are to be believed, then the corresponding rates for Ottoman Christians would be better than these figures. The Ottoman state encouraged and was delighted with high fertility, sometimes expressing its pleasure with cash bonuses for multiple births. In 1818, for example, it gave a Damascus-area mother a daily award of 10 *akçe*s for each of her new-born triplets.[21]

HOUSEHOLDS

Uncertainty about Ottoman households and their size is particularly frustrating. Households after all are an essential key to understanding manufacturing and agriculture and how families mixed the two activities in their survival strategies. The scant data, presented below, suggest that, at the macro level, a majority proportion of rural and urban households were simple or nuclear. Such patterns in the agrarian countryside acted to reduce cultivator plot size and also suggest considerable labor mobility. But the present lack of comparative data at the provincial or regional level prevent use of the household as a tool for investigating economic change.

There has been only one systematic analysis of nineteenth-century households in the Ottoman countryside, dealing with the Anatolian coast of the Black Sea, where the household average was c. 6.5 persons. Rural households elsewhere in Anatolia probably averaged between this number and 5.3 persons, figures that place Anatolian rural households just above the average in preindustrial Western Europe. Another estimate, however, claims that the rural Ottoman household of the nineteenth century averaged only four persons. Multiple family households in rural Anatolia probably never totaled more than 30 percent while simple or nuclear households averaged between 50 and 60 percent.[22] On this issue, much research is needed.

We similarly are in the dark regarding households in almost all Ottoman urban areas. In Nablus, an Arab town of some 8,000 persons, an analysis of 107 marriage contracts recorded between 1750 and 1858 offers a glimpse into certain marriage customs in this town, revealing considerable differences between wealthier and poorer women. Upper-strata women had virtually no choice in their marriage partners. Marriages between cousins and of minor girls, for example, were much more common among the wealthy than the poor, as such arrangements served to tie families together for political or economic advantage. For lower-class women in Nablus, marriage often was the sole opportunity, through the dowry (*mahr*) to accumulate wealth and improve status. Moreover, such women more frequently remarried than their wealthier counterparts. In Nablus, little importance was attached to virginity and remarriage carried no particular stigma, suggesting that the virtue of purity celebrated in the rhetoric did not mean much in the practice. Polygyny in Nablus was not the norm. In this Arab town, only 16 percent of the men enumerated had more than one wife and none possessed more than two.[23] These kinds of data suggest that many cherished suppositions regarding the Ottoman family are incorrect and in need of modification. But patterns at Nablus are not necessarily typical. In many areas of the empire, the combination of Sharia and local custom turned the "dowry" into a variant of the brideprice as members of the bride's family appropriated the *mahr*.

A different situation obtained in the Ottoman capital. Extensive research in the court records of İstanbul for the period 1884–1926 shows conclusively that the dowry (*mahr*) there had only symbolic significance, especially for the lower classes. Most frequently, the dowry paid was a nominal sum – 51, 101 or 201 piastres. Thus, in the case of İstanbul and its lower strata, the dowry could not have served as a vehicle for accumulating wealth or improving status.[24] Substantial and reliable data from the 1884 and 1906 enumerations permit some assertions about Muslim households in İstanbul. The famed extended family is not common and formed only 16 percent of the İstanbul households enumerated. The simple household, by contrast, accounted for 40 percent and individuals living alone and in non-family households formed an additional 21 percent of the total. The majority of İstanbul Muslims lived in fairly small households, an average of 3.6 persons. Women headed more households than might be expected, namely 14 percent. As in the case of Nablus, the household's place in the local social hierarchy was an important variable. In İstanbul, it affected household size. The poorer İstanbul household averaged 4.5 persons while 5.7 persons was the norm for elite households. The number of servants does not seem impressive since they existed in only 10 percent of all households. These servants overwhelmingly were young and female; here, clearly, was a pattern of young women serving as domestics until marriage.[25]

Hardly any men in the İstanbul survey married before their thirties. Just over 2 percent of all married men in the city married polygynously and these men, on the average, had two wives. Therefore, about 5 percent of the women at any one time were involved in such marriages.[26] This 2 percent polygyny rate is substantially smaller than the 16 percent figure given earlier for Arab Nablus, but the causes of the difference are unknown. Possible factors include local customs, differences in reporting reliability, time period or the small size of the Nablus sample. At present, there is little information about the marriage age of women. In the capital city around 1900, the female mean age at marriage was c. 20 years and the mean age at motherhood was about 28 years. At İstanbul, fertility began to fall sharply just before World War I, a pattern that continued into the post-Ottoman era. The fall derived from a very sharp rise in the female age at marriage and a decline in marital fertility, a combination of factors that probably was not replicated elsewhere.

And finally, there are suggestions that relatively low levels of fertility in İstanbul already were established by 1875.[27] A surprisingly large number of young people there headed households or lived alone: persons fifteen to nineteen years in age formed about one-third of all one-person households. Here, in part, one sees the impact of the great late nineteenth-century immigrations. In fact, between the two enumerations of the mid-eighties and 1906, there is a decreasing percentage of one-person, no-family, or solitary female households. This decline clearly demonstrates that the in-migratory waves were receding and that residential life was returning to normal.[28] But, in addition, the large number of solitary, no-family and youthful households points to the substantial number of migrant workers that the capital typically supported. These provided the labor pool for the low-wage and unskilled jobs. Many married and single men migrated from their home villages and towns to İstanbul, both for seasonal work and for employ lasting from one to ten years. Areas around Harput and Lake Van and the Cappadochian region are very frequently mentioned as sources of migrant labor.[29] In the capital, men from the provinces took on a vast variety of jobs in patterns of migratory work that reached back decades and, in some cases, centuries. Men from certain villages cooked for the sultan; others undertook certain specific artisanal and construction tasks. The Kastamonu area, for example, commonly provided launderers.[30] The most famous migratory workers, the porters, often came from villages of eastern Anatolia. These porters, and other migratory laborers as well, lived together in small groups, shared a cook and saved their money. They temporarily returned to their villages after several years, married, set up a home, and went back to İstanbul for perhaps five more years' work. Other Ottoman cities, such as Beirut, Aleppo and Salonica, similarly gave employ to migrant laborers "for the livelihood denied their numbers at home." Working at the ports or in construction, for example, the numbers of migrant laborers employed in these cities presently remains unknown.[31]

POPULATION RESTRAINTS

The four horsemen rode with birth control and emigration to restrain Ottoman population growth. After often-catastrophic visitations, some of the deadliest killer diseases disappeared or weakened during the post-1875 period. The first quarter of the century had been disastrous as plague combined with yellow fever and cholera swept through Ottoman territories. Bubonic plague, long-known in the region, caused very severe casualties at İzmir and other port cities during the late eighteenth and early nineteenth centuries. Between 1812 and 1818, virtually the entire empire was afflicted. In 1812, an estimated 300,000 persons (probably an exaggeration) in the greater İstanbul area died of the plague and, as late as 1836, it still had sufficient vigor to kill some 30,000 residents of the capital. Plague visited İstanbul and the nearby Balkan provinces nearly annually during the next thirty years, but the intensity apparently decreased. In its bubonic form, plague reappeared in every decade until the 1850s in the Egyptian, Syrian, Iraqi and Arabian provinces. On the

Aegean coast of Anatolia, it struck twenty-six times between 1801 and 1850; at İzmir, the 1812 outbreak reportedly carried off a full one-fifth of the city population. Plague visited the central and eastern Anatolian regions 28 times in this half century. In the Syrian lands, plague at Aleppo in 1827 killed some 20–25 percent of the inhabitants. At Baghdad, in 1831, some 7,000 persons died in two weeks and plague helped to end the rule of the last Mamluk in the besieged city. This eruption was part of the largest single incidence of the plague during the nineteenth century, visiting Iran and the Iraqi provinces as well as Syria, İzmir and Trabzon.[32] In the Balkans and Anatolia, plague recurred through the 1840s; while it gradually faded away in these regions, the Arabian and Iraqi provinces remained afflicted.[33]

As the plague faded in ferocity, a new killer – Asiatic cholera – appeared from the Orient. Entering the Ottoman world via Russia, cholera first struck the Iraqi provinces in 1821 and quickly moved into the Syrian and east Anatolian regions. During the next three decades, there were seven pandemics in the empire. In Anatolia, serious outbreaks erupted in 1847 and in 1865. At Salonica, in 1848, 3,000 persons died. Via the Holy Cities of Mecca and Medina, pilgrims from India and East Asia often spread epidemics of cholera, as well as other diseases. Cholera appeared in the Hejaz, reportedly for the first time in 1832, killing more than 10,000 persons before spreading to Egypt and Europe. Two new outbreaks in the 1830s were followed by a visitation in the 1840s, that killed some 10,000 in Mecca and reportedly 20,000 in Baghdad, and four more in the 1850s. In 1865, a very severe outbreak carried off at least 30,000 among the pilgrims as well as the wife, son and daughter of the Hejaz governor. Beginning in the 1850s, an increasingly rigorous international quarantine system fought the disease. Quarantine stations brought the Meccan-borne disease more or less under control and prevented major outbreaks from the 1860s through the 1880s. But disaster again struck in 1893 and up to 40,000 pilgrims died. Returning pilgrims carried cholera to İstanbul where it killed some 1,200 persons, as well as to İzmir and Trabzon. Another major empire-wide outbreak erupted in 1902.[34] There were other killers as well. Typhus raged during the middle and later decades of the century as it accompanied Muslim refugees from Russian territories. But, as these migrations faded, so did the disease. Typhus made a rare late-century appearance in 1892, when a shipload of laborers fled famine around Bengazi and brought a mild outbreak to Syria. Malaria, for its part, carried off large numbers, reducing and sometimes wiping out entire colonies of Tatar and Circassian immigrants settled in the Adana region and on the Syrian frontier of settlement. Syphilis and gonorrhea were common around large military garrisons and in mining communities with their transitory labor. But their impact on mortality rates is uncertain.[35]

Famine, as well as disease, declined in frequency during the nineteenth century. Iraq, for example, had suffered famines in 1801, 1827 and 1831 but, apparently, none of major consequence thereafter. In Anatolia, a great famine, caused by a combination of harsh winters, droughts and crop failures, erupted in 1873–74 and killed tens of thousands. Climatic crises recurred again, for example, in the late 1880s and again between 1906 and 1908, causing substantial crop failures and livestock deaths. But, by then, improved communications and transportation systems could bring in needed food supplies and prevent massive deaths. During World War I, however, military mobilization and, in some areas, drought and severe winters, neutralized these improvements. Severe famine struck again and even the capital city suffered. The situation was still worse in the Anatolian and Syrian provinces which suffered extraordinary death tolls.[36]

Wars destroyed vast numbers of Ottoman lives, particularly among the Muslims who formed the vast bulk of the military forces. Most affected were the young males needed to produce the next generation. The wars extracted tens and sometimes hundreds of thousands of young men from their homes, transported them to distant areas and then debilitated or killed them in vast numbers. There are no enumerations concerning even the military casualties but their numbers certainly were enormous.

Most Ottoman wars were doubly disastrous since they took place on home territory, inflicting serious losses upon the civilian populations as well. Non-combatants not only died violent deaths at the hands of soldiers, but also of malnutrition and its accompanists – plague, typhus and cholera. Infant and child mortality must have been very high in such circumstances while high death rates among women of childbearing age further impaired the ability of an Ottoman generation to reproduce itself. Those far from the battle zones also suffered when food supplies from the embattled countryside dwindled. Between 1821 and 1841, for example, the European, Anatolian and Arab provinces all were the scenes of major catastrophes: the Greek War of Independence, the 1827–29 war with Russia and the two wars with Mehmed Ali Pasha.

It seems startling to note that the Ottoman state was fighting at least one war during fifty-three of the years between 1800 and 1918 (45 percent). In the first half-century, wars were especially common and raged during thirty-two of the fifty years (nearly 66 percent), and on numerous occasions with more than one enemy. In the second half-century, until 1918, there were some twenty-one years of war.[37] The economic consequence of these wars seems obvious. Labor shortages worsened and became critical. When the Ottoman lands were battlefields, crops went unsown or unharvested, commerce was disrupted and work-shops and factories were destroyed. The 1870s economic crisis, for example, was extremely grave. For it derived not only from international financial panic but also the combination of killer famine followed imme-diately by the Russo-Turkish War.

Birth-control practices, ranging from *coitus interruptus* to abortion, must have been widely known in the nineteenth-century Ottoman world. The medieval Muslim world had learned of birth-control practices through a variety of means such as medical handbooks and, more import-ant, jurisprudence and erotica.[38] This and the widespread knowledge of birth-control practices in the modern Turkish and Arab worlds make it reasonable to assume a general awareness of the varying forms of birth control during the nineteenth century. But the prevalence of their use, that surely varied over time, locality and by social class, is unknown. Birth control, including an increasingly later age of female marriage, as seen, was common in İstanbul during the late nineteenth century and perhaps earlier.[39] Otherwise, there is little information.

Abortion certainly was not uncommon. In the 1820s, 1830s and 1840s, as the first conscription teams depopulated villages in their zeal to locate recruits for the reformed army, many village women apparently aborted in despair over their own lives and in fear for the futures of their unborn children. During the 1830s, the level of abortions so worried the state that it took a number of measures to prohibit its practice.[40] Reports in the 1850s at Rhodes and during the early 1860s at İzmir discuss Muslim abortions in Aegean coastal areas, carried out with the assistance of Jewish midwives. In the late nineteenth century, midwives at Mecca sold drug compounds to women seeking to prevent conception. The midwives were so confident in their prescription's effectiveness that they offered clients a money-back guarantee in case of failure.[41] At İstanbul, in the 1870s, Muslims were practicing abortion to "an alarming extent." The report continues, in a rare reference to Christians, that they frequently resorted to abortion as well. Abortion again attracted official attention towards the end of the century, when the state created a post to combat abortion in Bursa province, with plans to fund similar positions elsewhere in the empire.[42]

Emigration also checked Ottoman population levels. Some, probably very few, Ottoman immigrants came to the New World before mid-century, as early as the 1820s. Among these was one "Hi Jolly" (Hac Ali), a Syro-Lebanese who developed a camel corps in the American Southwest on the request of Secretary of War Jefferson Davis. His tomb, a pyramid topped with a camel, can still be seen in Quartzite, Arizona. Ottoman emigration rose sharply after the 1860s, as did out-migration from Italy, Greece and the Mediterranean basin in general. Record emigration levels were reached precisely when agricultural labor was most needed, at the time of the late nineteenth-century Ottoman boom in agrarian output. In a few regions, a deteriorating economic or social environment, such as the massacre of Armenians in the mid-1890s, triggered the population movement. In the Mount Lebanon area, large landholders had dispossessed many cultivators and focused on silk production, that came to form over one-half of total agricultural output. When fluctuations in the international silk market cut back on the employ of the now-landless workers, many opted for emigration.

But the peak years of emigration occurred after 1890, when poverty and economic desperation usually were not the critical factors. Most migration coincided with the era of prosperity at the very end of the period. Pull factors attracting Ottomans to new lands probably matched the push factors in importance. Everywhere in the Mediterranean world (and in northern Europe as well), emigrants left their homes in increasing numbers thanks to the increasing availability, simplicity and cheapness of steamship travel. In the 1890s alone, over four million persons emigrated from continental Europe while, in the subsequent decade, more than 7.5 millions left.[43] The building of railroads perhaps stimulated Ottoman emigration although overland routes had been well-traveled long before. Once begun, migrations acquired their own dynamic as the more cautious followed the example of successful emigrants and patterns of chain migration became well-established. The increasingly active American missionaries in the Middle East also played a role, providing migrants with destinations, introductions and, sometimes, educational opportunities in the United States. In addition, the reputation of the New World and the high salaries of its factories were powerful inducements to migrate. These kinds of factors probably explain the paradoxical coincidence of late nineteenth-century emigration increases and the post-1890 agrarian boom, when most cultivators benefited from rising prices for their crops.

Very many of the emigrants were cultivators. Some may have migrated first to Ottoman port cities, joined the urban under- or unemployed and then gone abroad. Just over half of the migrants from the Syrian provinces in 1911 were (to use the vocabulary of the U.S. enumerators) unskilled farm and factory workers, about one-fifth were engaged in trade and another one-fifth were in skilled occupations. Most emigrants, over three-quarters probably, were males. Sixteen percent of all Ottoman emigrants to the United States in 1899 were females; in certain years before 1900, 32 percent of Syrian emigrants were females. Thereafter, it seems that a larger number of Syrian women and children emigrated to join their husbands and fathers in the United States. Most males likely migrated at the peak of their reproductive lives, when they were between the ages of 15 and 40 years. The emigrants typically settled in cities in the Americas, Africa and Australia.[44] Between 1860 and 1914, an estimated 1.2 million Ottoman subjects migrated to the Americas alone, about 5 percent of its total population at the latter date. Comparatively, this was a small proportion. By contrast, Italy lost over 6 million persons during this period, some 18 percent of its population.[45] During the period 1869–92, 178,000 persons migrated from "Turkey-in-Asia" to the United States (the figures for the European provinces are not given). Between 1895 and 1914, 120,000 migrants from "Turkey-in-Europe" and another 150,000 from the Asian provinces arrived in the United States. The majority of all emigrants were Christian and about 15–20 percent were Muslim. Thus, the emigration helped to further tilt the Ottoman religious balance in favor of the Muslims. At some periods and in some areas, however, Muslim emigration loomed larger. In 1909, 43 percent of all Syrian immigrants to Argentina were Muslims; between 1901 and 1913, the United States specifically recorded some 43,000 Armenian and 17,000 Turkish arrivals. Overall, Syria and Lebanon provided about one-half of all emigrants while Macedonia, Albania, Thrace and western Anatolia ranked next in importance. Ottoman Armenians from the Harput area, for example, had established regular patterns of migration to America in the 1860s.[46]

The number of emigrants jumped sharply in the Young Turk period, a response to the push factors enumerated above and to the 1909 law that rendered Ottoman Christians eligible for military service. In 1910–12, record numbers left; some 45,000 Syrian/Lebanese emigrated to Argentina alone. These emigrant workers sent back impressive sums to their families and donated generously to the schools and religious institutions of their home districts. Annual emigrant remittances (that do not include the Syrian areas) averaged £300,000 in the 1880s and increased steadily, to £2,200,000 millions between 1910 and 1913.[47]

As elsewhere, e.g., in Portugal and Italy, Ottoman migration often was a strategy for social mobility as the migrants planned to return home. One-third of Ottoman emigrants, some 400,000 persons, ultimately returned home, a proportion somewhat higher than in Italy, where some 28 percent of all emigrants between 1900 and 1914 returned. Such temporary emigration had positive effects on the economy, as Ottoman subjects returned with new skills and technologies. A number of returnees, for example, opened factories in various locations after working in the United States and England.[48] Altogether, emigration permanently removed about 800,000 persons (exclusive of unborn children), primarily male and Christian and rural in origin, from the Ottoman lands.

IMMIGRATION AND ITS IMPACT ON OTTOMAN POPULATION

Malthusian obstacles such as disease and war, together with birth control and emigration, retarded overall Ottoman population growth until the 1860s. Thereafter, these impediments were overcome by huge waves of immigrants and the total Ottoman population climbed. The immigrants can be divided into two groups. The first, statistically not important, were those who came voluntarily, attracted by the immigration policies of the Ottoman state. The second and vastly more significant group were refugees fleeing into the sultan's realms. Easily the most important among them were Muslim refugees from the Crimea, the Caucasus and the Balkans, as well as lesser numbers from central Asia and Crete. Altogether, some 5–7 million Muslims immigrated into the Ottoman lands between 1783 and 1913.[49] Some of these were the sultans' subjects retreating from lost territories and thus were only a re-distribution rather than a net gain of population. Others, at least 3.8 million of the total, were former subjects of the Russian czar. Their settlement offset the effects of disease, war, birth control and emigration.

The Ottoman Empire never became an important locale for voluntary immigration although the government offered generous terms. An 1857 decree established the conditions under which many of the voluntary immigrants entered the empire. It welcomed all newcomers who possessed some property and were willing to become Ottoman subjects and submit to Ottoman laws. The settlers would obtain good arable land without fee, but they could not sell it for a period of twenty years. If they chose to settle in Rumelia, they were exempted from military service and all taxes for six years. If they opted for the less-populated Anatolian and Arab provinces, the exemption was valid for twelve years. Although many interested Europeans and Americans inquired, the number of actual settlers who voluntarily came seeking economic opportunity seems to have been quite small. The Arab provinces contained no more than a few thousand Europeans, while Anatolia held perhaps 20,000 in 1900. In the end, the Americas were more attractive and Europeans remained reluctant to place themselves under Ottoman jurisdiction.

Jews who migrated to Palestine formed the largest single group of voluntary immigrants. In 1880, there were an estimated 25,000 Jews in Palestine and, by 1914, they numbered as many as 100,000 persons. The new settlers included not only the better-known immigrants from Russia and Eastern Europe but also many Jews from other areas of the Ottoman Empire. While the Ottoman state welcomed immigrants generally, it came to fear the formation of a Zionist state and, towards the end of the century, unsuccessfully tried to restrict the flow of Jewish immigrants.[50]

Involuntary migrants, that is, refugee immigrants, included Balkan Christians seeking religious sanctuary, settled in small numbers in both Rumelia and Anatolia. Several hundred Old Believers who had fled from Russia to the Danubian areas during the late eighteenth century fled again to Anatolia in 1878 when those regions became part of the Rumanian state. At mid-century, groups of Poles, Magyars, and Cossacks settled near İstanbul and in the European and west Anatolian regions, often after failed revolutions back home. While the migrations of these Christians into the Ottoman state are fascinating, they pale in significance before the great Muslim immigrations of the post-1850 period.

As formerly-Ottoman territories in the Balkans became independent, their Muslim populations largely fled, causing ever-higher concentrations of Muslims in the remaining Ottoman lands. Each successive loss brought another population shift. The first Muslim immigration of any magnitude began in the 1770–84 period, with the flight of Tatars from the newly annexed Russian Crimea to Ottoman Bessarabia and the Dobruja. The Crimean migration acquired new significance after 1856, when forcible expulsion became official Czarist policy. Some 30,000 Nogay Tatars were relocated in the Çukurova area, near Adana, but the vast majority died in the malarial heat. Some 150,000 residents of the Crimea had left by 1860 while, in the next three years, an additional 228,000 migrated. Most settled in the Dobruja and moved again as the empire continued to shrink. In 1878, Rumania gained its independence, causing the Nogay Tatars and others to re-settle in western and central Anatolia. Altogether, by 1922, an estimated 1.8 million Tatars had migrated to Ottoman territories.

The Circassians formed perhaps the largest single group of involuntary immigrants into the Ottoman lands. With its final conquest of Circassia in the 1860s, the Czarist government triggered a wave of migration that, over the next half century, added at least two million persons to the Ottoman population. Some Circassians had fled as early as 1860 to escape the forced sedentarization and Christianization programs of the Russian state. To control the migrations, the Russian and Ottoman regimes reached an agreement in 1860, which İstanbul apparently believed would transfer only some 50,000 Circassians. But, by the end of 1864, the expected trickle had become a flood and the Ottoman state struggled to cope with an estimated 522,000 refugees from eastern Circassia alone. Another estimate states that perhaps one million Circassians successfully had moved to Ottoman lands by 1866. Embarking on ships from Russian ports, many traveled to the Danubian areas and then dispersed; for example, by 1876 some 600,000 Circassians had settled throughout the Balkan provinces. In common with the Crimean migrants, many re-located in Anatolia and the Arab areas as the Balkan provinces gained independence. By the end of the Russo-Turkish War of 1878, a total of 1.5 million Circassians had survived the migration and settled in the empire. As Russia continued its pacification policies, another half-million immigrated between 1881 and 1914. Fearing these refugees would become a security risk, St. Petersburg required İstanbul to settle them in regions distant from the borders. Thus the Circassians found new homes in places such as Aleppo and Bursa, and along the railroad lines being opened between İstanbul, Ankara and Konya. Others obtained uncultivated lands along the frontier of settlement in the Syrian provinces. At least 25,000 families re-located to the province of Damascus between 1873 and 1906. The government gave Circassian settlers land grants, tools and seeds.

These immigrants became an important factor in the agricultural explosion that accompanied Anatolian railway building and the reclaiming of the Syrian frontier. In these and many other areas, they brought new cultivation techniques and methods that provided a powerful stimulus to the improvement of late Ottoman agriculture. Even so, however, in areas as far apart as Samsun on the Black Sea and Palestine, tensions between Circassians and local inhabitants simmered for decades.[51]

NOTES

1 Issawi (1980), p. 11.
2 Trietsch (1910).

3 See sources used in Karpat (1985a), pp. 210–11.

4 Issawi (1980), p. 11.

5 Karpat (1985a), p. 21.

6 *Ibid.*, p. 15 and Ubicini (1856), I, p. 18.

7 Karpat (1985a), pp. 35, 168–9.

8 Trietsch (1910).

9 Mitchell and Deane (1962).

10 Issawi (1980), pp. 34–35.

11 Lampe and Jackson (1982), p. 238; Popoff (1920), p. 289.

12 Lampe and Jackson (1982), p. 280; Issawi (1982), p. 101.

13 Issawi (1980), pp. 34–35; Owen (1981), pp. 24–25; Issawi (1969); Fawaz (1983).

14 Karpat (1985a), pp. 148–49 and Issawi (1980), p. 18; Ubicini (1856), I, p. 12.

15 Karpat (1985a), p. 21, 72, 55, 148–49.

16 Bowring (1840), p. 3; Karpat (1985a), p. 148; McCarthy (1983), pp. 110–11.

17 Cem Behar, personal communication, 15 September 1987.

18 Karpat (1985a), p. 217.

19 McCarthy (1983), pp. 16–46.

20 *Ibid.* and Duben (1985), p. 93. Mitchell and Deane (1962), pp. 26–31.

21 BBA Cev Bel 4229, 8 B 1233.

22 McCarthy (1979); Duben (1985); Duben (1987).

23 Tucker (1987).

24 Cem Behar, personal communication, 15 September 1987.

25 Duben (1986).

26 Behar (1986).

27 Behar (1987).

28 Duben (1986). Unless otherwise stated, I have preferred the 1906–7 figures.

29 Sources cited in Quataert (1983), pp. 97–99.

30 BBA İ MV 1289, 25 Ş, 1261/1845.

31 Quataert (1986b); FO 195/8899, Taylor 18/4/1867 on Kharput.

32 Biraben (1975), I, pp. 438–39; Longrigg (1925), pp. 265–68; Issawi (1988), e.g. pp. 18–19, 103.

33 Dols (1979), Table on p. 189; McNeill (1976), pp. 151–58, states that the late nineteenth- early twentieth-century eruption from China did not affect the Mid-East.

34 Ochsenwald (1984), p. 65; Issawi (1980), p. 12. Panzac (1985) replaces previous scholarship on the subject.

35 McCarthy (1983), p. 12; Adams (1924) in Mears (1924), p. 164; Lewis (1987), p. 102; Quataert (1973), pp. 10–13; Şerif (1325/1907).

36 Issawi (1982), pp. 98–99. Quataert (1973); McCarthy (1983).

37 Issawi (1980), p. 4.

38 Musallam (1983) and Himes (1936), pp. 135–59.

39 Behar (1987).

40 BBA Cev Dah 5 Za 1254/1839.

41 Himes (1936), p. 159, citing C. Snouck Hurgronje.

42 Quataert (1973), p. 12; Issawi (1980), pp. 23–24.

43 Trebilcock (1981), p. 311. Unless otherwise noted, the emigration section is

based on Karpat (1985b), pp. 175–209. State policy mildly discouraged emigration until 1896, when a conditional liberalization took place, followed, in 1902, by a strict prohibition which remained unenforced.

44 Issawi (1988), e.g. pp. 19–21, 79. For a fascinating narrative of emigrants from the Lebanese village of Hadeth, see Touma (1958), pp. 105–10.

45 Trebilcock (1981), p. 309.

46 FO, AS, 1891, No. 930, Hampson at Erzeroum, 16 June 1891 citing Boyajian at Kharput.

47 Pamuk (1987), Table A6.4.

48 Öncü (1987); Issawi (1988), pp. 19–21.

49 Karpat (1987); Shorter (1985).

50 Mandel (1975, 1976); Issawi (1982), p. 84; Issawi (1988), p. 21; Karpat (1987).

51 Between the 1860s and the 1880s, immigrants into the Ottoman Empire annually sent back an average of £300,000; the sum fell to c. £100,000 and rose again, to one-quarter million pounds, in the period 1900–8. Pamuk (1987), Table A6.4.

31

TRANSPORTATION

The invention of the steam engine in the late eighteenth century and its application to transportation profoundly changed the way that people and goods were moved, both by water and land. As it developed during the nineteenth century, the new technology brought greater dependability, speed, carrying capacity and safety. Railroads conquered vast interior spaces, sharply reduced transport costs and thus linked inland regions as never before to the coast, its harbors and the global economy. Steamships eliminated the wild unpredictability of voyaging by sail, where a typically week-long journey might take three months with contrary winds.[1] And, with the increasing size of steamships over the course of the century, maritime transport costs plummeted. By 1900, the old technologies – animal transport and sailing ships – everywhere were in retreat.

The modern transport technologies, both land and sea, generally were foreign enterprises, capitalized in Europe and built by Western engineers. There are exceptions to this generalization (see below), but the emergence of steam technology meant increased foreign involvement in the Ottoman economy. For Ottoman cultivators, the new technologies meant new market opportunities, both around the port areas served by the new ships and in the regions tapped by railroads. But the innovations also meant the cultivators were competing on a world market. Thus, Ottoman grains fell sharply in importance on the international market over the century. Ottoman cultivators sometimes lost even local customers as foreign foodstuffs now could come from afar, for example, American flour from Duluth, Minnesota. The record also was mixed for Ottoman manufacturers. Thus, East Asian raw silk flooded into Europe and depressed prices, to the loss of Ottoman silk raisers. Local manufacturers also struggled to retain domestic markets as cheap bulk transport by sea and land reduced prices of European manufactured goods in Ottoman coastal and interior areas. On balance, modern transport probably worked against Ottoman industry as it evolved during the period (see below).

In this stress upon the new, we should not forget the existing transport forms against which steam technologies competed. If the ultimate outcome between new and old was certain, the struggle was prolonged. Even in the United Kingdom, the birthplace of steam power, the registered aggregate tonnage of sailing ships actually increased steadily between the 1820s and 1870s. Similarly, in the Ottoman Empire, sailing vessels remained important and were increasing in number well into the late nineteenth century. On land, camel caravans and other non-mechanized transport forms remained commonplace and, indeed, flourished, in the age of the iron horse. Hauleteers and wagoners fought the new competition with lower wages and often enjoyed the increased business that steam transport generated.[2]

SEA TRANSPORT

Sailing vessels and steamships

Small sailing ships transported most Ottoman goods and passengers in 1800 and, until the mid-nineteenth century, sailing vessels with hulls weighing more than 200 tons were unusual in the Mediterranean.[3] The volume of shipping in Ottoman waters during the early years of the century was unimpressive compared to the levels reached later on. The sea-lanes to İstanbul certainly were the most heavily traveled in the empire. In 1800, for example, the capital consumed some 92,000 tons of wheat and most of it came by sea, from the Moldavian and Wallachian provinces, from Salonica and Volos, and from the north Anatolian coast. In many areas, traffic was light. Basra, on the Persian Gulf, received only 80 ships per year in the 1840s, with a total tonnage of perhaps 11,000 tons.[4] The volume of foreign shipping also was low around 1800. The southern ports of France, then the most important foreign trading partner of the Ottomans, annually sent only 150 ships.

There is debate over the share of intra-Ottoman trade that depended on European ships since the proportions of trade goods carried in European or Ottoman-owned vessels are difficult to determine. Most presently available sources are European and do not adequately report Ottoman shipping. According to some historians, European shippers had dominated Ottoman Mediterranean trade, except for coastal shipping, for many centuries before 1800. At the turn of the century, however, thanks to the Napoleonic Wars, a prospering Ottoman Greek merchant marine captured much of the intra-empire trade. In the Red Sea, local Muslim shippers retained control until approximately the 1840s, sailing in two-masted vessels not larger than 80 tons.[5]

Steamships began entering Ottoman waters during the 1820s and, within several decades, became a familiar sight in most areas. A British steamer reached İstanbul in 1828; five years later, the Odessa Company sent a Russian steamer to İstanbul via the Black Sea and, in the following year, an Austrian steamer came down the Danube to the capital. In 1836, the first steamships entered Beirut harbor and, by 1840, the Red Sea. At the end of the 1840s, Britain was operating regular steamship transport on the Red Sea while several other major European nations offered this service in the eastern Mediterranean and the Black Sea. Regular steamship traffic to the Persian Gulf was not instituted until the early 1860s; the number of ships rose sharply with the opening of the Suez Canal in 1869. Steamship travel on the Tigris and Euphrates had begun in the late 1830s. From the 1860s, the Lynch Company concession provided regular, if relatively expensive, steam service.[6]

The advent of steam brought dramatic increases in the size of vessels. For example, the mean size of the Austrian Lloyd fleet rose fourfold, to 1,000 tons between 1836 and 1874. Ships calling at Trabzon averaged an eightfold rise in size, to 1,005 tons between 1830 and 1888. Similarly, steamships calling at İstanbul in the 1830s ranged between 130 and 530 tons but in the late nineteenth century averaged over 1,250 tons.

Steam vessels overwhelmed their sail competitors but the pace varied. At Samsun and Trabzon in the late 1880s, steam vessels accounted for 93 and 99 percent of all tonnage. In the 1860s, sailing ships serving İstanbul still carried more than four times as much total cargo (by weight) as steamships. At the capital, steam pulled even with sail tonnage in the early 1870s; by 1900 only 5 percent of all cargoes traveled there by sail. At Mersin, that had an open roadstead and was quite a different port than İstanbul, the results were similar: by the end of the century, steamers carried more than 95 percent of all goods. At Jidda on the Red Sea, sailing ships profited from the increasing trade and, between 1814 and 1861, their numbers rose from 250 to 600, averaging eight tons each. Thereafter, however, Jidda sailing ships suffered from steamship competition and, by 1900, steamships accounted for 90 percent of all shipping.[7]

Thus, the number of steamships rose remarkably and captured the vast majority of all goods transported by sea. Throughout the nineteenth century, this increase sustained and was supported by an extraordinary

Table IV:8. Shipping tonnage entering main Ottoman ports, 1830–1913
(thousand tons)

Port	1830	1860	1890	1913
Basra	10	—	100	400
Beirut	40	400	600	1,700
İstanbul	—	—	800	4,000
İzmir	100	600	1,600	2,200
Trabzon	15	120	500	

Source: Issawi (1982), p. 48.

rise in the volume of shipping (also see Ch. 32). Between 1800 and 1914, the total volume at Beirut rose from 40 to 1,700 tons and at İzmir from 100 to 2,200 tons. Trabzon's shipping soared from 15 to over 500 tons and that of Basra from 10 to 400 tons. The total at İstanbul quadrupled to 4,000 tons in the two decades before 1914. Vessels owned by Europeans carried increasing proportions of the total traffic and, by 1914, accounted for 90 percent of total tonnage. The Ottoman share of shipping at Trabzon, for example, fell from 69 to 33 percent between 1830 and 1874. But some Ottoman shippers benefited greatly. In the example just cited, although the relative Ottoman share of tonnage at Trabzon slipped, the absolute volume of Ottoman tonnage there actually increased by some sevenfold, from 11,000 to 71,000 tons. Ottoman ships at Jidda annually carried an average total of 100,000 tons in 1878–82 and 259,000 tons in 1900–4, an increase of over 250 percent. In other ports, such as Samsun, Trabzon and the roadstead at Tarsus, Ottoman shippers remained present in significant numbers (see Table IV:8).[8]

Thanks to the huge increases in commerce, more Ottoman sailing vessels probably were operating in 1914 than at any point in the nineteenth century. The boom in shipping meant new business for Ottoman sailing vessels and their crews and not just for the foreign steamships. Substantial numbers of Ottomans remained employed in civilian sailing vessels throughout the nineteenth century. Between 1879 and 1914, aggregate Ottoman sailing vessel tonnage increased from 164,000 to 202,000 tons.[9] Overall in 1914, sailing ships still accounted for two-thirds of the total tonnage under the Ottoman flag. At Jidda, Muslim merchants operated ten very large sailing ships, reportedly up to 1,000 tons each, into the 1890s, as well as 400–600 smaller vessels. Over 2,500 Ottoman sailing ships annually called at Beirut at the end of the nineteenth century.[10] Sailing vessels numbering 529 visited the port of Mersin in 1897 and, in 1906, 626 sailing ships arrived.[11] More impressively, some 8,000 sailing vessels annually visited Trabzon in the late 1880s while at İzmir, between 1908 and 1912, some 3,000 sailing ships annually were recorded. By contrast, only fourteen sailing ships anchored at Samsun in 1888.[12]

Port development and labor unrest

The growth in commerce and steamship tonnage placed severe strains on existing Ottoman port facilities. The amounts of cargo being handled and the ever-larger size of steamships created bottlenecks that caused delays, increased costs and frustrated merchants. Most Ottoman ports changed relatively little over the century. Mersin, for example, remained an exposed roadstead: railroad cargoes were onloaded via long, unprotected piers equipped with a light tram and small cranes. Steamers were becoming too large for many of the ports they visited. For example, in the 1880s, when the average size of steamships exceeded 1,000 tons, the Beirut harbor was only 150 meters long, 100 meters wide and 2 meters deep.[13] To load at such ports, larger ships anchored offshore and lighter boats ferried the goods between ship and shore, a slow procedure that often resulted in damaged merchandise. Foreign merchants protested and pressured the government for improvements. When İbrahim Pasha, the son of Mehmed Ali Pasha, visited Beirut in the 1830s, British merchants petitioned for an increase in the number of warehouses and lighterboats and for construction of a breakwater. He obliged by ordering a survey, building a new customs house and taking steps to construct the breakwater.[14]

But major improvements came very late and in only a few places. Foreign companies constructed and operated larger and more efficient port facilities at Salonica, İzmir, Beirut and İstanbul. Not coincidentally, these were the four leading Ottoman ports in 1909.[15] In the 1860s and 1870s, as the Salonica–Mitrovitza railroad quickened the commerce of Salonica, a quay of 1,800 meters in length was built to handle steamship cargoes. Nearly three decades later, the Salonica Quay Company and two railroad companies signed an agreement to permit freight trains to roll directly onto the quays for direct discharging of goods into the ships. This finally ended the need to carry merchandise the half-mile distance from the railroad station to the harbor.[16] Major improvements at the port of İzmir were begun in 1867 and completed in 1875. Facilities included a 4 km-long quay and some 32 hectares of dock space. A Paris-based company developed Beirut's port in 1894 by constructing a 800 m-long pier and 21 hectares of dock space, in addition to new customs and quarantine buildings.[17] Another French company nearly simultaneously erected quays at the port of İstanbul that permitted the direct handling of large steamships. In response, traffic rose a full 50 percent within a decade.[18] New facilities at the four ports vastly improved the flow of commerce but foreign merchants continued to complain about inadequate storage, handling facilities and customs processing. Most of all, they railed against the Ottoman port workers who, in turn, had their own reasons for complaint.

The activities of the foreign-owned port companies gravely threatened many Ottoman workers employed in the port zones. Prior to foreign development of the four ports, thousands of boatmen had earned livelihoods transporting passengers and cargo between ships anchored offshore and the dockside. Other boatmen placed cargoes into storage boats for future delivery. Porters carried goods from the shore to customs and to the warehouses. Some porters used their own backs or those of animals; others, the *sırık* porters, worked in teams and carried goods suspended from stout poles. In the major ports, most porters and boatmen belonged to guilds that were exceptionally cohesive. In return for the membership dues, guildsmen expected continued employment and exclusive access to the worksite. But the new port facilities destroyed their worksites and many of their jobs. The quays eliminated the jobs of many boatmen when ships tied directly to the quays for handling. (In at least İstanbul and İzmir, however, ships tied up perpendicular to the quays and the cargo was lowered onto floating barges for transfer to the quay. This maximized use of valued quay space and did preserve some boatmen's jobs.) Warehouses built by the companies eliminated the need for the storage vessels. When trams were installed on the quays, hundreds of porters were thrown out of work. And as railroad lines were extended into the port zones, such as happened at İzmir, still more jobs were lost. At Salonica, completion of the rail link between the central station and the quay saved transport time but cost porters' jobs. Moreover, the concessions that the foreign corporations received included provisions that gave them monopoly control of the port areas. The companies sought to exercise their monopolies by closely regulating the port workers. Moreover, these companies, and foreign merchants and shipping lines generally, preferred to hire port workers from abroad and/or Ottoman workers who were not members of any porters' or boatmen's guilds. Port companies' interests in monopoly control, their quays, trams, warehouses and employment practices gave rise to bitter struggles with the porters and boatmen of Ottoman port cities. Battles on the quays and wharves accompanied construction of the port facilities. Port workers prevented ships from offloading and sabotaged construction. Enraged foreign merchants and port company officials appealed to their consuls and the Ottoman government arrested its own subjects on behalf of foreign corporations. But the port workers fought a rearguard action with remarkable success and won major concessions from the companies.[19]

The port workers' cause received a considerable boost from the boycott of Austro-Hungarian goods during 1908–9, a response to the Habsburg annexation of Bosnia-Herzegovina. Young Turks managed the movement while boatmen and porters enforced the boycott on a day-to-day level. The port workers maintained the boycott when popular enthusiasm flagged. As a reward, workers at İstanbul gained back some of the jobs they had lost earlier to the Quay Company. More generally, the boycott boosted port workers' political power and enhanced their ability to fight against the port companies, foreign merchants and shipping firms. At Trabzon, where they had been particularly active during the boycott, the boatmen seized control of the local Unionist Party and effectively ran the city in the years before World War I. They also remained active at İzmir and Salonica. The lightermen's and porters' guilds repeatedly halted commerce at Salonica after 1908. Prolonged negotiations with them, the British consul said in frustration, were fruitless. Unless shipping companies were willing to import labor for port work, he said, little could be done to curb the guilds' power and improve the flow of commerce.[20]

RAILROADS

General

The Ottoman Empire came late to the railroad age. In 1850, not a single track had yet been laid anywhere in the area of Ottoman control.[21] Second-ranking European powers just then were acquiring railroads; Italy had 620 km of track and Spain possessed under 100 km. Among the Great Powers, Austria–Hungary already maintained 1,357 km while major railway nations such as Great Britain possessed 9,800 km and the United States some 14,480 km of track.

During the second half of the nineteenth century, mainly after 1890, Ottoman territories acquired some 7,500 km of track. This relative burst of activity came several decades after the great explosion of railroad building in the United States, where the track laid rose almost tenfold between

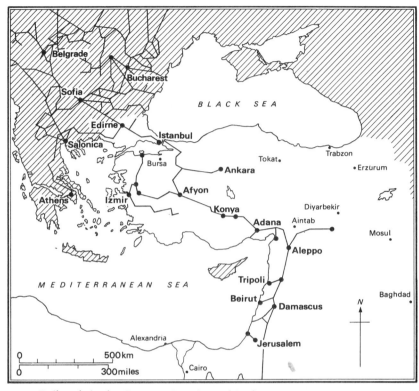

21 Railroads in the Ottoman Empire and its former European possessions, c. 1914.

1850 and 1880, more than twenty times the track that would be constructed in the Ottoman lands. As the American system reached maturity, railroad construction in many other lands quickened. The Ottoman rail-laying boom thus paralleled that in many countries, but was of more modest proportions. Railroad lines in the Habsburg Empire, for example, extended to nearly 23,000 km by 1913, over three times the Ottoman level. Former Ottoman territories in the Balkans – the independent states of Rumania, Bulgaria, Serbia, and Greece – together built about 8,000 km of track, or slightly more than in the empire itself.[22]

A statement of the Council of the Tanzimat from 1854, demonstrates how favorably impressed the İstanbul regime was by the economic future promised by railroads. One of the most important improvements which will do most to develop sources of wealth, is the building of connecting routes in the empire. . . . To achieve this, there must be great unifying arteries, that means a network of railroads that go from the agrarian areas to the sea, cutting across the most fertile provinces.[23]

Notably, the Council made no comment on the potential of railroads as stimuli to industrialization.

Foreign capital and workers played the critical role in the construction and initial operation of almost all Ottoman railroads. The building of railroads posed unusual financial and technological problems for the Ottoman Empire (as well as for all societies outside those of their birth). The technology was totally alien and thus initially had to be imported in its entirety. Likewise, the introduction of railroads required workers familiar with the technology. This meant foreign, imported labor, at least for a while. In addition, railroad building required vast sums to lay track and to purchase engines and cars, before operations could even be initiated.

The state used two methods of financing. In the first, less frequently used method, the government directly provided the funds for construction. It either made the necessary capital available to foreign companies or, in a very few cases, (the most remarkable being the Hejaz Railway, see below), it used domestic funds and built the line itself. In the 1870s, for example, the state built a short section between Kasaba and Alaşehir in west Anatolia and turned it over to a foreign company for operation. But, in 1914, state capital accounted for only 10 percent of all sums invested in Ottoman railroads. More commonly, the state awarded concessions to organizations that raised the capital, through the sale of bonds, for construction and operation. To encourage such ventures, the state usually offered some type of formal financial assurance to entrepreneurs. For the first few construction projects early in the rail-building period, the state guaranteed a certain rate of return on the capital outlay. But when it reneged on payments during the 1860s and 1870s, foreign investors declined to invest further in Ottoman railroad construction. State interest in railroads remained high, however, and, in 1872, İstanbul officials invited the German engineer, Wilhelm von Pressel, to submit a master plan for an Ottoman rail network. Pressel's ten-year plan (the blueprint for much of the subsequent construction) called for a great 2,700 km trunk line from the Asian shores of İstanbul to the Persian Gulf. In addition, he proposed an extensive feeder and branch system of 1,800 km. Abdülhamid's administration adopted the plan, but preferred to build the sections offering greater military and political benefits rather than those with high economic potential.

To encourage foreign investment, the government adopted a new financial technique, called the kilometric guarantee system. Commonly used in the later nineteenth century, this method assured the railway company a certain minimum revenue per kilometer of track in operation, the state pledging to make up any deficiencies. The system relieved the state of the need to provide start-up capital and left that burden with the private company holding the concession. But this advantage was offset by other, less desirable aspects; by providing a revenue floor for the company, kilometric guarantees could serve as a disincentive to more efficient operations. Foreign capital built only a few lines without such state guarantees, under 20 percent of all mileage in the Asian provinces; typically these were sections that the government considered without strategic value.[24]

Construction

Ottoman railroads were part of an ever-expanding network of rail construction that radiated steadily outward from Western Europe. From the lands of its West European origins, main arteries, often financed by French investors, simultaneously were built in several directions of the compass, e.g. Spain, Austria, Russia and Italy. As these networks filled in, investors turned to regions lacking rail systems; railroads thus spread southeastward into the Balkans and Anatolia. Finally, in the 1890s, rail laying reached into the Syrian provinces further east, followed by building in the Iraqi and Arabian peninsula areas after 1900.[25]

Railroad building began in the European and Anatolian provinces just after the Crimean War, when highway construction also accelerated. British capital built the first railway, in what became Rumania, followed quickly by construction on the İzmir–Aydın Railway in west Anatolia. The European provinces took the lead and most of the 2,000 km of track constructed in this area were laid before 1890. By contrast, the Anatolian provinces of 1890 contained only c. 900 km of rail and the Arab provinces none at all. Salonica in the Balkans was connected to Skopje in 1871 and to Belgrade in 1888. The greatest of the European lines was the Oriental Railway, begun in the early 1870s and completed in 1888. This system ultimately encompassed 1,300 km of track and connected İstanbul to Edirne and Sofia, with a branch from Edirne to Salonica. Military considerations shaped its final routing and some planned sections that were economically advantageous, from Skopje to Sofia, for example, never were built. To finance the Oriental line, the state borrowed tens of millions of *lira*. But, in the case of other Rumelian lines, such as the 219-km Salonica–Monastır Railway, it employed the kilometric guarantee method of financing. Most of this valuable infrastructure was lost, however, when the Balkan peoples broke away and became independent. In 1914, the İstanbul regime retained only 480 of the 2,000 km constructed in the European provinces.[26]

Anatolia acquired some 2,900 km of track. The earliest were two British-built lines, completed in the 1860s and later extended to include 1,300 km that tapped fertile river valleys in western Anatolia. In the 1870s, the state sought to build lines inland from the port towns of İzmit and Mudanya. These efforts failed, however, for want of technical expertise. In the latter example, the roadbed was improperly graded so that the new engines could not climb the hill. Later, these lines were rebuilt with foreign assistance. The great extension of railroads occurred between 1890 and 1895, with construction of the 1,000-km Anatolian Railway, from İzmit to Ankara, with a branch to Konya. Tortuous international negotiations finally yielded a plan to extend the Anatolian line to the southeast. In 1903, the İstanbul government issued a concession for the Baghdad Railway, from Konya in Anatolia to the head of the Persian Gulf. Construction of this railroad promised to fulfill the long-held dream of uninterrupted railway travel from Berlin (or, depending on the dreamer, Paris or London) to the ancient capital of the Abbasids on the Tigris. Diplomatic struggles among the European powers often delayed construction, but some 700 km were completed by the outbreak of the war. The Iraqi provinces held 122 km of the Baghdad line, the only track laid in those provinces during the Ottoman period.

Railroad building in the Syrian provinces began in earnest after completion of the Anatolian Railway. French capital built the first line, a short link from Jaffa to Jerusalem in 1891. The next, in 1894, linked Damascus with the rich Hawran wheat-growing districts. French-financed activity then connected this line to Beirut, further promoting the city's preeminence in the eastern Mediterranean just as, three decades earlier, the two British railways in western Anatolia had re-confirmed the commercial supremacy of İzmir. Other Syrian lines similarly connected important interior cities with the coast, for example, Aleppo to the port of Tripoli, in 1906. By 1914, Syria held 1,677 km of track. In relation to land mass and population, the Syrian network was twice as dense as the Anatolian system, but its impact was reduced by the use of three different gauges. In Anatolia, by contrast, all lines except the 42-km Mudanya–Bursa Railway employed the same gauge.

Unique among Ottoman railroads, the Hejaz Railway was built with Ottoman capital and largely by Ottoman labor. The sultan planned the line, intended to connect Damascus and Mecca, with several purposes in mind, including reinforcement of his Pan-Islamic claims as leader of the world's Muslims. Bogged down in a prolonged and bloody war in the Yemen, he saw the line as a means to bind this region and the distant Hejazi areas to the capital. The planners sought to rely on domestic savings only and not foreign loans or kilometric guarantees. And they wanted to employ only Ottoman materials, except for the railroad engines and cars. The internal financing was a great success thanks to voluntary donations, special taxes, contributions from non-Ottoman Muslims, and the use of army labor. With the sultan and grand vizier leading the way, government officials donated sums while, for several years, civil servants, including Christians, compulsorily gave one month's salary. Egyptian as well as Indian Muslims were also important contributors. The sums that they donated were not significant financially but they worried colonialists who saw a Pan-Islamic threat to British interests. Several new taxes, beyond the compulsory pledges of civil servants, provided much of the needed money. The use of large numbers of soldiers for construction helped balance the budget of the enterprise, since these expenses were carried on the ledgers of the military and not the railroad. At one stage of construction, for example, some 9,300 troops prepared the roadbed and laid track. But plans to avoid using foreign technical experts foundered on the reality of Ottoman technological backwardness. After some false starts, the state hired European engineers and let contracts to foreign companies for the more skilled work, such as building the bridges and tunnels. As the line extended into the Arabian peninsula and neared the Sacred Precinct, soldiers apprenticed to skilled European workmen assumed many tasks. Muslims from Egypt were utilized as well. Sultan Abdülhamid won an important propaganda victory with successful completion of over 1,500 km of track to the Holy City of Medina.[27]

The labor force

Laborers engaged in building Ottoman railways mainly were Ottoman subjects. Although the number of soldiers employed on the Hejaz line probably is unusually high, its use of military troops is not unique. In 1873, for example, soldiers helped in the unsuccessful effort to connect İzmit and Ankara. The extent to which corvée labor summoned civilian construction workers is uncertain but probably it was not routine. The corvée was employed to some extent, for example, in building the Hejaz Railway and the İzmit-Ankara line in 1873.

It seems likely that wage labor built most Ottoman lines. Account books for the building of the İzmit–Ankara and the Niş–Vidin lines in 1873 record the presence of Kurds, Turks, Armenians, Greeks, Slavs and Rumanians who received a daily cash wage. In addition, they obtained bread as well as tent shelters from the state.[28] How they were recruited is unknown but, once at the worksite, they received wages. Contract wage labor, directly hired by the companies, built most and perhaps all of the Anatolian and Baghdad Railways. In the first season of Anatolian railway construction, up to 6,500 workers labored for 1.6 million workdays to prepare the roadbed.[29] Many laborers walked hundreds of kilometers to obtain jobs, from as far away as Shiraz in Iran. In the case of the Baghdad line, headmen recruited labor gangs and brought them to the site, a practice that probably was common in the building of the other Ottoman lines.

Foreign workers were used, sometimes in large numbers, for the more skilled tasks. There were some 1,500 foreigners in a total of 5,000 construction workers in the early 1900s, while the Hejaz network used at least 600 foreigners at one point in the construction phase. The Anatolian, Baghdad and Hejaz railways each employed large numbers of Italians and Montenegrins, usually as stone cutters and masons. Fighting among workers was commonplace and occasionally serious incidents erupted: in 1896, Kurds murdered seven foreigners working on the extension of the İzmir–Kasaba line.[30]

A new Ottoman work force thus came into existence and, by c. 1914, the railways employed a permanent work force estimated at 10–15,000 persons.[31] Many were semi-skilled or unskilled, working to maintain the roadbeds or clean the stations. Other, skilled workers, serviced and ran the engines, repaired equipment, or worked in the traffic departments. Still others maintained accounts and supervised operations.

The railroad work force overall was sharply stratified by religion, ethnicity and nationality. Among railroad employees, Europeans held the highest ranking jobs. Europeans and Ottoman Christians filled the middle levels and Ottoman Muslims, either Turks or Arabs, depending on location of the line, dominated the lowest ranks. This stratification pattern hardly was accidental. At the very highest levels of management, the Western origins of the capital dictated that Europeans filled virtually all board memberships and the crucial management positions. Also, the novel nature of railway work in Ottoman society naturally meant reliance on European personnel in the early years, since most Ottoman subjects had been unfamiliar with rail technology. But some railroad companies restricted the skilled and managerial jobs to Europeans as Ottomans developed the necessary skills. The stratification patterns of the railroad workforce indeed closely resemble those of most other foreign-owned corporations in the Ottoman Empire. It was not only the novelty of rail technology but also company policy that impeded advancement of Ottoman workers. Still worse, the companies offered unequal pay for equal work; Europeans obtained salaries that were 50 percent higher than those that Ottomans received for the same tasks. While such a policy attracted and retained Europeans working far from their homelands, the aggrieved Ottoman worker understood the issue differently.[32]

Worker protests to improve conditions and obtain higher wages date from the early years of Ottoman railways and strikes occurred in the late 1870s. Railway employees and workers were powerfully influenced by developments in Europe. The direct physical links between the Ottoman and European rail systems promoted the easy flow of ideas among the engineers who ran and cared for the locomotives. Also, many of the engineers and more highly skilled employees were Europeans familiar with labor syndicates or unions. Thus, when these Ottoman workers formally organized, it is not surprising that they adopted European models. Workers on the İstanbul–Edirne–Salonica line formed the first Ottoman railway union in 1907, while the Anatolian Railway Union emerged just weeks after the July 1908 Young Turk Revolution. More than four-fifths of its elected officers were Ottoman Christians or foreigners, certainly a reflection of actual union membership. In 1908, strikes erupted on railroads in all regions of the empire. Thereafter, until 1914, railroads remained a center of labor agitation as workers regularly struck to promote their demands.[33]

Impact of the railroads, an assessment

Historians are fond of arguing about the relative worth of railroads. One American historian has taken the position, hotly disputed, that if canals had been built instead of railroads, the net economic impact would have been the same.[34] Hence, the argument goes, railroads were not that important. A definitive assessment of the economic impact of Ottoman lines similarly is difficult. Many other costs and benefits – social, political and military – are present and there is uncertainty about some of the economic gains. Ottoman railroads offered important economic, political and military advantages. But the price paid does seem extremely high, mortgaging the future to build in the present, with ever-more intricate

Table IV:9. Passengers transported on various Ottoman railways
(millions)

Line	1891	1895	1900	1910
Ankara–Konya	0.7	1.0	1.2	2.7
İzmir–Kasaba	–	1.5	1.7	2.4
Aydın	–	–	–	1.9
Mersin–Adana	–	–	–	0.3
Damascus–Hama	–	–	0.2	0.7
Hejaz	–	–	–	0.2
Baghdad	–	–	–	0.01

entanglements in the European financial web and, hence, additional losses of autonomy. By 1911, the Ottoman state had paid nearly 170 million francs in kilometric guarantee sums plus another 100 million francs for the Hejaz line. Increases in the amount of agricultural tithes collected in the newly opened railroad districts nearly offset this amount, according to one calculation. But almost all these tithe revenues were paid to the railroad companies and not into the coffers of the Ottoman treasury. Railroad building in the short run actually reduced the sums at the disposal of the state; but total kilometric guarantee sums did diminish over time, as the railroads carried more goods and became more solvent.[35]

For the monies spent, the Ottoman state and economy gained a number of important benefits. The railroads opened up interior regions to political control and economic development and they helped the state to shuttle troops quickly within the empire. The state used them with success in the 1897 war with Greece, the Balkan wars and World War I. Railroads helped to bring nomads under firm control in many areas, although during the Arab Revolt the Hejaz line was a fatal trap for the Ottoman military. Other benefits to the economy as a whole included substantially reduced transport costs. Despite sustained price-cutting by caravan operators, the railroad ultimately defeated animal transport on routes where they directly competed. But caravan operators benefited from the iron tracks as well; the railways stimulated the rise of new feeder networks of animal transport (see below).

By 1914, railroads reportedly carried one-half of all goods transported by land in Syria and 48 percent of all goods shipped in Anatolia.[36] These figures, however, are no more than informed guesses, since animal-back traffic cannot be calculated with any certainty. Since the lines in Syria were more densely built than in other Ottoman regions, this 50 percent share probably represents the maximum contribution of railroad to total land transport (Table IV:10).

Table IV:10. Goods transported on various Ottoman railways
(thousand tons)

Line	1891	1895	1900	1910
Ankara–Konya	—	118	357	585
İzmir–Kasaba	—	—	245	327
Aydın	—	—	—	342
Mersin–Adana	—	—	—	130
Damascus–Hama	—	—	—	309
Hejaz	—	—	—	66
Baghdad	—	—	—	28

Source: Tables IV:9 and 10 derived from Hecker (1914), pp. 1554–1565.

Railroads brought few additions to the Ottoman industrial sector. In Russia, Great Britain and the United States, for example, the expansion of railroads fostered the growth of heavy industries, such as iron and steel production. Some fairly extensive repair shops, at Eskişehir for example, did emerge, capable of working iron and steel parts. But builders of Ottoman lines remained dependent on imported rails and rolling stock; and so, these railroads generated few multiplier effects in the Ottoman economy. The wages that thousands of construction laborers earned certainly pumped in fresh supplies of money. More significantly, the 10,000 or more permanent jobs added new sources of income that provided increased demand for Ottoman (and foreign) goods and services.

Railroads also vastly increased the circulation of people within the empire. In 1911, all Ottoman railroads carried about 14 million passengers, with the Oriental Railway in the Balkans accounting for a full one-half of the total. In 1908, the Anatolian Railway transported 1.9 million passengers, while the İzmir–Kasaba and İzmir–Aydın lines respectively carried 2.4 and 1.4 million persons (Table IV: 9). The Baghdad line, by contrast, then carried only 53,000 passengers, a reflection of the sparse population of its hinterland. By comparison, the Damascus–Hama line reported 498,000 passengers and the Salonica–Monastır line transported some 332,000 persons.[37] Many passengers were commuters and these statistics thus also show the population re-distribution initiated by the railroads. Affluent residents of Ottoman cities began buying villas in the countryside, now more accessible. Thanks to railroads, a certain suburbanization occurred. Also, the population of railroad districts grew proportionately faster than in other areas. In part this was due to their greater safety, their potential for market agriculture, internal migration and the government settlement of refugees that took place, for example along the Anatolian and Rayak–Aleppo railroads and northern portions of the Hejaz line.[38] The total number of pilgrims to the Holy Cities increased sharply thanks to the greater speed, relative security and lower charges of the Hejaz Railway. The transport costs of a pilgrim from Damascus to Medina fell from 1,200 to 200 francs with the railroad. In the late nineteenth century before the railroad, perhaps 5,000 pilgrims journeyed on camel from Damascus to Medina; by 1913, they traveled by rail and sea and the number had doubled.[39]

Changes in the agricultural sector are frequently and justly associated with the railroad enterprise. And often these were quite dramatic. The post-1870 state emphasis on lines of strategic and military importance, however, reduced the potential impact on agriculture. For example, the government determined not to build a proposed line that would have tied the İzmit–Ankara section to the fertile and relatively densely populated regions around Sivas. Instead, citing strategic and military reasons, it pushed for the Eskişehir–Konya section, that passed through sparsely populated zones. Some lines were not significant economically. The Beirut–Damascus Railway, for example, reportedly did not play an important role in the continuing development of the Beirut economy. Nor is the Hejaz railway line considered an economic success since, in the richer agricultural zones through which it passed, it duplicated existing lines. But its tariff wars to attract customers did improve the export potential of local growers by reducing rail charges for wheat some 16 percent. Similarly, it enhanced the purchasing power of local consumers when it reduced sugar freight charges by 50 percent.[40]

Railroads promoted the flow of both imported finished goods and the export of Ottoman raw materials and foodstuffs. Manufactured goods, especially textiles, formed the vast majority of imports although, by volume, coffee, sugar and coal predominated. The completion of lines to interior towns such as Ankara damaged some local handicraft producers previously protected by distance. But some manufacturing centers, such as Aleppo, Damascus or Buldan in Aydın province, thrived in close proximity to railroads while others such as Amasya, Tokat, Arapkir and Diyarbekir continued to prosper in the absence of rail lines. Increased sales of imported goods were financed by rising exports from the railroad districts.

It is for their role as conduits for the export of agricultural commodities that Ottoman railways have been most noted. Foodstuffs, frequently cereals, and raw materials formed the overwhelming majority of exports, more than 90 percent, on most railroads. The volume of railroad exports far exceeded that of imports. Exports were 70 to 85 percent of all shipments on the Anatolian, Damascus–Hama and İzmir–Kasaba railways. But, in several cases, where lines penetrated short distances from the coast to an inland city, imports prevailed. This was true of the Jaffa–Jerusalem and the Mudanya–Bursa lines, where imports accounted for two-thirds of total traffic.[41] Sometimes there were spectacular economic increases in agricultural production as transport costs fell and prices received by cultivators increased. Within a decade of its completion, the Anatolian Railway caused the additional annual production of 400,000 tons of grain. İstanbul changed its provisioning patterns and Anatolia became an important factor in the city's grain supply. İstanbul millers began buying rail-shipped wheat from inner Anatolia instead of water-borne grain from Russia, Bulgaria and Rumania. Thereafter, under favorable circumstances, the Anatolian Railway provided over 90 percent of all wheat delivered in the capital city for local consumption. By substituting locally grown for imported grains, the railroad contributed important sums to the balance of payments, annually saving perhaps 700,000 *liras*. Overall, however, most of the railroad grain, perhaps 75 percent of the total, was exported abroad. Thus, some railroads offered import substitution benefits while reinforcing the role of the Ottoman economy as a supplier of raw materials.[42]

ROADS, HIGHWAYS AND CARAVANS

The drama of railroads has attracted attention away from the other important parts of the overland transport system, that is, the roads, highways, wagons and caravans. The story of the wagoners, hauleteers and caravan operators, however, is difficult to reconstruct. There is little completed research and, besides, these transporters have not left us many records. Thanks in large measure to the re-imposition of central authority, the overland movement of goods and persons became considerably more certain and secure as the century progressed. In some areas, with the expanded use of wheeled transport, it became faster and more efficient as well.

In the early decades of the century, before Mahmud II re-asserted imperial authority over the provinces, the empire held numerous, relatively small commercial zones under the control of local power figures, such as regional dynasts or tribes. As commercial travellers moved from one zone of jurisdiction into another, they negotiated the price of passage with those controlling the routes, sometimes called brigands and at other times notables. The presence of these zones and fees prolonged travel time and increased the costs of doing business. But, as we see from the following example, concerning the Salonica–Seres route in 1812, many notables actively sought to attract trade through their territories.

> The Pachas and Commanders desirous to secure so lucrative a business to their Country have endeavoured to improve the roads by avoiding steep and rugged mountains, by building kans (*sic*) and by establishing Guards in the most dangerous parts of the road. They have so far succeeded . . .[43]

The successful movement of merchandise sometimes had depended on good relations with nomadic tribes. Nomads' relations with caravans were not merely predatory, although their ability to slow or halt commercial traffic and the seriousness of the threat they posed to caravans should not be underestimated. Many nomads maintained and promoted commerce. Agreements often existed between tribes and merchants, since the continued flow of trade redounded to the advantage of both. Merchants obtained safe passage and the tribes received fees, adding to the income they earned from selling supplies and services. Tribes frequently provided animals for the caravans and often themselves were in the caravan business, furnishing workers and arranging for forage. They also provided security for transiting commercial traffic.[44] In addition, they often entered into agreements with government officials to guard commercial routes; in the early nineteenth century, for example, the pashas of Aleppo paid the Mawali tribe to protect the Aleppo–Hama road.[45] European merchants outside of such economic alliances complained bitterly about the rapacity of tribes and pashas, only occasionally remembering the services being provided and that their goods, in fact, paid very low duties.[46]

The system sometimes failed when the rewards of plunder outweighed those of passage. In 1842, for example, Bedouins sacked the caravan from Baghdad to Aleppo, that carried goods worth perhaps one-half million piasters. Similarly, in 1857, nomads plundered another caravan outward-bound from Baghdad, reportedly carrying five million *liras* of cargo.[47]

Plundering dropped sharply as the central state imposed its tribal pacification programs. Nomadic sedentarization seems to have been well advanced in west and central Anatolia before mid-century. The governor of Sivas, for example, had forced the settlement of local tribes during the 1830s. But pacification occurred later further east in Anatolia and in the Syrian and Iraqi provinces. Cevdet Pasha crushed and forcibly settled the Kozanoğlu tribes of the Adana region in 1865. Real restrictions on the Syrian tribes began in the 1840s and acquired momentum in the subsequent decade. By the 1880s, most tribes in the transition zone of the Syrian desert either had settled or had been driven away.[48] The impact of pacification on the tribes' caravan activities is uncertain but certainly reduced camel herd sizes and the ability to receive transit fees.

Even after a half-century of sedentarization and extension of government control into the countryside, highway travelers remained in peril. In the early twentieth century, bandits still were attacking individual travelers around İzmir, a relatively well-administered area. In the Hejaz as well as sections of the Syrian desert and eastern Anatolia, protection money from the government rather than its military forces assured tribal cooperation until 1914.

Overall, however, security on highways improved as the century grew older. The multiple customs barriers operated by the state gradually disappeared as the government dismantled its system of internal duties. Delays in moving through the jurisdictional zones of the notables, brigands and tribes generally faded from memory (see Ch. 32). This simplification of travel combined with improvements in security reduced travel time and encouraged commerce.

Animal backs were more common than wheeled transport in most areas and during most of the period. Routes often were suitable only to animal-back transport; shipment by wagon often damaged the goods. Generally, carts were restricted to travel within a village but became more common later in the period. In the areas where they settled, Circassian and Jewish immigrants re-introduced wheeled transport. Mules, donkeys and horses sometimes were preferable to camels for shorter trips because of their greater speed. For example, camels needed 5–9 days but mules only 4–5 days to carry a cargo between Aleppo and Latakia.[49] Camels were famed for their ability to carry cargoes of 550 pounds (and more) for distances of 24–32 km per day. By contrast, mules and horses could carry 420 pounds while donkeys transported about 170 pounds. Camels were more common in the Arab lands than in Anatolia and still less frequent in Rumelia.[50] In 1812, for example, horses carried most of the goods from Salonica north towards the German lands and some 20,000 animals were used. Great caravan networks extended across the length and breadth of the region. East–west routes included those from Iran to İzmir, across the Syrian desert, Tabriz to Erzurum to Trabzon, and from Baghdad to İstanbul. Other routes passed from Baghdad to Aleppo, or connected the Syrian provinces with the Black Sea or northwest Aegean regions. In 1838, caravans required 25–28 days to travel between Aleppo and Baghdad while, at the other end of the empire, the Salonica–Vienna caravans journeyed 50 days. At about the same time, caravans traversing the Aleppo–İstanbul route needed 40 days.[51] Shorter caravan routes included the 16-day trek between Alexandretta and Diyarbekir, and the 9-day journey between Diyarbekir and Erzurum.

The road system generally remained in poor repair, despite some improvements over time. Roads from the coast to Aleppo in the 1830s were said to be "formed almost by nature." The miserable state of roads in the earlier part of the century was due to the final disappearance of the *timar*-holders who had maintained them. Throughout the nineteenth century, however, the central state paid too little attention and gave too few resources. And so, the roads remained neglected and poor. There were bursts of activity, for example, in the period after the Crimean War and during the Young Turk era, when annual expenditures for roadbuilding quadrupled from their late nineteenth-century levels. But in most areas, few improvements were made.[52] In the Iraqi provinces during the final prewar years, there were no metalled roads outside towns, with the exception of a short portion of the Aleppo caravan route. This metalled portion may account for the apparent reduction in caravan travel time between Aleppo and Baghdad. In the 1830s, the journey required 25–28 days but only 22 days in 1910. In Anatolia, despite the vast growth in traffic on the Tabriz–Trabzon route through the first two-thirds of the century, the road remained in bad condition with few improvements. A wagon road begun in the late 1860s was constructed so poorly that operators preferred the old highway.[53] As trade at Beirut similarly boomed, business also was constrained by the land transport system. A single traveller journeyed two days between Beirut and Damascus while caravans, using a combination of mules in the mountains and camels in the desert, took three to four days. Then, in the early 1860s, a French-financed company constructed 110 km of road, permitting wagon transport and offering 13-hour stagecoach service between the two cities. By 1890, this road, that some historians credit with the rise of Beirut, carried 21,000 tons of goods.[54] But well-maintained roads remained the exception even in the Syrian areas and camel transport continued as the dominant form of moving goods on the highway.

Despite these shortcomings, caravans, highways and trails continued to bear one-half of all goods shipped overland in Anatolia and Syria. In 1904, the entire Ottoman world contained only 24,000 km of roads; three-quarters of these were within the borders of modern Turkey, poor in quality and badly maintained.[55]

Caravans provided most of the overland, non-mechanized links within and between regions. The actual volume of goods handled by caravans, difficult to measure, certainly was very substantial. In the 1830s, the single annual caravan that reportedly traveled from Baghdad to Aleppo counted as many as 5,000 camels, carrying a total of c. 1,250 tons. At that time, the Basra–Aleppo caravan ordinarily had 6,000 camels while the Diyarbekir caravan, that went more frequently, utilized 600 camels.

Caravans bore regional surpluses to domestic and foreign buyers as well as the full range of consumer goods required by sophisticated urban societies and their hinterlands. A Basra–Aleppo caravan in 1752 brought Indian textiles, various perfumes and drugs; pearls, rubies, glass and porcelain. A Mosul caravan of the same date carried Indian and Mosul textiles, "drugs" and gallnuts. In the mid-nineteenth century, by comparison, caravans from Baghdad to Damascus were carrying Iraqi, Persian and Indian goods, ranging from clothing to indigo and hides. In the reverse direction, Damascus sent local textiles, as well as cloth from England and Germany. The Damascus–Baghdad caravan contained 1,000–1,500 camels per year, carrying some 250–350 tons.[56] During the 1860s, the caravans between Tabriz and Trabzon annually transported as much as 12,000 tons, requiring perhaps 48,000 pack animals.[57]

Sometimes, the caravan engaged in one-way traffic, arriving (nearly) empty to haul out the harvest. In the early 1890s, an estimated 4–6,000 camels daily carried wheat from the Hawran fields to the coast. For the service, the caravaneers received, in kind, one-half of the wheat transported.[58] Similarly (see below), thousands of camels carried grain to railroad stations in western and central Anatolia. Concentrating on the grain traffic, the caravan operators probably bore some imported consumer goods on their journeys to the fields.

Overland freight rates long had formed a major part of the selling price of goods, particularly those of high bulk and low value. Except when crops failed, long-range shipment of cheap, bulk foodstuffs was not feasible. With the nineteenth-century technological revolution, animal shipment rendered many Ottoman productions unacceptably expensive. High shipping costs checked the development of Ottoman export agriculture and, more generally, restrained economic growth.

Freight charges varied considerably, depending on the commodity, season, destination, competition, distance and direction. For example, during the 1830s, merchants paid twice as much per unit of weight for goods sent on less competitive routes, such as Latakia–Aleppo, than on the more heavily traveled Alexandretta–Aleppo route. Similarly, in the

1860s, operators packed full cargoes going out of the great industrial center of Aleppo to Diyarbekir, but were more desperate for the return journey and dropped their fares 50 percent. Short hauls usually cost proportionately more than longer journeys. Even though less than half the distance, the per ton kilometer rate of the Aleppo–Alexandretta camel journey in the 1860s was twice that of the Diyarbekir–Mosul trip.[59]

The caravan business fluctuated dramatically, affected by the state of the crops, regional and international business cycles, war, epizootic diseases, and the development of alternative transport modes. Business could expand sharply. In the early nineteenth century, the Damascus–Baghdad route supported perhaps only one and not more than three caravans per year. But in the 1840s there were 12–15 departures in either direction on the route.[60]

Some caravan routes suffered severely as competing forms of transportation emerged or frontiers changed. The Trabzon–Tabriz route had flourished between the 1830s and 1860s, thanks to British merchants' efforts to reduce shipment costs for trade with Iran. At its peak, during the 1850s and 1860s, Trabzon–Tabriz caravans carried 40 percent of the total foreign trade of Iran. By 1900, however, tonnage had fallen by one-third, to less than 10 percent of the expanding Iran trade. On this route, serious competition had developed from two distinctly different sources. First, the opening of the Suez Canal in 1869 diverted goods from the northern Iran–Black Sea route to a Teheran–Basra network. Also, the Russian state embarked on an ambitious road-building program that hurt Ottoman transporters. A Russian route through Georgia first was improved and wagon traffic developed; while the Erzurum route temporarily maintained its traffic volume, the more valuable items passed through the Russian port of Poti. Thanks to further improvements, a network of good quality highways radiated outward from Tiflis by the early 1870s. And then came the Tiflis–Poti–Baku railroad that dropped freight rates by five-sixths. The volume of traffic through Trabzon fell accordingly.[61]

Other caravans encountered the competition of Ottoman railways. Railroad builders not surprisingly found themselves following trails long traced by caravan operators. The three main caravan routes leading northwards from Thrace today are marked by railroad tracks.[62] Similarly, the İzmir–Aydın, Aydın–Kasaba, Anatolian and Adana railroads, among others, all closely followed well-used caravan paths for much of their routes. When, for example, the Anatolian Railway began service to Ankara in 1892 and to Konya in 1895, it threatened the business of caravans traveling between these cities. In response, the operators dropped their fees by more than half and, for a brief period, undercut the rail transport charges by about 10 percent. The railway counter-attacked with discounted lower fares and eventually won most of the carrying trade on routes parallel to the caravans. Thus, railroads damaged or destroyed some caravan routes.

At the same time, the relative thinness of the Ottoman rail system left whole regions to the caravans. Merchants in the southern two-thirds of Konya province, again using the Anatolian Railway example, continued to caravan goods to the Mediterranean. Prevailing transport patterns here were maintained.

When spur lines or good highways to feed the trunk lines were lacking, railroads brought new vitality to the caravan business. Caravan traffic as well as rail freight grew as agricultural production for export soared in many railroad areas. Caravaneers found new work and prosperity transporting goods, particularly grain, short distances from developing agricultural districts to the railhead. After railroads were built in the Aegean region, caravan networks containing some 10,000 camels funnelled merchandise to these two lines.[63] Similarly, four decades later, over a thousand camels at a time waited their turn to be unloaded at the busy Ankara railway station where a

> large number of the camel and cart drivers are also middlemen, and buy wheat and barley from the farmers to sell to the agents at the station, covering the costs of the transport out of the small profits they make.[64]

Hence, the old and new transport systems sometimes meshed in fascinating syntheses that provided new employment and market opportunities for the Ottoman agricultural, mercantile and service sectors.

NOTES

1 Braudel (1966), I, pp. 246–53.
2 See Greenberg (1982); Mitchell (1978), pp. 313–49; Quataert (1977); Issawi (1988), pp. 203–67.
3 Braudel (1966), I, pp. 306–12.
4 Güran (1984–85); Issawi (1980), pp. 25, 152–53; al-Shaafi (1985).
5 See Issawi (1982), e.g. pp. 45–46; al-Shaafi (1985).
6 Batatu (1978), p. 238; Issawi (1982), pp. 45–48; Issawi (1988), e.g. pp. 160–68, 227–29, 249.
7 ZStA, AA 53739, Bl. 79; al-Shaafi (1985), pp. 68–73.
8 Issawi (1982), p.8; Eldem (1970), p. 165; al-Shaafi (1985), p. 62; Issawi (1980), p. 153.

9 Eldem (1970), p. 168; figures for the pre-1879 period are not available. Direct comparisons with other countries could not be made since Eldem's figures are gross and those in Mitchell (1978) net tonnage.

10 Eldem (1970), p. 168; Ochsenwald (1980); al-Shaafi (1985), p. 48; Fawaz (1983), p. 133.

11 GB AS 1964, Trade of Baghdad and Basrah for 1896; A&P 116, 1908, Long-worth, n.d., at Aleppo, for 1907.

12 GB (1920), p. 165. Issawi (1980), p. 170, states that, except for the coasting trade, sailing vessels virtually had disappeared from the port of Izmir by the 1870s.

13 Fawaz (1983), p. 72.

14 Issawi (1977).

15 See Eldem (1970), p. 169 for figures.

16 *BCF* 1883, Salonique, le 25 juillet 1883; GB 4579, AS, Trade for the Consular District of Salonica for 1909.

17 Issawi (1980), pp. 169–70; Fawaz (1983), p. 72.

18 İstanbul Ticaret Bahriye Müdürlüğü (1928), p. 75.

19 Quataert (1983), pp. 95–120.

20 Quataert (1983); GB AS 4797 for 1910 for Salonica.

21 Egypt, nominally in the Ottoman Empire but in reality independent of its control, is remarkable for the early development of railroads. In 1869, it had 1,338 km of track and some 3,000 by 1905. Issawi (1982), p. 54.

22 Mitchell (1978), pp. 581–85, Table F1; Licht (1983), pp. 10, 31.

23 Hecker (1914), p. 778.

24 Quataert (1983), pp. 71–93; Hecker (1914), pp. 790–91, 1085–86; Issawi (1982), p. 55.

25 Cameron (1961).

26 Hecker (1914), pp. 1076–77; Lampe and Jackson (1982), p. 302.

27 Ochsenwald (1980); also Arif (1971).

28 For example, BBA Nafia Nezareti 68–74 Demiryolları ve Limanlar, D 16 1290, 4–22, various dates, 1289/1873.

29 Anatolian Railway Company Reports for 1890 and 1891, see Quataert (1977).

30 Quataert (1983), pp. 74–75; Ochsenwald (1980), pp. 34–40; Hecker (1914), pp. 1582–83.

31 Estimate based on extrapolations from Hejaz Railway personnel data in Ochsenwald (1980), p. 93.

32 Compare stratification in Quataert (1983), pp. 76–80 and Ochsenwald (1980), pp. 93–97.

33 Quataert (1983) and Ochsenwald (1980).

34 Fogel (1964).

35 Quataert (1983), pp. 71–93 and (1977). A note of caution: kilometric guarantee sums paid were artificially low after 1912. Military traffic greatly increased railway company income and generated swollen receipts. GB (1920), p. 59.

36 Eldem (1970), p. 153, cited in Issawi (1980), p. 150; Issawi (1982), p. 56.

37 Hecker (1914), pp. 1553–67; Eldem (1970), p. 163; Pech (1911), p. 77.

38 Kolars and Malin (1970); Hecker (1914), p. 1549; Lewis (1987).

39 Hecker (1914), p. 1550; Ochsenwald (1980), p. 104 and Arif (1971), p. 159.

40 Fawaz (1983), pp. 70–71; Ochsenwald (1980), p. 109.
41 Hecker (1914), p. 1541 and *RCL*, #240, 31 mars 1907, pp. 479–82.
42 Quataert (1977).
43 Cunningham (1983), p. 108.
44 Lewis (1987), e.g. pp. 9, 27.
45 *Ibid.*, p. 8; also see Spooner (1977), p. 245.
46 Bowring (1840), p. 45.
47 Rafeq (1983); Owen (1981), p. 168; Lewis (1987); Issawi (1988), pp. 247–49.
48 Gould (1973); Lewis (1987).
49 Lewis (1987), p. 106; Bowring (1840), p. 45.
50 Quataert (1977); Issawi (1980), p. 177; Issawi (1988), pp. 212–20.
51 Cunningham (1983), p. 105; Bowring (1840), p. 38; Issawi (1988), pp. 247–49.
52 For state construction activities see the accounts in Shaw and Shaw (1977) and Göyünç (1983).
53 Owen (1981), p. 278; Bowring (1840), pp. 38 and 113; Issawi (1966), pp. 181–2; Issawi (1970), p. 21.
54 Fawaz (1983), pp. 67–69; Rafeq (1983).
55 Owen (1981), p. 246; Shaw (1977), p. 227; Issawi (1980), p. 150; Issawi (1988), pp. 231–40.
56 See Sauvaget (1941), pp. 229 n. 853 and p. 259; Rafeq (1983), p. 421; Bowring (1840), pp. 45, 47.
57 My calculations are based on Issawi (1970). Tonnage estimates based on Table, pp. 26–27. If all the animals were camels, which they were not, these traffic volumes would represent 10,000 camel trips in the 1830s and a peak of 48,000 camel trips in the 1860s. Some three trips per year were made: therefore 3,333 camels in the 1830s and 16,000 in the 1860s. Another source quoted in the article, p. 24, states that an estimated 15,000 pack animals made three round trips annually to deliver 8,200 tons of goods.
58 Elefteriades (1944), pp. 132–36.
59 Bowring (1840), p. 63; Issawi (1980), p. 177.
60 Owen (1981), pp. 53–54, refers to two to three operating between Damascus and Baghdad and four departing from Aleppo "for the principal towns of Iraq and Anatolia," while Bowring (1840), pp. 45–47, speaks of an annual caravan. Issawi (1982), p. 53.
61 Issawi (1970), pp. 26–27.
62 Cunningham (1983), p. 24.
63 Kurmuş (1974), p. 80.
64 Quoted in Quataert (1981), p. 77.

32

⌢

COMMERCE

International commerce has been the most widely discussed topic in Ottoman social and economic history while trade within the empire as well as Ottoman commerce with Egypt, Iran and India have been neglected nearly totally. The reasons for this distribution of emphasis are several. European merchants and diplomats wrote extensively on the flow of goods between the West and the Ottoman economy, reports that are well organized and readily available in the archives of the European states. Many have been published *in extenso* and are in wide circulation.[1] Moreover, since scholars of European origin have dominated historical writing until recently, these records have been used more often than the less-accessible sources in the Ottoman, Arabic, Armenian or Greek languages. This emphasis, in addition, also reflects a Eurocentric perspective that focuses on westernizers and the westernizing aspects of the economy. Also, international commerce grew extraordinarily; a longstanding consensus therefore has prevailed among Western scholars as well as their westernized Turkish and Arab colleagues about its singular importance in the Ottoman economy. This agreement, however, is collapsing and scholars now explore a variety of other topics, sometimes from purely internal Ottoman perspectives. Since international trade is relatively well documented in the secondary literature, it will be treated here only in a summary fashion.[2] To the extent possible and in the hopes of stimulating research on the subject, emphasis will be placed on trade within the empire. Even so, because the literature on international exchanges is so vast and that concerning domestic commerce so sparse, the bulk of this chapter remains weighted in favor of the foreign trade.

COMMERCIAL DUTIES AND OTTOMAN TARIFF POLICIES

Duties rose very sharply, five times and more above previous levels, during the first quarter of the century. Until the end of the eighteenth century the state had levied 3 percent duties on both imports and exports but raised them as the currency depreciated in value.[3] Other restrictive practices increased and the state created a number of prohibitions and monopolies, especially regarding exports. These policies clashed with European efforts to remove all remaining restraints on foreign commerce. The opening of the Black Sea, begun with the Treaty of Küçük Kaynarca in 1774, continued with the 1829 Treaty of Adrianople. Britain most of all needed the Ottoman economy for raw material imports and export markets for its vastly expanding industries, a need made critical because protectionism among its European customers was mounting at the time. Hence the famed Anglo-Turkish Convention of 1838. As seen above, the Convention did not radically depart from existing state policies but followed the path set by the government's destruction of the Janissary corps, the defender of guild monopolies and privileges. The 1838 Convention and the Imperial Rescript of the following year continued this new initiative towards economic liberalism and signalled the government's formal commitment to end industrial, commercial and agricultural monopolies.

The 1826 Auspicious Event, as the abolition of the Janissary corps officially was known, the Convention of 1838 and the *Hatt-ı Şerif* of 1839 all were hallmarks of further Ottoman integration into the world market, a reversal of previous decades of trade restriction and monopoly. These events did not mark a new direction in actual Ottoman commerce or economic development but rather affirmed and perhaps accelerated ongoing established trends. The Convention, for example, did not create a new pattern of British–Ottoman trade. Ottomans already were buying mainly finished (and colonial) goods and selling chiefly raw materials. In the last decades *before* the Convention, the remaining exports of manufactures, notably red yarn, fell precipitously. Commerce between the two states already was increasing dramatically: British exports to the empire had doubled in value during the late 1820s and doubled again before 1837.[4] The 1838 Convention, as well as the later agreements modeled on it, allowed foreign merchants to trade anywhere, subject only to the applicable import/export or interior duties. The *Hatt-ı Şerif* of the next year flatly prohibited monopolies.

Thus the monopolies officially vanished, in many cases within two decades of their imposition, while other, older, commercial restrictions disappeared as well. For example, the privileged access of Ankara mohair yarn and cloth makers to the raw mohair of their region had been eroded well before these two enactments. In the 1820s, nomadic tribes around Ankara routinely were making cash sales of mohair to European merchants at Aleppo, although Ottoman regulations stated it must be sold to the guild at Ankara. In the late eighteenth century, foreign merchants regularly were buying mohair as they and the officials at Ankara and in the export center of İzmir ignored the proviso that the Ankara artisans' needs be met first. Immediately after issuing the Gülhane decree, the state, in almost embarrassing haste, legally ratified current practices and informed Ankara manufacturers that their monopoly was null and void. İstanbul did not refer to the 1838 Convention, an international agreement, but rather to the "Blessed Tanzimat," a government decree issued to regulate the behavior of its subjects.[5]

The rapid implementation of the 1838 Convention usually is attributed to the attentiveness of European consuls and pressure from the Powers. But this view confuses cause and effect. The emergence of free trade already was well underway; it was not created but rather acknowledged by the Convention and the Rescript. Further, such a position does not credit the actions of officials in the İstanbul government, who sought free trade as in the best interests of the economy and treasury.[6] Duties now were fixed at 3 percent on imports and transit goods, 2 percent in lieu of other internal duties paid by importers, and 12 percent on exports. With the 1838 accord, the Ottoman trade regime became "one of the most liberal in the world."[7]

But ongoing monetary instability, treasury shortfalls and complaints from suffering manufacturers prompted immediate second thoughts on free trade and initiated efforts to change the rates. Unsuccessful attempts to gain the agreement of the Great Powers in the 1840s–50s gave way to some victories in the early 1860s. Accords in 1861–62 raised import levies from 3 to 8 percent, a move not merely to increase state income but to stimulate Ottoman manufacturing (see Ch. 34). The development of Ottoman protectionist policies dating from the 1860s is one of the earliest cracks in British global hegemony. In 1907, the Great Powers finally granted permission, stipulating that revenues from the 3 percent increase pay for reforms in Macedonia and that the Public Debt Administration regulate its collection. Again, in 1914, the import duty rose to 15 percent, too late, as it turned out, to help the treasury and still too little to afford meaningful protection for Ottoman manufacturers.

The 1861–62 conventions that raised import duties also sought to enhance the marketability of Ottoman produce by lowering the export tax from 12 to 1 percent by 1869. Such measures aided international trade. But the presence of internal duties until very late in the period (among a host of other factors) undermined the growth of domestic commerce. Most internal duties on overland commerce were abolished only in 1874. The İstanbul Chamber of Commerce finally succeeded, by 1894, in removing internal duties on the sea transport of most important cereals, belatedly eliminating a powerful deterrent to the intra-empire grain trade.[8] Other seaborne goods shipped within the empire, however, paid 8 percent duty until a reduction to 4 percent in 1889 and 2 percent in 1900. This duty did not disappear totally until 1909.

Customs duties were an important source of state income. In 1877, for example, they formed approximately 15 percent and, in 1911, some 16 percent of total Ottoman revenues.[9] There is an ongoing scholarly debate regarding the primary intent of the tariff policies. Was it to raise revenues or was it a development tool to stimulate exports and, after 1861–62, protect local manufacturers? Although most scholars have stressed revenue-earning as the motive, recent work challenging that view seems persuasive. If the government only sought to enhance tax revenues, why did it reduce export duties from 12 to 1 percent? Did it really expect to stimulate exports more than twelve-fold? Ottoman customs policies were not merely a response to foreign pressure, but also were an effort to stimulate the economy by enhancing exports and protecting local manufacturers.[10] The ranks of Ottoman officialdom may well have been divided, some seeing customs duties primarily as revenue sources, others considering them as instruments of economic growth. Perhaps most saw tariffs as an economic tool, but retained the duties despite their convictions because of fiscal insolvency.

TRENDS IN INTERNATIONAL TRADE

International trade probably formed a proportionately larger share of total Ottoman trade – that consisted of intra- and inter-regional and foreign commerce – in 1914 than it had in c.1800. Western and Central Europe loomed ever-larger in Ottoman international commerce over the course of the century, both in absolute volume of trade and in relative importance. Until c. 1820, trade within the empire and with Russia certainly was more important than that with Western and Central Europe. By the century's end, Britain, France, Germany, Austria and Italy accounted for over three-quarters of total Ottoman international commerce and for the bulk of aggregate increase in foreign trade that had occurred. But, despite the impressive changes, domestic commerce continued to overshadow foreign trade. In 1914, the flow of goods within and between regions of the empire still accounted for the vast bulk of all commodities exchanged (see below, domestic trade).

Between 1780 and 1830, a period of recovery and then growth, Ottoman–European trade increased at an annual rate below 1.5 percent. The growth rate likely was higher by about 1820, but it took a long time to recoup the war-induced losses of 1790–1815. Nor were the following years particularly peaceful: the wars of the French Revolution and Napoleon's invasion of Egypt were succeeded by the Russo-Turkish War of 1827–28, the Greek War of Independence and Mehmed Ali's invasions of Syria and Anatolia. The Arab provinces were more vulnerable to the disruption of sea traffic and an earlier thriving trade with Europe ceased.[11] On the other hand, the presence of Bonaparte's armies and their enemies in Egypt and Syria surely promoted strong grain and livestock sales. More generally, mobilization of vast armies in Napoleonic Europe stimulated substantial Western demand for foodstuffs from the nearby Middle East, especially the Balkan provinces and, secondarily, western Anatolia. In addition, long-distance caravans carried some goods from the Arab provinces to İzmir for water shipment to Europe.[12] During these first decades of the century, foreign trade of the Rumelian and Anatolian provinces was larger and grew faster than in the Arab lands, reversing the pattern of the eighteenth century. Despite the changes, Ottoman trade in 1840 (when exports formed approximately 4 percent of estimated gross national product) may not have surpassed the levels of 1800 (Table IV:11).[13]

After this period of recovery, foreign trade grew very rapidly between the early 1840s and 1870s. Imports and exports each annually increased at compound growth rates of c. 5.5 percent, nearly doubling in each successive decade. Despite the loss of the Rumanian Principalities, Ottoman trade with Western Europe doubled between the early 1850s and 1870s, thanks to the vast expansion of European industrial output, the food needs of its work force, and the requirements of the Crimean and American civil wars. During this trade boom, Ottoman foreign trade and export growth rates exceeded those of global trade. Soaring output,

Table IV:11. Ottoman foreign trade, 1830–1913 (annual average, in millions of current pounds sterling).

Period	f.o.b. exports	c.i.f. imports
1830s	4.2	5.1
1840s	6.0	6.9
1850s	9.8	12.3
1860s	15.4	18.3
1870s	18.6	20.8
1880s	15.5	16.0
1890s	17.7	18.6
1900s	23.0	26.0
1910–13	27.3	38.6

Source: Pamuk (1987), p. 149.

acceleration of the work pace and technological advances meant that prices for European industrial goods fell faster than those of primary commodities. During the mid-1870s, exports were about 6 to 8 percent of estimated Ottoman GNP, about double the proportions of the 1840s, and not more than 15 percent of total Ottoman agricultural production.[14]

Stagnation followed boom in the 1870s as fiscal crisis and government bankruptcy joined famine and the Russo-Turkish War to slow the growth of international trade. The relative stagnation of the 1873–96 price depression, for its part, reduced European industrial production and Western demand for foodstuffs and raw materials. Foreign trade continued to mount, but at rates below those of the preceding half century. Between the late 1870s and 1890s, imports and exports each increased at compound annual rates of c. 2.6 percent, half the pace of the three preceding decades (but twice that of the 1780–1830 era).

After the international depression ended, Ottoman prices resumed their upward climb and the terms of trade again turned favorable for primary commodity producers. The rates of relative increase during the period 1896–1914 were below those of the 1840–73 boom, but expanded from a much larger base. At locations as diverse as Salonica and Jaffa, imports leap-frogged over exports. Within a decade Ottoman exports grew by 3.4 percent as imports rose by 4.8 percent (compound annual rates). Subsequently, despite the huge territorial losses suffered in the Balkan Wars, exports in 1913 equaled and imports exceeded, by 25 percent, the levels of 1907. Foreign loans, made possible by the state's agreement to restructure its international debts and allow formation of the Public Debt Administration, financed the trade deficits.

In 1914, perhaps one-quarter of total agricultural production was exported; exports altogether formed nearly 14 percent of the gross national product and the "ratio of imports to GNP was around 18 per cent."[15] These figures are revealing. They demonstrate that, despite the relatively substantial increases of the nineteenth century, foreign trade remained a minor factor in Ottoman economic life.

Between 1840 and 1914, the value (in constant terms) of Ottoman exports increased nine times and imports ten times. Thus, per capita export increases were slightly below the global average. After steadily increasing in importance until the 1870s, the Ottoman Empire's relative international position as an exporter slipped. Overall, in terms of involvement in the international market economy, the Ottoman Empire ranked above Asia and Africa but below Latin America.[16]

TERMS OF TRADE

The terms of trade fluctuated sharply over time but generally moved against the Ottomans and in favor of the industrial nations as the latter retained most of the results of their productivity increases "in the form of higher wages and higher rates of profits."[17] Between c.1820 and the mid-1850s, Ottoman terms of trade improved, mainly because of rapid declines in the price of imported cotton manufactures. During the subsequent boom, Ottoman terms of trade fell perhaps 10 percent although they did rise during the Crimean War. They then deteriorated steadily during the Great Depression of 1873–96: the price of manufactures fell 35 percent but those of Ottoman primary goods fell 48 percent. And finally, the Ottomans benefited from the post-1896 rise in commodity prices and their terms of trade improved by 14 percent. Thus, fluctuations in the terms of trade (and in export levels) reveal periods of expansion and depression closely tied to changes in the world market.[18]

REGIONAL DISTRIBUTION OF INTERNATIONAL TRADE

Until c. 1850, the European provinces ranked first in international commerce, followed by Anatolia and the Arab provinces. The Anatolian region then moved to the first rank, probably after the Crimean War and final loss of the Rumanian Principalities, and experienced its greatest growth in international trade before 1870. At the mid-century point, three-quarters of all British exports to the Middle East (including Egypt) flowed through west Anatolian entrepôts. Exports from the four major ports of Anatolia– İzmir, Trabzon, Samsun and Mersin– rose 3.5 times between the early 1840s and the mid-1870s, while imports increased

Table IV:12. Relative importance of Ottoman ports, 1907 (% of total trade)

İstanbul	33	Alexandretta	5
İzmir	17	Edirne	4
Beirut	11	(via Dedeağaç)	
Salonica	11	Yanina	2
Trabzon	7	(Preveza)	
Baghdad	6	Hicazi	1
		Yemeni	1

Source: Derived from data in Turkey (1327a/1909), pp. 160–61; this source, however, excludes important commercial centers such as Samsun.

c. 4.3 times. Imports actually decreased until 1900 as exports rose very slightly; then they respectively rose 80 and 30 percent. In absolute terms, the value of the Anatolian trade c. 1914 was half again as great as the combined commerce of the Syrian and Iraqi regions.

The Arab port cities increased dramatically in importance late in the period. (This trend and other data suggest strong economic growth in the Arab provinces towards the end of the century.) Iraqi seaborne trade, in current values, doubled between the 1840s and 1860s, quadrupled again by 1900 and more than tripled in the subsequent decade. Overall, this trade increased 37 times in 75 years. Syrian commerce increased some twenty-fold overall but only very slightly after 1900. The seven principal ports of Syria/Palestine handled commerce whose worth rose 68 percent between the 1880s and 1913. The tonnage of Beirut, for example, more than doubled between 1895 and 1913. By the latter date, the value of Syrian trade exceeded that of the Iraqi provinces by 150 percent.

In the European provinces, exports from the Principalities tripled between 1818 and the Crimean War. After the Rumanian Principalities had gained *de facto* independence, their exports rose more than fourfold in the period until 1900 while imports increased more than ten times. Enjoying a positive balance of trade during the Ottoman era, imports of the Principalities surpassed exports during the late 1870s. In independent Serbia, exports tripled by the late 1840s and nearly tripled again in the subsequent three decades; imports rose similarly but remained below the value of exports through the 1870s.[19] Bulgaria, recently *de facto* independent, doubled its export trade between 1880 and 1900, as did post-Ottoman Rumania and Serbia.

By 1912, Salonica was the sole remaining important Ottoman commercial center in Europe (excluding, of course, İstanbul). Until 1878, both its imports and exports grew. Thereafter, in the period following Bulgarian independence, the value of Salonica exports actually declined somewhat. Imports, by contrast, doubled by 1900 and then rose another 50 percent by 1912. In the period as a whole, Salonica exports rose tenfold while its imports increased some 36 times. The economic loss represented by the loss of such regions was enormous. In 1912, the trade of Salonica alone approximated the total commerce of Samsun, Adana and Trabzon and was slightly more than one-half the trade of all Syrian ports[20] (Table IV:12). (Again, İstanbul is excluded from the commercial total of the European provinces.)

PROFILE OF INTERNATIONAL TRADE

Textiles, particularly cotton, led import growth until c. 1870 and remained important thereafter. During the early 1830s, cotton cloth formed two-thirds of all British exports to the Ottoman Empire while, in 1900, textile manufactures still accounted for a full 50 percent of imports into İzmir. After 1870, however, the relative share of foodstuff imports generally increased. But in some locations, such as Jaffa, the relative share of coffee, tea and sugar imports stayed the same.[21] By the end of the period, wheat, flour, rice, sugar, coffee and tea formed about one-third of all Ottoman imports. In exports, agricultural products usually were more than 90 percent of the total. A single commodity formed the bulk of exports from a few areas: for example, animal products in Serbia, cereals at Mersin and in the Iraqi seaborne trade, and silk from Lebanon. But, reflecting patterns in Ottoman agriculture (see below), no single item dominated Ottoman exports. Typically, the top eight-ranking items did not exceed 60 percent of the total. The export mix shifted over time, depending on international demand, and usually included important quantities of raisins, opium, cereals, hides, wool, cotton, tobacco, figs, and raw silk. Besides raw silk, carpets were the only manufactured products of any significance, and their export mounted quickly after 1860 (Table IV:13).

Until the revolution of 1789, France easily had dominated Ottoman foreign trade, holding as much as 60 percent of the total. French trade then nearly disappeared during the subsequent wars. As normal political and economic relations resumed, French merchants discovered that their longstanding superiority had given way to British domination. Britain thereafter retained first rank; it consistently was the largest single supplier of Ottoman imports and, in the early 1880s, provided a record 45 percent of the total. Although its relative share then slipped badly, Britain in

Table IV:13. Composition of Ottoman trade, 1897 (in millions of piasters)

Leading exports		Leading imports	
Grapes	177	Sugar	158
Silk	136	Coarse cloth	139
Figs	68	Cotton yarn	118
"Rifles"	65	Coffee	103
Olive oil	63	Rice	79
Opium	62	Flour	79
Nuts	58	Calico	70
Cotton	48	Petticoats	64
Barley	48	Wheat	62
Wool	47	Gauze	56
Sheepskin	35	Cashmere cloth	42
Sesame	32	Muslin	40
Tobacco	24	Linen	35
Dates	19	Felt	32
Wheat	15		

Source: Ottoman sources as quoted in Shaw and Shaw (1977), pp. 237–38.

1910–11 still shipped 24 percent of Ottoman imports, twice the share of its nearest rival. The Ottomans then ranked as Britain's third best customer for both cotton yarn and cotton piece-goods.[22] France, from the 1830s, usually provided about 10 percent of Ottoman imports but was more important as a buyer of Ottoman goods. During the early 1860s, for example, France received 30 percent of all Ottoman exports. In common with Britain, France also declined in relative importance after the 1880s, accounting for 8 percent of Ottoman imports and 24 percent of exports in c. 1914. Austria consumed 30 percent of the exports and shipped 17 percent of the imports during the 1830s. It declined in both categories after the mid-1850s and then recovered somewhat after 1900. In c. 1914, Austria furnished 24 percent of Ottoman imports and purchased 8 percent of all exports. German-supplied imports tripled between the 1830s and 1870s, reaching 14 percent of the total; they fell for a decade, and rose back to 14 percent in 1909–11. From less than 2 percent between the 1840s and the 1880s, the German export share increased to 7 percent in 1900 and 11 percent in 1909–11.

At the end of the period, Britain, France, Germany and Austria shipped three-quarters of all imports and consumed 60–70 percent of Ottoman exports. Other important trade partners included the United States, Russia and Bulgaria. Of the lost Balkan provinces, Bulgaria, Serbia and Greece retained measurable trade relations with the Ottoman economy. Bulgaria forwarded a steadily declining share of its exports, down to 16 percent by 1910. During the second half of the century, both Serbia and Greece sent stable proportions of their total exports, about 8 percent each.[23]

DOMESTIC TRADE

It is certain that the quantity and value of domestic trade surpassed that of international Ottoman commerce throughout the period 1800–1914. While the assertion is correct, proving it is an altogether different matter. Quantitatively establishing the changing levels of domestic Ottoman trade has been and will remain impossible. But we can apprehend its general significance. For example, international exports formed only 25 percent (maximum) of gross Ottoman agricultural production. Thus, 75 percent of all crops grown remained within the empire. These either were consumed on the spot, sold and consumed locally, or shipped to Ottoman buyers outside of the region. Ottoman urban dwellers, forming 20 percent of the population, were an important component of this domestic market. But so were other cultivators who, for various reasons, did not grow their own subsistence requirements. For example, as cultivators increased cotton and tobacco production at different periods (see below), their demand for foodstuffs grown by others also rose.

Statistics are scarce, particularly for goods that were produced, sold and consumed within a particular area. Literally millions of Ottoman cultivators and artisans either produced for their own subsistence needs or made a living growing or manufacturing goods for sale in the immediate vicinity. This trade perhaps exceeded the combined quantity and value of all commerce between Ottoman regions plus Ottoman international trade as well. And yet it is nearly invisible. Here, two examples suggest the importance of the trade in locally produced goods within a region. In a 1911 case of agricultural commodities, we find the increasing local population now consumed virtually the entire grain production of Aleppo province, that had expanded significantly. Where locally manufactured goods are concerned, there are good data from Diyarbekir province, an important industrial center. Detailed data from several districts of the province in 1903 offer statistics on local manufactures and their sale within the region. Consumers in Ergani district, for example, bought 100 percent of all the locally manufactured white cloth (*bez*), morocco leather, colored leather, sole leather and agricultural implements, as well as locally raised cocoons. Similarly, Mardin district consumers used 100 percent of its production of cocoons, handkerchiefs and caps; they also used one-half of the gauze (*gazliye*) and the wool cloth produced, 75 percent of both the red and the white cloth (*bez*) and three-quarters of all the shoes manufactured. The district of Diyarbekir was a major center of industrial production for export to other provinces. But even so, local buyers consumed important quantities of its manufactured goods. For example, one-third of the striped cloth (*manusa*), half the printed cloth (*basma*), 80 percent of the iron wares, more than two-thirds of the shoes and stockings, and all of the sole leather and agricultural implements produced in the district remained there.[24]

These data regarding intra-regional trade clearly demonstrate its importance but they are extremely scarce. In their absence, the following section stresses trade between various regions of the empire, commercial activities more frequently encountered in the historical record. Here, we propose a definition of inter-regional trade that is different from its more general meaning of goods, whether of domestic *or* foreign provenance, shipped from point to point within an economy. Instead, the focus is on goods that actually were manufactured, grown or raised inside the imperial borders and then transported and sold in another area of the empire.

Most of the available quantitative materials relating to such trade between regions are not very useful. Caravan transport statistics could be helpful but these are rarely available; and, they infrequently differentiate between goods of foreign and local origin. For another example, consider the data gathered by Ottoman customs officials as they itemized import, export and transit taxes. These official statistics show that, in the 1880s, the reported value of inter-regional trade equaled about one-quarter that of goods directly imported from abroad. But, by this date, many kinds of goods transported within the empire no longer paid duty; therefore they are not recorded in the statistics just reported. Also these figures include not only domestically made goods but also those of foreign origins shipped within the empire. And so the proportions derived from these data have little real significance.[25] Foreign consuls' reports occasionally specified the shipment or receipt of goods from another part of "Turkey," but they included foreign products imported at one point and re-shipped to another Ottoman area.[26] The limited usefulness of customs data, whether reported by Ottoman officials or foreign consuls, is reduced further since we know little about the changing efficiency of assessment and collection. Thus, only the crudest approximations of the importance of inter-regional trade can be offered at this time.

The data do indicate that the flow of Ottoman goods within the empire was important and must be better appreciated if we are to understand

Table IV:14. Goods of unspecified origin (foreign and domestic)
transported between Ottoman regions, 1883–1901 (% of total
value shipped)

Place	Date	To other Ottoman areas	From other Ottoman areas
Samsun	1883	24	13
Samsun	1901	48	37
Mersin	1898	52	20
Ankara province	1897		38
İzmir	1885	1	13

Source: GB A&P.

the workings of the Ottoman economy. In 1862, for example, the value
of Ottoman goods imported into the province of Damascus was five
times greater than the value of the merchandise it received from abroad
(16.2 versus 3.0 million francs).[27] Railroads, for their part, were not
merely the quintessential instruments of European economic penetration.
They also facilitated trade within the empire. Their freight data measure
imports and exports and also inter-regional commerce. Construction of
the Anatolian Railway stimulated a boom in grain exports; the new railway also altered the provisioning patterns of the capital and provided
İstanbul inhabitants with up to two-thirds of their total grain needs. This
domestic market in İstanbul consumed 25 percent of all grains that the
railroad transported while the Ottoman military consumed an additional
10 percent of all rail-shipped grains. Thus, over one-third of all the cereals
transported on the Anatolian Railway remained within the empire. (But
it also is true that, with the exception of the grain sent to İstanbul, hardly
any goods went from one station to another on the Anatolian line.)[28] The
Damascus–Muzayrib Railway, for its part, had been expected to export
the wheat of the Hawran district. Instead, much of it filled domestic
needs. In one sample year, residents of Damascus, Beirut and the Lebanese silk-raising districts consumed 58 percent of all the rail-shipped
Hawran wheat.[29]

The following tables show the inter-regional trade of several randomly
selected areas. Table IV:14 includes shipments of both foreign and Ottoman-produced goods between various Ottoman regions. Sometimes,
one-half and more of the goods sent remained within the empire. In other
areas, intra-Ottoman traffic averaged about one-quarter of all goods sent
or received. It is not surprising to see that İzmir, a city that literally came
to life because of international trade, scarcely was involved in inter-
regional commerce.

Table IV:15. Locally produced goods shipped (in thousand pounds sterling)

Place	Date	Abroad	To other Ottoman areas
Ankara[a]	1883	325	172
	1887	62	318
Diyarbekir[a]	1890	60	125
	1894	65	94
Harput[a]	1887	61	130
	1891	36	86
Harput province[a]	1906	100	50
Mosul city[b]	1884	206	398
	1896	219	888
	1897	203	583
	1909	363	356

Sources: [a] GB A&P; [b] Shields (1986).

Table IV:15 offers more satisfactory statistics. These report the value of only Ottoman-grown or Ottoman-manufactured goods that were shipped from one to another area within the empire. In some cases, the value of a district's inter-regional trade in goods of Ottoman origins vastly exceeded the value of its exports to foreign countries. At Mosul, in some years, the ratios were nearly three and four to one. During a typical year in the 1890s, Diyarbekir, Harput and Mosul together inter-regionally sent goods worth more than one million pounds sterling. Clearly, the value of aggregate Ottoman inter-regional trade is far above this figure, given the dozens of Ottoman centers that have gone unreported. (Total Ottoman exports abroad during the 1890s averaged 18 million pounds sterling.)

These data are from interior regions and suggest that inter-regional traffic in Ottoman-produced goods remained important in certain areas until the end of the period. The absence of such data from port cities, moreover, does not necessarily indicate that goods of local origin were not being shipped. It simply indicates that the data are not available presently. The above examples do stress the need to reconsider (and research) the problems posed by inter-regional commerce in locally made goods.

THE OTTOMAN MERCHANT COMMUNITY

At the end of the eighteenth century, Muslim merchants still dominated Ottoman trade in many areas. They seem to have been very strong in the Syrian provinces, less so in Anatolia and least of all in İstanbul. This pattern reflects the influence of European diplomats. The greater their presence, the better the protection that they and Western merchants could give to their non-Muslim Ottoman commercial protégés. Most local and inter-regional trade had remained in Muslim hands, as did the Eastern trade with Iran and India. But the secular trends of nineteenth-century commerce – the geometrically increasing trade with Europe and the relative decline of the Eastern trade – favored a transformation in the make-up of the Ottoman merchant community dealing with foreign commerce. A profound change resulted from struggles between Ottoman and foreign merchants and between Muslim and non-Muslim Ottoman traders for control of the international trade. But the change seems much less marked in the intra- and inter-regional merchant community.

The late eighteenth century and first decades of the nineteenth century were particularly important for the formation and growth of the Otto-man merchant community dealing in international trade. Non-Muslim merchants long had been acquiring foreign protection in the form of a certificate (*berat*) that endowed the tax benefits and privileges of a Euro-pean merchant.[30] As trade with Europe mounted in the late eighteenth century, the number of certificates granted to persons purportedly ser-ving as interpreters for the foreign legations increased dramatically. In 1793, over 1,500 non-Muslims in the city of Aleppo alone held these certificates and investigations showed that only six actually were inter-preters.[31] A stunning indication of the commercial profitability of holding certificates is the example of Russia that, by 1808, had enrolled 120,000 Greeks as protected persons.

During this crucial juncture, as international trade and its merchant community were being reshaped, the Ottoman state sought to stamp its own impress on the identity of the merchant group. Sultan Selim III feared the threat that an indigenous merchant class under foreign protec-tion posed to the Ottoman economy and state. And so, he sought to eliminate that class of merchant. In its stead, he created a new category of Ottoman merchants, the so-called "European merchant," licensed to engage in foreign commerce. These were non-Muslim Ottomans who paid a fee to the state and obtained essentially the same rights and privil-eges as foreign merchants or their Ottoman protégés. To further promote a takeover of international trade by Ottoman subjects, the sultan sought to provide his newly privileged traders with foreign bases of operation. Thus he established a number of consulates in Europe.

Not surprisingly, the already few Muslim merchants engaged in trade with the West complained of unfair competition at the hands of foreign and now this new group of non-Muslim traders. And so, Mahmud II created the "merchants of benefaction" (*Hayriye tüccarı*) category of traders. These merchants paid a license fee to obtain the privileges of the newly emergent "European merchants." Muslim merchants clearly understood the potential benefits. Soon after implementation of the system, they persuaded the government to substantially raise the number of such merchants allowed to operate in İstanbul and other cities. Despite this measure, however, they failed to compete either with the foreign traders or the non-Muslim "European merchants" and did not play a decisive subsequent role in commerce with the West.[32]

The struggle between Ottoman non-Muslim and Western merchants began in earnest when the Napoleonic wars ended. As is well known, foreigners, benefiting from their capitulatory privileges, had relied on non-Muslim intermediaries who spoke the languages of the area and knew the culture and the officials regulating the international trade. Towards the end of the eighteenth century, foreign merchants apparently controlled most of this international commerce.[33] But, during the early nineteenth century, in almost every area of the empire, they were pushed out by their erstwhile protégés. Within several decades, non-Muslims successfully seized the burgeoning European trade from the foreign merchants who had been its original beneficiaries and orchestrators. In c. 1815, 412 Ottoman merchants were registered in the major cities; twenty years later, their number had jumped to over 1,300.[34] By the late 1840s, the nineteen leading commercial cities in the empire contained only 80 British and 70 French merchant houses. For example, five British merchant firms remained in Damascus and four in Aleppo; by contrast, 110 Aleppine Muslim and non-Muslim trading establishments were doing business. In 1871, five British merchant houses remained in Beirut and none at all in Damascus or Aleppo. Ottoman Syrians settled in London and Manchester beginning in the 1870s and soon operated their own trading networks (Armenians had established bases in Europe much earlier, in the seventeenth century). In Iraq during the 1860s, local Arabs owned nine of the ten houses dealing in wool. Unusually, Jews dominated most commercial transactions in the Iraqi provinces and played an important role at Salonica as well. In sum, Ottoman non-Muslim merchants replaced the foreigners in almost all locations.[35] In 1911, only 3 percent of the 1,000 registered merchants in İstanbul possessed names that readily are identifiable as French, German or British. Yet, at this time, Britain, France, Germany and Austria accounted for at least one-half of the Ottoman international trade. Similarly, only one foreigner was among the 24 founding members of the İstanbul Chamber of Commerce in 1885.[36]

The position of foreign merchants, however, revived late in the period, at least in western Anatolia. After 1870, the general expansion of foreign capital, including the rail networks and the activities of the Public Debt Administration, served to undermine the position of local merchants. Various new banks, including the state-funded Agricultural Bank, began to offer loans and eroded their credit monopoly.[37]

Non-Muslims dominated the international trade in most Ottoman port cities, where conditions optimally favored them. Beirut, for example, owed its existence to foreign trade and, indeed, non-Muslims dominated its commercial affairs. But we also find that both Muslim and non-Muslim merchants in Beirut prospered.

> The most spectacular successes were Christians because their European ties made the transition easier for them but some of the old, established Muslim merchants were almost as successful . . . [38]

Similarly, Ottoman Christians, mainly Greeks and Armenians, easily were the majority of officially registered merchants at İstanbul in 1911. Readily identifiable Muslim names belonged to only 10 percent of the total. Two-thirds of the largest textile importers then active in İstanbul were Armenians and only one-seventh were Turkish.[39]

The continuing significance of Muslim merchants, however, has been under-estimated. In some major commercial centers, Muslims remained important throughout the century. They frequently dominated the trade between port cities and their hinterlands (at least in areas where Muslims were a majority of the population) and between urban centers of the interior. This important role has been overlooked. At Damascus in 1840, for example, Muslims formed the most important single group of merchants while, at Aleppo, Muslim mercantile firms outnumbered those of Christians and Jews by a margin of almost two to one (70 vs. 40). Muslim merchants retained considerable importance in both cities for at least another century, until after the Second World War probably, and played the leading commercial role. Returning to the example of Beiruti merchants, Muslims traded with Damascus, Baghdad and other inland centers while, by and large, the Christians dealt in exports.[40]

This division between Ottoman Christian/Jewish merchants in the port cities and Muslim traders in the interior also prevailed in Anatolia. The 1908–9 boycott of Austro-Hungarian goods was most successful in the Anatolian interior because Muslims dominated the trade there.[41] In the coastal ports, by contrast, boycott supporters had more difficulty; participation in boycott activities posed serious financial risks for the dominant Ottoman Christian merchant group.[42] The importance of Muslim merchants subsequently increased in many parts of Anatolia, at the expense of Ottoman Greeks, thanks to boycotts against goods of the Greek state. Also, the "national economy" policies after 1908 promoted the growth of a Muslim merchant group. Overall, Muslim merchants continued to play a more important role in Syria and Lebanon than in the Iraqi or Anatolian provinces.

Commercial rivalry among Christian, Jewish and Muslim merchants probably played some role in the rising domestic violence of the post-1850 period. The efforts of Muslim merchants to protect their inland trade from an Ottoman Christian takeover may help explain the 1850 attacks against Christians in Aleppo and the 1860 Damascus massacres as well. Before the massacres, some thirty Armenian merchant families worked in Damascus but in 1900 only five remained and none were involved in trade. Similarly, the number of Jewish merchants in Aleppo reportedly declined in the later nineteenth century.[43] The impact of the 1890s Armenian massacres on the Armenian and Muslim merchant communities of İstanbul is not clear at this time.

NOTES

1 See the printed consular reports cited in the bibliography, p. 935.
2 For additional information, readers are directed to the works of Issawi (1966, 1980 and 1988), Owen (1981) and Pamuk (1987). My debt to these studies is heavy and will be obvious to the reader. Trade with India, Iran and Egypt are major topics awaiting independent research.
3 This depreciation made Ottoman goods cheaper and thus more exportable; Frangakis (1986).
4 Urquhart (1833).
5 For example, BBA Cev İkt 52, 6 XI 1241/July 1826 and Cev İkt 694, 6 XI 1244/June 1829.
6 Sayar (1986).
7 Issawi (1980), p. 76.
8 Quataert (1973).
9 Shaw (1975), pp. 451–52.
10 Issawi generally holds for the revenue view; the latter view recently has been put forward by Bağış (1983). Also see Sayar (1986).
11 Tabak (1988).
12 Schatkowski-Schilcher (1985), p. 39; Tabak (1988).
13 Pamuk (1987), p. 26.
14 *Ibid.*

15 *Ibid.*, pp. 17, 26.
16 *Ibid.*, Ch. 2.
17 *Ibid.*, p. 48.
18 *Ibid.*, pp. 49–52 is discussing the period 1840–1913. Issawi (1980), pp. 277–78 uses 1800–1914 as his period of analysis and concludes that the terms of trade moved in favor of the Ottomans. Also see Quataert (1973); Issawi (1988), pp. 147–51.
19 Lampe and Jackson (1982), pp. 103, 122.
20 Fawaz (1983), p. 133.
21 Gilbar (1986), pp. 188–210.
22 GB A&P, for example, AS 2950, Constantinople for 1902.
23 Lampe and Jackson (1982).
24 Diyarbekir VS, 1321/1903, pp. 194–96, 204, 212.
25 Turkey (1327a/1909).
26 *Ibid.*
27 Quataert (1977).
28 Elefteriades (1944), pp. 132–36.
29 Tabak (1988).
30 Sources important for the merchant section include the following. Sousa (1933); Issawi (1981); Bağış, (1983); Toprak (1982); Kurdakul (1981); and Çadırcı (1980).
31 İnalcık (1971).
32 Bağış (1983) for the above paragraph. Merchants of benefaction operated until at least 1855, see BBA İ MV 14194, 20 S 1271/1855.
33 Frangakis (1986); Goffman (1986) shows foreigners' difficulties penetrating into the interior. And compare with Stoianovich (1960).
34 Bağış (1983), p. 93.
35 Issawi (1980), pp. 62–71; Delbeuf (1906); Kasaba (1988b); Tabak (1988); Schatkowski-Schilcher (1985), pp. 68–69.
36 Hoell (1973), pp. 50–51; Turkey (1911).
37 Tabak (1988).
38 Turkey (1911).
39 Fawaz (1983), p. 95.
40 Bowring (1840); Braude and Lewis (1981); Tabak (1988).
41 Tabak (1988); Çadırcı (1980); Maoz (1980). Vatter (c. 1987), however, holds a different view.
42 İndzhikyan's figures, cited by Issawi (1966), showing that "Turks" in 1912 constituted only 15 percent of the total merchant community in internal trade, certainly are incorrect.
43 Quataert (1983), pp. 121–45.

33

ॱ

AGRICULTURE

Until its death after World War I, the Ottoman Empire remained an agrarian empire, as it always had been. From certain vantage points, the nature of agriculture and its importance in the economy appear to have changed only slightly. In both 1800 and 1900, for example, four-fifths of the population, more or less, lived on the land and drew some portion of their livelihoods from the soil.

Beneath this placid surface of continuity, however, extraordinary changes had taken place. The crop mix certainly was different and richer in 1914 than in 1800. Total agricultural output had risen exceptionally and so had the relative importance of agricultural exports to foreign countries. In 1914, agricultural production, export levels and export-production ratios, were far greater than ever before in the nineteenth century. Huge increases in the amount of land under cultivation mainly were responsible for the rising output. Vast untilled regions were brought under the plow, especially in the interior of Anatolia, Syria and Iraq, in response to a combination of foreign and domestic factors. Thus, the changes derived from the extension of agriculture, not its intensification. Although the introduction of new implements was impressive in some areas, there generally were few technological improvements. Productivity rates remained approximately the same. The overall use of natural fertilizers did not increase and there was almost no adoption of chemical fertilizers.

Many more cultivators grew crops for sale than ever before, a trend that should have reverberated throughout the rest of the economy. The impact of this commercialization, however, was muted by the continued presence of tax-farmers who probably marketed most of the produce. Thus, much of the cash generated from farm sales remained in these few hands. In those instances when the peasants directly sold their produce for cash, ripples spread outward to merchants and manufacturers alike, as well as to other cultivators. The peasants bought more goods, sometimes foodstuffs, if they were growing non-food crops for sale. They also purchased luxury food imports, such as coffee and sugar, and also domestic and foreign manufacturers, such as yarn and cloth, or perhaps sewing machines and plows.

Both the domestic and foreign markets increased substantially. Trends in agriculture increasingly followed rhythms set by the international market that, over the century, gained considerably in relative importance. Cultivators steadily increased production for foreign consumers and larger proportions of total output went abroad.[1] But, at the same time, various domestic forces also drove production upwards.[2] The influx of up to seven million immigrants, the settlement of tribes, and relative as well as absolute increases in the Ottoman urban population all contributed to rising agrarian production. In some areas, improving security and successful tribal sedentarization were more significant than foreign demand in stimulating aggregate agricultural output. But for all these foreign and domestically driven stimuli, agriculture in the Ottoman Empire (as in the rest of the Mediterranean basin) slipped in relative global importance as new agricultural nations arose, particularly the United States. In 1800, Ottoman agriculture had been of major significance in the international economy. At the end of the century, it occupied no more than a niche, and was of only regional importance.

CROP PROFILE

The term "Ottoman Empire" camouflages the tremendous diversity of soils and climates that formed the essential conditions for Ottoman agriculture. Overall, the region only marginally is suited to agriculture, of a precarious type usually surviving on slight and undependable rainfalls. Vast deserts in the Iraqi, Arabian and east Syrian regions contrasted sharply with lush if limited plains, for example, around Adana and in many Balkan and west Anatolian riverain regions. The high plains of central Anatolia and Syria offered unpredictable harvests, unlike the compact oases of western Syria. The general sparsity of rainfall usually matched the sparsity of population.

Ottoman soils nourished a wide range of crops including roses in the Bulgarian lands and dates around Basra. But cereals easily predominated (see Tables IV:16 and 17). Grains, primarily wheat and barley, accounted for approximately 90 percent of all cultivated land, under a system of

Table IV:16. Crops being cultivated, 1863 (in % of area of all crops)

Area	Wheat	Grains	Cotton	Tobacco	Vines	Other
Edirne	30	53			5	12
Salonica	38	50				12
Seres	20	48	10	15		7
Cavalla		55	3	8		34
Diyarbekir	40	55	5			2
Trabzon	6	58		10	1	25
Acre	40	16	6	2		36

Sources: Issawi (1980), p. 199. Area units are not necessarily comparable with Table IV:17 below.

either biennial or triennial rotation. Even in districts with a highly commercialized and diversified agriculture, such as Aydın province, cereals occupied two-thirds of the cultivated land. In the European provinces, cereals provided an average 81 percent of all tithes collected in 1909: they were 67 and 89 percent respectively in the provinces of Salonica and Edirne. Other statistics show that, in 1907, cereals accounted for 76 percent of the value of agricultural production and grew in 88 percent of cultivated land in Ottoman Macedonia and Thrace. In Anatolia, cereal tithes formed 81 percent of all tithes collected. Cereals were 84 percent of Anatolian cultivated land and, in value, some 77 percent of its production. In Syria, cereals provided 76 percent of all tithes collected; e.g., 88 and 77 percent in Aleppo and Damascus provinces but only 43 percent in the area of Jerusalem. In the Iraqi provinces, cereals furnished 88 percent of all tithes.[3] Crops besides grains could be regionally important. For example, cotton and tobacco fields covered one-quarter of the cultivated lands around Seres in 1863 and nearly one-third those at Adana in 1909. Grapes were important in coastal areas such as Aydın and also in interior regions, such as Diyarbekir (Tables IV:16 and 17).

MEASURES OF PRODUCTION

A variety of statistics measuring production and tax revenues underscore the vital place of agriculture in the Ottoman economy. One educated guess suggests that, in 1914, agriculture contributed 56 percent of Ottoman "national" income. Agricultural taxes were the most important single set of imperial revenues. Tax-revenue data provide a very imperfect and indirect measure. But they are much more available than production figures and thus form our main means of measurement.

Table IV:17. Crops being cultivated (in % of area of all crops), in selected areas

Areas	Cereals	Vegetables	Industrial crops	Vines
Adana	64	1	32	3
Ankara	90	1	–	8
Aleppo	79	3	4	14
Aydın	73	4	6	17
Baghdad	96	–	1	3
Basra	98	1	1	–
Beirut	79	9	10	2
Bitlis	95	1	1	3
Bursa	79	2	3	16
Damascus	89	3	–	8
Diyarbekir	81	4	3	13
İstanbul	79	–	14	7
Konya	91	2	2	6
Mosul	87	1	4	8
Van	95	–	3	2

Source: Turkey (1327b/1909), p.p.
– = less than 1 percent. Errors due to rounding. This table is reproduced in Nickoley (1924), p. 285.

Moderately reliable data become available c. 1850 but cannot be used with any assurance until the end of the period. By mid-century, İstanbul had regained control over most areas and the tithe, standardized at 10 percent, had been in place for about two decades. During the 1850s, the tithe formed 30 percent and the land tax another 27 percent of all taxes collected. A quarter-century later, the two taxes respectively totaled 27 and 13 percent while, in 1910, the tithe and land taxes formed 28 and 11 percent of total revenues. Although the absolute amount of the tithes collected increased by more than 40 percent during a 50-year period, their relative share remained more or less the same, about one-quarter to one-third.[4]

The share that the tithe contributed to the revenues of the individual provinces varied considerably, a reflection both of regional productivity and governmental ability to collect taxes. In the Danubian province, during the 1860s, the share of agricultural revenues was said to be the highest in the empire. There, in several sample years, the tithe and live-stock taxes respectively were as much as 45 and 18 percent. By contrast, the tithe of Edirne province during the 1870s accounted for 28 percent of provincial revenues while, in 1891, with different borders, the tithe was 45 percent of budgeted total revenues.[5] During the 1890s, the tithe respectively formed 47 and 29 percent of the revenues collected in Bagh-dad and Mosul provinces. The various land taxes in the Iraqi provinces, in 1911, provided 44 percent of all receipts. In the Anatolian provinces, the tithe averaged 31 percent of all revenues during the 1890s, respectively ranging from 46 to 27 percent in Erzurum and Aydın provinces.[6]

The European provinces certainly contributed the lion's share of imperial agricultural taxes for most of the century. Even in 1910 (before the Balkan Wars), they still provided one-quarter of all Ottoman tithes and animal taxes collected in the empire. Anatolia by then had taken the lead and contributed 57 percent of the total. Syria yielded 11 percent, while Iraq and the Hejaz respectively provided 6 and 3 percent of all agricultural tithes in the empire.[7]

The scant statistics on actual production reveal patterns very similar to those suggested by the tithe data. Overall, total output certainly increased sharply between 1820 and 1860, when rising European demand and improved security were the major factors. Thereafter, until 1914, gross agricultural production at least doubled (in the area within the 1911 borders of the empire). During this latter period, foreign demand probably played a less crucial role and other factors, such as nomad sedentarization, immigration and the growth of urban centers, especially port cities, came to the fore. Anatolian production, for example, then expanded substantially so that, by 1909, 5.5 million hectares of land were under cultivation. Just prior to the Balkan Wars, the European provinces contained 24 percent and Anatolia held 55 percent of the total estimated value of Ottoman agricultural production. After the Balkan Wars, Rumeli's share plummeted to 2 percent. Syria accounted for only 9 percent and Iraq for 7 percent of total output.[8]

Fluctuations in the production of the major crops followed a variety of patterns. Aggregate grain output rose one-third between 1888 and 1913, despite substantial territorial losses. Anatolian wheat production increased by some 50 percent between c. 1850 and the early twentieth century.[9] The production of many crops rose sharply between 1897 and 1909, and even more impressively in the final years before World War I. For example, the production of İzmir figs nearly doubled, that of tobacco tripled and the output of Adana cotton quadrupled between 1897 and 1913.[10] In the Syrian provinces, the expansion of cultivation under Egyptian occupation probably gave way to some retrogression for several decades. Subsequently, substantial amounts of new acreage came under cultivation in the Syrian and Jordanian lands. By contrast, there was comparatively little new cultivation in Lebanon and Palestine after 1850, despite Jewish settlements in the latter area. In Iraq, very large increases in grain exports clearly indicate the expansion in cultivated lands since the 1860s, but no production figures are available.

Table IV:18. Cultivated land, 1909, selected areas (thousands of hectares)

Province	Total area	Area cultivated
Adana	4,000	467
Aleppo	7,560	353
Ankara	7,500	571
Aydın	5,700	600
Baghdad	14,121	41
Basra	13,880	44
Beirut	3,050	298
Bitlis	2,985	258
Bursa	5,130	506
Diyarbekir	4,680	308
Erzurum	7,672	338
Harput	3,780	182
İstanbul	400	10
Kastamonu	6,000	245
Konya	9,160	633
Mosul	9,100	232
Sivas	8,370	424
Suriye	10,000	348
Trabzon	3,130	366
Van	4,770	76

Source: Turkey (1327b/1909), p.t.

Thus, there were vast increases in agricultural output over the period. Even so, only tiny fractions of the total land mass came under cultivation in late Ottoman times. Table IV:18 compares cultivated to total land areas and shows how little land fell under the plow, even in the early twentieth century. While the data surely are faulty, they nonetheless unmistakably underscore the combined impact of poor soils and continuing underpopulation.

DOMESTIC AND INTERNATIONAL MARKETS

Production increases reflected a mix of internal and exogenous factors. As seen in Chapter 32, domestic consumers accounted for at least three-quarters of all Ottoman agricultural production, in 1913 when exports had reached their maximum. The point needs to be stressed – even in the heyday of export agriculture, domestic consumption remained more important, by several orders of magnitude. Most food crops traveled only short distances to the final consumer. The market for highly perishable products, such as fruits, was even more restricted and generally remained so, given the nature of the Ottoman transport network.

Demographic changes directly affected production and consumption of agricultural commodities. The presence of large cities such as İzmir,

İstanbul and Beirut and dramatic increases in their size provided important domestic markets. (These port cities also were major consumers of imported foodstuffs.) Sedentarization and immigration, not foreign markets, provided the major motor of agricultural expansion in some interior regions. The successful sedentarization of nomads and their transformation into cultivators provided agriculture with many scores of thousands of new laborers and gave agricultural production a major spurt. The flood of refugees created new urban consumers as well as vast numbers of additional producers. The Aleppo region provides a clear example of the impact of tribal pacification and immigration. By the mid-1860s, the tribes around Aleppo had been pushed east into the desert and, after 1880, rarely caused problems for the state. At about this time, large numbers of Muslim refugees settled in the province; for example, some 15,000 Circassians in 1878 alone. Agriculture boomed in Aleppo province and virtually all of its increased cereal production fed a growing local population. Exports actually fell.[11] There were many other similarly important domestic markets for agricultural produce. Thus, the estimate that only one-quarter of the overall increase in agricultural production derived from rising domestic demand surely understates the significance of these local factors.[12]

Important proportions of the increases in agricultural output derived from foreign demand and were exported. Already bound to the global market as the period opened, the Ottoman agrarian economy thereafter followed the international cycles of expansion, depression and recovery. As Western demand for specific commodities fluctuated, many Ottoman growers correspondingly reduced or expanded the production of a particular crop. Overall, agricultural exports from the Arab lands probably experienced the highest *relative* rates of increase in the empire between 1840 and 1913. The Anatolian share of aggregate Ottoman exports slipped, from 35 percent to 29 percent, and the European territories were rapidly escaping from the control of İstanbul.[13]

Export ratios – the share of total production exported – certainly increased over time, at both the imperial level and in many regions. But the actual ratios are not certain. By the late 1880s, exports perhaps accounted for 18 percent of agricultural production, then rose swiftly from 22 to 26 percent between 1910 and 1913. But another source, drawing upon a five-year sample during the early twentieth century, states that exports formed only c. 10 percent of the value of imperial agricultural production.[14]

Marketing ratios varied considerably by region and crop and date. For example, perhaps 90 percent of raw-silk production was exported from Bursa but rural subsistence and consumption in local urban centers certainly accounts for the entire grain production of Van province. Marketing ratios for cotton fluctuated wildly over the century, in tandem with the boom–bust cycle of the world market. Given the chronic labor shortages in the Ottoman economy, there was a surprisingly large number of labor-intensive export crops, notably tobacco, cotton, opium and raisins/grapes.

Ottoman agriculture displayed little tendency towards monoculture. On the contrary, over time, agricultural production and exports abroad not only were greater in quantity but were more diversified as well. In the first part of the century, cereal exports had increased exceptionally in many provinces and the proportions of grain to overall exports probably reached record heights. Cereal growers in the Aegean and Mediterranean littoral long had exported their surpluses to Europe. For example, in 1800, the Hawran region of Syria supported a flourishing export trade in good quality wheat and barley. The northern Balkan provinces came to play a more important role in supplying European grain needs as the Ottoman hold on the Black Sea slipped away between 1768 and 1829. This trend developed real momentum with the final disappearance of Ottoman monopolistic control over the Black Sea trade and the repeal of the British grain laws in the 1840s. The Salonica region, however, did not participate in the grain boom. Many of its Greek merchants departed for the newly formed Greek state while others suffered from heavy losses during the revolution. Cereal exports from the Rumanian provinces responded instantaneously to the new market opportunities of free trade. In 1843, seven ships left the Principalities for England, carrying 7,000 imperial quarters of grain; by 1849, 128 ships freighted 298,000 quarters of grain. Bulgarian production similarly responded to the removal, by the 1839 Gülhane decree, of all vestiges of the Ottoman grain monopoly. By 1842, grain exports had risen severalfold. The Bulgarian lands maintained these new high levels throughout the 1840s and then doubled shipments in the next two decades. This boom provided Bulgarian peasants with the profit incentives to buy up the lands of the departing "*sipahis*."[15] The rise of the United States as a highly efficient grain producer, beginning in the 1840s and acquiring real momentum after 1850, reversed the pattern of booming Ottoman cereal exports. The relatively labor-intensive Ottoman grain suppliers found it increasingly difficult to compete on the international market, particularly in the supply of wheat. By the second half of the century, Ottoman wheat growers had slipped to second-rank status, as incidental suppliers to the world market. In common with other Mediterranean areas, Ottoman export agriculture increasingly shifted away from wheat in favor of fruits and vegetables. In some regions, grain producers came to favor barley exports, for beer brewing. This was true along the Anatolian Railway and in the Iraqi provinces during the last decades of the century.[16]

Grape exports, often in the form of raisins, increased markedly after 1850, particularly from west Anatolia, and producers were able to compensate for their grain market losses. But a late nineteenth-century combination of phylloxera, a grapevine disease, and unfavorable tariff policies of France, a major consumer of Ottoman grapes, stifled the rising trend. Other food crop exports included figs and dates. In the early part of the century, the few exports from the Iraqi areas mainly had been dates, grown near Basra and thus shipped with relative ease. After the Suez Canal opened direct trade with Europe, the list of exports from areas some distance north of Basra expanded to include bulk goods such as wool and cereals.[17]

Non-food exports ranged from valonia cups for tanning to cotton and tobacco. Cotton exports from many areas faded in importance during the first half of the century as the American South and Egypt increased production. Drooping production picked up during the American Civil War, that cut off Southern suppliers, and then slumped for the remainder of the century. As the post-1900 needs of global textile production became nearly insatiable, Ottoman cotton exports from many but not all areas soared again. Syria, that commonly had exported cotton during the eighteenth century, subsequently shifted to other crops. Among non-food crops, the export of raw or reeled silk acquired new importance in the Lebanon, around Bursa, and in a few other areas. The production of raw silk for foreign suppliers mounted early in the period and then rose again in the 1850s and 1860s, with the opening of steam-driven silk spinning mills to reel the uniform quality silk needed by French and Italian weavers. Silk raising already had become so important in Lebanon by 1800 that the region no longer grew enough food for its own subsistence. The narrow terraces nourished mulberry bushes at the expense of cereals and cattle. Therefore, silk profits bought food from Egypt, the Hawran and Zahle, and thus fueled commercial agriculture in those areas. By the 1890s, mulberry trees covered about 50 percent of the cultivated land in the Mountain; raw silk then accounted for nearly one-half of the value of Beirut's exports. Raw-silk production employed perhaps 50,000 Mountain families and another 20,000 in the Bursa silk-raising districts. In contrast to the Lebanon, Bursa agriculture remained diversified and diversified and most, perhaps all, west Anatolian silk-raising families remained self-sufficient in food production[18] (also see Chapter 34).

The production and sale of dyestuffs such as madder root and yellow berries remained important until the 1860s but then dropped away sharply and permanently with the invention of chemical synthetics. Yellow berry bushes that once had covered hilltops in central Anatolia vanished; in the province of Konya, yellow berry production dropped from 60,000 to 1,000 *okes* between the 1860s and the early twentieth century. Ironically, this occurred just as west Anatolian carpet production began its spectacular late nineteenth-century spurt.

Tobacco exports from most production centers, excluding Lebanon, dramatically increased during the second half of the century. With the invention of mechanically rolled cigarettes, Ottoman tobacco became highly prized for blending, especially by American producers. Tobacco, by 1914, had become the leading single export from Anatolia. By then, however, some of the best Ottoman tobacco-growing lands, located in the Balkans, had been lost. Bulgaria profited immediately from its acquisition of tobacco-growing lands during the Balkan Wars and the contribution of tobacco to Bulgarian exports rose from 1 to 18 percent.[19] Ottoman Bulgaria also had been a center for the lucrative business of growing roses and extracting their attar essence.

Non-food exports – notably wool, mohair and opium – were important from the beginning of the century. During the period, there appears to have been some trend in favor of non-food crop exports at the expense of food crop exports. Ottoman cereal exports, even with the building of lines into the grain-growing plateau of Anatolia and the rich Hawran area, never recovered their former relative importance. But the rise in other non-food exports more than compensated. The example of the Lebanese silk raisers suggests, however, that emphasis on growing such products could leave cultivators dependent on others for food supplies. More positively, the rising emphasis on non-food crop exports meant enhanced domestic markets for Ottoman food crop producers, e.g. booming tobacco exports triggered increases in demand for Ottoman cereals and other foodstuffs.

AGRICULTURAL TECHNOLOGY

Dry farming prevailed on the overwhelming majority of cultivated land. Irrigation, when used, boosted productivity three to eight times but irrigated lands formed a small minority of all land under cultivation. And it is possible that the extent of irrigated land even declined after 1800 because of problems with security. Although these were resolved by mid-century in most areas, insecurity persisted in the Iraqi provinces until 1914. More generally, a fall in rice production probably accounts for the decline in irrigation. Cheaper and better varieties of imported rice and higher profit margins of other crops diminished the production of rice in Macedonia and Thrace, that had supplied İstanbul and Salonica. During the nineteenth century, the empire lost its longstanding self-sufficiency in rice production.[20] Just before World War I, however, several great works boosted the extent of irrigated lands in the empire. Perhaps the most notable project was at Konya that, in 1913, opened 50,000 hectares of irrigated land. Similarly noteworthy were the vast irrigated date plantations in the Basra region and the opening of the Hindiya dam in 1913.[21]

The Anatolian and Arab areas particularly suffered from a lack of trees. Most cultivators used animal and human wastes for fuel and its use as fertilizer remained exceptional. In the adoption of modern agricultural tools and machinery, the Balkan provinces were far more advanced than almost all areas of Anatolia and the Arab provinces. By 1900, for example, iron plows were in a two to one majority in the Sava and Morava river valleys of former Ottoman Serbia. But fertilizers were not used regularly there, crop rotation was inconsistent and peasants used the sickle more than the scythe. In post-Ottoman Bulgaria, iron plows increased tenfold between 1893 and 1910 and, by the latter date, were present in 18 percent of all peasant households.[22] The use of iron plows and modern implements also gained substantial momentum in Anatolia after 1890 but likely did not equal that in the Bulgarian lands. Thanks to individual initiative, government programs, and various railway companies, inexpensive American reapers became fairly common while annual sales of plows exceeded 4,000 before World War I. Adoption of steam threshers and plows also increased but only on the large private and imperial estates in the Aydın, Adana and Syrian regions. Improved equipment remained the exception in Anatolia. As late as the 1950s, only 24 percent of farms had iron plows in Turkey, then agriculturally the most advanced country of the modern Middle East. The rest employed wooden plows with iron tips.[23] Yield ratios reflect these radical differences in the levels of technology regionally employed. Wheat yields in the European provinces equaled two tons per hectare but only about one ton in the central Anatolian lands. Overall, productivity changed little, if at all, and increases in output levels derived from the extension of cultivation.[24]

THE OTTOMAN LAND REGIME

Throughout the nineteenth century, the central government struggled to reassert its claims to the land and control over collection of the surplus. With the Janissaries safely eliminated, Sultan Mahmud II's centralizing government continued its assault on alternate sources of power, targeting the provincial notables who had accumulated fiscal or landed power. In 1813, for example, the state broke the fiscal monopoly of the Karaosmanoğlu family in western Anatolia. Instead of appointing a family member to succeed the deceased Karaosmanoğlu Hüseyin as tax collector/administrator, Mahmud II designated an outsider for the post. Then, using the army mobilized for the 1828 Russian War, he attacked the notables.[25] In 1831, İstanbul moved to displace the 2,500 *sipahi*s who remained in the Anatolian and European provinces. It introduced a plan to pension off the remaining *timar*-holders, eliminate their tax-collection rights and lease out the lands to tax-farmers. Thus, the *timar*-holders were to lose their revenues as tax collectors, the vital fiscal base of their autonomy. The plan proceeded in stages between 1838 and 1844. The state abolished many existing dues, services and taxes and categorically prohibited forced labor. And it insisted on a 10 percent maximum for the tithe. Stripped of their incomes as tax collectors, most *sipahi*s fell back on the revenues from the core holdings. These, however, appear to have been small and only marginally profitable. In Ottoman Serbia, the power of the *sipahi*s had vanished by 1839 and the Gülhane decree gave the Christian peasants legal rights to former *timar* lands. Almost everywhere, the central government successfully wrecked the claims of the great landholders, and restored those lands to its own titular possession.[26] The military campaigns of Mahmud II against the notables assured that they would not have *de jure* control of the land. This was a crucial achievement for the state in the nineteenth century.

In asserting control over the land, the government intended to win the unchallenged right to fiscal exploitation of the agrarian economy. Beginning with Mahmud II and continuing throughout the century, it repeatedly but ultimately unsuccessfully attempted to replace tax-farming with direct collection by salaried state employees. Success would have gained the central treasury more effective control over cultivators and a greater share of the surplus. The government officially abolished tax-farming for the first time in 1839, at the very moment it was relying on tax-farmers to collect former *sipahi* revenues. Not surprisingly, it abandoned the effort in 1842 and the rescinding order (*firman*) noted the financial losses that had accrued with the use of government agents for direct collection. (İbrahim Pasha in Syria similarly had tried to abolish tax-farming and faced rebellion as a result.) Hence, tithe collecting again was awarded to local administrators and prominent men, in return for a lump sum.[27] The 1856 *Hatt-ı Hümayun* ordered the "final" abolition of tax-farming but with no better results than the Gülhane rescript. In the early 1880s, the state again abolished tax-farming; but reassessing its position in 1886, concluded that the reformed system was too costly and abandoned the experiment. Tax-farming, not direct collection, remained the norm throughout the empire. Even in the early twentieth century, tax-farming accounted for more than 95 percent of all tithe revenues collected.[28]

Thus, the İstanbul government never won direct access to the agrarian surplus of an agrarian empire. The continued prevalence of tax-farming vividly illustrates the tenacious power of local notables in almost every area throughout the century. In many respects, İstanbul did impose its will on the notables. It did reassert itself as the single most important factor in domestic politics. It often appointed once-autonomous dynasts to government posts at a distance from their former seats of influence. In the later nineteenth century, for example, Karaosmanoğlu family members from western Anatolia served as governors of Jerusalem and Drama. But the central administration did not destroy the political, economic and social power of most notables. Instead, it reached accommodations, winning the cooperation of local groups by allotting them, for example, continuing political privileges. The former notables and their descendants officially served as regional administrators and commonly were on the local councils created as part of the İstanbul reform programs.[29] And, when further reforms changed council memberships from salaried to unpaid status, continued domination by the local upper strata was assured. In very many instances, these elites also continued to control tax-farming and thus access to a substantial share of the agricultural surplus. Former *sipahis* and other local notables, Christian and Muslim alike, served as members of regional administrative councils and retained control over the farming of taxes in most areas.[30] In "the provinces feudal lords still flourish but under different names now . . . influential and rich local people, such as council members and other urban notables."[31]

But competition as well as accommodation marked the relationship between the central state and provincial holders of power. Throughout the century, as seen in the efforts to eliminate tax-farming, İstanbul sought to garner more of the surplus and reduce the notables' share. There was continuous friction as well as cooperation. But the alliance between the two forces remained and for this Ottoman cultivators surely paid. In c. 1800, local cultivators with their dues and services maintained the notables who forwarded some, small, portion to İstanbul. In the early stages of centralization, the cultivators sometimes paid both the new taxes demanded by İstanbul and the rents and dues traditionally owed the notables.[32] The latter imposts subsequently were often eliminated but cultivators continued to support notables who served as tax-farmers under İstanbul's nominal supervision. The cultivator payments that now flowed to İstanbul were far vaster than before, monies needed to maintain the ongoing centralization and bureaucratization. Towards the end of the period, the agricultural tax rate itself increased sharply, by over 25 percent, rising from 10 to 12.63 percent, between 1883 and 1900.[33] It is likely that the average cultivator family in 1900 handed over more of its gross production to local and imperial overlords than ever before in the nineteenth century.[34]

The emergence of the Ottoman Public Debt Administration after 1881 jeopardized the position of the tax-farmer notables and thus upset the relationship between İstanbul and the provincial elite. When the Debt Administration hired its own army of tax collectors to gather the various revenues under its jurisdiction, these agents thus took over functions and monies that had been the monopoly of the tax-farming notables.[35] Such displacement and loss of income helps to explain the notables' participation in early twentieth-century insurrections against the state, such as those at Erzurum and Uşak. It thus serves to explain the involvement of some provincial elites in the Young Turk movement.[36]

THE 1858 LAND LAW

The Land Law of 1858 is like the elephant of the blind man as it appears to scholars in different guises.[37] Some insist on the code as the instrument of the government to reassert its fiscal domination over the peasantry. Others have stressed its character as a catalyst that transformed state land (*miri*) into private property. Arguments about the Land Law focus on two issues – the intended purpose of the legislation and its actual impact. In regards to intent, the code has political, fiscal, and economic dimensions. A key feature is the demand that individuals possess a title deed to have legal use of state land. To achieve complete registration, the state intended to survey all lands and provide title deeds to those who possessed them. By insisting on delivery of title deeds to the actual cultivators, the state sought to regain firm control over Ottoman growers and eliminate the sway of the notables. Hence, article after article of the code reiterated that government officials must record land transfers of whatever kind.

When it offered title even to those who illegally had been tilling state land, the code strove to maintain and promote agricultural development. It provided a clear and gratuitous title to those who *de facto* had seized and cultivated otherwise untilled land for a period of ten years. To retain title, moreover, the deed-holder had to continuously cultivate the land, either personally or via shares or lease to another. If a cultivator allowed land to remain unproductive for three years, its title became subject to transfer. Thus, the state promoted production, bringing and keeping the land under cultivation and on the tax rolls. The list of heirs established by the 1858 law was extended substantially in 1867. Here, most scholars have emphasized how such inheritance provisions resembled those of private property. In balance, however, it seems that the code's role in converting state to private land has been exaggerated. Scholars' insistence on a supposed evolution to private property tells more about their biases or misperceptions than about actual patterns of landholding and usage. It seems more important to stress how the rules governing inheritance and many of the other provisions dramatically increased the likelihood that land would remain occupied and cultivated. Thus, the 1858 code promoted greater stability of tenure, increased production of crops and the continued flow of taxes.

While most of the code discusses title acquisition by the actual cultivator, a few provisions favored large landholders and actually undermined state–small-cultivator relations. For example, those who leased land from the title-holder acquired no rights to it at all, no matter how long the lease tenure (Art. 23). Similarly, a single individual could acquire title to an entire village if no alternative means were available to maintain production. The issue, however, does not seem to be one of large versus small landholder. Instead, these provisions, in common with the inheritance regulations, reflect state concern to maintain stability of tenure and/or the maintenance of cultivation, in this case by large holders. The government generally preferred small cultivators to the potentially dangerous great landholder, but permitted land aggregation to maintain production and tax levels.

The Land Law was deeply concerned with the fiscal health of the imperial treasury and some scholars argue that here, indeed, is the essence of the code. In this argument, the state granted title deeds neither to register actual cultivators, nor to promote agricultural development but rather to identify taxpayers. With a list of title deed holders in hand, the state could find those responsible for paying taxes. Hence the provisions that title-holders who leased land to others still retained clear title and the insistence on the presence of state officials to effect land transactions of whatever sort. Other provisions of the law, however, argue against this view. For example, the state declared that it would remove fruit trees or grape vines if they had been planted without official permission (the time limit was three years, thereafter the plants remained). This proviso sacrificed production potential and the (probably) higher taxes from such land use so that the government would retain its right to control the land. Similarly, another provision insisted on the title deed rights of persons already cultivating the land, even if others offered to pay more for the deed. Higher deed prices also were to be ignored so that possessors, families or co-villagers could have first claim on land, subject to title-deed sale.

The argument for the code as fiscal instrument, however, is undermined by the relative absence of direct exploitation by large landholders. These instead usually employed sharecropping arrangements. Often verbal in nature, the contracts varied according to crop, region, market conditions and labor availability. Although the deed-holders were responsible for the taxes, cultivators typically paid the tithe before dividing with deed-holders. Title-holders employed these arrangements to forestall confiscatory state actions for non-payment of the taxes. Since, in this case, the state received taxes from cultivators who were not deed-holders, is not the fiscal interpretation of the code invalid?[38]

Overall, the character of the Land Law as an instrument to maintain rural stability and continuity stands out. While the concern for revenues hardly can be exaggerated, the state sacrificed revenues to maintain stability. It focused on the small cultivator, but it countenanced large estates to initiate or maintain cultivation. In some of its guises, the code appears as another example of the increasingly intrusive role played by nineteenth-century administrations. But, from another vantage point, the code appears as a resumption of ancient Ottoman *kanun*s seeking close control over the land and the cultivators.[39] In this respect, the state appears as un-modern and pre-capitalist, atavistically asserting ownership over land in the manner of ancient Near Eastern empires. And yet the code also displays the modern and capitalist aspects of the evolving Ottoman state, striving to divest itself of concern for production and focus on the flow of taxes. In certain respects, the law reflects laissez-faire notions that we already have encountered in governmental customs policies (Ch. 32) and will see in state attacks on guild privileges (Ch. 34). Referring back to the elephant simile: we should not be surprised to find a capitalist trunk and a mercantilist foot on the land code, for these reflect the transitional nature of the state itself.

For many economic historians, the impact of the Land Law is a more relevant issue than the real or imagined intent of the state. Most scholars assume that large holdings became the rule in the later nineteenth century: a consensus, that seems partially ill-founded, has emerged along the following lines. Basically, this interpretation argues, the upper strata rather than the actual cultivators registered the land and became its legal possessors. Peasants everywhere allegedly either were too ignorant to know the value of registration or feared government intentions and refused to register the land in their own names. Consequently, cultivators implored or permitted local notables, who saw the advantages of registration, to place their names on the title deeds. Thus, the peasants lost title to land they had been cultivating to more sophisticated and market-wise elites. Similarly, in this interpretation, tribal sheikhs saw the profits of a market economy and personally registered lands once held communally.

However plausible these scenarios may seem, there presently is little substantiating evidence for most regions of the empire. In the Vidin area, it is true, notables in c. 1850 were the owners of state land; but they had already achieved this in the eighteenth century, long before the Land Law. The oft-cited research by one scholar documents well the usurpation of tribal lands by sheikhs in Iraq.[40] This account seems accurate but it is incorrect to generalize from this one example to the whole empire. Indeed, landholding patterns in Iraq probably were quite atypical.

The absence of research on landholding and actual land registration prevent us, at this time, from saying a great deal about the impact of the Land Law. But there are a number of cases that demonstrate widespread registration by small cultivators and their eagerness to use the system to their own advantage. In the village of Hadeth in Mount Lebanon, officials recorded land transfers for some 2,291 holdings during the period 1866–1914, showing some 4,614 acts of transfer. These figures may not be reflective of any larger reality: the area is Lebanon, unusual in itself, and the example only concerns one village. But still, it hardly suggests a peasantry reluctant to use the land registry office.[41] Peasants of the al-Al village of Jordan during the 1860s and near Damascus in the 1870s similarly had frequent recourse to the new method of land registration.[42]

Preliminary findings for the Jerusalem region indicate that all the persons requesting land registration were smallholders. In the sample, no urban notable, money lender or absentee landlord is indicated to have registered land. Instead, all the applicants for registration were the occupants of the lands in question and inhabitants of the villages on which the lands were situated.[43] Thus, these examples reveal precisely the opposite pattern of the research on the Iraq region. Land surveys, that were undertaken in most regions, could show us the actual patterns of registration and landholding but these remain largely unstudied.[44] At least three such surveys were carried out – in 1878, 1886 and 1907 – that may provide the basis for research.

In any event, it is a mistake to credit land laws *per se* with the landholding patterns that prevailed in the final Ottoman period. This would be to confuse cause with effect. The pattern of landholding at the end of the Ottoman Empire derived from a complex interaction among a long list of variables. These include soil and climate, previous patterns of landholding, the changing availability of labor, capital and land, the presence of sedentarized and nomadic tribes, transport systems, regional and international market opportunities for both agricultural and animal products, the coercive power of local notables, the degree of centralized political control, and the land legislation itself. If the land codes of the state had been a decisive influence, we would find a certain uniformity of landholding patterns throughout the Ottoman realm. But it is clear that there was *not* a single pattern of landholding in the Ottoman Middle East. We do not find a single pattern dictated by state fiat, but differing sets of customs, practices and landholding patterns in the various regions.[45] Upon these, the state attempted to imprint its legislation. And it is not sufficient to argue that the landholding variety stems from ineffective or incomplete application of the laws; this simply is a variation on the argument that gives primacy to the state in determining landholding patterns. While state policy is important, it was not the primary variable in forming patterns of landholding.[46]

In sum, the 1858 code should not be seen as the initiator of trends. Rather, it confirmed, verified and sometimes accelerated tendencies prompted by other factors. By conferring legal title on sheikhs, urban notables and others who reclaimed abandoned or uncultivated land, the code provided a more secure legal context for entrepreneurial investors. At the same time, on a vaster scale, it provided small cultivators with legal title and affirmed their hold on the land. This is important and should be emphasized. In providing for secure registration, the law aided in the consolidation and further development of private landholding. Doubtless the security of tenure prompted by these processes raised production, increased the flow of revenues and helped the state to order its fiscal house.

LANDHOLDING PATTERNS

In the presence of extraordinary diversity in the Ottoman lands, few valid generalizations about landholding patterns seem possible. On the one hand, there are the serf-like conditions of Wallachia and Moldavia; one the other hand, we see the egalitarian *mushaa* practices in Palestine and the similar *lazma* system in lower Iraq. And these systems again differed from the individually held small plots in areas such as Serbia, Lebanon and Anatolia. After careful reflection, the following assertions seem fair. Smallholdings prevailed throughout the Ottoman lands for the entire period, before and after commercialization. There were great estates everywhere (see below) but they were not particularly common in any single region – the Balkans, Anatolia, or the Arab lands. Overall, most holdings were and remained small in size, although large estates became more common, particularly in the Arab provinces at the end of the period.

The amount of land under cultivation generally expanded, thanks to the resumption of tilling on abandoned lands and the opening of new regions to settlement. Particularly in the coastal areas and near urban centers, newly cultivated lands were interspersed among those already tilled. Here, the pattern of new cultivation resembled filling in the blank squares on a checkerboard. But in many interior regions, travellers once had crossed extensive zones of almost empty lands. Vast regions, previously the domain of nomads, now came under cultivation for the first time in centuries. Until c. 1850, while their fringes were cultivated, the great basins of central Anatolia were nearly devoid of permanent settlements. Similarly, nomads controlled the semi-arid steppes and deserts from a point 10–40 km east of the Aleppo–Homs–Hama line. In western and southeastern Anatolia, fertile but malarial swamp lands largely were unexploited in the early nineteenth century. This situation rapidly changed under the twin impetus of refugee settlement and tribal pacification. The government gave land, without fee, to refugees who formed permanent agricultural communities. Often they settled on lands already claimed by tribes that had been using them for seasonal animal pasturage and/or occasional cultivation. The government granted title to these refugees who, following time-honored *çift-hane* patterns, divided the parcels into equal-size plots for each family. Over time, however, in the Syrian and Anatolian lands alike, inequalities in landholding developed according to the varying subsequent fortunes of the individual immigrants. In Anatolia, the nomadic inhabitants sought to protect their claims and lands by settling in permanent new villages close to those of the immigrants.[47] Nomadic settlement was further encouraged by the policies of the Anatolian and Baghdad railway companies and the new market opportunities that they offered. Even so, vast uncultivated and empty lands remained, thanks to the meagerness of the Ottoman population base and, sometimes, successful tribal resistance. On the plateaus of inner Anatolia, the nomads were able to block the establishment of refugee settlements and maintained their very large animal herds that provided substantial quantities of wool to the burgeoning carpet industry.

In the northern portions of Syria, the zone of cultivation moved steadily eastward along the Euphrates towards Raqqa. By the 1860s, some tribes had abandoned their former summer pastures close to Aleppo since there were too many settlements. Instead, they pastured their animals north of the Euphrates. But, by c. 1900, there were some 57 new villages in the area of Raqqa alone and pasturage was disappearing.

Government pacification of Palestine began in earnest during the late 1850s. The state established new garrisons, and thus encouraged villages on the plains that had been sparsely settled. Villagers who had lived in the hills for safety now flocked to the plains to assert their claims to these lands, based on seasonal or occasional cultivation. Other new settlers included tribesmen, both those who saw the advantages of settled life and others who forcibly were placed on the land.[48] And finally there were the Christian and Jewish religious settlers from abroad. Between 1882 and 1908, 26 Jewish agricultural colonies purchased some 400,000 *dönüm*s of land from the government and large estate owners. Thus, Palestine became the only Ottoman area of significant foreign settlement. In the Iraqi provinces, with the opening of the Suez Canal, there were extraordinary increases of cultivated land. The land under cultivation reportedly increased at least ninefold between 1860 and 1913, while agricultural tithes nearly doubled.[49]

Unlike many contemporary states that forbade land usage to certain ethnic or religious groups, the Ottoman regime permitted any subject (and, after 1867, any foreigner who conformed to Ottoman laws) to hold land. This legal principle was borne out in practice and we find Albanian and Arab, Circassian and Armenian, Druze, Slavic, Turkish and Jewish cultivators. The ethnicity and religious background of landlords also varied widely. In provinces where Christians were a majority, survival of the classical land regime into the nineteenth century often meant Muslim landlords and Christian peasants. Tax-farming, for its part, meant that persons of any ethnic or religious group could be in a position to dominate Muslim and Christian cultivators.

Sharecropping, as seen, was very common and most often was based on a 50-50 division, with the sharecropper usually paying the taxes before dividing the produce. Sharecroppers rather than wage laborers commonly exploited large estates, whose owners usually granted less favorable terms than smallholders. There were some important exceptions, such as the large estates on the Cilician plain during the second part of the century, that employed wage laborers to pick cotton. There, owners of large grain harvesters traveled about, offering their equipment and services for a fee. Variations in sharecropping arrangements abounded according to crop, region and date. For example, in some areas of Mount Lebanon, the landholder turned over a land parcel to a cultivator who planted it with trees. After 5–10 years, the peasant acquired one-quarter or one-half of *both* the land and trees in question as his own holding.[50]

Generally, the varying legal classification of land as *vakf* or *miri* or *mülk* (pertaining to pious foundations or to the state or freehold) had little impact on the method of its cultivation. Likewise, large and small holders generally exploited the land in similar ways, using combinations of wage labor and sharecropping. Large commercial estates – extensive lands held by an individual who employed sharecroppers and/or wage laborers to produce for the market – were unusual and economically unimportant except in Moldavia, Wallachia, the Çukurova plain, much of the Iraqi regions, and in the Hama area. Usually, these workers tilled small plots; vast fields with plantation-like labor gangs were rare. There were capital-intensive, mechanized, large holdings in a few areas but these were exceptional. The added input usually was in labor rather than capital. The significance of large holdings increased later in the century and they played a significant role in the production of some export crops. Small landholdings predominated in almost all areas, a pattern that seems remarkably stable over time despite major increases in population and agricultural commercialization. One estimate suggests that smallholdings accounted for 82 percent of all Ottoman cultivable land in 1859 and

about the same proportion in 1900 (see Table IV:19).[51] Free cultivators
accounted for most agricultural production and exports, even on the
largest estates.

Land distribution is well-documented for the Anatolian provinces[52]
where smallholdings prevailed throughout the century. In c. 1840, over
four-fifths of the cultivated lands were held in small plots of less than 8
hectares, the amount an average household could cultivate without outside help.[53] Scattered data for 1863 show small ownership dominance
while, in 1869, 82 percent of Anatolian cultivated lands were in holdings
of 6–8 hectares, representing some 80 percent of all peasant households.[54]
In 1907, holdings of 4.5 hectares and less constituted 81 percent of all
Anatolian cultivated land and in 1910, holdings under 5 hectares numbered over one million, constituting 75 percent of all landholders.[55]

In the Rumelian regions c. 1907, holdings smaller than 10 *dönüm*s
formed 34 percent of all holdings and those under 50 *dönüm*s amounted
to 81 percent of all holdings. In Ottoman Serbia, family–owned small
peasant holdings, "dwarf farms," had become almost the only form of
land tenure by the early nineteenth century. This pattern sustained itself
through the breakaway and remained characteristic of the independent
Serbian state. In 1914, 70 percent of all peasant households in post-
Ottoman Serbia owned more than 2 hectares of land (the minimum
required for the Serbian peasant to break even in a money economy). In
Bulgaria, c.1800, large estates covered less than 20 percent of the cultivated lands and employed under 10 percent of the peasant labor force.
One sample shows the land distribution among some 385 village households in central-north Bulgaria during the 1840s. Holdings of 50 *dönüm*s
or less formed 60 percent of the "total land owned" (compare with Table
IV: 19).[56] After mid-century, the limited number of Bulgarian *çiftlik*s
further declined, thanks to the İstanbul takeover of tax collection from
the *timar*-holders. Muslim holders began to withdraw from the Bulgarian
region and, in the third quarter of the century, much *çiftlik* land was
transferred to the peasants. In 1878–79, before the mass flight of Muslims
from the new state, Russians carried out a land survey that found barely
200 *çiftlik*s north and south of the Balkan Mountains. About one-half of
the 108 estates whose size they recorded encompassed less than 6 hectares. In independent Bulgaria, c. 1900, holdings smaller than 20 hectares
remained characteristic: they accounted for 80 percent of privately held
rural land and 96 percent of all landowners. In the Macedonian and
northern Greece areas, *çiftlik*-holders did not transfer their lands to peasants but instead rented them, usually to Greek merchants. Unlike in
Bulgaria, the *çiftlik* tended to remain intact.[57]

Table IV:19. Landholding patterns: selected districts (*kazas*) in the Anatolian and Arab provinces, c. 1909, where more than 50 percent of cultivator households possessed lands greater than 50 *dönüms*

Kaza	No. households with 50+ *dönüms*	Total no. households	In sancak of	In province of
Alasgird	2,500	3,500	Bayezid	Erzurum
Adana	2,862	2,987		
Arifiye	3,700	4,202	Adana	
Kara Isralu	3,400	4,680		Adana
Yarpuz	4,000	4,000	Cebel Bereket	
Karas	2,300	·3,000	Kozan	
Haymana	3,507	6,507	Ankara	
Çorum	5,200	7,200	Çorum	Ankara
Mecidiye	1,600	3,200	Kırşehir	
Söke	5,500	6,000	Aydın	
Denizli	2,000	3,000	Denizli	Aydın
Bitlis	1,525	3,100	Bitlis	
Ahlat	1,000	2,000		
Siirt	700	700	Siirt	Bitlis
Vartu	1,000	2,000	Muş	
Sokut	5,507	10,017	Ertuğrul	
Yenişehir	2,097	4,239		
Gemlik	700	1,000	Bursa	Bursa
Buldan	3,565	7,130	Karahisar-Sahib	
Diyarbekir	8,500	9,000	Diyarbekır	
Siurgi	8,000	12,000	Siurgi	Diyarbekır
Cizre	1,000	1,500	Mardin	
Nisbin	1,500	2,000	Mardin	Diyarbekır
Ayvacık	900	1,571	Biga	Biga *sancak*
Merzifon	1,500	2,000	Amasya	Sivas
Bafra	8,000	15,000	Canik	Trabzon
Aksaray	10,632	12,632	Niğde	Konya
Dilbin	7,230	8,180	Baghdad	Baghdad
Sevir	6,345	7,330	Beirut	
Haifa	1,080	1,150	Ala	Beirut
Nasra	3,000	3,000		
Bab ul-Cebul	2,900	5,000		
Cebel Saman	2,738	5,238		
Harem	4,146	6,146	Aleppo	Aleppo
Raqqa	1,820	3,320		
Minbiç	2,000	2,000		
Elbistan	5,433	9,433	Maraş	
Salt	4,500	5,000	Krak	Suriye
Bazyan	1,000	1,000	Sülemaniye	Mosul
Total in "Asya ve Afrika-yi Osmani"	8,400	29,771		

Source: Turkey (1327b/1909).

In Wallachia and Moldavia, landholding evolved in ways more reminiscent of the east Elbian lands than the Ottoman Balkans in general. Unusually, a form of serfdom flourished in Moldavia and Wallachia. There, in the post-Ottoman era, 4 percent of landowners held over one-half the land.[58] The Rumanian Principalities had been outside of effective

Ottoman control and tendencies towards land agglomeration, that elsewhere were blunted or reversed by the centralizing efforts of İstanbul,
here went unchecked. This factor combined with good transport facilities
and market opportunities, especially after the 1829 Treaty of Adrianople
lifted Ottoman trade restrictions, to produce a unique set of landholding
patterns. Overall, the condition of Wallachian and Moldavian peasants
deteriorated considerably in the first half of the century as boyar-
dominated administrations systematically stripped small cultivators of
their land. The plundered lands were not exploited as great plantations
but rather were sharecropped in a particular fashion.[59] Over time, the
boyars evolved into absentee landlords. They placed their properties in
the hands of agents. These in turn rented out lands to peasants who
paid increasingly burdensome rents, taxes and labor services. In the late
eighteenth century, for example, peasants paid a tithe of 10 percent and
worked six to eight days per year for the lord. Boyar-sponsored legislation in 1818 effectively doubled the tithe; by mid-century, the amount
of labor legally required had increased to 24 days in Wallachia and over
50 days in Moldavia! These methods account for the vast expansion of
Wallachian and Moldavian agricultural production: for example, the
threefold to sixfold increase in corn and wheat acreage between 1830 and
1848.[60]

> The country was but a big estate, administered like an estate – a complex
> of latifundia in which private law is public law, the inheritance of landed
> wealth the inheritance of power in the State.[61]

Scholarly assessments concerning landholding patterns in Palestine and
Syria currently are mixed. Most scholars had believed that cultivators
employed the *mushaa* system of collective ownership to redistribute the
land among themselves. It once had been held that the *mushaa* system
prevailed throughout Syria and Palestine and, more generally, the Middle
East, generalizations long discarded in the absence of supporting data.
More recent information even suggests that the *mushaa* system may have
been unimportant in parts of Syria and Palestine. The communal system
may not be of an ancient age after all. Nor, according to some, was it
very common. Rather, *mushaa* seems to have been present mainly on
newly reclaimed lands. Even there, it reportedly fell into disuse because
the 1858 land code did not acknowledge the registration of communal
land. But there is some recently collected evidence of a conflicting nature.
In one Jordanian village, cultivators obeyed Ottoman law and registered

the land in the names of individuals. They also continued to follow the *mushaa* system in practice for another fifty years.[62]

On the question of great or small holdings in the Syrian provinces, there also is considerable debate. Smallholdings certainly were characteristic of the Lebanon region throughout the period.[63] But the situation is less clear elsewhere. The Bedouin had moved almost at will before being restrained by Mehmed Ali's son, İbrahim Pasha. The resumption of Ottoman rule at first meant chaos in the land tenure regime but, after 1850, matters improved. A few scholars argue that large estate consolidation was well underway before mid-century, a response to increasing market opportunities of the post-1750 era.[64] Others argue that smallholdings gave way to large estates only after 1850; a process that quickly accelerated, leaving only a quarter of the land in peasant hands by 1907.[65] Proponents of the post-1850 argument point to events such as the acquisition of seventeen villages by the great merchant families of Hama or the Sursuq family's purchase of 230,000 *dönüms* in northern Palestine or the Jumbalats' ownership of 35 entire villages.[66] In the Hawran, also, the al-Atrash Druze chiefs amassed land, evicted the previous cultivators and adopted sharecropping. Also, some argue that urban notables, merchants or the sultan himself acquired most of the newly cultivated lands east of the Euphrates. In Syria, Sultan Abdülhamid steadily acquired land, especially to the south and east-north-east of Aleppo, totaling some 1.25 million hectares by 1908. These estates were rented out in small parcels to peasants, in some cases Circassian refugees.[67]

Thus, there has been consensus on the prevalence of large estates in Syrian agriculture, with some disagreement about its timing. Recently, however, this has been challenged by the assertion that scholars have projected landholding patterns of the mandate period backwards onto Ottoman Syria and have generalized solely on the example of Hama and its large holdings. This single example, the argument continues, repeatedly has been cited to demonstrate the predominance of large holdings in Syria, "but it would be quite erroneous to consider Hamah representative of a larger pattern."[68]

In fact, there seem to be two different discussions taking place. The first concerns the timing of the rise of significant market-oriented agriculture: was it before 1800 or after 1850? And the second revolves around the engine of the commercial agriculture that did develop: large estates or smallholdings? Many scholars assume that the dynamic of commercial agriculture required large estate formation. In a recent and excellent study, one scholar describes the various forms of landholding and taxation in Damascus province during the 1840s. He calls the state of landholding confused and states that "a good part" of the land was in large estates. But the evidence that he presents clearly shows a multiplicity of land exploitation forms that characteristically were in smallholdings. There is a pattern, that of smallholders cultivating land under a variety of arrangements.[69] As seen, research concerning other Ottoman areas (as well as in Europe) has shown that smallholdings very often generated the marketed surplus. In Syria, smallholders produced a great deal of the produce sold on regional and international markets. Some were working their own lands, for personal profit. Others tilled their own plots and rented additional land or worked as sharecroppers. Still others, as seen, lost their lands and cultivated only for others. It is true that, after 1850, much new land in the northern parts of Syria was brought under cultivation in large holdings. And it may be that large estate formation was the most visible change in Syrian landholding. But it does not prove that large estates had become the dominant form of commercial agricultural exploitation and accounted for most of the marketed surplus. The importance of large holdings in Syria is not at all clear at this time. Smallholdings likely occupied most of the cultivated lands throughout the century and accounted for the bulk of the market surplus.[70]

In the Iraqi provinces as in parts of Syria, Sultan Abdülhamid II acquired vast lands through a variety of tactics, ranging from purchase to coercion. By the early 1890s, he owned some 30 percent of the cultivated land in Baghdad province. Many of the imperial estates here and in Syria were well managed. Military personnel designed, built and maintained the irrigation works and soldiers collected the rent and taxes. To keep them on the land, cultivators were well treated and received a variety of benefits, including interest-free loans and exemption from some taxes and from conscription. They rented or sharecropped most of the lands. Tribes continued to exploit some lands as they had before the sultan's takeover but his acquisition in turn improved security, encouraged settlement and stimulated greater production. The tithes collected flowed to his personal, not the imperial treasury.[71]

In lower Iraq, landholding before 1858 functioned primarily within the framework of the *lazma* system, another form of communal landholding similar to the *mushaa* pattern. The *lazma* system was well adapted to the tribal and natural conditions of the region. A tribe reserved exclusive rights of possession to itself, for cultivation or pasturage. Or, it might choose not to exploit the lands at all but instead to hold them in reserve.

The group brought reserve lands under cultivation to make up for the soils lost to salinization, floods, or changes in the river course. Imbedded in this tribal land tenure system were a "striking" number of individual rights that offered very secure tenure of property. For example, the tribe often distributed the cultivated areas in parcels; the sheikh received from one-sixth to one-half of the total and the members equal shares of the remainder. Individual holdings were not contiguous but frequently scattered throughout the tribal *lazma*. These (and other forms of) individual holdings could be sold, rented, inherited and mortgaged, so long as the transaction was within customary tribal law. (This *lazma* system continued unchanged on the lands that Abdülhamid II acquired.)

It quickly was noticed that many provisions of the 1858 code, notably the basic principle of individual land registration, directly conflicted with aspects of the *lazma* system. Also, the code required cultivation of land as a condition of its possession, while the *lazma* system encouraged the maintenance of uncultivated reserve lands. Moreover, there are clear indications that Ottoman officials unimaginatively sought to enforce the code without regard to its impact on local conditions.

Here in lower Iraq, as well as elsewhere, local practices and land–labor–capital ratios were more powerful molders of landholding patterns than the 1858 law. But the conflict between the two systems meant failure to implement the code and worse, major confusion in landholding itself. Tribes either were prevented from communally registering their lands or they avoided the land registry office. Consequently, usurpation of tribal land rights occurred on a perhaps unprecedented scale and large holdings became predominant in most of lower Iraq. Urban elites, Sultan Abdülhamid and others acquired legal title to lands that tribes felt to be theirs. Tribal leaders sometimes abused their position and, among these, the al-Sadun family is a remarkable example. The al-Sadun family of sheikhs ruled the Muntafik tribes probably since before the Ottoman conquest and had defended Ottoman Iraq against the Wahhabis. In the 1870s, representatives of the family began acquiring title deeds to vast tracts of Muntafik land, reportedly for a political objective, to buttress the power of their emirate. These efforts to solidify a local power base, however, clashed with Ottoman centralization. When İstanbul broke the family's military power in 1881, it fell back on the financial resources of the title deeds. Thus began the fragmentation of the Muntafik that led, during the mandate period, to land agglomeration in the hands of the al-Sadun's agents and to massive tribal landlessness.[72]

Foreign ownership was unimportant, despite the contemporary

consular attention lavished on European acquisition of Ottoman land. Foreigners had held land prior to the 1867 legislation that extended formal approval to the practice. Mehmed Ali, for example, encouraged foreign holdings during his control of Syria. While there is much discussion about the legal rights that the 1867 law may or may not have given,[73] the law had little practical effect. Foreign settlements were of consequence only in Palestine and even there formed a tiny percentage of the land and population. Western hopes of vast plantations with docile labor foundered on the reality of hostile Ottoman officials and scarce agricultural labor. The reportedly impressive British holdings around İzmir area at the mid-century never fulfilled their potential.[74] Foreigners did not have the same access to labor as Ottoman subjects nor could they compel tribes to the task. And, as the consuls tirelessly complained, the Ottoman courts opposed foreign landholders. Thus, foreign settlements were few and far between. One, at Amasya, seems to have thrived for 75 years before World War I, while a German-Jewish community established a colony along the Anatolian Railway very late in the period. But, generally, German plans for Anatolia to become a colonization field remained a fantasy.[75] Most of the relatively few resident foreigners lived in cities and towns. The Ottoman Empire never developed into a European colonial settler state.

THE QUESTION OF LARGE ESTATE FORMATION

As seen, large commercially run estates existed in all areas and in all parts of the period. Those serving domestic markets often were near the urban centers and thus could tolerate poor transport facilities. For example, in the 1850s, one Seyid Mehmet Salahaddin Agha, who began his career as a tax-farmer in Ankara, amassed a considerable estate, including entire villages, just one and one-quarter hours' horseback journey from the outskirts of the town.[76] Estates producing for the international export market, however, had to be near good transport. Thus, in the early period, commercial estates concentrated in areas within easy reach of sea transport; later on, railroads helped them to expand into interior regions.

But a variety of factors continuously retarded large estate formation. Low population densities and lack of labor certainly played a critical role. In the land along the Anatolian Railway, brought into cultivation by new market opportunities, small not large holdings predominated. Even here, labor shortages sometimes were so acute that the profitability of livestock raising surpassed that of crop growing.[77] The heritage of the *timar* system also was important in blocking large estate formation. In most areas where the *çift-hane* patterns had flourished, large holdings did not proliferate. Where the *timar* pattern never had been deep rooted, for instance in the Arab provinces, big farms were more likely to develop. The unwillingness of the central government to cooperate in the enserfment of cultivators also powerfully blunted tendencies towards large estate formation. Thanks to state action, the combination of scarce labor and abundant lands usually did not lead to debt peonage and enserfment. For example, when officials stationed in Bulgaria complained, in 1816, that *sipahis* were skimming off tithes at the expense of İstanbul, the central government broke the *sipahi* group. As seen, the importance of *çiftliks* in Ottoman Bulgaria actually declined at the very time when international demand for its grain mounted.[78]

Tax-farming rather than large estates probably brought most Ottoman produce onto the domestic and foreign market. Tax-farmers obtained produce from cultivators and directly sold it to export houses or merchant intermediaries. They (and merchants) also employed debt mechanisms to control peasants and extract the agricultural surplus. Their power over the cultivators probably increased after 1873. Much of the period between 1820 and 1873 had been favorable to cultivators as terms of trade improved. Such conditions had encouraged cultivators to buy more imported goods and gradually they became involved in market agriculture. This favorable period for primary producers ended abruptly with the onset of the 1873–96 price decline. Prices of primary goods fell faster than those of manufactured products and cultivator indebtedness probably mounted. The 1873–96 depression thus may have caused the anti-Armenian violence that occurred in the mid-1890s. As the price depression and indebtedness deepened during the 1870s and 1880s, Muslim peasants attacked Armenian money-lenders, violence that then spread to the Armenians in general.

To stem the mounting agrarian crisis, the government intervened with unprecedented agricultural development programs. State-sponsored efforts to enhance agriculture and assist peasants dated back to the 1830s Council for Agriculture and Industry and its reconstitution as the Council for Agriculture in 1843. These programs had included sending agronomists into the provinces and granting state loans worth 13 million piasters. Local notables, however, dominated the councils that distributed the funds and probably received most of these credits. In the late 1840s, the state tried but failed to establish an agricultural school. Subsequent programs to stimulate production often were few and shortlived, for example, the distribution of American cotton seeds during the U.S. Civil War.[79] State intervention in the rural economy increased in the 1870s and accelerated during the 1880s and 1890s. Several agricultural schools opened to train Ottoman subjects in the theory and practice of agriculture; some graduates then went on to staff model fields and farms founded in over half a dozen locations. There, they demonstrated improved seed types, modern tools and fertilizers, hoping to interest local cultivators.

More important, the state formed the Agricultural Bank (*Ziraat Bankası*) in 1888 to provide cultivator loans and help finance development programs. The bank can be traced back to the 1840s loan program and to Midhat Pasha's 1863 formation of agricultural cooperatives in the Danubian province. The Agricultural Bank, with some administrative modifications, generally followed this pattern. In the next several decades, its 400 offices offered 6 percent loans to over 800,000 cultivators in Anatolia alone. Equally important, two-thirds of its net profits financed the agricultural schools, the model farms and fields, the seed distribution programs and the experiments with improved machinery and tools. But local elites ran the provincial bank branches at the expense of smaller cultivators, while high state officials siphoned off profits for other purposes.[80]

The record of agrarian credit institutions similarly was mixed in the various Ottoman successor states. In Bulgaria, for example, there were 1,400 agricultural cooperatives in 1911, while Rumania contained some 3,000 similar cooperatives in 1913. In common with the Ottoman institution, the Bulgarian and Rumanian operations also offered too small loans and mainly served the more prosperous peasants.[81]

The flowering of these programs during the 1880s and early 1890s certainly can be understood as the maturation of an agrarian bureaucracy, a building upon earlier efforts. From this development perspective, the Ottoman state as capitalist acted at the worst possible time in the nineteenth century, seeking to raise revenues by fostering production during a period of falling prices. The programs take on an additional significance, however, when considered in the context of a social and political crisis that the state was trying to mitigate. In this view, the reforms can be seen as efforts to prevent smallholders from falling more fully under notable domination and preserve central government–cultivator relations, in common with some sections of the 1858 Land Law.

Following this quarter-century of falling prices, primary commodity prices increased sharply between 1896 and 1913, faster than those of manufactured products. This certainly was an era of prosperity for many cultivators. It also is the period when large estate formation increased in some regions. Some cultivators likely had succumbed to the indebtedness brought on by two decades of agricultural price declines. Thus, their lands became available for agglomeration and, willingly or not, they came to work on great estates as sharecroppers or wage laborers. The final Ottoman boom after 1896 thus benefited money-lenders as well as the mass of smallholders, although labor scarcity, land abundance and state concern about powerful landed notables continued to protect many small cultivators.

The market-oriented large estates of the nineteenth century generally form two distinct groups. The first consists of estates that emerged before the recentralization of Ottoman power, roughly before 1830. In the absence of effective countervailing pressure from İstanbul, market demand had encouraged large farms on the water routes to Europe. These estates were more common in the Balkan areas and remained quite rare in Anatolia before c. 1850.[82] Although central impotence gave way to power, many of these large Balkan holdings survived into the Tanzimat era. In certain districts of Macedonia through the 1870s, *çiftlik* villages still constituted a one-half to two-thirds majority. Around Salonica, 42 percent of all villages were attached to big farms. Similarly, in Thessaly, *çiftliks* formed at least one-half of all arable land.[83] Overall, it seems, an increase in sharecropping accompanied the formation of such estates to provide the necessary labor. In Anatolia, by contrast, the central state successfully confiscated most of the large holdings that had accumulated in the era of decentralization.[84] The apparent absence of confiscation in the Balkan provinces may be due to concerns that it would disturb relations between the Christian cultivators and Muslim landholders.

The second group of large estates consists of those formed in the later nineteenth century, at the apex of central state power. These primarily were founded in the northern Arab provinces and in adjacent areas of southeastern Anatolia. The key to understanding this second group of estates lies in the pacification and sedentarization of tribal groups. Large estate formation in Syria, Iraq and southeast Anatolia primarily derived from tribal settlement and the opening of new lands to cultivation.

Contemporary (European) sources often explained late-century estate formation as a function of dispossession. On examination, this dispossession most frequently was not of settled agriculturalists who were being driven from their land or enserfed. The takeover of settled villages (e.g., at the hands of the Azms and Sursuqs) certainly did occur but probably took place earlier in the century. From c. 1850, peasant insurrections (see below) and the central government helped to block the lords and preserve smallholders' claims. In this later period, dispossession usually involved nomads who had lost their customary rights to land. In the eyes of the state, tribal holdings often were waste (*mevat*) lands that, because of insecurity, had not been cultivated regularly. During the second half of the century, however, tribal pacification brought improved security, as domestic and foreign demand mounted. Entrepreneurs now entered these all but empty lands in safety to develop agriculture. Unable to coerce enough villagers, they instead obtained some surplus peasant labor through wage and sharecropping arrangements. Thus, some peasants used the opportunity to gain additional income and preserve their own holdings during the difficult times of the price depression. The notables also used the labor of sedentarizing tribesmen. Over them, probably, they established greater social and economic control.[85] Thus, the later estate formation took place on newly tilled land, used mainly tribal labor and was not based on the exploitation of the existing peasantry.

Dispossession of tribes, however, was not always a foregone conclusion. During the 1880s, for example, in the Middle Euphrates region of Iraq, there is an example of a tribe that refused to pay taxes. As punishment, the state then sold the tribe's land to a notable. Government troops sought to push out the tribe but it kept returning; in the end, the notable did not gain control of the land.[86]

The dispossession of tribes was more common than peasant expropriation because reclamation of former waste lands and the use of tribal labor presented fewer social costs than coercing existing village communities. This solution was possible in the first place because the state had pacified the tribes and provided the security. The government also preferred tribal to villager exploitation since it preserved existing village taxpaying communities, the financial backbone of the empire, while bringing additional lands into cultivation and onto the tax rolls. The cultivation of new lands accelerated late in the century because of two additional factors. Railroad construction in Syria, Iraq and Anatolia during the 1890s substantially increased sedentarization pressures and cost the tribes considerable freedom of movement.[87] And, simultaneously, the upswing in agricultural prices after 1896 vastly enhanced profitability in agriculture. Thus, many more tribal members than ever before became available precisely at a time of rising profit margins.[88] It may well be that the creation of large estates in the Arab lands became important only in the very late nineteenth and early twentieth centuries.

Similar kinds of processes brought the Çukurova plain of southeast Anatolia/northwest Syria into cultivation. Beginning in the late 1860s, Cevdet Pasha's Reform Division broke the tribes that had dominated the region. Private entrepreneurs then brought the vacant lands of this plain into cultivation. Thanks to its great expanses, emptiness and proximity to the sea, entrepreneurs employed an otherwise-rare combination of vast estates, sophisticated machinery and masses of wage laborers. These workers came for seasonal labor, taking advantage of the differing crop cycles of the Anatolian plateau and the coastal plains. Great imperial estates emerged here too, as they had on the Syrian and Iraqi vacant lands.

RURAL UNREST

Natural, economic and political forces all shaped the pattern and frequency of rural unrest in the nineteenth century. Droughts, famines, or locust infestations, a familiar part of life for most of the period, often caused bread rioting but usually not sustained violence or rebellion. The growing commodification of agriculture certainly was important, bringing increasing responsiveness to market conditions and changes in the business cycle. Thus, it is no surprise to find the international financial crisis of the mid-1890s mirrored in rural violence within Ottoman borders. Shifting demand for Ottoman crops, such as the bust in cotton exports after 1865 or the post-1900 boom in tobacco exports, also must have affected the level and frequency of unrest in the countryside. Similarly influential were the changing terms of trade: between 1820 and 1873, for example, these favored cultivators but then worsened before turning around again after 1896.

State policy often aggravated conditions in the countryside. When it settled immigrants, the state inadvertently challenged the position of established villagers in areas as widely scattered as Ottoman Bulgaria, the Black Sea coast of Anatolia and southern Syria. The Land Law of 1858 had destabilizing effects, for example, dispossessing smallholders in some regions. Tribal pacification policies that otherwise benefited the body politic and the economy could bring the settling tribes into conflict with village communities – a notable example being the Kurdish settlement in eastern Anatolia. Overall, state policy, often in the form of the centralization of power, exercised a decisive impact on the timing, frequency and intensity of rural unrest in the nineteenth century.

During the nineteenth century, the state began to encroach upon life in the countryside in a manner hardly seen, if ever, during the long centuries of the Ottoman imperium. This encroachment was part of the larger Tanzimat program of centralization and westernization in which the central state intervened against the autonomy of local notables and sought to regain control over the land, the peasants and their surplus. Hoping to increase aggregate revenues, İstanbul ordered that everyone pay the same agricultural tax rate. In some respects, these reform programs ironically accelerated the pace of Ottoman destruction. For they tore at the loyalty of its long-privileged Muslim subjects while straining relations between Ottoman Muslims and Christians. Vast waves of rural (and urban) unrest were unleashed, shaking the state to its very foundation and recasting whole provinces as independent states.

These great cycles of rebellion and destruction hardly were unique examples of nineteenth-century rural discontent in the Ottoman Empire. Protest indeed was a non-exceptional part of everyday Ottoman life. Nonetheless, it often has escaped the notice of historians because they mainly were examining imperial institutions, reform programs and westernizers. It also is because the protest was located in the largely illiterate countryside, distant from governmental and other record keepers. Examples occasionally do appear in the written record. In 1880, central Anatolian villagers murdered several government officials seeking to collect arrears in taxes while further west in the same area, other peasants resisted administrators seeking to transfer grain from their famine-stricken village.[89] Official attention came usually only when unrest became very large, widespread or violent, or caused substantial declines in state revenues. Most protest was neither violent nor widespread and so it has remained largely invisible and undocumented.

Peasant avoidance certainly was the most common form of protest, a refusal, sometimes ending in flight, to perform duties or pay taxes or enter the military. But, unless very large numbers were involved, such as the mass movement of Christian peasants from the Ottoman Bulgarian provinces to independent Serbia in the mid-nineteenth century, this avoidance remained unrecorded. Other forms of protest included the actions of social bandits who often articulated the grievances of villagers and/or nomads. There also were frequent open insurrections against state and rural elites, both by peasants and by tribes. Inter-sectarian violence, when Ottoman cultivators fought with one another instead of against the rulers, sometimes was a degeneration of social banditry or insurrection that had begun as anti-elite protest.

There seem to have been three clusters of rural unrest that were particularly widespread and violent. The first covers the years from 1839 until about the mid-1860s, characterized by resistance to the Tanzimat reforms. These rebellions were, quite probably, the greatest of the nineteenth century. In the Balkan areas, they mutated into nationalist revolutions. In the Arab provinces, there were important uprisings around Aleppo, Damascus and in the Hawran, and particularly the Kisrawan rising of 1858–61, that also derived from the Land Law of 1858. The next cluster of violence was directed against the Armenians in eastern Anatolia. Beginning in the 1890s and reaching its climax two decades later, in 1915–16, this violence owed much to the settlement of the Kurds and to Tanzimat promises of equality. The third cluster includes the growing disorders in the Balkan, Arab and Anatolian rural areas during the years immediately before the Young Turk Revolution.

Between c. 1863 and the early 1890s, rural rebellions probably were less widespread than they had been before or would be later on. The notable exception is in Bulgaria where violence reached new heights in 1875–76, just before its final break from Ottoman control. It seems unlikely that the overall decline in rural violence is only apparent, due to reporting flaws. If anything, the sources for the late nineteenth century are incomparably richer than for the earlier part of the period. Instead, the quiescence derived from several factors. Much unrest had been in the Balkan areas that, by the mid-1860s, had won *de facto* independence. Macedonia, where rebellions continued into the twentieth century, is an exception.[90] In the Arab and Anatolian areas, the decrease in social unrest between the 1860s and early 1890s remains somewhat of a mystery, at least to this writer. Increasing central control and taxation had been in effect for over three decades and had become institutionalized. More concretely, the military power of the central state was vastly greater than it had been. The regular army consisted of not more than 24,000 soldiers in 1837; their number soon had risen to perhaps 120,000 regular troops and came to be supported by the telegraph and, in some areas, by railroads as well.[91] Thus, the peasants had become accustomed to taxes that evolved from being a novel to a normal part of the rural landscape; and, in any event, they were less able to resist. The case of the notables is slightly different. In the face of Tanzimat policies, the latter almost everywhere lost direct control over the land, some revenues and, to boot, their tax-exempt status. But they retained considerable local prominence, power and wealth, attributes that were powerful disincentives to rebellion. Toward the end of the century, however, many notables resisted

Abdülhamid's regime because their position had been deteriorating in the face of increasingly effective central rule and because the Public Debt Administration had weakened their fiscal hold as tax-farmers.

Among the insurrections arising from implementation of the Tanzimat, the Bulgarian peasant rebellions are the best known. Their origins are well documented and arise directly out of the 1839 Reform decree. The land regime in the Vidin area combined pre-Ottoman practices with a distorted version of the *timar* system. In a turn of events almost unique in Ottoman history, Muslim lords, descendants of *sipahi*s, and urban notables became the true owners of state land during the eighteenth century, when they also seized control of the local administration.[92] In return for a cash payment to a strapped central treasury, these groups emerged as a class of great landlords and took over "all" state lands. The lords were Muslim because the lands earlier had been classified as frontier territories. By customary practice predating the Ottoman arrival, the *sipahi*s collected certain extra dues and taxes not demanded in most other provinces, such as one or two months' sowing labor, a cart of wood, or a cartload of corn. Indeed, the peasants owed as much or more to the lord than to the state. When the 1839 decree abolished compulsory services, peasants in the Vidin region quickly tried to refuse to perform them any more. When called in to decide, the state straddled the fence. Like the Czar's emancipation of the serfs, the sultan's decree attempted to reconcile the irreconcilable, seeking to abolish the services due but without harming the landowners. As a result, landholders generally had their way and, the reform regulations notwithstanding, services and feudal-like dues continued.

Confusion and disorder in the land system was the underlying cause of the 1850 revolt that erupted in Vidin. In the intervening ten years since proclamation of the Tanzimat, İstanbul had stabilized peasants' possession of state lands by increasing the number of family members who could inherit. The lords, for their part, continued to take dues and services by force. They dominated the local councils and thwarted the actions of the governor sent to control them. Peasants demanded abolition of the lords' rule and, apparently, title deeds granting them direct ownership of the land. The governor of Vidin concurred. But the authorities in İstanbul required a three-step procedure: continuation of state ownership of the land; abolition of certain obligations to the lords which it deemed illegal; and retention of other obligations that cultivators would render for life, partly to the lords and partly to the central treasury. This plan flew in the face of peasants' expectations since they intended to keep the lords' former revenues and pay nothing either to the government or the lords. The state vacillated but finally, in 1851, decided to sell the lords' lands to the peasants. But it was too late. The peasants by now were seeking to obtain the land without compensation. These discontents then meshed with mounting Bulgarian nationalism and culminated in the great revolt of 1875–76 that brought effective Bulgarian independence.[93]

A parallel set of events occurred further west in the Balkans, in Bosnia and Herzegovina. There, as in Bulgaria, a three-way struggle pitted Muslim notables interested in retaining tax revenues against the state, while Christian peasants sought to take over the land that the notables held. Unrest began immediately after proclamation of the Gülhane decree. The notables orchestrated the first rebellions against the centralizing state but, later on, peasants rose against the lords. In 1858–59, long-established feudal families manipulated the peasants into revolting and prevented imposition of Ottoman central control. With the help of the peasants, these families opposed the Tanzimat reforms and retained their *timar*s or, where they had been converted, their tax-farms. The lords thus kept the majority of the surplus and dominated both Muslim and Christian peasants, despite strong state efforts in the early 1860s to break their power. Over time, however, the programs of the central government weakened the notables. In 1874–75, Herzegovinian Christian peasants rose against Muslim landowners in a number of villages where tax-farmers had been trying to collect taxes during a time of bad harvest. The rebellion then spread all over Bosnia and Herzegovina. The Great Powers became involved and the rebellions ended in the elimination of Ottoman authority, similar to the process that brought about the loss of Bulgaria.[94]

Widespread unrest in Anatolia seems to have been relatively unusual. Perhaps this is due to the manifest disinterest of most historians. More likely, it derives from the moral economy of the Anatolian peasantry that itself was tied to the continuing dominance of small family holdings in the region. This is not to say that Anatolia was devoid of unrest since its rural history was one of incessant active and passive protest. What seems different about Anatolia is that the protests there were small-scale in nature.

Implementation of the Tanzimat reforms there brought immediate and varying forms of resistance. Sometimes the sumptuary aspects of the new state policies were opposed passively: in the small town of Bergama, for example, most of the people ignored the example of the westernizing bureaucracy who adopted the fez and continued to wear their turbans and conical hats. Against the new fiscal measures, the protests could be more active: in 1841, for example, a low-ranking member of the ulema in Adapazarı called on the populace not to pay the new, higher, imposts since they already were unable to pay their present taxes. At the same time, notables at Yalvaç, who themselves were subject to heavier taxes under the new policies, sought to gain allies and urged the populace at large to resist the new levies. A notable in the Bala area south of Ankara understood that the Tanzimat's removal of tax exemptions meant taxes on large state properties in his possession. And so he incited a tax revolt among some 400 villagers. When arrested, he complained that, although his taxes had increased sharply, those of poor villagers had more than doubled.[95] During the early part of Sultan Mahmud II's reign, social bandits had been common, often the unpaid military forces responsible for maintaining order. By the 1830s, thanks to the reimposition of central authority and the rise of the larger, salaried military force, many had vanished from western and central Anatolia.[96] But social banditry persisted throughout the period, sometimes focusing on foreign travellers with the connivance of local cultivators and authorities.

Tribal unrest, for its part, faded as the century progressed and had ceased to be an important factor in most areas by the 1870s. But, in the Armenian massacres of the 1890s, several factors seem to have been at work. The power of the Kurdish beys over their tribes was fading just as Tanzimat pledges of equality and an awakening nationalism caused some Armenian villagers to become increasingly assertive. The famous Sasun massacre, for example, occurred when the local Armenians refused to continue yielding to the extortionary demands of nearby Kurdish chieftains. Their authority over both the villagers and the tribesmen threatened, the chiefs used massive force. Using a variety of appeals that may have included a shared ethnicity as well as economic advantage, the chiefs mobilized the tribesmen against the peasants and thus kept themselves in control.

The Muslim refugees' encroachment on common lands also contributed to disorders all over Anatolia. In the 1870s, for example, considerable friction existed between newly arrived settlers and established villagers in the coastal areas around Black Sea Samsun. The worst, however, probably was over by the early 1880s.[97] Factory burnings also are an integral part of the social history of nineteenth-century Anatolia, although these protests remained specifically focused on particular establishments and never developed into a Luddite-like protest against factory *qua* factory. There were factory sackings at Bursa in the 1860s, Bergama in the 1880s and Uşak in 1908, to name but a few.[98] Crop cycles, by themselves, were not catalysts of major protest. The terrible killing famine of 1873–74 provoked only a few bread riots in various regions. Later, however, a broader series of bread riots accompanied crop failures and shortfalls in 1906–8. For example, in June 1908, Sivas-area villagers marched into the town, joined the urban discontented and together sacked local granaries. The response at nearby Kayseri was more pacific as 12,000 gathered and prayed for rain.[99] At Erzurum, however, fears about food shortages combined with an ongoing taxpayers' protest over increased poll and animal taxes. The revolt, that joined rural and urban dissidents, persisted until the 1908 Young Turk Revolution. These protests occurred in the context of failing or threatened crops. But the crop conditions themselves do not appear to have been as critical as the cadre of revolutionaries who mobilized, organized and articulated the discontents. That is, peasant discontent was a constant, but usually required some outside variable to erupt in open revolt or insurrection. These last demonstrations eloquently expressed the weakened legitimacy of the state and helped pave the way for the Young Turk seizure of power.[100]

In the Arab provinces, rural unrest erupted with considerable frequency until the 1860s. In 1834, for example, the fellah of Palestine rebelled against the conscription of Muslims into Mehmed Ali's army, against forced labor and against the *ferde*, a levy like the poll-tax previously reserved for Christians that he imposed on Muslims. Lebanon had four or five rural uprisings between 1820 and 1861. Among these were 1840 revolts in Mount Lebanon, Alawi risings during the 1850s and Druze insurrections in the Hawran in the late 1870s. Many revolts fought primarily against remnants of the old agrarian regime and against the increasing fiscal pressures of the centralizing state: for example, numerous insurrections in Palestine and Syria between 1852 and 1866. Peasant rebellions in the Fertile Crescent were most common in remote districts where villages usually were more prosperous than on the plain or near important cities. In many mountainous districts, the local lords, who usually were the tax-farmers, led peasant revolts against the centralizing efforts of the state. In this case, the protests were like the early ones in Bosnia and Herzegovina, from c. 1839 to the 1860s. But, in other instances, peasants rebelled against local lords or intermediate tax-farmers who had been weakened by the intrusion of central power.[101]

Perhaps the best documented example is the 1858–61 revolt of the Maronite peasants of Kisrawan against their Maronite overlords. In Kisrawan, after the Emir Bashir II had removed the tax-farmers' judicial authority, Mehmed Ali and then the Ottomans further weakened the power of the Khazin family of Maronite sheikhs. The revolt began as some prosperous cultivators connected to the Beirut silk trade sought more land to grow mulberries and meet the demand for cocoons. The Khazin overlords, however, refused to alienate land and thus blocked this expanding peasant group. Khazin power had weakened substantially but, increasingly strapped for money, they demanded all kinds of feudal presents. Still worse from their perspective, massive quantities of European-made arms recently had flooded into peasants' hands. When the revolt erupted, its leaders appealed to the call of the *Hatt-ı Hümayun* for universal equality.[102] The rebellion was a great success for the peasants since, by its end, the Khazins had lost much of their land. In addition, the state abolished feudal privileges and proclaimed equality before the law. Unlike the Kurdish chiefs in facing opposition from the state and their own followers, the Khazin lords had not maintained military superiority and lost the day.[103]

The Kisrawan demands for changes in traditional lord–peasant relations closely paralleled those of the Vidin peasants during the 1850s and their efforts to gain full control over the land. They also are echoed by the Druze peasants' actions in the Hawran during 1889–90. These rebelled against their Atrash lords as the Ottoman state sought to subdue the district. As in the Kisrawan, the Druze rebellion here ended feudalism and extended new relations of production.[104]

Generally, the peak of open unrest occurred between the 1840s and the mid-1860s. Much of the discontent can be traced to government fiats. The imposition of the Tanzimat reforms meant a changed agrarian order, with greater central control of land and of the surplus, and higher taxes for the peasantry. The notables continued to hang on with considerable success, using their memberships in local councils and other bodies to maintain their influence and power over the peasantry. Extreme confusion reigned in the countryside, everywhere in the empire, since the state had declared the new, but could not fully eliminate the old, order.[105] As in the Vidin case and that of the Kurdish beys, it may have been unwilling to do so. Tax increases angered peasants as well as notables. Responding to conscription laws, Muslims abandoned villages in the first decades of the reform era just as Ottoman Christians fled the empire after 1908. The expansion of sharecropping, for its part, took place when taxes on peasants were increasing faster than agricultural productivity. And so, the peasants demanded that landlordism be abolished and rebelled against a state that was not willing to sacrifice the estate owners. In the Vidin region, the fact that peasants were Christians and the owners were Muslims gave the social conflict a religious and finally a national dimension.[106] Social conflict indeed played a vital role in many of the nineteenth-century nationalist movements. Peasants hoped to gain from the reform legislation and resented state efforts to acquire notable lands that they coveted. Thus, *çiftliks* undermined Ottoman control of the Balkans.[107] The social struggle between the Kurds and Armenians also took on a religious dimension that incompletely evolved into a national struggle. But in this last example, tendencies toward land agglomeration and market agriculture do not seem to have played a catalytic role.

Lebanon and the Bulgarian lands each were important seats of insurrection. Each possessed unusually high population densities and a strong commitment to commercial agriculture, but it is not clear if their feudal-like relations were stronger than elsewhere. The relative lack of risings in Anatolia, as seen, probably is not due simply to an absence of research. Central state control in Anatolia, both civil and military, was greater than in Bulgaria and Lebanon and this surely helped to minimize open rebellion. Other factors were present, such as the prevalence of small peasant family farms and comparatively lower growth rates and levels of agricultural commercialization after 1850. The relative lack of open insurrection hardly suggests the absence of serious discontents or oppression. Peasants employed avoidance to cope with crisis or difficulties. In Anatolia as in many cultures, open revolt remained the exceptional method of expressing rural discontent.

NOTES

1 Pamuk (1987).
2 See, for example, Shields (1986).
3 Quataert (1973); various *vilayet salnameleri*; Cuinet (1890–94); Eldem (1970), p. 272; and Pamuk (1987), p. 85; convenient table in Verney and Dambmann (1900), p. 480; Issawi (1988), pp. 271–73.
4 The slippage between the 1850s and the late nineteenth century surely is only apparent. Shaw (1975), pp. 451–52; Eldem (1970), pp. 267ff; Ubicini (1856), I, p. 266.
5 Lampe and Jackson (1982), p. 150; Turkey (1938), appendix, n.p.
6 Cuinet (1890–94), III, p. 84; *ibid.*, II, p. 805; Batatu (1978), p. 96; Quataert (1973), p. 347.
7 Eldem (1970), pp. 78, 86–87.
8 Pamuk (1987), p. 83. Eldem (1970), p. 283; on p. 81 he offers different statistics that show a nearly identical regional distribution of empire-wide

agricultural production: Rumeli with 24 percent in 1910 and 3 percent in 1913; Syria with 8 percent in 1910, Iraq with 6 percent, Anatolia with 54 percent and the Hejaz with 3 percent.

9 Issawi (1982), p. 133. Unfortunately, the accuracy of an official agricultural survey in the early twentieth century is not assured since its figures are higher, by a factor of three, than other contemporary estimates. Turkey (1327b/1909) and Quataert (1981).

10 Quataert (1973) and Eldem (1970), p. 77.

11 Lewis (1987), pp. 41, 55, 98; Owen (1981) p. 259; Issawi (1988), pp. 128–33.

12 Quataert (1981), p. 80.

13 Pamuk (1987), p. 85.

14 Compare Pamuk (1987), p. 83 and Eldem (1970), p. 71.

15 Owen (1981), p. 29; Puryear (1935), pp. 292ff; Lampe and Jackson (1982), p. 138 who state that the export increase took place in the context of declining *çiftlik* production. See below in landholding section.

16 Owen (1981), p. 279; Quataert (1973) and (1977); Issawi (1988), pp. 272–73.

17 Quataert (1973); Owen (1981), pp. 182–83; Issawi (1988), pp. 279–81.

18 Owen (1981), pp. 30, 249; Quataert (1983), pp. 481–503; Issawi (1988), pp. 275–78.

19 Quataert (1973), p. 333; Lampe and Jackson (1982), p. 346; Issawi (1988), p. 278. Ger *BuHI*, 5 Dezember 1912, Bd. XVIII, Heft 7, is an excellent report on tobacco production and manufacture in the European provinces.

20 İnalcık (1982).

21 Issawi (1982), p. 131; Issawi (1988), pp. 283–84, 353–59. See Owen (1981), pp. 186–88 for struggles among various groups for water resources. Also see Suleiman Sırrı Bey (1924), pp. 265–79.

22 Lampe and Jackson (1982), pp. 184–85.

23 Quataert (1973); Issawi (1982), p. 31.

24 Quataert (1973), pp. 186ff; Issawi (1980), 214.

25 Kasaba (1988b); Issawi (1988), pp. 284–85.

26 Berend and Ránki (1974), p. 38; Lampe and Jackson (1982), p. 135; Issawi (1980), pp. 202, 220–24.

27 İnalcık (1973), p. 20.

28 Turkey (1327a/1909), pp. 80–81; Quataert (1973), p. 27; Baer (1983), p. 262; Jwaideh (1984), pp. 340–41.

29 Mordtmann (1925) consists of a series of reports, during the decades of the 1850s, from scores of Anatolian locations. When the author met the local administrative officials, he frequently made note of the fact that they were former *derebeys* or their children. See, for example, pp. 109, 113–16, 206, 246 and 482. Also, Şerif (1325/1907).

30 İnalcık (1973); Arıcanlı (n.d.), pp. 25–26.

31 Ziya Pasha, *Arzıhâl* (İstanbul, 1372 sic), cited in İnalcık (1973), p. 16.

32 e.g. GB FO 78/1396, Guarraino at Samsun, 4 October 1851. See below for the revolts this triggered.

33 Quataert (1973).

34 Aktan (1950) and in Issawi (1966).

35 Arıcanlı (1976). Even if the Debt Administration hired these notables as its

agents, a presently unresearched topic, their gross income certainly would have declined.

36 Sources cited in Quataert (1979), nn. 22–23 and Quataert (1986a). The difference between the taxes reported to the treasury by the Debt Administration and earlier by the tax farmers, in a crude way, approximates the surplus formerly skimmed off by the notables.

37 Sources cited in Quataert (1973), pp. 36–48. In this discussion, the focus is on state land, that formed the vast bulk of all land in the empire.

38 The practice can be seen as a vestige of the *timar* system in which the *sipahi* extracted the tithe before sharing. Halil İnalcık, private correspondence, 15 May 1988.

39 *Ibid.* İnalcık states that "the code followed in the main [the] rules of the *miri* regime as applied in the classical period."

40 Jwaideh, e.g. (1984).

41 Touma (1958), p. 23.

42 Reilly (1987); Al-Sa'di (1989).

43 Rafeq (1984).

44 Gerber (1987), p. 77.

45 Reilly (1987).

46 Gerber (1987), pp. 67–90; McGowan (1981); Sluglett and Farouk-Sluglett (1984); Issawi (1988), p. 286, sees the law as the cause of land agglomeration.

47 Gould (1973); Hütteroth (1974) gives much credit to the 1858 Land Law, pointing to the security of property that it established.

48 Lewis (1987); Owen (1981), pp. 254–55.

49 Owen (1981), pp. 174–75, 270, 273, 284.

50 Buheiry (1984), p. 294.

51 Pamuk (1987), tables on pp. 92, 94, 96.

52 In part this is due to the larger number of Turkish scholars researching these topics and to the research of Albertine Jwaideh on Iraq. Roger Owen says that the Syrian land records were lost in World War I; but it is possible that copies exist in the Tapu ve Kadastro Müdürlüğü Archives in Ankara. A note on land prices: during the period of the first land registration, carried out between 1840 and 1859, land values rose 75 percent. Thereafter, the data are very sparse. Average land values were 70 piasters in 1859 and 76 piasters in 1910, but we know nothing about fluctuations in between. Eldem (1970), p. 70.

53 Kasaba (1985), p. 229.

54 *Ibid.*, quoting Pamuk (1987), p. 88, who is citing the British consul Palgrave's conclusion that 70 percent of all cultivated land was *mülk*. This statement is incorrect.

55 Turkey (1327b); Nickoley (1924), p. 295; Kasaba (1985), p. 229; Issawi (1982), pp. 146–47, argues that the 1858 Land Law played a decisive role in the predominance of smallholdings.

56 Eldem (1970), p. 70; Lampe and Jackson (1982), pp. 196, 135; Draganova (1988).

57 Lampe and Jackson (1982), pp. 135, 137.

58 *Ibid.*, pp. 184–85.

59 *Ibid.*, p. 85.

60 Lampe and Jackson (1982), p. 92; also see Berend and Ránki (1974), pp. 35–37.

61 The Rumanian author Michael Eminescu, quoted in Stavrianos (1958), p. 344.

62 Gerber (1987), pp. 147–48 and Owen (181), p. 256. Al-Sa'di (1989).

63 Bowring (1840); Naff (1972), pp. 546–47.

64 Sluglett and Farouk-Sluglett (1984); İnalcık (1973), p. 414; Vatter (c. 1987).

65 Owen (1981), p. 255; Issawi (1988), pp. 286ff, 331.

66 For example, Owen, pp. 267–68.

67 Owen (1981), p. 255; Lewis (1987), see map on p. 16 and also pp. 53–54; Hütteroth (1974), p. 20; Issawi (1988), p. 286.

68 Gerber (1987), p. 97.

69 Rafeq (1984), p. 374.

70 Here, I am parting company with Gerber (1987), pp. 99–100, who suggests that large estate formation was the dominant trend of the latter part of the century.

71 Jwaideh (1965); Owen (1981), pp. 280–81; only a small proportion of these estates were exploited directly by the *Daire-i Seniye*. Lewis (1987), pp. 53–54; Issawi (1988), pp. 288–90.

72 Jwaideh (1984); also see Batatu (1978), pp. 53–88, for a different view. Gerber (1987), pp. 73–75; Issawi (1988), pp. 363, 366.

73 For example, du Velay (1903).

74 The conclusion of Kurmuş (1974), pp. 105–6, that the British held over 200,000 hectares in Anatolia, is based on very shaky statistical calculations and probably is a gross over-estimate.

75 Quataert (1973); Arıcanlı (n. d.), p. 21.

76 Mordtmann (1925) p. 529.

77 Şerif (1325/1907), pp. 149–54.

78 İnalcık (1983); Owen (1981), p. 274.

79 Güran (1980).

80 Quataert (1973), pp. 129–54.

81 Lampe and Jackson (1982), pp. 194 and 199.

82 Kasaba (1985), p. 233.

83 Lampe and Jackson (1982), p. 135; Faroqhi (1987), p. 32.

84 Kasaba (1985), p. 234. The subsequent fate of these holdings is a subject requiring additional research.

85 Lewis (1987), e.g. pp. 49–52.

86 İnalcık (1983); Hütteroth (1974); Owen (1981), pp. 282.

87 See Ch. 32. Caravan business certainly declined in some areas and gained in others; thus the railroads respectively depleted or increased the incomes of tribes.

88 Arıcanlı (n.d.), p. 34.

89 Halil İnalcık helped to clarify this discussion and my thanks to Fatoş Kaba of the SUNY Binghamton Anthropology Department for these references, drawn from the Great Britain Foreign Office, reports.

90 Adanır (1984–85), however, does not believe that socio-economic factors

were the cause of the Macedonian rebellions.

91 Engelhardt (1882), p. 89; (1884), pp. 281–82.
92 Meriwether (1987), pp. 55–73.
93 İnalcık (1943, 1973).
94 See sources cited in Shaw and Shaw (1977), II, pp. 149–60.
95 İnalcık (1973) and Bayatlı (1957), p. 7.
96 Çadırcı (1980); Uluçay (1955).
97 GB, FO, reports.
98 Quataert (1986a), pp. 473–89; and Bayatlı (1957), p. 7.
99 Quataert (1979, 1986a).
100 *Ibid.*
101 Baer (1982), pp. 253–323. Buheiry (1984), p. 299; Burke (1986a) pp. 27–32.
102 Buheiry (1984), p. 299.
103 Account based on Baer (1982). See Article 6 of the 1861 "Regulation for the Administration of Lebanon" in Hurewitz (1975), pp. 347–49.
104 Burke (1986a, 1986b). In an otherwise very useful analysis, Baer overly stresses the uniqueness of the Kisrawan affair. "Only once in Middle Eastern history did poor and wealthy peasants revolt together against a feudal aristocracy." Baer (1982), p. 294. Here, Baer is excluding the Anatolian and Balkan areas of the Ottoman Empire from his Middle East.
105 See, for example, the 1850s reports in Mordtmann (1925), e.g. pp. 116 and 139; İnalcık (1943, 1973).
106 İnalcık (1973).
107 Faroqhi (1987), pp. 32–33, discussing the research of Stoianovich and İnalcık. As mentioned above, Adanır (1984–85) holds a dissenting view with regard to the causes of the Macedonian risings.

34

MANUFACTURING

In the literature on Ottoman manufacturing, the story of Ambelakia in Thessaly long symbolized the plight of Middle East industry during the age of the European Industrial Revolution. The town's industry had enjoyed a vigorous prosperity thanks to substantial exports of red yarn. Its population tripled in the final two decades of the eighteenth century as local factories strained to meet booming European demand. Ambelakia merchants founded commercial houses in Buda, Vienna, Leipzig, Dresden and Bayreuth, as well as Salonica, İzmir and İstanbul. By 1800, they were selling over 6,000 hundredweights of the yarn. Two decades later, however, the town stood deserted. The industry had "been out-stripped by Manchester" and collapsed because of "the revolution in commerce that English cotton yarn was beginning to effect."[1]

From this narrative, we are intended to understand that the relationship between the European and Ottoman manufacturing sectors was that of efficient producer taking over the markets of a hapless competitor. Once set, the relationship continued along a linear path: Ottoman manufacturing steadily deteriorated, becoming ever-weaker and less competitive over time. The story is one of remorseless collapse. By implication, the Ottoman manufacturing sector is seen as irrelevant by c. 1850.

The details of the Ambelakia story are not inaccurate. But the conclusions drawn are misleading. The history of nineteenth-century Ottoman manufacturing is more complex and fascinating than this account suggests. A tide of European manufactured goods did flood Mid Eastern markets and cause severe dislocations, destroying many thousands of jobs. It is true that the thriving industry of Ambelakia vanished and that production of other Ottoman manufactures declined sharply. But these examples are not the whole story of Ottoman manufacturing; they are only part of its beginning chapter.

The European impact was most devastating in its initial phase, when local producers were bewildered by the sudden influx of imported manufactures and the taste changes they often represented. Most Ottoman and foreign observers have focused on these first moments of the encounter between the two industrial sectors. There is another story, however, that of Ottoman industry after the initial shockwave, when many manufacturers restructured their industries and survived. Vigorous and ongoing adaptation to changing conditions, not collapse, is the main characteristic of nineteenth-century Ottoman manufacturing. Output in some sectors in fact reached record-high levels in the early twentieth century. These examples of dynamism and of growth, however, have been overlooked in the literature because their success ran contrary to the value systems concerning the fate of Ottoman industry that prevailed among European observers and the Westernizing Ottoman elite. Contemporaries believed that industry as properly understood existed in factory settings possessing machinery and a vast proletarianized work force. Other forms of industrial organization were invisible, archaic, backward and unworthy of mention. Since there were few big, mechanized Ottoman factories, by definition there was no industry in the Middle East. Ottoman manufacturing thus failed the litmus test of modernity because it lacked the acceptable forms of industrial organization. It was easier to support the argument of remorseless decline with selected examples from specific points in time than to wrestle with issues of dynamic adjustment and change.

From the perspective of manufacturing, the period roughly divides into three parts: c. 1800–26, 1826–70 and 1870–1914. In the first era, export of Ottoman industrial products already was dwindling. As the Napoleonic wars ended and political stability returned, British manufactures rose and were imported into the eastern Mediterranean in increasing quantities. Between 1826 and 1870, the destruction of Ottoman industries was at its greatest, particularly in textile manufacturing; but even then new Ottoman industries were being born. Subsequently, until 1914, manufacturing output in many sectors expanded relatively and absolutely both for the domestic and export markets.

The growth in some industries serving Ottoman buyers occurred as manufacturers learned to make the new styles and fashions, often aided by new and simple technologies imported from Europe. Ottoman textile makers, for example, became more familiar with synthetic dyestuffs. They increasingly imported plain yarns and cloth and had them dyed locally, taking advantage of dyers' labor that cost some 55–60 percent less than in Europe.

On top of enhanced production for domestic sales, there were several emerging industries devoted to the international export market, particularly carpet and lace making and silk reeling. Carpet making for export, long-familiar in the Ottoman lands, reached unprecedented heights late in the century while lace making for Western consumers was a new activity. Export-oriented silk reeling, for its part, had emerged in the darkest days of Ottoman industry during the 1840s and 1850s. The presence of these export industries but not their importance generally has been acknowledged in Ottoman economic literature. Did they compensate for vanished manufactured exports, such as, we will see, mohair textiles from Ankara? Aggregate measurement of Ottoman manufacturing c. 1800 and 1914 is difficult. The value of exported manufactures in the early twentieth century probably exceeded that in 1780 or 1800; but it is uncertain if the proportion of exports in the manufacturing sector had risen or fallen. Similarly, the gross volume of early twentieth-century manufacturing for the domestic market may well have surpassed that of 1800. That is, the present chapter argues that we need to more carefully consider our assumptions regarding the decline of Ottoman industry.

GUILDS AND THEIR DECLINE: A CRITIQUE

Much discussion of Ottoman manufacturing focuses on the craft guilds and their demise, an emphasis deriving from the critical place of these organized groups of workers in the political centers. Guilds were of major importance to the state. They produced many of the goods that the government needed to maintain its civilian and military components and provided considerable tax revenues as well. The state thus took great care in recording guild members' activities. Since we historians rely on written documents, the focus of the Ottoman government's attention became our own.

The studies of Osman Nuri have played a decisive role in shaping our notions about the collapse of guilds. His monumental opus includes a report on the Industrial Reform Commission of the 1860s that sought to revive several flagging industries in the capital, including silk weaving, gold and silver wire making as well as tanning, shoe making and iron working.[2] The İstanbul guild of silver and gold wire makers, for example, had counted some 1,500 members in c. 1825. This group had enjoyed a privileged position, obtaining its precious metals at subsidized prices from the state treasury. But in the second quarter of the century, production and sales fell sharply with changes in the international market for these metals and the guild became impoverished. The silk-weaving industry, for its part, employed some 10,000 persons during the first half of the century, as skilled artisans in metropolitan İstanbul and in Bursa wove the richly variegated cloths required by Ottoman officialdom and beloved by the population at large. Propped up by this steady demand, the weavers also had profited from state intervention to assure supplies of raw silk from Bursa. Government fiat fixed its price and permitted shipment only to İstanbul.[3] But, between c. 1825 and 1850, higher prices for European raw silk overrode official enactments and siphoned away the needed raw materials.[4] As the silk weavers struggled with these supply problems, the official dress code changed to Western-style clothing, overnight eliminating the major domestic market. Simultaneously, the introduction of inexpensive Manchester cotton yarn and cloth encouraged taste changes among Ottoman consumers, away from silk to ever-cheaper cotton clothing. Silk weavers sought to compete by dropping prices, often at the expense of quality. Thus, they offended their remaining buyers. By the 1860s, these silk-weaving guilds were in an advanced state of decline.[5]

The mohair weavers of Ankara, possessing some 1–2,000 looms in c. 1815, offer another example of a collapsed guild.[6] Here, too, competition with foreign buyers for the raw material posed grave problems. European merchants increasingly bought only the raw mohair for export, despite government prohibitions against its sale to anyone except Ankara artisans. At the same time, European machine-made mohair textiles drove down prices. By c. 1850, the mohair weavers were said to have disappeared, but for a few in the small town of Istanos who continued to weave until the end of the century.[7]

With such disarray and collapse in famous and highly visible guilds, it was easy to conclude that Ottoman manufacturing overall had declined. Their disappearance has been considered the end of a process, and there has been no research into what came after the collapse of a particular guild. Mohair weaving and the weaver's guild at Ankara did vanish. But, as seen below, silk weaving revived and in fact expanded at Bursa and other locations. The example of the pipestem makers' guild (*lüleci esnafı*) further suggests that we need to employ great caution in assessing the meaning of a guild's decline. By 1865, this group of workers had fallen on difficult times. The number of its workshops had dropped from 180 to 30 and only some old and poor men remained employed.[8] This reduction certainly is significant, but what conclusions should we draw? We cannot assume a net loss of jobs to the Ottoman economy since, in this instance, a large new industry emerged, that of cigarette making. By 1913, cigarette factories in İstanbul and İzmir alone employed 923 women and girls and 1,071 boys and men.[9] This example suggests that, while the deaths of certain Ottoman industries have been noted, little study has been accorded to the births of others.

This example further demonstrates that little attention has been paid to non-guild labor. The contribution of such manufacturing labor has been grossly understated, both before and after the decline of the guilds. It seems likely, for example, that unorganized labor made up the bulk of all textile-making labor in c. 1800. This includes production for immediate consumption in the household as well as commercial manufacturing. The inattention to this work force derives from several factors. First of all, the state had little institutional interaction with workers outside guild structures. Hence, their activities usually are unrecorded in the central state documents that most historians have been consulting. Only rarely, for example in times of unrest, do non-guild labor groups find their way into these records.[10] Also, this is a more diffuse working group, often in the home, and, to boot, in the countryside. Thus its activities were more difficult to follow and record. For example, a group of female weavers near Erzurum briefly appear in the documents in 1841, only because they pleaded exemption from certain taxes. These were Muslim rural women who were engaged in part-time commercial manufacture, of linen cloth, three months per year.[11] The rural population of the Black Sea provinces in Anatolia similarly played a critical role in the manufacture of textiles, especially coarse cottons, for export to the north shore of the Black Sea.[12] Or, to give another example, village manufacturers played a vital role in the mohair textile industry of Ankara; it was not a monopoly of guilds in the town itself.[13] The outlying districts of Aleppo also were vital textile-production centers in the period before 1850. Thus, manufacturing in the rural sector by non-guild labor must be included in any analysis of manufacturing.

Our confusion regarding Ottoman industry is aggravated still further by misperceptions of the guilds themselves, viewed frequently as state anachronisms that continued unchanged from the sixteenth century before fading away in the new era of free trade. Ottoman and European sources frequently discuss guilds in terms of their restrictive practices, ossified ideas and rigid hierarchies, with limited memberships, fixed prices, and protected sources of supplies that hindered adaptation to foreign competition. This often is the picture presented by guild regulations; but such rules were not descriptions of reality, rather they expressed the state and guild's shared vision of an ideal working environment.[14] In real life, guilds' structures and activities varied considerably from place to place. In many cases, their reality does *not* conform to the standard view. Moreover, guilds in some areas did not vanish but survived and flourished well into the twentieth century. The use of free, market-valued, labor was not rare and guild membership sometimes meant little more than participating in a certain manufacturing activity, not unlike a modern-day chamber of commerce.

Guilds commonly were religiously mixed, non-egalitarian associations; they usually were male in membership and employed females. When guild membership involved hereditary transfers of the workshop, women likely were guild members since they could inherit the workshop. However, there is no concrete information on this point. While there were İstanbul guilds with exclusively Muslim or non-Muslim membership, inclusion of both Muslims and non-Muslims (*Müslim ve reaya kulları*) in a single guild was more usual, at least in the capital.[15] In Salonica, only about one-quarter of the guilds were mixed, but then, two-thirds of the population was from a single *millet*, in this case Jewish. Aleppo weavers' guilds contained both Muslims and Christians.[16] Despite the mixed nature of guilds, only co-religionists would band together and act collectively on certain occasions, such as petitions to the state. In those activities, they excluded fellow guild members who were not of the particular religious community.[17] Considerable income differences often separated members of the same guild: in the late 1820s, some artisans in certain İstanbul silk-weaving guilds paid fourteen times more in taxes than their fellow guildsmen. In other similar guilds, differentials of five and six were common.[18] Female labor played an important role in the operation of many guilds, in the capital as well as the provinces, throughout the century. Although we do not always know if the women participated as guild members or as outside hired labor, the latter is the more likely case. For example, as the Ankara mohair-weaving guildsmen struggled to meet European competition during the early 1840s, they implemented what contemporaries hailed as an innovation. Previously, the guild sheikh had bought raw mohair at fixed prices in regional markets and then distributed it to the spinners. Now, however, the guild entered into a contract with the "poor women" of the Ankara district (*kaza*). These women purchased the raw mohair at local markets, spun it and then sold it to the guild (*sof ve şalcı esnafı*) for whatever price they could obtain. This method did not replace but supplemented the previous method of supply, an effort to meet the "cheap price" of European-made mohair cloth.[19]

Despite the claims that the practice was brand-new, reliance on inexpensive female spinners in fact is evident much earlier. During the early eighteenth century, for example, the higher-grade yarn (guild-made?) was sold in the market-place but women spun the lower qualities, that were some 50 to 75 percent cheaper, and sold it to the customs official (*kolcu*).[20] Similarly, male braid makers at Karlovo, in the southern Balkan Mountains, belonged to a guild (*gaitancı esnafı*), but the women who spun the woolen yarn for them did not. Around the middle of the nineteenth century, reportedly "all" the İstanbul guilds that made clothing or furniture employed women embroiderers. Some 5,000 women, for example, then worked for the bonnet makers' guild and another 1,000 labored for the shoe makers' guild.[21]

Earlier in the century, many craft guilds were minutely divided, both horizontally and vertically, according to the commodities they produced. For example, separate guilds made the different kinds (and sometimes even colors) of cotton, wool and silk cloths as well as the various twists and yarns. Makers of the soles of shoes had their own guild, as did producers of the uppers. Sometimes, individual guilds making related products, such as the various silk textiles, or providing a similar service, such as porters (*hamals*), also belonged to a larger organization encompassing several guilds. In other instances, however, workers providing a particular service or product were divided into separate guilds for each city district. This fragmentation remained characteristic of guilds engaged in transport services and retail sales. But, where the craft guilds were concerned, organization on the basis of city districts apparently faded as the century progressed. By the 1860s, some weakened guilds that produced similar goods had merged together into single organizations. Notably, several once-separate cloth weaving guilds (*kumaşçı, kemhacı* and *çatmacı esnafları*) joined together in a single unit. Reflecting the more limited sales for its products, the newly organized group wove not only silk but also wool, cotton and linen cloth as well as furniture covers.[22]

No estimate presently is possible for the number of guilds and guild members. Salonica, in the 1860s, contained some 116 separate guilds. An 1887 tax register lists some 287 separate guilds in the İstanbul metropolitan area. This enumeration probably is not complete and reflects the guilds in a relatively advanced stage of consolidation. Most of the guilds listed contained masters, journeymen and apprentices among its members.[23] This survey is one statistical indicator that guilds hardly had disappeared from the capital, even at this late date.

GUILDS AND MONOPOLIES

In principle, the exclusive guild right to produce and/or sell a good offered advantages for both the state and the artisans. Some guild leaders helped collect and forward taxes; guilds also facilitated the channeling of goods and services for government use and general consumption. The guilds obtained some obvious benefits, including sole access to the market and, sometimes, official help in obtaining raw materials. The strength and effectiveness of monopolies varied by region and, for a particular guild, over time as well. Guilds sought to maintain or extend their own monopolies and, as seen below, hesitated little in encroaching on another guild's activities during the nineteenth century. They constantly pressured the state for assistance since, ultimately, privilege depended on official cooperation, that by no means was assured. Government maintenance of guild monopolies depended on the circumstances of the moment. For example, in c. 1805, the government concluded far-reaching agreements with guilds in many urban textile production centers, a reflection of the increasingly restrictionist atmosphere at the time. By 1816, in diverse locations such as İstanbul, Bursa, Damascus and Diyarbekir, all weavers had agreed to take their textiles to a single location (*mengenehane*) for polishing (*perdah*). There the state recorded and taxed textile production; only cloth bearing its stamp (*damga*) legally could be sold. Thus, in the arrangement, the guilds more easily prevented competition. But, in 1839, a profit tax (*temettü vergisi*) began to replace this stamp tax as part of the Tanzimat effort at economic de-regulation. İstanbul imposed the new profit tax in stages across the empire, gradually abandoning the stamp tax and the system of summoning all textile manufactures to a single polishing establishment. Finally, in 1878, the cloth-polishing monopoly system officially was abolished throughout the whole empire.[24]

Government regulation of manufacturing took additional forms. Beginning in c. 1750, İstanbul artisan and merchant guilds, with the cooperation of the state, gradually created a certification process for those wishing to practice a particular craft or operate a retail store. By the end of the eighteenth century, possession of the certificate (*gedik*) had come to mean the exclusive right to carry out a craft. The number of certificates issued for each activity became fixed, sometime during the reign of Mahmud II.[25]

Here, in using the example of İstanbul guilds, we again encounter a familiar problem in Ottoman economic history, namely the bias in favor of the capital city. Unfortunately, the abundant data available for the economic life of İstanbul are not matched for other regions. The experiences of guilds in the capital surely were quite different from those elsewhere; but the available evidence often seems to compel frequent use of İstanbul examples.

Just as monopolies were becoming entrenched, state policy reversed course in the Anglo-Turkish Convention of 1838 and the 1839 Gülhane decree. Accordingly, all monopolies were to be abolished. These two enactments inaugurated an era of extreme confusion for both the guilds and the government. On the one hand, monopolies in trade definitively were smashed. Raw materials now could be exported without reference to the needs of local artisans, e.g., the mohair or silk weavers, and thus their livelihoods were jeopardized further. To mention another example, the state informed the İzmir tanners' guild that the Tanzimat decree deprived it of the right to buy hides from the butchers' guild at a fixed price. Instead, the tanners henceforth had to pay the market price and the butchers were free to sell to anyone. The government made exactly the same argument to the İstanbul tanners, who lost their exclusive right to buy hides from the local butchers' guild. These practices were against the Tanzimat, it said, and the trade was open to anyone.[26]

With the abolition of monopolies, a free-for-all among craft guilds in the capital immediately developed as they tested the meaning of the new enactments. While trade was to be free, the situation in manufacturing was less certain. For example, one group of cloth printers, in the Üsküdar area of İstanbul, earlier had won the exclusive right to make a particular kind of cloth (hassı yemeni). Within a year of the 1839 Imperial Rescript, another group of cloth printers elsewhere in the capital (at Yenikapı), successfully challenged the monopoly on the grounds that it was contrary to the Tanzimat. At this time, major fashion changes were occurring, adding to the confusion in the printed cloth industry. By 1852, the monopoly had been broken totally and, in various sections of the city, as many as ten printing factories were operating. This is an excellent example of a particular guild suffering while the industry as a whole flourished.[27] In this case, although the state broke the monopoly on production, it still sought to maintain regulated retail prices.[28]

Other guilds were more successful than the Üsküdar cloth printers in fending off competitors. In 1841, the fez dyers in İstanbul argued that the certificate (gedik) empowered them to prevent others from entering the craft. The headgear in question, it should be recalled, was de rigueur wear for the reforming bureaucracy and its consumption was expanding at the time. In the case of fez dyeing, the state agreed with the petitioning guild and ruled in favor of the fez dyeing monopoly. This decision was the direct opposite of that given in the cloth printers' case. Two decades later, in 1862, the fez dyers again appealed to the government that reiterated support for the exclusive right to dye fezzes. Comparably, indigo dyeing at Mosul remained a monopoly until at least 1853, with active assistance from the state that benefited from the sale of indigo.[29]

Despite the late 1830s enactments that attacked monopolies, the certificate system remained, another indication of the continuing struggle for and against a free market economy. But the certificates did not necessarily retard the expansion of manufacturing. In the 1840s, for example, certified places were created for those making a new, embroidered textile, a product for which there had been no places (see below). In return, new workshops paid double the usual tax. Thus, manufacturing expanded while the guild kept a monopoly and the government gained revenue. In 1861, the state prohibited the issuance of new certificates but, at the same time, continued to endorse monopolies. Thus, in 1865, the tinners' guild (*kalaycı esnafı*) appealed for help, complaining that the number of certified places (*gediks*) remained limited despite a boom in business. In response, the state permitted the guild to open additional but uncertified shops, with the proviso that they pay double the taxes of a certified shop.[30] Again, the guild expanded its activities and maintained its monopoly.

During the 1860s, several important İstanbul guilds lost their monopolies when the Industrial Reform Commission sought to revive a number of important manufacturing activities. The commission was active between 1867 and 1874, just after the government had managed to wrench Great Power agreement to increased import duties. This state effort to stimulate industrial production contained both pro- and anti-monopolistic features. It reorganized a number of the existing guilds into companies (sing. *şirket*) to make commodities such as machine parts, silk cloth, leather, and sperm oil and provided them with capital and tax privileges. The commission also eliminated the distinctions that had existed among many guilds. Thus, as seen, the various kinds of silk cloth makers (such as *kumaşçı, kemhacı,* and *sandalcı*) all became part of the *kumaşçı* company. *Anyone* could join the newly created organization, whether or not the person previously had belonged to a guild. The regulation required the person be an Ottoman subject and buy shares in the cooperative enterprise. Access to membership was open to all but, in a measure reminiscent of the certificate system, only the shops of company members could sell the goods. In addition, the new companies had subsidized access to raw materials and to factory work space.[31]

Other Ottoman guilds adopted new forms of production and distribution but remained within a guild framework. In the Bulgarian lands, "guilds continued to be an obligatory form of organization for the commodity producers" not only in the long-established but also in "the new branches of production that appeared in the first half of the nineteenth century."[32] Such bodies hardly were the monopolistic monoliths of the idealized guild type. Rather, in common with Aleppo guilds at the end of the century, these Bulgarian guilds were loosely organized associations, with few restrictive powers or monopolistic privileges. At present, we do not know how this pattern developed at Aleppo but its emergence in the Bulgarian area is better documented. There, the woolen cloth (*aba*) guild had struggled with a member who sought unrestrained production. Finally, the guild lost out and the manufacturer won the right to produce without limit. In this case, the guild changed its character but did not collapse with the defection of one of its prominent members. Externally, the organizational form of the guild remained the same, and the rebel manufacturer continued as a member, but now the guild no longer placed restrictions on production.[33]

THE RESTRUCTURING OF MANUFACTURING

Factories and their importance in Ottoman industry

In the telling of Ottoman manufacturing history, much emphasis has been placed on mechanized factories or, more accurately, on their comparative absence. Since factories remained few in number, even after the rapid progress of the late nineteenth century, it was easy to assume Ottoman manufacturing generally was unimportant. Factories are only one measure of Ottoman industrial output, however, a short chapter in the larger story of Ottoman manufacturing. Mechanized factory output was and remained relatively insignificant when compared with domestic and handicraft production. "Large industrial establishments" of all kinds employed only c. 35,000 workers in 1914. This is a very small number when compared with the handicraft work force; a single hand manufacturing sector, that of Anatolian carpet making, for example, possessed far more workers, as did the cotton and cotton-silk cloth weaving industries.[34] In this section, we trace the development of a fascinating but not central manufacturing activity.

State initiatives accounted for most factories built or attempted before 1840 and almost all were located in the İstanbul area. Thereafter, private entrepreneurs played an increasingly important role, starting with the foundation of silk reeling mills at Bursa and in the Lebanon. After the 1870s, they became the dominant group in factory formation and operations. Government efforts had begun with Sultan Selim III, who built or modernized a number of factories, mostly to arm or equip the military, during the period c. 1790–1804. A second state initiative to introduce European machine manufacturing methods began after 1826 and continued into the 1830s. This included foundation of a spinning mill in the Eyüp section of İstanbul in 1827, and a tannery and boot works at Beykoz. In addition, the state founded a fez-making factory in 1835 to replace the previous hand-manufacture of the headgear. A wool spinning and weaving mill at Sliven (İslimiye) in the Balkan provinces opened c. 1836, about the time that the cannon and musket works at Tophane and Dolmabahçe in the capital were converted to steam. All of these were state funded projects aimed at transferring European technology.[35]

Another distinct, officially sponsored program of industrialization spanned the decade between the early 1840s and 1850s. Noteworthy was the construction of an "industrial park" just to the west of İstanbul, a complex containing a foundry and machine works, a spinning, weaving and printing mill and a boatyard. It also included a number of existing factories, e.g., some gunpowder works. Other factories were established or planned for various locations outside the capital, such as a wool cloth mill for the military at Balıkesir in western Anatolia. Despite efforts to acquire equipment and machinery from France, the mill remained incomplete in 1849.[36] Other state factories dating from the mid-1840s included a powder mill at Baghdad and a large factory near İzmit, to make wool cloth and fezzes. At Hereke, a cotton-weaving mill utilizing English machines and workers changed over, by the late 1840s, to silk-cloth production for the palace.[37]

Some of these factories failed; others, such as the Hereke and İzmit mills, outlasted the empire. For many of the factories, the state sought to assure domestic sources of raw material, such as a merino sheep flock near Bursa.[38] It also contracted with nomads to provide wool for the Balıkesir plant and it built a steam-powered silk-spinning mill at Bursa. As a part of this 1840s–50s effort, the government surveyed the European and Anatolian provinces to find the best sources of mineral dyes and reduce imports.[39] With trivial exceptions, these factories enjoyed protected markets, producing for the military and civilian bureaucracy and for the palace.[40]

Altogether, state factories during the 1850s employed some 5,000 workers – girls, women and men. Initially, at least, Europeans managed them and also performed most of the skilled tasks. At some plants, for example, the İstanbul arsenals at Tersane and Tophane, foreigners remained in significant numbers throughout the century. The early state factories relied on a variety of sources for their labor. During the mid-1830s, orphaned children worked at a yarn factory (*rişte-hane-i amire*) to maintain uninterrupted production for the Ottoman fleet. These were "suitably paid" and brought in on a rotational basis for a specified time. At first, Armenian Orthodox children from the areas of Erzurum, Van and Sivas were recruited but their numbers proved insufficient. So, the government summoned some 100 Catholic and 100 Greek orphans from the mohair-weaving districts around Ankara and from Ürgüp and Niğde as well. In the 1850s, a yarn factory (*iplikhane*) employed adults who had committed misdemeanors – bakers who had sold short weights, as well as boatmen, grocers, stonemasons and weavers – with sentences of one and two months.[41] To staff an alum factory (*şaphane*) in the Gördes area, the government exempted local workers from certain taxes and from military service, and, in addition, paid piece-work wages. Legislation in 1845–46 eliminated these exemptions and only the wage compensation remained.[42] The wool-cloth factory at Balıkesir employed spinners from the Haremeyn tribe.[43] State sponsorship of factories sometimes conflicted with guilds' interests; for example, a paper factory at İzmit threatened the paper-makers' guild (*kağıtçı esnafı*). To blunt their opposition, the state turned over all the products of the factory to the guildsmen who later sold them for a fixed price and retained one-tenth of gross production. By the early 1850s, however, the factory manager broke the arrangement, finding it excessively costly.[44]

Before 1850, a number of private entrepreneurs sought to establish factories. In the main, these are poorly documented, for example, İzzet Pasha's importation of looms and other machinery from Europe for silk weaving at Bursa.[45] Also, two merchants, one of them a "merchant of benefaction" (*Hayriye tüccarı*), promoted rug and *kilim* production at Uşak and obtained certain tax advantages, planning to import machinery from Europe (whether for spinning yarn or weaving rugs is not certain).[46] In 1852, an official inspector toured the carpet-making districts and argued against mechanical rug weaving. Coal was unavailable in the area, he said, and mechanization would create unemployment. "And besides, it will be more expensive than the wages which are now given to the workers."[47] Another entrepreneur sought to build an indigo factory near

Anatolian İznik to check rising imports of the dyestuff. A retired military officer planned to build a wool-weaving mill in the town of Van, with uncertain results.[48]

Between 1847 and 1868, private investors founded at least 21 steam reeling mills in the Bursa region. At Trabzon, in 1862, a private entrepreneur opened a factory for the manufacture of high-quality, European-style, sole leather.[49] In the later 1860s, the İstanbul government launched perhaps its most ambitious program to stimulate manufacturing. Not surprisingly, it concentrated on factory-based production. To revive industry in the capital city, it reorganized guilds into cooperative associations that sold shares (see above, pp. 899–98). The capital raised would buy Western machinery in order to "constantly lower prices" of the manufactures. The government founded seven associations between 1867 and 1873, with plans for more in the future. But it abandoned the effort, perhaps from discouragement over results or because of the financial crisis that struck during the early 1870s.

At long last, in 1874, the state inaugurated a standing policy of tax exemptions for machinery and tools to be used in factories. Two years later, it exempted factory-made yarn from all internal and export duties, and offered entrepreneurs other fiscal privileges and tax exemptions.[50]

Many Ottoman entrepreneurs suffered from fiscal disadvantages. Take for example, a nail-making factory at İzmir that competed with imported nails. The imports paid 8 percent duty when brought into the country, but the factory paid 8 percent duty on the imported bar iron and another 4 percent on shipping its manufactured nails elsewhere in the empire. This kind of situation certainly encouraged investors to make their profits from negotiating and selling the concession rather than constructing or operating a factory.[51] But there were sufficient numbers of actual entrepreneurs so that each increase in the import duty – in 1861–62 and again in 1907 – sparked a modest spurt of factory-building.[52]

After the 1870s, the number of Ottoman factories increased very rapidly, thanks mainly to private capital. Many factories used imported raw materials, e.g., the sugar for the refineries and the paper for cigarette making. In most instances, the new factories produced foodstuffs for local consumption, such as flour, ice and macaroni as well as beer, products that enjoyed "natural protection" from European competition.[53] There were exceptions to this rule and certain industrialists directly competed with imports. At İzmir, for example, the largest iron works in the Ottoman world contained a forge, boiler makers and a foundry and employed some 200 workers. Ottoman and foreign entrepreneurs also founded wool spinning and dyeing factories in western Anatolia to supply the carpet industry. Machine-made cotton yarn, for its part, developed significantly, usually in locations close to major sources of raw cotton. The processing of tobacco and cigarette making employed large numbers of factory workers. In 1875, the tobacco monopoly factory in İstanbul contained 70 employees and 1,400 "workmen" (who actually were mainly women). In the early twentieth century, the tobacco factory at Cibali in the capital employed 1,600 persons. There were 180 male sorters and 100 cutters (of undetermined gender); most of the remaining were female packagers and cigarette makers. At İzmir, Samsun and Salonica, tobacco monopoly factories together employed about 1,400 women and men.[54]

Towards the end of the period, Salonica, İstanbul and the Adana area, as well as the Bursa and Lebanon silk-reeling districts, contained the major concentrations of mechanized factory production. Other major manufacturing centers such as Aleppo and Damascus remained the domain of small workshop producers. At the turn of the century, for example, some Aleppo entrepreneurs tried but failed to introduce jacquard looms; at the same time, other industrialists successfully adopted these at Diyarbekir.[55]

Salonica experienced a remarkable burst of factory-building activity during the early 1880s. Entrepreneurs founded a whole range of new enterprises: a distillery, six soap factories, one factory each for tile and bricks, nails, and cigarettes, as well as ten other factory establishments.[56] The cigarette factory, for example, doubled production between 1888 and 1892, and employed almost 400 workers. Raw wool exports from Salonica declined sharply because of rising woolen cloth production for the army and for local and Syrian consumers. By the mid-1890s, local factories consumed four-fifths of total regional wool production. Two cotton-spinning factories, established in 1878 and 1884, employed 800 workers. These mills, and another at nearby Naoussa (Niausta), began competing successfully with foreign yarns in the lower counts. By the early 1890s, there were four factories – two each at Salonica and Naoussa – that exported yarn to Macedonia, Albania, Bulgaria, Serbia, Anatolia and the archipelago. In 1907, one Salonica cotton mill remained closed after a decade of neglect but the other increased production to 1.5 million lb of twist per year. Nearby, at Veroia (Karaferia), cotton yarn mills annually produced 300,000 lb while another mill at nearby Edessa (Vodena) yielded double that amount. Elsewhere in the European region, at Edirne, spinning mills consumed 30 percent of local raw cotton production in 1889. At that time, Edirne also had two silk mills and two

steam flour mills.[57] At İstanbul, the Yedikule spinning mills used Ottoman cotton and began producing yarn in the early 1890s. By 1914, most
army cloth no longer came from Britain but from government factories,
one with 125 looms and 1,500 workers. A pair of Bosnian and Albanian
entrepreneurs opened a military cloth mill at Karamürsel, with 100
modern looms and 500 workers, chiefly fellow countrymen. Two factories founded at Trabzon in 1885 made soap and substantially reduced
imports.[58] Impressive steam-powered mills were founded at Adana in the
later 1880s, spinning both silk and cotton. By 1912, two cotton-spinning
mills there held 15,000 spindles and two weaving mills had 230 looms.
Nearby, at Tarsus, two spinning factories contained 26,000 spindles. Each
spinning mill owned ginning mills to supply the raw materials. Three-
quarters of the yarn produced went to the Archipelago and the Black
Sea region, while local buyers accounted for the balance. In one factory,
the weaving section consumed up to one-half of the yarn made in its
spinning division.[59]

These were impressive gains. By 1898, for example, seven cotton spinning factories in the empire had eliminated foreign yarn in the lower
numbers. But the factories filled only a small proportion of Ottoman
cotton textile needs. Taken together, all Ottoman cotton-spinning mills c.
1911 annually were producing 4,000 tons of cotton yarn, approximately
one-quarter of the total then consumed in the empire. Cotton-cloth production from Ottoman factories averaged 1,000 tons per year, estimated
at perhaps 2 percent of the cotton cloth being imported.[60]

The contribution of Ottoman factories to total industrial output cannot
be determined more precisely because the statistics are unreliable.
According to one calculation, 56 factories were founded before 1880,
another 51 during the 1880s and 1890s, and an additional 107 between
1901 and 1915.[61] These figures, at least for the period until the 1890s,
cannot be correct; the number of Bursa silk mills founded until that date
alone exceed the total indicated. Similarly problematic are two government surveys of factory enterprises, carried out in 1913 and 1915. These
are too defective to be of more than limited use. The surveys were made
after the substantial losses of European territory during the Balkan Wars
and thus do not include the significant industrial base in the Salonica
region and Macedonia. By the definitions employed in the enumeration,
the survey excluded the smaller workshops, both handicraft and mechanized. Moreover, it counted only those establishments located in İstanbul
and western Anatolia – İzmir, İzmit, Bursa, Bandırma, Manisa and Uşak.
Thus, it ignored the major industrial mechanized development that had
taken place around Adana as well as smaller factories at Harput, Trabzon,

Diyarbekir, Afyonkarahisar, Amasya, etc. The usefulness of the data is hampered still further by the poor statistical base of the survey. A full one-third of the establishments surveyed did not keep proper books. In one factory, employing 100 workers, the owner allegedly kept his accounts written on the wall, in pencil.

These incomplete surveys show that İstanbul contained just over one-half and İzmir one-quarter of the factories counted. Eight percent of the factories were state property, 11 percent were joint stock companies and 81 percent were privately owned. The founding, mostly foreign, capital of all counted factories totaled an estimated 1,193 million piasters. Most owners were Ottoman subjects, usually merchants, but their capital investments scarcely equaled 10 percent of the numerically fewer foreign investors. Foreign capital investment occurred mainly after the 1870s, as surplus European funds increasingly became available for investment abroad.[62]

The concentration of factories around İstanbul and in the European provinces hardly was coincidental. İstanbul's enormous population offered a rich labor pool and consumer market. In the province of Salonica, population densities were the highest in the empire, some 75 persons per sq. km. Both cities, furthermore, possessed comparatively well-developed rail and sea links to other parts of the empire and to Europe. The areas around Adana also had excellent rail and sea transport and close linkages with the raw cotton production of the Çukurova plain. Labor in the Adana industrial area, however, was not abundant. In some cases, factory owners, merchants mainly, brought Armenian workers from Hacın, Zeytun and Aintab and provided them with housing. Dormitories were common at many other factory sites, for example, the government carpet factory at Hereke and the silk-reeling mills at Bursa. In many other cases, such as the Uşak wool spinning mills and some İstanbul and Salonica factories, the workers lived at home and daily walked to their jobs.[63]

Child labor was common not only in Adana but also at all the factories for which we have any information on the workers. Young girls formed an important proportion of the overall Ottoman factory work force and their low wages helped make these factories competitive. They usually remained employed for brief intervals, however, forcing the management to continuously train new workers and retarding the emergence of a more highly skilled work force. In this regard, the Ottoman factory work force closely resembled its counterpart in the U.S. and Europe.

The case of cotton yarn production

Ottoman homes and workshops, not factories, were the locale of the most impressive changes in Ottoman textile production during the nineteenth century. The import of European yarns, cloth and synthetic dyestuffs played a vital role in the transformation of Ottoman industry. Sold by local merchants and used by Ottoman artisans, these imports destroyed and created manufacturing activities in patterns of considerable regional and temporal variation. Imports of cotton yarn and cloth, for example, undermined and then wrecked a once-prosperous putting-out network centered on Anatolian Kayseri.[64] During the 1830s, Kayseri merchants continued to supply raw Adana cotton to spinners in some northern Anatolian towns, such as Zile, Merzifon and Vezir Köprü. The merchants then either sold the yarn to larger manufacturing centers, such as Bursa, or distributed it on the spot for the manufacture of coarse calicoes (in imitation of the once-dominant Indian product) for local consumption or export to the Crimea. A decade later, these merchants still were active, supplying indigo, cochineal and Adana cotton to weavers at Bor in southeastern Anatolia who made cloth for export to nearby Kayseri and to Gümüşhane further to the north.[65] They competed, however, with the continuously declining prices of British manufactures and, by the 1860s, had succumbed. This decade probably marks the end of the Kayseri putting-out empire.

New activities created by British yarn imports include the cotton cloth weaving industry in the town of Arapkir. In this town near Malatya, weaving enterprises developed in the 1820s and early 1830s and flourished for the remainder of the century. This was an entirely new industry in the town, one based on the import of British yarn. By 1836, some 1,000 Arapkir looms were using about 210,000 lb of British yarn.

> The quantity is not important but the fact of so many looms being employed is remarkable as the manufacture has sprung up within about six years, previous to which the looms were few and the yarn was the produce of the country. This manufacture has in this part of Turkey superseded the use of the nankeens of Great Britain, the native are found cheaper as well as more durable in texture and colour.[66]

Then occupying 4,800 Muslim and 1,200 Armenian households, the industry was "in a thriving condition." The construction of a new dyehouse in the 1860s suggests continuing activity.[67] In 1888, its 1,000 hand looms still wove a coarse cotton cloth and the town was "thriving." At that time, annual cloth production reportedly was mounting rapidly, having doubled, to c. 120,000 pieces, during the mid-1880s. Ottoman consumers continued to prefer these locally made goods to the British because of their greater durability and color fastness, and because they were price competitive.[68] In the subsequent two decades, the town's weaving capacity expanded and, by 1907, over 1,200 looms were operating.[69]

Prior to its adoption of British yarn, Arapkir was not an important manufacturing center. Its rise to prominence seems important for several reasons. First, the example demonstrates that European textile imports did not necessarily cost Ottoman jobs. In this case, contrariwise, yarn imports created and then maintained 1,200 new jobs (assuming a low figure of one worker per loom). Also, the development of Arapkir contradicts assumptions about the connection between geography and the impact of Western imports. Distance from the coast was not always the crucial variable. Arapkir is considerably *further* from the coast than Zile, Merzifon and Vezir Köprü but it adopted British yarn as the other three towns held onto their traditions of spinning yarn from Adana raw cotton. The important factor was not geography but rather the interests of established yarn makers in the three towns and of the Kayseri merchants who stood to lose if British yarn replaced Adana cotton. In Arapkir, these obstacles to innovation were absent and so the new manufacturing patterns emerged. This town consequently rose to manufacturing prominence as the other three declined.

In some areas, hand spinning of cotton yarn had vanished by 1840. British yarn, after all, was cheaper and of higher quality. Its adoption permitted Ottoman cotton cloth makers to reduce costs as textile prices were falling in Europe. Use of this yarn freed workers from a time-consuming and poorly paid job. Overall, yarn spinning ranked lowest in skills and in remuneration, a weaver earned many times more for each hour worked.

Nevertheless, the hand spinning of cotton yarn persisted, in some regions until World War I. "All" of the Kurdish women near Diyarbekir spun yarn in the winter season during the 1850s. These women were too poor to buy the imported yarn or even the cotton from which they were to spin the twist. So they picked cotton and received their wages in kind. The women spun the raw cotton they had earned into yarn and sold it in town for more raw cotton. They repeated the cycle until their husbands had enough yarn to weave cloth for the family, selling the surplus on the market.[70] During the 1870s, village women in eastern Anatolia provided rural weavers with yarn and received finished cloth in exchange.

Harput weavers still were using hand-carded, hand-spun thread into the 1890s. Near Sivas, hand spinning was commonplace during the late 1880s, made at home by women using spinning wheels.[71] At the end of the century, village spinners around the city of Mosul annually supplied urban weavers with over 1.5 million lb of cotton yarn. In times of economic downturn, Mosul textile producers gave up buying thread from these villagers. Instead, they saved labor costs by purchasing raw cotton from Aleppo and spinning it themselves.[72] Both men and women spun, "during times when they are not employed in other profitable occupation(s)."[73] Cotton (as well as wool and goat hair) spinning also was extensive at nearby Aintab in the early twentieth century. Using Adana cotton as well as Indian, and even some shipped via Europe, women at home spun an estimated 100 tons per year.[74] The widespread prevalence of hand spinning in such quantities is a striking reminder that the transformation of Middle East manufacturing proceeded unevenly, over a prolonged period that extends well beyond the limits of this study.

The example of the Bursa silk industry

The silk industry of Bursa also illustrates the intricate ways that Ottoman entrepreneurs and workers adjusted to shifts in technology and market. The fate of the Bursa industry also encourages a closer examination of Ottoman industry and a challenge to cherished notions of "decline" and forces us to re-evaluate the meaning of the term.

Competition from European silk weavers, the reform decrees of the state, taste changes and sharply declining prices for cotton goods combined against the ancient silk-weaving craft of Bursa during the first half of the nineteenth century. Towards the end of the 1810s, Bursa annually produced more than 100,000 pieces of manufactured silk goods, ranging from cloth for women's blouses to velvets. This apparently was an output record, a substantial jump in production that had occurred only after 1808.[75] An important technological breakthrough in the finishing of silk cloth probably accounts for the leap. Introduction of the new technique, using stone rather than fire to provide the final finish, occurred as the state and guilds formed the monopoly on cloth finishing. The new method produced a higher-quality cloth that also was cheaper in price. In the early stages of its adoption, İstanbul silk weavers moved to monopolize the process. When it spread to Bursa, Damascus and Diyarbekir, they demanded that the state dismantle the finishing plants erected by guilds in the three cities. The government, however, rejected the petition, siding with those who sought to make the best product at the cheapest price.[76]

The Bursa region also furnished spun silk for the warp (meşdud) to local weavers and in substantial quantities (some 5,000 okka per month) for manufacturers in metropolitan İstanbul and Aleppo. State officials required the sale of raw silk and at a price that they fixed. Foreign purchasers offered higher prices, however, and continuously interrupted supplies. At times, shortages of raw silk became critical. To eliminate this problem, İstanbul weavers in 1810 petitioned for the right to produce their own raw silk.[77] More generally, the government sought to solve the problem by decreeing that no raw silk be sold to any foreign or domestic weavers except those of İstanbul and Bursa.[78]

European textile manufacturers also undermined the position of Bursa silk cloth makers by bidding up natural dyestuff prices. On the one hand, dyestuffs produced within the empire, such as madder root for "Turkey red," were siphoned off by the higher prices prevailing in Europe. On the other, prices of dyestuffs that Ottoman manufacturers had been importing jumped very sharply, or the goods altogether disappeared from the market. During the late 1830s and early 1840s in particular, guild dyers complained of rising prices for imported stuffs such as salamoniac and indigo and that logwood had become unavailable. In a five-year period during the 1830s, the price of dyestuffs increased 100 percent.[79] By the 1840s, silk-cloth production had fallen to approximately 20,000 pieces, almost all of it for domestic consumption. In the subsequent decade, output dropped to 12–15,000 pieces.[80] During this crisis, İzzet Pasha from the district of Bursa sought to reorganize local silk weaving. Initially he sought only local weavers and formed a partnership with them, sharing equally in the profits. He also tried to raise capital for the importation of European weaving and finishing machinery to produce imitations of Western silk textiles. After five years of trying, the pasha had obtained a dozen looms on the Italian model as well as the services of an Italian master weaver. But the goods "not at all" resembled European textiles.[81]

Important occupational changes took place in Bursa during the first four decades of the century. The 80 percent fall in local silk cloth output certainly undermined silk weavers' livelihoods. The raw-silk producers, on the other hand, faced a rapidly expanding export market just as British cotton yarn "entirely superseded" domestic yarn at Bursa. Thus, silk weaving and cotton yarn spinning faded in importance and other manufacturing activities arose to take their place. Many silk weavers switched over to cotton cloth production, based on British yarn. The expanding silk-reeling industry absorbed increasingly important quantities of labor, including those who once had spun cotton yarn.[82] Indeed, the ready availability of high paying jobs in the emerging raw silk industry of the 1810s–40s probably accelerated the decline of both silk weaving and cotton-yarn spinning. British cotton thread found a particularly ready market since it released labor for the silk reeling sector, then in its initial expansionary phases and offering premium wages to attract workers. Between c. 1815 and 1845, the international market price of raw silk climbed dramatically and Bursa raw silk production quadrupled, without changing technologies.[83] During this period, probably c. 1838, Bursa silk reelers changed from the so-called long reel to the short reel method, one that produced raw silk better suited to the needs of European factories. To encourage the shift, reelers received a 25 percent bonus to produce according to the short reel method. Between 1840 and 1845, the aggregate payroll of silk reelers rose ten times as they strained to meet foreigners' demands, employing manually operated reels.[84]

Between the mid-1840s and mid-1850s, raw silk output doubled again, but this time with a new technology. In a remarkably rapid shift that was completed in fifteen years, the once-manually powered silk-reeling industry became located in steam-driven factories, employing thousands of workers. French silk workers, probably beginning with the Glaizal family that came to Bursa in 1834 and established a spinning mill, carried the new technology and the initial capital. By 1850, the French colony at Bursa numbered 67 members; all of them had been in the French silk industry, working as mechanics, reelers, dyers and weavers. (İzzet Pasha or Lyons merchant houses perhaps played a role in summoning these French experts but this cannot now be determined with certainty.) In 1844 or 1845, M. Falkeisen from Basle opened what most historians believe was the first steam-powered mill in the region. Falkeisen, under contract to a Lyons firm, founded the enterprise in partnership with Taşçıyan Ohannes, an interpreter at the local British consulate, and one Bayoğlu Osip. In 1850, steam-powered mills were spinning 10 percent of total raw silk output. By 1860, manual reeling essentially had vanished, accounting for only 2 percent of total production. Some 46 steam mills employed at least 4,200 persons.[85]

At the outset, mill operators had difficulties attracting workers. They recruited only from among the Greek population and paid wages that were considered "remarkably high," as had other entrepreneurs during the boom of the manual-reeling period. To find cheaper labor, factory managers turned to other sources, some outside the city of Bursa. They built dormitories near the factories and recruited mainly "very" young girls from surrounding rural areas. The girls stayed near the mills through the spinning season and returned home with "practically all" their wages. After c. 1855, Turkish girls and women also were employed, as were some Jews. At about this time, the Pope in Rome issued a decree permitting Armenian girls to work in the mills.[86] With a variety of labor sources available, wages fell sharply. An approving European observer put it another way: "The level of wages progressively stabilized with the true value of labor. . . . All is for the best in the most beautiful of cities."[87] Thereafter, until World War I, wages in the reeling mills were among the lowest in Ottoman industry.[88]

The pattern of female labor seasonally working for low wages in steam factories to produce a semi-finished good primarily for export prevailed until the end of the period. In the half-century after 1860, raw-silk production fluctuated with the demands of a volatile international market, competition from Far Eastern producers and diseases afflicting silkworms.[89] Output fell drastically in the 1860s, 1870s, and into the later 1880s. Production then recovered thanks to international demand, an anti-disease treatment developed by Louis Pasteur and imported from France, and the efforts of silk merchants, the government and the Public Debt Administration. The recovery, however, occurred in the context of prices that fell by more than one-half between 1850 and 1900.[90]

Over the century as a whole, Bursa raw-silk output increased some tenfold, mostly before 1870 when production rose perhaps eight times. The subsequent history primarily is one regaining former levels, with perhaps a 15 percent net increase in raw-silk output between 1870 and the pre-World War I peak. At its apogee, c. 1910, Bursa province and the adjacent district of İzmit possessed some 165 reeling mills, producing 700,000 kg of raw silk. Most mills were located outside the city of Bursa in smaller towns and villages, near cocoon sources and where labor was cheaper. Some thirty-two towns and villages outside the city contained over 75 percent of the productive capacity of the steam-powered mills in 1909.[91]

Silk-cloth production in Bursa, moreover, had staged a comeback. As seen earlier, annual cloth output had fallen to under 20,000 pieces by the 1850s, woven on a maximum of 200 looms. By the mid-1890s, however, cloth output had increased. Some 500 looms with unchanged technology used 13,000 kg of raw silk to weave 40,000 pieces of cloth for domestic consumers. By 1908, 800 town looms used 37,000 kg of raw silk to produce 110,000 pieces of silk cloth, perhaps a record for the post-1800 period.[92] By 1910, six mechanized looms were operating and they alone consumed 10,000 kg of raw silk, adding to the record levels set two years before.

At the end of the period, the many different stages of the Bursa silk industry employed substantial numbers of workers. An estimated 130,000 families raised cocoons, a part-time activity interspersed with other tasks. The silk-reeling factories employed another 19,000 persons, also seasonal workers. And silk weaving, for its part, may have employed 2,000 individuals. In c. 1810, by comparison, cocoon raising occupied perhaps 25,000 families, while reeling and weaving together employed c. 10,000 persons.[93] Thus, there had been a recovery of skilled jobs in the weaving sector later in the period, to about the levels of the early nineteenth century. Overall the industry employed substantially more workers in 1900 than in 1800. The new jobs, however, mainly were low skill, low wage, dead-end tasks. Many cocoon raisers carried out their work as a sideline, to bring in a bit of cash; the majority of the reelers were young girls, in the work force only until marriage. Neither group accumulated cash or skills and the industry did not stimulate development of other Ottoman manufacturing activities.

THE POST-1870 MANUFACTURING REVIVAL

An overview of hand manufacturing

As the Bursa silk example suggests, labor moved readily from one textile manufacturing activity to another. In the silk industry case, cotton-yarn spinners became silk reelers, pulled initially by the more attractive wages. In one sense, the raw-silk industry grew at the expense of cotton-yarn production. Thus, in assessing changes in manufacturing, we need to keep the various branches in focus. The decline of one activity did not always mean an overall diminution of industrial output; sometimes there was a compensatory increase in the production of another textile.[94] In the city of Trabzon, a modest silk-weaving industry had survived at home, done by Christian and Muslim women who were paid by the piece, manufacturing outer body and head wraps (*çarşafs*). During the first decade of the twentieth century, this industry grew by a third, adding some twenty looms to the total. At precisely this time, the local weaving of cotton aprons (*peştimals*) declined and twenty cotton looms reportedly were abandoned. Thus, it appears, cotton weavers shifted to silk-cloth production. Both in Trabzon and the coastal zone stretching to Samsun, silk-cloth production "has shown an extraordinary growth in recent years."[95] Increases in silk weaving occurred empire-wide: substantial output increases took place not only at Bursa but also at other major centers such as Diyarbekir and Aleppo.

Alongside rising imports of European and American cloth, Ottoman production of cotton and wool textiles continued in many areas, both rural and urban, domestic and workshop, for home consumption and for sale. During the 1870s, some 12,000 looms wove commercially in the districts of Erzurum, Diyarbekir and Harput. One-third of these were in towns and wove the more expensive fabrics, employing silk weavers for c. 100 days per year and cotton and cotton-silk weavers for 290 days per year. But most weavers, working on some 8,000 cotton looms, lived in rural areas. In city and countryside, the weavers were men and boys under 16 years of age and, invariably it seems, piece work prevailed.[96] In the 1890s, "almost every family" in Anatolia reportedly still owned a hand loom.[97] The city of Mosul then held nearly 800 looms that wove a variety of cloths, mainly cotton. Twenty years later, an estimated 1,000 looms were working in Mosul and an approximately equal number operated elsewhere in the province.[98] In the Sivas region, women worked on some 10,000 home looms, using imported thread to make coarse, striped cotton cloth while another estimated 10,000 looms wove in western Anatolia.[99] One estimate, surely too low, suggests that the Anatolian districts contained 30,000 looms while the Syrian regions held at least 14,000 looms.[100] When prices for agricultural products were high, rural families might neglect weaving, while in less favorable times, they again would make cloth for family and market. Household manufacturing fluctuated with the harvest; family labor ebbed and flowed between industry and agriculture, depending on market conditions and income opportunities.

An authentic industrial revival occurred in the manufacture of textiles, shoes and other goods, beginning in the 1870s and continuing into World War I. This growth, it is important to note, accompanied a continuing rise in Ottoman imports of European textiles. That is, both domestic production and the import of textiles simultaneously increased. In part, the manufacturing revival derived from the removal of most internal duties that had plagued domestic industry within the empire. The 1873–96 global price depression played an important role. When the terms of trade turned against agricultural goods, rural incomes and the ability to buy imports fell abruptly. But, in some areas, "a great manufacturing revival" already was evident before the internal duties were lifted and prior to the onset of the price depression.[101] A number of factors were involved. During the final third of the century, the domestic market certainly was larger, thanks to natural population increases, immigration, and the swelling population of the port cities. Events within Europe had their effect. European workers finally reaped some benefits from industrialization and their real wages rose. Thus, the price of Ottoman labor correspondingly declined after c. 1850. The growing wage gap, however, was offset to some degree by the continuing rise in European industrial productivity. Much credit for the revival must go to the manufacturers themselves, who adapted to changing environments with a variety of strategies. They accepted lower wages and further cut production costs by calibrating the proportions of different inputs from labor, domestic and imported materials. Thus, in some cases they cut costs by substituting foreign, machine-made, yarn for the domestic hand-made product. In other instances, thanks to the invention of synthetic dyes, Ottoman workers dyed imported yarns and cloths and thus replaced Western with (cheaper) Ottoman labor inputs. Entrepreneurs increasingly imported plain rather than colored yarn and undertook the local dyeing and printing of plain imported cloth. Often lamented for their low quality and lack of fastness, synthetic dyes lowered production costs. They were quick and simple to apply and cheap as well. Their adoption probably further undermined monopolies among guild dyers since spinners and weavers could use the novel technology on their own. In addition, Ottoman entrepreneurs successfully imitated European manufactures that earlier had displaced local and, at a still earlier time, Indian textiles on the Ottoman market. They also created new fashions and styles for a very local market, making it difficult, if not impossible, for European producers to compete. Many of the new styles involved the extensive use of embroidery, a low-wage, labor-intensive decoration that Manchester could not competitively replicate. By encouraging the consumption of new kinds of embroidered cloth (the fabric itself might be imported), Ottoman manufacturers created a market for a unique product that could be sold cheaply, thanks to the vast pool of women available for work at low wages.

Hand manufacturing for international export

Lace making Several export industries emerged after 1870, aimed at the Western market. Antique dealers in İstanbul founded the first of these, almost by accident. They had been selling old lace to customers in Europe but, sometime after 1850, depleted the available supplies. So, to satisfy their customers, they began selling copies of old patterns and invented new styles as well. To maintain this now-thriving enterprise, the merchants annually imported 80,000 kg of yarn from Britain, Austria and Germany, and delivered it to women working at home in the capital. These women made the yarn into lace and turned over the finished product to the merchants who paid for it by weight. The merchants exported the entire output, mainly to Paris and London. The amount of lace produced, calculations show, would have employed 7,600 women full-time for a year; since the lace makers interspersed this work with household and other tasks, the number of women employed in the industry certainly was much higher.[102] Lace making demonstrates that yarn imports, as in the case of Arapkir, often represented a net employment gain for the Ottoman economy.

Towards the end of the century, other Ottoman artisans began producing and exporting "Irish" lace, as well as embroideries and other textiles. Following the 1890s Armenian massacres, foreign Christian missionaries in several Anatolian and Arab provinces established textile centers based on cheap labor, usually oriented towards the international market. At the important Merzifon mission in the Black Sea area, missionaries used American and British charitable donations to encourage an allegedly new industry. Many hundreds of people annually manufactured 150,000 yards of narrow gingham cloth, in addition to some toweling.[103] Near Adana, children at the Hacın orphanage and many of the "poorer" inhabitants were put to work weaving cotton stuffs and carpets, again with capital from American and British donors. At Urfa, Aintab and Maraş, Armenian women and children worked under the direction of the American mission, embroidering for English and American buyers. By 1910, women using cambric, silk and high-grade linen from Belfast were exporting "ladies handkerchiefs, doyleys, table centres, collars and scarves," as well as men's silk girdles, to the United States and Egypt. At Aintab, the agent of an Irish firm in 1911 employed several hundred women and girls. They produced linen handkerchiefs and lacework and soon were competing with small "native" firms that exported directly to the United States. On the eve of the war, the Syrian region "was rapidly taking the first place in the production of Irish lace."[104]

Carpet making Knotted rugs and carpets certainly are the best-known Ottoman manufacture and they occupy a beloved place in numerous

American and European, as well as Middle Eastern, homes and businesses.[105] Already in the mid-eighteenth century, foreign buyers were affecting local production and marketing practices. Western demand began moving to new plateaus around 1850. A series of international expositions held in London, Paris, Vienna and Philadelphia between 1851 and 1876 stimulated the rapidly growing Western interest in Oriental rugs.[106] Carpets became nearly a mass consumption item by 1900, used in the homes of middle-class and even working-class families, both in Europe and the United States.

Ottoman carpet exports soared. In the first decade of the nineteenth century, Uşak was the leading carpet-producing town in Anatolia and it exported 50–60,000 sq. meters of carpets to Europe.[107] At the end of the century, its carpet exports were over 440,000 sq. meters, to Europe and America. Carpet shipments from the Ottoman Empire as a whole jumped from c. 17 million piasters in the late 1870s to over 32 millions by the mid-1890s. Most carpet exports went through İzmir. During the 1870s alone, the value of rug exports from İzmir doubled and then tripled over the next thirty years.[108]

Commercial carpet making centered in western and, to a lesser extent, central Anatolia. Back in the sixteenth century, tribes such as the Kaçar, Karakeçli, Kızılkeçli, Tekeli and the Kınıklı had settled in western Anatolia and brought along carpet making. The Kaçar became the most sedentarized and made rugs in the town of Uşak. During most of the nineteenth century, the major centers of carpet export production were the towns of Uşak, Kula, Gördes and Demirci. Until the 1890s, Uşak accounted for at least two-thirds of all Anatolian commercially made carpets. Rug production there doubled between 1870 and 1890 and rose another 50 percent during the following decade.[109] In 1850, the industry already had difficulty maintaining standards; shoddy knotting and dyeing practices were not rare. Demand pressures had become so great that Uşak artisans largely abandoned weaving *kilims* to concentrate on knotting rugs.[110] (Gördes had been famous for a coarse cotton cloth but gave it up in favor of carpet making earlier in the century.) Putting-out was firmly in place during the 1860s and the most important Uşak merchant had some 3,000 homes annually producing 84,000 sq. meters of carpets.

Beginning in the 1850s, European chemists began to develop dyes that produced colors once obtained only from nature; by the end of the century, synthetic dyes were available for most colors. These synthetics were cheaper and easier to use than the natural materials and they created color schemes preferred by European and American buyers.[111] The abandonment of natural dyes seems to have been immediate in many areas and must have caused important income losses to the villagers who had been supplying them to merchants. For example, Kula workers in the 1860s had used only natural dyestuffs, and yellow berries in the adjacent province of Konya were selling for 40–50 piasters per *okka*. By c. 1906, synthetic dyes had depressed the price to one piaster and Konya production plummeted from c. 60,000 to 1,000 *okkas*.

In the context of booming foreign demand, there was the potential for much profit: for example, Uşak carpet prices rose by at least 50 percent between the 1840s and 1870s. Great profits brought great temptations. Some producers rushed rugs to market with little concern for quality and the often-careless adoption of aniline dyes damaged the reputation of traditional production centers such as Uşak.[112] By the end of the century, cotton had replaced wool in the woof at Gördes, Demirci and partially at Isparta.

The quality decline prompted quick responses in some quarters. In the 1840s, local entrepreneurs and the İstanbul government attempted to halt the abandonment of traditional patterns. In the next decade, some producers called for the import of European chemical dyes.

During the transition to synthetic dyes, foreigners became more active and increasingly took control of rug making. Dyers from Europe were brought to the carpet centers of Uşak, Kula and Demirci. Many dyehouses fell under the domination of the İzmir-based merchant houses and frequently were owned by their agents. The agents distributed the merchants' rug orders among local producers for a 3 percent commission. But they made most of their money from the dyehouses, requiring that all rug producers under contract to them utilize only the dyes produced in their particular dyehouse.

There were an estimated eight large-scale dyehouses in Uşak alone, and others of importance at Kula, Gördes, Akhisar and Demirci. Some still used natural dyestuffs c. 1900 while others worked with aniline dyes. Uşak producers predominantly used aniline dyes from Germany and France. Around the turn of the century, however, dyehouses of the larger İzmir merchant firms began employing only natural dyes and the high-quality red synthetic, alizarin, as part of their effort to improve quality.

The various steps in carpet making – washing, spinning, dyeing and knotting – can be performed by one or several persons. In Anatolia, the number of different persons engaged in making a rug varied in relation to the involvement in market production. The greater the commitment to export, however, the more refined the division of labor became. The earliest nineteenth-century records show Sivrihisar as the vibrant center for the supply of wool to the knotting towns. In the early 1870s, men from villages near Uşak were washing and bleaching the wool. Women, sometimes referred to as old, then spun the wool at home. Although the use of spinning wheels was known in the Uşak area, most yarn was spun by hand since this method produced a loosely made yarn more suitable to carpet production.[113] Local domestic industry exclusively provided the rising amount of yarn required at Uşak until the 1890s. By the previous decade, virtually every house in the town already was laboring in some aspect of carpet making. But the need for yarn continued to rise as Uşak carpet output tripled between 1885 and 1896. During the 1890s, men took over the spinning tasks once the prerogative of females, leaving the women more time to knot. Nomads (yürüks) also made warp threads for sale to Uşak producers and villagers (*Gedizliler*) some 40 km away from the town spun the weft.[114]

After spinning, the yarn was dyed, both in independent dyehouses and those of the commission agents. Dyers had recipe books, each page containing a separate written recipe for a color; attached to the page was a sample of the colored yarn. At some important centers, such as Kula, women continued to dye the yarn. At Uşak, women also had performed this task but, at some point in the nineteenth century, it became the preserve of a separate group of male workers. In Uşak, but apparently not at the other production centers, the yarn dyeing became separated from the knotting functions, a result of rising demand and, perhaps, increasing European control of the dyeworks. This differentiation of function at Uşak probably occurred in the 1880s, when synthetic dyes were adopted wholesale and when European dye masters arrived on the scene. Knotting was done on looms that were wider in town houses than at nomads' tents. At Uşak, these were very large, reportedly up to 8 meters in width. The carpet knotters of Uşak exclusively were women and young girls. In contrast, men as well as women and girls knotted and wove carpets at Kula and Gördes.[115] The number of loom operators rose steadily at Uşak during the nineteenth century, underlining a growing dependency on the carpet trade. In the early 1880s, some 3,000 women and 500 girls worked more or less year-round on 600 looms. By 1900, their number had increased to c. 6,000, working on approximately 1,200 looms. Thus, the number of looms and workers doubled as production levels tripled. The town had reached its maximum production levels, given its population and the prevailing technologies.

Without exception, the knotters had worked in private homes, where they adjusted the workpace to family considerations and the needs of the agricultural cycle. Neither the knotting techniques employed nor the loom itself changed over the century. Uşak knotting families owned their looms and some houses possessed two, three and even four. Depending on the size of the rug, up to eight persons worked side by side on a loom. The work days varied by season, usually 5–7 hours in the winter and 9–12 hours in the summer. When a new pattern was introduced, a more experienced knotter directed the others. The mistress of the house supervised operations. Workers who were not members of the loom owner's family received either daily or piece wages; both systems of payment coexisted. Typically, young girls of 7–8 years were apprenticed to a master craftswoman. The apprenticeship lasted from two to three years depending on the child. At Uşak, Turkish Muslims dominated the knotting tasks and rug making in general; elsewhere, Greeks and Armenians played a more important role. Turks reportedly comprised 75 percent of knotters in the industry overall.[116]

An almost bewildering series of additional changes took place at the end of the century. In 1895, the Ottoman government sought to profit from the boom and founded a carpet factory in the town of Hereke, where a government industrial complex had existed since the 1840s. Within a decade, rug making had taken hold and over 1,000 female knotters from the area produced custom-ordered carpets in the state factory. The yarn came from a mechanized government spinning mill at Karamürsel and a German-trained master dyed it on the premises. Turkish and Greek girls from four to fifteen years of age worked in three great knotting halls, on 150–180 knotting frames of varying sizes. The factory worked only with pre-ordered patterns, thus it did not develop its own designs. These knotters followed instructions that specified not only the number of knots but also the color arrangements. Photographs or sketch patterns were widely employed not only at new production centers such as the Hereke factory, but also at Uşak, from at least the 1850s. This de-skilling of a craft reduced it to a process accessible to a larger number of workers and, therefore, lower wages could be offered. At Hereke, the knotters worked 11 hours per day, except for the very youngest girls. The factory provided a school and a hospital for the employees. Some of the female workers walked to work from their nearby homes but others came from more distant villages and lived in factory furnished dormitories. Greek and Turkish girls lived apart, in separate dormitories, under the supervision of "old" women.[117]

Other mechanized yarn-spinning factories, in addition to the one at Karamürsel, furnished wool yarn for the rugs. The first near Bandırma opened before 1890, followed by three mechanized factories at Uşak. Within several years, these latter three produced more than 1,000 kg of yarn per day and employed some 2,000 persons, mainly women. The factories threatened the business of merchants competing with the three entrepreneurs who had established the mills; they also jeopardized the jobs of the village and tribal women (and men) who had supplied the yarn. As a result, unemployed spinners attacked the three factories in 1908. A crowd mainly of women and children smashed the engine rooms and carried off great quantities of stored wool.[118]

Other methods bolstered carpet production besides mechanized factories and synthetic dyes. Ottoman and foreign merchants and a number of Ottoman officials all promoted the industry. The governors of Sivas and Konya provinces each sponsored carpet exhibitions in their provincial capitals. Later rising to prominence as the minister of the interior and grand vizier respectively, the governors sought to impose quality control over the production of rugs in their areas and stimulate production for export. Commercial rug making outside the traditional centers sometimes was situated in private homes but, more frequently, entrepreneurs established work sites outside the home. Since the 1850s, İzmir and İstanbul merchant houses had encouraged production outside the traditional centers and had boosted the volume of rug making by substantial proportions. In some regions, e.g., Kütahya and Kayseri, the merchants employed large numbers of Greek and Armenian women. Many of these new workers did not even own a loom and received it and production supplies from the merchants. Moreover, the new rug makers worked longer hours under controlled conditions at a faster pace and earned less than knotters at established centers such as Uşak.

The diffusion of rug making to areas outside the four traditional centers at Uşak, Gördes, Kula and Demirci is very similar to the European experience, where merchants established production networks in the countryside to escape the urban guilds. The four towns virtually had monopolized rug production. Although it is not yet known if the labor was organized into guilds, this seems unlikely. But the towns did have a stranglehold; to break it, merchants set up production networks in lower-wage areas. As their counterparts in Europe, the merchants found a cheaper and more pliant work force that expanded production at lower costs. These new areas and workshops account for the continuing increases in Anatolian carpet production after the 1890s. During the first years of the twentieth century, the traditional centers of Uşak, Kula, Gördes and Demirci together contained 3,600 carpet looms. Elsewhere in western Anatolia, the carpet merchants had established a new export nexus with over 12,000 looms.[119]

The final change occurred in 1908, when a group of İzmir-based rug merchant houses, all European, formed a trust – called the Oriental Carpet Manufacturers, Ltd. – to corner the market and control production processes still more tightly. This carpet trust became the major single factor in the Anatolian rug industry and, by 1913, it controlled as much as 75 percent of total rug production. It drove many competitors from the field and, before World War I, employed 50,000 knotters of both sexes. In a number of towns and cities, the company established additional centralized workshops using, typically, Greek and Armenian knotters who gathered outside the home to make rugs. The company provided dyed yarn from its factories and dye-houses that employed vegetable dyestuffs in Bandırma and İzmir. At 14 other locations, including Uşak, the trust found it easier to establish agencies. These agents required loom operators to use only yarn that had been dyed in the factories of the trust.[120]

Control of the two most important export industries – carpet making and raw silk reeling – had evolved in precisely opposite patterns. At Bursa, foreigners had completely dominated the raw-silk export industry at its outset, bringing in the new technologies and founding the first factories. But then, over the century, ownership of the steam-powered mills moved into Ottoman hands. By 1914, foreigners owned only a few silk-reeling factories. In carpet making, by contrast, Ottoman subjects (mainly at Uşak) had fully dominated the industry through its long development until the mid-nineteenth century. Although they seem to have hung onto the means of production at Uşak, ownership and control of the industry largely passed into the hands of the Oriental Carpet Manufacturers. The bulk of the profits in the largest export industry flowed out of the country, to the corporate offices of the trust in London.

Hand manufacturing for domestic markets

The surge in the domestically oriented industrial sector that took place after 1870 was real enough, but aggregate statistics are not available to measure its scale and intensity. In their stead, the following extended series of examples suggests the nature and pattern of the expansion in the Anatolian, Arab and European provinces. With the exception of the first example – shoe making in İstanbul – all are from textile manufacturing, because of its central place in Ottoman industry and the abundance of documentation.[121]

The shoe-making industry in the capital had been important. During the 1860s, when it reportedly was on the verge of disappearing, some 1,000 women and an unspecified number of men still labored in the industry. Fashion changes were creating unstable market conditions and European producers supplied increasing quantities of the new, Western-style footwear. To compound the problems for Ottoman shoe makers, mechanization in the European and American shoe industries advanced rapidly after 1850. Thus, foreign makers seemed to be taking over the local markets. The İstanbul shoe makers, however, began a "surprising recovery" c. 1875, producing better quality shoes at a lower price than foreign suppliers could provide. By 1900, they had fully recaptured their local customers, supplying the "entire demands" of the capital and exporting substantial quantities of shoes to the provinces and to Egypt. Imports ceased except for limited quantities of the very highest quality and most recent fashions. Supplied by local tanneries, competition against the İstanbul shoe makers became impossible, even from automated factories located in the capital.[122]

During this shift from moribundity to vitality, guild labor declined in importance, replaced by free labor. Shoe making in İstanbul evolved into a highly decentralized craft dominated by small manufacturers employing non-guild workers. Workshops were scattered about in various quarters of the city; the ethnicity of the work force varied by neighborhood. In one quarter, for example, the shoe makers were all Greeks while in another they exclusively were Armenians. Each quarter seems to have specialized in different footgear. Merchants and exporters gave orders to small workshops run by a master, to whom they provided the necessary materials. The master usually employed 5–10 male and female workers, but sometimes there were as many as 50 persons. The workshops maintained a minute division of labor. There was a special worker at a certain piece-work rate for each step – the cutting, sewing, hole punching, heel and sole making, lining and assembly. The work was of quite high quality but the wages were extremely low by the standards of the time.[123]

Turning to textile production, the bustling hinterland of İzmir reported substantial increases in the number of looms and dyeing facilities after 1900. The "importation of British water twists is increasing owing to the larger number of looms in the interior, while the coloured yarns are declining on account of the natives doing more and more their own dyeing themselves."[124] At Buldan, for example, the number of looms perhaps doubled during the 1890s, reaching 1,500 at the turn of the century. Quite nearby, in the remote and large village of Kadıköy, the 10,000 inhabitants imported yarn from Britain and dyes from Germany to make a strong cotton cloth sold everywhere in Anatolia, at a lower price than imports.[125] In the city of İzmir, by 1901, printers annually were making over 1.2 million head scarves from English cotton cloth and shipping them inland.[126] Cheap labor at Kayseri in the Anatolian interior made it an important supplier of wool yarn for the carpet industry in 1900; the region also supplied wool thread to weavers around Adana. At Mardin, "where a few years ago there was nothing of the sort," a new industry emerged in the late 1880s, with 500 looms weaving cotton cloth. In 1893, the town held 600 looms "where a few years ago there were none."[127] Cotton-cloth production orchestrated by the Kayseri merchants had disappeared from Amasya and Merzifon by c. 1860. In the later 1870s, however, "the numerous looms which are now at work" marked an industry that had "been gradually revived" using 5,000 bales of British yarn to weave cotton goods. The area also possessed a major handkerchief printing industry. Somewhat later, however, cheaper Russian imports won away some Trabzon consumers from Merzifon (and Aleppo) textile products.[128] In the early twentieth century, Gürün, a town near Sivas, began exporting the *şal* textile to Diyarbekir for the first time in living memory. An active manufacturing center, the town contained some 3,500 looms in 1911, weaving a large quantity of cotton and woolen goods with British yarn, as well as producing chairs, shoes and rugs.[129]

European (particularly Swiss) imitations had destroyed, by c. 1850, Ottoman production of the thin printed cottons (*kalemkâr*) that some women used to cover their heads or faces. Subsequently, however, Ottoman entrepreneurs recaptured the industry. Armenian merchants imported plain British gauze-like cloth and distributed it to women in their homes. In villages along the Bosphorus, women painted delicate works of art on both sides of the cloth. Elsewhere, in the Balkans and Anatolia, lesser qualities were stamped on primitive wood blocks. By the 1890s, European imports had ceased completely, unable to compete in price. Thanks again to very low wages (a maximum of 1.2 piasters per day), Ottoman producers had regained the local markets and exported substantial quantities to Persia as well.[130]

At Erzurum, consumption of Ottoman textiles increased during the mid-1880s, in the midst of the price depression. The city imported 20,000 pieces of cloth from Diyarbekir and Mardin, another 40,000 pieces from Erzincan and 100,000 pieces from Arapkir, the town whose prosperity was created by British yarn in the 1830s.[131] At the end of the decade, however, Erzurum purchases of Ottoman textiles reportedly were declining as foreign cloth sales increased.

The manufacture and local consumption of "native-made stuffs" at Harput increased sharply between the mid-1880s and World War I, because they were considerably cheaper and more durable. At the earlier date, the province annually exported 121,000 pieces of silk and cotton cloth and 45,000 pairs of shoes to other Ottoman areas. The number of cotton looms then increased: the value of cotton yarn imports rose 50 percent during the late 1880s while purchases of finished cloth and prints fell. Similarly, indigo imports increased because of the "revival of the manufacture of native cotton and silk cloth."[132] Local cotton cloth manufacture climbed again in the 1890s, prompting further rises in indigo and yarn imports and declines in the import of prints. In the late 1890s, Harput province exported 130,000 pieces of striped cloth (*manusa*) to Erzurum, Trabzon, Sivas and Bitlis and 90,000 pieces of its red cloth and prints to Erzurum, Diyarbekir and Sivas. Between the early 1890s and 1910, the value of cloth exports to Sivas, Trabzon, Erzurum and Bitlis had more than quadrupled.[133]

The Diyarbekir region endured its share of vicissitudes and yet remained a vibrant exporter of textiles as well as of shoes and shoe leathers. In the 1830s, its normal markets in Syria and Iraq were closed because of Mehmed Ali's economic policies. Only a "few hundred looms half employed" reportedly remained of the 2,000 said to be the norm. By this date, the cotton and cotton silk weavers were using British yarn. During the 1860s, some 1,200 looms in the city exported £74,000 of textiles to Anatolia, Aleppo and Baghdad. Villages in the district (*sancak*) of Diyarbekir contained an additional 2,700 looms weaving for the market. This district, c. 1884, exported 84,000 pieces of unspecified size (*top*) and an additional 64,000 "pieces" of various textiles, ranging from red yarn to woolen cloaks to silk cloth. And, "in sympathy with the revival of the manufacture of native cotton and silk stuffs," indigo imports rose substantially. The total number of textile looms operating in the city of Diyarbekir was said to have doubled between 1888 and 1908, to 800. Since 1,200 looms were working in the city during the 1860s, a severe decline in cloth production must have occurred during the 1870s to account for the "doubling" of the 1888–1908 period. Thus, Diyarbekir provides another example of dramatic fluctuations in production over time. Over 60 percent of the looms working in 1908 wove cotton cloth, worth 30,000 Turkish *liras*, partially to satisfy rising Baghdad demand. The number of silk looms had risen from 200 to 300, including 50 jacquard looms that were introduced in 1903. "This industry is well on the road to progress." Small silk-reeling mills employed about 500 persons. The increasing local manufacture of silk cloth eliminated cocoon exports, and, "is year by year giving employment to more and more Christian workmen, who would otherwise be without work."[134]

Van in the 1870s exported 5,000 pieces of locally spun and dyed mohair cloth, as well as 10,000 pieces of red morocco leather. In the following decade, workers in 200 city homes made both striped and checkered cloth (*manusa* and *satranç*) and 67 others wove coarse wool cloth (*aba*). In addition, seven "factories" manufactured a fine textured mohair cloth (*şal*). At this time, city weavers also produced 50,000 pieces of mainly white calico for sale in nearby markets. In the same vicinity, at the town of Çatak, 60 factories produced mohair cloth. Both towns also manufactured another kind of wool cloth (*şayak*). By the late 1880s, Van-area cloth production as well as the local consumption of Ottoman textiles imported from other regions reportedly was declining, in the face of "superior" imported goods. Nonetheless, in 1896, 700 looms in the regional town of Bitlis, using Persian cotton, manufactured 120,000 pieces of cloth for export to Russia and eastern Anatolia. In 1901, Bitlis shipped £18,000-worth of red and white canvas cloth to Russia and, in 1908, two-thirds of that amount to Ottoman markets.[135]

The history of the textile industry at Aleppo has been abundantly documented but misused to illustrate the decline of Ottoman manufacturing.[136] Aleppo textile output did not decline over the course of the century as alleged. The statistics actually show that production fluctuated, falling and rising in concert with changing market and political conditions. This pattern holds true for most of the nineteenth century. After remaining at relatively constant levels through the 1890s, Aleppo textile manufacturing then enjoyed two decades of very strong growth.

The weavers tenaciously held onto their looms, putting them aside in bad times, and resuming work when the market improved. A remarkably constant number of looms remained available in this ancient cloth production center between the 1840s and c. 1900. Altogether, between 8,000 and 10,000 looms were on call and went into use on demand. After 1900, the number of looms available absolutely increased, by at least 20 percent.

Table IV:20. Production of selected textiles at Diyarbekir, 1857–1903

	kutni	çitari	gazliye	şeytan bezi	canfes	bez (coarse)	manusa	basma	çarşaf	şal aba
1857[a]	15,000	15,000	25,000	5,000 pcs	30–40,000 yds	large qty				
1863[a]	21,000	10,000		7,000	15,300 yds	100,000 pcs			3,500 yds	15,000 pcs
1884[b]	3,000	16,000	24,000 top			30,000 pcs	30,000	20,000	3,000 top	4,000 pcs
1903[b]	3,200	17,500	25,000 top			2,000 pcs	32,400	21,500	3,400 top	4,700 pcs

Sources: [a] FO 195/459 and 799 for town of Diyarbekir; [b] Diyarbekir VS 1302/1884 and 1321/1903 for district (*sancak*) of Diyarbekir. *Top* and piece are not necessarily the same unit of measure.

As the following statistics show, when the various historical sources reported declines in the number of looms at Aleppo, they actually were recording merely the temporary withdrawal of these looms from production. The number of looms operating at any particular moment varied radically. In 1829, some 6,000 looms were at work but, a decade later, their number had fallen to 1,200. In 1846, Aleppo weavers petitioned the government for relief from internal duties, claiming that the 8–10,000 looms they usually worked had been reduced to 800 because of unfavorable tariffs. But, c. 1852, 10,000 looms reportedly were functioning while some 5,600 were at work just a few years later. In 1861, the number of looms operating had increased by 1,000, thanks to the riots that temporarily eliminated competing textile production in Damascus. In 1868, only 800 looms were operating in January, but at the end of the year, there were 3,000 in operation, weaving for the Egyptian market. Between 1871 and 1872, the number of working looms rose from 5,000 to 6,500, thanks to strong Anatolian and Egyptian demand. In the following year, the reported numbers reached 8,000 and sometimes 11,000 looms. When killer famine struck Anatolia in 1873 and 1874, the number of Aleppo looms employed fell sharply, to 2,400. But the famine ended and, in 1875, the government lightened the customs duties paid on Aleppo silk cloth. In the late 1880s, drought struck Anatolia and famine visited adjacent Adana province, boosting unemployment at Aleppo. In the cotton-weaving industries, weavers worked "12 hours a day for a pittance." But harvests improved and industrial revival came quickly in 1889 as customers in Anatolia resumed purchases of Aleppo manufactures. In 1898, 3,300 of a stated 8,000 looms operated; as the important Egyptian market slumped, only 1,700 looms worked during the following year. In 1903, Egyptian and Anatolian demand for cotton and silk manufactures mounted substantially and 12,000 looms worked between July and November. In 1906 and 1907, a record 14,000 and 12,000 looms respectively were in operation. Overall, the total number of available looms increased by two or three thousand during the post-1890 output rise.

Changes in the number of cloth printing factories and dye-houses similarly point to significantly increasing textile production at the end of the century. In 1845, an estimated 100 dyeing and printing establishments employed some 1,500 persons while, in 1899, there were 129 dyehouses and 27 printing factories.[137]

Rising cloth production at nearby towns – Aintab, Maraş, Antioch/Antakya and Urfa – paralleled that of Aleppo and, in some ways, derived from it as well. As labor costs in Aleppo rose, the number of new looms in the other towns increased substantially. The various communities came to specialize in the production of particular fabrics; Aintab producers, for example, created a red cloth industry at the expense of Aleppo producers.[138]

The patterns displayed in the example of the Aleppo industry often seem to hold for Ottoman manufacturing in general. Thus, slumping red cloth production in the context of a generally prosperous textile industry in the city reinforces the point that we need to retain the broad view in considering the fate of Ottoman manufacturing. Also, the Aleppo example illustrates how the various kinds of textile production were affected differently by changing conditions. A slump, triggered by war, political instability or international finance might depress output in all branches of textile making or in one particular branch. For example, silk cloth weaving everywhere in the empire suffered during the 1860s and 1870s because of the very high prices for cocoons that silkworm diseases had induced. Alternatively, high prices for raw cotton in the early twentieth century, prompted by world-wide shortages, hurt cotton weavers and promoted silk-cloth manufacture. Also, as seen, a substantial proportion of the total looms that actually were present in an area might *not* be working at a particular time. A reserve army of looms existed that came into use under certain conditions.

More generally, the details in this enumeration of hand manufacturing collectively demonstrate *activity* and *change* in Ottoman manufacturing over the century. This was not a stagnant sector and it hardly was moribund. Moreover, there was unquestioned expansion. In production for the domestic sector, growth was more impressive in the second half of the century and was very widespread. Manufacturing for export grew at several different points. The first, at the mid-century, was associated with silk reeling – a rare example of mechanized production. Later on, silk reeling increased slightly while lace and, particularly, carpet exports mounted very sharply.

Ottoman manufacturing for the domestic market, as stated, has been overlooked in the economic literature because it did not conform to existing definitions (that required mechanization) and because it often was rural and household based and not readily visible. Contrariwise, both of the major Ottoman export industries, silk reeling and carpet making, received much attention both from contemporary and late-twentieth-century scholars. But they have been seen as unimportant. This is in marked contrast to the export manufactures of the eighteenth century, for example, red yarn and mohair cloth, that have been given their due. The differing emphasis does not derive from the relative values of the exports in question. Silk, carpet, lace and other manufactured exports in 1914, as seen, likely were worth more than Ottoman export manufactures c. 1800. Nineteenth-century exports have not been emphasized because the European and Ottoman economies had become far more complex and, in the European case, vaster by very many orders of magnitude. Ottoman exports of the final Ottoman century might well have been greater than before, but they were of far less relative importance to the Western economy. This should remind us of the need to remember the internal perspective when examining the question of late Ottoman manufacturing and economic change.

NOTES

1 Urquhart (1833), pp. 47 and 52. For additional information on the subject of manufacturing, see my *Ottoman manufacturing in the age of Industrial Revolution* (Cambridge, 1993), written after the present chapter was completed.
2 The account of nineteenth-century Aleppo similarly has been used as an ideal type in the decline typology; see Ubicini's (1856) widely quoted comments on the collapse of silk cloth production in Aleppo between 1800 and 1850, decreasing in value by over 90 percent.
3 e.g., BBA Cev İkt 996, 1241/1826.
4 Genç (1987) shows that European purchases of raw materials had caused serious problems well before the nineteenth century began.
5 Nuri (1330–38/1911–19); Sarç (1940) and in Issawi (1966); BBA e.g. İ ŞD 32, 1284/1868; Ubicini (1856).
6 Corancez (1816), p. 403, says that each loom occupied 5–18 workers. This seems unlikely given the population of Ankara at the time.
7 BBA Ankara eyaletine dair mesâili mühimme #2073. Also, Sahillioğlu (1968); USCR *Monthly*, February 1909, pp. 113–14 says there were 1,000 looms with 10,000 weavers.
8 BBA İ MV 24072, 1282/1865.
9 Ökçün (1970), p. 72, does not include the factories in Samsun, Adana, Damascus or Aleppo.
10 For example, the Uşak rioters, see below. An important source for labor unrest are company archives but, outside of Egypt, they have not been exploited very systematically except for Beinin and Lockman (1988).
11 BBA Cev Mal 16795, 1257/1841.
12 İnalcık (1979–80), pp. 39–42.
13 Sahillioğlu (1968), pp. 65–66.
14 Baer (1970).
15 See the 1805 declaration of the Plovdiv *abacı* guild in Todorov (1983), p. 224.

16 BBA HH 48311 Dah, 1254/1838–39.
17 BBA Cev İkt 2024; information provided by Professor Dimitriadis.
18 BBA Kepeci 54 1243 7465.
19 For example, BBA MV 25281, 1283/1866, from the merchants of Aleppo and Damascus. The significance of this tendency is not clear at present.
20 BBA Ankara eyaletine dair mesâili mühimme #2073.
21 Sahillioğlu (1968), pp. 65.
22 Todorov (1983), p. 228; Salaheddin Bey (1867), p. 129.
23 BBA İ ŞD 32, 1284/1868 and 1284/1867; also Nuri, (1330–38/1911–19), I, pp. 760–63.
24 BBA, İ MM 4031, 12 cr 1304/March 1887; information provided by Professor Dimitriadis.
25 BBA Cev İkt 347, 1220/1805–6. For locations, see Cev İkt 1642, 1231/1816; I ŞD 2196, 1295/1878 and 2580, 1296/1879. Thanks to the late Jean-Pierre Thieck for his guidance on this matter of the *mengenehanes* and for his (1985).
26 Akarlı (1986) and BBA Cev Bel 1674, 1226/1811 and HH 57568, 1212/1797.
27 BBA İ MV 7788, 1268/1851; Cev Bel 5672, 1267/1851.
28 BBA İ MV 505, 1257/1841; MV 8392, 1268/1852. See the 1887/1304 tax register in İ MM 4031. For another example of state acquiescence in the destruction of a guild's previous monopoly, see İ MV 672, 1258/1842.
29 BBA İ, Dah 2874, 1258/1842.
30 BBA İ MV 403, 1257/1841 and MV 21191, 1279/1862; Shields (1986), p. 77.
31 BBA İ, MV 636, 1258/1842; MV 24162, 1282/1865.
32 BBA İ, ŞD 45, 19 XII, 1284/1868; Nuri (1330–38/1911–19), I, pp. 748ff; Sarç (1940), pp. 423–40 and quoted in Issawi (1966), pp. 48–59.
33 Todorov (1983), pp. 230, 269.
34 For an account of eighteenth-century factory production, see Genç (1987); Eldem (1970), p. 286.
35 Clark (1974), pp. 65–67; Eldem (1970), pp. 117–20.
36 See sources in n. 115.
37 See Clark (1974), pp. 67–69, for other factories established at this time and for the role of the Dadian family in factory building. See Eldem (1970), p. 120, for other details.
38 BBA İ MV 1269/1852.
39 BBA İ Dah 5253, 1261/1845; İ MV 1460, 1262/1846. In the mid-1850s, the government brought Damascus hand weavers to Baghdad to revive its weaving industry and manufacture cheap copies of Indian textiles. And, it obtained indigo samples from Egypt to encourage local efforts to raise indigo and reduce imports. BBA İ MV 14224, 1271/1855.
40 Clark (1974). A shop was opened to sell fezes not required by the military, see BBA HH 51587, 1834–35.
41 BBA İ MV 13393, 1271/1855.
42 BBA İ MV 19941, 1277/1861.
43 BBA İ MV 23874, 1282/1865; İ ŞD 42, various documents, e.g. 1279/1863, show the factory still was operating.

44 BBA İ MV 12510, 1270/1854. He, however, was ordered to reach a negotiated settlement with the guild.

45 BBA İ MV 99, 1256/1840; Cev İkt 424, 1251/1835.

46 BBA Hüdavendigâr eyaletine dair mesâili mühimme #2282, 1263/1846; Cev Ikt 1520, 1262/1846.

47 BBA İ MV 8422, 1268/1852.

48 BBA İ MV 1183, 1260/1845; MV 7746, 1268/1851.

49 BBA İ MV 20885, 1278/1862.

50 BBA İ ŞD 32, 42, 45, 60 and 67, 1284–85/1867–68; Nuri (1330–38/1911–19), I, pp. 748ff, 764–65; Sarç (1940) and as quoted in Issawi (1966).

51 Thobie (1977).

52 GB FO 195/889, 18 April 1867, Issawi, e.g. (1988), p. 373.

53 Owen (1984).

54 US CR, 1875, #1692–166, 24 November 1875. Stern (1909), 69–71; Quataert (1983), p. 18; Issawi (1988), p. 378.

55 A centralized workshop, in 1902, began the hand manufacture of silk rugs for the American market. GB A&P 1903, 89, 6699, Aleppo for 1901.

56 GB A&P AS Salonica, 1883–4; AS 1888 and 1889, Salonica for 1887 and 1888.

57 GB A&P 1908, 17, 7253; GB A&P AS Adrianople for 1888.

58 GB A&P 1892, 84, 16 June 1892; also one at İzmir. GB A&P 1899, 103, c. 1899; GB AS 1887, Trabzon province for 1886.

59 GB A&P AS 1889 and 1890, Adana for 1888 and Aleppo for 1889; A&P 1900, 96, 6353, Sivas for 1899; A&P 1913, 73, 7781, Constantinople for 1912.

60 Pamuk (1987), pp. 108–29.

61 Issawi (1980), p. 177 quoting Eldem (1970), p. 121.

62 Turkey (1333/1914) and Ökçün (1970). For an analysis of the survey method and techniques see Hoffmann (1909). Eldem (1970), table after p. 122.

63 Adana VS 1319/1903, p. 189; GB A&P and Ger *BuHI*, 1902–12; *RCL* 31 Octobre 1910, pp. 502–5.

64 See Faroqhi, Part II above.

65 GB FO 195/253, 1844.

66 GB FO 78/289, 8 November 1836.

67 GB FO 78/289, Brant, 22 May 1836; BBA İ MV 21959, 1279/1863.

68 US CR, Reel T 681, Jewett at Sivas, 1 March 1888; GB A&P AS 2886, Devey at Erzerum, 7 July 1886.

69 Ger *BuHI*, 20 August 1907, p. 691. There were considerable fluctuations in production over time. But this does not detract from the main point, that imports benefited some communities while damaging others.

70 GB FO 195/459, Holmes at Diyarbekir, 14 April 1857.

71 US CR, Reel T 681, Jewett at Sivas, 6 June 1893 and 26 May 1893; GB A& P (1870–71), pp. 795–97.

72 Shields (1986), pp. 72–73.

73 *Ibid.*, p. 74.

74 Ger *BuHI*, 1907, Heft 9, p. 740.

75 Compare Hammer (1818), p. 69 and Genç (1975), p. 273, who shows the *muaccele* was 58,000 *kuruş* in the 1740s and 50s, 60,000 *kuruş* in 1808, but 76,000 between 1811 and 1833.

76 BBA HH 16756, 1225/1810; Cev İkt 1642, 1231/1816.

77 BBA HH 16756, 1225/1810; HH 16756, 1225/1810.

78 For example, BBA Cev İkt 996, 1242/1816.

79 BBA Cev İkt 1487, 1255/1839; I MV 505, 1257/1841.

80 Various FO reports of Sandison at Bursa. But Texier (1862) asserts that Bursa annually was exporting 100,000 pieces, about the same level reported by Hammer.

81 BBA Cev İkt 424, 1251/1835; İ MV 99, 1256/1840 and Dah 1606, 1256/1840–41.

82 GB FO, various Sandison reports; but Stich (1929), p. 96, flatly asserts that silk weavers became silk spinners.

83 The following is based on GB FO reports by Sandison at Bursa, 1840–45.

84 GB FO 195/113, Sandison at Bursa, 15 February 1840; FO 195/240, 27 March 1846.

85 Hüdavendigâr VS 1324/1906, 278; Dalsar (1960), pp. 410–13; Delbeuf (1906), pp. 166–69; US CR, Reel T 194; GB A&P 1862, 58; Farley (1862).

86 GB FO 195/299, Sandison at Bursa, 24 May 1851. FO 195/393, Sandison at Bursa, 13 August 1855 and author's interview with Rânâ Akdiş at Bursa, June 1986.

87 Delbeuf (1906), p. 142.

88 Ökçün (1970), p. 22.

89 See Quataert (1983).

90 Fr AE CC, Brousse, 1853–1901, 31 Mars 1897. Raw silk was 120 Fr. in 1850 and 55 Fr. in 1900.

91 Quataert (1983). *RCL* 30 Novembre 1909; also see Hüdavendigar VS, 1324/1906, p. 278.

92 MacGregor (1847), p. 107, quoting 1841 GB FO consular reports; Fr AE CC for 1895; *Revue Technique d'Orient*, Decembre 1911; Quataert (1983), pp. 499–500. But, at the last date, this represented only 5 percent of total output.

93 Quataert (1983); Rânâ Akdiş, see n. 57, stated that the average village family in contemporary Turkey annually raises 30 kg of cocoons.

94 See Vatter (n.d., c. 1987) for an excellent discussion of this point.

95 Aus, *k und k*, 1906, Trapezunt, Februar 1909. Trabzon VS, 1322/1904, p. 101.

96 GB A&P (1870), pp. 795–97.

97 US CR, Reel T 681, Jewett at Sivas, 30 June 1893.

98 Shields (1986), pp. 75–78.

99 Ger *BuHI*, 19 Juli 1904, Bd. VII, Heft 4, p. 300.

100 Eldem (1970), p. 145.

101 GB A&P 1873, 67, 14 November 1872, p. 685.

102 Ger *BuHI*, 19 Juli 1904, Bd. VII, Heft 4, pp. 273–74. This probably is the same group as reported in Dumont (1981) p. 220.

103 Hall (1918), p. 155, suggests these production levels were surpassed by other missions. The industry certainly was not new, but based on local traditions of cloth manufacture.

104 GB A&P 1900, 96, Aleppo for 1899; A&P 1898, 94, 6195; A&P 1905, 93, 6884; also A&P 1907, 93, 7127; A&P 1911, 96, 7579; A&P 1914, 95, 7883. Hall (1918), p. 157.

105 The following section is based largely on Quataert (1986b) and sources cited therein.

106 See, e.g., Stoeckel (1892).

107 Cunningham (1983), p. 45.

108 See Table 1 in Quataert (1986a).

109 See Table 2 in Quataert (1986a).

110 Turkey (1968), pp. 276–77.

111 Işıksaçan (1964), p. 12.

112 RCL Juliet 1900, "Lettre d' Ouchak," 5 Juillet 1900.

113 Atalay (c. 1952), p. 48.

114 Aus HHStA, PA, XI, Türkei, Karton 272, 4 Januar 1896.

115 In the midst of the west Anatolian textile zone, at Balıkesır, the government founded a factory to make military uniforms during the 1850s. Most details about the factory are unknown. But in exchange for spinning yarn and delivering it to the factory, we know that the Haremeyn tribe of the Karası district (sancak) received wages and tax exemptions. The tribe bought wool from others in the area and spun it into yarn, receiving a fixed rate per unit of weight. More generally, there were intimate and complex economic relations between the nomadic and settled populations. When discussing textile production, most sources refer to town residents as the suppliers of certain materials, e.g., dyestuffs or yarn, leaving the implication that the individuals lived in settled towns or villages. On closer examination, some turn out to be nomads whose exchange of goods played a vital role in the economic life of sedentary communities. The significance of nomads has been under-estimated and we may need to revise still further our understanding of nineteenth-century manufacturing. Also, we need to consider the likelihood that the economic role of nomads in Anatolia and Syria, as well as other regions, changed over the course of the century, affected by a number of variables. Among these, certainly, is the issue of tribal pacification by the government that began in the 1820s. At this time, however, we don't know how this forcible sedentarization influenced the tribal role in rug making. Some of the villagers producing commercial carpets in the later nineteenth century had been nomads. BBA Cev İkt 499, 1264/1848; İ MV 4003, 1265/1849.

116 Ger BuHI, 9, 1906, 'Die anatolische Teppichindustrie'; Pittard (1931).

117 Stoeckel (1892), p. iv.

118 BBA BEO 693/22, s. 1–40, 80–81 and 132.

119 Ger BuHI, 9, 1906, 'Die anatolische Teppichindustrie'.

120 Annual Reports of the Oriental Carpet Manufacturers, Ltd., 1909–18. One source states that aniline dyes were being used.

121 The following section is more detailed because it offers data not available in the published sources.

122 Salaheddin Bey (1867), p. 129. Herlt (1918), 58; Ger *BuHI*, 1902, 10 April 1902 and 1904.

123 Ger *BuHI*, 1904, pp. 306–8; Junge (1916), p. 446, asserts that a shoe-making guild of Turks survived into the twentieth century.

124 GB A&P AS 3170, Smyrna for 1902–3, p. 11.

125 Fitzner (1902) was translated in edited form and published as GB, Naval Staff Intelligence Department, *A Handbook of Asia Minor*, July 1919. Also see GB A&P AS 5247, Smyrna for 1912–13.

126 Ger *BuHI*, 1902, Smyrna.

127 Fr RCC 1900, Reel 33, pp. 9–10. GB A&P 1892, 84, 16 April 1892.

128 UPA FO vol. 7, 31 December 1878 Trabzon report; GB A&P AS 1888, Trabzon for 1887 and AS 1890, Trabzon for 1889.

129 GB A&P 1908, 117; Fr RCC 1901, Reel 34 and RCC 1911, Reel 40.

130 Ger *BuHI*, 1904, p. 302.

131 GB A&P 195/2584, 1887 at Erzerum.

132 GB A&P AS 1886, Kharput for 1885, 11 September 1886; FO 195/1887, Kharput province for 1886.

133 GB A&P AS 1889, Erzerum for 1887–88; A&P AS 1891, Erzerum for 1889–90 and various FO 1891–1911.

134 GB FO 78/289, 8 November 1836; FO 195/799, 31 March 1864; FO 195/799, July 1864.

135 GB A&P 1905 and 1906, p. 129; UPA FO Vol. 16, 1908 report and compare with Diyarbekir VS, 1302/1884–85 and 1321/1903, pp. 195–96. Diyarbekir exports of silk and cotton cloth to Ottoman areas equaled £14,000 and £13,000 in 1892 and 1893.

136 GB A&P 1873, 67, 14 November 1872; GB A&P AS 1887 Van and Hekkiari for 1885–86; A&P AS 1891, Erzerum for 1889–90, reporting on Van and Bitlis.

137 See note 2 above.

138 Bowring (1840), p. 20. BBA İ MM 2276, 1292/1875; GB A&P AS 1889, Aleppo for 1888 and other FO and A&P reports from Aleppo. The rapid revival in part, perhaps, is due to the abolition of the 4 percent duty for export by sea. GB A&P AS 1890, Aleppo for 1889; A&P 1905; Halep VS, 1317/1899, pp. 191–92 and Aus *k und k* Aleppo, 1901. Also, Issawi (1988), pp. 372–81. BBA Cev İkt 2024; MacGregor (1847); various GB A&P and FO 195.

∴

BIBLIOGRAPHY

Archives

Turkey: Başbakanlık Arşivi, Prime Ministry Archives, İstanbul
   Bab-ı Ali Evrak Odası
   Cevdet Tasnifi, Belediye
   Cevdet Tasnifi, Dahiliye
   Cevdet Tasnifi, İktisat
   Cevdet Tasnifi, Maliye
   Cevdet Tasnifi, Nafia
   Hatt-ı Hümayun Tasnifi
   Kamil Kepeci Tasnifi
   İradeler Tasnifi
   Yıldız Tasnifi
   Ankara eyaletine dair mesaili mühimme
   Hüdavendigâr eyaletine dair mesaili mühimme

Austria: Haus-Hof und Staatsarchiv, Vienna

France: Archives du Ministère des affaires étrangères, Paris
   Correspondance consulaire et commerciale, 1873–1901
   Constantinople, 106–7, 115–17
   Trebizonde, 9–13
   Smyrne, 55–57
   Brousse, no nr.
   Erzeroum, 4

Germany, (formerly) Democratic Republic: Zentrales Staatsarchiv, Potsdam
   Auswärtiges Amt

Great Britain: Foreign Office, The Public Records Office, London
   FO 195 and 424

United States: National Archives, Washington, D.C.
   Brusa, 1837–40

Constantinople, 1820–70
Salonica, 1832–40
Smyrna, 1802–75.

Published consular reports

Austria: *Berichte der k. u. k. Österr.- Ung. Konsularämter über das Jahr.* ...
Herausgegeben im auftrage des K.K. Handelsministeriums vom K.K. Österr.
Handelsmuseum. Vienna, 1900–1912.
Politisches Archiv, Türkei XII, K 195, 196, 352.

France: *Bulletin consulaire français. Recueil des rapports commerciaux adressés
au Ministère des affaires étrangères par les agents diplomatiques et consulaires
de France à l'étranger.* Paris, 1877–1914.

Germany: Deutsches Reich. *Handel und Industrie. Berichte über Handel und
Industrie.* Berlin, 1900–15.

Great Britain: Parliamentary Papers, *Accounts and Papers.* London, 1876–1913.

United States: Department of State. *Commercial Relations of the United States.*
Washington, 1856–79.
Daily Consular Reports. Washington, 1901–2.
Department of Commerce and Labor, Bureau of Manufactures, *Monthly Con-
sular and Trade Reports.* Washington, 1907–14.

Contemporary newspapers and journals (selected)

Aydın, 1297–1301
Board of Trade Journal, 1906–14
Bursa, 1310–11
Levant Trade Review, 1911–15
İtidal, Adana, 1327
Bursa Sergisi, 1325
Diyarbekir, 1327
*La Revue commerciale du Levant, bulletin mensuel de la chambre de commerce
française de Constantinople,* 1896–1912
Revue de Constantinople, 1875–76
Revue Technique d'Orient, 1910–14
Sivas, 1902–8

Secondary sources

Adams, Walter Booth (1924). "Public health" in Mears, ed., pp. 155–176.

Adanır, Fikret (1984–85). "The Macedonian Question: the socio-economic reality and problems of its historiographic interpretations," IJTS, Winter, III (1), 43–64.

Akarlı, Engin Deniz (1986). "Gedik: implements, mastership, shop usufruct, and monopoly among Istanbul artisans, 1750–1850," Wissenschaftskolleg Jahrbuch, 225–31.

Aktan, Reşat (1950). "Agricultural policy of Turkey," Ph.D. dissertation, University of California, Berkeley.

Arıcanlı, Tosun (1976). "The role of the state in social and economic transformation of the Ottoman Empire, 1807–1918," Ph.D. dissertation, Harvard University.

(n.d.). "Agrarian relations in Turkey: state, peasant property and the question of landlordism," unpublished paper.

Arif, Muhammad (1971). al-Sa'ada al namiye a-abadiyya fi'l-sikka al-hadidiyya al Hijaziyya, manuscript trans. and ed. by Jacob Landau as The Hejaz railway and the Muslim pilgrimage. A case of Ottoman political propaganda, Detroit.

Atalay, B. (c. 1952). Türk Halıcılığı ve Cihan Halı Tipleri Panoraması.

Bacqué-Grammont, Jean-Louis and Paul Dumont (1983a), eds. Économies et sociétés dans l'Empire ottoman (fin du XVIII–début du XX siècle), Paris.

(1983b), eds. Contribution à l'histoire économique et sociale de l'Empire ottoman, Paris–Louvain.

Baer, Gabriel (1970). "The administrative, economic and social functions of Turkish guilds," IJMES, I, 28–50.

(1982) "Fellah rebellion in Egypt and the Fertile Crescent," in Gabriel Baer, ed. Fellah and townsman in the Middle East. Studies in social history, London, pp. 253–323.

(1983) "Landlord, peasant and the government in the Arab provinces of the Ottoman Empire in the 19th and early 20th centuries," in Bacqué-Grammont and Dumont, eds. (1983a), pp. 261–74.

Bağış, Ali İhsan (1983). Osmanlı Ticaretinde Gayri Müslimler. Kapitülasyonlar-Beratlı Tüccarlar, Avrupa ve Hayriye Tüccarları (1750–1839), Ankara.

Bairoch, Paul (1975). The economic development of the Third World since 1900, trans. by Cynthia Postan. Berkeley.

(1976). "Europe's gross national product: 1800–1975," JEEH, Fall, 273–340.

(1983). "A comparison of the levels of GDP per capita in developed and developing countries, 1700–1980," JEH, March, 27–41.

Batatu, Hanna (1978). The old social classes and the revolutionary movements of Iraq, Princeton.

Bayatlı, Osman (1957). Bergama'da Yakın Tarih Olayları, XVIII.–XIX. Yüzyıl, İzmir.

Behar, Cem (1986). "Some data on polygyny in İstanbul, 1885–1926," unpublished paper, İstanbul.

(1987). "Evidence on fertility decline in İstanbul, (1885–1940)," unpublished paper, İstanbul.

Beinin, Joel and Zachary Lockman (1988). *Workers on the Nile. Nationalism, Communism, Islam and the Egyptian working class, 1882–1954*, Princeton.

Berend, Ivan T. and György Ránki (1974). *Economic development in East-Central Europe in the 19th & 20th centuries*, New York.

Biraben, Jean-Noel (1975). *Les hommes et la peste en France et dans les pays européens et méditerranéens*, I, Mouton and Paris.

Bowring, John (1840). *Report on the commercial statistics of Syria*, London (reprint, New York, 1973).

Braude, Benjamin and Bernard Lewis (1981), eds. *Christians and Jews in the Ottoman Empire*, I, New York.

Braudel, Fernand (1966). *The Mediterranean and the Mediterranean world in the age of Philip II*, New York.

Buheiry, Marwan (1984). "The peasant revolt of 1858 in Mount Lebanon," in Khalidi, ed., pp. 291–301.

Burke, Edmund III (1986a). "Changing patterns of peasant protest in the Middle East, 1750–1950," paper presented to the 1986 annual meeting of the Middle East Studies Association.

(1986b). "Understanding Arab protest movements," *Maghreb Review*, XI (1), 27–32.

Cameron, Rondo (1961). *France and the economic development of Europe, 1800–1914*, 2nd ed., Princeton.

Clark, E. (1974). "The Ottoman Industrial Revolution," *IJMES*, V, 65–76.

Corancez, L.A.A. (1816). *Itinéraire d'une partie peu connue de l'Asie Mineure*, Paris.

Crafts, N.F.R (1984). "Economic growth in France and Britain, 1830–1910: a review of the evidence," *JEH*, March, 49–67.

Cuinet, Vital (1890–94). *La Turquie d'Asie: géographie administrative, statistique, descriptive et raisonné de chaque province de l'Asie Mineure*, 4 vols., Paris.

Cunningham, A.B. (1983). "The journal of Christophe Aubin: a report on the Levant trade in 1812," *AO*, VIII, 5–131.

Çadırcı, Musa (1980). "II. Mahmud Döneminde (1808–1839) Avrupa ve Hayriye Tüccarları" in Okyar and İnalcık, eds. (1980), pp. 237–41.

Dalsar, Fahri (1960). *Bursa'da Ipekçilik*, İstanbul.

Davison, Roderic (1968). *Turkey: a short history*, New Jersey (1981 edition).

Delbeuf, Régis (1906). *Une excursion à Brousse et à Nicée*, Constantinople.

Dols, Michael (1979). "The second plague pandemic and its recurrence in the Middle East," *JESHO*, XXII (2) (May), 162–89.

Draganova, Slavka (1988). "Documents of the 1840s on the economic position of the villages in central north Bulgaria," *Bulgarian Historical Review*, XVI (2), 87–104.

du Velay, A. (1903). *Essai sur l'histoire financière de la Turquie depuis le règne du Sultan Mahmoud II jusqu'à nos jours*, Paris.

Duben, Alan (1985). "Turkish families and households in historical perspective," *Journal of Family History*, Spring.

(1986). "Muslim households in late Ottoman İstanbul," unpublished paper.

(1987). "Locating the household in late Ottoman İstanbul," unpublished paper.

Dumont, Paul (1981). "Jewish communities in Turkey during the last decades of the XIXth century in the light of the archives of the Alliance Israelite Universelle," in Braude and Lewis, eds., I, pp. 209–42.

Eldem, Vedat (1970). *Osmanlı Imparatorluğunun İktisadi Şartları Hakkında Bir Tetkik*, İstanbul.

Elefteriades, Eleuthère (1944). *Les chemins de fer en Syrie et au Liban*, Beirut.

Engelhardt, Ed (1882 and 1884). *La Turquie et le Tanzimat*, 2 vols., Paris.

Farley, J.L. (1862). *The resources of Turkey*, London.

Faroqhi, Suraiya (1987). "Agriculture and rural life in the Ottoman Empire ca. 1500–1878," *New Perspectives on Turkey*, Fall, 3–34.

Fawaz, Leila (1983). *Merchants and migrants in nineteenth-century Beirut*, Cambridge.

Feis, Herbert (1930). *Europe, the world's banker*, New Haven.

Fitzner, Rudolf (1902). *Anatolien. Wirtschaftsgeographie*, Berlin.

Fogel, Robert W. (1964). *Railroads and American economic growth*, Baltimore.

Frangakis, Elena (1986). "Western merchant and financial capital in eighteenth-century İzmir," paper presented to the 1986 meeting of the American Historical Association.

Genç, Mehmet (1975). "Osmanlı Maliyesinde Malikane Sistemi" in Ünal Nalbantoğlu and Osman Okyar, eds., *Türkiye İktisat Tarihi Semineri, Metinler, Tartışmalar*, Ankara, pp. 231–91.

(1987). "Entreprises d'état et attitude politique dans l'industrie ottomane au XVIIIe siècle," in Jacques Thobie and Jean-Louis Bacqué-Grammont, eds., *L'accession de la Turquie à la civilisation industrielle. Facteurs internes et externes*, İstanbul.

Gerber, Haim (1987). *The social origins of the modern Middle East*, Boulder, Col.

Gilbar, Gad G. (1986). "The growing economic involvement of Palestine with the West, 1865–1914," in David Kushner, ed., *Palestine in the late Ottoman period*, Jerusalem, pp. 188–210.

Goffman, Daniel (1986). "A European commercial network in seventeenth-century western Anatolia," paper presented to the 1986 meeting of the American Historical Association.

Gould, Andrew G. (1973). "Pashas and brigands: Ottoman provincial reform and its impact on the nomadic tribes of southern Anatolia 1840–85," Ph.D. dissertation, University of California, Los Angeles.

Göyünç, Nejat (1983). "The procurement of labor and materials in the Ottoman Empire (16th and 18th centuries)," in Bacqué-Grammont and Dumont, eds. (1983a), pp. 327–33.

Güran, Tevfik (1980). "Tanzimat Döneminde Tarım Politikası (1839–76)," in Okyar and İnalcık, eds., pp. 271–77.

(1984–85). "The state role in the grain supply of İstanbul: the grain administration, 1793–1839," *IJTS*, Winter, 27–41.

Great Britain (1920). *Anatolia*, London.

Parliamentary Papers, Accounts and Papers (1870 and 1871). "Report on the Condition of Industrial Classes [in Turkey]," vols. 66 and 68.

Greenberg, Dolores (1982). "Reassessing the power patterns of the Industrial Revolution: an Anglo-American comparison," *AHR*, LXXXVII (4), 1237–61.

Hall, W.H. (1918). *Reconstruction in Turkey*, New York.

Hammer, Joseph V. (1818). *Umblick auf einer Reise von Constantinopel nach Brussa und dem Olympos, und von da zürück über Nicäa und Nicomedien*, Pest.

Hecker, M. (1914). "Die eisenbahnen der asiatischen Türkei," *Archiv für Eisenbahnwesen*, pp. 744–800, 1057–87, 1283–321, 1539–84.

Herlt, G. (1918). "Die industrialisierung der Türkei," *Das Wirtschaftsleben der Türkei*, II, 41–80.

Himes, Norman E. (1936). *Medical history of contraception*, New York.

Hoell, Margaret S. (1973). "The *Ticaret Odası*: origins, functions, and activities of the Chamber of Commerce of İstanbul, 1885–99," Ph.D. dissertation, The Ohio State University.

Hoffmann, Friedrich (1909). "Die industrie in der Türkei," *Weltwirtschaftliches Archiv*, XIV (7) Januar, 1–23.

Hütteroth, Wolf-Dieter (1974). "The influence of social structure on land division and settlement in inner Anatolia," in P. Benedict, E. Tümertekin and F. Mansur, eds., *Turkey. Geographic and social perspectives*, Leiden, pp. 21–38.

Hurewitz, J.C. (1975), ed. *The Middle East and North Africa in world politics. A documentary record*, 2nd ed., I, New Haven.

İnalcık, Halil (1943). *Tanzimat ve Bulgar Meselesi*, Ankara.

— (1971). "İmtiyazat," *EI²*, III, Leiden, pp. 1179–89.

— (1973). "Application of the Tanzimat and its social effects," *AO*, V, 97–128.

— (1979–80). "Osmanlı pamuklu pazarı, Hindistan ve Ingiltere: pazar rekabetinde emek maliyetinin rolü," *TITA*, 1–65.

— (1982). "Rice cultivation and the çeltükci-reaya system in the Ottoman Empire," *Turcica*, XIV, 140–41.

— (1983). "The emergence of big farms, *çiftlik*s: state, landlords and tenants," in Bacqué-Grammont and Dumont, eds. (1983b), pp. 105–26.

Işıksaçan, Güngör (1964). *Batı Anadolunun Başlıca Halı Merkezlerinde İmâl Edilen Halıların Desen ve Kaliteleri Üzerinde Araştırmalar*, İzmir.

Issawi, Charles (1966). *The economic history of the Middle East, 1800–1914*, Chicago.

— (1969). "Economic change and urbanization in the Middle East," in Ira Lapidus, ed., *Middle Eastern cities*, Berkeley, pp. 102–21.

— (1970). "The Tabriz–Trabzon trade, 1830–1900: rise and decline of a route," *IJMES*, I, 18–27.

— (1977). "British trade and the rise of Beirut, 1830–60," *IJMES*, VIII, 91–101.

— (1980). *The economic history of Turkey 1800–1914*, Chicago.

— (1981). "The transformation of the economic position of the *millet*s in the nineteenth century," in Braude and Lewis, eds., pp. 261–85.

— (1982). *An economic history of the Middle East and North Africa*, New York.

— (1988). *The Fertile Crescent 1800–1914. A documentary economic history*, New York.

İstanbul Ticaret Bahriye Müdürlüğü (1928). *İstanbul Limanı*. İstanbul.

Junge, Reinhard (1916). "Türkische textilwaren," in *Balkan-Orient-Sonderausgabe der Zeitschrift, die Textile Woche*, 1916–17.

Jwaideh, Albertine (1965). "The sanniya lands of Sultan Abdul Hamid II in Iraq," in George Makdisi, ed., *Arabic and Islamic studies in honor of Hamilton A.R. Gibb*, Leiden.

(1984). "Aspects of land tenure and social change in Lower Iraq during the late Ottoman times," in Khalidi, ed., pp. 333–56.

Karpat, Kemal H. (1983). "Population movements in the Ottoman state in the nineteenth century: an outline" in Bacqué-Grammont and Dumont, eds. (1983a), pp. 385–428.

(1985a). *Ottoman population 1830–1914. Demographic and social characteristics*, Madison, Wisconsin.

(1985b). "The Ottoman emigration to America, 1860–1914," *IJMES*, XVII (2), 175–209.

(1987). "The immigration of Ottoman Jews into the Ottoman Empire 1860–1914," unpublished paper.

Kasaba, Reşat (1985). "Peripheralization of the Ottoman Empire," Ph.D. dissertation, State University of New York at Binghamton.

(1988a). "Migrant labor in Western Anatolia, 1750–1850," unpublished paper.

(1988b). "Was there a compradore bourgeoisie in mid nineteenth-century Western Anatolia?" *R*, Spring, 215–28.

Khalidi, Tarif, (1984), ed. *Land tenure and social transformation in the Middle East*, Beirut.

Kolars, John and Henry Malin (1970). "Population and accessibility: an analysis of Turkish railroads," *The Geographical Review*, LX (2), 229–46.

Kurdakul, Necdet (1981). *Osmanlı Devletinde Ticaret Antlaşmaları ve Kapitülasyonlar*, İstanbul.

Kurmuş, Orhan (1974). *Emperyalizmin Türkiye'ye Girişi*, İstanbul.

(1983). "The 1838 treaty of commerce re-examined," in Bacqué-Grammont and Dumont, eds. (1983a), pp. 411–17.

Lampe, John R. and Marvin R. Jackson (1982). *Balkan economic history, 1550–1950. From imperial borderlands to developing nations*, Bloomington, Indiana.

Lewis, Bernard (1961). *The emergence of modern Turkey*, London, and later editions.

Lewis, Norman (1987). *Nomads and settlers in Syria and Jordan, 1800–1980*, Cambridge.

Licht, Walter (1983). *Working for the railroad: the organization of work in the nineteenth century*, Princeton.

Longrigg, Stephen (1925). *Four centuries of modern Iraq*, Oxford.

MacGregor, J. (1847). *Commercial statistics*, 4 vols., London.

Maddison, Angus (1964). *Economic growth in the West*, New York.

Mandel, Neville J. (1975). "Ottoman practice as regards Jewish settlement in Palestine, 1881–1908," *MES*, II (1), 33–46.

(1976). *The Arabs and Zionism before World War I*, Berkeley.

Maoz, Moshe (1980). "Intercommunal relations in Ottoman Syria during the Tanzimat era: social and economic factors," in Okyar and İnalcık, eds., pp. 205–10.

McCarthy, Justin (1979). "Age, family and migration in the Black Sea provinces of the Ottoman Empire," *IJMES*, X, 309–23.

(1983). *Muslims and minorities. The population of Anatolia and the end of the Empire*, New York.

McGowan, Bruce (1981). *Economic life in Ottoman Europe. Taxation, trade and the struggle for land, 1600–1800*, Cambridge.

McNeill, William (1976). *Plagues and peoples*. New York.

Mears, Eliot Grinnell (1924). *Modern Turkey*, New York.

Meriwether, Margaret L. (1987). "Urban notables and rural resources in Aleppo, 1730–1830," *IJTS*, Summer, 55–73.

Mitchell, Brian (1978). *European historical statistics*, abridged ed., London.

Mitchell, Brian and Phyllis Deane (1962). *Abstract of British historical statistics*, Cambridge.

Mordtmann, A.D. (1925). *Anatolien. Skizzen und Reisebriefe aus Kleinasien*, ed. Franz Babinger, Hanover.

Musallam, B.F. (1983). *Sex and society in Islam. Birth control before the nineteenth century*, Cambridge.

Naff, Alixa (1972). "A social history of Zahle, the principal market town in nineteenth-century Lebanon," Ph.D. dissertation, University of California, Los Angeles.

Nickoley, E.F. (1924). "Agriculture," in Mears, ed., pp. 280–301.

Nuri, Osman (1330–38/1911–19). *Mecelle-i umur-u belediyye*, 5 vols., İstanbul.

Ochsenwald William (1980). *The Hijaz railroad,* Charlottesville, Va.

(1984). *Religion, society and the state in Arabia: The Hijaz under Ottoman control*, Columbus, Ohio.

Okyar, Osman and Halil İnalcık (1980), eds. *Social and economic history of Turkey, 1071–1920*, Ankara.

Orga, Irfan (1950). *Portrait of a Turkish family*, London.

Owen, Roger (1981). *The Middle East in the world economy*, London.

(1984). "The study of Middle Eastern industrial history: notes on the interrelationship between factories and small-scale manufacturing with special references to Lebanese silk and Egyptian sugar 1900–30," *IJMES*, 475–87.

Ökçün, A. Gündüz (1970), ed. *Osmanlı Sanayii: 1913, 1915 Yılları Sanayi Istatistikleri*, Ankara.

Öncü, Ayşe (1987). "Turkish migrants return from Europe: a review of research," *TSAB*, September, 55–64.

Pamuk, Şevket (1987). *The Ottoman Empire and European capitalism, 1820–1913. Trade, investment and production*, Cambridge.

Panzac, Daniel (1985). *La peste dans l'empire Ottoman 1700–1850*, Louvain.

Pech, E. (1911). *Manuel des sociétés anonymes fonctionnant en Turquie*, 5th ed., İstanbul.

Pittard, Eugène (1931). *Le visage nouveau de la Turquie*, Paris.

Popoff, Kiril G. (1920). *La Bulgarie economique, 1879–1911*, Sofia.

Puryear, Vernon J. (1935). *International economics and diplomacy in the Near East*, Stanford.

Quataert, Donald (1973). "Ottoman reform and agriculture in Anatolia, 1876–1908," Ph.D. dissertation, University of California, Los Angeles.

(1977). "Limited revolution: the impact of the Anatolian Railway on Turkish transportation and the provisioning of İstanbul, 1890–1908," *Business History Review*, Summer, 139–60.

(1979). "The economic climate of the 'Young Turk Revolution' in 1908," *JMH*, September, D1147–D1161.

(1981). "Agricultural trends and government policy in Ottoman Anatolia, 1800–1914," *AAS*, XV (1), 69–84.

(1983). *Social disintegration and popular resistance in the Ottoman Empire, 1882–1908*, New York.

(1986a). "Machine breaking and the changing carpet industry of western Anatolia, 1860–1908," *Journal of Social History*, Spring, 473–89.

(1986b). "Ottoman households, Ottoman manufacturing and international markets, 1800–1914," unpublished paper.

Rafeq, Abdul Karem (1983). "The impact of Europe on a traditional economy: the case of Damascus, 1840–1870," in Bacqué-Grammont and Dumont, eds. (1983a), pp. 419–28.

(1984). "Land tenure problems and their social impact in Syria around the middle of the nineteenth century," in Khalidi, ed., pp. 371–96.

Reilly, James (1987). "*Sharia* court registers and land tenure around nineteenth-century Damascus," Middle East Studies Association *Bulletin*, December, 155–68.

Al-Sa'di, Essa Ali (1989). "Migration and social change in a Jordanian village: a socio-cultural perspective," Ph.D. dissertation, State University of New York, Binghamton.

Sahillioğlu, Halil (1968). "XVIII. Yüzyıl Ortalarında Sanayi Bölgelerimiz ve Ticâri imkânları," *BTTD*, 11, 61–66.

Salaheddin Bey (1867). *La Turquie à l'exposition universelle de 1867*, Paris.

Sarç, Celal Ömer (1940). "Tanzimat ve Sanayiimiz," in *Tanzimat*, İstanbul, pp. 423–40. Translated as "Ottoman industrial policy" in Issawi (1966), pp. 48–59.

Sauvaget, J. (1941). *Alep*, Paris.

Sayar, Ahmet Güner (1986). *Osmanlı İktisat Düşüncesinin Çağdaşlaşması*, İstanbul.

Schatkowski-Schilcher, Linda (1985). *Families in politics: Damascene factions and estates of the 18th and 19th centuries*, Stuttgart.

Sencer, Oya (1969). *Türkiye'de İşçi Sınıfı*, İstanbul.

al-Shaafi, Muhammad S. (1985). *The foreign trade of Jiddah under Ottoman rule, 1840–1916*, Riyadh.

Shaw, Stanford J. (1975). "The nineteenth-century Ottoman tax reforms and revenue system," *IJMES*, VI, October, 421–59.

Shaw, Stanford J. and Ezel Kural Shaw (1977). *History of the Ottoman Empire and modern Turkey*, II, Cambridge.

Shields, Sarah (1986). "An economic history of nineteenth-century Mosul," Ph.D. dissertation, University of Chicago.

Shorter, Frederic C. (1985). "The population of Turkey after the War of Independence," *IJMES*, November, 417–41.

Sluglett, Peter and Marion Farouk-Sluglett (1984). "The application of the 1858 land code in Greater Syria: some preliminary observations," in Khalidi, ed., pp. 409–21.

Sousa, Nadim (1933). *The capitulatory regime of Turkey, its history, origin and nature*, London.

Spooner, Brian (1977). "Desert and sown: a new look at an old relationship," in Thomas Naff and Roger Owen, eds., *Studies in eighteenth century Islamic history*, Carbondale, Ill.

Stavrianos, L.S. (1958). *The Balkans since 1453*, New York.

Stern, Bernhard (1909). *Die moderne Türkei*, Berlin.

Stich, Heinrich (1929). *Die weltwirtschaftlich Entwicklung der anatolischen Produktion seit Anfangs des 19. Jahrhunderts*, Kiel.

Stoeckel, J.M. (1892). "Modern Turkey carpets. A monograph," in C. Purdon Clarke, ed., *Oriental Carpets*, Vienna.

Stoianovich, Troian (1960). "The conquering Balkan Orthodox merchant," *JEH*, 234–313.

Suleiman Sırrı Bey (1924). "Irrigation," in Mears, ed., pp. 265–79.

Şerif, Ahmet (1325/1907). *Anadolu'da Tanin*, İstanbul.

Tabak, Faruk (1988). "Local merchants in the peripheral areas of the empire: the Fertile Crescent during the long nineteenth century," *R*, Spring, 179–214.

Texier, Charles (1862). *Asie Mineure. Description géographie, historique et archéologique*, Paris.

Thieck, Jean-Pierre (1985). "Décentralisation ottomane et affirmation urbaine à Alep à la fin XVIIIème siècle," in Zakaria *et al.*, eds., *Mouvements communautaires et espaces urbains au Machreq*, Beirut, pp. 117–68.

Thobie, Jacques (1977). *Intérèts et impérialisme dans l'empire ottoman (1895–1914)*, Paris.

Todorov, Nikolai (1983). *The Balkan City, 1400–1900*, Seattle, Wash.

Toprak, Zafer (1982). *Türkiye'de 'Milli İktisat' (1908–18)*, Ankara.

Touma, Toufic (1958). *Un village de montagne au Liban (Hadeth el-Jobbé)*, Paris.

Trebilcock, Clive (1981). *The industrialization of the continental powers, 1780–1914*, New York.

Trietsch, Davis (1910). *Levante-Handbuch*, Berlin.

Tucker, Judith (1987). "Marriage and family in Nablus, 1720–1856. Towards a history of Arab marriage," unpublished paper.

Turkey (1327a/1909). Maliye Nezareti. *İhsaiyat-i Maliye, 1325*, İstanbul.

(1327b/1909). Orman ve Maden ve Ziraat Nezareti, İstatistik Şubesi. *1325 Senesi Asya ve Afrika-yi Osmani Ziraat İstatistiği*, İstanbul.

(1911). Direction Genérale du Commerce. Ministère du Commerce et de l'Agriculture, *Listes indiquant les noms, genre de commerce et adresse des commerçants de Constantinople*, Constantinople.

Ticaret ve Ziraat Nezareti (1333/1914). *1328, 1331 Seneleri Sanayi İstatistiği*, İstanbul, rendered into modern Turkish by Gündüz Ökçün (1970).

(1938). *Türk Ziraat Tarihine Bir Bakış*, İstanbul.

(1968). *Uşak İl Yıllığı 1967*, İstanbul.

Ubicini, M.A. (1856). *Letters from Turkey*, 2 vols., London.

Uluçay, M.Ç. (1955). *Saruhan'da Eşkiyalık ve Halk Hareketleri*, İstanbul.

Urquhart, David (1833). *Turkey and its resources; its municipal organization and free trade; the state and prospects of English commerce in the East*, London.

Vatter, Sherry (c. 1987). "The European capitalist impact upon the textile industry of Ottoman Damascus, 1820–80," unpublished paper.

Verney, N. and G. Dambmann (1900). *Les puissances étrangères dans le Levant, en Syrie et en Palestine*, Paris and Lyon.

Part V

MONEY IN THE OTTOMAN EMPIRE, 1326–1914

ŞEVKET PAMUK, BOĞAZIÇI UNIVERSITY

أ

EVOLUTION OF THE
OTTOMAN MONETARY SYSTEM

This chapter surveys the evolution of the Ottoman monetary system from the earliest coins until World War I. Since the the world economic environment and the Ottoman monetary system changed substantially during these six centuries, it will be necessary to identify distinct time periods and treat the basic problems of each separately. For each time period, I focus on both the supply of money and the demand for money. With respect to the former, I examine the types of coinage and money in use in different parts of the empire; government policies and administrative practices; and European and other foreign coins which were a permanent part of the Ottoman scene. With respect to the latter, the focus will be on the long-term structural and institutional changes in the Ottoman economy in order to identify the evolving sources and types of demand for the use of money.

Tables show the specie content of the Ottoman units of account, the silver *akçe* and *kuruş*, the gold *sultani* and *lira* as well as their rates of exchange against other leading currencies. A summary table and graph are provided at the end of the chapter, while more detailed tables are presented in the text separately for each time period. One important purpose of these tables is to assist readers in inter-temporal comparisons of prices, wages and other monetary magnitudes. It is also hoped that they will prove useful in a future construction of the price and wage history of Ottoman lands.

Five time periods are defined:

1 *1326–1477:* from the minting of the first silver *akçe* until the minting of the first known Ottoman gold coin; the silver-based and relatively stable currency of an emerging state.

2 *1477–1585:* a bimetallic system based on silver and gold during a

period of economic fiscal and political strength for the empire; problems associated with the arrival of large quantities of silver from the Americas to the Old World.

3 *1585–1690:* disintegration of the monetary system due to fiscal, economic and political difficulties compounded by the adverse effects of inter-continental movements of specie; invasion of Ottoman markets by foreign coins and their debased versions.

4 *1690–1844:* attempts to establish a new silver standard around the Ottoman *kuruş*; relative stability of the *kuruş* until the 1760s, followed by severe fiscal crises and rapid debasement.

5 *1844–1914:* a new bimetallic system based on the silver *kuruş* and gold *lira*; rapid expansion of trade with Europe, heavy borrowing in the European financial markets and the abandonment of debasement as a means of creating fiscal revenue; adoption of a "limping" gold standard in the 1870s.

In view of the changing economic and institutional structures, it is clearly difficult to make sweeping generalizations regarding the basic features of the Ottoman monetary system during these six centuries. Nonetheless, a few conclusions may be attempted here.

First, it is significant that after the fifteenth century the central government could not impose a single monetary system for the entire empire. Different types of Ottoman coinage circulated in different regions from Crimea and the Balkans to Iraq, Syria, Egypt and northwest Africa. Perhaps even more significantly, foreign coins always circulated widely in different parts of the empire, occasionally exceeding in importance their local counterparts. The Ottoman experience was certainly not unique in this respect; many other countries faced similar problems during these centuries. Nonetheless, the absence of a unifying monetary standard does bring into question some larger issues regarding the economic and political unity of the empire.

Secondly, the stability of the Ottoman monetary system in each period was closely linked with the strength and well-being of the state finances and the economy, the nature of economic and institutional change and the political power of the empire. It may not be surprising, therefore, that the early and middle part of the sixteenth century was one of the more stable periods monetarily. On the other hand, the seventeenth century witnessed rapid debasement/depreciation of the currency and the disappearance of Ottoman coinage, especially in the provinces.

Thirdly, world economic and monetary developments often had

important consequences for the Ottoman monetary system. As Fernand Braudel has emphasized, money and bullion flows, often accompanied by commodity flows in the opposite direction, constituted one of the strongest links between different regions of the world economy linking the Americas to Europe and Asia during these centuries. Yet, the Middle East was often merely a transit zone for these inter-continental flows. As a result, the monetary system of the empire was often vulnerable to and adversely affected by the large movements of gold and especially silver.

Fourthly, it is now possible to establish the long-term trends in the specie content and exchange rate of the Ottoman currency. In the core areas of the empire from the Balkans to Anatolia and Syria, *akçe* and its successor *kuruş* remained the basic units. Since they were linked at 120 *akçe* = 1 *kuruş* after the 1680s, it is possible to calculate the total rate of debasement of the Ottoman currency for the six centuries under study here. As shown in Table V:10 and Fig. V:1 at the end of the chapter, from the earliest coins in 1326 until 1914 the silver content of the *akçe* declined from about 1.03 grams to 0.0083 grams, which corresponds to a long-term average rate of debasement of 0.8 percent per year. In comparison to the standards of the twentieth century, this may appear low. In relation to the rates of debasement observed in different parts of Europe during the same time period, however, this was a relatively rapid pace of debasement.[1] Not surprisingly, rates of debasement were not uniform over time. The specie content of the currency was relatively stable until 1560 and after 1844. In contrast, the century after 1580 and especially the interval 1760 to 1844 witnessed the highest rates of debasement.[2]

The exchange rate of the Ottoman currency showed similar trends against the benchmark Venetian ducat, whose gold content changed by only 1 percent during these six centuries. Following the decline in its silver content and the decline in the relative value of silver against gold, the exchange rate of the *akçe* against the ducat declined from about 1:30 (30 *akçes* = 1 ducat) in the fourteenth century to 1:6,000 (50 *kuruş* = 1 ducat) in the mid-nineteenth century, again as shown in Table V:10 and Fig. V:1.

Fifthly, in a long-term survey of this type, debasement inevitably occupies center stage. Fiscal pressures are presented here as an important determinant of the decline in the specie content of the currency. As Carlo Cipolla has argued eloquently, however, fiscal pressures constitute only one of the many causes of debasement. Moreover, debasement often constitutes only one of a number of possible responses to a particular economic, fiscal or monetary problem.[3] Future research needs to examine more carefully these other causes and dimensions of debasement in the Ottoman context.

Finally, it should be stressed that the monetary historiography of the Ottoman lands is still in the early stages of development. On many basic questions, such as how the monetary system worked in different parts of the empire, and the short-term fluctuations in the specie content of coinage, we still have limited knowledge. What follows, therefore, needs to be read with these qualifications in mind.

1326–1477: THE SILVER-BASED CURRENCY OF AN EMERGING STATE

It is well known that the eastern Mediterranean and the Middle East experienced an acute silver famine during the eleventh, twelfth and thirteenth centuries. Coins minted during this period were made from gold bullion and base metals. At the same time, Europe was relatively abundant in silver, and coinage there relied mostly on silver. It appears that this pattern began to change towards the end of the twelfth century. Just as gold was becoming more readily available in Europe, silver reappeared in abundance in the Middle East, soon to displace gold as the basis of many currencies. Silver coinage spread throughout Seljuk and Mongol Anatolia during the thirteenth century. The well-known hyperperon of the Byzantine Empire was one of the last gold coins to resist but it declined in importance.[4]

It is usually believed that the first silver Ottoman coin was minted in 1326 (727 H) during the reign of Orhan.[5] It was called *akçe* or *akça*, which has the connotation of "white." Western sources also refer to it as *asper*. *Akçe* remained the basic Ottoman unit and money of account until it was replaced by the Ottoman *kuruş* at the end of the seventeenth century. Evidence from the available coins indicate that the first *akçe* weighed approximately 1.15 grams. Until late in the seventeenth century, successive Ottoman administrations changed its weight but continued to instruct the mints to use clean silver only. In practice, of course, for technological reasons and because government control over the mints varied considerably in time and space, neither the weight nor the degree of fineness of the silver could be fully controlled. In addition, during periods of severe shortages of silver, even the mints in İstanbul were forced to produce sub-standard coinage.[6]

The basic unit of the *akçe* system was the small one-*akçe* coin. Other denominations were rarely minted.[7] In addition, for small daily transactions copper coinage called *mangır* or *pul* was minted in each local economy. While the purchasing power of the *akçe* was determined basically by its silver content, the copper coins were exchanged on the basis of their nominal value. In this early period, eight of the large copper coins and twenty-four of the small copper coins were accepted in small transactions as equaling one *akçe* in value. The state did not accept copper coinage as payment.[8]

The earliest Ottoman coinage was minted in Bursa, Edirne and in other unspecified locations around the Marmara basin. They circulated together with the coinage of the other Anatolian *beyliks* and the Byzantine Empire. As the Ottoman state began to expand its territories, new mints were established in commercially and administratively important cities and close to silver mines.[9] By the middle of the fifteenth century *akçe* had become the basic monetary unit of the southern Balkans, western and central Anatolia.

As it is the case with most pre-industrial societies, the Ottoman economy periodically faced shortages of specie. The government often exempted silver and gold imports from customs duties and prohibited their exportation. Ottoman laws also required that all bullion produced in the country or imported from abroad be brought directly to the mints to be coined. Under the circumstances, the rich silver mines of Serbia and Bosnia, which had for long been an important source of silver for the Byzantine Empire, Hungary and Italy, provided an additional incentive to the Ottomans to bring these areas under their control during the late fourteenth and fifteenth centuries.[10]

The central government auctioned off the operation of the mints and their revenues to private individuals. It then tried, through a representative of the local kadi, to maintain close control especially of the specie content of the coinage.[11] Under the open mint system, in practice, holders of bullion and old coins could always bring them to the mints and have new coins struck in return for payment. In addition, with each new sultan or whenever new coinage was to be issued, those possessing the old *akçes* were required to surrender them to the mints at rates often below those prevailing in the market.[12] The owners were then paid with the new coins. Needless to say, as the difference between the official and the market rates increased, so did the tendency for the holders of coins to evade state demands to surrender them.

It may be useful at this point to review briefly the sources of demand for money in the Ottoman economy and society. We start with the countryside, where close to 90 percent of the total population lived. It is well known that in response to the scarcity of specie and coinage, the institutions developed by most medieval societies for collecting the agricultural surplus attempted to reduce the demand for money. The *timar* regime was not an exception in this respect. First, by relying on a provincial army, it reduced the need to transfer large monetary resources to the capital. Secondly, the collection of the larger part of rural taxes in kind, most notably through the tithe, reduced the need for money for the rural population.

It is difficult to estimate what share of rural taxes were paid in kind under the *timar* regime during the fifteenth century. This proportion certainly showed significant variations from one region to another and also depended upon the crops cultivated.[13] On the basis of the evidence gathered from provincial regulations (*kanunname*s) by Halil İnalcık, it appears that the *çift resmi* and other fixed obligations of the rural households accounted for perhaps one-fifth of their total tax burden, on the average.[14] It is possible and even probable that some of these fixed taxes were also paid in kind to the *sipahi*, depending on the region, proximity to the markets and the type of crops cultivated by the rural producers. The *sipahi* was the most market-oriented member of most rural settlements.

On the other hand, the detailed lists in the provincial regulations regarding the rates at which labor and other obligations of the peasantry could be converted to money, and vice-versa, suggest that money was not beyond the reach of the rural population. Moreover, villages in the vicinity of towns specialized in the production of cash crops and were, in many ways, integrated to the urban economic life.

Money was used extensively in the urban economy during the fifteenth century. The artisanal activity organized around the guilds, money-lending and long-distance trade generated considerable demand for coinage and other forms of money. There is a good deal of evidence that credit was used widely within both the urban economy and to some extent by the rural population. Moreover, long-distance trade was often facilitated by the use of a special type of bill of exchange called *süftece* which reconciled Islamic Law with the exigencies of commerce.[15] In addition, the state used the *mukataa* and the *iltizam* system to collect some of its revenues in cash in order pay salaries and meet other expenditures. High-level bureaucrats who were engaged in a variety of economic activities and investments accumulated large fortunes and held at least part of their wealth in money form.

The *akçe* was fairly stable during the fourteenth and fifteenth centuries. Its silver content remained basically unchanged until the 1440s. During the two reigns of Mehmed II, however, debasement was used as regular state policy to finance the costly military campaigns and expand the role of the central government. Between 1444 and 1481, the silver content of the *akçe* was successively reduced for a total debasement of approximately 30 percent (see Tables V:1, V:2 and Fig. V:1 on p. 975). Contemporary observers, both Ottoman and European, emphasize that the debasements of Mehmed II were linked directly to fiscal pressures. With each debasement, the state obtained additional revenue, at least temporarily.[16] Nonetheless, more research is needed to examine other possible causes of this policy, such as the specie shortage faced by most economies of the period and the growing demand for money in an expanding economy.[17]

It would be incomplete to examine the Ottoman monetary system in the early period in terms of silver and copper alone. Evidence from court records makes abundantly clear that the rather limited supplies of the small-sized *akçe* and the locally circulating *mangır* could not meet the monetary demands of the growing economy. For larger transactions of trade, credit and for hoarding, gold coins were used extensively.[18] While no direct evidence is yet available regarding the minting and circulation of Ottoman gold coins in this early period, gold coins of other states circulated freely and the Ottoman government accepted them as payment. Most important was the Venetian ducat called the *efrenciyye*. Other gold coins in circulation had been designed after the popular ducat: those of the other Italian city states, the Egyptian *ashrafi* (*eşrefiyye*) and the Hungarian gold coin (*ongari* as it was known in Europe and called *engurusiyye* locally) which circulated mostly in the Balkans. (For the exchange rates of the *akçe* against these coins, see Tables V:1 and V:3.)

1477–1585: BIMETALLISM AND THE MONETARY
PROBLEMS OF AN EXPANDING EMPIRE WITHIN THE
SIXTEENTH-CENTURY WORLD ECONOMY

Starting as early as the 1420s, European sources make repeated references to Ottoman gold coins circulating in the markets of Italy and southeastern Europe, even though neither the actual coins nor Ottoman documents referring to such gold pieces have yet been recovered. It is also

Table V:1. The Ottoman *akçe* and its exchange rate, 1326–1477

	Akçes per 100 dir.	Akçe (gr.)	Exchange rate vs. Ven. ducat	Gold:silver ratio (calculated)
1326	266	1.15	—	—
1388	260	1.18	30	9.0
1410	266	1.15	35	10.2
1431	260	1.18	35–36	10.6
1444	305	1.01	39–40	10.1
1451	315	0.98	40–41	10,0
1460	330	0.93	42–43	10.0
1470	350	0.88	44	9.8
1475	370	0.83	45	9.4

Notes: (1) From some early date until late in the seventeenth century, orders from the central government to the mints specified the number of *akçes* to be struck from 100 *dirhams* of pure silver. According to Sahillioğlu, the weight measure used in defining the standards for the *akçe* until the second half of the seventeenth century was the *dirham* of Tabriz which weighed 3.072 gr. Sahillioğlu (1958, 1965a, 1983).
(2) Evidence from government sources and mint archives regarding the legal weight of the *akçe* is scarce for this early period. The information presented here is based mostly on the weight of coins in numismatic collections. Column 1 is derived from the gram weights of column 2.
(3) Even when information regarding government standards for the *akçe* are available, it is not clear to what extent these standards were followed by the mints. The weight and fineness of the coins varied considerably, due to the imprecise nature of the available technology. In addition, government control over the mints varied over time and space.
(4) Following most numismatic catalogues, calculations for the last column assume that the standard or proper (*sağ*) *akçe* contained 90 percent silver, on the average.
(5) The Venetian ducat weighed 3.559 grams with a fineness of 0.996 during this period.
(6) In view of the quality of the available data, the gold:silver ratios calculated here should be taken as no more than approximations. These ratios serve the additional purpose of providing an indirect check on the other figures. The average gold:silver ratio in Europe remained close to 10 during the second half of the fifteenth century. Braudel and Spooner (1967), p. 459.
Sources: Sahillioğlu (1958), pp. 1–58, (1965a), pp. 1–17 and (1983); Sultan (1977); Galib (1889–90); Edhem (1915–16); Refik (1921–23); Beldiceanu and Beldiceanu-Steinherr (1988).

known that the Ottomans often minted the Venetian, Genoese and Egyptian gold coins during the mid-fifteenth century, especially during the war with Venice (1463–79).[19] In any case, after the establishment of peace with Venice, the Ottomans began in 882 H (1477–78) to strike their own gold coins, called *hasene* or *sultani*, with the weight and fineness very close or slightly superior to those of the ducat. Despite two small adjustments in the sixteenth century, the weight and fineness of the *sultani* remained basically unchanged until late in the seventeenth century.[20] The *sultani*s exchanged mostly at par against the ducat until early in the seventeenth century (see Tables V:2 and V:3).

Starting in the middle of the fourteenth century, gold coins had become the prime means of international settlement in the Mediterranean basin.[21]

Table V:2. *The silver* akçe *and the gold* sultani, *1477–1584*

	Akçes per 100 dir.	Akçe (gr.)	Sultani (gr.)	Exchange rate akçe/sultani	Gold:silver ratio (calculated)
1477	370	0.83	3.572	45.5	9.5
1481	400	0.77	3.572	47	9.2
1491	420	0.73	3.572	52	9.6
1512	420	0.73	3.572	55	10.2
1526	420	0.73	3.544	59	11.0
1550	420	0.73	3.544	60	11.2
1566	450	0.68	3.517	60	10.4
1582	450	0.68	3.517	65–70	11.8

Notes: (1) See notes 1, 3 and 4 in Table V:1.
(2) The *sultani* was reduced in weight twice, first in 1526 following a similar reduction in the ducat, and also in 1564. Its fineness remained unchanged at 0.996 – the same as the ducat.
(3) The official rate of exchange of the *sultani* as well as the ducat remained at 60 until 1585. Their market rates began to increase, however, during the 1570s as the gold:silver ratios increased, apparently with some regional variations. As should be expected from the prevailing west–east differentials in the gold:silver ratio, gold coins were more expensive in the Balkans and silver was more valuable in the eastern parts of the empire.
(4) In view of the quality of the available data, the gold:silver ratios calculated here should be taken as no more than approximations. These ratios serve the additional purpose of providing an indirect check on the other figures. The average gold:silver ratio in Europe declined from 11.3 in 1470 to 10.6 in 1520 and then increased to 11.7 by 1580. Braudel and Spooner (1967), p.459.
Sources: Sahillioğlu (1958), pp. 1–58, (1965a), pp. 1–17 and (1983); Sultan (1977); Galib (1889–90); Edhem (1915–16); Refik (1921–23).

In addition, the stability of gold coins in contrast to the steady depreciation of silver currencies had turned the former into units of account. The Venetian ducat had for long dominated the markets of the eastern Mediterranean. The decision to strike Ottoman gold coins designed after the ducat was undoubtedly facilitated by the increasing availability of gold and the growing monetary needs of the Ottoman economy. This move also had political overtones: in effect, the emerging Ottoman Empire was signalling its intention to challenge the commercial and maritime supremacy of Venice in the eastern Mediterranean. At the same time, however, the Ottomans did not interfere with the circulation of the ducat or other foreign coins in their domains.

A limited amount of gold was mined in the Balkans under Ottoman control during the fifteenth and sixteenth centuries. It was the conquest of Egypt, however, which gave the Ottomans access to abundant supplies of gold from Egypt and the Sudan. The tax revenues from Egypt were received in gold coins, mostly in an Egyptian version of the *sultani* called *şerifis* which replaced the *ashrafis* of the Mamluk period.[22] As a result,

Table V:3. Exchange rates of other coins expressed in *akçes*, 1477–1584

	Venetian ducat (gold)	Egyptian ashrafi (gold)	Hungarian engurusiyye (gold)	Spanish 8 real (silver)	Dutch rixdale (silver)
1479	45.5	42.5	42–43		
1481	47				
1491	52	50			
1500	54	52	52		
1512	55	50–55	53	40	35
1526	59				
1550	60				
1566	60		57		
1582	60 (official) 65–70 (market)		57 (official)	40–42?	

Notes: (1) The Venetian ducat was reduced in weight from 3.559 to 3.494 gr. in 1526. Its fineness remained unchanged at 0.996. This new standard continued until the end of the eighteenth century. The exchange rate of the ducat and the *sultani* was identical during this period.
(2) The Egyptian *şerifi*, which replaced the Mamluk *ashrafi* after the Ottoman conquest, was intended to have the same value as the *sultani*. The *şerifis* of Cairo were often lower in weight, however, and they exchanged below par against the *sultani* and the ducat.
(3) For more information on the Spanish *real* and the Dutch rixdale (*thaler*), see Table V:6.
Sources: Based on Sahillioğlu (1958), pp. 140–64 and (1983).

the Ottoman domains were relatively abundant in gold until the third quarter of the sixteenth century.

It is thus possible to characterize the Ottoman monetary system after 1477 broadly as bimetallism. The mints were kept open for the coinage of both silver and gold subject to seigniorage payments to the state. The government announced the official rates at which coins of both metals would be accepted as payment. Similar rates were made available for foreign coins as well. On a day-to-day basis, the economy functioned in a similar fashion. The *akçe* and *sultani* as well as foreign coins changed hands on the basis of their market rates of exchange.[23] The silver content of the *akçe* remained relatively stable between the 1480s and the 1580s (see Table V:2).[24]

As the emerging Ottoman state became a full-fledged empire, however, the relatively simple Ottoman monetary system based on the *akçe* and the *sultani* became increasingly more complex. The newly conquered territories, each of which was subject to different economic forces, already had well-established currency systems of their own. In most cases, the Ottoman governments did not attempt to change them as they wished to avoid economic disruption and possibly popular unrest. Although the coinage minted in these territories began to bear the name of the sultan, Ottoman authorities in İstanbul could not fully control the evolving monetary structures, each of which remained distinct from the İstanbul-based *akçe/sultani* system. In addition, in most parts of the empire, foreign coins circulated extensively and without any form of free government intervention.

The Balkans, together with western and central Anatolia, remained as the core regions of the *akçe/sultani* system.[25] In outlying Wallachia, Moldavia and Hungary, on the other hand, Austrian, Polish, Hungarian and German coins were used more widely than Ottoman coins.[26] In Crimea, coins were minted in the name of the local khans, even though İstanbul exerted some influence in monetary affairs, especially since the prices of agricultural imports from Crimea played an important role in the economic life of İstanbul.[27]

When the Ottomans conquered Egypt, they retained the standard small silver coin called *medin*, *nisf* or *nisf fidda* which dated back to the early fifteenth century. Over time this unit began to be called *pare* or *para*, and remained the basic silver standard in Egypt until the end of the eighteenth century. As the exchange rates and the legal silver content of the Egyptian *para* shown in Table V:4 confirm, İstanbul exerted considerable influence on monetary policy in Egypt. From the mid-seventeenth century until the end of the eighteenth century, the silver content of *para* remained broadly linked to the *akçe*.[28] During the sixteenth century the *medin* also circulated in Arabia and Yemen. Other Ottoman coins were also minted in Yemen from the 1520s to the middle of the seventeenth century, but they do not appear to be significant economically.[29] In Syria, which remained as a transitional monetary zone between Egypt and Anatolia until the eighteenth century, *akçes* circulated together with *medins*.

The areas neighboring Iran, from eastern Anatolia to Iraq, were especially sensitive for the Ottoman government. In this region, Ottoman mints produced a coin called *dirham* by the numismatists and *shahi* by the Ottoman documents and the local population. Its weight and silver content was similar to the *shahis* of Persia.[30] Political factors may have contributed to this strategy of having a separate monetary zone next to Safavid Persia. Perhaps more importantly, trade with the east exhibited large deficits during the sixteenth century and the outflow of specie occurred mostly through this region. The minting of the *shahi* might therefore be interpreted as part of unsuccessful Ottoman attempts to control the outflow of specie to the east.[31] *Shahis* or *dirhams* continued to be minted in Baghdad until the 1730s.

Finally, in northwest Africa the political and economic ties to İstanbul were rather weak. Even though local coins, such as the square-shaped

Table V:4. The *para* or *medin* of Egypt, 1524–1798

	Silver content (gr.)	Silver content *para/akçe*	Exchange rate vs. Ven. ducat	Exch. rate against *akçe* based on rates vs. Ven.ducat
1524	1.05	1.4	?	—
1564	0.73	1.1	41	1.5
1582	?	?		1.5*
1584	?	?	43	1.5
1588	?	?	85	1.4
1618	?	?		3.0*
1641	?	?		2.0*
1670	?	?	90	2.8
1685	0.54	2.4	105	2.9
1688	0.52	3.1	105	2.9
1705	0.44	3.1	130	2.3
1720	0.35	2.7	120	3.1
1740	0.34	2.8	160	2.8
1760	0.18	2.0	168	2.8
1789	0.14	2.7	235	2.9
1798	0.079	1.5	350	2.7

Notes: * See below, n 5.
(1) The silver content of the *para* refers to the legal standard. The coins in circulation often contained less silver: in the eighteenth century *para*s often contained 20 to 30 percent less silver than the legal standard.
(2) Column 2 gives the ratio between the silver content of the *para* and that of the *akçe*. The data for the silver content of the *akçe* is taken from Tables V:2, V:5 and V:7.
(3) Little is known about the silver content of the *para* between 1525 and 1685. Based on official Ottoman records, Sahillioğlu (1983), Appendix Tables indicate that the standard for *medin* was set in 1524 at 1.224 gr. of 84 percent pure silver. According to the same sources, in 1564 the standard for *medin* was at 1.054 gr. of 70 percent pure silver. Whether there was a 30 percent devaluation in Egypt in 1566 (or earlier?) as stated by Braudel (1972), I, p. 539 (based on Hammer) and whether the debasement of 1585–86 in İstanbul had any impact on the *medin* remains to be established.
(4) Column 4 is calculated by dividing the exchange rate of the *akçe* against the ducat by the exchange rate of the *para* against the *ducat*. The exchange rates of the İstanbul *akçe* and *kuruş* against the ducat are taken from Tables V:3, V:6 and V:7.
(5) The exchange rates for 1582, 1618 and 1641 (*) refer, however, to the official rate at İstanbul. It appears that the official exchange rate between the *medin* and the *akçe* remained at 1 *medin* = 1.5 *akçe* until the end of the sixteenth century. The silver content of the *akçe* during this period is shown in Tables V:2 and V:5.
Sources: Based mostly on Raymond (1973–74), I, ch. 1; also Sahillioğlu (1983), Appendix Tables and (1958), pp. 84–88; Hansen (1981), p. 513; Shaw (1962).

silver *nasri*s, carried the name of the Ottoman ruler, İstanbul exerted little influence over the evolution of the monetary system in Algeria, Tunisia and around Tripoli. European coins circulated extensively in this region.[32]

During the sixteenth century the Ottoman economy came under the influence of other powerful forces, which had far-reaching consequences for the entire Mediterranean basin and beyond. For one thing, the six-teenth century was a period of considerable increases in population and economic activity in the eastern as well as the western Mediterranean regions. In the Balkans and Anatolia rural–urban economic ties were strengthened as local and long-distance trade flourished. Suraiya Faroqhi has shown, for example, that not only long-distance trade but also the activities of periodic local fairs increased during the sixteenth century both in the Balkans and in Anatolia. These trends point to an expansion in the demand for and use of money both by the rural and urban population.[33]

Large amounts of gold and especially silver began to arrive from the Americas to the Old World after the 1520s. The silver from the Potosi mines was minted into large coins and gradually found its way to Asia as Europe preferred to use it as payment for the spices, cloth and other wares of the East. These coins, commonly called *guruş* (after *grosso* or *groschen*), began arriving in the Balkans as early as the 1550s.[34] In other words, during the mid-sixteenth century not only demand for money was growing but this demand could be met by increased supplies of silver. The remarkable increases in the numbers of active mints in the Ottoman domains during this period provides strong evidence for the growing monetization of the Ottoman economy.[35]

In many ways, however, the Middle East was only a transit zone for these inter-continental bullion flows. The Ottoman government welcomed the arrival of large amounts of silver from the West as the trade with Europe showed surpluses. At the same time, however, it could not prevent the outflow of the same silver towards Iran and India because of the trade deficit towards these areas.[36] The form of payment depended on the West-East differences in the relative values of gold and silver or gold to silver. With the arrival of large amounts of silver from the Americas, its price relative to gold declined in Europe. As the relative price of silver remained higher in Asia, European trade deficits towards the East continued to be paid in silver.

There has been an extensive debate in the literature over the consequences of the arrival of silver. Ever since Hamilton, one side has argued that the world-wide inflation of the sixteenth century was mostly or purely a monetary phenomenon and was caused by the increasing availability of specie. Others in the debate have shown that prices of agricultural commodities rose faster than the prices of manufactures and emphasized the importance of real causes such as population growth and the population pressure on land in explaining the price inflation.

This problem has preoccupied the historians of the Ottoman Empire, especially since Fernand Braudel demonstrated the strong linkages between the western and eastern halves of the Mediterranean. In an important study, Ö.L. Barkan attempted to examine the extent and causes of the increases in food prices in İstanbul during the sixteenth and early seventeenth centuries.[37] His findings suggest that food prices in İstanbul expressed in *akçes* tripled between 1490 and 1580. Since the silver content of the *akçe* was mostly stable, food prices expressed in grams of silver registered a similar increase during this period. The available evidence also indicates that food prices increased even more rapidly after 1585 and these increases were related to the dramatic debasement of the Ottoman currency after that date (see Tables V:2 and V:5 for the silver content of the *akçe*).

Barkan's work did not resolve the debate regarding causes of the Ottoman inflation until the 1580s. This increase could be due to real factors such as population pressure, or the transmission of the price revolution from Europe via increased demand for Ottoman commodities or a combination of both. Before that answer can be established, however, a good deal remains to be learned about the history of prices as well as trends in population, agriculture and manufacturing.

Whatever the causes of the Ottoman price inflation up to the 1580s may be, there is considerable evidence that Ottoman state finances were adversely affected by these price movements, most importantly because many of the state revenues were fixed in *akçe* while its purchasing power declined with inflation.[38] Moreover, the slowdown in territorial expansion together with the revenues it generated and the need to maintain larger permanent armies tended to exacerbate the fiscal difficulties during the 1570s and 1580s. Against this background, the long and costly war with Safavid Iran put state finances under a severe strain. In addition, it appears that in 1584 there was a substantial debasement/devaluation in Iran, which had come under the influence of similarly adverse developments.[39] It is possible that the debasement in Iran may have played an important role in determining the timing and extent of the debasement on the Ottoman side.[40]

The precise date of the Ottoman debasement/devaluation is yet to be established.[41] It was undertaken some time after 1584, probably in 1585 or 1586. The debasement was the largest to date and one of the largest in Ottoman history. Whereas 450 *akçes* were legally struck from 100 Tebriz *dirham*s up to 1584, 800 *akçes* began to be struck from the same amount of silver after 1586. In other words, the silver content of the *akçe* was reduced by about 44 percent. The official exchange rate of the *akçe* against the ducat and the *sultani* was accordingly lowered from 60 to 120 (see Tables V:2 and V:3 and Fig. V:1, p. 975). This debasement/ devaluation constitutes an important turning point not only in Ottoman monetary history but also in economic and fiscal history. It signals the beginning of a new era of instability for the Ottoman currency. Since the debasement was not followed by increases in many of the fixed-rate taxes, it played an important role in the disintegration of the *timar* system, with long-term economic and fiscal consequences.[42] Many important questions remain to be resolved regarding the debasement of 1585–86 and the price history of the period.

1586–1690: THE DISINTEGRATION OF THE OTTOMAN MONETARY SYSTEM

The monetary history of the seventeenth century offers sharp contrasts with that of the previous century. The sixteenth century had been characterized by relative fiscal stability, economic expansion and growing monetization of the economy, matched by the increased availability of gold and silver. These trends were all reversed after the 1580s. Fiscal crises remained a recurring problem during the seventeenth century. The internal problems, such as the Celali rebellions, were often accompanied by external wars. The campaigns against Austria and Iran were followed by the long and costly war with Venice for Crete and the second siege of Vienna, leading to a series of military defeats in Europe. In addition, it appears that the long-term increases in population and economic activity came to a halt towards the end of the sixteenth century. Combined with the social and political upheavals, both urban and rural economic activity stagnated if not declined during the seventeenth century. One would expect that, despite exceptions in certain regions, rural–urban economic linkages, long-distance trade and credit were all adversely affected by these trends. This stagnation if not downward trend in economic activity after the 1580s must have reduced the demand for the use of money.

At the same time, however, with the decline of the *timar* regime and the increasing importance of *iltizam* during the seventeenth century, a larger part of the rural taxes began to be collected in money form, although the extent of this shift showed considerable variations between regions.[43] Moreover, even the taxes collected in kind had to be converted to money and sent to the provincial centers and the capital. As a result, the expansion of *iltizam* tended to increase the demand for money by both the rural and urban economy.

Due to the problems created by the inter-continental silver flows and the severe fiscal difficulties of the state, the period from the 1580s until the 1640s was one of exceptional instability for the *akçe*. Its silver content fluctuated sharply and often. In addition, since the government was not always successful in collecting the earlier coinage or adjusting the official rates of exchange after each debasement, the clipped versions of the old *akçes* often circulated together with the new versions, leading to further confusion. Not surprisingly, the counterfeiting of silver coins flourished in this environment. Each time these problems reached crisis proportions with adverse effects for the economy, the government attempted to establish a new standard for the *akçe*. These operations, called *tashih-i sikke* (correction of coinage), were carried out in 1600, 1618, 1624 and 1640.[44] As the series of debasements turned the *akçe* into a very small coin, starting in 1624, the *para*, originally an Egyptian coin, began to be minted also at İstanbul and elsewhere in the *akçe* region. The İstanbul *para* contained three times as much silver as the *akçe*.[45] (Compare the silver content and exchange rates in Tables V:5 and V:6 with those in Tables V:2 and V:3; also see Fig. V:1.)

One of the most important monetary developments of the seventeenth century is the decline in mint activity and the closing down of many of the mints. Numismatic evidence suggests that by the third quarter of the century only a handful of mints remained open in the empire. By contrast, more than forty had been active during the mid-sixteenth century.[46] The reasons for this trend have not been adequately examined. However, a decline in the volume of silver flows from the Americas may now be ruled out as a potential cause since the recent work of Michel Morineau has shown that, contrary to earlier views, the volume of precious metals coming from the Americas to Europe actually increased during the seventeenth century.[47] At the same time, there is a good deal of evidence that the Ottoman government found it increasingly more difficult to locate supplies of silver during this period. The fiscal crises of the state, and the closing down of many of the silver mines after the arrival of cheap American silver must both have contributed to the shortages. Many of the mines were not re-opened in the seventeenth century. Moreover, the role of external trade deficits, if any, and the resulting outflows of specie from the empire need to be considered, although an empirical estimation of external trade balances may be an impossible task. Finally, the extreme instability of the *akçe* earlier in the seventeenth century and the resulting loss of confidence in the currency may have contributed to the decline of mint activity and the virtual disappearance of the *akçe* in many parts of the empire.

Table V:5. The silver *akçe* and the gold *sultani/şerifi*, 1584–1690

	Akçes per 100 *dir.*	Akçe (gr.)	Sultani (gr.)	Exchange rate akçe/sultani	Gold:silver ratio (calculated)
1584	450	0.68	3.517	60	10.4
1586	800	0.38	3.517	120	11.8
1596	1400?			220	
1600	950	0.32	3.517	120	10.0
1612	950	0.32		120	
1618	1000	0.31	3.517	150	11.8
1621	1000	0.31		150	
1623	?			210	
1624	1900?	0.17	3.517	310	
1625	1000	0.31	3.517	130	10.3
1632	1400	0.22	3.517	220	12.3
1636	?			240	
1640	?			250	
1641	1000	0.31	3.490	160	12.7
1659	1250	0.26	3.490	180	11.9
1669	1400	0.23	3.490	225	13.3
1672	1400	0.23	3.490	270	16.0
1683	1400	0.23	3.490	270	16.0

Notes: (1) See notes 1, 3 and 4 of Table V:1.

(2) This was an especially unstable period for the *akçe*. Due to the frequent debasements during which the earlier coins were not completely retired, coins with different silver content often circulated simultaneously. The problems were compounded by the existence of counterfeit coinage. On the other hand, archival information regarding the silver content of *akçe* is scarce. For these reasons, the figures in Columns 1 and 2 should be accepted only as approximations.

(3) The exchange rates presented in Column 4 include both the official rates which were applied in many parts of the empire and market rates at İstanbul. There were often regional differences within the empire in the market rates of exchange. New coinage and the changes in the exchange rates often reached the provinces with a time lag. For example, in Ankara the exchange rate of the *akçe* against the *sultani* remained at 60 *akçes* until 1593 despite the debasement of 1585–86 in İstanbul. Ergenç (1978–79).

(4) 1624 was an exceptionally poor year for the *akçe*. Its market rate against the *sultani*, available from the court records at İstanbul, declined from 270 to 400 *akçes*. On the basis of this information, it appears that the silver content of the *akçe* fell from about 0.19 grams to 0.13 gr. during that year. This rapid decline culminated in a major correction of coinage at the end of the year. Weight and exchange rate figures presented here for 1624 are averages for that year.

(5) In view of the quality of the available data, the gold:silver ratios calculated here should be taken as no more than approximations. These ratios serve the additional purpose of providing an indirect check on the other figures. Since the official exchange rates given in Column 4 often did not keep pace with the changing silver content of the *akçe*, short-term changes in the gold:silver ratio given in Column 5 are not significant. The average gold:silver ratio in Europe increased from 11.7 to 15.0 during this period. Braudel and Spooner (1967), p. 459.

Sources: Based on Sahillioğlu (1965a), pp. 38–53, (1965b, 1983).

When the Ottoman government could not or did not meet the economy's demand for money, this need was met increasingly by European coins. Although foreign coins had always circulated in Ottoman lands since the fourteenth century, they played a qualitatively

Table V:6. Exchange rates of European coins expressed in *akçes*,
1584–1731

	Venetian ducat	Spanish 8-*real* (*riyal guruş*)	Dutch rixdale (*esedi guruş*)	Polish isolette (*zolota*)
1584	60			
1588	120	80	70	
1600	125	78	68	48
1618	150	100		
1624	310	240		
1625	120	80	70	50
1632	220	110	100	70
1641	168	80	70	
1650	175	90	80	
1659	190	88	78	48
1668	250	110	100	66
1683	300	130	120	
1691	300–400		120–160	88–107
1698	300–400	120–160		88
1708	360			
1725	375	181	144	88
1731	385	181	144	88

Notes: (1) See notes 2, 3 and 4 of Table V: 5.
(2) The exchange rates presented here include both the official rates which were applied in many parts of the empire and market rates in İstanbul. Market rates showed regional differences within the empire.
(3) The gold content of the ducat is given in note 1 of Table V: 3. In the 1640s, 5 percent difference emerged between the exchange rates of the ducat and the *sultani* in favor of the former. This difference increased to 10 percent by the 1660s. It is not clear whether this was due to a decline in the gold content of the *sultani* (compare Column 1 above with Column 4 of Table V: 5).
(4) The Spanish 8-*real* was a stable coin and contained close to 25.6 gr. of pure silver. It appears that the silver content of the other coins fluctuated and declined over time as the exchange rates presented here confirm. The silver content of the Dutch rixdale declined at least to 74–77 percent. Late in the century the *isolette* contained 60 percent silver.
(5) Starting in 1691 the government, in order to generate additional revenue, began to apply different rates to coins received and coins used as payment by the government. It appears that the rates at which the coins were accepted reflected the market rates more closely.
Sources: Mantran (1962); Sahillioğlu (1965a, 1965b and 1983); Belin (1931); Baykal (1967).

different role during the seventeenth and early eighteenth centuries. As Ottoman coinage disappeared, official transactions continued to be expressed in *akçes*, but the *akçe* was reduced to little more than a unit of account, an invisible unit in which monetary magnitudes were cited and the values of actual coins were measured.[48] Foreign coins became the leading forms of actual money. Local court records, European commercial reports and the observations of travelers provide ample evidence in this respect.

One of the more prominent silver coins in circulation from the Balkans to Egypt was the Dutch *thaler*. It was called *esedi guruş* or *aslanlı guruş*, pas it had the inscription of two lions.[49] Even more important was the Spanish 8-*real* (*reales de a ocho*), called the *riyal guruş*, a large coin containing close to 25.6 grams of pure silver. The *riyal guruş* was in fact the most widely used coin of the world economy during the sixteenth and seventeenth centuries. There were others, such as the Polish isolette or *zolota*, which was later imitated by Dutch and English merchants and brought into the Levant markets. The Venetian gold ducat together with the Hungarian gold coin in the Balkans remained the most important gold coinage.[50] The Ottoman government did not attempt to restrict the circulation of these coins. In fact, in many instances it demanded payment in European coinage. It also published regularly the rates at which these coins would be accepted by the treasury (see Table V:6).

Towards the middle of the century, as shortage of coinage intensified, counterfeits or debased versions of European coins began to arrive literally in shiploads to flood the markets of the Levant. The Dutch, the English, the Venetians and the French were all involved in this lucrative trade. European observers were often incredulous how easily these debased coins could be accepted. The local markets were certainly not unaware of their low intrinsic values. Because the Ottoman government could not provide a stable currency, however, these debased coins were accepted at substantial premia. In effect, the European counterfeiters were taking advantage of the absence of local coinage. In return for the service of providing money for daily transactions, they enjoyed substantial profits. Needless to say, these debased coins caused considerable confusion and instability in the local markets.

Foreign coins prevailed not only in the *akçe* region but around the entire empire from the Balkans to Iraq, from Egypt to Tunisia. Not surprisingly, the role of credit and reliance on alternative forms of money increased in direct proportion to the shortages of coinage.[51] Bills of exchange and multilateral clearing mechanisms became increasingly more common in the conduct of long-distance trade with Europe.[52]

Copper coinage was minted and used in limited amounts during the seventeenth century.[53] Towards the end of the century, however, there was a brief period when, under pressure of war, large amounts of *mangır* were struck in İstanbul to raise fiscal revenue. Each *mangır* was given the value of one *akçe* and the government began to accept these coins as payment. This experiment was discontinued after three years due to counterfeiting and inflation.[54]

1690–1844 : THE NEW OTTOMAN *KURUŞ* AND ITS DEBASEMENT

The decline of the *akçe* posed serious challenges to the Ottoman administration. Without control over the currency, its control over the economy diminished considerably. In addition, without its own currency, the government could not use debasement as a means of obtaining fiscal revenue in times of difficulty. Perhaps most important of all, the disintegration of the monetary system and the increasing reliance on foreign coins had serious political implications.

As the series of demanding wars began to wind down towards the end of the seventeenth century, the government renewed efforts to establish a new system around a new unit, called the Ottoman *kuruş* (piaster) with 1 *kuruş* equaling 40 *para*s or 120 *akçe*s. The first set of large silver coins based on this system was minted in 1690.[55] The earlier principle of minting coins mostly from clean silver was also abandoned after 1690, if not earlier. It appears that the early *kuruş* and their fractions were struck from alloys which contained approximately 45 to 60 percent silver[56] (see Table V:7).

It is also significant that the minting of silver coins became increasingly centralized during this period. Continuing a trend which had started in the seventeenth century, the numbers of mints in operation remained limited. After the middle of the eighteenth century, the *kuruş* and its fractions were minted almost exclusively in İstanbul. Provincial mints struck a limited amount of copper coinage. *Kuruş*-type coins were not minted anywhere in the Balkans or Syria while the mint in Baghdad was used only occasionally. At the same time, mints in Cairo, Tripoli, Tunis and Algiers continued to operate regularly minting silver, copper and gold coinage for local use.[57]

As for gold coins, the *sultani* or *şerifi* had changed very little for more than two centuries, remaining close to the ducat standard. It was discontinued, however, late in the seventeenth century. In its place a number of new gold coins called *tuğralı*, *cedid İstanbul*, *zincirli*, *fındık* and *zer-i mahbub* were initiated between 1697 and 1728. All but the last of these started close to the standard of the ducat. Orders were also sent to Egypt to mint coins with the same names and standards. The gold content of the Egyptian coins ended up consistently lower than that of their İstanbul

Table V:7. The silver *kuruş* and its exchange rate, 1690–1844

	Weight (gr.)	Approx. fineness	Pure silver content (gr.)	exchange rate of Ven.ducat	Calculated gold:silver ratio
1690	29.5	0.60–0.68	18.9	2 *k*. 60 *ak*.	13.6
1696	28.2	0.60–0.68	18.1	2 *k*. 60 *ak*.	13.0
1708	25.6	0.56–0.68	15.9	3 *k*.	13.7
1720	26.4	0.52–0.58	14.5	3 *k*. 20 *ak*.	13.2
1731				3 *k*. 25 *ak*.	
1740	24.1	0.52–0.58	13.7	3 *k*. 80 *ak*.	14.4
1752				3*k*. 108 *ak*.	
1758				3 *k*. 105 *ak*.	
1766	19.2	0.52–0.58	10.6	4 *k*.	12.2
1772	19.2	0.46–0.56	9.8	4 *k*. 15 *ak*.	11.6
1780	18.5	?		4 *k*. 70 *ak*.	
1788	15.2	0.46	7.0	5 *k*. 60 *ak*.	11.1
1790	12.6	0.46	5.9	5 *k*. 90 *ak*.	9.7
1794	12.6	0.46	5.9	7 *k*.	11.8
1800	12.6	0.46	5.9	8 *k*.	13.5
1810	10.0	0.46	4.6	10–11 *k*.	13.9
1824	4.0	0.60	2.4	16–18 *k*.	11.4
1829	1.5	0.83	1.25	30–32 *k*.	11.1
1834	2.0	0.44	0.86	45 *k*.	11.1
1844	1.2	0.83	1.0	50–52 *k*.	14.6
1844 to					
1922	1.2	0.83	1.0		15.09

Notes: (1) Based on 1 Ottoman *kuruş*=40 *paras*= 120 *akçes*.
(2) In view of the quality of the evidence, the estimates for the silver content of the *kuruş* should be accepted as approximations, especially until the 1780s.
(3) For the late seventeenth and early nineteenth century, whenever new *kuruş* coins were not minted, the silver content of the *kuruş* was calculated from that of other large coins in circulation such as the 30 *para* (*zolota*), 60 *para* (2 *zolota*), 2-*kuruş* pieces.
(4) See note 1 of Table V: 3 for the gold content of the ducat. The exchange rates presented here are either official rates which were applied in many parts of the empire or market rates at İstanbul. Market rates showed regional differences within the empire.
(4) In view of the quality of the data, the gold:silver ratios calculated here should be taken as no more than approximations. These ratios serve the additional purpose of providing an indirect check on the other figures. Since the official rates of exchange given in Column 4 often did not keep pace with the changing silver content of the *kuruş*, short-term changes in the gold:silver ratio given in Column 5 are not significant. The *tashih-i sikke* operation of 1844 set this ratio officially at 15.09. The average gold:silver ratio in Europe remained around 15 during the first half of the eighteenth century. Braudel and Spooner (1967), p. 459.
(5) For the Egyptian silver currency in the seventeenth and eighteenth centuries, see Table V: 4.
Sources: Sahillioğlu (1965a), pp. 68–122 and (1983); Sultan (1977); Krause and Mishler (1984); Artuk and Artuk (1974); Schaendlinger (1973), pp. 63–74; Beaujour (1800), pp. 366–72; Svoronos (1956), pp. 82–3, 114–18; Genç (1975); and archival notes provided by Mehmet Genç.

Table V:8. Exchange rates of other coins and currency expressed in
Ottoman *kuruş*, 1720–1844

	Fındık (gold)	Zer-i mahbub Istanbul (gold)	Hungarian (gold)	Pounds sterling
1720	—	—	3 k.	
1736	3 k. 40 ak.	2 k. 90 ak.	3 k. 20 ak.	5–7 k.
1758	3 k. 105 ak.	2 k. 90 ak.	3 k. 80 ak.	
1768	4 k.	3 k.	3 k. 50 ak.	8 k.
1774	4 k.	3 k.	3 k. 50 ak.	9–10 k.
1780	4 k.		4 k.	
1788	5 k.	3 k. 60 ak.	5 k.	11 k.
1798	7 k.	5 k.	7 k.	15 k.
1805	8 k.	5 k. 60 ak.	8 k.	15–17 k.
1810	9 k.	6 k. 60 ak.	9 k. 75 ak.	19 k. 90 ak.
1816				19 k.
1820	11k.	8 k.	13 k.	25 k.
1822	11k.		15 k.	40 k.
1825				53.5 k.
1828				57–62 k.
1830				75–77.5 k.
1832				87–94 k.
1834	33 k. 60 ak.		45 k.	98–100 k.
1844				108–11 k.

Notes: (1) The exchange rates presented here include both the official and market rates. Market rates are given mostly for İstanbul. The rates for gold coins are mostly official rates. The rates for the British pound sterling are all market rates.
(2) The *fındık* weighed close to 3.5 gr. and the *zer-i mahbub* weighed more than 2.6 gr. The gold content of these coins declined over time as exchange rates presented here confirm.
(3) The *fındık*, *zer-i mahbub* and other gold coins of Egypt contained less gold and exchanged at a discount against their İstanbul counterparts. For example, in 1731 the official rate at İstanbul for *tuğralı* of İstanbul was 3k. and for *zincirli* of İstanbul 3k. 40ak. During the same year, the official rates at İstanbul for *tuğralı* of Egypt was 2 k. 75 ak. and for *zincirli* of Egypt 2k. 90 ak., indicating that the value of the Egyptian coins was 15–20 percent lower.
(4) The Hungarian gold coin weighed 3.47 gr.
(5) The first exchange rate for pounds sterling presented above is for 1740. During most of the eighteenth century, the British pound was linked primarily to gold. Reed (1930).
Sources: Belin (1931); Baykal (1967); Pere (1968); Michoff (1971); Artuk and Artuk (1974); Issawi (1980).

counterparts, however.[58] In subsequent years, the gold content of coins struck both in İstanbul and Cairo fluctuated and declined. By mid-century, only the *fındık* and the smaller *zer-i mahbub* with their fractions and multiples and Egyptian counterparts remained in circulation. These coins continued to be minted until early in the nineteenth century. *Fındık* of İstanbul exchanged at a discount against the ducat and close to par against the Hungarian gold coin (*ongari*) for most of the century (see Table V:8).

While *kuruş* emerged as the leading currency in areas close to İstanbul, the Ottoman government struggled, with mixed results, to establish it in the provinces. On the one hand, there is evidence that the volume of minting activity increased considerably during the eighteenth century. This trend was in part due to the operation of new silver mines in Anatolia, in Gümüşhane, Keban and Ergani while the mines in the Balkans declined in importance. The annual output of the mines in Anatolia reached 35–40 tons during the 1730s, providing considerable support for the state treasury. It appears, however, that the periodic scarcity of coinage continued in the provinces. Moreover, the silver content of the new coins fluctuated frequently, causing a considerable amount of confusion and eroding the confidence towards Ottoman coins. As a result, the popularity of the European coins persisted. Their influence increased directly with the distance from İstanbul. In many parts of the empire, the Ottoman *kuruş* did not become the leading currency until the second half of the eighteenth century.[59]

Para remained the basic silver coin and the unit of account in Egypt. Despite weak political ties, its silver content was controlled by İstanbul. Its rate of debasement followed fairly closely the rate of depreciation of the İstanbul *kuruş* during the eighteenth century (see Table V:4). European coins, such as the Spanish *real*, Dutch *thaler*, the Venetian ducat and the German *thaler* continued to play an important role in Egypt.[60] In Syria, on the other hand, it appears that the *kuruş* and its fractions minted in İstanbul constituted the basic silver currency. In addition, the *para* of Egypt (*misriyya*) and European coins were widely used. Similarly, the gold coins of İstanbul and Cairo were used together with the Venetian ducat. There were, of course, considerable regional variations within Greater Syria.[61]

In Tunisia and Algeria, the locally minted silver coins remained mostly independent of the standards in İstanbul even though they carried the name of the Ottoman sultan until the nineteenth century. In gold coins, however, the standards of İstanbul were followed more closely. European coins such as the Spanish 8-*real*, the Venetian ducat and others circulated widely both in Tunisia and Algeria.[62] As the scarcity of coinage occasionally intensified in different parts of the empire, debased versions of European coins arrived by ship to flood the local markets. Scarcity of money helped bills of exchange play an important role especially in the trade with Europe.

The *kuruş* was relatively stable until late in the eighteenth century. The evidence summarized in Tables V:7 and V:8 indicate that its silver content declined by about 40 percent between 1700 and the late 1760s. As Mehmet Genç has argued, there were extended periods of peace during the early part of the century.[63] In addition, revenues from the silver mines provided considerable support for state finances. In fact, what might need an explanation in this period is not the relative stability of the currency, but the fact that its silver content declined at all. Increasing demand for money may be an important reason for the debasement of the *kuruş* until the 1760s. The expansion of trade between coastal regions of the Balkans and Europe, increasing commercialization of agriculture and the collection of as much as half or more of the agricultural taxes in money form in the more commercialized regions contributed to the growing use of money.

Starting in the late 1760s, however, the Ottoman Empire entered a series of exhausting wars and the debasement of the *kuruş* gained momentum. From the late 1760s, until 1808, the *kuruş* lost about 50 percent of its silver content. It declined in value even more rapidly during the reign of Mahmud II (1808–39). During these three decades, the silver content of the *kuruş* fell from 5.9 grams to less than 1 gram for a total debasement of 85 percent. It is clear that the reign of Mahmud II witnessed the most rapid debasement in Ottoman history (see Fig. V:1) (p. 975). Ten successive sets of silver coins, each with different and mostly lower silver content for the *kuruş*, its multiples and fractions, were produced during these three decades. Gold coins were also changed often both in style and gold content. New gold coins called *rumi*, *adli*, *hayriye* and others each with varying gold content were initiated during this period.[64] Not suprisingly, available evidence indicates that this was also the most inflationary period in Ottoman history.[65] The fiscal crisis of the state was the primary cause of these dramatic trends. Between the late 1760s and the 1840s, the Ottoman Empire was engaged in frequent wars against Austria, Russia, France, Greece, Egypt and others. In addition, the internal political problems and military campaigns proved equally demanding for the state finances.[66]

1844–1914 : FROM A NEW BIMETALLIC SYSTEM TO THE "LIMPING" GOLD STANDARD

From the perspective of Ottoman economic and monetary history, the nineteenth century constitutes a period quite different from the earlier era. On the one hand, it was characterized by major efforts at Western-style reform, in administration, and in economic, fiscal and monetary affairs. It was also a period of integration into world markets and rapid expansion in foreign trade, particularly with Europe. It is estimated that the foreign trade of the core areas of the empire increased by more than tenfold between the 1840s and World War I.[67] This process was facilitated by the construction of ports and railroads and by the establishment of modern banking institutions by European capital. As a result, the commercialization of agriculture proceeded rapidly in Macedonia, western Anatolia and along the Syrian coast. The rural population was drawn to markets not only as producers of cash crops but also as purchasers of imported cotton textiles. These developments substantially increased the demand for and the use of money in these more commercialized regions of the empire.

From early in the nineteenth century, monetary stability was perceived as an important pre-requisite for reform and commercial development both by the Ottoman government and by European interests. After decades of frequent debasements and instability, another *tashih-i sikke* operation was undertaken in 1844 which established a new bimetallic system based on the silver *kuruş* and gold *lira* with 1 gold *lira*= 100 silver *kuruş*.[68] The gold *lira*, the silver *kuruş* and the silver 20-*kuruş*, often called the *mecidiye*, became the leading coinage. After this date, debasement of the coinage was abandoned as a means of raising fiscal revenue. All silver and gold coinage minted in İstanbul adhered to these standards until 1922. In addition, copper coinage of small denominations continued to be minted for daily transactions. Nickel coinage was introduced for the same purpose in 1910.

The stability of coinage did not mean the end of fiscal difficulties, however. Throughout the century the Ottoman government resorted to a variety of methods to deal with its fiscal problems. These efforts had important implications for the monetary system. One method of raising fiscal revenue which began to be used in 1840 was the printing and circulation in the İstanbul area of interest-bearing paper money called *kaime-i muteber-i nakdiyye*, or *kaime* for short. As their volume remained limited until 1852, the *kaime* performed reasonably well despite problems with counterfeiting. During the Crimean War, however, large amounts of *kaime* were printed and the market price expressed in gold *lira* declined to less than half the nominal value. One gold *lira* began to exchange for 200–220 *kuruş* in *kaime*. As a result, this first experiment in paper money resulted in a major wave of inflation. The *kaimes* were finally retired in the early 1860s with the help of short-term loans obtained from the Imperial Ottoman Bank.[69]

Another method used by the Ottoman government to deal with the budget deficits was borrowing in the European financial markets, which

Table V:9. Exchange rates of other currencies expressed in Ottoman
gold *liras*, 1850–1914

	1850	1914
British pound sterling	1.10	1.10
French franc	0.0433	0.044
Austrian florin/kroner	0.11	0.046
German mark	—	0.0542
Russian rouble	0.175	0.116
Egyptian *lira*	1.0	1.146
U.S. dollar	0.229	0.229

Note: Between 1844 and 1878, the gold *lira* weighed 7.216 gr. with a fineness of 22/24 or
91.67 percent, containing 6.6 grams of gold. The gold *lira* was also set equal to 100 silver
kuruş each of which contained 1.0 gram of pure silver. The implicit gold:silver ratio was,
therefore, set at 15.09. After 1878 the link with silver was severed and gold became the
only standard for Ottoman currency.
Sources: *Tate's modern cambisit, a manual of foreign exchanges and bullion*, 9th ed.,
London, 1858, and "The statistical abstract for the principal states and foreign countries"
in A&P, 1914; Eldem (1970), pp. 225–26.

started during the Crimean War. In the following two decades, large
sums were borrowed in London, Paris, Vienna and elsewhere under very
unfavorable terms. When the financial crises of 1873 led to the cessation
of overseas lending in the European financial markets, the Ottoman government was forced to declare a moratorium on debt payments. The
Ottoman Public Debt Administration was established in 1881 to ensure
European control over Ottoman finances.[70]

After the establishment of the Imperial Ottoman Bank by French and
British capital in 1863, the monopoly of issuing paper money within
the empire was given to that institution. The Ottoman Bank used this
monopoly rather conservatively, issuing only a limited amount of paper
notes until World War I. These notes, which were convertible to gold,
circulated primarily in the areas close to İstanbul.

There were two other occasions when the government resorted to
non-convertible paper money as a fiscal measure. The war of 1877–78
with Russia exacerbated the fiscal problems already made acute by the
crisis of 1873–76. Under the circumstances, *kaime*s were issued once
more to help finance the war. Because of their large volume, however,
they declined to one-quarter of their nominal value within two years,
even though the government agreed to accept some payments in paper
currency. Similarly, during World War I, non-convertible paper circulated regularly and was one of the leading sources of fiscal revenue. By
1917 one gold *lira* equaled six paper *lira*s. Once again, the use of *kaime*
resulted in a considerable rise in prices expressed in paper currency.

Table V:10. Ottoman currency and its exchange rate, 1326–1914:
a summary

	Weight of akçe (gr.)	Exchange rate vs. Ven. ducat	Pure silver content of kuruş (gr.)	Exchange rate vs. Ven. ducat	Silver content (index; 1500=100)	Exchange rate
1326	1.15	n.a.			157.5	n.a.
1410	1.15	30			157.5	180.0
1444	1.01	39–40			138.4	136.7
1481	0.77	47			105.4	114.9
1512	0.73	55			100.0	101.9
1550	0.73	59			100.0	91.5
1582	0.68	65			93.2	83.1
1588	0.38	120			52.1	45.0
1625	0.31	130			42.5	41.5
1669	0.23	225			31.5	24.0
1687			18.9	2k. 60 ak.	24.0	18.0
1708			15.9	3k.	20.2	15.0
1740			13.7	3k. 80 ak.	17.4	12.3
1766			10.6	4k.	13.4	11.3
1788			7.0	5k. 60 ak.	8.9	8.2
1810			4.6	10–11 k.	5.8	4.3
1834			0.86	45k.	1.1	1.0
1844			1.0	50–52 k.	1.3	0.9
1914			1.0	n.a.	1.3	n.a.

Notes: (1) 1 *kuruş* = 120 *akçe*.
(2) It is assumed that the *akçe* was minted from 90 percent pure silver until the end of the seventeenth century (Column 1). Column 3, on the other hand, refers to pure silver content of the *kuruş*. Column 5 is adjusted accordingly.
(3) Columns 2 and 4 give the exchange rate of the Venetian ducat expressed in *akçe* and *kuruş*. Column 6 is derived by taking the inverse of Columns 2 and 4.
(4) For other details and sources as well as the qualifications and limitations of the available data, see other tables in this chapter.

In the 1870s the price of silver in relation to gold declined sharply in the world markets leading to the adoption of the gold standard by many countries. The Ottoman government was also forced to move away from a bimetallic system. In 1878 the link between silver and gold was severed and gold was accepted as the standard for Ottoman currency. The government also stopped minting silver coins of large denominations, most notably the 20-*kuruş mecidiye*. Nonetheless, it continued to accept unlimited amounts of silver coinage as payment until 1916. Receiving primary support from gold and partial support from silver, the Ottoman currency system became another example of the "limping" standard (*topal mikyas*). With the decline in the price of silver world-wide, this policy resulted in considerable inflows of silver and counterfeit silver coinage. In the provinces the silver *kuruş* declined in value, often exchanging at 120 *kuruş* and even more against the gold *lira*. The premium for gold over silver usually increased with the distance from İstanbul.[71] Carrying Adrien Billiotti's earlier estimates forward, Vedat Eldem has estimated that the total money supply in the Ottoman Empire was approximately 50 million *liras* in 1914, including Ottoman coinage, paper notes and some foreign coinage. Gold coins in circulation accounted for approximately two-thirds of this amount.[72]

The expansion of trade with Europe also increased the circulation and acceptance of the leading European currencies, especially the British pound and the French franc in many parts of the empire. In addition, different coins and currencies were popular in different regions. For example, Russian coinage circulated in the Trabzon area because of seasonal migration, Austrian currencies and the Russian rouble in the Balkans, the Iranian *kran* and the Indian rupee in Iraq and the Marie-Theresa *thalers* in Yemen[73] (for the exchange rates of other currencies, see Table V:9).

The Egyptian currency remained linked to the Ottoman *lira* at par until the British occupation in 1882. Egyptian coinage continued to bear the name of the sultan until World War I. Elsewhere in North Africa, silver and gold coinage continued to be minted with the name of the Ottoman sultan despite the nominal nature of the political ties; in Algeria, until the French occupation of 1830 in Algiers and until 1837 in Constantine; until 1840 in Tripoli and until 1881 in Tunisia.[74]

NOTES

1 For the rates of debasement of various European currencies from the fifteenth to the eighteenth centuries, see Braudel and Spooner (1967), Fig. 4, p. 458.

2 It appears that prices increased somewhat more rapidly than the rate of debasement. For example, our preliminary calculations indicate that food prices in İstanbul increased approximately 300- to 500-fold between 1490 and 1914. This total increase corresponds to a long-term average inflation rate between 1 and 1.3 percent per year. Again, low by our standards, but not insignificant by the standards of these centuries. It appears that the highest rates of inflation were experienced during the sixteenth century, especially towards its end and the interval 1760 to 1844.

3 Cipolla (1963).

4 Watson (1967) and Spufford (1988), Part III. Specie flows between Western Europe and the eastern Mediterrenean were closely related to the trade balances between the two regions. Especially important in this respect were the trade balances between Venice and Egypt. For estimates of the trade balances, and mostly surpluses, of the eastern Mediterranean during the late Middle Ages, see Ashtor (1971).

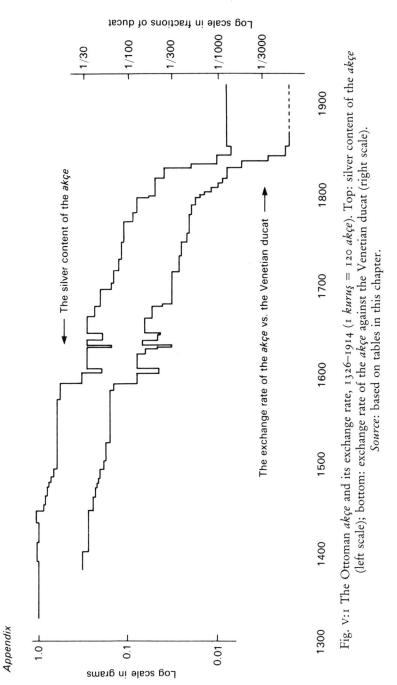

Fig. V:1 The Ottoman *akçe* and its exchange rate, 1326–1914 (1 *kuruş* = 120 *akçe*). Top: silver content of the *akçe* (left scale); bottom: exchange rate of the *akçe* against the Venetian ducat (right scale).
Source: based on tables in this chapter.

5 There is some controversy regarding this date. Recently, the numismatist İbrahim Artuk argued that the first *akçe* was actually minted by Osman I (c. 1290–1324): Artuk (1980).

6 It appears that until the late seventeenth century the standard or proper (*sağ*) Ottoman coins contained 85 to 90 percent pure silver. However, more evidence regarding the metallic content of the existing coins is necessary to resolve this and other similar problems in Ottoman numismatics.

7 Amongst the known exceptions are the 5-*akçe* piece struck by Orhan and the 10-*akçe* coins struck by Mehmed II and Bayezid II. In the late sixteenth and early seventeenth centuries, 10-*akçe* pieces called *osmani* were minted more regularly: Schaendlinger (1973), pp. 87–105.

8 Sahillioğlu (1962–63). The ornamentation of the copper coinage became an art form in the fifteenth and sixteenth centuries. These *nakışlı mangırlar* were minted mostly in Anatolia but also distributed in the Balkans: Ölçer (1975).

9 During the fifteenth century, the more important mints were in Bursa, Edirne, Amasya, Serez, Novar (Novaberda) and İstanbul.

10 İnalcık (1965, 1978); also Godinho (1969), Ch. 8; Spufford (1988), section VI.

11 Sahillioğlu (1962–63); İnalcık (1965) and (1978).

12 This operation was called *tecdid-i sikke* (renewal of coinage).

13 While the tithe for wheat and barley was almost always collected in kind, it was collected in money form for many of the cash crops.

14 Author's calculations based on the survey of *raiyyet rüsumu* obligations presented by İnalcık (1959) and data on the prices of agricultural commodities during the fifteenth and sixteenth centuries.

15 Sahillioğlu (1975); also İnalcık (1981).

16 In a well-recorded incident called Buçuktepe Vakası (Halfhill Incident), the Yeniceri soldiers who were paid with the debased coinage revolted after the first debasement of 1444 and succeeded in having their daily salaries raised from 3 *akçes* to 3.5 *akçes*: Sahillioğlu (1958), pp.40–41. The policy of frequent debasements was also opposed by other groups with fixed incomes who extracted from the next sultan, Bayezid II, the promise for a more stable currency.

17 Sahillioğlu (1958) and (1965a); also see İnalcık (1951) and Kafadar (1986), Ch. 2. It should also be noted that mid-fifteenth century was a period of severe silver shortages in many parts of Europe. Spufford (1988), Chs. 13–16.

18 For example, İnalcık (1981); Sahillioğlu (1975).

19 Babinger (1956); Sahillioğlu (1962–63); Beldiceanu and Beldiceanu-Steinherr (1988).

20 Sahillioğlu (1958), pp. 105–22, (1965a), pp. 18–37 and (1983).

21 Spufford (1988), pp. 814 ff.

22 The gold content of the Egyptian *şerifis* was often lower and they exchanged below par against both the ducat and the İstanbul *sultani*. For the exchange rates of the Egyptian *ashrafi* in the early sixteenth century, see Table V:2.

23 For a succinct discussion of bimetallism, see Reed (1930).

24 In contrast, Akdağ has argued that the silver content of the *akçe* fluctuated frequently during this period because of specie shortages and the inability of the government to control the mints: Akdağ (1974).

25 In the Balkans Ottoman mints were located primarily in Serbia and Mace-
    donia, although *akçes* were minted as far west as Banjaluka in Bosnia. On the
    basis of numismatic evidence, it appears that the Ottomans minted *akçes* only
    rarely north of the Danube. (I am indebted to Kenneth M. MacKenzie for
    this last point.) See also Erüreten (1985).
26 Beldiceanu (1959), Maxim (1975), Gedai (1988), Sahillioğlu (1983).
27 Sahillioğlu (1958), pp. 92–93.
28 For the Egyptian *para*, see Raymond (1973–74) and the other sources cited
    in Table V:4.
29 Poop *et al.* (1988).
30 Starting in the 1520s this coin weighed more than 4 gr., exchanging for 7
    or 7.5 *akçes*. In the 1580s, the silver content of the *shahi* was reduced by
    approximately half to more than 2 gr. following the debasements in Persia and
    İstanbul: Sahillioğlu (1958), pp. 89–91 and (1983), Maxim (1975), Steensgaard
    (1973), pp. 419–21.
31 Geographically, a good deal of overlap existed between the three units, *akçe*,
    medin or *para* and the *shahi*. For example, mints in the cities of Amid
    (Diyarbekir) and Aleppo struck all three of these coins and a number of other
    mints struck two of them during the second half of the sixteenth century.
    Schaendlinger (1973), pp. 99–105.
32 Sadok (1987), pp. 77–83; Valensi (1985), Ch. 7.
33 Faroqhi (1979).
34 For a more detailed discussion of these coins, see text above.
35 The numbers of active mints reached their peak during the reign of Süleyman
    I (1520–66) when silver coins were struck in at least 43 cities around the
    Ottoman domains. Erüreten (1985) and Schaendlinger (1973), pp. 96–113.
36 Spooner (1972), Ch. 2, Braudel and Spooner (1967) and Braudel (1972), I.
37 Barkan (1975).
38 İnalcık (1951, 1978). For a discussion of how the increased availability of
    silver and the increases in prices may have caused the Ottoman debasement,
    see Çizakça (1976–77); for a more recent perspective, Sundhaussen (1983).
    Kafadar (1986) provides a detailed account of the monetary turbulences of
    the late sixteenth century as well as their impact on Ottoman thought.
39 The exact date of the debasement in Iran remains to be established. Braudel
    (1972), I, p. 540 places it just before the Ottoman move; Steensgaard (1972),
    p. 419 is inclined to push it back in time and İnalcık (1951) states that the
    two debasements occurred around the same time.
40 Faced with bullion shortages, the Ottoman government was particularly sens-
    itive to the outflow of specie towards the East especially through its border
    with Iran. If the debasement in Iran had not been matched in the Ottoman
    Empire, the outflow of silver towards Iran would have only accelerated,
    bringing additional monetary difficulties at a time of war. Recently, Kafadar
    (1991) has also emphasized the importance of these bullion flows in under-
    standing the Ottoman debasement.
41 In simple terms, debasement refers to the decline in the specie content of
    a monetary unit. Devaluation means the decline in the value of a currency
    against other currencies in a fixed-rate regime. Clearly, the two are related.

A debasement often necessitates a devaluation as was the case in 1585–86.

42 İnalcık (1980). İnalcık has also argued that the desire to realign the official gold : silver rate in the face of large inflows of silver into the Levant played a role in the debasement decision: İnalcık (1978), pp. 90–96. In a recent essay, Kafadar (1991) examines the impact of the monetary turbulences and the debasement of 1585 on Ottoman consciousness of decline.

43 Suraiya Faroqhi states, for example, that in the Konya area in central Anatolia it appears that all taxes except the tithe on wheat and barley were collected in money in the early part of the seventeenth century. Faroqhi (1984), Ch. 8. This pattern probably represents a substantial change from the earlier situation when the *timar* regime prevailed.

44 Terms like *çürük, hurda, züyuf* were all used to refer to sub-standard *akçes*. Amongst other adjectives used for *akçes* in circulation were *kalb* (counterfeit), *sağ* (proper), *atik* (old) and *cedid* (new). Sahillioğlu (1958), (1965a); Gerber (1982); Mantran (1962), pp. 233–71. After each *tashih-i sikke*, new *narh defterleri* were published providing detailed lists of government controlled prices for large numbers of goods using the new standard for the *akçe*: Kütükoğlu (1983).

45 Kolerkılıç (1958), p. 57; Schaendlinger (1973), pp. 110ff. For the silver content of the *para* minted in Cairo and its relation to *akçe*, see Table V: 4 above.

46 For example, during the 40-year reign of Mehmed IV (1648–87), only six locations are known to have minted *akçe* and *para*: İstanbul, Belgrade, Amid (Diyarbekir), Aleppo, Damascus and Cairo. Schaendlinger (1973), pp. 112–13.

47 Morineau (1985).

48 For discussions of the term "unit of account," see Braudel and Spooner (1967), pp. 378–83 and Spufford (1988), Appendix II.

49 Most European silver coins were called *guruş*, which was the local adaptation of *groschen*, a diminutive for *gross* or *grosso*, a term used for silver coins in many European countries going as far back as the thirteenth century. The *esedi guruş* was called *ebukelb* in the Arab provinces, apparently because the lions were taken for dogs.

50 Mantran (1962), pp. 233–71; Sahillioğlu (1965a), pp. 38–53 and (1965b); Masson (1896), pp. 492–94; Spooner (1972), Ch. 1; for the monetary system in Egypt see Raymond (1973–74), I, Ch. 1; for Tunisia see Boubaker (1987), pp. 77–83 and Valensi (1985), Ch. 7.

51 Jennings (1973) has documented the widespread use of credit and interest by both the urban and rural population in seventeenth-century Kayseri.

52 In recent years Frank Perlin has argued forcefully that the use of money in the rural areas of India expanded steadily during the seventeenth and eighteenth centuries. His analysis has shed considerable light on the broader social and economic role of money in pre-colonial India. At the present, it is not clear whether similar developments were in progress in the Ottoman Middle East during the same period. See, for example, Perlin (1987).

53 For the short list of Ottoman mints striking copper coinage in the seventeenth century, see Schaendlinger (1973), pp. 106–15. In the literature, the debasement of the *akçe* and the decline in the need for even smaller coins have been cited as the principal reasons for this trend. In view of the disappearance of

the *akçe* and the silver shortage, however, other explanations need to be considered. It is noteworthy that copper coinage was widely used in Europe during the latter part of the seventeenth century, after the decline of silver. Spooner (1972), Ch. 1.

54 Sahillioğlu (1982).

55 Sahillioğlu (1965a), p. 91. These coins carried the date of 1099 H (1687–88), the year of accession to the throne of Süleyman II. the largest of these weighed 6 *dirham*s or approximately 19.2 gr. Later in 1703 a larger coin weighing approximately 8 *dirham*s or 25–26 gr. and its fractions were minted. It is not clear whether the first large coin of 1690 was intended as a *kuruş* or merely as a 30-*para* piece which came to be called *zolota* or *cedid* (new) *zolota* to distinguish it from the popular Polish coin. Numismatic catalogs suggest that the 6-*dirham* piece minted in 1690 was the first Ottoman *kuruş* and the weight of the Ottoman *kuruş* was revised upwards to 8 *dirham*s in 1703. On the other hand, Sahillioğlu has argued that the earlier large coin was intended as a *zolota* and the first Ottoman *kuruş* was minted in 1703: Sahillioğlu (1965a), pp. 94–122. Our calculations in Table V: 7 regarding the silver content of the *kuruş* are based on the latter argument. It should be noted that the early Ottoman *kuruş* was also called the *esedi kuruş* since its standards were close to those of the Dutch *thaler*. This term for the Ottoman *kuruş*, which has caused considerable confusion in the literature, was eventually abandoned: Sahillioğlu (1983).

56 Additional evidence is necessary to establish more clearly the silver content of the *kuruş* during the late seventeenth and eighteenth century.

57 Schaendlinger (1973), pp. 112ff.

58 As a result, the exchange rates of the gold coins minted in Cairo were always quoted separately. For eighteenth-century gold coins, see Sahillioğlu (1965a), pp. 94–122; Pere (1968); Artuk and Artuk (1974); Krause and Mishler (1984); for the Egyptian gold coins, Raymond (1973–74), I, Ch. 1; Walz (1983); and Krause and Mishler (1984).

59 For monetary conditions in the Balkans during the eighteenth century, see, for example, Svoronos (1956), pp. 82–83, 114–18 and Beaujour (1800), pp. 366–72. New *kuruş*-type coins began to be minted in the autonomous Crimea in the 1780s: Agat (1982).

60 The *kuruş* was not minted in Egypt until the third quarter of the eighteenth century. Raymond (1973–74), I, Ch. 1 is the best source for the monetary system of Egypt in the eighteenth century.

61 For the coinage in circulation in eighteenth-century Palestine, for example, see Cohen (1973).

62 For a review of the monetary system in eighteenth-century Tunisia, see Valensi (1985), Ch. 7. Also Boubaker (1987), pp. 77–83; Ismail Galib (1889–90); Ölçer (1970); and Schaendlinger (1973), pp. 112ff.

63 Genç (1984).

64 For Ottoman coinage during the reign of Mahmud II, see Ölçer (1970); Krause and Mishler (1984); Sultan (1977); Pere (1968); Artuk and Artuk (1974).

65 A detailed price history of the period has not been undertaken. For an overview of price changes, see Issawi (1980), pp. 321–37.

66 Cezar (1986) provides a comprehensive examination of the fiscal difficulties and reforms of this turbulent period.

67 Issawi (1980), Ch. 3; Pamuk (1987), Ch. 1.

68 The silver *kuruş* weighed 1.2027 gr. with a fineness of 83 percent. It contained 1.0 gr. of pure silver. The gold lira weighed 7.216 gr. with a fineness of 22/24 or 91.67 percent, containing 6.6 gr. of gold. As a result, *tashih-i sikke* of 1844 established the official gold : silver ratio at 15.09. Ferid (1914); Eldem (1970), pp. 225–29; Ölçer (1966).

69 Davison (1980).

70 Blaisdell (1929) remains the classic treatment of this topic. For the magnitudes of funds flows arising from external borrowing, see Pamuk (1987), Chapter 4 and Appendix III.

71 Billiotti (1909); Ferid (1914); Kuyucak (1947); Tekeli and İlkin (1981), Ch. 2.

72 Billiotti (1909) and Eldem (1970), pp. 228–29. In a later manuscript which remains unpublished, Eldem indicated that the estimates which appeared in the 1970 volume exaggerate the amount of nickel and copper coinage by a factor of ten. The figure given here is adjusted for that error. See V. Eldem, "Cihan Harbi, Mütareke ve Milli Mücadele Yıllarında Osmanlı Ekonomisi," unpublished and undated manuscript, p. 148.

73 Cohen (1976); Gerber and Gross (1980); Eldem (1970), pp. 226–27.

74 Schaendlinger (1973), pp. 129–55; Ölçer (1970).

ȧ

BIBLIOGRAPHY

Ağat, Nurettin (1982). "Kırım Hanlarının Paralarının Nitelikleri ve Işık Tuttukları Bazı Tarihi Gerçekler," reprints of three earlier articles, *The Turkish Numismatic Society Bülten*, No. 7, 6–43.

Akdağ, Mustafa (1974). *Türkiye'nin Iktisadi ve Içtimai Tarihi*, I: 1243–1453; II: 1453–1559, İstanbul.

Artuk, İbrahim (1980). "Osmanlı Beyliğinin Kurucusu Osman Gazi'ye Ait Sikke," in Osman Okyar and Halil İnalcık, eds., *Social and economic history of Turkey (1071–1920)*, Ankara, pp. 27–33.

Artuk, İbrahim and Cevriye Artuk (1974). *Istanbul Arkeoloji Müzeleri, Te'şhirdeki Islami Sikkeler Kataloğu*, II, İstanbul.

Ashtor, Eliyahu (1971). *Les metaux precieux et la balance des payements du Proche-Orient a la Basse Epoque*, Paris.

Babinger, F. (1956). "Goldpragungen im 15. Jahrhundert unter Murad II und Mehmed II", *SF*, XV, 550–53.

Barkan, Ömer Lütfi (1975)."The price revolution of the sixteenth century: a turning point in the economic history of the Near East," *IJMES*, VI, 3–28.

Baykal, Bekir Sıtkı (1967)."Osmanlı İmparatorluğunda XVII. ve XVIII. Yüzyıllar Boyunca Para Düzeni ile İlgili Belgeler," *Bl*, No. 7–8, 49–77.

Beaujour, Felix (1800). *A view of the commerce of Greece . . . from 1787 to 1797*, trans. from the French, London.

Beldiceanu, N. (1959)."La crise monetaire Ottomane au XVIe siècle et son influence sur les principautes Roumaines," *SF*, XVI, 70–86.

Beldiceanu, N. and Irene Beldiceanu-Steinherr (1988)."Les informations les plus anciennes sur les florins ottomans," in The Turkish Numismatic Society, pp. 49–58.

Belin, M. (1931). *Türkiye Iktisadi Tarihi Hakkında Tetkikler*, trans. from French by M. Ziya, İstanbul.

Billiotti, Adrien (1909). *La Banque Imperiale Ottomane*, Paris.

Blaisdell, Donald C. (1929). *European financial control in the Ottoman Empire*, New York.

Boubaker, Sadok (1987). *La régence de Tunis au XVIIe siècle: ses relations com-*

merciales avec les ports de l'Europe méditerranéen, Marseille et Livourne, Zaghouan.

Braudel, Fernand (1972). *The Mediterranean and the Mediterranean world in the age of Philip II*, 2 vols., London.

Braudel, Fernand and Frank Spooner (1967). "Prices in Europe from 1450 to 1750", in E.E. Rich and C.H. Wilson, eds., *The Cambridge economic history of Europe*, IV, pp. 374–486.

Cezar, Yavuz (1986). *Osmanlı Maliyesinde Bunalım ve Değişim Dönemi (XVIII. yy.dan Tanzimat'a Mali Tarih)*, İstanbul.

Cipolla, Carlo M.(1963). "Currency depreciation in medieval Europe," *EcHR*, XV, 413–22.

Cohen, Amnon (1973). *Palestine in the eighteenth century*, Jerusalem.

Cohen, David (1976). "La circulation monetaire entre les principautes Roumaines et les terres Bulgares (1840–78)," *Bulgarian Historical Review*, IV (2), 55–71.

Çizakça, Murat (1976–77). "Osmanlı Ekonomisinde Akçe Tağşişinin Sebebleri Üzerinde Kısa Bir İnceleme," *Boğaziçi University Journal, Administrative Sciences and Economics*, IV-V, 21–27.

Davison, Roderic (1980). "The first Ottoman experiment with paper money," in Osman Okyar and Halil İnalcık, eds., *Social and economic history of Turkey (1071–1920)*, Ankara, pp. 243–51.

Edhem, Halil (1915–16/1334H). *Meskukat-ı Osmaniyye*, İstanbul.

Eldem, Vedat (1970). *Osmanlı İmparatorluğunun İktisadi Şartları Hakkında Bir Tetkik*, İstanbul.

Ergenç, Özer (1978–79). "XVI. Yüzyılın Sonlarında Osmanlı Parası Üzerine Yapılan İşlemlere İlişkin Bazı Bilgiler," 86–97.

Erüreten, Metin (1985). "Osmanlı Akçeleri Darp Yerleri", *The Turkish Numismatic Society Bülten*, No. 17, 12–21.

Faroqhi, Suraiya (1979). "Sixteenth century periodic markets in various Anatolian sancaks", *JESHO*, XXII, 32–80.

(1984). *Towns and townsmen of Ottoman Anatolia, trade, crafts and food production in an urban setting, 1520–1650*, Cambridge.

Ferid, Hasan (1914/1330H). *Nakid ve Itibar-ı Milli, 1: Meskukat*, İstanbul.

Galib, İsmail (1889–90/1307H). *Takvim-i Meskukat-ı Osmaniyye*, İstanbul.

Gedai, Istvan (1988). "Turkish coins in Hungary in the 16th and 17th centuries," in The Turkish Numismatic Society, pp. 102–19.

Genç, Mehmet (1975). "Osmanlı Maliyesinde Malikane Sistemi," in O. Okyar and H.Ü. Nalbantoğlu, eds., *Türkiye İktisat Tarihi Semineri, Metinler/ Tartışmalar*, Ankara, pp. 231–96.

(1984). "XVIII. Yüzyılda Osmanlı Ekonomisi ve Savaş," *Yapıt*, Ankara, 4, 52–61.

(1989). "Osmanlı İktisadi Dünya Görüşünün İlkeleri," *İstanbul Üniversitesi Edebiyat Fakültesi Sosyoloji Dergisi*, 3. Dizi, 1.

Gerber, Haim (1982). "The monetary system of the Ottoman Empire," *JESHO*, XXV (3), 308–24.

Gerber, Haim and Nachum T. Gross (1980). "Inflation or deflation in nineteenth-century Syria and Palestine," *JEH*, XL, 351–57.

Godinho, Vitorino M. (1969). *L'économie de l'empire portugais aux XVe et XVIe siècles*, Paris.

Hamilton, Earl J. (1934). *American treasure and the price revolution in Spain, 1501–1650*, Cambridge, Mass.

Hansen, Bent (1981). "An economic model for Ottoman Egypt: the economics of collective tax responsibility," in A.L. Udovitch, ed., *The Islamic Middle East, 700–1900: studies in economic and social history*, Princeton, N.J., pp. 473–520.

İnalcık, Halil (1951). "Osmanlı İmparatorluğunun Kuruluş ve İnkişafı Devrinde Türkiye'nin İktisadi Vaziyeti Üzerine Bir Tetkik Münasebetiyle," *B*, XV, 629–90.

(1959). "Osmanlılar'da Raiyyet Rüsumu," *B*, XXIII, 575–608.

(1965). "Dar al-Darb," *EI²*, II, 117–19.

(1970). "The Ottoman economic mind and aspects of the Ottoman economy," in Michael Cook, ed., *Studies in the economic history of the Middle East*, London, pp. 207–18.

(1978). "The impact of the Annales School on Ottoman studies and new findings," *R*, I(3/4), pp. 69–96.

(1980). "Military and fiscal transformation in the Ottoman Empire, 1600–1700," *AO*, VI, 283–337.

(1981). "Osmanlı İdare, Sosyal ve Ekonomik Tarihiyle İlgili Belgeler: Bursa Kadı Sicillerinden Seçmeler," *Bl*, X (14), 1–91.

Issawi, Charles (1980). *The economic history of Turkey, 1800–1914*, Chicago.

Jennings, Ronald C. (1973). "Loan and credit in early 17th century Ottoman judicial records," *JESHO*, XVI (2–3), 168–216.

Kafadar, Cemal (1986). "When coins turned into drops of dew and bankers became robbers of shadows: the boundaries of Ottoman economic imagination at the end of the sixteenth century," Ph.D. dissertation, McGill University.

(1991). "Les troubles monétaires de la fin du XVIe siècle et la prise de conscience Ottomane du déclin," *Annales, ESC*, II, 381–400.

Kolerkılıç, Ekrem (1958). *Osmanlı İmparatorluğunda Para*, Ankara.

Krause, Chester, L. and Clifford Mishler with Colin R. Bruce II (1984). *Standard catalog of world coins*, 10th ed., Iola, Wis.

Kütükoğlu, Mübahat S. (1983). *Osmanlılarda Narh Müessesesi ve 1640 Tarihli Narh Defteri*, İstanbul.

Kuyucak, Hazım Atıf (1947). *Para ve Banka*, Cilt I, İstanbul.

Mantran, Robert (1962). *Istanbul dans la seconde moitié du XVIIe siècle*, Paris.

Masson, Paul (1896). *Histoire du commerce français dans le Levant au XVIIe siècle*, Paris.

Maxim, Mihai (1975). "Considerations sur la circulation monetaire dans les pays roumains et l'Empire Ottoman dans le seconde moitié du XVIe siècle", *RESEE*, XIII, 407–15.

(1983). "O lupta monetara in sec. al XVI-lea: padişahi contra aspru," *Cercetari Numismatice* (Bucharest),V, 129–52.

Michoff, Nicolas V. (1971). *Contribution à l'histoire du commerce de la Turquie et de la Bulgarie*, VI, Sofia.

Morineau, Michel (1985). *Incroyables gazettes et fabuleux metaux: les retours des trésors americains d'après les gazettes hollandaises (XVIe–XVIIIe siècles)*, New York and Paris.

Ölçer, Cüneyt (1966). *Son Altı Osmanlı Padişahı Zamanında İstanbul'da Darp Edilen Gümüş Paralar*, İstanbul.

(1970). *Sultan II. Mahmud Zamanında Darp Edilen Osmanlı Madeni Paraları*, İstanbul.

(1975). *The ornamental copper coinage of the Ottoman Empire*, İstanbul.

Pamuk, Şevket (1987). *The Ottoman Empire and European capitalism, 1820–1913: trade, investment and production*, Cambridge.

Pere, Nuri (1968). *Osmanlılarda Madeni Paralar*, İstanbul.

Perlin, Frank (1987). "Money-use in late pre-colonial India and the international trade in currency media," in John F. Richards, ed., *The imperial monetary system of Mughal India*, Delhi. pp. 232–74.

Poop, V., R. Puin and H. Wilski (1988). "Ottoman coins of the Yemen," in The Turkish Numismatic Society (1988), pp. 251–62.

Raymond, André (1973–74). *Artisans et commerçants au Caire au XVIIIe siècle*, 2 vols., Damascus.

Reed, Harold (1930). "Bimetallism and monometallism," in *Encyclopedia of social sciences, 1st ed.*, II, pp. 546–49.

Refik, Ahmet (1921–23). "Osmanlı İmparatorluğunda Meskukat," *Türk Tarih Encümeni Mecmuası*, XIV (1340 H/1921–22), 358–79; XV (1341 H/1922–23), 1–39, 107–27, 227–54.

Richards, J. F. (1983), ed. *Precious metals in the later medieval and early modern worlds*, Durham, N.C.

Sahillioğlu, Halil (1958). "Kuruluştan XVII. Asrın Sonlarına Kadar Osmanlı Para Tarihi Üzerine Bir Deneme", doctoral dissertation available in Library of the Faculty of Economics, University of İstanbul.

(1962–63). "Bir Mültezim Zimem Defterine Göre XV. Yüzyıl Sonunda Osmanlı Darphane Mukataaları," *IFM*, XXIII (1–2), 145–218.

(1965a). "Bir Asırlık Osmanlı Para Tarihi, 1640–1740," Ph.D. dissertation, University of İstanbul.

(1965b). "XVII. Asrın ilk Yarısında İstanbul'da Tedavüldeki Sikkelerin Raici," *Bl*, I (2), 227–34.

(1975). "Bursa Kadı Sicillerinde İç ve Dış Ödemeler Aracı Olarak "Kitabü'l-Kadı" ve "Süftece'ler," in O. Okyar and H.Ü. Nalbantoğlu, eds., *Türkiye Iktisat Tarihi Semineri, Metinler/Tartışmalar*, pp. 103–44.

(1982). "Bakır Para Üzerine bir Enflasyon Denemesi (H 1099–1103/1687–91)", *The Turkish Numismatic Society Bülten*, 10, 7–40.

(1983). "The role of international monetary and metal movements in Ottoman monetary history," in Richards, ed., pp. 269–304.

Schaendlinger, Anton C. (1973). *Osmanische Numismatik*, Braunschweig.

Shaw, Stanford J. (1962). *The financial and administrative organization and development of Ottoman Egypt, 1517–1798*, Princeton, N.J.

Spooner, Frank C. (1972). *The international economy and monetary movements in France*, Cambridge, Mass.

Spufford, Peter (1988). *Money and its use in medieval Europe*, Cambridge.

Steensgard (1973). *Carracks, caravans and companies, the structural crisis in the European–Asian trade in the early seventeenth century*, Copenhagen.

Sultan Jem, (1977). *Coins of the Ottoman Empire and the Turkish Republic, a detailed catalogue of the Jem Sultan collection*, 2 vols., Thousand Oaks, Calif.

Sundhaussen, Holm (1983)."Die 'Preisrevolution' im osmanischen Reich wahrend der zweiten Hälfte des 16. Jahrhunderts," *SF*, XLII, 169–81.

Svoronos, N. G. (1956). *Le commerce de Salonique au XVIIIe siècle*, Paris.

Tekeli, İlhan and Selim İlkin (1981). *Türkiye Cumhuriyeti Merkez Bankası*, Ankara.

Toprak, Zafer (1988). "İktisat Tarihi," in Sina Akşin, ed., *Türkiye Tarihi*, III: *Osmanlı Devleti, 1600–1908*, İstanbul, pp. 191–246.

The Turkish Numismatic Society (1988). *A Festschrift presented to Ibrahim Artuk on the occasion of the 20th anniversary of the Turkish Numismatic Society*, İstanbul.

Valensi, Lucette (1985). *Tunisian peasants in the eighteenth and nineteenth centuries*, London and New York.

Walz, Terence (1983). "Gold and silver exchanges between Egypt and Sudan, 16th–18th centuries," in Richards ed., pp. 305–28.

Watson, Andrew M. (1967). "Back to gold and silver", *EcHR*, XX, 1–34.

ة

GLOSSARY

HALİL İNALCIK

These terms apply primarily to the period 1300–1600. They are listed here without transliteration as found in the text, and then in their original form in the transliteration alphabet used in *Encyclopaedia of Islam*, 2nd edition. Terms whose meaning is clear in the text or are to be found in an English dictionary are not included.

ABBREVIATIONS

A Arabic   P Persian
G Greek   Sl Slavic
It Italian   Sp Spanish
L Latin   T Turkish

ahdname (P. *'ahdnāma*): A written pledge under oath by the sultan granting a privilege, immunities or authority to a community, ruler or person.

akça or *akçe* (T): Ottoman silver coin, see Part V.

askeri (A. *'askarī*): (1) Literally "of the military class"; (2) All those groups belonging to the military or religious elite with complete tax exemption; a non-Muslim, when granted such a status by a royal diploma also becomes an *askeri*.

avarız (A. *'awārid*): Extraordinary levies or services introduced by the state on emergency situations, mostly to support the navy; a certain number of households of *reaya* is registered as *avarız* tax units (*hane*).

azeb (A. *'azab*): (1) An unmarried young man; (2) An auxiliary footman recruited for the imperial army, whose expenses were met by the local people under the *avarız* system; (3) Fighting man in the navy.

bac (P. *bādj*): Market or transit dues taken on goods for sale per container.

barca or *barça* (Old Venetian:*barca*): Large ships with a capacity of 600 × 8 tons, equipped with guns.

bashtina (Sl): A peasant family farm in the Balkans corresponding to the Ottoman *raiyyet çiftlik*. The Ottomans retained the Slavic term with groups whose pre-Ottoman status and services were maintained.

bayt al-mal (A. *bayt al-māl*): (1) The public treasury; (2) An inheritance without heir, hence belonging to the public treasury.

bedestan or *bedesten* (T. from P. *bezzāzistān*): Synonym of *ḳayṣariyya*, or Roman *basilica*, a covered strong stone building in the center of a bazaar, where imports such as precious textiles, jewelry and arms are stored and sold; the leading merchants have shops, and trust money is preserved in a *bedestan*.

beg or *bey* (T): (1) Ruler in central Asian Turkish states and in the early Ottoman centuries; (2) Commander; (3) Title of the governor-commander of a *sancak*, or of a *ziamet*.

beglerbegi or *beylerbeyi* (T): Synonym of *mīrmīrān*: it designates the governor-general of a *beglerbegilik*.

beglerbegilik (T): Synonym of *eyālet* or *vilāyet*; all these terms stand for the Ottoman province, the largest administrative unit under a *beglerbegi*.

berat (A. berāt): A sultanic diploma bearing his official seal, *tughra*; also called *manshūr*.

bogasi or *bohassi* (T): A fine cotton textile manufactured in large quantities in Hamid-eli and exported to the Balkans, the Crimea, Hungary and other European countries.

Boz-Ulus (T): Turcoman tribal confederation in eastern Anatolia.

cebelü (T): A fully armed retainer of a *timar*, *ziamet* or *hass* holder.

Celali (T): Mostly *sekban* and *saruca* mercenary bands, which turned into bandit gangs when unemployed; they infested Anatolia during the period 1596–1610.

cihad (A. *djihād*): Islamic Holy War.

cizye (A. *djizya*): Islamic poll-tax imposed upon a non-Muslim male adult, originally at the rate of 12, 24 or 48 *dirhem* of silver according to his means; the three categories are: working poor man, those of medium income and the well-to-do in the tax registers; however, the Ottomans mostly levied the tax per household uniformly, at the rate of one gold, or its equivalent in silver *akça*.

çift-hane system: Under this system the state organized rural society and economy by appropriating grain-producing land and distributing it under the *tapu* system to peasant families (*hane*). Each family in theory in possession of a pair of oxen was given a farm (*çiftlik*) sufficient to sustain the family and to meet its tax obligations. This was the basic fiscal unit which the state endeavored to maintain. Families with less than half a *çift* or *çiftlik*, or unmarried peasants, were separately categorized as *bennak* and *mücerred* (or *kara*), and subjected to lower rates of *çift*-tax.

çiftlik (T): (1) Land workable by a pair (*çift*) of oxen, or a farm in which the fields make up a unit workable with a pair of oxen by a peasant family within the *çift-hane* system; (2) A big farm consisting of several *raiyyet* *çiftliks* under the control of an absentee landlord; (3) Any plantation-like agricultural exploitation.

çift-tax (T): A tax under the *çift-hane* system, assessing a peasant's labor capacity in combination with the land in his possession.

devşirme (T): Levy of boys from Christian rural population for services at the palace or the divisions of the standing army at the Porte; also see *kul*.

divan (P. *dīwān*): (1) Imperial council which functioned as the government and the supreme court in İstanbul: (2) The government; (3) The state treasury.

dolab (P. *dōlāb*): (1) A turning device; (2) Water wheel; (3) A vortex of affairs, bank.

Eflaks (Ottoman name for Vlachs): In the fifteenth century Vlachs, mostly pastoralist nomads, were organized for military or other public services under the Ottomans.

ekinlik (T): See *mezra'a*

emin (A. *amīn*): (1) A man of trust, a superintendent; (2) An agent of the sultan appointed to carry out a public work with financial responsibility; (3) The head of an office in the palace or government responsible to provide provisions, etc., or to supervise a public work.

eşkünci (T): (1) "Campaigner"; (2) Those *timar*-holders assigned to take part in military expeditions, or *eşkün*.

fay' (A. *fay'*): The inalienable property (land) of Muslims as a community, or of the Islamic state.

faytor (Sp. *feitor*): The representative in Basra of the Portuguese *capitaõ* of Hormuz in the sixteenth century.

ferag (A. *farāgh*): Legal transfer of property or possession of rights in it.

fetva (A. *fatwā*): Formal written legal opinion by an authority in Islamic Law.

gaza (A. *ghazā*): Fighting for the cause of Islam, Holy War against the infidels.

gazi (A. *ghāzī*): A Muslim warrior fighting for Islam.

gulam (P. *ghulām*): See *kul*.

hane (P. *khāna*): (1) A house; (2) A family; (3) A household as tax unit.

harac (A. *kharādj*): (1) Djizya; (2) A combined land–peasant tax levied from a non-Muslim possessor of state-owned agricultural land; (3) Tribute in general; (4) a Tribute paid by a non-Muslim state to an Islamic state.

haraci land: In early Islam those state-owned agricultural lands left in the possession of non-Muslim farmers in return for a higher rate of tithes.

hasil (A. *ḥāṣil*): (1) Product, total revenue or income; (2) In the *tahrir* registers the total sum of the revenues estimated for a village or other units.

hass or *hassa* (A. *khāṣṣ*): (1) Belonging to a member of the elite or to the sultan; (2) Those prebends pertaining to the elite or to the sultan; (3) A farm or vineyard assigned to the direct control of a *timar*-holder.

havass-i humayun (A. *khawāṣṣ-i humāyūn*): Sources of revenue in the *timar* system reserved for the sultan, actually for the central state treasury; *havass* are collected directly by the sultan's agents or through tax-farms.

hawala (A. *ḥawāla*): An assignation of a fund from a distant source of revenue by a written order, used in both state and private finances.

hayduk or *haydud*: (1) Originally a Hungarian irregular foot-soldier; (2) A brigand.

hutba (A. *khutba*): Sermon delivered in the mosque by the *khaṭīb* or leader of the community at the Friday service or at religious festivities; the custom was established to mention the name of the ruling sovereign at the prayer; Ottoman sultans appointed shaykhs of religious orders as *khaṭīb*s to major mosques; the mentioning of the name became a symbol of the recognition of the legitimacy of his sovereignty.

icaratayn (A. *idjāratayn*): The "dual" lease system in which the tenant of a *vakf* property paid, first, an immediate substantial amount to dispose of the property and then a second monthly rent; under the system the renter enjoyed extensive possession rights on the property.

imam (A. *imām*): (1) Prayer leader; (2) A successor of the Prophet, Caliph; (3) The chief of a Muslim state.

imaret (A. ʿimārat): Soup kitchens attached to *vakf* complexes.

irsalat or *irsaliyye* (A. *irsālāt, irsāliyya*): (1) Goods destined for the consumption of military units, or shipments belonging to the state; (2) Revenue in cash sent to the central treasury from the surplus of a province.

ispence (originally Sl, *jupanića*): Poll-tax paid to feudal lord in pre-Ottoman Serbia; continued under the Ottomans as a customary tax, it is mostly included in *timar* revenue.

istimalet (A. *istimālat*): Literally to make someone inclined to accept; an Ottoman term for winning over the population in conquered lands or enemy territory.

kapan (A. *ḳabbān*): (1) A large public weighing device; (2) Caravanserai or mart in which such a device is placed to weigh goods and collect dues.

kaza (A. *ḳāḍā*): (1) Jurisdiction of a kadi; (2) An administrative unit corresponding to the kadi's jurisdiction in a province.

Kara-Ulus (T): A Kurdish tribal confederation in eastern Anatolia.

kethüda (P. *katkhudā*): (1) A steward; (2) The head or member of the governing body of a military, professional or social group, elected by the group and certified by the local kadi or the sultan.

kılıç (T): (1) A sword; (2) Registered *timar* unit, not to be divided and assigned in parts.

kirbas (Sanskrit *karpassa*): A coarse cotton cloth manufactured in various regions in Asia Minor and exported to the Balkans and Black Sea countries in great quantities.

kışlak (T): Winter pastureland.

Kızılbaş (T): (1) Literally "red-head," it designated Turcoman soldiers in Anatolian emirates who wore red caps; (2) A member of the sect in central and eastern Anatolia, mostly of Turcoman origin, following heteredox beliefs, often rebellious against the centralist and orthodox Sunni policy of the Ottoman state.

kul (T): (1) A slave; (2) A tax-paying subject of the state (cf. *reaya*); (3) *kuls* (plural) designate the sultan's servants and soldiery at the Porte.

kulluk (T): (1) The state of a slave; (2) Labor service, or its monetary compensation, which an Ottoman subject owes to the state (cf. *çift*-tax); (3) Special services and dues a peasant with state-owned land had to give to the state or *timar*-holder (cf. *çift resmi*).

levend (P. *lawand*): Privateers who joined the Ottoman navy with their ships when their services were needed.

liva (A. *liwā*): see sancak

maktu (A. *maḳṭūʿ*): A lump sum agreed upon for payment of rent or taxes.

malikane (P. *mālikāne*): Belonging to a landlord.

martolos: A pre-Ottoman group of militia maintained by the Ottomans, mostly serving on the frontier for raids and intelligence in the neighboring country.

mashlah (A): A large cloak of camel wool made in Arabia.

mevat (A. *mawāt*): Legal term for "dead" land; a "dead" land is either one abandoned and left uncultivated for a long time or wastelands such as deserts, forests or marshes.

mezra'a (A. *mazra'a*): (1) A field under cultivation; (2) A large farm with no permanent settlement; it may be originally a deserted village or land reclaimed by a nearby village.

millet (A. *milla*): A community, the religious autonomous organization of which is formally recognized by the Islamic state; *millet*s in the Ottoman Empire obtained their own charters in the reform period in the 1860s, which extended their autonomous status and gave their organization a formal secular character.

miri (P. *mīrī*): Belonging to the ruler or to the state.

muaf (A. *mu'āf*): Exempt from taxation.

mudaraba (A. *mudāraba*): Corresponding to the Western *commenda*, *mudaraba* is a contract between a person providing capital and a caravan trader; they shared the profit equally.

muhtesib (A. *muhtasib*): An inspector helping the kadi of a town to see that the Muslims' conduct in their public lives and transactions conformed to the prescriptions of Islamic Law; he was particularly active in the bazaar area, inspecting weights and measures, prices and the quality of goods.

mukataa (A. *mukāta'a*): (1) A renting contract, tax-farm; (2) The rent itself; (3) A source of revenue estimated and entered into the registers of the finance department as a separate unit.

mukataalu (T): State-owned land leased under the *mukataa* system.

mukus (A. *mukūs*): (1) Customs or excise duty; (2) All kinds of small dues and taxes outside those approved by Islamic Law.

mülk (A. *mulk*): Freehold ownership as opposed to state ownership; see *miri*.

müsellem (A. *musallam*): (1) Exempt from taxation; (2) A group of militia of *reaya* origin, enjoying various tax exemptions in return for military service.

musha' (A. *mushā'*): (1) Collective ownership; (2) Communal land.

narh (P. *narkh*): The maximal price list on necessities, periodically established by the local kadi.

nişancı (T): A member of the imperial council responsible for the chancery, checking all diplomas and putting the imperial seal (*nishan*) on them; responsible in particular for the administration of *miri* land and the *timar* system.

nüzul (A. *nuzl*): (1) Food served to a guest; (2) A tax, mostly in kind, imposed upon the fiscal units of households for provisioning the army or navy, see also *avarız*.

ocak (T): (1) Hearth; (2) The unit of households in military organizations such as *yaya* or *voynuk*; (3) Corps or the whole body of a military organization such as *Yeniçeri Ocağı*.

ortakçılık (T): Sharecropping; as opposed to *reaya* in possession of land under the *tapu* system, a sharecropper cultivates land belonging to another person who as a rule supplies means of production and sometimes also shelter, and shares the product equally; an *ortakçı kul* is a slave working for his owner on the same basis.

paroikoi (G): A dependent peasant, serf; in Turkish texts *parikoz*, in Italian *parici*.

pishkesh (P. *pīshkesh*): A gift presented to a superior as a symbol of recognition of his authority and protection.

poliçe (It. *polizza*): A letter of credit.

proniar (G): Provincial military elite in the Byzantine Empire, enjoying a prebend in return for military or administrative service, as in the Ottoman *timar* system.

raiyyet (A. *raʿiyya*): See *reaya*.

rakaba (A. *raḳaba*); (1) Eminent domain; (2) *proprietas nuda*; (3) State ownership (of land); see also *miri*.

reaya (A. *raʿāyā*): All those groups, Muslim or non-Muslim, outside the *askeri* elite, engaged in economic activities and thus subject to taxes.

rikab (A. *riḳāb*): See *rakaba*.

salgun (T): See *avarız*.

sancak (T): A sub-province; administrative unit under a *sancak-begi* (*beyi*); a *beglerbegilik* is divided into several *sancaks*.

sekban (P. *sagbān*): (1) Literally a keeper of hounds; (2) In the Janissary army: divisions originally of the keepers of the sultan's hounds, who were incorporated to the corps of Janissaries under Mehmed II; (3) A particular mercenary organization, equipped with muskets, organized as companies of 50 to 100 under a Janissary officer; in the sources, usually mentioned together with a similar group called *saruca*.

serbestiyet (P. *sarbastiyyet*): (1) Freedom, full immunity; (2) Full immunity from government control in *vakf* and *temlik* lands.

Shi'i (A. shīʿī): As opponents of the Sunni, the Shi'is follow the *shīʿa*, claiming that the legitimate imamate or the religio-political leadership belonged after the death of Muhammad to ʿAlī, the cousin and son-in-law of the Prophet, and to his descendants. In general, Shi'is believe that with the Shi'i Imam divine revelation and mediation between God and His creatures continues, and until the day the Mahdi, or the hidden Imam, reappears the *mudjtahids*, as spokesmen of the hidden Imam, have the supreme religio-political authority over the Islamic community. In Iran, with the accession of the Safavids in 1501, such a regime was believed to be achieved. This gave the old rivalry between the Ottoman state and Iran a religio-ideological character as a fight between Sunnis and Shi'is. The rivalry became particularly fierce when the Safavids were supported by the Kızılbash Turcomans of Asia Minor throughout the sixteenth century.

simsar (L. *censarii*): The head of brokers in a bazaar.

sipaşı (P. *sipāhī*): (1) A mounted soldier; (2) A member of the noble class; (3) A member of the cavalry divisions at the Porte; (4) The lowest rank in the provincial *timariot* (see *timar*) army.

sipahi-oğlanları (T): The top division among the six salaried cavalry divisions at the Porte.

subaşı (T): (1) Commander, originally a compound of *sü*, soldier and *bash*, head; (2) In the Ottoman provincial administration it designates a commander in the *timariot* army above *sipahi* and below *sancak-begi*; (3) An agent appointed by a governor to take care of the collection of his revenues and other resposibilities; see *voyvoda* and *ziamet*.

Sunni (A. sunnī) or *ahl al-sunna*: Those Muslims who refrain from deviating from the *Sunna*, or the dogma and practice as established by the Prophet, the companions (*ashāb*) and the traditions of the community. Sunnis consider Shi'is as heretics deviating from the *Sunna*. Turkish states, including the Ottoman state, made Sunnism a state policy, which entailed serious social and political consequences and brought the government into a fierce struggle with the Turcoman Kızılbash sect in Asia Minor in the sixteenth century.

sürgün (T): (1) A term for the Ottoman method of relocation or forcibly deporting and settling population from one region to another; (2) An individual subjected to this operation.

tafviz (A. *tafwīḍ*): (1) To give full power and authority; (2) Full possession rights entrusted to a peasant on state-owned land.

tahrir (A. *taḥrīr*): (1) Enregisterment; (2) Ottoman system of periodical surveying of population, land and other sources of revenue. Survey registers called *defter-i khākānī* were of two kinds: *mufassal*, registering the sources of revenue "in detail," and *idjmāl* that register only their distribution among the military.

tahtacı (T): A generic name for the Yörük Turcoman tribes on the Taurus mountain range who were occupied with cutting and trading in timber (*tahta*); in eastern Asia Minor they are known as *ağaç-eri* or "woodmen."

taife (A. *ṭā'ifa*): See *millet*.

tamga: See *bac*.

Tanzimat (A. *Tanzīmāt*): (1) Reforms; (2) Radical Ottoman westernizing reforms introduced in the period 1839–76.

tapu (T): (1) An act of homage; (2) Permanent patrilineal lease of state-owned land to a peasant family head in return for his pledge to cultivate it continuously and meet all the obligations in tax or services; (3) The title deed certifying *tapu* rights.

tapulu (T): A state-owned farm leased to a peasant family head under the special conditions of the *tapu* system.

tasarruf (A. *tasarruf*): (1) Free disposal; (2) The exercise of actual possession rights on state-owned land.

temlik (A. *tamlīk*): Sultan's grant to a member of the elite of state-owned land as freehold property with complete tax immunity and autonomy.

timar (P. *tīmār*): (1) Any kind of care; (2) A prebend acquired through a sultanic diploma, consisting as a rule of state taxes in return for regular military service, the amount of which conventionally was below 20,000 *akça*: also see *sipahi*, *hass* and *ziamet*.

ulufe (A. *'ulūfa*): Salary in cash paid, as a rule, to the military.

umma (A. *umma*): The Muslim community as a whole.

urfi or *örfi* (A. *'urfī*): (1) Customary; (2) Based on the sultan's command; (3) State taxes mostly based on pre-Ottoman dues confirmed by the sultan, as in the term *rusum-i 'urfiyya* or *takalīf-i urfiyya*.

uthmani (A. *'uṣmānī*): (1) Of the Ottoman sultan; (2) The Ottoman silver coin *akça* or *akçe*, as called in Arab lands.

vakf (A. *waḳf*, plural *awḳāf*): Synonym of *hubs*, namely a pious foundation or an endowed thing, as a rule real estate, but sometimes also an amount of cash, which "while retaining its substance yields a usufruct and of which the owner has surrendered his power of disposal with the stipulation that the yield is used for permitted good purposes" (*Shorter Encyclopaedia of Islam*, p. 624).

valā (A. *walāʾ*): (1) Legal control; (2) A master's legal rights on the inheritance of a manumitted slave.

vekil (A. *wakīl*): (1) An agent; (2) A proxy.

voynuk or *voynug* (Sl. *voynik*, warrior, soldier): A pre-Ottoman militia from the peasant population of Slavic states in the Balkans, maintained by the Ottomans.

voyvoda or *voyvode* (Sl): (1) Slavic title for prince, used in particular for the rulers of Wallachia and Moldavia; (2) A military agent appointed by a governor to take care of the collection of his revenues in the *kada* area; the title *subaşı* is sometimes used instead.

yasakiyye (T): Fee for Janissary in charge of enforcing law.

yaya (T): (1) Footman; (2) Peasant militia organized in *ocak*.

Yörüks: A bureaucratic name for Turcoman pastoralist nomads when they came in the territories controlled by the Ottomans, mostly in western Anatolia and the eastern Balkans.

yurt (T): An area reserved for a pastoralist nomadic group with summer and winter pasturelands.

Ziamet (A. *ziʿāmat*): (1) Military leadership; (2) A prebend bestowed by a sultanic diploma to the commander of *timariot sipahi*s in a district, conventionally from 20,000 to 100,000 *akça*; synonym of *subaşılık*.

ﯼ

INDEX

In the organization of this index, the modern Turkish alphabet is followed, according to which ş comes after c, ç after s, ü after u, and ö after o.